About this book

This book focuses on the provision of basic social services – in particular, access to education, health and water supplies – as the central building blocks of any human development strategy. The authors concentrate on how these basic social services can be financed and delivered more effectively to achieve the internationally agreed Millennium Development Goals.

Their analysis, which departs from the dominant macroeconomic paradigm, deploys the results of the broad-ranging research they led at UNICEF and the UNDP, investigating the record on basic social services of some thirty developing countries. In seeking to learn from the new data from this research, they develop an analytical argument around two potential synergies: at the macro-level, between poverty reduction, human development and economic growth, and at the micro-level, between interventions to provide basic social services. Policymakers, they argue, can integrate macroeconomic and social policy. Fiscal, monetary, and other macroeconomic policies can be compatible with social-sector requirements. The authors make the case that policymakers have more flexibility than is usually suggested by orthodox writers and international financial institutions, and that if policymakers engaged in alternative macroeconomic and growth-oriented policies, this could lead to the expansion of human capabilities and the fulfilment of human rights. This book explores some of these policy options.

Eliminating Human Poverty also argues that more than just additional aid is needed. Specific strategic shifts in the areas of aid policy, decentralized governance, health and education policy and the private–public mix in service provision are prerequisites to achieving the goals of human development. The combination of governance reforms and fiscal and macroeconomic policies outlined in this book can eliminate human poverty in the span of a generation.

About the authors

Santosh Mehrotra is a human development economist educated at the New School for Social Research, New York, and the University of Cambridge, where he did his doctorate. He was Associate Professor in Jawaharlal Nehru University, New Delhi, before moving to the United Nations in 1991. For the past fifteen years he has worked on the human impact of macro-economic policy. He led UNICEF's research programme on economic and social policy on developing countries at the Innocenti Research Centre, Florence, 1999–2002. He was a co-author of the *Human Development Report 2002–4*, and Regional Economic Adviser for Poverty for the Asia region, 2005–6. His books include *India and the Soviet Union: Trade and Technology Transfer* (Cambridge University Press, 1990), *Development with a Human Face: Experiences in Social Achievement and Economic Growth* (edited, with Richard Jolly, Clarendon Press, 1997), *Le Développement à Visage Humain* (Economica, 2001), *Universalizing Elementary Education in India: Uncaging the Tiger Economy* (co-authored, Oxford University Press, 2005), *The Economics of Elementary Education in India* (edited, Sage Publishers, 2006), and *Asian Informal Workers: Global Risks, Local Protection* (with M. Biggeri, Routledge, 2006). He is currently adviser to the Planning Commission, Government of India, and is involved in writing India's eleventh Five Year Plan (2007–11). Website: http://santoshmehrotra.org/.

Enrique Delamonica is an economist and political scientist educated at the University of Buenos Aires, Columbia University, and the New School for Social Research, New York. He has worked for almost fifteen years as a consultant for UNICEF and UNDP and a policy analyst in UNICEF headquarters, focusing on the impact of macroeconomic policies on children, poverty-reduction strategies, financing of social services and budget allocations, the analysis of trends in socioeconomic disparities, child poverty measurement, and social protection policies. He has published widely, including two co-edited books on issues of social policy, particularly as they affect children. He has also taught economics, international development, policy analysis and research methods at New York University, Columbia University, the University of Buenos Aires, the Institute for Social and Economic Development (Argentina), and the New School. Currently he teaches at Saint Peter's College in New Jersey.

About CROP

CROP, the Comparative Research Programme on Poverty, is a response from the academic community to the problem of poverty. The programme was initiated in 1992, and the CROP Secretariat was officially opened in June 1993 by the director-general of UNESCO, Dr Federico Mayor.

In recent years, poverty alleviation, poverty reduction and even the eradication and abolition of poverty have moved up the international agenda, and the CROP network is providing research-based information to policymakers and others responsible for poverty reduction. Researchers from more than a hundred countries have joined the CROP network, with more than half coming from so-called developing countries and countries in transition.

The major aim of CROP is to produce sound and reliable knowledge that can serve as a basis for poverty reduction. This is done by bringing together researchers for workshops, coordinating research projects and publications, and offering educational courses for the international community of policymakers.

CROP is multidisciplinary and works as an independent non-profit organization.

For more information contact:

CROP Secretariat
Nygårdsgaten 5, N5020 Bergen, Norway
tel: +47 55589739 fax: +47 55589745
email: crop@uib.no
website: www.crop.org

CROP INTERNATIONAL STUDIES IN POVERTY RESEARCH
PUBLISHED BY ZED BOOKS IN ASSOCIATION WITH CROP

David Gordon and Paul Spicker (eds), *The International Glossary on Poverty*, 1999.

Francis Wilson, Nazneen Kanji and Einar Braathen (eds), *Poverty Reduction: What Role for the State in Today's Globalized Economy?*, 2001.

Willem van Genugten and Camilo Perez-Bustillo (eds), *The Poverty of Rights: Human Rights and the Eradication of Poverty*, 2001.

Else Øyen et al. (eds), *Best Practices in Poverty Reduction*, 2002.

Lucy Williams, Asbjørn Kjønstad and Peter Robson (eds), *Law and Poverty: The Legal System and Poverty Reduction*, 2003.

Elisa P. Reis and Mick Moore (eds), *Elite Perceptions of Poverty and Inequality*, 2005.

Robyn Eversole, John-Andrew McNeish and Alberto Cimadamore (eds), *Indigenous Peoples and Poverty: An International Perspective*, 2005.

Lucy Williams (ed.), *International Poverty Law: An Emerging Discourse*, 2006.

Maria Petmesidou and Christos Papatheodorou (eds), *Poverty and Social Deprivation in the Mediterranean*, 2006.

Paul Spicker, Sonia Alvarez Leguizamón and David Gordon (eds), *Poverty: An International Glossary*, 2nd edn, 2007.

Santosh Mehrotra and Enrique Delamonica, *Eliminating Human Poverty: Macroeconomic and Social Policies for Equitable Growth*, 2007.

Eliminating human poverty

Macroeconomic and social
policies for equitable growth

**SANTOSH MEHROTRA
AND ENRIQUE DELAMONICA**

International Studies in Poverty Research

International Social Science Council

Z

Zed Books
LONDON & NEW YORK

Eliminating Human Poverty was published in 2007 by Zed Books Ltd,
7 Cynthia Street, London N1 9JF, UK, and Room 400,
175 Fifth Avenue, New York, NY 10010, USA

www.zedbooks.co.uk

CROP International Studies in Poverty Research
CROP is a programme under the International Social Science Council,
which has also helped finance this publication

Designed and typeset in Monotype Bembo
by illuminati, Grosmont, www.illuminatibooks.co.uk
Cover designed by Andrew Corbett
Printed and bound in Malta by Gutenberg Press Ltd

Distributed in the USA exclusively by Palgrave Macmillan,
a division of St Martin's Press, LLC, 175 Fifth Avenue,
New York, NY 10010

A catalogue record for this book is available from the British Library
Library of Congress Cataloging-in-Publication Data available
Library and Archives Canada Cataloguing in Publication Data available

ISBN   978 1 84277 772 5 Hb
ISBN   978 1 84277 773 2 Pb

Contents

List of tables and figures   x

Foreword by Kemal Dervis   xiii

Preface   xv

1   Introduction   1

PART I   Macroeconomic policies

2   Integrating macroeconomic and social policies to trigger
    synergies   13
2.1 The theoretical foundations of mainstream macroeconomic
     policies: a critique   16
2.2 An alternative approach   31
2.3 The industrialized countries: the state, the market economy
     and the capabilities of labour in historical perspective   40
2.4 Concluding remarks   55

3   Macroeconomic policies and institutions for pro-poor growth   57
3.1 Redistribution to reduce income poverty and manage
     distributional conflict   61
3.2 Industrial policy for technological/structural change   68
3.3 Alternative macroeconomic policies   81
3.4 The historical significance of the current conjuncture in the
     macroeconomic policy debate   87

PART II   Public expenditure on basic social services

4   The (in)adequacy of public spending on basic social services   97

4.1   Neoclassical basis for state financing of basic services   97
4.2   The synergy among social services   102
4.3   Measuring and assessing public expenditure on
      basic social services in developing countries   113
4.4   Concluding remarks   132

5   The distribution of benefits of health and education spending   134

5.1   Disparities in health and education outcomes   134
5.2   The distribution of benefits of public spending on education   137
5.3   The distribution of benefits of public spending on health   142
5.4   Explaining the incidence of benefits of health and education
      expenditure   148
5.5   Conclusion   151

**6   Policies to enhance efficiency and improve delivery
     in the public provision of basic social services   154**

6.1   Allocative efficiency   156
6.2   Technical efficiency   173
6.3   Conclusion   208

**7   Governance reforms to address the systemic problems of
     state provision of basic services   211**

7.1   The nature of the state as a factor in state failure in
      service delivery   211
7.2   Capabilities, democracy and decentralization   215
7.3   Case studies   220
7.4   Summing up   233

**8   Promoting complementarity between public and private
     provision   235**

8.1   Why has private provision increased?   236
8.2   Education   238
8.3   Health   247
8.4   Water and sanitation   258
8.5   The private sector – full speed ahead?   270
8.6   Conclusions   271

PART III Mobilizing domestic and external resources

**9   Taxation and mobilization of additional resources for
      public social services   277**
9.1   Intra-sectoral reallocation of public spending   280
9.2   Inter-sectoral restructuring of public spending   287
9.3   Enhancing revenues   299
9.4   Earmarking of funds (or hypothecated taxes)   307
9.5   Public expenditure effectiveness and performance budgeting 310
9.6   Concluding remarks   314

**10   The consistency between aid and trade policies
      and the Millennium Goals   319**
10.1 Aid policies and poverty reduction   321
10.2 ODA for basic social services: the quantitative evidence 322
10.3 Aid to basic education, basic health and water and sanitation:
      some qualitative issues   332
10.4 Modality of aid to basic services –
      whither the sectoral approach?   337
10.5 Improving the consistency of donor government policies   342
10.6 Concluding remarks   349

11   Conclusion   358

Notes   369

References   395

Index   426

List of tables and figures

Annex 1.1	The scale of human poverty	8
Annex 1.2	Millennium Development Goals and targets	10
Table 2.1	Economic growth by level of income-poverty and enhancement of functionings	38
Table 2.2	A heuristic schema of development strategies and synergies	39
Figure 2.1	Mortality in the UK, France and Germany, 1840–1905	44
Figure 2.2	GDP per capita, adult literacy rate and mortality: UK 1840–1905	45
Figure 2.3	GDP per capita, adult literacy rate and mortality: Germany 1840–1905	49
Table 2.3	Historical education expenditure in now-industrialized countries	54
Figure 4.1	Education and health feedback effects	103
Figure 4.2	Life cycle of an educated girl	106
Figure 4.3	Defence expenditure: selected high achievers versus developing countries	109
Table 4.1	Sequence of investment in high-achieving countries: health breakthrough followed by or simultaneous with education breakthrough	110
Figure 4.4	Sequence of investment in education and health in high-achieving countries (Costa Rica and Korea)	111
Table 4.2	Women's status in selected high-achieving countries	112
Figure 4.5	Women's agency: employment outside the household, women as % of men	113
Table 4.3	Basic social service spending as % of national budget	117
Figure 4.6	Share of basic services in public spending on health and education	119
Table 4.4	Education, health and demographic indicators	120

Table 4.5	Index of real per capita expenditure on BSS	121
Table 4.6	Trends in real per capita expenditure on BSS	122
Table 4.7	Trend of BSS share in total public spending	123
Figure 4.7	Under-5 mortality and public spending on health	126
Table 4.8	Public expenditure as a percentage of GDP	128
Table 5.1	Urban and rural enrolment by income group	135
Table 5.2	Benefit incidence of public spending on education	138
Table 5.3	Benefit incidence and primary education needs	139
Figure 5.1	Distribution of primary education spending and enrolment	140
Figure 5.2	Côte d'Ivoire: enrolment by income level and gender	141
Table 5.4	Distribution of public health spending benefits	143
Figure 5.3	Distribution of primary health-care benefits and child mortality	144
Figure 5.4	Distribution of public spending on hospitals and child mortality	145
Table 5.5	Distribution by quintile of subsidies for different health services	146
Table 5.6	Health services unit costs by quintile	147
Table 5.7	Health services expenditures per person by region and race, South Africa	148
Figure 5.5	Enrolment increase in Malawi after elimination of fees and uniforms	150
Figure 6.1	Selected high achievers by geographic region: higher education as a share of current public expenditure on education	157
Figure 6.2	Selected high achievers: % per capita income spent on each primary (and pre-primary) pupil, *circa* 1980	158
Figure 6.3	Selected high achievers by geographic region: per pupil expenditure as a multiple of primary education	159
Figure 6.4	Education costs and enrolment for primary schools	161
Table 6.1	Expenditure on health globally by households, governments and donors	169
Table 6.2	Who may be spending too much on teachers' salaries?	177
Figure 6.5	Female teachers as a percentage of all teachers	183
Table 6.3	Interventions with a large potential impact on health outcomes	190
Table 6.4	Access to drinking water and sanitation by rural/urban population and public expenditure on basic water and sanitation as % of total public expenditure, 1995–97	191
Table 6.5	High achievers versus low achievers: doctors and nurses per 100,000 persons	195
Table 6.6	Decline in total fertility and population growth rate, by region, 1960–99	198
Table 6.7	Size and structure of government and NGO expenditure on population activities, 1996	200

Annex 6.1   Trend of BSS share in total public expenditure   209

Table 8.1   Students enrolled in private schools (1965 and 1975)
             and adult literacy (1980) in some developing countries   240

Table 8.2   Types of PPP contracts in the water and sanitation sector   260

Table 8.3   Two alternative systems of social service delivery   272

Table 9.1   Resource requirements to universalize access to BSS   278

Figure 9.1   Per-pupil expenditure ratios by region, 1995   282

Table 9.2   The now-industrialized countries: share of public education
             expenditures by level, *circa* 1900   284

Figure 9.2   Basic services versus defence in public expenditure   288

Table 9.3   Share of basic social services, defence and debt service
             in public expenditure   289

Figure 9.3   Basic services versus debt service in public expenditure   291

Table 9.4   Public expenditure as a percentage of GDP, selected countries   311

Table 9.5   Types of accountability   313

Annex 9.1   International taxation and other potential international sources
             of development finance   315

Table 10.1   Net flows of ODA to direct recipients and intermediaries,
             1990–98   323

Figure 10.1 Official development assistance   324

Table 10.2   Share of BSS in total (bilateral) ODA commitments   326

Table 10.3   Share of BSS in ODA of selected multilateral agencies, 1996   327

Table 10.4   ODA to drinking water and sanitation sector by recipient:
             project-wise distribution, mid-1990s   331

Table 10.5   ODA to BSS by IDA and regional development banks,
             1995–98   332

Table 10.6   Technical assistance in SIPs   338

Annex 10.1a Bilateral ODA commitments (grants and loans) to education   351

Annex 10.1b Share of education in total bilateral ODA commitments
             (grants and loans)   352

Annex 10.2   Bilateral ODA commitments to basic education   353

Annex 10.3   Share of health and population in total bilateral ODA
             commitments   354

Annex 10.4   Bilateral ODA commitments to basic health   355

Annex 10.5   Bilateral ODA Commitments (grants and loans)
             to population/reproductive health   356

Annex 10.6   Bilateral ODA Commitments (grants and loans)
             to water supply   357

Foreword

For many developing countries, particularly least developed countries in sub-Saharan Africa, the prospects for achieving the Millennium Development Goals seem bleak unless the pace of economic growth increases, and such growth becomes more equitable, including through the provision of universal basic social services. Changing the pace and quality of economic growth is critically dependent upon changes in public policies, in both donor and developing countries. For the poorest countries, the Poverty Reduction Strategy Papers are an advance, but as currently conceived they are insufficient in their degree of ambition, as well as lacking scope for home-grown policies. For several emerging market economies – home to the majority of the world's poor – high debt levels coupled with the volatility of international capital markets limit their ability to formulate home-grown macroeconomic policies.

This book presents the results of broad-ranging analysis led by two policy experts at UNICEF and UNDP. It investigates the record on basic social services of some thirty developing countries. In seeking to learn from the data, the book develops an argument around two potential synergies: at the macro-level, between poverty reduction, human development and economic growth; and at the micro-level, between interventions to provide basic social services. The book explores policy options that could enable policymakers to have more flexibility to engage in growth-oriented, distributive macroeconomic policies and the provision of social services that could lead to the expansion of human capabilities.

It also argues that more is needed than just additional aid. A strategic blend of domestic governance reforms and macroeconomic policies could contribute significantly to the reduction of human poverty. Equally important, the book argues that there is an inconsistency between the increased aid that donors have committed since 2001 and their trade policies. Only a minority of governments have taken tangible steps to ensure that their domestic policies, and their position in international trade negotiations, are consistent with poverty-reduction goals.

The book also discusses concerns with lack of country ownership of economic reforms recommended by the international financial institutions, and how this may relate to the governance structures of these institutions. The reliance of emerging market economies upon international capital markets is also addressed. The possibility that global and regional development banks could offer long-term financing to social programmes to achieve the Millennium Development Goals to complement purely private flows, and at a cost that should reflect some 'blending' of concessional with non-concessional resources, is discussed.

As UNDP's recent *Human Development Report*s have warned, despite the development gains made by many Asian countries – in particular by the world's most populous countries, China and India – globally, the world is lagging behind in meeting the Millennium Development Goals. This book is an important contribution to the debate on policies, national and international, that could put countries back on track.

Kemal Dervis

UNDP Administrator and UN Under-Secretary General;
former Vice-President, Poverty Reduction and
Economic Management, World Bank

Preface

Except for a minority of countries in Asia, most developing countries have not made a dent in reducing income poverty. The prospects for achieving improvements in human development and capabilities seem dim as well unless macroeconomic policies, economic growth and social expenditures become more equitable.

In this book we deploy the results of broad-ranging research we led at UNICEF and UNDP, investigating the record on basic social services of some thirty developing countries. In seeking to learn from these new data, we develop an analytical argument around two potential synergies: at the macro-level, between income poverty reduction, human development and economic growth; and at the micro-level, between interventions to provide basic social services. Policymakers, we suggest, should integrate macro-economic and social policy; policymakers have more flexibility than usually presented by orthodox writers to engage in macroeconomic and growth-oriented policies that could lead to the expansion of human capabilities. This book explores some of these policy options.

We fully recognize in this book that over the past decade the international financial institutions have been articulating in their official publications a less hard-edged open economies/free markets/small states agenda. However, we also demonstrate that there is a difference between what is said and what is done. The Policy Framework Papers of yesteryear are now called Poverty Reduction Strategy Papers. But the macroeconomic policies remain the same or similar in content. The World Bank's International Development Association, whose loans are based on the Country Policy and Institutional Assessment, evaluates country performance and thus allocates loans on the basis of compliance with a neoliberal development agenda.

Part I of the book traces the problems of capability deprivation partly to the dominant orthodox paradigm in macroeconomic policy and its deficient record in terms of economic growth and volatility, income distribution and poverty reduction over the last quarter of the twentieth century. Elements of an alternative strategy are also offered in Part I.

Part II of the book is then devoted to an examination of fiscal policies for the poor. It deals primarily with level, efficiency and equity of public spending on basic social services. In addition, it discusses the private sector's role in health, education and water services – which many bilateral and multilateral organizations advocate for. It also devotes considerable space to what can be done to improve dramatically the capacity of the state to deliver these services – through deep democratic decentralization – in ways in which over a decade of experience with decentralization has failed to do so far. But such organizational changes alone will not be sufficient. Additional finance is needed.

Part III examines the sources of domestic and external resources for achieving the Millennium Development Goals. External resources are needed in least developed countries for basic services; it examines the evidence on this international support – with a view to determine whether the reality of aid has matched the rhetoric in favour of the Millennium Development Goals. Developing-country governments, however, have also to mobilize additional domestic resources: the sources of domestic resource mobilization are discussed, as well as the constraints on such resource mobilization.

This book has benefited from detailed comments by a number of friends: Mario Biggeri, Bob Deacon, Robert Cassen, Mick Foster, Gerry Helleiner, Sir Richard Jolly, K.S. Jomo, John Langmore, David Lewis, Peter Lindert, Edward Nell, John Micklewright, Seethaprabhu, Ajit Singh and Jan Vande-moortele. Participants at a number of seminars (in Florence, Italy; Hanoi; Cambridge, UK; Hamilton, Canada), where different chapters were presented, also influenced the evolution of the argument.

The views expressed herein are those of the authors, and should not be attributed to their respective organizations.

1

Introduction

Human development is a goal, an objective and an aspiration. The goal gives salience to the well-being of the individual and the individual's full participation in society. It is a goal towards which economic policies should lead.

The notion of human development also provides an alternative framework beyond the traditional approach of economic analysis at the theoretical level. This notion is firmly grounded in the capabilities approach (Sen, 1982, 1985; Nussbaum, 2000). It requires an explicit and constant recognition of the need to integrate economic and social policy, which alone will ensure the goals of human development. This has at least two implications. First, by integrating and linking the human dimension with the analysis of growth and development, it should no longer be sufficient to look at macroeconomic variables, such as investment and trade, to assess or predict a country's performance or growth in the near future or the long run. Elements such as gender equity, and the health, nutrition, and education levels of the population are as significant as the macroeconomic variables.

There are practical policy implications of such a theoretical framework. It could be argued, for instance, that the international financial institutions should be evaluating country performance differently over a loan period (e.g. the period of applicability of the joint IMF–World Bank–Government Poverty Reduction Strategy Papers in low-income countries).[1] This would not be merely in terms of macroeconomic indicators, or governance indicators, but also in terms of human development outcomes. This does happen increasingly at meetings of the Consultative Group of donors, but ultimately the most important indicators remain macroeconomic ones. The weight of 'Policies for Social Inclusion' in the evaluation of country policies is only

25 per cent. The Poverty Reduction Strategy Papers, initiated in 1999, are an attempt to address this problem. Whether this change in name from the erstwhile Policy Framework Papers means a substantive change in direction in the IMF remains to be seen; but the evidence so far does not suggest that there has been much substantive change (IMF, 2003; 2004).

Second, while there has been an increase in literature focused on many of these issues (i.e. the link between social and macroeconomic variables) (World Bank, 1980, 1990, 2000a), studies usually apply standard economic tools to non-economic issues. We believe that this approach gives a distorted picture of what human development is and how it can be achieved. In particular, the analysis of health and education sectors as if they were competitive markets could lead to seriously misguided policy recommendations. As a result, we suggest that Human Development, as a theoretical lens, is more naturally associated with various strands of non-orthodox economics, such as structuralist macroeconomics and evolutionary growth theories.

We do not pretend to cover all aspects of human development in this brief book. Our goal is more modest, as we concentrate on one fundamental piece: the provision of basic social services (BSS) to expand what Sen calls capabilities and functionings. We concentrate on how basic social services can be financed and delivered more effectively than hitherto in order to ensure universal and equitable access to high quality basic social services – so that the Millennium Development Goals (MDGs – some set for 2005, but mostly with a target date of 2015) can in fact be achieved (see Annex 1.1 to this chapter for a brief discussion of the magnitude of human poverty and Annex 1.2 for a list of the goals and targets of the MDGs). This provision of basic services is also related to other dimensions of human development, and we touch upon them along the way, especially when our analysis implies policy recommendations that differ from those of the dominant development paradigm.

Mainstream economic theory is the framework explicitly or implicitly used by most analysts of development. It is based on the assumption that given preferences and technology, production and distribution take place in such a way as to maximize welfare and to distribute income to the owners of the factors of production in proportion to their contribution to output. Thus, efficiency is maximized, and growth is determined by savings – that is, individuals/households prefer to exchange present for future consumption. This is not the place to engage in a critique of such a view, whether applied to industrialized or developing countries.[2] Our approach is different. It can be summarized as follows.

First, production takes time. During the period of production, transactions must be carried out. These transactions include purchases of subsistence goods by workers and purchases of production inputs. These exchanges imply that enough commodities exist to sustain workers and facilitate production. These commodities can only come from previous production,[3] and, at the very least, producers expect that at the end of this period enough commodities will again exist in order to sustain workers and production in the future.

Second, profits and accumulation (and consequently growth) are expected by producers. Otherwise, there would be no incentive to produce. Although individual producers may fail, society as a whole must produce enough commodities for its survival (to sustain workers and production, i.e. social reproduction as described in the previous paragraph). Moreover, at the aggregate level, a surplus (loosely interpreted as production beyond 'social reproduction') is needed as an incentive for production and to allow accumulation (i.e. economic growth).

Third, all commodities (those needed for social reproduction and those representing a surplus) need to be distributed. This distribution may or may not reflect contribution to output. It rarely does, as it is based on relative bargaining power of different groups and sectors. Assuming, in order to simplify, that the commodities used to sustain workers and production are distributed in a way that guarantees social reproduction,[4] the distributional conflict revolves around the surplus.

The distribution of this surplus affects economic growth, social development and income-poverty reduction. As it is widely recognized, there are one-way direct linkages as well as feedback mechanisms connecting these spheres. Thus, the provision of basic social services directly reduces poverty (albeit not necessarily its income dimension). It has also been argued that lower poverty (income and non-income) can result in higher economic growth, as it limits the possibility of underconsumption by generating a higher demand for goods.[5] It is particularly important to emphasize the role of improvement in the distribution of assets (both physical and human capital) in reducing income-poverty.

As we attempt to understand the positive experience of recently industrialized countries or of high-achieving developing countries (as we do in Chapters 2 and 3), we are struck by the difficulty of establishing causality relationships. For example, despite widespread literacy within a population, many countries have not achieved rapid growth,[6] although education is a major determinant of such economic growth. There are also examples of countries with relatively rapid economic growth but persistent income-poverty.[7] Thus, no single element can be specified as the main cause (or 'development magic bullet') for success in all areas. Rather, interventions that increase income and improve the quality of human capital support each other in a synergistic way or through various feedback loops.

This synergy can be succinctly expressed as the enhanced impact a change in an independent variable has on the rate of growth of a dependent variable, given the presence of a third variable. This leads to several important, and often overlooked, interrelated effects in terms of policy at a macro-level. The impact of a policy (e.g. to promote economic growth) on another variable (say income-poverty reduction) crucially depends on the level of a third variable (e.g. previous investment in basic social services). In other words, economic growth will be more effective in reducing (income) poverty (the elasticity of poverty reduction will be higher) when the capabilities of citizens are more widespread.

It is hard to identify the necessary and sufficient conditions for achieving the desired outcomes of economic growth, income-poverty reduction and expansion of human functionings. Given sufficient inputs for BSS, the non-income dimensions of poverty can be reduced without economic growth; well-being is enhanced as ill-health and illiteracy are reduced. However, in the absence of sufficient investment in BSS, economic growth may not reduce the income or non-income dimensions of poverty, primarily because the poor may be unable to take advantage of market opportunities on account of ill health or poor education or limited skills. Actions on several fronts are needed.

Related to the previous point, standard tools of marginal analysis, rates of return, or linear regressions are not adequate to establish the importance, relative weight or priority of interventions to promote one or the other of the three desired outcomes or ends, because the presence of the synergies creates non-linearities. For instance, trade liberalization in a context of a weak human development level will have a very different impact than the same policy (all other elements being equal) in a situation where the labour force has high mean years of schooling, is well-trained and healthy.

Thus, the goals and the theoretical foundations of human development assume that there is integration of economic and social objectives and policies. Consequently, a different strategy from the one consciously or unconsciously followed by most developing countries is needed. We say 'most' and not 'all' developing countries because some of them (those we term 'high achievers') succeeded in developing education and health standards comparable to those of industrialized countries despite having a fraction (sometimes just a tenth) of their level of income per capita.

These experiences (summarized in Mehrotra and Jolly, 1997) strongly influence our analytical lens and are presented for reference and comparison purposes throughout the book.[8] These countries also illustrate another well-known synergy, or feedback loop, among social interventions in basic health care, reproductive health care, education, nutrition, and water and sanitation. This synergy takes place at a micro-economic level, as illustrated by the positive influence of better nutrition on school attendance and learning. Better education also leads to improved health outcomes and lower fertility rates. Increased access to water also improves health outcomes and school attendance. Education improves the effective usage of water resources. Thus, a web or mesh of interaction takes place. For synergies to exist at the macro-level, actions on several fronts are again needed. This should not be taken to mean that 'everything matters'; quite the contrary. If everything matters, nothing does. The implication of the subtitle of the book, 'Macroeconomic and Social Policies for Equitable Growth', means that while the ends at macro-level are the three objectives (economic growth, expansion of functionings, and income-poverty reduction), priorities have to be set at the level of *means* such that there is a balance between macroeconomic and social policies, rather than a hierarchy between them (see Chapters 2 and 3 for further discussion).

To summarize, there are two synergies present. One takes place at the macro-level among income-poverty reduction, expansion of human functioning and economic growth. The other synergy of outcomes, at the micro-level, occurs as a result of interventions to provide the basic social services that are the foundation of expansion of functionings. These two synergies are linked by the synergies among good health, nutrition and education – which are ends in themselves, but also means to other ends at a macro-societal level, and hence common to both sets of synergies. This conceptually underlines the need to integrate social-sector policies with macroeconomic ones.

In order to achieve this integration, it is crucial that fiscal, monetary and growth policies be compatible with social-sector requirements. The latter must also be compatible with macroeconomic constraints and supportive of the long-term growth process. A natural starting point for discussion of this integration and compatibility is the budget. On the one hand, total revenues and spending are at the core of fiscal polices. On the other hand, public expenditure supports the provision of basic social services (BSS). The importance of BSS in this synergetic connection requires that a deeper look be taken at their provision and financing. This implies that the case for the state's active role in this area needs to be made. In addition, the level, distribution and efficiency (quality) of public spending on BSS needs to be analysed.

The structure of this book follows the logic presented in the last few paragraphs. Part I (Macroeconomic Policies) has two chapters. Chapter

2 (Integrating Macroeconomic and Social Policies to Trigger Synergies) presents a conceptual macroeconomic framework. In order to do that, it examines the dominant framework for economic and social policymaking. Finding it wanting, the chapter proposes an alternative based on the two synergies. The two-synergy analysis is a theoretical construct with policy implications and builds upon certain specific antecedents in development theory. It is also a conceptual framework that can guide the analysis of, and assist in understanding, specific country examples of success or failure in human development and poverty reduction. In light of this conceptual framework, the experience of the now industrialized countries in respect of social provisioning is discussed. Chapter 3 then goes on to spell out macroeconomic policies consistent with achieving pro-poor, employment-intensive growth and achieving the Millennium Development Goals.

Part II (Public Expenditure on Basic Social Services) comprises five chapters. Chapter 4 examines the data on the inadequacy of public spending on basic services in the majority of developing countries. Prior to the UNICEF/UNDP country studies, summarized in this chapter, almost no developing country was able to assess how much it was spending on basic social services – basic health (including reproductive health and family planning), drinking water and sanitation, and basic education. No donor, until 1994, knew how much official development assistance (ODA) was going to basic social services despite the increasing emphasis in recent years on the need for both public spending and aid focused on poverty reduction. Chapter 4 also examines the debate about the impact of public spending on the actual outcomes of health and education.

Chapter 5 examines the benefit incidence of health and education spending in over twenty developing countries and finds that spending on education and health services is not equitably shared. Very little of this data was available before it was collected for our study. Typically, the rich gain twice as much as the poor from education and health budgets. Primary education spending appears to be best distributed. The implication is that there is considerable scope for reaching the poor through budget reallocation from higher levels of service (hospital-based health care and tertiary education), which are used mainly by the better-off, to basic services used by the poor (primary health facilities and primary education).

Chapter 6 examines the allocative and technical efficiency in the delivery of basic services – health, education, water and sanitation (and briefly reproductive health and nutrition). The need for additional resources is far from the only problem preventing universal access to basic services. We examine what kinds of sector-specific policies need to be put in place to improve access and delivery of health, water/sanitation and education services. Both aspects of allocative as well as technical efficiency are examined for each of three sectors.

Of course, there are many examples of state failure in the provision of basic social services over the last several decades. That is why Chapter 7 shows that decentralization and the articulation of voice by the poor can address these failures and ensure accountability and effective provision of services for the poor. Examples of democratic decentralization that have been demonstrated to be effective in improving state provision of basic social services are presented. A new model of deep democratic decentralization is presented to demonstrate, with empirical evidence from countries around the world, that it is possible for the state to improve dramatically its delivery of basic services.

Chapter 8 is devoted to private provision and examines the possibility of building complementarity between private and public provision. The chapter first re-examines the case for state financing and provision (as opposed to the private sector or civil society) in theoretical terms. It also examines the question as to what extent private or NGO provision can substitute for, or complement, state provision. The role of civil society organizations in the provision of social services is examined. There has been an increase in privatization of health and urban water services since the 1990s. The experience with privatization and with public–private partnerships is assessed.

In Part III (Mobilizing Domestic and External Resources), the last two substantive chapters deal with the mobilization of additional resources for basic services – domestic (Chapter 9) and external (Chapter 10). Chapter 9 presents the gap between existing resources allocated to basic services, and the additional requirements for resources – at a global level – in order to achieve universal coverage of basic services. However, most of the chapter is devoted to an analysis of the main instruments for the mobilization of additional public resources for social investment – including various tax instruments and innovative sources of financing. It also addresses the political economy underlying the decision-making process for various instruments.

In Chapter 10 the adequacy and efficiency of ODA to basic services is analysed, drawing on data that has not been analysed so far in the literature. Given the size of the gap between what is currently being spent and what is required, it will be very difficult for many low-income countries, especially the least developed ones, to achieve universal access to BSS without some assistance by donor countries. This is true in particular during the period when countries restructure their budgets in order to allocate more resources to BSS. However, although it has risen since 2001, ODA was declining in the 1990s and, on average, donor allocation to BSS remained only about

10 per cent of ODA – inadequate to reach universal coverage within the foreseeable future. The chapter examines in detail the subsectoral composition of ODA to health education and water and sanitation. In addition to the quantitative evidence, it also discusses new qualitative developments away from project-aid towards programme assistance and sector-wide programmes. Finally, it examines the lack of consistency between aid policies and the trade/economic policies of industrialized countries (i.e. Millennium Development Goal 8, calling for a partnership between rich and poor countries), which makes the international environment hostile to achievement of basic services for all.

Of the nine substantive chapters (2–10), three (4, 5 and 10) draw on new data for this book, and not analysed elsewhere so far, while Chapter 2 presents a conceptual framework within which the rest of the book's analysis is framed.

Implicit in the approach we adopt in this book is the belief that good governments can be made better in their economic decision-making, and 'bad' governments can be made good. The experience of high-achieving countries (Mehrotra and Jolly, 1997) demonstrates that there are a significant number of good governments. In both types of government, there are, fortunately, many senior politicians and bureaucrats who do not need convincing – for them the arguments above would serve to strengthen their arsenal. But the governing elite in many 'bad' governments do need convincing, if not for the sake of the poor, then for their own long-term self-interests. In such cases, social conditionality from the international financial institutions could help, since it is to the Ministry of Finance that the social conditionality is addressed.[9] Unfortunately, in most governments, there is a hierarchy of policy, with macroeconomic policy being determined first and social policy following (Atkinson, 1999). Social conditionality could help to bridge this gap.

Annex 1.1   The scale of human poverty[10]

Although the governments of the world have committed themselves to halving income poverty between 1990 and 2015 (the Millennium Development Goals), the number of people living on less than $1[11] a day fell only slightly between 1990 and 1999, from 1,276 million to 1,151 million, and their share fell from 29 to 23 per cent (UNDP HDR, 2002). Most of this decline was accounted for by China and India. Lack of progress in other countries can be attributed to fast economic growth with increasing income inequality or declining per capita income with steady distribution.

Another goal is to halve the proportion of people suffering from hunger (i.e. those who consume less than 1,960 calories a day) between 1990 and 2015. According to the UN's Food and Agriculture Organization (FAO), that number hardly declined at all globally by 2000 from around 800 million in 1990; the increase in Africa more than compensated for the decline in China. In fifty countries with almost 40 per cent of the world's people, more than one-fifth of children are underweight – that is, suffering from protein energy malnutrition. Half of child deaths are accounted for by malnutrition – which is preventable (as we discuss in Chapter 6).

Every year about 11 million children die of preventable causes, usually for want of simple improvements in nutrition, sanitation and maternal health and education. Similarly, half a million women die every year as a result of pregnancy and childbirth. Increasing the number of births attended by skilled health personnel, having access to emergency obstretric care and reducing the number of pregnancies are simple interventions – but they can only be provided by a functional health system, which can reduce both child and maternal mortality. Every year there are more than 300 million cases of malaria, and 60 million people are infected with tuberculosis (TB). Current medical technology can prevent these diseases from being fatal, but lack of access to health services implies that TB kills 2 million people a year and malaria kills 1 million.

While current medical technology cannot cure HIV/AIDS but only slow its progression, given the high cost of treatment, prevention is the best way forward. Countries like Thailand, Uganda and Senegal have already demonstrated what the effective means of prevention are. Yet the disease continues to spread: by the end of 2000 almost 22 million people had died from AIDS, 13 million children had lost their mother or both parents to the disease, and a total of 40 million people were living with the HIV virus – 90 per cent in developing countries, 75 per cent in sub-Saharan Africa.

In 2000, 1.1 billion people – a sixth of humanity – lacked access to safe drinking water, and 2.4 billion people – over a third of humanity – did not have access to any form of improved sanitation services. Over the 1990s these numbers did not fall much, on account of growing population.

At least in respect of schooling, the ratio of primary enrolment has been increasing, but the number of primary-school-age children out of school has actually risen to 115 million in 2000 – even though the enrolment ratio has been rising. At the same time, the number of illiterates (currently around 900 million, or just under a sixth of humanity) is still rising, primarily because the enrolment ratio at primary and junior secondary levels is not rising fast enough to absorb the growing population.

Annex 1.2 Millennium Development Goals and targets

Goal 1: Eradicate extreme poverty and hunger

Target 1: Halve, between 1990 and 2015, the proportion of people whose income is less than $1 a day.

Target 2: Halve, between 1990 and 2015, the proportion of people who suffer from hunger.

Goal 2: Achieve universal primary education

Target 3: Ensure that, by 2015, children everywhere, boys and girls alike, will be able to complete a full course of primary schooling.

Goal 3: Promote gender equality and empower women

Target 4: Eliminate gender disparity in primary and secondary education, preferably by 2005 and in all levels of education no later than 2015.

Goal 4: Reduce child mortality

Target 5: Reduce by two-thirds, between 1990 and 2015, the under-5 mortality rate.

Goal 5: Improve maternal health

Target 6: Reduce by three-quarters, between 1990 and 2015, the maternal mortality ratio.

Goal 6: Combat HIV/AIDS, malaria and other diseases

Target 7: Have halted by 2015 and begun to reverse the spread of HIV/AIDS.

Target 8: Have halted by 2015 and begun to reverse the incidence of malaria and other major diseases.

Goal 7: Ensure environmental sustainability

Target 9: Integrate the principles of sustainable development into country policies and programme and reverse the loss of environmental resources

Target 10: Halve by 2015 the proportion of people without sustainable access to safe drinking water.

Target 11: Have achieved by 2020 a significant improvement in the lives of at least 100 million slum dwellers.

Goal 8: Develop a global partnership for development

Part I

Macroeconomic policies

2

Integrating macroeconomic and social policies to trigger synergies

This chapter explores, from both a theoretical and an empirical perspective, an alternative to the mainstream view of development. At its core, the mainstream view stresses that markets are (or tend to be) efficient and, consequently, that the best course of action for the state is to eliminate (in some sectors) or minimize (in other sectors) government interventions. Thereby economic growth will be maximized, poverty will be reduced, and increases in welfare will ensue. This should take place in a more or less automatic fashion.

We critique this traditional view and focus on some of its theoretical problems (section 2.1). We then present a sketch of an alternative view based on the two synergies mentioned in the introduction, one occurring within BSS and the other linking BSS to income-poverty reduction and economic growth (section 2.2). In the final section, we show that this alternative framework provides a better description of the path followed by the now-industrialized countries (section 2.3).

Although the book is primarily about basic social services, it is essential to engage in a discussion centring on the mainstream policy paradigm, and its foundations in the neoclassical and information-theoretic framework. This results from a fundamental argument of the book that economic and social policy must be conceived in a more integrated manner than currently occurs within the orthodox paradigm.[1] Without this, there is little likelihood that poverty will be reduced; nor is there a probability that growth will benefit the poor and access to basic social services will be universalized. The provision of basic services must be part of an economic and social policy package, in which social policy does not trail economic policy. Atkinson (1999) notes that at present much policymaking occurs under a leader–follower hierarchy model, where macroeconomic policy is determined first, while social policy is left to address the social consequences.[2] Atkinson notes that this leader–follower model applies not only to national governments but also to international agencies. 'It makes no sense', he states, 'for macroeconomic stabilization policies to be determined by Bretton Woods institutions, and then for the social consequences to be addressed by other agencies.'

The separation of the 'economic' from the 'social' discourse is inherent in the leader–follower hierarchy model of the orthodox policy recommendations. This approach has several shortcomings. It is inefficient in achieving macroeconomic objectives, as we will discuss below. Also, it underplays the human welfare outcomes, often unintended, or inadequately anticipated, on account of initial conceptual errors in the model (as we discuss below). In such circumstances, Social Funds and education and health ministries are left to take care of the consequences of macroeconomic policy mistakes – essentially, to pick up the pieces.

The recognition of the goal to expand human capabilities and functionings, on the other hand, allows this separation of the 'economic' and 'social' goals to disappear, as capabilities and functionings are intrinsically important to the well-being of the population. In other words, we are taking an explicitly normative stance. Although economists tend to argue that their science should be positive (i.e. value-free), in practice it is not, and cannot be freed from conscious or unconscious ethical and political judgements (Myrdal, 1953; Sen, 1989). In that case, it is better to be explicit about normative positions. The capabilities approach has placed human beings and their well-being at the centre of its concerns – not only their well-being, but their freedom to choose a life one has reason to value. Thus, Sen has argued that for many evaluative purposes, the appropriate 'space' is not that of utilities (as claimed by welfare economists) but that of substantive freedoms and capabilities.

Underlying the continuing separation of 'social' and 'economic' discourse are certain key differences in framework. A salient one is the perspective shared by international financial institutions and many policymakers and economists in the finance ministries. A different perspective is offered by analysts and advocates in civil society and throughout some of the specialized agencies of the United Nations. On the state versus the market debate, the first group has increasingly tended (over the last two decades) to take a minimalist view of the role of the state and a benign view of the market (Kanbur, 2001). The first group typically takes a competitive view of market structure, while the second group believes that there are strong elements of monopolistic power, especially in the corporate sector. Those in the first group tend to take a much more aggregated view of outcomes, while those in the second group are concerned with the disaggregated outcomes of economic policy (by region, income-group, gender and age). When the former group worries about poverty, it is only at the national level. The first group has a strong belief in the power of economic growth to transform the lives of the poor; while the second, although not opposed to growth, is far from convinced of market power being able to deliver the poor from poverty.

In support of the second point of view, in this chapter we argue that the theoretical foundations of the capability approach lead to the integration of economic and social objectives and policies. Consequently, a different strategy from the one consciously or unconsciously followed by most developing countries is needed. We say 'most' and not 'all' developing countries because some of them (those we note as 'high achievers') succeeded in developing education and health standards comparable to those of industrialized countries despite achieving a fraction (sometimes just a tenth) of their level of income (Mehrotra and Jolly, 1997). These countries illustrate a well-known synergy, or feedback loop, among social interventions in basic health care, reproductive health care, education, nutrition, and water and sanitation.[3] This synergy takes place at a micro-economic level, as illustrated by the positive influence of better nutrition on school attendance and learning. Better education leads to improved health outcomes and lower fertility rates. Increased access to water also improves health outcomes and school attendance. Thus, a web or mesh of interactions takes place.

As we will argue, in the process of development there is a second synergy. The second one takes place at the macro-level among income-poverty reduction, enhancement of functionings at the aggregate level, and economic growth. We are, obviously, borrowing the expression 'functionings' from Sen. However, in this context we are interpreting it in a narrower sense than he does. Instead of all the important activities that people may value engaging in, we concentrate on those functionings which come about from the provision of basic social services – that is, the ability to lead healthy, literate, knowledgeable lives. While an achieved functioning (e.g. of being healthy) is an attribute of an individual, we are here interested in achieved functionings at an aggregate or societal level. For synergies to be realized at an aggregate or macro-level, actions on several fronts are needed. These two synergies are linked by the presence of basic social services (BSS) found in both. The difference is that in the first synergy basic services are inputs; in the second, BSS interventions appear in the form of health and educational outcomes. However, this difference is highlighted merely for expository purposes, since in fact poverty reduction, economic growth and health/education outcomes cannot be realized without independent inputs/interventions. These inputs, when transformed into outputs or outcomes, have a synergistic effect in continuous feedback loops. This supports the need to integrate social policies with macroeconomic ones, which is not possible to achieve within the conceptual confines of the orthodox paradigm.

In section 2.1 we critique this paradigm and the policies emanating from it on theoretical and empirical grounds. The critique is essentially that the prescriptions of the international financial institutions often go much beyond what can be supported by careful theoretical reasoning or empirical information. The critique we make is fully cognizant of the fact that governments facing large domestic and external imbalances often cannot continue with 'business as usual', and sometimes have to take action to contain those imbalances. The argument we are making is not that macroeconomic imbalances were a good thing for the poor, but that a different kind of adjustment was needed (Cornia et al., 1987). Economies that performed well in the last half century (China, several East and Southeast Asian countries, India in the last fifteen years) have done so via their own distinct version of heterodox policies (for our menu of options available to countries on heterodox policies, see the next chapter). Macroeconomic stability and high investment rates have been common, but apart from that many details vary (Rodrik, 1999a; Stiglitz, 1998a; Bird, 1999). In section 2.2, we spell out our alternative dual synergies framework, and examine the empirical evidence for the conceptual framework. The final section then uses this approach to interpret the historical experience of the now industrialized countries in order to give further empirical support to the discussion.

2.1 The theoretical foundations of mainstream macroeconomic policies: a critique

In order to achieve macroeconomic stability, the IFIs propose limiting the supply of money, and lowering both government expenditures and budget deficits, in addition to the current account deficit (Williamson, 1990; Stiglitz, 2002; Kuczynski and Williamson, 2003). For growth, they recommend structural reforms, which imply reducing the size and role of the government in the productive sectors as well as services, and the liberalization of trade in both the product and the capital markets (in addition to investment in the basic services and infrastructure, though not necessarily by the state). Both the stabilization and the structural reform recommendations are based on the same premiss grounded in neoclassical thinking: markets are efficient and any attempt to reduce their influence can only have deleterious effects.[4] This policy environment facing developing countries through the 1980s and 1990s was dominated by the prescriptions of an 'alliance' among traditionally powerful local interests and the international financial institutions (IFIs).[5]

When a country approaches the IMF for finance, it does so when there is a macroeconomic crisis – in the external or domestic balances, or both. To be fair to the IMF, one has to note that it prescribes policies which it believes will restore market confidence, especially in capital markets, so that funds will flow back into the country facing the crisis. The confidence of international financial markets is particularly important for emerging market economies[6] (though the prescribed policies are not dissimilar for low-income countries which are normally unable to access international financial markets). But as Krugman (1998) rightly notes,

> The overriding objective of policy must therefore be to mollify market senti-ment. But, because crises can be self-fulfilling, sound economic policy is not sufficient to gain market confidence; one must cater to the perceptions, the prejudices, and the whims of the market. Or rather, one must cater to what one hopes will be the perceptions of the market. In short, international economic policy ends having very little to do with economics.[7]

While market feeling about what constitutes sound economic policy is not arbitrary, there is little doubt that investors do tend to link the public interest with their private interest. Not surprisingly, high interest rates, open capital accounts and free entry for foreign financial service firms are seen as desirable, since they are good for foreign creditors and investors (Rodrik, 1999a; Eatwell, 1997).

We discuss these policy prescriptions by first addressing their theoretical limitations. As the theoretical shortcomings of the policy stance of the IFIs tend to be muffled in international policy dialogue, despite their continued use as the basis for policies, we briefly touch upon some of them. We then analyse what actually happened over the 1990s in respect of economic growth and poverty as a result of the implementation of orthodox policies. Further, we examine to what extent the Post-Washington Consensus, which emerged at the beginning of this decade, has really changed the character of the policy advice available to developing countries.

Some theoretical considerations

To begin with the most basic microeconomic discussion, neoclassical eco-nomics, which underlies the practice and policy advice of international (financial and) development institutions, is built on the premiss that self-interested individuals maximize utility. From this seemingly innocuous assumption follows that public policy should attempt to obtain the most utility for the maximum number of people. At the theoretical level, there have been numerous critiques of such a simplistic view of human behaviour. As Nussbaum (2000) says: 'We have to grapple with the sad fact that contemporary economics has not yet put itself onto the map of conceptually respectable theories of human action.' At the normative level, it has resulted in overreliance on the principle of Pareto optimality, which severely hinders any redistributive attempt. Sen, in various writings, has shown some of the contradictions of this approach. For instance, that a rich person may obtain very little utility from having several houses and many cars, while a poor person may be content with a small hut and a bicycle, leading to the conclusion that redistribution from the latter to the former would increase aggregate utility. The attempt to solve these paradoxes by stressing that fairness should be analysed at the level of commodities, however, also leads to some dead-ends. Actually, people need different goods and services, and more or less of them – for example, if they are sick or they live in different climates. Thus, Sen argues for a 'middle space' between commodities and utilities, which he calls 'capabilities'.[8]

Moreover, as we turn to the macroeconomic level, many other theoretical problems arise. For instance, the orthodox paradigm recommended strict monetary policies and market-determined interest rates. These should encourage savings and, hence, be a source for investment. However, investment is mostly financed with profits or borrowing, not previous savings (Minsky, 1975; Moore, 1988; Nell, 1998). As Keynesian and structuralist economists have argued (Dutt, 1990; Taylor, 2006), banks and financial institutions can lend without the existence of previous savings, leading to an endogenous-type of credit creation that ultimately undermines the strict monetary policy as proposed by the IFIs. Thus, existing high interest rates can damage investment and raise the cost to the state of public borrowing (resulting in a high budget deficit).

For limiting budget deficits, the orthodox recommendations are usually straightforward: reduction of spending and reduction of tax rates (the latter with the expectation that they will increase total revenues). Tax reductions are usually promoted because mainstream authors emphasize the effects of taxes on production efficiency. Taxes, however, play another important role that is usually unnoticed. Taxes affect the distribution of income, both directly through disposable income, and indirectly through the advantages or disincentives created to either favour or discourage the production of certain commodities (or production in certain geographical regions). Given a tax rate structure, tax rate reductions are seldom neutral. The kind of tax reduction usually advocated for 'efficiency gains' tends to lower taxes on the income of the wealthiest groups. Also, by not increasing taxes in order to reduce fiscal deficits, limits are imposed on possible future expenditures.[9]

In addition, the arguments that privatization, free trade and lower taxes promote growth and efficiency are based on dubious grounds. It is well known that the sources of prolonged growth are innovation and productivity increases, and that these, rather than efficient, highly competitive markets, characterize industrialized economies (Abramovitz, 1989; Chakravarty, 1982; Schumpeter, 1934; Solow, 1997). To understand how innovation and productivity increases come about, a model such as the evolutionary one, rather than one involving firms with absolute knowledge concerning static production functions, is needed. Such a model would stress that both inventing and adapting new technologies are a process of discovery characterized by uncertainty, rather than by probabilistic risk (Nelson and Winter, 1982). In this case, markets are not efficient and have no tendency to reach equilibrium, as they tend to change (Anderson et al., 1988; Lesourne and Orléan, 1998). Endogenous growth models of the New Growth Theory kind fail to incorporate these elements and retain the assumptions of competitive markets, leading to very weak empirical results (Pack, 1992; Verspagen, 1992). Thus, the efficiency in markets is in the eye of the beholder.

Markets, in the orthodox model, could dynamically move to an equilibrium where consumers and producers simultaneously maximize their objective functions, subject to given constraints. However, if markets are in constant flux as firms try to alter those constraints through innovation, then the very notion that taxes or import restrictions introduce distortions lacks foundation − unless, of course, the tax rates or tariff barriers are very high. In fact, some degree of protection from international competition, balanced with export opportunities and market access, is the best source of learning by doing and increasing the capacity to adapt, and eventually innovate. In fact, the emphasis on free trade tends to ignore the possibility of an economy acquiring dynamic comparative advantage as a result of this process of learning.

As part of the drive to promote economic growth, and given the ideological bias against the state, mainstream economists have recommended the privatization of state enterprises to increase efficiency. But if privatization is pushed without policies to promote competition, it can result in monopolies, which are unlikely to benefit consumers or accelerate economic activity (Stiglitz, 2002). Privatization is usually pushed by groups that wish to see their taxes reduced and perceive no benefits from government services such as education, food subsidies or water and sanitation provision (or could easily acquire them in the private market at non-subsidized prices due to their purchasing power). The proceeds of privatization also eased the budget deficit with a once-off increase in revenues. This effect is, by definition, only temporary. More permanent is the reduction in the fiscal burden of the state companies that had deficits. However, in most cases, no serious analysis has been done of the social benefits of these deficits, as long as they are not excessive[10] (e.g. maintaining low unemployment and high capacity utilization throughout the economy and, consequently, favouring investment and economic growth), or of the activities of the state companies themselves (e.g. whether the social benefits more than compensate the firms' accounting losses). We are not denying the fact of government failure, which we address in Chapters 6, 7 and 8, only discussing the pros and cons of privatization.

Besides innovation, the key to growth is continuing investment – which is financed by profits or by sustainable inflows from abroad. The latter may be more volatile than the former. Further, the focus on freeing up financial markets in mainstream policy advice may have had the adverse effect of contributing to macroeconomic instability by weakening the financial sector (Grabel, 2003). Also, the focus in orthodox policies on reducing inflation led to macroeconomic policies that may not be the most conducive for long-term economic growth. It has also distracted attention from other major sources of macroeconomic stability – that is, weak financial sectors (Stiglitz, 1998a). Bruno and Easterly (1995) have demonstrated that inflation rates of up to 40 per cent are not necessarily inimical to growth, and rates up to 15 per cent are consistent with growth. Palley (1998) has demonstrated the pernicious effects of a monetary policy that attempts to drive the inflation rate to zero.[11]

Moreover, growth is an overwhelmingly important determinant of profits, but deflationary adjustment policies driven by the desire for regaining the confidence of international capital markets (e.g. high, market-determined interest rates) may be self-defeating, as deteriorating growth sharply reduces investment, equally due to lower profits and to the expectation of lower profits in the future. As Rodrik notes,

> When the IMF acts as if markets' judgment of economic policy is independent of its own, it ends up entrenching its own vision of economic policy in the name of restoring market confidence. Just as governments often hide behind the IMF in explaining that they have no choice but to cut fiscal expenditures and raise interest rates (and do a myriad other things on top), the IMF can hide behind markets and argue that 'market confidence' requires it all. But of course this is all circular. Indeed, the interdependence between market

confidence and IMF policy preferences can lead in the limit to self-fulfilling equilibria of a rather undesirable kind. (1999a: 15–16)

The vast majority of the population need to work to earn a living. In the formal sector, people either work at the established wages and institutional arrangements (hours per day, days of the week, etc.), or they do not – there is no continuous choice set from which to pick the 'optimum' amount of work to offer. The same is true in the informal sector, the existence of which cannot be construed as an example of good practice (even if the informal sector is closer to the idealized model of the unfettered and unregulated labour market proposed by neoclassical economists). As most developing countries are without welfare or unemployment insurance mechanisms, the choice to work or starve undermines the simple choice-theoretic labour supply curve of the textbook competitive labour market. Yet it is the assumption of such a labour supply curve that underpins the high flexibility of the labour market proposed by IFIs.

There are many additional issues related to the supply of labour, which are also absent in the mainstream discussion, but which are of utmost importance when describing the real world, and in particular when thinking about policies. These are related to the role played by women in social reproduction. Not only is this role not valued economically, it is often assumed to be the 'natural' job of a woman. Not incorporating these activities, the differentially gendered roles played by women and men, and the concomitant topic of intra-households allocation in the analysis of the impact of adjustment policies, for instance, has had pernicious effects both for women and for the economy as a whole.[12]

Based on an alternative to the marginalist theory of distribution of income, it can be argued that the demand for workers is not based on the equalization of the actual existing wage to the marginal product. Rather, it is determined by a bargaining process where the number of workers required by employers depends on current and expected output (Taylor, 1991; Dutt, 1990). In other words, there are many reasons why the neoclassical explanation of how the labour market works does not quite correspond to reality.

In conjunction with the non-existence of the 'labour supply', it is not obvious that unregulated labour markets will ever attain the level of full-employment equilibrium. In this case, labour flexibility (recommended by the IFIs and their local allies) is no guarantee of full employment.[13]

Given these weak theoretical foundations, it is not a coincidence that these policies failed. Orthodox policies (based on neoclassical assumptions) have almost invariably resulted in no growth advantage, higher volatility, increased inequality, little social progress, higher unemployment and financial crises

(Barbato, 2001; Boron et al., 1999; Rodrik, 2002). A central tenet of the orthodoxy is the notion that trickle-down mechanisms exist (e.g. that growth will bring a reduction of poverty), and, therefore, no state action is necessary to ensure poverty alleviation. The faster the growth, the more quickly poverty diminishes. In this view, it is a fallacy to suppose that 'the removal of poverty requires 'direct' anti-poverty programmes, not growth' (Bhagwati, 1993). In this view, state intervention in economic affairs, inasmuch as it retards growth by assumption, will perpetuate poverty. However, there is some tension and ambiguity about the role of the public sector in the social services. Thus, it is not uncommon to find references to some cases where public action can be useful (World Bank, 1997a, 2004). Nevertheless, first, the practice rather than the precepts are biased against state involvement. There has been increasing emphasis in policy advice by the IFIs in the 1990s on privatization of social services (World Bank, 2002; IFC, 2002). Second, our position is that the separation between social and economic policies is precisely part of the problem.

The trickle-down hypothesis assumes society is composed of homogenous people with equal chances of participating in the market and finding jobs. As this assumption is not valid, empirical studies testing the trickle-down hypothesis suggest growth has not trickled down. When they do indicate the existence of trickle-down, it is because they draw inappropriate inferences from cross-sectional data about dynamic processes (Srinivasan, 1985).

Although neoclassical models based on rational choice tend to minimize the role of the state in social policy, this need not be the case, at least theoretically. Individual rationality[14] is used in these models to show the advantages of markets (efficiency, equilibrium, etc.). However, there is also an extensive literature dealing with the interaction of 'rational individuals' which leads to free-riding, Nash equilibrium, and so on. This implies the need for collaboration. Collaboration needs to be enforced, resulting in rules and regulations. To be effective these rules and regulations should emanate from a (hopefully democratically elected, participatory and representative – see Chapter 7) state which sets up and has the capacity to enforce laws. Thus, collective efforts of society are institutionalized through the state.[15]

Some empirical considerations

The reality is that in recent decades a very large number of countries have become dependent upon international policy advice, which usually comes tied to financing. The prolonged use of IMF resources has increased dramatically over the last three decades (IEO, 2003a). The Internal Evaluation Office

(IEO) of the IMF, created in 2000, has defined a prolonged user as a country that has been under IMF-supported programmes for seven or more years in a ten-year period. On this basis, 44 countries were prolonged users at some point during 1971–2000; a further 7 countries were prolonged users if precautionary arrangements are included. While 29 of them are low-income countries eligible for the Poverty Reduction and Growth Facility, that still leaves some 16 countries which would be emerging market economies. It is interesting that this growth in IMF reach was happening precisely at a time when bilateral official development assistance declined consistently, from 0.35 per cent of OECD countries' GNP in 1990 to 0.22 per cent of GNP in 2000 (see Chapter 10 for a further discussion). Naturally, the power of a multilateral institution is much greater than of any single donor in bilateral discussion with a recipient, and IMF intervention in domestic policymaking has increased commensurately.

The real issue is: what has been the experience with poverty-reduction economic growth, income distribution and economic stabilization since the orthodox economic policies became dominant? The empirical evidence over the last two decades since these orthodox policies became the dominant paradigm of economic policy (and countries privatized, liberalized trade and reduced taxes, as described above) is that it has failed to encourage growth, promote stability or reduce poverty.[16] Data from the World Bank World Development Indicators show that while GDP in developing countries grew at an annual average rate of 5 per cent (with a population growth of 1.7 per cent) between 1990 and 1997 (before the slowdown which followed the East Asian crisis), from 1965 to 1980 the GDP of developing countries increased by 6.1 per cent (while the population increased by 2.3 per cent). This indicates that in spite of the two oil crises and the stagflation of the 1970s, the earlier period characterized by state-led industrialization and restrictions on capital flows had higher per capita growth.

In spite of economic growth in developing countries (excluding China), the incidence of income-poverty (as measured by the World Bank[17]) was static between 1987 and 1998 (Ravallion, 2002). The decline from 28 to 26 per cent of the population, based on the controversial US$1-a-day measure (see, e.g., Reddy and Pogge, 2002), can be considered within the margin of error of the estimates.[18] Regionally, the same pattern applies. The 1990s saw a strong economic recovery in Latin America with average per capita income increasing by one-sixth between 1990 and 1998. The former chief economist of the World Bank noted that the region 'followed our advice and carried out some of the most successful macroeconomic stabilization programs the world has ever seen' (Stiglitz, 1998a). Nevertheless, the ranks of the income-poor increased by 6 per cent over that period, as much as the total population, which leads to a constant incidence. Hence, a decade of sustained reforms and economic liberalization has resulted in a meagre harvest in terms of social progress and equitable growth. In other words, the growth elasticity of poverty reduction was zero for this region during the 1990s.

Morley et al. (1999) constructed an index of structural reform for Latin America that quantifies the policy changes in the areas of trade liberalization, tax reform, financial liberalization, privatization, and opening up to capital flows. The average value of this index for the continent rises from around 0.47 (the maximum being 1) in the early 1970s to around 0.55 in the early 1980s, and then jumps up to 0.82 by 1995. Yet economic performance in Latin America was quite disappointing during this period. In fact, there are hardly any countries that did better in the 1990s than they did during 1950–80. And of those, only Chile is a genuine success. Of course, the relationship between 'reform' and growth is a complex one, and there is only a limited conclusion that one can draw from such a quick examination of the evidence. But the Latin American experience does suggest that the growth in the most ambitious reformers has been limited (Bustelo, 1991; Damill and Fanelli, 1994; Ocampo, 2004).

More important evidence comes from the high-performing economies of the last two decades. China and India stand out here. These two large countries have experienced a significant increase in their growth rates – China since the late 1970s, and India since the early 1980s – in a period when most other developing countries have gone the opposite way. Indeed, China's and India's performance overshadows the disappointing outcomes elsewhere, making the last two decades a developmental success on a population-weighted basis. Mukand and Rodrik (2005) note that the policies that have enabled this performance present a very awkward fit with the orthodoxy.

> China's reforms have been marked by partial liberalization, two-track pricing, limited deregulation, financial restraint, an unorthodox legal regime, and the absence of clear private property rights. India's reforms have been less distinctive, but still marked by significant departures from the rulebook. Even after the trade reforms of the early 1990s, for example, India remained one of the world's most protected economies.

India was the world tenth fastest growing economy in the 1980s, and the twelfth fastest in the 1990s. China was second (behind Korea) in the 1980s and the first in the 1990s.[19]

Thus the evidence is that the orthodox framework has not worked well either on growth or on poverty reduction. What about income distribution? Cornia (2000) argues that while within-country inequality declined in several countries during the 'Golden Age' (1950s to early 1970s), this trend was reversed with increasing frequency over the 1980s and 1990s. The rise of within-country inequality was universal in Eastern Europe and CIS, almost universal in Latin America, common in the OECD, and frequent in South, Southeast and East Asia. Trade liberalization, the rise of financial rent and changes in labour institutions have tended to increase inequality (Wood, 1994; Cornia et al., 2003).

In a market economy, people who are better educated, enjoy better health, and are already better off financially have a greater probability of contributing to growth and benefiting from it. Thus women, who in many developing countries receive little or no education, are at a serious disadvantage when it comes to the benefits of a trickle–down structural system. The same applies to those who grow up in poverty. The experience of the presently industrialized countries in the early stages of their growth suggests that the inegalitarianism of the development process derives not so much from failure to trickle down as from the failure of horizontal growth from the enclaves to the traditional sectors (Lewis, 1978). The benefits of rapid growth in the now industrialized countries accruing to the lower income groups were rather limited during the nineteenth century. Income inequality declined in these countries in the first half of the twentieth century, but not due to growth (Sundrum, 1990). Instead it was due to significant changes in the education, organization and political power of workers.

The arguments of mainstream economists stand on two platforms: that growth has no measurable effect on income distribution, and that a more egalitarian income distribution may have a positive influence on growth. Consequently, the analysis is strictly linear: equitable income distribution (and, by extension, human capital formation) helps to improve growth, and growth reduces poverty without affecting income distribution. Thus no feedback loop is possible. This is quite unlike the notion of dual synergy that we posit in the alternative approach (discussed in the following section). Moreover, both premises are factually wrong. Deininger and Squire (1996) concluded, on the basis of data for 108 countries, that 'aggregate growth was associated with an increase in the incomes of the poorest quintile in more than 85 per cent of cases'. The same authors concluded in 1998 that the 'accumulation of new assets is likely to be a more effective way of reducing poverty than efforts to redistribute existing assets'. However, the fact that income distribution changes seem orthogonal to income growth does not necessarily imply that there is no association between growth and income distribution, as Bruno, Ravallion and Squire (1996) conclude. Rather, it signifies that some policies lead to growth with worsening income distribution, and other policies lead to both improving income distribution and growth. We discuss below what some of the latter policies may be.

It is not uncommon for countries to experience a significant economic recovery during which not everyone benefits. For instance, the top decile enjoys large consumption increases, while the bottom quintile experiences an absolute decline in expenditure. Not only are the poorest fifth of the population often excluded from the benefits of growth; they actually see the depth and severity of their income-poverty increase – in other words, the number of people in extreme poverty increases. Although the inability of growth to reach the poorest groups are common in Africa (Demery and Squire, 1996; World Bank, 1997a), in East Asia the benefits of growth have been shared more widely (Ahuja et al., 1997). Only inclusive, equitable, employment-generating growth can reduce poverty in a sustained manner.[20]

On recent critiques of mainstream economic policies

So far we have argued against the policy prescriptions of the dominant paradigm by highlighting their weak theoretical underpinnings and unfavour-able actual outcomes. We showed that the neoclassical models that underlay the policy advice emanating from that paradigm are incomplete. Also, empirical evidence shows that the long years of reforms based on mainstream orthodoxy have resulted in higher economic instability (Stiglitz, 2002; Fine et al., 2001), lower per capita income growth and imperceptible declines in poverty when compared to previous decades or countries, like those in East Asia, which flouted the traditional advice.

The improvement upon the orthodox consensus that prevailed until the 1990s comes from the recognition of the damage caused by pro-cyclical policies (e.g. the IMF recommendation to cut expenditures during the East Asian crisis, when output should have been expanded through fiscal policy). Regarding this policy stance and criticism of the IFIs, mostly associated with Joseph Stiglitz, it is clear that it is similar to the critique of adjustment by, *inter alia*, Cornia, Jolly and Stewart (1987), almost two decades ago. Thus, Stiglitz (2002) concentrates on the negative impact of contractionary measures on wages and unemployment. These result in lower household income, which leads to undesirable health and education outcomes. He also criticizes the way some trade liberalization, capital account opening, and privatization have taken place because they failed to include provisions to protect the poorest segments of society.[21]

The main thrust of what Stiglitz proposes is in line with orthodox thinking (smaller state, safety nets, etc.) (Standing, 2000), not an alternative view based on a different concept of society (based on capability expansion at the individual level and equity in terms of distribution of income and assets at the societal level). Certainly, he consistently advocates for a more equitable distribution of income (although less often about the distribution of assets), with people enjoying more freedom, a better standard of living, and the opportunity to participate in decision-making. He also introduces the need to protect the environment. But none of these is a serious threat to orthodox thinking, nor is any a new idea (Srinivasan, 2000).

In addition, Stiglitz's theoretical writings (on asymmetric and imperfect information) are basically a refinement/extension of orthodox models. Many people would consider asymmetric and imperfect information merely 'accidents' or 'imperfections', not as pervasive as Stiglitz claims them to be. Theoretically the problem is that the way markets, left to themselves, are and behave results in inefficient, wasteful and inequitable outcomes; these are not imperfections based on lack of information (Eatwell and Milgate, 1983; Fine, 2001).

There is controversy in the literature about how radically different or traditional the Post-Washington Consensus thinking is, whether the theoretical model actually underpinning its policy prescriptions is fundamentally different from the orthodox one, and the extent to which orthodox policy advice actually changed (Mukand and Rodrik, 2005; Jomo and Fine, 2005; Jomo, 2005; Standing, 2000). In that context we may ask: are critical comments by Stiglitz, and a few other mainstream economists (e.g. Sachs, 2005), merely debates about implementation issues?

There is, indeed, a mutation in the language. Erstwhile Policy Framework Papers are now called Poverty Reduction Strategy Papers (PRSPs), and the Extended Structural Adjustment Facility is called the Poverty Reduction and Growth Facility (PRGF). Poverty reduction concerns are built into the PRSPs now. We recognize that substantively, too, what has changed is that, on average, PRGF-supported programmes target a smaller and more gradual fiscal consolidation than under ESAF, and give more weight to revenue increases than to expenditure contraction (IEO, 2004). However, even here the Internal Evaluation Office of the IMF finds that the outcomes are not very different between Extended Structural Adjustment Facility loans and its renamed successor, the Poverty Reduction and Growth Facility. Furthermore, the IMF's traditional approach to programme design does not take sufficient account of the underlying determinants of growth, nor of the factors that influence the response of the real economy to macroeconomic policies, nor of potential feedback of macro-policy on poverty. PRGF programmes are still calling for rapid state-owned enterprise (SOE) reform, on the assumption of a rapid 'crowding in' of private-sector aggregate demand – regardless of whether the evidence for rapid crowding in from private agents exists. Besides, even the IMF's Internal Evaluation Office observed after interviews and questionnaires with authorities of prolonged users of IMF resources: 'The views expressed regarding the impact of prolonged use on the policy formulation process were generally negative, in particular because program negotiations were often characterized as proceeding in a way that left too little space for policy debate and the formulation of homegrown policies' (IEO, 2003a).

Why should this matter, especially for the poor? For at least three reasons. One, the evidence on growth – which is taken axiomatically to be as good for the poor – is rather mixed in most countries that have followed the economic policies recommended since 1980. Without faster growth whereby the incomes of the poor grow proportionally faster than those of the non-poor, poverty cannot be reduced. Hence, if economic policies are failing in terms of growth, with an increased health/education emphasis in PRSPs policies may be giving with one hand what they are taking from the poor with another.

Two, since financial liberalization restricts the scope and space for domestic fiscal and monetary policies, there is a case for limiting the degree of financial liberalization expected in orthodox policy advice. As Dervis (2005) notes: 'It is now again increasingly recognized, not only by left-wing critics but also by mainstream economists, that capital markets are not the incredibly efficient processors of information that market fundamentalists would have us believe. Instead, capital markets display substantial amounts of herd behaviour' (2005: 105–6), where a reversal of capital inflows may lead to economic collapse (as happened in Thailand in 1997 followed by a number of East Asian economies, and in Russia, followed by a number of Latin American ones in 1998, and in Turkey in 2001). These economic collapses following upon financial outflows proved damaging for the poor in each of these countries.

Three, the hierarchy of 'economic policy first, then social policy' means that policy performance is determined not by whether human well-being or child well-being has been enhanced but by whether, as in the 20 Country Policy and Institutional Assessment indicators (see Chapter 1 n1), average tariffs have fallen to as close to 10 per cent or not, the investment climate has provided a level playing field between foreign and domestic investors, and how many state-owned enterprises have been privatized – regardless of whether these policies are home-grown or not, and regardless of their impact on the poor. Policies are recommended without clarifying or analysing this macro–micro linkage. In fact, the IEO (2004) clearly states that IMF staff admit that the impact of macroeconomic policies upon the poor (the macro–micro linkage) is not fully understood by the IMF, and actually the IMF does not have enough staff strength to monitor that impact in any case for each country.

No one is suggesting here that donors, and especially Bretton Woods institutions (BWIs), do not set minimum criteria for lending; the point is that those should be *minimum* criteria, and they should enable donors to choose *between* countries when trying to allocate resources, and not try to overdetermine an individual country's macroeconomic policy, once a decision has been taken to allocate resources to that country (over another country). Nor is one suggesting that countries should not be encouraged and supported to ensure that basic health and basic education are prioritized. In fact, they should be. Yet at the same time, in both Highly Indebted Poor Countries and high-debt emerging market economies which are dependent on external resources, there needs to be greater scope for determining macroeconomic policies based on a domestic consensus.[22]

What we have now is the opposite. As ODA fell from 0.35 per cent of OECD countries' GNP in 1990 to 0.22 of GNP in 2000, the magnitude of BWI, especially IMF, funding increased. The number of prolonged users of IMF funds rose – as we noted above. It is ironic that the IMF was always intended, in its core operational approach, to focus on achieving a restoration of external and domestic balance and sustainability *within a short period of time.* It was the World Bank that was meant to be the development institution. However, the IMF has become involved in prolonged lending to the same group of countries. Thus, over time, the IMF has become embedded in local policymaking. As the IEO of the IMF notes:

> the reluctance of donors to maintain their aid flows at a level consistent with the intended diminished reliance on IMF lending, implied that the IMF would have to remain involved either through repeated programs until a sustainable external situation could be reached, or withdraw from the country concerned midway in the process before external viability could be achieved. (IEO, 2003a)

Given that orthodox policies failed in terms of their own criteria of promoting economic growth and stability, it might be worth taking seriously the IEO's suggestion which would expand the space for local decisions in macroeconomic policymaking. The IEO says, first, that the IMF should let domestic 'authorities ... have the initial responsibility for proposing a reform program, which should be the starting point for negotiations'; second, that the core elements of the programme should be 'subject first to a domestic policy debate within the member country's own policymaking institutions'; and, third, that Article IV surveillance reports should 'actively seek to present alternative policy options and to analyse the trade-off between them so as to encourage an open debate on alternative policy options'.

If until the early 1990s international financial institutions focused on making the case that market incentives are critical to economic development, by the late 1990s there was a strong recognition that market incentives alone are not enough, and that they have to be 'underpinned by strong public institutions' (see e.g. World Bank, 1997a, 2000a, 2004). However, after the Asian economic crisis of 1997, IMF programmes in the region prescribed a series of structural reforms in the following areas: banking, business–government relations, corporate governance, bankruptcy laws, labour-market institutions, and industrial policy. In fact, these prescriptions were part of a new financial architecture with a set of codes and standards – on fiscal transparency, monetary and financial policy, banking supervision, data dissemination, corporate governance and structure, accounting standards – which were meant to be applicable to all countries, but directed particularly at developing countries. In addition, the Uruguay Round of global trade agreements – on intellectual property rights, subsidies and investment-related measures – harmonizes practices in the developing countries with those in the industrialized countries (Rodrik, 2000). This new view of development means an increase in conditionality and a restriction of the domestic space within which policy is formulated and conducted – a concern that the IMF's IEO itself is raising, as we noted above. This view also ignores the fact that the historical evidence of high-performing economies suggests, first, that market economies can coexist with a diverse range of institutional arrangements, not just the ones that are being recommended; and, second, when market-oriented reforms fit well with pre-existing institutional capabilities, the chances of success are demonstrably greater.

If income poverty generally has declined sharply in much of Southeast Asia, China, Vietnam, and now in India, the question worth asking is whether the economic policies and the institutional arrangements that they have followed are what mainstream economists were recommending. The consensus of the literature, starting with Stiglitz, is that they are not. Instead, they followed selective industrial policies; instead of financial liberalization, South Korea used its heavily controlled financial system to channel credit to industrial firms willing to undertake investments. They import-substituted until such time that it was unnecessary. In the social sectors they did not apply user charges (see next chapter for further discussion). China reduced its tariffs only at the end of 1990s, and mostly after joining the WTO in 2001, long after its industrial boom was well in place. India carried out partial and gradual reforms. The contrasts between East Asia and Latin America here are instructive; just as the contrasts between China and Russia have been rightly drawn attention to by many economists (e.g. Nolan 1995).[23] In fact, Chang (2003) has argued, the industrialized countries inappropriately expect developing countries today to have institutions that took the rich countries a century to acquire.

2.2 An alternative approach

As growth did not improve after liberalization but volatility ensued while the poverty incidence barely changed outside China and India through the 1990s, the theoretical basis of orthodox policies has been increasingly questioned. Thus, an alternative framework for policies is necessary. In this alternative framework, we posit that two kinds of synergies could exist – and the state could actively intervene to trigger and take advantage of them. One exists between interventions in health, nutrition, family planning, water and sanitation, and basic education. The other is between interventions resulting in income growth, the reduction of poverty and access to basic services. With these ends in view, we propose an alternative approach to integrate economic and social policies.

One may well wonder why we propose income-poverty reduction as a goal, rather than reduction of inequality. That is because not all reductions in inequality will reduce poverty, particularly if the reductions in inequality are among those in the richest six or seven deciles of the population. Ravallion (2004) defines pro-poor growth as any increase in GDP that reduces poverty. Such a definition is too broad: it implies that most real-world instances of growth are pro-poor, even if poverty decreases only slightly and income distribution worsens during a period of strong growth, or inequality improves but leaves the incomes of the poorest where they were. A more appropriate definition has growth as pro-poor if in addition to reducing poverty it also decreases inequality. Despite being an improvement, this definition still does not reflect well what should be understood as 'pro-poor growth' and falls short of providing straightforward answers to various plausible combinations of growth, poverty reduction and inequality changes. Kakwani et al. (2004), van der Hoeven and Shorrocks (2003) and others have proposed a simple and sensible definition, according to which growth is pro-poor, relatively speaking, if it benefits the poor proportionally more than the non-poor.[24]

We suggest that the state has a critical role to play in ensuring all three desirable outcomes (economic growth, income–poverty reduction and access to basic services). The policy implications that derive from these two synergies are quite distinct from the policies proposed by the IFIs. We elaborate on alternative policies consistent with the alternative framework, which fundamentally derive from the need to incorporate a social dimension in the formulation of economic policies.

The synergy among the expansion of functionings, income-poverty reduction,[22] and economic growth

In attempting to understand the positive experience of recently industrialized countries or of high-achieving developing countries, we are struck by the difficulty of establishing causality relationships. For example, despite widespread literacy within a population, many countries (e.g. Sri Lanka) have not achieved rapid growth, although education is a major determinant of such economic growth. There are also examples of countries with relatively rapid economic growth but persistent income-poverty (e.g. Botswana). Thus, no single element can be specified as the main cause (or 'development magic bullet') for success in all areas. Pritchett and Woolcock (2002), Easterly (1999) and Levine and Radelet (1992) discuss various shortcomings of econometric estimates that attempt (and fail) to establish these relationships.

We would argue that interventions to promote expansion of human functionings, reduction of income-poverty and economic growth support and strengthen each other in a synergistic way or through various feedback loops. This synergy can be succinctly expressed as the enhanced impact changes in an independent variable have on the growth rate of a dependent variable, given the presence of a third variable. This leads to several important, and often overlooked, interrelated effects in terms of policy. The impact of a policy (e.g. redistribution to reduce poverty directly) on another variable (say economic growth) crucially depends on the level of a third variable (e.g. health and educational status). In other words, economic growth will be faster and more sustainable if (income) poverty is reduced simultaneously through direct policies aimed at the income-poor and the health and educational status of the population is higher. A widely recognized example, and one often mentioned even by mainstream economists, is that economic growth will be more successful in reducing income-poverty – that is, the elasticity of poverty-reduction will be higher – when human capital is more equitably distributed. We do not deny this. We simply stress that this is only one of the interactions among interventions. What we have in mind can be expressed algebraically in three separate equations:

(1) GNP per capita growth = f_1 (technical/structural change, macroeconomic policies, expansion of functionings, income-poverty reduction)

GNP per capita growth is determined by the expansion of functionings, the pace of poverty reduction, by sustainable macroeconomic balances as well as by productivity increases through technical/structural change. Investment will generate growth by utilizing additional factors of production (land, labour, capital), and/or by using existing productive factors more efficiently, and thus more productively. Technical change within existing economic activities can enhance productivity. Structural change occurs in the economy when sectors which are more productive (e.g. industry or certain kinds of services are compared to most traditional agriculture) come to occupy a higher share of output than agriculture. Thus, GNP per capita growth is not chosen by governments, but is the result of public policies and private decisions. Moreover, the latter are not independent of the former. Public investment, especially in infrastructure, will often crowd in private investment. Consequently, public policies do need to take into account the effects on private decisions. Contrary to what many traditional economists think, the engine of growth (its main determinant) is not macroeconomic policy but technological change. Of course, stable prices and low interest rates contribute to a favourable context in which firms would invest. However, this does not mean that macroeconomic stability per se results in economic growth, as evidenced by the standard error of the regressions that try, but fail, to establish this point. In fact, a privately led boom could result in imbalances. Simply stated, economic growth is usually irregular.

Now consider the determinants of income-poverty.

(2) Income-poverty reduction = f_2 (GNP per capita, expansion of functionings, asset distribution)

As with economic growth, the primary income distribution is not in the hands of government to decide, but emerges from market results and relative bargaining power between the owners of factors of production. The distribution of income, in turn, affects the incidence of income-poverty. Nevertheless, the government through both regulation and overall management of macroeconomic policies[26] (captured in the GNP per cap growth variable) can also affect income distribution. It can use fiscal policy to affect the after-tax income streams (the secondary income distribution), correcting the excesses of the market and reducing income-poverty. Moreover, the distribution of assets can be altered (e.g. land reform, titling, distribution of shares, etc.), which in turn will affect income distribution (more on this in section 3.1). Finally, a fundamental way in which the government can also influence distribution is through the provision of services and transfers (the tertiary income distribution), which builds and enhances functionings and provides a modicum of security (of work and income, during working life and during old age). This requires separate treatment, as it affects what we call the second synergy.

(3) Functionings expansion = f_3 (GNP per capita growth, income-poverty reduction, social policy)

This is the better-known synergy. Education, health, sanitation, the elements which enable people to enjoy the functionings that make life worth living, have myriad interaction effects among them (see UNICEF, 1998b; UNDP HDR, 1998, for details on this synergy). Obviously, additional resources (at the household level and nationally) through economic growth help. However, as many country experiences show, 'unaimed opulence' is not sufficient. Public action in terms of social policy is fundamental in enhancing functionings. Social policy here refers specifically to three elements: health, education and social insurance/assistance. Appropriate social and fiscal policies are the strongest card in the suite of policies available to impact the level of functionings.

A simple example linking these three equations, only for illustrative purposes, would work as follows. Both technological change and appropriate macroeconomic policies are needed for economic growth and tend to reinforce each other. Similarly, macroeconomic policies and the expansion of functionings through social policy should work together. Macroeconomic stabilization policies that increase unemployment and reduce wages do not induce positive synergies. On the contrary, they tend to reduce welfare and functionings, undermining the feedback loop.[27] Fiscal policies should be implemented to channel resources to the poorest (where they will have the largest impact in enhancing functionings), thus the need to integrate macroeconomic and social policies. Policies to distribute assets and income are fundamental for poverty reduction and economic growth, which we discuss below. It can be perceived intuitively, then, that a series of small, strategic interventions can unleash a powerful virtuous circle. This example shows not only the importance of jointly devising economic and social policy, but also how the three-equation framework can highlight deficiencies in traditional policymaking, with macroeconomic policy determined first, and social policy in a follower role meant to pick up the pieces.

Empirically, there is evidence supporting the view synthesized in the three synergetic equations. Not all countries that made great strides in health and education achieved substantial and long-lasting reductions in income-poverty. This is partly the result of slow economic growth. Indeed, the relationship between economic growth, income-poverty and enhancement of functionings is a complex one. A simple framework to describe these linkages and some empirical evidence is presented below.

This problem can best be described if one takes two of the variables at a time. Starting with economic growth and income-poverty, four possibilities exist:

- Economic growth is accompanied by income-poverty reduction (the one combination highlighted in the literature; for example, Republic of Korea during the 1960s–1980s).
- Economic growth is not accompanied by income-poverty reduction (if income distribution deteriorates significantly; for example, Argentina during the 1990s).
- Stagnation or negative economic growth is accompanied by income-poverty reduction (in the presence of redistributive policies; for example, Nicaragua in the 1980s).
- Stagnation or negative economic growth is not accompanied by income-poverty reduction (a more common occurrence; for example, Indonesia in the late 1990s).

There are also four potential outcomes of interactions between economic growth and functionings enhancement:

- Economic growth and enhancement of functionings happen at the same time (a sort of ideal case; for example, Malaysia during the 1970s and 1980s).
- Economic growth occurs but there is no advance on capability enhancement (economic growth with little spillover on human capital formation; for example, Brazil during the 1970s).
- Stagnation or low economic growth but significant capability enhancement happens (when public policies allow expansion of effective and inexpensive social services; for example, Sri Lanka in the 1980s, the Indian state of Kerala over 1960–90).
- Stagnation or low economic growth with limited advance in capability enhancement (a tragically all too common case, especially in many sub-Saharan countries, characterized by retrogression in health outcomes partly due to HIV/AIDS).

As in the previous set of combinations, all these possibilities actually are observed among developing countries. One thing is clear: there is no need to wait for economic growth in order to achieve improvements in enhancement of functionings. Also, although it is true that enhancement of functionings (especially education) is conducive to economic growth, its presence does not always lead to economic growth (e.g. if excessively open trade policies destroy jobs). Moreover, economic growth can take place even if there is not much enhancement of functionings, primarily if the income growth occurs in only a few sectors or certain enclaves, but growth is unlikely to be sustained under the circumstances.

Finally, the relationship between income-poverty and the level of functionings could take any of the following forms:

- Enhancement of functionings and income-poverty reduction go hand in hand (as individuals have more capabilities or human capital, their capacity to earn higher income and lift themselves above the poverty line increases; for example, China in the 1980s).
- Enhancement of functionings occurs but there is limited reduction in income-poverty (unequal asset distribution and/or jobless growth prevents income-poverty reduction; for example, Botswana in the 1980s and early 1990s, or Brazil in the 1990s).
- Enhancement of functionings does not take place but income-poverty is reduced (as when income or asset redistribution policies are implemented; we found no empirical evidence for this theoretical possibility).[28]
- Enhancement of functionings does not take place and income-poverty is not reduced (the most common case, especially in sub-Saharan Africa).

This set of combinations, like the two previous ones, highlights that enhancement of functionings is neither necessary nor sufficient for income-poverty reduction, nor is income-poverty reduction necessary nor sufficient for enhancement of functionings. The same applies to the other combinations between economic growth and income-poverty reduction and between economic growth and enhancement of functionings.

In spite of our dual synergy framework solving some puzzles (i.e. why does a country with high human capital seem unable to generate growth?[29]), the lingering question is: if there are no sufficient or necessary conditions linking these ends, are they unrelated? The answer is, yes they are related, but in a complex way. Although neither element is necessary or sufficient for the advancement of the other, they help each other. Thus, for instance, the effectiveness of industrial policy in inducing economy-wide productivity growth, or non-agricultural employment in rural areas, will be enhanced in the widespread presence of functionings, in turn resulting in higher rates of income growth. Similarly, in the presence of rapid enhancement of functionings, economic growth will have a much stronger impact on income-poverty as the poor take advantage of market opportunities.

The argument is supported by empirical evidence. As we argued above, using bivariate analysis, some countries experienced strong linkages between economic growth and enhancement of functionings. Resources generated by economic growth were used to enhance functionings, which in turn furthered economic growth. However, in several other countries these linkages were weak. Lack of economic growth prevented investment in health and education, which in turn undermined economic growth.

We can now turn that bivariate analysis by incorporating all three variables. An empirical exercise can help to underscore these interactions.[30] There are serious restrictions on the availability of data on changes in income-poverty. Nevertheless, there are close to fifty countries for which data are available on the incidence of income-poverty (based on national poverty lines) at the beginning of the 1990s. For these countries, the *under-5 mortality rate* (U5MR) in 1990 was used as a proxy for enhancement of functionings.[31] Also, the *average annual per capita income growth rate* for the period 1990 to 2000 is available. The countries were classified according to their *initial incidence of income poverty* as: high (a head count ratio of over 50 per cent of the population), medium (between 50 and 30 per cent), and low (less than 30 per cent). Also, they were grouped in terms of their levels of U5MR: high (over 170 per 1,000 live births), medium (between 170 and 70), and low (less than 70).

With these classifications, nine groups of countries can be formed (Table 2.1). The findings are revealing, and tend to confirm our earlier theoretical framework of dual synergies. Few countries combined low U5MR and high income-poverty or high U5MR and low income-poverty. An interesting pattern emerges when the growth rates of per capita income are compared among the remaining seven groups. Countries with high U5MR experienced negative growth in per capita income. Even countries with medium U5MR but with high income-poverty experienced negative economic growth (the top-left three figures in Table 2.1), suggesting that poverty and low levels of human capital are actually inimical to economic growth. Countries falling in the other combinations (medium or low levels of both U5MR and income-poverty) experienced positive growth. Moreover, the rates of growth were highest when the initial level of income-poverty and U5MR was lowest (the bottom-right cell).

In other words, countries with rapid enhancement of functionings (low U5MR) and low income-poverty experienced faster growth than countries with low U5MR and medium levels of income-poverty. Nevertheless, it

Table 2.1 Economic growth by level of income-poverty and enhancement of functionings (average annual growth rate of per capita income, 1990–2000)

Income-poverty	U5MR		
	High	Medium	Low
High	−1.6	−0.5	0.5
Medium	−2.6	0.9	1.9
Low		0.6	2.7

Sources: Tabatabai, 1996; UNICEF, *State of the World's Children*, various issues; and World Bank, *World Development Report*, various issues.

cannot be stated, as it was explained above, that either (or their joint presence) is necessary or sufficient.

Although these figures show only correlation, they strongly suggest that basic social services are of fundamental importance in triggering the virtuous circle between economic growth, income-poverty reduction and enhancement of functionings.

A fundamental point about synergy between the three types of intervention is that in strategies where one is absent, the effect of interventions to achieve the other goals is less than what it would otherwise be (see Table 2.2). Policies that focus largely on *economic growth* without much regard for income-poverty reduction or enhancement of functionings are doomed to unequal income distribution or lower levels of functionings (than otherwise possible), which will dampen economic prospects in the long run. This policy of 'unaimed opulence', as Sen (Drèze and Sen, 1989)[32] calls this strategy, represents a failure of a development plan in converting the benefits of output growth into enhancement of functionings or poverty reduction.

Policies that focus only on *enhancement of functionings* (poverty reduction), and ignore economic growth and income-poverty reduction (enhancement of functionings), will lead to outcomes that are not sustainable. Depending on initial conditions, these policies could eliminate poverty and/or provide minimum access to high quality basic social services. However, in the absence of economic growth the situation could be unsustainable or, if achieved and sustained, it could preclude further progress (e.g. if the rest of the world continues discovering new health improvements). These policies could also imply a politically unfeasible redistribution of income.

A 'growth-mediated' strategy, following Sen's terminology, could be translated into enhancement of functionings (poverty reduction) through

Table 2.2 A heuristic schema of development strategies and synergies

Enhancement of functionings	Poverty reduction	Economic growth	Result
–	–	–	Disaster
–	–	+	Unaimed opulence
–	+	–	Sustainability at risk[†]
–	+	+	Growth mediated[*]
+	–	–	Sustainability at risk[†]
+	–	+	Growth mediated[*]
+	+	–	Support-led[*]
+	+	+	Synergy

Notes: A + sign implies an active policy is present, while a – sign implies no active interventions to enhance functionings, reduce poverty or promote economic growth. * These strategies could eventually work, but are risky and may take too long to impact the lives of the poor. † For political as well as economic reasons; also further progress could be curtailed (see text).

supportive social policy (transfers), which eventually could lead to poverty reduction (enhancement of functionings). A growth–mediated strategy may also help people expand their functionings as higher income may enable command over goods and services and to make use of them if growth leads to more jobs. However, a growth–mediated strategy is a risky proposition, as many elements may not materialize in this long causal chain. Moreover, it could represent unconscionable delay for those at the bottom of the socioeconomic pyramid.

Policies that focus mainly on direct *income-poverty reduction* (e.g. asset re-distribution or food-for-work programmes, or cash transfers, or social security arrangements for workers, as discussed in section 3.1 below) and enhancement of functionings and ignore macroeconomic balances or interventions promoting technological change that are critical to economic growth (i.e. a 'support-led' strategy according to Sen) run the risk of both economic and social stagnation or reversal, especially if the economy suffers from an exogenous shock.

Mainstream economists tend to suggest that 'economic growth typically does promote human development, and a strong positive relationship is evident from the line of best fit (the 'regression')' (Ravallion, 1997; see also World Bank, 2001a, and the critique by Stiglitz, 2002). When growth and poverty or growth and enhancement of functionings indicators are modelled, it is usually argued that it is growth that influences health indicators or poverty, and rarely the other way around. In other words, a policy of 'unaimed opulence' is assumed. 'Economic growth typically promotes human development' is usually the hypothesis, which is proven by the use of regressions, where the regression line is (by its construction) the expected effect of growth on a human development indicator or on poverty. Where growth failed to deliver income gains to the poor, or to promote non-income dimensions of welfare (e.g. access to schooling and health care), such cases are called 'quite untypical' (Ravallion, 1997). It is rarely stated that correlation never proves causation. It is acknowledged that 'there are deviations (the 'residuals') around this line; these are cases with unusually low, or unusually high, performance in human development at a given level of income or a given rate of economic growth' (Ravallion, 1997). It is also argued that the human development approach, which we espouse, devotes 'more attention to residuals' and 'the regression line is ignored'. Indeed, orthodox policy analysis has traditionally placed faith in the outcomes of cross-country (or inter-temporal) regression analysis, rather than explaining the reasons why some countries divert from these average trends and are 'outliers'. To us, the outliers demonstrate that it is possible for countries to relieve the non-income dimensions of poverty and achieve social indicators comparable to those of industrialized countries regardless of the level of income (Mehrotra and Jolly, 1997).

The poor should not have to wait for the benefits of economic growth. We do not downplay economic growth; but as economic growth is such a predominant part of the orthodox paradigm, the pace at which social outcomes improve appears to be at a discount. A synergy exists between poverty-reduction, enhancement of functionings and economic growth, which does not put increasing the growth rate on a pedestal higher than the other two variables (i.e. enhancement of functionings and direct poverty reduction). Instead, it calls for the integration of social and economic policy – with the main instruments in the hands of the state being consistent fiscal and macroeconomic policies, which promote all three desired objectives or ends simultaneously.

2.3 The industrialized countries: the state, the market economy and the capabilities of labour in historical perspective

In the previous section, an alternative framework to the neoclassical model of the interaction between economic and social development was presented. This approach, which is based on the synergy among basic social services (discussed further in the next chapter), as well as income-poverty reduction, economic growth and human capital formation, is used here to interpret the historical experience of presently industrialized countries in order to give empirical support to the theoretical discussion. Also, a major conclusion of the previous section – the need for state involvement in this process – is highlighted by the industrialized countries.

In this section, we begin by briefly discussing the role of the state in the emergence of market economies in the presently industrialized countries. We then tackle the two arguments concerning the interplay of the synergies and the role of the state in industrialized countries during the nineteenth century. We focus initially on the UK with a discussion of the evolution of the labour market and laissez-faire. This is subsequently complemented with a third line of argument interwoven in the country-by-country discussion, which suggests that the process involved important political conflicts. The emphasis is again on the UK and relates to developments in education and health.

The market economy in the currently industrialized countries would not have come into existence but for the state; the state was critical in establishing key institutions of the market economy (Polanyi, 1944). In the UK, the state was responsible for bringing land into the market economy through its programme of enclosing common land; thereby it also set in motion a process which ultimately led to the creation of a national market for labour (Barrington Moore, 1966).

While the Industrial Revolution began in England in the last quarter of the eighteenth century, it can hardly be said that an integrated national economic system existed until the second quarter of the nineteenth century. No market economy was conceivable that did not include a market for labour; but to establish such a market, especially in England's rural civilization, a complete transformation of the traditional fabric of society was needed. In fact, during the most active period of the Industrial Revolution, from 1795 to 1834, various laws, rules and traditions prevented the creation of a labour market in England. A national market for labour did not form because of strict legal restrictions on its physical mobility, since the labourer was practically bound to his parish. The Act of Settlement of 1662, which laid down the rules of so-called parish serfdom, existed until 1795. When it was loosened that year, it was replaced by another law (Speenhamland Law, 1795), which lasted until 1834 and reinforced a paternalistic system of labour organization. It granted subsidies in aid of wages, so that a minimum income was assured to the poor, irrespective of their earnings through wage labour, and thus encouraged them to stay on the land. This was financed from parish-based rates (taxes). Thus, on the one hand, a new gigantic wave of enclosed common land was bringing land into the market economy and producing a rural proletariat compelled to earn a living by offering their labour for sale. On the other hand, the laws mentioned above precluded them from earning a living by their labour. However, this changed with the repeal of those laws, and a national market for labour was created by the action of the state, which enabled labour to offer itself for employment in the factory system and the 'satanic mills'.

'The road to the free market was opened and kept open by an enormous increase in continuous, centrally organized and controlled interventionism' (Polanyi, 1944). Witness the complexity of the provisions in the innumerable enclosure laws; the amount of bureaucratic control involved in the administration of the New Poor Laws, which were supervised by a central authority; or the increase in governmental administration entailed in municipal reform. Yet this government interference was meant to organize simple freedoms, such as that of land, labour and municipal administration. The introduction of free markets, far from doing away with the need for control, regulation and intervention, enormously increased their range.

As Polanyi puts it aptly, 'While the laissez faire economy was the product of deliberate state action, subsequent restrictions on laissez faire started in a spontaneous way. Laissez faire was planned; planning was not' (1944: 141). He also makes clear this is not to be interpreted as a conscious planning exercise. He means that the emergence of laissez-faire was not a natural development, but one led by state policies. These state policies in turn responded to different interests and pressures and was against the views of those who thought that a society based on the pursuit of self-interest was unworkable (Hirschman, 1977).

The voices of those who opposed the 'rule of the market' changed after the implementation of free markets. This growth of administration over the market was reflected in Jeremy Bentham's utilitarianism. When industrial capitalism was in full swing, the liberal creed, intent on the spreading of the market system, was met by a protective counter-movement leaning towards its restriction. However, this counter-movement did not appear to be due to any preference for socialism or nationalism on the part of concerted interests, but seemed, rather, to be a practical reaction prompted by the expansion of the market mechanism.

Adam Smith (1776) pointed out the role of the state in 'erecting and maintaining those public institutions and those public works, though they may be in the highest degree advantageous to a great society, are, however, of such a nature, that the profit could never repay the expense to any individual.' Such works were 'those for facilitating the commerce of the society, and those for promoting the instructions of the people' (1937: 681). Each of the

European countries passed through a period of free trade and laissez-faire, followed by a period of 'anti-liberal' or social legislation and measures in regard to public health, education, public utilities, municipal trading, social insurance, trade associations and factory conditions (Polanyi, 1944). This was as true of Victorian England as of Bismarck's Prussia, of France (Third Republic) and of the postbellum United States.

There is an amazing diversity of matters on which action was taken by the state, including basic health, sanitation and education. Herbert Spencer cited a list of interventions when accusing liberals of having abandoned and deserted their principles. In 1860, authority was given to provide 'analysts of food and drink to be paid out of local rates'. There followed an Act providing 'the inspection of gas works' and an extension of the Mines Act 'making it penal to employ boys under twelve not attending schools and unable to read and write'. In 1861, power was given to 'poor law guardians to enforce vaccination'. In 1862, there was an Act giving the Council of Medical Education exclusive right 'to furnish a Pharmacopoeia, the price of which is to be fixed by the Treasury', and in 1863 came the 'extension of compulsory vaccination to Scotland and Ireland'. There was also an Act appointing inspectors for the 'wholesomeness, or unwholesomeness of food'; a Chimney Sweeper's Act, meant to prevent the torture and eventual death of children set to sweep too-narrow slots; and a Contagious Diseases Act. Spencer used these as evidence of an anti-liberal conspiracy.

Nevertheless, these were helpful in both establishing and strengthening capitalism through the mitigation of social costs (their most visible and direct objective), but also by promoting growth through a healthier, better trained workforce, safer markets for consumers and newer areas of investment. Thus, social and economic development occurred together and reinforced each other as growth transformed societies and states took up different and expanding roles (Nell, 1992).

From a human development perspective, two fundamental outcomes were achieved in education and health. One was that most European countries saw a consistent rise in the literacy rate during much of the nineteenth century, most notably during the second half. In the early nineteenth century, learning became equated with formal, systematic schooling, and 'schooling became a fundamental feature of the state' (Green, 1990). The second was that child mortality declined simultaneously, most notably after the last quarter of the century (see Figure 2.1). The two other trends that characterized this period were rising per capita income and increasing state involvement in social services (e.g. health, education and water provision). The rest of this section presents four country narratives (the UK, the USA, France, Germany) to

Figure 2.1   Mortality in the UK, France and Germany, 1840–1905
(crude death rate/1,000)

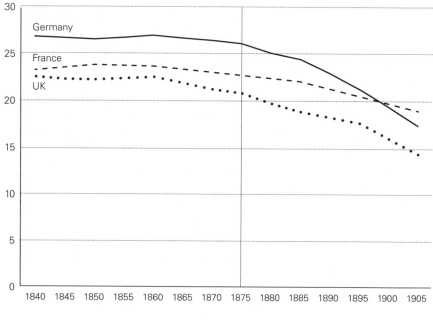

Source: Maddison, 1982.

illustrate some common themes regarding the conflicts and arguments about state involvement, the financing of social services, their impact on well-being, and their relationship with economic growth.

The United Kingdom

Throughout the nineteenth century, the economy grew, driven by industrialization. It is estimated that GDP per capita almost doubled between 1820 and 1850, and doubled once more between 1850 and 1900. However, as observed in Figure 2.1, it was not until after the 1870s that the mortality rate declined appreciably. Two elements could help to explain this: increases in education levels and the introduction of health policies.

The motives of both the educators and the educated need examination. The drive for mass literacy occurred particularly over the period 1830 to 1870. First, churches were concerned with the salvation of souls and the winning back of the non-believing working-class urban populations. The Established Anglican Church not only interpreted the behaviour of many

Figure 2.2   GDP per capita, adult literacy rate and mortality, UK
1840–1905

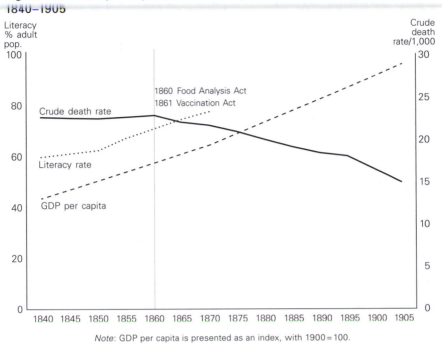

Note: GDP per capita is presented as an index, with 1900 = 100.

Source: Maddison, 1982.

of its lower-class members as 'unchristian', but also felt itself under attack
from a revival of Nonconformity and Catholicism in the 1830s. Second, at a
more secular level, the long period of endemic social unrest from the 1790s
to the 1840s, from food riots to Chartism, had created a deep anxiety about
order and social control. 'The early Victorian obsession with the education
of the poor is best understood as a concern about authority, power, and the
assertion (or the reassertion) of control' (Sanderson, 1983).

However, there existed arguments against the education of the poor as
well. Those arguments suggested that schooling and literacy would make
the poor unfit for the performance of menial labouring tasks.[33] To make
matters worse, the acquisition of literate skills would make the working
classes receptive to radical and subversive literature. Despite the dilemma,
the ideology that education would be an agency of social control finally
won by the 1830s. What dominated the minds of policymakers by then
was that education could be a means of reducing crime and the resulting
expenditures on punishment. With the prison system costing £2 million a

year in 1847 and the Poor Law another £7 million in 1832, any expenditure on education that kept a child out of prison and the workhouse as an adult became a social investment.

A third reason for encouraging education came when the victories of Prussia (in 1870) and the Union Forces in the United States civil war (1860–65) suggested that good levels of education contributed to military efficiency. Fourth, the Reform Act of 1867 prompted a concern to ensure the education of those who would soon wield political power through the extended suffrage. Fifth, it also came to be appreciated that education had important implications regarding the creation of an industrial society. By making it possible for people to read notices, they could become aware of available possibilities, jobs for labourers, products for consumers, or of safety issues in dangerous mines and factories. It enabled the efficient functioning of an urban industrial society marked by letter writing, drawing up wills, apprenticeship indentures, passing bills of exchange, and advertisement reading (Sanderson, 1983).

As in all countries, the question of financing education remained. In the UK, the first factor that drove up the literacy rate was the injection of public money for the building and maintenance of elementary schools (Sanderson, 1983).[34] The state was also determined to stimulate school growth by subsidizing two religious bodies (Anglicans and Nonconformists) with an annual grant from 1833. These grants were raised and their administration placed in the hands of a committee supervised by civil servants – the forerunner of the government education department. The grants were extended from limited capital grants for building, equipment, teacher training, to per pupil grants for the actual running of schools. The rising levels of government expenditure pumped life into the societies and drove up the literacy rate even before the beginning of secular schools built and run by local government with local finance. Despite the role of the state and religious societies, there existed a large sector of cheap private education where the working classes bought education for their children outside of the church and state system. In 1851, there were still twice as many private as public day schools for the working class, though only one-third of pupils attended these private schools.

Besides subsidizing the private sector and setting up schools in the public sector, the state undertook other actions that helped schooling. The Factory Act of 1833 obliged factory owners to ensure that their child workers were receiving a regular education either in a factory school or outside. Fifty years later, in 1880, the state made general education compulsory.

Schooling was far from universal through the third quarter of the nineteenth century. The imposition of compulsory education was necessary to achieve universal school attendance and reduce gross educational disparities between classes, communities and sexes. Attendance rates for working-class children rose from 68 per cent in 1871 to 82 per cent by 1896. Resistance to compulsion was overcome partly by the abolition of school fees, but also by legal enforcement of attendance. In fact private working-class schools virtually disappeared after the introduction of free public schooling. The public school system was funded from locally levied taxes, a fact which gave them a huge financial advantage over the voluntary (mostly denominational) schools. By 1900, many voluntary schools were unable to compete with rate-supported board schools, yet had to charge higher fees to keep running while still providing an inferior education (Stephens, 1998).

To summarize, schooling before 1833 was entirely private (no government subsidies were available). It also involved fees, and there was no element of compulsion. Male literacy stood at 67 per cent and female literacy at 51 per cent in 1841. By 1858, education was predominantly private and church-aided, but some schools were subsidized and inspected. There was no compulsion, yet male literacy had improved to 75 per cent, and female to 65 per cent. By 1882, one-third of pupils were in rate-supported government schools (board schools), compulsion had been introduced, fees reduced, and the UK was near total literacy and moving towards universalization of schooling.

Simultaneously, the move towards the development of *public health* was greatly assisted by the concern of the wealthy middle class of being infected by the poor. Because of rising migration from the rural areas to cities in England, the poor were the first to become the subject of health campaigns.[35] For instance, the scientifically informed campaign against the infected individual had a strong tendency to bear hardest upon the most disadvantaged.[36] The financially better-off evaded more readily all policies of disease notification, disinfection and segregation (Webster, 1993).

The period between 1848 and 1918 in England was the era of public health. The era began with the erosion of lay care of the sick and elderly, as self-help systems gave way under strain. Lay care for the chronically sick was affected by the absorption of married women into the paid labour force. The charitable societies began to wilt under pressure from the changing demographic regime, in which adults lived longer (as income and nutrition levels rose), but were not necessarily in better health. Hospitals for the care of the sick developed. The number of hospital beds per 1,000 jumped sharply from 3.2 in 1861 and 3.9 in 1891 to 5.5 in 1911 (Webster, 1993). It is of interest, for the purposes of this study, that in regard to financing health care, four-fifths of the hospitals in 1861 were public hospitals, with others being voluntary (for which money was raised through private charity and the introduction of paid beds).

Public health also meant the rise of the sanitary movement, which expanded legislation on public health, created a medical department in the government, focused on water supply and drainage in urban areas, and introduced the small-bore sewer pipe (thanks to Chadwick). It also involved building up a formidable system of controls on food production, workplaces, shops, housing, schools and hospitals. Combined with the rise of enrolment and literacy, these actions promoted mortality reductions (see Figure 2.2). This figure shows that growth, by itself, was not helpful to reduce mortality, as can be seen by several decades of constant high mortality rates in spite of increasing income levels. However, once high levels of education were achieved, and combined with health interventions as a result of state activities in the 1860s, mortality started to decline.

Germany

Analysis of nineteenth-century Germany is complicated by the fact that it did not unify until 1870. Nevertheless, the regions comprising what is now Germany were growing at a compound rate of 10–15 per cent per decade from 1820 to 1900. As in the UK, however, higher incomes did not automatically result in lower mortality, which finally did decline with the introduction of massive literacy and health policies.

Education was centralized, compulsory and free from the early part of the nineteenth century, which showed in the high level of literacy and enrolment in Prussia well before the unification of Germany (1870). In fact, by the 1830s (i.e. much earlier than most other European countries) there was a full national system of public elementary and secondary schools, which provided universal, compulsory schooling up to 14 years, and secondary education for the elite thereafter. Schools were public institutions, controlled by the state educational bureaucracy and financed largely through taxation. Public elementary schools greatly outnumbered private schools and by 1861 they did so in the proportion of 34:1 (Green, 1990). Free elementary tuition was made into law in 1868.

There were some military considerations underlying state action in favour of *health*. After the unification of Germany in 1871, the deteriorating state of workers' living conditions loomed as one of the most urgent priorities of the new nation. This could be reflected in the emigration of an annual average of 62,500 Germans to the USA between 1871 and 1880 (Knox, 1993). Bismarck and his ministers were worried about the military implications of

Figure 2.3 GDP per capita, adult literacy rate and mortality: Germany
1840–1905

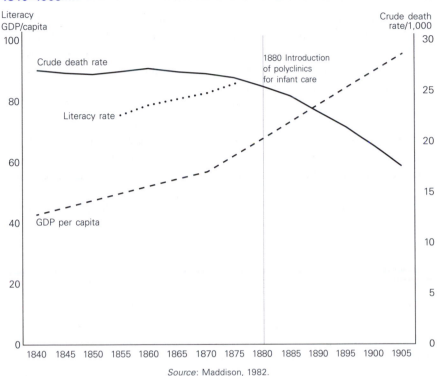

Source: Maddison, 1982.

poor health due to alarming reports that recruits from industrial areas were unfit for service. 'Welfare socialism', they concluded, 'was essential if the fatherland was to survive in a hostile world' (cited in Knox, 1993).

Germans were already making strides in science and technology, and under Bismarck the German government fostered public health as a means of strengthening the state. In 1854 Prussian law obligated all mines and foundries to have sickness funds, and required funds to offer sick pay, medication and rehabilitation. This marked the first compulsory, regulated health insurance system. Church-sponsored charity could not support the task, although the Roman Catholic Church and the Catholics' influential Centre Party (until the 1890s) strongly resisted state intervention on philosophical grounds. The Church said intervention was against the 'natural law' that required individuals to be responsible to themselves and dependent only on God, but it also knew that state-sponsored social relief would undercut the Church's power (Knox, 1993).

Welfare clinics and home-visiting schemes were devised in Germany and modelled after pioneer French dispensary clinics[37] started in the early part of the nineteenth century. Whereas the French clinics provided treatment, pressure from the German medical profession limited the role of the German equivalents to diagnosis and the provision of welfare benefits. Networks of urban 'polyclinics' (organized for infant welfare, alcoholism and sexually transmitted diseases) supplemented the French and German municipal hospital systems from the 1880s. By the turn of the century, a broad social spectrum was making use of new children's hospitals.

Figure 2.3 shows that growth, by itself, was not helpful to reduce mortality, as can be seen by several decades of constant mortality in spite of increasing income levels (measured as an index, 1900 = 100, on the left axis). However, once high levels of education were achieved (the percentage of literate adults is also measured on the left axis) and combined with health interventions as a result of state activities in the 1870s and 1880s, mortality started to decline (crude death rate on the right axis).

France

In France progress in schooling had been relatively slow, as peasants in rural areas were opposed to the education of their children, regarding it as a *luxe inutile* (useless luxury) through to the middle of the nineteenth century. Although school enrolment increased from 58 per cent in 1840 to 65 per cent in 1850, seasonal variations were very high as children worked on farms in the summer. France, in 1870, launched a big public effort after its defeat at the hands of Prussia. In fact, the share of government expenditure allocated to education and science increased sharply between 1872 and 1880, and then nearly doubled between 1880 and 1890. There was increasing centralization as a law of 1881 made education free, and another made it compulsory in 1882 for all children between the ages of 6 and 13.

The United States

As in most federal countries today, each state in the USA had sovereign powers for education. The Southern states did not generally develop public education systems until after the Civil War, while most Northern states did so during the 'Era of Reforms' between 1830 and 1860 (Green, 1990). In 1860, the common school system was based predominantly on local finances. Fees were a significant element in several states, and typically there was little compulsion. Enrolment at all ages (with a population base of 5–19 years) was 50 per cent.

However, by 1890 most of the US states had established public-school systems, and a large number of children were obtaining an elementary education. In addition, some youth in Massachusetts, New York, Pennsylvania, and a few others were receiving free secondary education. By then, three principles had been established. One was that education was a primary responsibility of the state instead of an obligation traditionally assumed by the family. The second was that the state had both the right and the power to raise funds through taxation on a citizen's property for school support. Third, the bitter struggle for free (non-fee-paying) schools established the principle of a non-sectarian system open to all youth, regardless of creed or financial status.

In several states in 1860, the charging of parental fees was certainly a feature of the common school system and there was also a significant tradition of private schooling. Between 1860 and 1880, however, most of the common schools became 'free' (West, 1994). By 1880, fees had been largely abolished; and about half the states had compulsory education laws, as reflected by the enrolment figures. By 1890, 78 per cent of 5 to 17-year-olds were in school; schooling was free and compulsory nearly everywhere.[38] By 1900, the number of public high school students outnumbered those in private secondary institutions.

This pattern of enrolment increase was consistent with the pattern of government spending. Over the latter half of the nineteenth century, the share of public spending in total spending on formal education rose consistently. In 1850, that share was 47 per cent; in 1860, it was 57 per cent; by 1880, it rose to 77 per cent; and in 1900, it stood at 79 per cent. The state and local government were the principal financiers of public education, as is clear from the high share of education costs in their total expenditures: education was already 21 per cent in 1850, and rose slightly to 25 per cent by 1900 (Fishlow, 1966).

In the USA, the expanding economy created a perennial labour shortage that attracted immigrants from Europe. Before the large influx of immigrants in the 1880s and 1890s little concern had been shown for industrial *health* (Duffy, 1990). However, since the Civil War, health reformers were beginning to point out that health was the sole property of the wage earner, and that, as property, it required a measure of government protection. 'It is both bad politics and bad economy to leave this work mainly to the weak and spasmodic efforts of charity, or to the philanthropy of physicians.' Furthermore, the federal government should 'provide more and greater laboratories for research in preventive medicine and public hygiene' (cited in Duffy, 1990). It is no accident that such views achieved prominence in a period marked by a resurgence of mercantilist ideas and policies in the USA, and efforts to acquire colonies to secure markets and sources of raw materials, and to have a large productive population. This view was reinforced during the First World War when the consequences of neglecting the national health became evident in the large number of rejected draftees, which was an experience England had already endured at the time of the Boer War in the last decade of the nineteenth century.

It was a similar recognition of economic and military uses of a healthy labour force that led to action in the USA. In 1909, Irving Fisher prepared a report for the Conservation Commission in which he urged the federal and state governments, as well as municipalities, to undertake vigorous action to protect the people from disease, and thus conserve a basic national resource.

The common threads: the pro-active state and the economic growth–human development relationship

While the preceding discussion highlights the role of public health measures in reducing mortality in a variety of countries, for the UK some scholars (McKeown, 1976) have downgraded the role of medical care in improving life expectancy in favour of improved nutrition. Szreter (1988, 1994) has revised the account of McKeown and has emphasized the role of public health measures in improving health.

An interesting question is how important general improvements in the standard of living were to lower infant mortality. The historical question posed by Preston and Haines (1991) is relevant to present-day problems surrounding childhood mortality in developing countries (but also industrial-ized ones):

> In 1900, the United States was the richest country in the world…. On the scale of per capita income, literacy, and food consumption, it would rank in the top quarter of countries were it somehow transplanted to the present. Yet 18 per cent of its children were dying before age 5, a figure that would rank in the bottom quarter of contemporary countries. Why couldn't the United States translate its economic and social advantage into better levels of child survival?

Preston and Haines took the coexistence of high levels of child mortality with relative affluence as proof of the inadequacy of the influential thesis pro-posed by McKeown that emphasized improvements in material resources.[39]

Despite growing education and increasing per capita income the infant mortality rate (IMR) does not decline in most of Europe until about 1900. After 1900, there is a dramatic decline in IMR (and crude birth rates) in all

European countries (although a slow decline in child or under-5 mortality had been taking place during the latter half of the nineteenth century). There is no country in Europe that does not experience a sharp decline in IMR between 1900 and 1949. After the declines, by 1949, Germany, Austria, Italy, Portugal and Spain ended up with the highest IMRs, in the range of 60 (e.g. Germany) to 115 (e.g. Portugal), while the Netherlands, Norway, Sweden and the UK had the lowest (in the range of 23 to 32).[40]

The reduction in IMR came with the introduction of maternal and child health (in four stages) (Corsini and Viazzo, 1993) with the 'gradual medicalization of motherhood'. First, the two world wars gave an impetus to the organization of mother and child health care. After the First World War came the first large-scale attempts to organize local child health clinics and, in some countries, provide nutritional supplements by means of milk depots (Masuy-Stroobant, 1999). Second, there was an acceleration of the hospital delivery system in the years following the Second World War, with the spread of social security systems in Europe. In this way, a permanent decline in post-neonatal mortality started in the early 1920s, and improvements in maternal mortality and the first signs of an early neonatal mortality decrease emerged in the early 1950s. Third, stillbirth rates began to decline in the inter-war period when antenatal clinics were organized on a systematic basis. Finally, during the 1980s, the provision of neonatal intensive-care units led to a further drop in early neonatal mortality.

It is important to stress that the state interventions were due to very different reasons from those proposed by neoclassical models: no rates of return were estimated, no market failures were identified and no public goods were defined based on production or commercial properties. Rather, social objectives and political considerations were driving state involvement.

The modern school system developed without much reference to the needs of the Industrial Revolution, and much after the latter was well under way. There is evidence that 'few intellectual requirements were necessary to make the industrial revolution' in the last quarter of the eighteenth century (Hobsbawm, 1969). In fact, literacy grew in the European countries in advance of the industrial need for it. 'It was less an effect of industrialization than a prior-facilitating agent. It was not until the second stage of the industrial revolution that education became more essential for the provision of new skills.'[41]

In fact, in the early nineteenth century a modern schooling system was only just emerging for the industrialized countries (other than Prussia, where elements already existed). However, by the end of the nineteenth century, most European countries (except Britain) and the USA had consolidated

Table 2.3 Historical education expenditure in now-industrialized
countries

Fiscal years	France (as % of GDP)	United Kingdom (as % of GNP)	Germany (as % of NNP)	United States (total expenditure as % of GNP)
1860	0.4		1.0	0.8
1880	0.9	0.9	1.6	1.1
1900	1.3	1.3	1.9	1.7

Note: These data are to be regarded as only approximate because of deficiency in the original sources. They should be, hence, read only for inter-temporal comparison for a country, not cross-country comparison. For the USA they are only total outlays relative to GNP. For Germany, while labelled public, they cover total outlays (public + private). For France and Britain they may be too large even for aggregate expenditures (Fishlow, 1966). The use of net national product exerts an upward bias on the German ratio.

Source: Fishlow, 1966.

a system of elementary education while secondary education too had expanded. While the beginnings were entirely due to private effort, it was the intervention of the state that led to universal elementary education. This process occurred unevenly and in different forms from country to country, as some made more rapid progress than others did.

Thus, there were a number of measures common to all states. First, the state created a public system of schooling financed by taxes. The rising tide of public investment is evident from Table 2.3. In 1860, Germany (then Prussia) was spending 1 per cent of net national product, a share that nearly doubled by the end of the century. The total outlays (public and private) relative to GNP rose from 0.8 per cent in 1860 to 1.7 per cent in 1900 (i.e. more than doubled). In the UK, outlays increased from 0.9 per cent (1880) of GNP to 1.3 per cent (1990), as prior to 1880 the state had mainly subsidized private schools with grants. France too showed a rise in expenditures.

Second, the state worked gradually towards the elimination of tuition fees. Third, the state made elementary education compulsory. Fourth, varying degrees of centralization emerged, with bureaucracies running the public school system, the training of teachers and the creation of an education department in government. Countries which developed state-funded systems of public education earlier (e.g. Prussia, northern USA, Switzerland, the Netherlands) achieved higher levels of enrolment and literacy. Countries (e.g. England and Wales) with no public system until quite late fared worse in terms of those indicators (an issue we pick up again in Chapter 7).

2.4 Concluding remarks

The separation of the 'economic' from the 'social' discourse that we commented upon at the beginning of the chapter is inherent in the mainstream development literature, as well as in policy advice. The emphasis of the Consensus on increasing income (economic growth) as a means of reducing poverty is partly inherent in the definition of inadequate income as a strong predisposing condition for an impoverished life.

Such a separation fades away in our approach, which is based on the capabilities normative framework (Sen, 1985, 1999) as well as different heterodox theoretical visions. It has long been known that separate interventions in health, nutrition, water and sanitation, fertility control, and education complement each other, and thus increase the impact of any one from interventions in any other. We noted that gender equality and women's functionings are central to the triggering of this first set of synergies (or feedback loops among the interventions). But we identified another set of synergies (of which the first one is a subset) between the enhancement of functionings, income–poverty reduction and economic growth. Policies should target all three ends.

As a theoretical construct this notion of the dual synergies needs to be distinguished from some antecedents along similar lines in the development economics literature. First, the synergy notion has to be distinguished from the concept of linear stages of development that was characteristic of the writings of Rostow (1959, 1960). Nor do we uncritically accept Kuznets's notion of non-linear relationship between economic growth and income inequality – that the link between income inequality and per capita income may be described by a curve (an inverted U), with an upward phase in which income inequality increases with increases in per capita income, and a downward phase in which income inequality declines with increases in per capita income (Taylor et al., 1997). Rather, the dual synergy model is built upon more recent theoretical and empirical literature, which has demonstrated the benefits for growth of low initial levels of asset/income inequality and reducing poverty. Moreover, by concentrating on the dual synergies, development patterns of countries can be understood by locating countries along these three axes of desirable outcomes.

Second, following the classical development theorists, who recognized that long-run economic growth is a highly non-linear process, our dual synergy model is similar to the Rosenstein–Rodan (1943) idea that posited the need for a government-financed series of interdependent investments, to take advantage of external economies and economies of scale and propel developing countries from a low-level equilibrium trap, with limited growth of per capita income, to a high-level equilibrium path, characterized by self-sustaining growth. In the view of the classical development economists, and in ours, development could not be induced by a minimalist state.

Third, our dual synergy construct is not only grounded in the normative capability approach but also emphasizes women's agency. With Sen and Nussbaum, we strongly believe that women's agency is critical to triggering the first set of synergies.

Fourth, the recognition of such synergies or virtuous circles by policymakers has the potential to improve considerably policy effectiveness in addressing the multifaceted dimensions of poverty. Above all, the recognition of such synergies will help to end the currently predominant separation of macroeconomic policy and social policy formation.

Finally, we have suggested that the experience of the industrialized countries not only confirms the role of state action but also shows that income growth did not always result in improvements in education/health indicators. Public action again played a key role, both in the expansion of educational opportunities in the nineteenth century, and in the decline of child mortality in the twentieth century. In fact, much research effort in recent years has gone into examining the effects of educational and health improvements on economic growth. Robert Fogel (1994) showed that better nutrition and improved health and sanitation explained 50 per cent of economic growth in the UK between 1790 and 1980.

The recognition of such synergies or virtuous circles by policymakers has the potential to improve policy effectiveness considerably, in addressing the multifaceted dimensions of poverty. Above all, the recognition of such synergies will help to end the currently predominant separation of macroeconomic policy and social policy formation. The current approach has shortcomings: it is inefficient in achieving macroeconomic objectives and in giving macroeconomic outcomes and indicators predominance; it makes social policies derivative, with unfortunate human consequences.

3

Macroeconomic policies and institutions for pro-poor growth

A central idea in the previous chapter was that markets and the state are complementary. This central idea emerges from the historical experience of growing prosperity based on the recognition of this complementarity of markets and the state in Western Europe, the USA and parts of East Asia in the last half of the twentieth century. The market economy was the result of deliberate state action, as we noted in the previous chapter, and later restriction on the market economy started spontaneously; so with Polanyi, we would emphasize that the market economy 'was planned; planning was not'.

The successes of the Soviet Union in the first half of the twentieth century instilled in developing countries the need for state action. Markets already existed in developing countries, though in very incomplete forms structurally; what had been missing until then was comprehensive state action. Hence, developing countries started out on a development path in the second half of the twentieth century with a strategy of state-capitalist development. This was true not only in the post-colonial states of Asia and Africa, but also in Latin America (where independence from colonial rule had come in the first quarter of the nineteenth century). In Latin America the structuralist view was that market incentives would not evoke a supply response. State capitalism did have its successes. Until the oil shock of 1973, developing countries grew at very respectable rates. The GDP growth for all developing countries was 3.8 per cent per annum in per capita terms over 1965–80, and it fell sharply thereafter.

What is equally interesting is that the most well known aspect of state-led development – import-substitution policies – did not result in widespread inefficiencies in the economy (as later attempts to rewrite history have attempted to show). Both Rodrik (1999b) and Collins and Bosworth (1996) have shown that the productivity performance of many Latin American and Middle Eastern countries was very good when seen in comparative terms. Over the period 1960–73, Brazil, the Dominican Republic and Ecuador in Latin America; Iran, Morocco, and Tunisia in the Middle East; and Côte d'Ivoire and Kenya in Africa, all demonstrated more rapid total factor productivity growth than any of the East Asian countries. Mexico, Bolivia, Panama, Egypt, Algeria, Tanzania and Zaire showed higher total factor productivity growth than all except Taiwan. In 1973, East Asia was still not perceived as a 'miracle' region. The pre-1973 period was one of not only rapid economic growth, but also sharp increases in efficiency of production.

After the mid-1970s the growth experiences of different groups of countries diverged quite sharply. In Africa and Latin America there was a general collapse of growth after the oil shock of 1973, though not in East and South Asia. The real difference was between those countries that managed the series of external shocks in the 1970s effectively and those that did not; between those that adjusted their macroeconomic policies cleverly (without sacrificing social expenditures) and those that did not. All countries faced the same or similar external environment: two oil shocks of 1973 (quadrupling oil prices) and 1979 (doubling them), the abandonment of the Bretton Woods system of fixed exchange rates, and the interest rates rise of the early 1980s. Of course their magnitude might have been felt differentially by countries, depending upon their dependence on oil imports and their reliance on external funds. But while all of them experienced the same shocks, they differed in later performance on macroeconomic indicators as those of human well-being.

The problem was not with state-led development per se. In fact some countries that were strong followers of state-led development and import-substituting industrialization policies were either able to maintain growth rates (e.g. Pakistan) or to increase growth rates (e.g. India) after 1973. The countries that managed to sustain progress on human development were also those that followed unorthodox macroeconomic adjustment policies in response to external shocks (e.g. South Korea and Costa Rica), as we have argued elsewhere (Mehrotra, 2000, 2004a). In fact, a similar argument has been made in a OECD study examining the experiences of several countries with adjustment and equity (Bourguignon and Morrison, 1992).

Those countries that adjusted their macroeconomic policy in response to the external shocks while preventing serious distributional conflicts prevented economic collapse and maintained growth after 1973. The ability to manage the social conflicts that emerge during a process of macroeconomic adjustment are critical to economic growth being maintained. Or, as Rodrik puts it, the differential performance of different countries on economic and social indicators had very little to do with trade and industrial policies. In other words,

> the main difference between Latin America, say, and East Asia was not that the former remained closed and isolated while the latter integrated itself with the world economy. The main difference was that the former did a much worse job of dealing with the turbulence emanating from the world economy. The countries that got into trouble were those that could not manage openness, not those that were insufficiently open. (2000: 11)

Over two decades have passed since the emergence and dominance of the orthodox paradigm in economic policymaking, with its emphasis on openness and export-orientation in response to the collapse in economic growth of the mid-1970s. However, there is very little evidence of a renewal of the growth of the pre-1973 period. The orthodoxy has also been on the back foot on account of the series of failures in the 1990s – the failure in Russia of privatization and price reform, and the Asian financial crisis that demonstrated the risks of financial liberalization – and, since the 1980s, the collapse of economic growth in much of Africa (despite prolonged use of IMF policies and resources even in countries that were not suffering from civil conflict), and extreme dissatisfaction with economic reforms in Latin America. However, all this does not mean that there exists a new consensus on macroeconomic policies which will revive growth while reducing poverty. Hence, this chapter is devoted to the institutional changes and macro-economic policies necessary to address human poverty in the twenty-first century.

The dual synergies framework presented in the previous chapter is not only useful as a heuristic model for description of actual patterns and an analytical framework; it can also be used to devise polices. A menu of policies that can be derived from the model are discussed in this chapter. Governments today have a panopoly of instruments available to achieve pro-poor growth.

Policies are needed that ensure that growth benefits the poor dispropor-tionately; in other words, any growth that benefits the poor is for us an inadequate definition of pro-poor growth, as we discussed in the previous chapter. We take the normative position that economic growth can be called pro-poor only if it disproportionately benefits the poor, both in terms of income, and in terms of financing of social services, improving working conditions and protecting the environment (especially in the areas where the lowest socioeconomic strata live). We take this position because the empirical evidence (discussed in the previous chapter) is that the pattern of growth since the early 1980s has in many regions tended to increase within-country income inequalities, and has not produced policies that improve the standard of living of the whole population. Hence growth that does not benefit the poor should be unacceptable to governments. Growth that benefits the income-poor proportionately (i.e. growth that is distribution-neutral) should be only barely acceptable to governments from an ethical and normative perspective.

In principle governments committed to pro-poor growth could also be concerned with rural–urban income inequalities – a phenomenon that has particularly affected two of the fastest-growing economies in the world in the last couple of decades, China and India. Increasing interpersonal inequalities in income in any country is likely to be correlated with increasing differentials in average incomes between rural and urban areas. In many developing countries, relying on 'free markets' for social and physical infrastructure has resulted in low investments which are largely concentrated in those urban areas serving higher income groups. This becomes another source of inequality in already unequal societies. This rural–urban differential will be an important concern throughout this book, though not so in this chapter for reasons of space.

In principle, another aspect of pro-poor growth could be whether intra-country (rural–urban and inter-regional) inequalities are decreasing or increasing. While these are legitimate issues that are central to managing distributional conflicts in any diverse society – especially ethnically diverse society – this chapter will steer clear of these discussions. Therefore, we will keep the definition of pro-poor growth restricted to the normative one of growth which raises the income of the poor disproportionately (i.e. greater than it raises income of the non-poor).

Part II of the book looks at the social services (what we call the first synergy). In this chapter we deal briefly with the other policies that help in the feedback loop between income poverty reduction, expansion of functionings and economic growth. This chapter spells out the menu of policy options available to governments to ensure that growth is pro-poor. The presence of a number of options essentially implies that one size does not fit all. Section 3.1 examines actions which will reduce income poverty directly, as well as measures which ensure 'redistribution with growth' (the title of a famous book by Chenery et al., 1974). Section 3.2 examines industrial policies needed for technological and structural change. Section 3.3 examines some alternatives to the macroeconomic policies that have dominated the orthodox paradigm. In every section, we give examples of specific countries where policies have been both innovative and unorthodox, and have resulted in positive outcomes in poverty reduction, economic growth and human capital formation. The concluding section examines the current conjuncture in macroeconomic policies, with all its attendant risks for the Millennium Goals.

3.1   Redistribution to reduce income poverty and manage distributional conflict

We noted above that the countries that continued to grow even after the external shocks of the 1970s were those which adjusted their macroeconomic policies in response to the shocks while containing the distributional conflicts resulting from the adjustments. But the ability of countries to manage social conflict when the economy suffers an external shock is itself contingent upon initial conditions – that is, how unequal the society is to start with. Hence one of the unfinished tasks of governments in the twenty-first century is to address a fundamental cause of inequality: inequality in assets. And in countries with surplus labour in rural areas, the asset that remains the major source of income and livelihoods is land.

In a world of increasingly integrated economies, external shocks are a stochastic variable – they may strike any time, and threaten economic growth if governments fail to adjust macroeconomic policies accordingly. As we noted above, the failure to adjust to external shock often follows on from the inability of governments to manage the distributional conflicts arising from an adjustment process which will inevitably contain winners and losers. Hence, addressing long-standing inequalities has become a political as much as an economic imperative. This requires addressing inequalities already in place before the adjustment that follows a macroeconomic shock, as well as those inequalities that may emerge during growth; we discuss each in turn.

Addressing land ownership/tenancy and landlessness

An unequal distribution of assets is not only a source of unequal income distribution at a particular point in time; it also produces rising income inequality with economic growth, characteristic of the early stages of growth in the now industrialized countries (i.e. the Kuznets hypthesis, on which see Sundrum, 1990). On the other hand, when there is a more equal distribution of income to start with, income inequality may actually decline with economic growth, as happened in many East Asian countries. Land, the main asset at the time, became equally distributed through a programme of land reforms in such countries as Japan, the Republic of Korea, Taiwan, and many socialist countries (e.g. China, Vietnam). The unequal distribution of assets also helps to explain why Latin American countries failed to make major dents in income poverty in spite of periods of robust economic growth.

At the beginning of the twenty-first century, the rural poor are either small, marginal farmers or landless labourers. We shall discuss each in turn.

The rural landless

The landless labourers in rural areas number 450 million today, and they are by far the largest segment of the world's labour force (FAO, ILO and IUF, 2005). The three major trends in agricultural labour markets in the 1980s and early 1990s reflected in ILO data have been: (1) an increase in the share of agricultural waged employment in total rural economic activity; (2) an increase in the share of women in agricultural waged employment; and (3) growing casualization of agricultural waged labour. (As we discuss later, the last two are trends evident for non-agricultural employment as well.) There are more workers in waged employment in agriculture today than at any time. The share of waged employment in agriculture, including the number of wage-dependent smallholders in agriculture, is continuing to increase in virtually all regions. The share of waged employment seems to have an inverse relation to the size of the agricultural labour force (IFAD, 2002). As more workers move into industry and services, and the agricultural labour force drops, production units in agriculture are transformed from small family holdings to large units relying on wage labour; in other words, the number of smallholders decreases.

If 1.1 billion people subsist on less than US$1 a day, nearly half that number can be classified as rural landless labour. Yet despite the sheer number of people involved, the issue of the income determinants of waged agricultural workers, and of their land tenancy rights, has remained on the back burner for policymakers. The income determinant of full-time workers is the wage level, and that of casual workers is number of days worked, wage level, and the share of income derived from plantation/farm wage work. Ultimately, the rural wage level in conditions of surplus labour will be determined by the speed at which rural workers are leaving agriculture for non-agricultural employment (a subject we will return to later). However, in the short run, the rural wage level will be determined by growth in agricultural productivity. In turn dependent upon public investment (e.g.

in irrigation, feeder roads, electricity) in most developing countries, higher productivity will create work in agriculture, in addition to the productive work generated off-farm in rural areas that services agricultural production. In other words, fiscal space (an issue we will return to in the final section of this chapter as well as in Chapter 9) has to be available for the state to maintain public investment in agriculture and rural areas, if agricultural productivity is a goal.

For landless workers, the number of days worked is critical. Unless non-farm employment is growing, it is possible for the state to increase the days that casual agricultural workers are employed, provided it is willing to invest in public works (e.g. pest control, watershed management, building water tanks, building feeder roads, flood control measures, afforestation, and actions to prevent soil erosion). There is hardly a developing country in the world that does not need additional infrastructure in rural areas; and construction is a highly labour-intensive activity. Such investments must be planned with rural local governments in partnership with the community if they are to survive (an issue we return to in Chapter 7). In 2005 India introduced legislation to guarantee in the poorest districts of the country that such work will be available for at least one member of the household for a hundred days in the year (see Mehrotra, 2004a; Patnaik, 2005).

The small landholders

A significant share of the extremely poor are those with very small landholdings. Concentration of landholdings as a cause of rural poverty is particularly acute in parts of South Asia (especially parts of India, Nepal, Pakistan) and parts of east and southern Africa (e.g. Kenya, South Africa, Namibia, Zimbabwe) (Moyo, 2004), as well as Latin America (de Janvry and Sadoulet, 2002). But although 70 per cent of developing country populations live in rural areas, and a significant part of those are dependent upon agriculture directly or indirectly (52 per cent of China's population depend on agriculture, 59 per cent in India, but higher in Africa), the issue of land reform and land tenancy is not central to the concerns of governments. (Given that bilateral donors have also ignored the issue, agriculture's share in bilateral ODA has declined sharply in the 1990s.)

A well-known literature has established that, in conditions of surplus labour, small farms are both efficient (because the cultivation per unit of land is much more intense compared to larger farms) and equitable (Bharadwaj, 1974). In other words, land reforms can not only promote growth of agricultural output, but also prove directly poverty-reducing. Yet, land reforms remain outside the purview of the reforming governments which need such reform most. The West Bengal government in India in the 1980s and Kerala in the 1950s remain exceptions. China's reforms of 1979 were another exception, as were South Africa's post-apartheid efforts. South Africa's land reform programme, beginning with a 1996 White Paper on the subject, has the following priorities: restitution for those forcibly removed from their lands, tenure security for those presently on farms, and land redistribution.

Similarly, it has been argued that the single most important economic factor affecting women is the gender gap in command over property. In rural South Asia, the most significant form of property is arable land, which is a critical determinant of economic well-being, social status and empowerment. However, few women own land and fewer control it (Agarwal, 1994). Women's inheritance claims regarding land are often opposed because they would decrease agricultural output by reducing farm size and increasing land fragmentation – but that argument applies as much to land when only men own it. Recent work in sub-Saharan Africa has also argued that one of the factors constraining growth and poverty reduction is the gender inequality regarding access to and control of a diverse range of assets (World Bank, 1999b, 2005).

The nature of institutional changes required in agrarian relations will naturally vary with the history of landholding and land settlement patterns (for a general argument to this effect, see Mann, 1990; for empirical evidence on South India, see Kumar, 1965; and de Janvry and Sadoulet, 2002, on Latin America). In Africa, the legacy of racially unequal land control afflicts the main agricultural settler areas of Namibia, South Africa and Zimbabwe, but also Botswana, Malawi and Swaziland. Most settler agriculture is on large farms, which is still claimed to be more efficient than the small subsistence farms of black farmers. As in South Asia, the fact that large farms provide most of the agricultural surplus for export and urban consumption ignores the well-established research in agricultural economics cited above that shows, in conditions of surplus labour, small farms to be more efficient than large ones. Yet colonial land expropriations continue to be reinforced by new land concessions to foreign investors. Some of the biggest landowners in southern Africa are multinational companies with cattle ranches and mining concessions. The companies control the wildlife and safari parks which – under the guise of ecotourism – are growing in Mozambique, Namibia, South Africa, and Zimbabwe (Moyo, 2004; UNDP HDR, 2004).

Exclusion on the basis of land often coincides with exclusion on grounds of ethnicity. Just as land issues cannot be separated from those of caste in South Asia, and with racial conflict in parts of Africa, land issues are still relevant to race relations in Latin America (especially in the Andean and

Mesoamerican countries of Bolivia, Ecuador, Guatemala, Mexico and Peru). The issues of social exclusion of the indigenous peoples in Latin America are linked to land issues (Yashar, 2004). Hence, addressing land issues will also mitigate social conflicts with ethnic overtones.

A major international trend that has been driving increasing land concentration in many developing countries that export agricultural products is the fact that supermarkets are now the main gatekeepers to developed-country markets for agricultural produce. To sell in world markets, especially markets for higher value crops, means selling to a small number of large supermarket chains. Suppliers must also meet high product standards, which smallholders are likely to find it difficult to meet. This means that more farms are either owned or leased by large international companies (especially in Latin America, but also some African countries, especially Kenya) (UNDP HDR, 2005).

De Janvry and Sadoulet (2002) identify four broad categories of approaches to land reform that can be considered: negotiated recuperation of land; expropriation; assisted land purchases; and assisted land rentals. Except under situations which were political turning points in history (revolutions in Russia, Cuba, Vietnam, China; US occupations in Taiwan and Korea's post-Japanese departure), expropriations are increasingly less of an option today. Hence negotiated distribution of public lands or settlement of inconclusive earlier land reforms (the first option), or assisted land purchases or rentals are a way forward. Land rental is still today a very important means of gaining access to land. Besides, demographic factors remain a consideration. The fact that even the large landholdings in South Asia are relatively small by international standards (e.g. Latin America), and that the land–population ratio is far more adverse in South Asia than in Latin America does not mean that land concentration is not an issue in South Asia (as some policymakers contend).

Eventually, agriculture will be unable to absorb the surplus labour in rural areas; hence the need for off-farm rural employment outside of agriculture. In the short term, many of the new regular wage jobs are for low-skilled workers. This implies a growth strategy based on exports of manufactured goods, but also production of low-skill-intensity goods for the domestic market (especially in countries which have large domestic markets; less in those with smaller ones). But given the large numbers involved, even a fast transfer out of agriculture will not pull all the working poor up out of poverty. This remains an issue in such large countries as India, Pakistan and China, which together have more of the world's poor than any other part of the world (including Africa).

Besides, the maximum attainable share of industry in total employment in late industrializers is lower than it was in the now industrialized countries at their manufacturing peak. In the UK it was 55 per cent (1901), in Japan 37 per cent (1973) and in Korea 33 per cent (1994). In China it is 22 per cent (2000) and in India 16 per cent (Ghose, 2004). Late industrializers borrow technology from early industrializers, and the labour intensity of technology always declines with time. Hence, regular wage employment in total employment will not rise significantly. Thus the share of self-employment will remain significant into the foreseeable future in most developing countries, including India. This underlines even further the need to reduce the scope of casual labour and hence the need for policies supporting entrepreneurial activity in labour-intensive manufacturing (through small and medium enterprises) and investment in rural infrastructure. It also implies a strategy that the service sector, which inevitably will absorb the surplus labour migrating from rural areas, will provide employment that is more productive than hitherto, since growing productivity of work will become the only basis for rising wages in the service sector.

Redistribution with growth

Apart from addressing agrarian issues, governments can follow other policies, in the short term, to improve the distribution of income. One policy (other than land reform, public works and public investment in rural infrastructrue) would be to influence the overall structure of production in the economy in favour of *commodities largely consumed by the lower-income sections* of society. A key aspect of this policy is the expansion of agricultural production, so that overall growth is not constrained by the agricultural sector (Taylor et al., 1997). Rapid agricultural growth will contribute to industrial growth in many ways: by generating demand for industrial goods, and by making available wage goods and thus keeping the low price of wage goods. In fact, one of the reasons why industrial growth has been slower in South Asia than in East Asia is because the rate of growth of agriculture in South Asia has been over three decades (1960–90) consistently lower than in East Asia (Saith, 1996). In sub-Saharan Africa it is even lower. In fact, the remarkable success of China in reducing income poverty after 1979 had two bases: the increasing productivity of agriculture founded upon an egalitarian distribution of land, and employment increase in labour-intensive town and village enterprises (Nolan, 1995). As we noted above, protecting and promoting small-landowner agriculture is better not only for income distribution, but also for growth, as the experience of the smaller East Asian countries also demonstrates.

Two aspects of income distribution need to be favourable for accumulation: the functional income distribution (i.e. between wages, profits and rent) for physical capital formation and the household (interpersonal) income distribution for human capital formation. The centrally planned economies had a highly egalitarian household income distribution, combined with high investment rates, which were financed by the socialist equivalent of profits, the planned surplus. The East Asian success in capital accumulation was based on a high profit share in the functional distribution of income and low inequality in the distribution of human capital. However, since high profit share and low inequality in household income distribution usually do not go together, the question is: how was it possible for Japan, Korea and Taiwan to have both at the same time? The combination of policies they followed are particularly relevant in the twenty-first century because personal income distribution has been worsening over the last two decades (as we saw in Chapter 2).

A major reason for the low inequality in household distribution in these countries was the unusually even distribution of wealth, especially land (as mentioned above). A second reason was the early investment in basic services for all and the widespread distribution of human capital. A third reason was that a relatively important and vibrant small-scale business sector also existed, which was the engine of employment and reduced overall income inequality. However, many countries have a high profit share in income, but are unable to convert the profit-oriented income distribution into high savings and investment. The difference in Japan, Korea and Taiwan is accounted for by institutional mechanisms and policies that facilitate the translation of profits into savings and investment.

Foremost, the corporate financing system in these three countries had a heavy reliance on bank loans and the relatively insignificant role of the stock market. The controlling shares remained in the hands of other firms within the group, and the firms were able to retain profits and reinvest them, rather than pay dividends. Second, the government (in Korea) admonished conspicuous consumption by the rich, restricted imports of consumer goods and restricted consumer financing. Third, tight foreign exchange controls prevented capital flight until the balance of payments equalized. Fourth, financial institutions (e.g. postal savings) existed to maximize the mobilization of savings (You, 1995; Chang, 2002). These policies ensured high savings and investment, which in turn led to employment expansion and real wage increases. These then played a critical role in reducing inequality at the earlier stage of rapid growth. In other words, this process involved much more than the *free labour market, free trade factor price* equalization process. It involved an active industrial policy and strong protection of domestic markets, especially of consumption goods, and was least receptive to foreign direct investment.[1] This experience highlights the connection between distributive policies, institutional arrangements and macroeconomic policies. In other words, poverty-reduction is more likely to succeed in the presence of policies and institutions conducive to redistribution before and with growth.

3.2 Industrial policy for technological/structural change

If redistribution before and during growth is essential for triggering synergies in human development, then industrial policy is equally critical to triggering poverty-reducing growth. Debates have raged about the value of industrial policy. We shall review the most recent version of these debates – post-publication of *The East Asian Miracle* (World Bank, 1993b) – before arguing why industrial policies are essential to economic growth and technological/structural change. However, we believe that the growing informalization of employment in all countries, both developed and developing, implies that the conception of industrial policy even in the current heterodox literature has to be supplemented with specific policies directed at the informal sector (including social insurance in the informal economy). Employment in un-registered informal enterprises in developing countries has grown in industry as well as services. In other words, even the most recent positions around industrial policy – of both mainstream and heterodox economists – have tended to ignore the large and growing issue of the informal sector.

Industrial and trade policy does have to be discussed together, so that the international labour-cost advantage of most low-income (LICs) and middle-income countries (MICs) in world trade will help generate employment and incomes for the poor. However, it will be argued here that, in contrast to the recommendations of the Bretton Woods institutions, developing countries should actively seek 'strategic' rather than 'close' integration with the international economy (Singh, 1994). Governments in almost all market-economy countries intervene to a greater or a lesser degree in the operation of their industries. For example, even the US government intervenes in industry through anti-trust laws, industrial standards, pollution regulations, and labour laws. No one would contend that the United States has an 'industrial policy'; but Japan and East Asian countries did. What makes interventions by the three East Asian states (Japan, South Korea, Taiwan) into an 'industrial policy' is that their interventions are generally coordinated and viewed as a coherent whole.

The World Bank's *The East Asian Miracle* (1993b) did recognize that there was widespread state intervention in the East Asian economies. But it argued that industrial policies in these countries were mostly unsuccessful, with the exception of Japan. It also emphasized that the second-tier newly industrialized countries (NICs) – Malaysia, Thailand, Indonesia – of Southeast Asia grew fast in the absence of such industrial policy, implying that industrial policy is not necessary for rapid economic development. It was also sceptical that industrial policy could be practised in other developing countries, since they have weaker bureaucracies. Moreover, the international environment in which today's developing countries are operating is unlikely to accept the interventionist industrial and trade policies that prevailed in the second quarter of the last century.

For these reasons it is necessary to restate the rationale for industrial policies, since we believe they remain relevant in the first decade of the twenty-first century. Chang (2003) noted that the *Miracle* study did recognize three justifications for industrial policy. The first, in its view, was the need to coordinate complementary investments when there are significant economies of scale and capital market imperfections. In other words, industrial policy is needed for a big push in investments – something the East Asians were able to achieve. Second, industrial policies are needed to address learning externalities, such as subsidies for industrial training. Third, the state can play the role of organizer of domestic firms into cartels in their negotiations with foreign firms or governments – a role that has become particularly relevant in the twenty-first century after the big business revolution of the 1990s (following mega-mergers and acquisitions among TNCs) (Nolan, 1995). In fact, given that China is one of the few late industrializers unable to create a large number of mega-firms with an international reputation, one of the objectives of China's industrial policies since the 1990s has been to support the growth of such firms (with some limited success, e.g. Lenovo computers, Haier home appliances).

Three other very important reasons are provided by Chang (2003) and Rodrik (2000). First, the role of industrial policy is not only to prevent coordination failures (i.e. ensure complementary investments) but also to avoid competing investments in a capital-scarce environment. Excess capacity will lead to price wars, adversely affecting profits of firms and forcing the scrapping of assets. The East Asian states managed this role successfully. Second, industrial policy can ensure that the industrial capacity installed is as close to the minimum efficient scale as possible, through policy measures such as investment licensing, forced mergers and export requirements. Choosing too small a scale can mean a 30–50 per cent reduction in production capacity (Chang, 2003). This is another role industrial policy performed in East Asia. Finally, when structural change is needed, industrial policy can facilitate that process. In a fast-changing market the losing firms will resist and block structural changes that are socially beneficial but will make their own assets worthless. Under these circumstances, industrial policies must help such firms. East Asian governments assisted such firms to prevent them from undermining the process of structural change, using orderly capacity-scrapping between competing firms and retraining programmes to limit such resistance.

Unfortunately, however, the potential role of industrial policy has been consistently downplayed ever since the early 1980s after the growing dominance of the orthodox paradigm – with well-known consequences in much of Latin America and also sub-Saharan Africa.

Foreign direct investment

There is a great emphasis in the current literature on the need for appropriate policies to attract foreign direct investment. In fact, one could argue that in spite of the distaste for industrial policy in the orthodoxy, two policies that stand out as proxies for industrial policy are the push for export-orientation and policies to attract FDI. Yet, with the exception of the two island city-states (Singapore, Hong Kong) and Malaysia, the ratio of FDI inflows to gross domestic capital formation over 1971–99 in East Asia was not particularly high by international standards. In Taiwan, Indonesia and particularly Korea, the contribution of FDI to capital accumulation has been much below the developing country mean. In Latin America, on the other hand, with a much lower growth performance, FDI's share in capital formation has been consistently higher than the developing country mean over the three decades (Chang, 2003).

For the second tier of Southeast Asian newly industrialized countries – Indonesia, Thailand – the optimal degree of openness was different from that of the East Asian countries. In the Southeast Asian economies, foreign direct investment has played a more important role than it did in Japan or South Korea. The rapid development of the East Asian countries led to a different historical situation in the second-tier NICs. It is advantageous for them to attract industries which are no longer economic in the first-tier countries because of the growth of real wages there – as suggested by the so called 'flying geese' model of Asian economic development (Singh, 1994). This model and the associated intra-regional pattern of trade and investment in Asia are themselves partly products of the industrial policy in Japan, Korea and other countries. Unlike many other advanced countries which try to protect declining industries, the Japanese practised a 'positive' industrial policy of encouraging structural change by assisting the replacement of old industries by the new. This, however, involves an orderly rundown of the older industries, including *inter alia* their transfer to less developed countries in the region, which is a function of effective industrial policy (as we noted earlier).

As a result, Felix (1994) suggests that East Asian FDI in the region has been structurally more conducive to sustaining backward linkage development in the participant economies than has been the case of FDI in Latin America. He ascribes this to the fact that the East Asian intra-regional pattern has evolved along a dynamic comparative advantage path dominated by cost-minimizing trade and investment. The Latin American pattern, he suggests, has been shaped largely by mercantilist market access rather than by cost-minimizing objectives. As a result, it is more vulnerable to disruptive shifts of trading advantages deriving from changes in the marketing and financial strategies of foreign firms.

Given China's recent growth experience, what lessons can be drawn from the Chinese policies towards FDI? Until 1990, well into the reforms, China's ratio of FDI inflows to gross fixed capital formation was well below the developing country average. However, after that it increased sharply: it was 11.1 per cent over 1991–95 (compared to the developing country average of 6.4 per cent), and 13.3 per cent over 1996–99 (against 11.4 per cent). Thus, China's opening up to FDI was very gradual indeed. Two other special factors need to be remembered in regard to China's FDI inflows. First, China's success in attracting FDI is exaggerated because of misreporting and round-tripping. The latter refers to capital originating in China that is sent to other economies and then returns disguised as FDI to take advantage of tax, tariff and other benefits given to foreign but not domestic investment (Heytens and Zebregs, 2003). Second, 59 per cent of all FDI into China over 1983–99 was from Hong Kong (51 per cent) and Taiwan (8 per cent) (Braunstein and Epstein, 2002), and there is a clear link between the first phenomenon and the second. Other developing countries may find it difficult to replicate these two rather special conditions that account for the phenomenal increase in FDI inflows into China. Two-thirds of all FDI inflows into China are in fact accounted for by Hong Kong, Taiwan, Singapore and South Korea. FDI from Europe and the USA has taken off only during the 2000s.

Another aspect relevant to our industrial policy concerns is the form that FDI has taken in China, and its evolution. Early in the reform period, China allowed FDI only in the form of joint ventures (except in the Special Economic Zones), because the authorities felt this form was better suited to tapping advanced foreign technology. It was not until 1986 that wholly foreign-owned enterprises were permitted outside the SEZs. Accordingly, equity and co-operative joint ventures accounted for over 60 per cent of contracted value of FDI in 1990. However, even though the share of foreign-owned enterprise went up in the 1990s to about 45 per cent, the balance still remained in the joint venture form (Heytens and Zebregs, 2003).

There is other evidence that China used its FDI inflows in a strategic manner to increase exports. Most of the earlier FDI inflow (from Taiwan and Hong Kong) for the first two decades after economic reforms began was export-oriented, not directed at the large domestic market. In fact, this FDI was concentrated in small, labour-intensive export-oriented manufacturing (Lai, 2002). By the early 1980s Hong Kong's economy was so developed and its cost structure so high that the transfer of export-oriented labour-intensive manufacturing from Hong Kong to neighbouring Guangdong province became profitable – a pattern consistent with the flying geese paradigm. Taiwan as a source of FDI into China treads the same path as Hong Kong, with a time lag (starting in 1992).

In 1986, the share of foreign-invested enterprises in total exports was only 2 per cent, and rose to 12.6 per cent in 1990. However, by 2000 this ratio had increased to 48 per cent. But until the late 1990s these exports were only marginal net suppliers of foreign exchange, since the objective of foreign firms was (and is) to import duty-free materials and parts for processing or assembly and subsequent re-export. Only since 1998 have net exports of foreign-invested firms exceeded net imports. European and US FDI, which increased only from the end of the 1990s, has in any case been mainly aimed at the large domestic market. It is the sum of export earning and FDI that was much larger than the value of imports – this explains why foreign-invested firms were major net suppliers of foreign exchange on the Chinese foreign exchange market (Lai, 2002).

Yet another aspect of China's industrial policy has been the strategic selection of sectors. Starting out in labour-intensive manufactures for export, the Asian FDI into China shifted to more technology-intensive sectors over the years. In the second half of the 1990s, FDI increased in capital- and technology-intensive sectors, especially chemicals, machinery, transport equipment, electronics and telecommunications; finally, the information technology sector became a key focus of new FDI (Lai, 2002). In the services, China has welcomed FDI only in real estate, which is where most of service-sector FDI is concentrated. But FDI in sectors such as banking, insurance, wholesaling and retailing has remained severely restricted in terms of geographical location and business scope.

Governments compete for FDI because it is commonly thought to be an important source of economic growth, employment generation and technological upgrading. China, as the largest recipient of FDI and one of the world's fastest growing economies, is often presented as evidence for the benefits of FDI – this is one reason why we have spent a disproportionate amount of space here on China's case. China's size and its large market size would lead one to believe that, more than any other country, it has a bargaining advantage in negotiating with large foreign firms. So the natural question arises as to whether FDI inflows into China have delivered the expected benefits. This question has spawned an interesting literature (Graham and Wada, 2001; Zebregs, 2003; Braunstein and Epstein, 2002).

Empirical studies have demonstrated that the causality need not merely be from FDI to growth, but also the other way around. In other words, a two–way causality exists between industrial growth and FDI: FDI leads growth, and growth draws FDI. This evidence holds in China too, at both the national and the provincial level: that causality between the two variables runs in both directions (Zebregs, 2003). Heytens and Zebregs (2003) and Zebregs (2003) find that FDI flows contributed to China's economic growth in at least two ways. First, increased capital formation is estimated to have contributed about 0.4 percentage points to annual GDP growth in the 1990s. The direct contribution of FDI to GDP growth has been highest in those provinces that have attracted the most FDI (e.g. the maximum of 4 percentage points in Guangdong). The other contribution is through higher total factor productivity, raising TFP growth by 2.5 percentage points a year during the 1990s. Thus, in total FDI contributed nearly 3 percentage points to potential GDP growth for China.

In addition, Braunstein and Epstein (2002) present empirical evidence (through an econometric exercise) on the impact of FDI on wages, employment, domestic investment and tax revenues. They find that the impact on employment growth and wage growth has been positive but rather limited. For instance, ILO data reveal that, over 1995–99, foreign enterprises contributed barely 0.8 per cent of total industrial employment. They also find it has a negative impact on domestic investment, in the sense of crowding it out, and on provincial tax revenues. They find that the decentralization of the FDI bidding process in China to the township and county governments (with neighbouring local governments competing in a decentralized system rife with corruption)[2] contributes to these negative outcomes.

Braunstein and Epstein (2002) argue that with China's bargaining strength, one would have expected that FDI leads to most of the anticipated benefits – that is, higher domestic tax revenue, higher wages and significantly more employment, and greater technology and productivity spillovers. The fact that the evidence is mixed suggests that the majority of developing countries that have a fraction of China's bargaining power are unlikely to be able to do much better. While FDI in China has contributed to growth, it has also contributed to increasing inter-regional income inequality as well as personal inequality.

However, all this quantitative discussion underestimates the wider effects of FDI on the Chinese economy. When reforms began China did not have a private sector, and there was also an institutionalized ideological hostility to private firms; not until 1988 was the China constitution (1982) amended to include a clause to permit establishment of private companies with more than eight employees, as a 'supplement to the socialist state-owned economy'. And it was not until 1999 that the constitution recognized the private sector as a component of, rather than as a supplement to, the economy. For credit allocation, the pecking order that the banking system was instructed to follow had the state-owned enterprises at the top, collective firms in the middle and the private firms at the bottom (Ghosh, 2005). Until 1998 the largest Chinese banks were under instruction not to lend to private firms. In this situation, foreign-invested firms filled the gap by providing entrepreneurship, and a separate enclave that could be controlled easily by the Chinese state. Town and village enterprises (TVEs), actively sponsored and assisted by local governments, became initially the major medium for foreign investment (Naughton, 1995). Wider ripple effects followed.

First, the remarkable growth of these rural industries was primarily due to their connection to the international market. The presence of foreign invested enterprises (FIEs) became pervasive in labour-intensive and export-processing industries such as electronics and telecommunications, garments and footwear, leather products, printing and record processing, cultural products and plastics. Some 1,504 manufacturing FIEs (about one-third of which came from the overseas ethnic Chinese) were operating in 1995 (Yasheng, 2003); in 1995 they accounted for over 60 per cent of Chinese exports in these industries. These projects were very small, and the parent firms making these investments were also small. TVEs commanded about 25 per cent of China's total export earnings and joint ventures by 1991, increasing to 36 per cent in 1996. In these TVEs the areas of highest growth were also the areas of deepest foreign penetration.

Second, FDI created an upsurge in private entrepreneurship. Throughout the 1980s until the mid-1990s, foreign investors were freely allowed to play the role of venture capitalists. They provided equity financing to private entrepreneurs shunned by China's formal financial institutions. FDI thus helped the Chinese private firms, directly and through joint ventures (Ghosh, 2005). Without the support of FDI these ventures would have atrophied under the weight of China's inefficient financial and economic institutions

(Yasheng, 2003). The domestic private sector increased output fivefold from 1998 to 2003. During this period it created 18 million jobs, while SOEs shed 22 million (and added 9 million in 2004). Now the private sector's share in China's economy is as much as two-thirds (OECD, 2005). For a country that had no privately owned companies before 1980, this remarkable achievement would have been impossible in the absence of the catalytic role of FDI.

Third, FDI's benefits led the political regime to make relaxations in the credit regime mentioned earlier. Domestic entrepreneurs were now given greater access to the banking system to finance contractual arrangements. Lack of finance had earlier driven these units to work out financial collaborations with foreign investors. Following this relaxation, a rapid increase occurred in contracting and export processing operations by private firms, which increased 82-fold from 1996 to 2000 (from $6.3 million to $526 million). In the garment industry, in particular, the decline of the share of FDI was large: the FDI share falling from 7.8 per cent to 4.5 per cent (Yasheng, 2003). All these are beneficial spillovers of a highly effective FDI policy.

Fourth, in the initial stages, FDI was mainly restricted to the collectives and joint ventures, but with growing confidence the SOEs are also receiving foreign investment. As benefits started flowing from FDI, with the surge of domestic entrepreneurship, the regime could afford to shift gear (Ghosh, 2005). The Communist Party declared that the state did not have to dominate every sector or have majority ownership in every enterprise in order to maintain broad control of the economy and decided to focus only on a few enterprises and privatize the rest. The policy now is 'grasping the big and letting go the small' – in other words, restructuring and consolidating China's largest SOEs and privatizing of small SOEs. The focus is now on the heavy industries, oriented to mining and defence, or some five hundred or so key SOEs. In several cases, management of specific assets to ensure greater efficiency is going to joint ventures, with restrictive rights for foreign investors (Yasheng, 2003).

Clearly, the broadest lesson from the Chinese experience is that with a strategic vision and effective regulation, FDI can play a very important role in restructuring the economy.

Supporting small enterprises and the informal sector

There are at least two major differences between the conditions under which developing countries are industrializing today, and the conditions faced by the now-industrialized countries over a century ago. First, there have been massive changes in technology. The techniques of industrial production in developing countries being used now, usually borrowed from industrialized countries which currently have a rather different factor endowment, means that the employment elasticity of manufacturing output in developing countries is much lower than it was over a century ago in the now industrialized ones. The technologies imported by developing countries today were the product of a second industrial revolution in the advanced capitalist countries. In most developing countries, in the phase of import-substituting industrialization, import- and capital-intensive products and inappropriate technologies entrenched a situation wherein formal sector manufacturing output has grown, but manufacturing employment has not grown commensurately (Stewart, 1974). The employment growth in the formal sector is insufficient to absorb even the growth in the labour force. In fact, as population has grown and the agriculture sector sheds its surplus labour, the slow growth of manufacturing employment has contributed to labour absorption in the informal economy in urban areas. In other words, in comparison with the shift from craft to mass production in developed countries during the second industrial revolution (Nell, 1992, 1998), middle-income countries got 'stuck in between' – their industrial firms use 'modern' technology, but at a much lower level of throughput and efficiency.[3] The result is not what Lewis (1955) had anticipated – that the formal, modern, industrial economy will absorb the labour in the traditional rural, agricultural economy (the 'dual economy') – but there has been the emergence of a differentiated informal economy.[4]

The second great difference is the demographic pressure faced by developing countries in the phase of their first industrial revolution, compared to the now-industrialized countries at an earlier comparable phase of development. During the first century after the start of the Industrial Revolution, the total population of Europe grew only from 185 million in 1800 to about 400 million in 1900. However, over the next century (1900–2000), when developing countries were attempting their own industrial revolution, populations multiplied several times.[5] The ability of formal industry or services to absorb this growing labour force is very limited indeed (as we have argued in section 3.1 above). Under the circumstances, growth in the informal economy, and with it industrial outwork and home-based economic activity, seems inevitable (see Mehrotra and Biggeri, 2006 for further discussion).

In the phase of import-substituting industrialization, the response of governments to this process was similar. Almost all countries had (and still have) some policies for small and medium enterprises (SMEs), since they are seen as engines of job creation. Japan, Korea and Taiwan made particular efforts to support SMEs, while at the same time supporting large firms using capital-intensive techniques. It should be noted, of course, that the protection of small-landowner agriculture and small businesses in these economies is market-distorting according to the perception of neoliberals. Korea protects the small-landowner farms, not only by trade protectionism, but also by restricting the size of individual farms, banning absentee ownership and numerous other measures in addition to land reform conditions (You, 1995). Taiwan vigorously promoted small-scale industries through the establishment of industrial parks and districts with financial and technical support, as well as agriculture and rural industries.

The three East Asian tigers managed to switch from a capital-intensive import-substituting industrial strategy to a strategy of labour-intensive manufactured exports, rapidly absorbing labour, and avoiding the formation of a large informal sector. But the majority of the remaining Asian countries, as well as Latin American and African economies, face a different historical situation today. Demographic pressures are severe, and the labour force is expanding faster than the formal economy is absorbing it in either industry or services. That is why we would stress, for agriculture, diversification of agricultural output into new labour-intensive products (e.g. horticulture, vegetables, flowers – as in India and Thailand) and rural infrastructure (so successful in absorbing rural labour in Indonesia and China). This would encourage the growth of rural non-farm activities and labour absorption – apart from raising rural wages for the landless in agriculture. Thus, one-third of rural incomes in India already come from non-agricultural sources. However, this agricultural diversification and rural infrastructure would not be enough to absorb the growing labour force. An industrial policy is needed that takes into account the non-transitory nature of the informal sector.

Apart from the two structural factors underlying the growth of informal enterprises/employment, an international force has also been at play – that is, increasing global integration and competition in the 1990s. To improve their global competitiveness, capital investing globally has increasingly shifted production to countries with lower labour costs, or has adjusted employment practices in rich countries to more informal arrangements. In other words, in recent years the expansion of the informal economy can be linked not only to the *capacity* of formal firms to absorb labour but also to their *willingness* to do so (Portes, 1990).

This lower willingness has manifested itself in the increased international role of subcontracting through commodity chains. The post-World War II period saw the development of essentially two types of international subcontracting: producer-driven commodity chains, and buyer-driven commodity chains, with the difference lying in the location of the key barriers to entry

(Gereffi, 1994). In producer-driven chains, large transnational companies play a central role in coordinating a production network, including backward and forward linkages. Such chains operate in capital and technology-intensive commodities like automobiles, aircraft, semiconductors, electrical machinery (for example, the Ford Escort is manufactured and assembled in fifteen countries). There is little scope for subcontracting to households in such industries. Buyer-driven commodity-chains, however, are usually operated by large retailers and brand-name merchandisers. Such large retailers as K-Mart, Gap and Wal-Mart play a central role. Such chains operate in labour-intensive consumer goods like garments, footwear, toys and houseware. These now extend to fruits, vegetables, non-timber forest products, and many more. The production of such goods is usually located in developing countries, while the high-value activities (e.g. design and marketing) are in industrialized countries. Often such chains extend all the way to the industrial outworker based at home. The trend of global manufacturing is to move from producer-driven to buyer-driven chains in international subcontracting (Gereffi, 1994). In fact, Wal-Mart, the world's biggest retailer, has driven this model, buying products from 65,000 suppliers worldwide and selling to over 138 million consumers every week through its 1,300 stores in ten countries (Oxfam, 2004).[6]

This is the new international environment in which industrial policy must operate to support the dynamic segments of SMEs and informal micro-enterprises. We suggest that the growth and the development of informal and formal micro-, small and medium enterprises and the development of local systems of development can be considered a direct approach to poverty reduction and human development, contributing at the same time to economic growth and complementing other industrial policy for certain industries essential to long-term country development (see Mehrotra and Biggeri, 2006 for further discussion). The strategy should thus consist of policies to remove the constraints for the upgrading of the informal activities into microenterprises and SMEs without forgetting the demand side, domestic and international.[7] One of the most successful strategies – followed, with different paths, by some late industrializers (e.g. Italy) and by some developing countries (e.g. China through its township and village enterprises) – is to develop the economy at local level through clusters of SMEs.[8]

It is worth pointing out that small firms can have a central role in local development not only because they generate more employment than large ones, but because healthy small enterprises in a cluster can foster the sub-contracting system, and by reducing the 'missing middle' also benefit large and medium-sized firms. Further, Mead and Liedholm (1998), after reviewing the evidence, also argue that growth-oriented small firms generally create employment of good quality, in that jobs created by expanding existing small firms are more productive than those that result from new small start-up firms. Moreover, they also show that returns per hour of family labour are substantially higher in firms with 2–5 workers (and even higher in those with 6–9 workers) than in those with one person working alone.

Reasons of space preclude a detailed discussion of the policies needed to upgrade microenterprises and promote the development of clusters. Suffice it here to say that informal activities need not be perceived as a symptom of economic dysfunction (as it is in the 'modernization' view), but as an opportunity. Indeed the informal actor's role (and that of SMEs in conjunction) can go beyond survival, and can enhance employment generation and poverty reduction (through income diversification), output creation, internal/domestic trade expansion, entrepreneurship formation, the transformation of savings into local investment, the use of appropriate technology in relation to local resources, and skills creation and production oriented to satisfy local demand. Too often, better integration of the economy is interpreted only as integration into the world economy; however, economies that are better integrated domestically are also able to access export markets. However, this positive role of informal activities need support to avoid what Tendler (2004) aptly calls the 'devil's deal'.[9] Some ways to provide this support are discussed next.

Social protection in the informal economy

Consistent with our view that policies to promote growth and human development have to fit together hand in glove (and that macroeconomic policies should not be determined without considering their microeconomic impacts carefully), one institution that will be required if the modern market economy is to become legitimate in the eyes of the poor is social insurance for the majority of developing countries' labour force – who are in the informal economy. As Rodrik rightly notes: 'A modern market economy is one where change is constant and idiosyncratic (i.e. individual-specific) risk to incomes and employment is pervasive....One of the liberating effects of a dynamic market economy is that it frees individuals from their traditional entanglements – the kin group, the church, the village hierarchy. The flip side is that it uproots them from traditional support systems and risk-sharing institutions' (2000: 17). Hence the modern market economy characterized by a large and growing informal sector needs a system of social insurance. A major reason why the market-oriented model has elicited an adverse reaction from the poor in developing countries – especially Latin America, which embraced the model most forcefully following the debt crisis of the 1980s – is that they have neglected social insurance.

However, social insurance does not mean unemployment insurance in urban areas. We exclude unemployment insurance, since the share of those in informal employment is so large in the developing countries that it is unrealistic to speak of such insurance on a wide enough scale; let us recall that even in the advanced capitalist countries unemployment insurance was resisted most by employers and came after other social reforms (Korbi, 2000). We believe, therefore, that a realistic programme of social insurance applicable to informal economy wage workers in developing countries, including home-based industrial/agricultural outworkers, would be one that in the first instance encompasses only a limited set of benefits: maternity benefits for women workers, disability and death benefits for all workers, and old-age pensions (or a savings/provident fund scheme). In the short run, if a universal, citizenship-based scheme for all workers in the informal economy is not feasible, we argue for practical steps towards such a goal. A universal scheme can only work if the government of the day is willing and able to use general government revenues to finance such a scheme; beneficiary contributions alone from low-paid and casually employed informal workers will not suffice to cover the costs of such a scheme, especially on a universal basis. The defining characteristic of wage work in the informal economy is sub-minimum wages and unstable income, since work availability is uncertain and often seasonal.

Yet, the needs of informal workers for some minimal forms of social insurance are undeniable and urgent. Even in countries with high economic growth, workers are increasingly in less secure employment, such as the self-employed, casual labour and homeworkers (ILO, 2005). Hence the gradual extension of formal social security programmes that currently cover a fraction of the labour force cannot be a solution for the social insurance needs of those in the informal economy. The labour force is expanding faster than formal sector employment.

Hence, we make a case here for a product-group or trades-based social insurance mechanism that is not primarily financed by beneficiary contributions. Sector- and even product-group-specific social insurance funds, financed mainly from a tax levied on the product produced by informal workers, could be a significant way forward for all informal sector manufacturing activities. The point is that the tax on the product does not go into the general treasury, but is actually earmarked specifically for the purpose of creating such social insurance funds. The same mechanism for protection that we propose here could also apply to agricultural products and hence the agricultural sector. However, the mechanism for those who work in the services would be trickier, and hence could be more difficult to implement.[10] Several state governments in India, as well as the central government, have several such funds – all in the informal sector. The Philippines already has such a welfare fund in agriculture for plantation workers. Such product- or activity-based social insurance mechanisms can be an important precursor to the more universal citizenship-based social insurance mechanisms, characteristic of industrialized countries (see Mehrotra and Biggeri, 2006: ch. 12; also Mehrotra and Biggeri, 2002b).

Such an institution has the potential of reducing economic insecurity and reducing the backlash against market-oriented reforms. They may also promote the social cohesion needed during the structural adjustment process, as we noted at the beginning of this chapter.

3.3   Alternative macroeconomic policies

Here we discuss briefly the areas in which the orthodox paradigm needs revision, with a view to ensuring that macroeconomic balance (an objective to which economists of all persuasions subscribe) is consistent with equity and poverty-reducing growth.

Broadly conceived, macroeconomic policies can be clustered under four heads: fiscal policy, monetary policy, external policies (trade, foreign investment and exchange rate policy), and domestic deregulation/privatization/ property rights (following Williamson's (1990) famous characterization of the ten elements of the Consensus policies). In regard to fiscal policy, the Consensus suggested that public spending should be allocated to activities 'with high economic returns and the potential to improve income distribution'. It is impossible to disagree with the need to shift public spending away from unproductive subsidies (an issue we discuss further in Chapter 9) and towards health and education. However, the reality during the stabilization periods generally was that the stress on overall fiscal discipline meant that in practice health and education expenditures did not increase in most countries, and the bias against *basic* health and education continued (see the World Bank's own publication, Jayarajah et al., 1996). The Millennium Development Goals (MDGs) agreed by all governments in the year 2000 can only be achieved if allocative efficiency in public social spending improves.[11] In addition, while reducing unsustainable fiscal deficits was an unexceptional objective, there was no mention of the need to finance counter-cyclical social programmes and social funds, which could also mitigate the adverse social impact of stabilization. When these programmes were introduced, they appeared as add-ons, not integral to the objective of expanding functionings (Cornia, 2004). In industrialized countries, the role of fiscal policy has been counter-cyclical; unfortunately, in emerging market economies, it has been cyclical and constrained, as fiscal policy in these countries is burdened by debt servicing as well as its dependence upon the international financial institutions for aid when a foreign exchange crisis hits.

As a means of fiscal deficit reduction, the Consensus focused mainly on public expenditure reduction, rather than tax revenue mobilization. However, achieving the MDGs is crucially dependent upon states mobilizing additional domestic resources (and, in the least developed countries, additional official development assistance from abroad). The tax base, according to the Consensus, was meant to be broad and marginal tax rates moderate. However, despite falling tax rates, the reality is that of widespread tax evasion in most low- and middle-income countries. Hence tax policy in the future needs to focus much more on enforcement and compliance of existing tax laws (see Chapter 9 for a further discussion of this issue).

In monetary policy, the requirement of the Consensus that public programmes should stop providing cheap loans to the well-connected or only to those who have collateral to offer and eliminate controls on interest rates paid to depositors, was appropriate. However, there was no need to throw the baby out with the bath water. In the future, the emphasis should be to prevent interest rates from rising inordinately, which negatively affects budget deficits and the cost of both private and public investment. The latter will affect growth prospects, impacting negatively on the poor. How high real interest rates can seriously dampen both public investment is demonstrated by the rise in real interest rates in India in the second half of the 1990s, just when inflation rates were low and falling – a 'failure of monetary policy in India of monumental scale'. Not only did public investment fall, but in fact this regime of tight money effectively killed off the quite dramatic and immediate response of private investment to the change in policy regime in 1991 (Balakrishnan et al., 2006).

The emphasis of the Consensus on controlling capital flight, which reinforces existing inequalities of income apart from diminishing the stock of savings, was appropriate – but financial market liberalization, which the Consensus promoted, facilitated capital flight (Grabel, 2003). The recent shift in emphasis towards gradual liberalization until regulatory and supervisory capacity improves is appropriate.

Contemporary economic crises differ from traditional episodes of balance-of-payments problems in important respects (Ahluwalia, 1999). The latter typically originated in the current account, with a macroeconomic policy imbalance, or an external shock or domestic-supply shock causing a widening of the current-account deficit which needed to be financed. Contemporary crises, on the other hand, originate from the capital account and are caused by a loss of confidence, which leads to a large outflow of capital and a denial of access to new financing. This becomes particularly relevant on account of the increase in private capital flows in the 1990s. Private capital flows were half of net official flows in the period 1984–89, but they had increased to more than eight times the level of official flows in 1995. However, this has also made these countries vulnerable to the volatility of private capital flows. Free mobility implies that capital can move out if there is a sudden loss of confidence, and the frequency of crises in the 1990s suggests that many developing countries have not been able to manage the risks arising from this situation in an effective manner. Hence the current shift in focus towards gradual financial liberalization is appropriate.[12]

In regard to external sector policies, the emphasis of the Consensus on competitive exchange rates is necessary, since that encourages employment creation in internationally competitive sectors of activity. However, trade liberalization was not the way in which either industrialized countries or, more recently, the East Asian countries built up their industrial capacity. Theoretically, rapid trade liberalization is assumed to increase a country's income by shifting resources from less productive to more productive uses, based on static comparative advantage. However, the real world works differently. Shifting resources from low productivity to no productivity does not increase incomes, which is precisely what happened under rapid trade liberalizations induced by Fund policies (on Africa, see Reinert, 2003). The orthodoxy's belief in the market also drives the belief that new, more productive, jobs will replace the erstwhile inefficient jobs that existed under protected barriers. However, creating new firms takes financial capital and entrepreneurial capacity, and limited bank capital and poor quality higher education restrict both. High interest rates, which normally accompanied Fund policies, will limit the demand for capital.

The East Asian countries dropped protective barriers only slowly, after years of systematic support for import-substituting industrialization, and then later forcing firms to export while providing subsidies. China is only just reducing its trade barriers, twenty years after its market-oriented reforms led to rapid growth of manufacturing exports (Nolan, 1995).[13] In fact, the relationship between trade policy and economic growth remains very much an open question, and the issue is not settled on empirical grounds. As Rodrik notes:

> The relationship [between trade policy and growth] is likely to be a contingent one, dependent on a host of country and external characteristics. The fact that practically all of today's advanced countries embarked on their growth behind tariff barriers, and reduced protection only subsequently, surely offers a clue of sorts. Note also that the modern theory of endogenous growth yields an ambiguous answer to the question of whether trade liberalization promotes growth. The answer varies depending on whether the forces of comparative advantage push the economy's resources in the direction of activities that generate long-run growth (via externalities in research and development, expanding product variety, upgrading product quality, and so on) or divert them from such activities. (2000: 30)

Besides, for the poorest countries, without enhanced market access to industrialized country markets in goods where they have a comparative advantage, reducing trade barriers will merely reduce the revenues of government, and worsen current account deficits. In fact, consistent with this prediction, current account deficits of developing countries were higher in the 1990s compared to the 1970s by 2 percentage points of GDP (UNCTAD, 2001).

Besides, open trade policies do not necessarily imply open capital markets. Convertibility on the current account should not automatically imply convertibility of the capital account. Opening capital markets exposes countries to the risk of financial contagion, thus making growth more volatile (as in many Latin American countries), affecting the poor adversely (Birdsall et al., 2001). When one combines the debt burden of many emerging market economies (discussed further below) with the volatility of capital markets, the resultant mixture can be explosive, as we have seen repeatedly since the Asian economic crisis. As Dervis notes:

> The interaction of volatile international capital markets with large accumulated stocks of debt have created chronic macroeconomic vulnerability in a whole class of emerging market economies, constraining their growth, reducing their capacity to fight poverty, and, at times, constituting a systemic threat to the entire world economy. (2005: 105)

The privatization advocated by the Consensus has become the basis of reinforcing existing inequalities in wealth and income (a phenomenon that has been particularly noticeable as privatization proceeded rapidly in much of Latin America (Bulmer-Thomas et al., 1996) and the former Soviet Union (Cornia, 2004) in the 1990s) – a process which is bound to break the links between growth and poverty reduction, and also between growth and human development. Privatization was undertaken primarily in order to reduce the drain on budgets from subsidizing state-owned enterprises, and for the sake of the one-off earnings from the sale. It was rarely undertaken with the objective of promoting competition, which could have encouraged efficiency (Stiglitz, 2002).

Several additional concerns arose. Privatizations proceeded too rapidly on the assumption that markets would arise quickly. However, as Karl Polanyi (1944) had noted in respect of the transformation in Europe in the nineteenth century, markets do not emerge spontaneously; the state has to play an important role in helping them emerge. A second concern is that privatization, as often practised, has been accompanied by corruption, hardly surprising given that the same politicians and bureaucrats that oversaw public enterprises also supervised the privatizations (Stiglitz, 2002). Hence, where possible, alternatives to privatization should be pursued. For instance, many state-owned companies in China were reformed and made profitable before being privatized, belying the argument of inherent public sector inefficiency.

Foreign direct investment (FDI) was another element in the Consensus. Privatization, liberalization and stabilization were meant to create the right environment for foreign investment. FDI can bring technical expertise and foreign capital. FDI is part of the story of successful export-oriented manufacturing in Singapore, Malaysia and also China – though not in the traditional East Asian tigers. However, is FDI creating new productive capacity? A significant proportion of all FDI over the 1990s has involved the mere takeover (mergers) of firms, instead of involving the actual creation of new productive capacity (UNDP HDR, 1999). Cross-border mergers and acquisitions (M&A) were 42 per cent of FDI in 1992, and 59 per cent of FDI in 1997, at the same time that the total value of M&A rose from $55 billion to $236 billion (increasing further in East Asia after the 1997 economic crisis).

The Consensus rightly emphasized property rights, but ignored the most important potential asset for poor rural households: land. As we argued in section 3.1, land reforms (as well as policies to redistribute other assets) will be needed in a large number of Latin American, South Asian and some African contexts if equitable growth is to take off in these countries, especially but not only in the agricultural sector.

Finally, it is not obvious that unregulated labour markets and labour flexibility (recommended by the Consensus) will ever resemble a full employment equilibrium. Since the majority of developing-country workers are engaged in informal employment, there is a case for at least a minimal social protection (involving social insurance for death and disability) for *all* workers – as we noted in the previous section.[14]

There is currently great pressure on developing countries to adopt a set of 'good policies' and 'good institutions' to foster their economic development. However, curiously, even many of those who are sceptical of the applicability of these policies and institutions to the developing countries take it for granted that these were the policies and institutions that were used by the developed countries when they themselves were developing countries. Chang (2002), on the basis of a detailed and careful review of historical evidence, argues that this cannot be further from the truth – the developed countries did not get where they are now through the policies and the institutions that they recommend to the developing countries today.[15] Most of them actively used 'bad' trade and industrial policies, such as infant industry protection and export subsidies – practices that are discouraged, if not actively banned, by the WTO these days. Very interestingly, the UK and the USA, which most of us think of as the paragons of free-trade and free-market policies, were the most ardent users of such policies in the earlier stages of their development. In terms of institutional development, until they were quite developed (say, until the early twentieth century), the developed countries had very few of the institutions deemed essential for developing countries today: democratic political institutions, a professional bureaucracy, and a central bank. Indeed, when they were developing countries themselves, the developed countries had much lower quality institutions than today's developing countries at comparable levels of development. The point here is not that developing countries should not attempt to develop some of these institutions today; only that those institutions have to be in keeping with the local conditions and address their current problems, as we have emphasized in this chapter (for example, land reforms; social insurance; government support for industrial policy to encourage formalization of informal enterprises, including clusters and microenterprises). The international community also has to be willing to accept institutional diversity, although that cannot become an argument in developing countries for authoritarian rule and undermining of participatory democracy.

Summing up, the state has many policies at its disposal if it wishes to promote economic growth along with the synergies to make it pro-poor.[16] State interventions in social sectors and the productive structure to promote and regulate economic growth, and redistributive policies, are part of this set and are interrelated. Unfortunately, as we saw above, most developing countries have focused not on distribution but rather on economic growth, for more than three decades (Birdsall and Londono, 1997; Kanbur and Squire, 1999).

The dominant paradigm has not ensured economic growth since the onset of the external debt crisis and the rise of orthodox thinking in the early

1980s, based on open markets and privatization. If anything it has reinforced inequalities of income, on which there has been increasing evidence (Cornia, 2004). At the same time, it has completely marginalized the poorer countries, and the poorest among them.

3.4   The historical significance of the current conjuncture in the macroeconomic policy debate

We cannot conclude this chapter without noting the historical significance of the current conjuncture – first in relation to the poorer low-income countries, and then to the emerging market economies of the world. Nations committed themselves to achieving the Millennium Goals of halving income-poverty and other social and environmental indicators by 2015 (see Annex 1.1), but by all accounts progress has been slow (UNDP HDR, 2003, 2005). Without faster economic growth the goals seems unachievable, except in a minority of Asian countries. While the poorest countries do need a large injection of foreign assistance, as the UN Millennium Project (2005) has argued strongly – an issue we discuss at length in Chapter 10 – we are suggesting that most countries will remain underachievers in respect of the goals unless there is a significant shift in macroeconomic policies and also major institutional changes, as discussed in this chapter.

For the least developed countries, a major change occurred in 1999 with the introduction by the IMF and the World Bank of the Poverty Reduction Strategy Papers (PRSPs). The change occurred out of the need to ensure that debt relief would be devoted to poverty reduction. It was the biggest change in international development cooperation since the introduction of the first structural adjustment loan in 1980. The change occurred because internal evaluations had concluded that the adjustment programmes were not effective for several reasons: there was a lack of national ownership of policy reforms; social elements were not incorporated in them; and poor donor coordination was causing transaction costs for governments and donors alike. The real issue today is: has this reform solved the problem?

The evidence from the reviews does not suggest that this new reform has made much difference (as we have already hinted in earlier chapters). Two reasons are noted by Dervis (2005). First,

> the existing framework created by the Heavily Indebted Poor Country/Poverty Reduction Strategy Papers initiative is appropriate as an *approach*, but it is insufficient in its *degree of ambition* and in the *amount of resources* available to make it work. As argued in detail in the Zedillo Report, resources deployed

worldwide in the fight against extreme poverty must be doubled, with most of these resources going to the poorest countries, if the MDGs are to be achieved (2005: 146).[17]

The UN Millennium Project Report has made strong proposals about integrating the Millennium Goals into PRSPs, costing sector investment strategies, and mobilizing additional ODA to finance the investment. After declining through the 1990s, official development assistance (ODA) has indeed risen since 2001. Yet ODA growth has not matched donors' economic growth, and a large part of the ODA increase over 2001–04 was in the form of debt relief and emergency and reconstruction aid.

The second reason for the scepticism about the credibility of the PRSP approach noted by Dervis cuts deeper. One of the main reasons for lack of ownership of PRSPs and macroeconomic reforms is that 'for the comprehensive conditionality required to be at all acceptable, the governance of the Bretton Woods institutions and of the whole international process with regard to the poorer countries will have to be perceived as much more legitimate' (Dervis, 2005: 145). The profoundly important point he makes is that a better globalization requires legitimate global governance.[18] The current process lacks legitimacy because, as noted in an IMF external consultation on conditionality, 'the PRSP is a compulsory process wherein the people with money tell the people who want the money what they need to do to get the money' (IMF, 2001: 147). This is not an environment that fosters home-grown policies.

If PRSPs were genuinely home-grown, they should reflect a diversity of national approaches. However, they are remarkably uniform (Stewart and Wang, 2003; Oxfam, 2004). We have noted in an earlier chapter that this uniformity is most evident in their macroeconomic policies, which are rarely subject to national dialogue or debate during the period of PRSP formulation (Vos, 2003).

The IMF's Poverty Reduction and Growth Facility (PRGF), which sets most macroeconomic policies for borrowing countries, should be based on the PRSPs. But the reverse is usually the case. Because most PRGFs have been negotiated before PRSPs, they have not benefited from national dialogue and debate, in which various policy options could be evaluated (Mckinley, 2004). The PRGF macroeconomic framework has been imported with limited alterations into many PRSPs. And national policy autonomy has suffered as a consequence. As we have argued in the current as well as the previous chapter, since governments have tailored their policies to satisfy external priorities, it is no wonder that PRSPs exhibit little variation. In recognition of this problem, the World Bank's Operations Evaluation Department has recommended that the World Bank should 'reduce or eliminate uniform requirements and foster better customisation' of PRSPs to country circumstances (World Bank, 2004: xiii).

If poor countries had more policy leeway, they could adopt more growth-oriented policies. One of the constant concerns of IMF programmes has been the rate of inflation – a legitimate concern given the reality of the 1980s in much of Africa and Latin America. However, the evidence is that in the 1990s and since the inflation rates around the world have fallen sharply. The World Bank's *Global Development Finance 2005* finds that in upper-middle-income countries the inflation rate averaged 7.3 per cent over 1991–2000, and under 3.9 per cent over 2001–03; in the lower-middle-income countries 8.3 per cent over the 1990s, and around 4 per cent since then; and 10.2 per cent in the 1990s and about 4.5 per cent since then even in the low-income countries. Such low inflation rates also have a deflationary impact since they are accompanied by tight monetary policies and high real rates of interest. Such a restrictive stance is of particular concern now with the rise in international oil prices. As a result, the IMF moderated its stance in 2005 to accommodate inflation rates of 5–10 per cent, instead of insisting on rates in low single digits (IMF, 2005b: 19). Allowing inflation to rise to moderate levels stems from the recognition that a dramatic scaling up of ODA, as envisaged for the MDGs, will expand domestic demand pressures, at least in the short run.[19]

The emerging market economies face problems of a slightly different character than the poorest countries (though not entirely dissimilar since they also derive essentially from their external indebtedness). The threat from macroeconomic policies to the Millennium Goals could not be clearer in the case of the twenty-nine emerging market economies of the world, which actually account for a majority of the world's poor.[20] The IMF's *Global Economic Outlook 2005* found for these twenty-nine countries (which include the largest developing economies of the world) the mean public-debt-to-GDP ratio was 69.1 per cent in 2002 (64.1 per cent in 1992), compared to the 25 per cent that the IMF determined was a warranted ratio.[21] Apart from the high debt stock, they also have interest payments which amount to 5 per cent of GDP. These are conditions that can precipitate a 'debt event', since most of this debt is commercial, not concessional. Governments have borrowed from international capital markets. The IMF shows that the median public-debt-to-GDP ratio in the year before a default was about 50 per cent.

Dervis and Birdsall (2006) rightly note that this is a structural situation that makes both economic growth and social investment highly vulnerable to international confidence in the developing country. There is a large difference in the interest rates that developing countries pay versus developed countries on foreign debt. Because of the difference in yields between developing and developed country foreign debt, the higher interest rates in the emerging market economies create an attractive short-term investment opportunity for international investors with high real returns on their bonds. As the exchange rate appreciates due to capital inflows, even if real interest rates decline in domestic currency terms when the demand for bonds goes up, real returns remain high for foreign investors because of the exchange-rate appreciation. This leads to further capital inflows, leading to a further appreciation of the exchange rate. When the cycle reverses itself, the real exchange-rate apprecia- tion hurts exports, and the current-account deficit deteriorates. Short-term capital flows out, and a debt event could occur. If international capital markets lack confidence in an emerging market economy with high debt, it has to approach the IMF for a bail-out; an IMF programme seems to accord that credibility to capital markets – regardless of whether the programme is consistent with growth and poverty-reduction objectives.

The biggest problem is that when a debt event does occur, two phe- nomena prove particularly damaging to the interests of the poor. The first is that a debt event disables fiscal policy. Unfortunately, in high-debt emerging market economies, fiscal policy is pro-cyclical, not anti-cyclical as it is in industrialized countries. Not concerned about debt events, rich countries can expand public spending by more than national income in a recession. The same does not occur in a normal emerging-market economy, as the income fall worsens debt-to-GDP ratio, and the government cannot borrow even more under the circumstances. If anything, the IMF will call for a larger primary surplus to restore international market confidence. The public expenditure cuts will undermine the social wages of the poor most. As Dervis and Birdsall rightly note:

> The procyclical austerity policies that the global capital market demands are the opposite of what industrial economies implement when there is lack of growth – including not only reduced interest rates and increased public spending in general but also unemployment insurance, increased availability of food stamps, emergency public works programmes, and other ingredients of a sound and permanent social safety net. (Dervis and Birdsall, 2006: 8)

Not surprisingly, these are some of the same measures that we have called for earlier in this chapter. Most strikingly, if the fiscal pressure is long-drawn-out (e.g. in Latin America in the 1980s), it weakens the institutional capacity of public service delivery systems (e.g. drug procurement systems collapse).

The second structural problem that emerging market economies face when they encounter a debt event is that income inequality is higher in many high-debt countries. High debt burdens tend to make the growth process disequalizing. To cite Dervis and Birdsall, 'Structurally high real interest rates caused by sovereign default and currency risk act as a mechanism constantly redistributing income to the rich, to both foreign fund owners across borders and domestic owners of liquid wealth' (2006: 7–8).

Their answer to this structural problem is that these emerging market economies should not have to rely exclusively upon international capital markets for borrowing: the Bretton Woods institutions need to create a new facility for countries which are no longer IDA-eligible. For a transitional period, those countries where incomes have increased to make them IDA-ineligible should be able to access funds from this new facility at less than market terms, though not on concessionary terms. This transitional facility will reduce the dependence of high-debt emerging-market economies on international capital markets, thus enabling them to overcome many of the problems discussed above.

An alternative view could be that in emerging market economies the IMF has lost its influence in any case (Weisbrot, 2005). After their experience with the fund in 1997–98, Asian countries began sharply to increase their international foreign exchange reserves – partly so they would never have to rely on the IMF again. But a serious challenge to the fund came in the 2000s from another emerging market economy: Argentina.

Argentina suffered through a terrible four-year depression, beginning in 1998. A country that until recently had among the highest living standards in Latin America soon saw the majority of the country falling below the poverty line. Many Argentines pointed a finger at the IMF, which had played a major role in actively supporting the policies that led to the collapse, and seemed to prescribe just the wrong policies during the crisis: high interest rates, budget tightening and maintaining the Argentine peso's unsustainable link to the US dollar. In December 2001 the government defaulted on $100 billion of debt, the largest sovereign debt default in history. The currency and banking system collapsed, and the country sank further into depression – but only for about three more months. Thereafter, the economy began to recover.

The recovery began and continued without any help from the IMF. In fact, on the contrary, in 2002, the Fund and other official creditors (including the World Bank), actually took a net $4.1 billion – more than 4 per cent of GDP – out of Argentina. But the government was able to chart its own economic course, rejecting IMF demands for higher interest rates, increased budget austerity and utility price increases. Argentina also took a hard line with foreign creditors holding defaulted debt, despite admonitions from the Fund. In September 2003, Argentina did what had rarely been attempted before – a temporary default to the IMF itself, until the Fund demurred. The result was a rapid and robust recovery, with a remarkable 8.8 per cent growth in GDP for 2003, and 9 per cent for 2004. With a projected 7.3 per cent economic growth rate for 2005, Argentina is currently the fastest growing economy in Latin America.

This development has been regarded as marking a new trend in the decline of the influence of the IMF in emerging-market economies. Before Argentina's showdown with the fund, only failed or 'pariah' states with nothing left to lose – like the Congo or Iraq – had defaulted to the IMF, because of the IMF's power to cut off not only its own credit but also most loans from the larger World Bank, other multilateral lenders, industrialized-country governments and even much of the private sector. This has been the source of the IMF's enormous influence over economic policy in developing countries. As Weisbrot puts it,

> It was, in effect, a creditors' cartel led by the fund, which is answerable primarily to the U.S. Treasury Department. But Argentina showed that a country could stand up to the IMF, and not only live to tell about it but even launch a solid economic recovery. This changed the world. Although the IMF still carries a lot of weight in poorer countries, its influence in the middle-income countries has plummeted. The fund is now a shadow of its former self. Reformers over the past 15 years debated whether change would come about through the IMF altering its policies, or through the fund losing influence. That debate has now been settled by history. The IMF has not been reformed, but its power to shape economic policy in developing countries has been enormously reduced. (2005)

In our view, this understanding is somewhat exaggerated, even though it recognizes a trend in Asia to rely on one's own foreign exchange reserves and turn to inter-country monetary cooperation within Asia (witness the swap arrangements arrived at in the Chiang Mai initiative), as has happened systematically after the Asian economic crisis of the late 1990s. It was during this crisis that Japan made the proposal for the creation of an Asian Monetary Fund to assist countries facing crises – given that most resources to bail out the East Asian economies in crisis were, in any case, mobilized in the Asian region.

A far more realistic understanding of the current conjuncture would perhaps be as follows. The IMF's role has obviously changed dramatically from the days when it was the centrepiece of the Bretton Woods architecture.

The shift to floating exchange rates in the 1970s, and the enormous growth in private capital markets since then, eliminated the Fund's role as a source of finance for industrialized countries. It has also become less important for those emerging-market countries which have access to capital markets and can therefore handle the more usual balance-of-payments problems on their own, though even these countries may need support from the Fund for large-scale crises, because their access to capital markets is subject to sudden interruption in times of difficulty. For the least developed countries, which do not have significant access to capital markets, Fund financing remains important.

The elimination of the Fund's financing role for industrialized countries inevitably weakened its ability to influence policies in the industrialized economies, even though these policies can have adverse effects on the rest of the world – an issue we return to in Chapter 10. The surveillance function of the Fund was at one stage projected as a possible mechanism for overseeing the consistency of macroeconomic policies of the industrialized countries, but this has not happened in practice.[22] Its contribution to the process of policy coordination among industrialized countries since then is also limited.

Policy coordination among industrialized countries is now conducted, if at all, only in the G7 forum. The position of these countries on international economic policy issues is usually decided as part of this process, and decisions which concern the Fund and the Bank are then presented at Interim Committee (renamed the Financial and Monetary Committee) and Development Committee twice-yearly meetings, more or less as a *fait accompli*. This governance structure is not very democratic, to say the least, since developing countries are excluded from this process during its early and formative stages, and they do not have the power to force reconsideration at later stages.

As the emerging-market economies integrate more fully with the world economy, problems in emerging-market countries will grow in scale and could also have larger potential effects on markets in industrialized economies. There is a need for a forum which can consider these issues in a more holistic manner and in which emerging market countries are adequately represented. The establishment of the G20 in September 1999, convened by the USA after the East Asian crisis to discuss international stability issues, achieved the objective of creating a forum for informal consultation with the systemically important developing countries. However, as Ahluwalia (1999) points out, it is not a substitute for a more formal structure which would involve these countries and which would be linked to the Bretton Woods institutions, and to the two committees which supervise them. The creation of a new overarching Ministerial Group, with a direct supervisory role over the Bretton Woods institutions, and a linkage to other international institutions concerned with the functioning of the financial system, could provide an opportunity to create a top-level governance forum with a more representative membership. In fact, the proposal of Dervis and Birdsall (2006) and Nayyar (2002) is also that a more representative governance structure is needed for the Bretton Woods institutions. That may finally create the space for the more nationally owned, country-differentiated macroeconomic policies that the Internal Evaluation Office of the IMF has itself been calling for in its work since its creation in 2000 (as we have noted earlier).[23]

Meanwhile, the external indebtedness of both the poorest countries and the emerging market economies poses a serious and continuing challenge to the achievement of the Millennium Goals. The difference between the two is mainly that while the former are dependent upon official sources of external finance, the latter are dependent upon private capital markets. The constraints upon macroeconomic policies that such high levels of debt impose upon these countries will need to be addressed by visionary joint action by governments in both North and South.

Part II

Public expenditure on basic social services

The (in)adequacy of public spending on basic social services

In this chapter, we follow a similar route to that adhered to in the previous chapter, but apply it to the synergy within the social sectors. First, we explore the theoretical and empirical shortcomings of the traditional economics approach to social policy (section 4.1). We proceed by presenting our alternative synergetic model (section 4.2). Subsequently (section 4.3), we explore spending patterns in developing countries and attempt to gauge their impact.

4.1 Neoclassical basis for state financing of basic services

Some theoretical issues

In regard to the social sectors, the neoclassical theory of public finance argues that when there are positive externalities,[1] market mechanisms alone will not ensure universal provision. Rather, there will tend to be an undersupply of goods that have positive externalities and an oversupply of goods that have negative externalities. Theoretically (in a tradition which dates back at least to Pigou), it would be possible to estimate the social benefit of the goods. The social benefit could be compared with its private one in order to calculate the amount of the subsidy required to bring the total quantities demanded and supplied equal to the social optimum. For instance, with immunization, assuming that the price (i.e. the cost to the consumer) of a vaccine equals the perceived private benefits (i.e. the utility of reducing the risk of infection), one segment of the population will buy the vaccines, while others will not (based on needs and budget constraints).

However, the benefits of immunization not only transcend one's own protection against the disease (the private benefit) but also extend to the lesser possibility of contagion among the general population (the social benefit). Because individuals do not need to (and usually do not) count these additional social benefits when deciding whether or not to pay for the vaccine, the price in the market is equalized to the private benefit, which is lower than the total benefit. This results in a sub-optimal (from a societal point of view) level of immunization. To increase this level in order to obtain the total benefits (both private and social), the price would have to be lowered. This could be done by subsidizing producers so they charge a lower price, or by providing funds to consumers to alleviate the cost of the vaccine. In both cases, the same subsidy has to be given by the state and would be based on the discrepancy between the private and social benefits – that is, the size of the externality.

There are, of course, serious limitations to calculating this subsidy in practice in terms of the information requirements. As a result, it has been argued (e.g. by neo-institutionalist authors who follow Ronald Coase, 1988) that, rather than state bureaucrats calculating the subsidy precisely, the state should allow and promote more complete markets. In other words, people who do not want to be infected would 'pay' not only for their vaccines but also for those who find it optimal not to get immunized. The difficulties involved in this approach can be as important as those in the calculation of the subsidy. Moreover, the approach assumes an enormous faith in the capacity of markets actually to perform as well as their theoretical counterparts in a relatively short period of time. Most societies have adopted a different and much more practical route, which is to provide the vaccination for free to everybody and cover the cost through other mechanisms (health insurance, general taxation, donations, etc.). Although informed by the model of externalities, this is a simpler approach much closer in spirit to the idea of merit goods.

Another element from the public finance literature that is often invoked for state involvement in the financing and/or provisioning of some services is the concept of 'public goods'. There are two distinctive characteristics of public goods: non-rivalry in consumption and non-exclusion. The first indicates that if one person uses the goods, it does not preclude others from also using them. Knowledge, which is not protected by property rights, falls under this category – for example, once patents expire, their usefulness remains intact and widely accessible on a universal spectrum. The second characteristic means that once the service is provided, consumers who do not pay for it cannot be prevented from consuming it. An example would be street lightning. Once lamp-posts are installed, they provide light for everybody; non-payers cannot be forced into the shadows.

It is usually claimed that due to the merging of these two features, private suppliers would not be able to generate any substantial profit from providing these goods. Consequently, the state has to intervene.

There are two aspects of public goods worth mentioning in the debate about basic social services (BSS). First, there are few examples of genuinely pure public goods in general, and within the social services in particular (Malkin and Wildavsky, 1991). Most public goods are of a mixed character, only partially non-rival or non-excludable. Roads and parks are generally non-rival, up to a congestion point, as are the air and the environment, in general. Firefighters potentially protect all of us at the same time – that is, non-rival. If more than one fire erupts, however, they cannot be at different places at the same time (rivalry in consumption). The same applies to the justice system, which, although available for all citizens, can be very slow in imparting justice to any single individual when the system itself is overburdened, as is all too often the case in most developing countries. In addition, roads and parks are excludable. Moreover, even some of the most obvious examples of public goods, such as the transmission of signals (whether from lighthouses, radio or television), can clearly be run for profit by the private sector.

When thinking of BSS, the examples of goods which are really non-rival and non-excludable are harder to find. Basic education, as all education, is obviously non-rival (up to a congestion point in the classrooms), but is certainly excludable. Although the social benefits of immunization are non-excludable, vaccines are rival in consumption. So are primary health-care centres.

The second point is that basing the limits of what goods should be financed/provided by the state on the notion of public good is a narrow view. It is questionable in normative terms and inaccurate historically. As we discussed in the previous chapter, states took up the provision of these goods as the market economy evolved. The state also defined what elements should be provided to all members of society (or the polity, i.e. those with a capacity to participate in political decisions), and how those goods and services should be financed. In other words, there have been other, more important, determinants of public spending and of state involvement than the technocratic definition of public goods. From the normative point of view, the limitation of state intervention, merely as it applies to pure public goods, would reduce state involvement quite considerably.

Thus, the role of the state in the mainstream discussion of public goods is rather narrowly conceived – and, above all, seems overly instrumental. A far more sophisticated analysis can be attempted within the realm of political economy. This would be attained by examining the state's provision of social services as, in fact, being central to the development of capitalism and the market economy in the now industrialized countries (as it was shown in the previous chapter). In fact, since the eighteenth century, the rise of tax-based social spending in rich countries has been central to government growth. 'It was social spending, not national defense, public transportation, or government enterprises, that accounted for most of the rise of governments' taxing and spending as a share of GDP over the last two centuries' (Lindert, 2004: 20).[2]

Attempts to measure the impact of expenditure

Several authors (Hanmer et al., 1999; Cornia and Mwabu, 1997; among others) have attempted exercises to gauge the impact of public social spending. As some of them seem to find that public expenditure has no impact on health outcomes (and this has sparked a rapidly growing debate), it might be interesting to review their arguments and empirical results. For instance, Filmer and Pritchett (1997), and Filmer et al. (1997), emphasize the lack of relevance of public health spending for the under-5 mortality rate (U5MR). Their theoretical arguments rest on several questionable assumptions, which in turn derive from the issues discussed in the previous section. Moreover, their arguments do not deny the relevance of public spending on health in general and primary health care (PHC), or BSS, in particular. Consequently, their empirical results do not prove that public health interventions are insignificant.

Filmer et al. (1997) argue, in line with the theory described in the previous section, that when health interventions are public goods, they should be financed by the state. However, as we argued earlier, this severely limits the interventions they would favour. All other health interventions undertaken by the state, they claim, would either be inconsequential or negative. As this is a strong argument, and it is quite common, it might be worthwhile to understand its rationale.

They introduce a simple optimization model where consumers, with a given level of exogenous income, maximize their utility subject to prices and a 'health production function'. They assume, but do not prove, that an internal solution to such an optimization problem exists and is unique. It is not recognized, however, that this 'optimal' consumption level of health 'inputs' may be insufficient to purchase the inputs needed to survive.[3] In other words, even the routine curative care they claim should only be provided by the private sector could be unaffordable or not supplied at all (if there is not enough effective demand).

When addressing the demand side, they claim that analysis of demand for health services should distinguish between 'serious' and 'non-serious' cases. Customers would be 'willing to pay' for care in the first case, and, consequently, there is no need to subsidize these services. They fail to realize, though, that if this reasoning were correct, there would be a rationale for public provision (or at least regulation). This is because private providers would enjoy rents from treating life-threatening illnesses, when customers have no choice but to purchase their services.[4]

Besides presenting anecdotal examples where public provision is of low quality,[5] they estimate several regressions, but do not have a model from which to choose their variables. It is then claimed that when all the variables used are included, the effect of public spending is statistically insignificant. However, most of the other variables are statistically insignificant too. This does not seem a good basis on which to assert that public spending is not relevant for health outcomes.[6] Moreover, in their regressions, public expenditure is, in fact, significant (with the correct sign) at 10 per cent, which is not bad, in two out of their six regressions.[7]

Other authors dispute their results. For instance, Hanmer et al. (1999) propose a counter-argument. Their approach is based on a review of existing literature and their own regressions. From their literature review, it is clear that using different data sets and model specifications, the empirical evidence is inconclusive about the effect of most variables. Nevertheless, per capita income does appear as one of the most robust, being significant in a majority of studies, but other input variables (which are assumed correlated to public expenditure) are robust too. Similar results are obtained by Anand and Ravallion (1993) and Cornia and Mwabo (1997).

These authors also estimate all possible combinations of several variables to gauge the effect of gender inequality, education and health inputs on health outcomes. Along with income, these variables also appear to be robust. Unfortunately, they have not included a direct measure of public expenditure on health services.

Neither externalities nor the notion of public goods allows the neoclassical framework to arrive at acceptable descriptions of what governments actually do in regard to basic social services. Not surprisingly, there are serious empirical shortcomings in the attempts to measure the impact of public expenditure in these sectors using these theoretical lenses. Thus, in the next section, we introduce an alternative model based on synergies, which expands and complements the model developed in the previous chapter.

4.2   The synergy among social services

Interventions in health, nutrition, water and sanitation, fertility control, education and income complement each other. Thus, the impact of any intervention is enhanced by investments in any other one.

Figure 4.1 represents this notion of synergy. On the horizontal rows, the various social services are represented as inputs or interventions – education, family planning, health, nutrition and water, and sanitation. The vertical columns represent the human development outcomes or outputs – knowledge, family size, health status, nutrition status, and healthy living conditions. The shaded cells are the ones where there is a relationship between a certain intervention and an outcome; for example, the use of contraception helps the spacing of children, which benefits the health status of the mother as well as the child. The arrows represent feedback effects from human development outcomes to the inputs/processes. For example, the improved health status of a child improves her ability to learn, just as improved nutritional status does. Similarly reduced family size improves the chances that a poor family will be able to afford education for all the children rather than merely the boy(s) in the family, and so on.

Since the connections presented here are central to our arguments about synergies, a more in-depth review of these connections is needed. First of all, it has to be recognized that none of these relationships is based on evidence discovered in the last few years. However, probably in part due to overspecialization within the disciplines represented on the matrix, they are all too often presented separately. By integrating them, it becomes clear that their separate effects, the ones often reported, are only partial. Interventions in health, nutrition, water and sanitation, fertility control and education not only affect a child's well-being but also complement and reinforce each other. Thus the impact of any one form of investment is increased in the presence of the others, proving the advantages of integrated approaches.

Notice that *educational inputs* have an impact on all types of human development outcomes.[8] The positive effects of education are intuitive and well known. First, parents, especially mothers, make better use of information and reproductive health-care facilities if they are more educated. Thus, more widespread education is associated with lower fertility. Better nutritional and health care is provided by educated parents for themselves and their children. Various routes ensure this result. The general knowledge acquired at school increases understanding of modern health practices and scientific beliefs, which make mothers (and fathers) more open to using health-care centres. Households with educated mothers spend a higher proportion

Figure 4.1 Education and health feedback effects

Social services inputs/ processes	Human development outcomes/outputs				
	Knowledge	Family size	Health status	Nutritional status	Healthy living conditions
Education		↵	↵	↵	↵
Family planning	↵				
Health	↵	↵		↵	↵
Nutrition	↵	↵	↵		
Water and sanitation					

of their income on food and health services. In addition, the capacity to acquire new knowledge and change behaviour accordingly is higher among those who attended school, as evidenced by the differential diffusion of HIV/AIDS among educated and uneducated women (Vandemoortele and Delamonica, 2000). As a result, health investments are more efficient in the presence of a more literate population (Caldwell, 1986). In countries where parents have been exposed during their school years to nutrition information, they combine different foods to obtain better nutritional outcomes. Also, mothers take better care of their nutritional needs during pregnancy, avoiding low-birth weight (ACC/SCN, 2000). Basic education also facilitates the rapid adoption of improved hygienic behaviour. This not only improves health outcomes but also enhances the impact of investments in water and sanitation systems.

In summary, education, and in particular girls' education, contributes to enhance the impact of other sectoral interventions. All of these, in turn, result in good nutrition and health, increasing the likelihood children will attend school and become better students. For instance, with lower fertility, parents can devote more attention to their children's studies and afford more food and school supplies, which improve learning. In addition, when girls need less time to help in household chores like fetching water, they have more opportunities to attend school. Also, they have more time and energy to study and do well in school, avoiding repetition or dropping out.

Family planning, by providing easy access to contraceptive means, enables the mother to space births, thus lowering the health risk to herself and the child, reducing infant and maternal mortality, and improving the healthy development of the child. Thus, lower fertility has positive implications for improving health and increasing life expectancy. Another important complementary outcome of intervention in health, education, water/sanitation and family planning is the rapid demographic transition. As children survive, families voluntarily curtail the number of children. This is not the place to enter the debate on the relative impact of supply of contraceptives versus desired family size in family planning (Bongaarts, 1994; Pritchett, 1994a, 1994b; Cassen, 1994). However, it is clear that lower infant and child mortality plays a major role in reducing fertility rates (Caldwell, 1986), as does education, the availability of information on reproductive health care, and its accessibility.

As population growth slows down, school systems find it easier to absorb all children. Teacher–pupil ratios can be reduced, increasing quality, without unduly burdening budgets; construction costs can also be reduced, releasing resources for other measures to enhance school quality.

As in the case of the health and nutrition sectors, the availability of information on and access to family planning services will not, on their own, reduce fertility as much as it might be needed or desired. They are more effective when couples are more educated and child survival rates are higher.

It is also very well established that lack of good *nutrition* critically interacts with *health*. For instance, control of diarrhoea and measles is very important not only for health outcomes but also in reducing malnutrition (by improving the capacity to absorb and retain caloric intake). By the same token, an insufficient intake of total calories, vitamins and protein weakens children's immune systems. This would make them vastly more vulnerable to the onset and consequences of infectious disease. Interventions in health promote good nutrition, and interventions in nutrition promote good health.

Moreover, micronutrient deficiencies and illness can have devastating consequences for the cognitive development of a child. For instance, iron-deficiency anaemia reduces cognitive functions, iodine deficiency causes irreversible mental retardation, and vitamin A deficiency is the primary cause of blindness among children. Girls are unfairly disadvantaged in many of these cases. They are more likely to suffer from iodine or iron deficiency. In addition, there are many contexts where girls' education is valued less than that of boys; consequently, girls miss school when they have to stay home to look after sick relatives. Also, boys are usually better fed and more likely to be taken to a health facility when ill.

While it is clear that good health and nutrition have benefits which reinforce each other, the above examples also show that they impact positively on fertility control and education. Yet it is also clear that good health, the protection against disease, and proper nourishment cannot be produced by health services or food alone.

Safe water and adequate sanitation also play a fundamental role in determining health conditions. Access to safe water and sanitation dramatically reduces the incidence of diarrhoea and many other diseases that kill millions of children and adults each year. Another effect of better access to water takes place through the reduced effort in carrying water, which is usually unduly borne by women and girls. Given the traditional roles they play in most societies, when women and girls have more time, they can apply it to better infant and child care. This leads to positive health results. Finally, especially for women, more time is available for pecuniary productive activities. This direct impact of water and sanitation improvements on income-poverty reduction is less well publicized than the effect of higher levels of education and better health on productivity.

The interaction between education, on the one hand, and safe water/sanitation, on the other, to strengthen each other and spill over to other sectors should be highlighted. The presence of toilets, safe water and hygienic conditions at school can reduce some constraints on sending children, especially girls, to school. Separate toilets for girls are known to be a consideration for parents (Mehrotra et al., 2005). Backed by proper hygienic behaviour such as hand washing and the use of soap, access to safe water and adequate sanitation reduces morbidity from infectious diseases and increases the nutritional status of children, which furthers their learning abilities.

Figure 4.2 also illustrates this synergy between interventions within the social sectors by presenting the impact in the form of a life cycle of an educated girl (Cochrane 1979, 1988; World Bank, 1996a). An educated girl is likely to marry later than a girl who remains without any education – this is especially true if the girl's education extends to at least a few years beyond primary level and she engages in economic activity outside the home. Also, an educated girl will have fewer children, will seek medical attention sooner for herself and her children, and is likely to provide better care and nutrition for herself and her children (Carnoy, 1992). This would reduce the probability

Figure 4.2 Life cycle of an educated girl

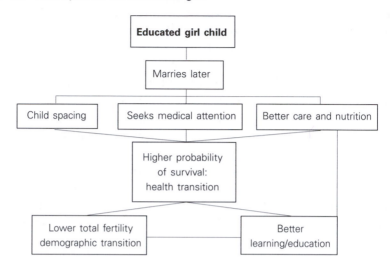

of morbidity through disease and hence the survival of her children beyond the age of 5. Over time, the survival of her children will change the family's behavioural pattern in respect to fertility and contraception – thus lowering the overall fertility rate. Smaller household size improves the care of children, and lower fertility reduces the size of the school-age population. These benefits of girls' education accrue from generation to generation. In other words, in order to maximize the complementarities among basic social services, it is crucial to focus on universal primary education early on, particularly for girls – but it also assumes that health/family planning/water and sanitation services are available (UNICEF, 2000).

In summary, each intervention has ramifications that lie outside its 'sector' and adds up to a virtuous circle of social and economic development. This is different from the existence of an externality, although they are of course present. Unlike the traditional treatment of externalities, which are usually exceptions and consequently can be dealt with (at least theoretically) by (re)specifying property rights, these interactions are pervasive.

Moreover, they do not just affect another sector; they all impinge on each other, resulting in a mesh of interactions. In other words, it is a multidimensional synergetic system. No wonder it results in a complex system, at which most developing countries have not yet succeeded. From an instrumental point of view, the benefits do not automatically accrue to all and markets alone would not ensure universal access – hence the need for the public sector to step in and finance these services.

Moreover, the case for government financing in these sectors also derives from equity considerations. It is the poor who usually lack these services, or if they have to pay for them they will underconsume them, and hence find it difficult to pull themselves out of the vicious cycle of a poverty trap – as the basic functionings of ability to read and write and lead a healthy life are essential to widening choices in life.

While the above arguments form the case for government financing of these services, the case for government provision rests on other grounds. The first is economies of scale. Water supply is in many ways a natural monopoly, and while in a large metropolis there may be a case for provision by two separate bodies (public or private), duplication and hence higher unit costs per volume of water supplied will result if several companies operate in the same locality. The second is improved coverage of services. Private physicians/nurses tend to concentrate in cities, while most of the population in low/middle income countries lives in rural areas. Similarly, private schools are more plentiful in urban as opposed to rural areas, partly in response to the higher incomes/demand in the cities and towns. If reducing interregional inequalities was a goal of government, the state would have to supply these services in rural areas as this would usually be cheaper than subsidizing private providers. Third, in social services, the practical contracting problems are particularly severe: even if private providers were willing and able to provide these services, asymmetric information between the government (which currently owns these services) and the private party interested in purchasing the public provider can lead to contracting problems.[9] A fourth reason is that the synergies may not be realized without simultaneous interventions in the different sectors. The risk of coordination failure is much greater if the state is merely financing these services, rather than providing them itself. Most states in developing countries suffer from capacity constraints, and coordination problems of pluralistic provision can prove overwhelming for a poorly trained civil service.

Another reason for ultimate state responsibility for provision of these basic services is that access to them is a fundamental human right, enshrined in the UN Declaration on Human Rights as well as subsequent conventions on social and economic rights and child rights. While citizens have rights, it implies a corresponding obligation on the part of the state to provide these services. These obligations entail respect, protection and fulfilment of rights by the state. In other words, the state not only must avoid doing harm (respect) and prevent others from infringing human rights (protect), it also ought actually to provide the means to ensure everybody can enjoy their rights (fulfil).

We would add one very strong cautionary note. While advocating state provision, we are keenly aware of the failures of the state in providing basic social services over many decades. That is why a whole chapter (Chapter 8) is devoted to private provision and examines the possibility of building complementarity between private and public provision. Second, another chapter (Chapter 7) is devoted to answering the question, how can the failure of state provision be addressed by decentralization and the articulation of voice as a means of ensuring accountability and effective provision of services for the poor? That chapter does not merely advocate decentralization – as has been done by the IFIs for at least a decade; it also puts forward a different model of democratic decentralization that has been demonstrated to be effective in improving state provision of basic social services – based on empirical evidence from a variety of sectors and countries in the developing world.

Policy lessons from high achievers – how to trigger the synergies

High-achieving countries, which made large improvements in their health and education indicators early in their development process, attest to the critical role played by the state in triggering the synergies between various social interventions. At least ten developing countries, drawn from every developing region, demonstrate this role of the state (Mehrotra and Jolly, 1997).[10] A number of principles of good practice in social and economic policy stand out as the way to launch this synergy. First, the role of the state in the provision of social services for the population was overwhelming. Whether it was the socialist state of Cuba or the market economy of the Republic of Korea, the provision of basic social services was not left to the free play of market forces, nor to the concept of economic growth trickling down to the poor in order to give them access to services. As in the case of industrialized countries (see Chapter 2), so for the high-achieving developing countries: the growth of per capita income was no guarantor of human development. For instance, in Brazil the income per capita is a multiple of Kerala's or Sri Lanka's, but the country has a lower life expectancy. Thus, the state ensured a high macroeconomic and fiscal priority to health and education spending compared to other countries in the region. At the same time, defence expenditure as a percentage of GDP is much lower for the high achievers than for developing countries as a whole (Figure 4.3).

Another principle, which emerged from the experience of the high achievers, was that the importance of the synergies within the social sectors

Figure 4.3 Defence expenditure: selected high achievers versus developing countries (defence expenditure as % of GNP)

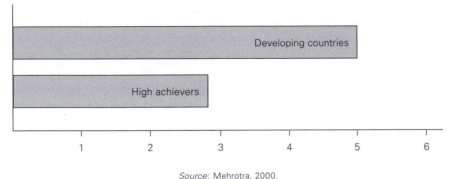

Source: Mehrotra, 2000.

is as critical as the size of the investment. Countries that achieved rapid and sustained advances in social indicators approached universal primary education and widespread access to basic health before achieving a 'breakthrough' in mortality reduction. The breakthrough in health status – the largest percentage decrease in IMR in the preceding three or four decades – was strongly assisted by nearly universal primary enrolment (see Table 4.1). The synergies between interventions in health and education are critical to the success of each and increase the return to each investment. The examples of the Republic of Korea and Costa Rica in Figure 4.4 are illustrative in this regard. In both cases, the fastest decline in infant mortality occurred when the returns to investments in health infrastructure were multiplied by the widespread attainment of primary education (see shaded areas in the graphs).[11]

This lesson of the predominant role of the state in funding the social services in the high achievers, and of the synergy of interventions, is central to our thesis in the rest of the book. The argument for the central role of the state in financing BSS derives from the potential for benefiting from synergies which comes from coordinated public action. In fact, if the state strongly encourages a policy of multiplicity of providers – private, NGO – there is a risk of coordination failure, resulting in the loss of benefit from the synergy of simultaneous interventions. This is especially the case since the regulatory capacity of the state remains weak – and has been demonstrated to be so (see Chapter 8 on the private sector in service delivery). While there is risk of government failure in social service delivery as well, there is

Table 4.1 Sequence of investment in high-achieving countries: health breakthrough followed by or simultaneous with education breakthrough

	Education breakthrough	Health breakthrough	IMR reduction (%)
Rep. of Korea	1960–70	1970–80	68
		esp. 1975–80	58
Malaysia	1947–60	1960–70	40
		1975–85	50
Kerala	1956–60	1975–85	40
Sri Lanka	1947–60	1940–50	40
Botswana	1970–80	1980–90	37
Mauritius	Before 1950 (m)	1945/9–1950/4	40
	1950–60 (f)		
Zimbabwe	1980–85	1980–90	30
Barbados	Before 1938	1950–60	50
	1970–80	1970–80	50
Costa Rica	Before 1960	1970–80	68
		1940–50	30
Cuba	1958–60	1970–80	40
		1975–85	50

Source: Mehrotra, 1997.

increasing evidence that such failure can be successfully addressed through deep democratic decentralization – which we explicitly address in Chapter 7. Problems of state provision do not result from resource constraints and allocative inefficiencies alone, but are also due to the bureaucratic and organizational context that prevails. However, the evidence from high achievers on the role of the state in achieving synergies should be treated with respect, not only by policymakers in the developing world but also by donor agencies.

Finally, the high-achieving countries demonstrate that it is important to shift the focus from 'welfare' approaches, which treat people as objects of development, to approaches which see them as active agents of change (Sen, 1995). This was particularly true for women. Sen (1995, 2000) argues that once women attain certain freedoms, they not only become agents of their own well-being, but of society as a whole: freedom to work outside the home, freedom to earn an independent income, freedom to have ownership rights, and freedom to receive an education. Thus, we find that in the high-achieving countries girls' enrolment has been very high, and on a par with that of boys, for several decades (Table 4.2). But we also find other evidence of gender equality.

Figure 4.4 Sequence of investment in education and health in high-achieving countries (Costa Rica and Korea)

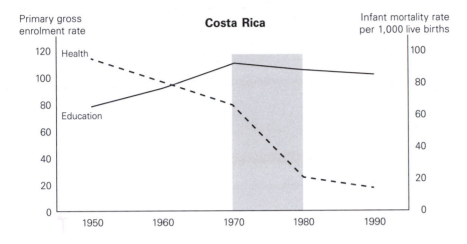

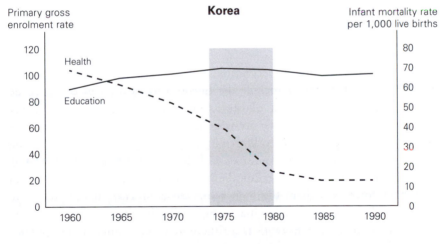

Source: Mehrotra, 2000

Table 4.2 Women's status in selected high-achieving countries
(primary enrolment, women as % of men)

Region	1970	1992	1970	1990
East Asia and Pacific				
regional average	74	81	87	96
high achievers	77	88	94	100
South Asia				
regional average	43	54	60	75
high achievers	76	91	92	100
Sub-Saharan Africa				
regional average	50	66	72	85
high achievers	76	85	98	103
Latin America/Caribbean				
regional average	91	97	101	98
high achievers	99	99	100	100

Sources: UNDP HDR, 1995; UNICEF, 1995a.

Women's participation in economic life can be measured in different ways.[12] Two main elements include the freedom to earn an income outside of the household and a lack of restrictions on owning productive assets. Unfortunately, data on the latter are very limited. However, female participation in the non-agricultural workforce in the labour force of high-achieving countries is higher than in countries with less social progress (Figure 4.5). Similarly, in professional and technical employment, women's participation in the labour force is high in the high-achieving countries. In Chapter 7 we further dwell on the agency of citizens, especially their political participation and their voice as a means of ensuring greater accountability in service delivery by the state.

In summary, various simultaneous actions can and should be taken to trigger the synergies. Private providers, looking (as they are supposed to do) only at their profits may both underinvest in these sectors and also misallocate investment only in certain geographical areas. Consequently, the state has a responsibility to engage in the provision of social services. This, evidently, requires public expenditures. In the next section we turn to measuring public expenditures and assess their impact.

Figure 4.5 Women's agency: employment outside the household, women as % of men, selected countries

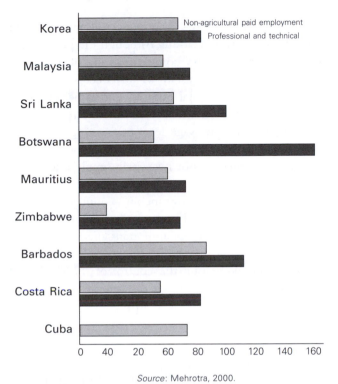

Source: Mehrotra, 2000.

4.3 Measuring and assessing public expenditure on basic social services in developing countries

Having discussed an alternative conceptual framework, focusing especially on the synergies connected to basic social services, we turn our attention in the rest of the chapter to assessing the current levels of public spending on BSS in selected developing countries. Unfortunately, this is an area where there is a dearth of information, in particular regarding public spending on *basic* social services, which constitute the core interventions to trigger the synergies. As a result, we have relied on evidence from a series of studies financed by UNICEF and UNDP in the mid- to late 1990s.

Comparing public spending across countries: some methodological issues

There are various ways to assess the importance of public spending for social services. All of them have limitations. Although the public expenditure literature is replete with cross-country comparisons in dollar terms, absolute figures (in dollar terms) are not as useful as macroeconomic priority (the share of public social spending in total output). This is because the bulk of the costs of delivery of basic social services are directly related to the level of development – in particular the wage level of teaching and nursing staff. Since BSS delivery is a labour-intensive activity, low expenditures in dollar terms in a low-income country do not necessarily imply a low priority for BSS. Moreover, given the preponderance of local inputs, interventions in BSS can be relatively inexpensive in low-income countries.

However, the proportion of national budgets allocated to the social sectors – that is, the fiscal priority – is a more important measure as it is directly determined by the government (while macroeconomic priority may be affected by changes in output beyond the control of the government). We used this measure, fiscal priority, to test for the impact of public action on health outcomes, which were proxied by U5MR.

Measurement issues

To calculate the ratio of government expenditure to basic social services (BSS), a manageable definition of basic expenditure is needed. The following definition was used in the studies mentioned above (see Annex 1.1 for further details on each category):

- primary health care (including preventive, promotion, and basic curative care);
- reproductive health and family planning;
- basic education (including pre-school, primary, literacy, life skills);
- water and sanitation for rural and peri-urban areas;
- nutrition support (including community-based approaches, and micronutrients).

Budgets are often not sufficiently transparent to allow an easy calculation of these categories. Consequently, when estimating the ratio, research required a detailed recalculation of parts of the budget.

The studies were also constrained by the fact that, in some cases, they were looking at budgeted expenditures rather than actual expenditures. In fact, public expenditure reviews carried out by the World Bank have tended to follow this practice as well, since actual spending data are not always readily available (Ablo and Reinikka, 1998). The trouble is that budgetary allocations can be rather misleading in explaining outcomes or in making policy decisions in a weak institutional context. Actually, it could well be the case that existing service delivery (and hence output) is much worse than budgetary allocations may suggest, since government spending (inputs) does not reach the intended facilities, as expected. The latter could happen because there are other priorities for the expenditure (i.e. other than basic health and basic education) or leakage.

Comparison issues

In the following section we present trends in public spending on BSS. One objective in presenting trends in public spending on BSS is to compare intertemporal changes in BSS allocations and real per capita spending, and their impact on outcomes across countries. However, making comparisons of public spending allocation across countries is fraught with problems. There are three main bases for comparison, and all are imperfect. One is to compare spending in absolute terms per capita in US dollar figures. The benchmark used for comparison could be compared to a global average, or the average in countries deemed to be successful in terms of their social indicators, or some similar international standard.[13] However, such comparisons can be misleading. There are problems translating expenditure in local currency to dollars. Basic social services, especially basic education, are labour-intensive. Many other inputs are also non-tradable. Thus, conversions at the exchange rate might distort the comparison. Besides, comparing dollar expenditures across countries with outcomes in those countries may not be fruitful; high or low levels of expenditure today would not necessarily be reflected in present-day social outcomes, but rather in those occurring in the future. This is due to the time lag between some of the major interventions and their effects. Moreover, countries that show high levels of expenditure may be using resources inefficiently or inequitably. In this case, the benchmark of per capita spending in other countries might not be very illuminating. Fixed international benchmarks, which by definition would apply across countries, would fail to take into account national variations, also limiting their usefulness. Hence, we do not estimate the absolute expenditure in dollars. We do not present per capita expenditures in dollar terms (though for countries where data permit, we do have time-series in real terms in local currency).

The second yardstick is to avoid absolute figures and concentrate on ratios – for example, the share of public spending on BSS as a proportion of GDP or total government spending. However, if total output or government spending decreased, while public spending decreased at a lower rate, the share would increase, although in real terms per capita spending would decline. Despite this limitation, we concentrate our analysis on the share of public expenditure on BSS (see Table 4.3), since it is a variable that the government can determine (while the level and trend of GDP is not entirely in the control of government). Nevertheless, there are limits as to what governments can 'decide' in terms of the allocations to BSS. Some of these relate to other claims on the budget that result in varying allocations to health and education, in general. Other limits relate to the size of the government sector (in terms of both revenues and expenditures), as a proportion of GDP.

A third gauge is the comparison between expenditures on BSS and the needs of a country, as determined by its social indicators. However, it is impossible to indicate exogenously what the needs of a country are. Nevertheless, a criterion based on social outcomes in countries at similar levels of income could be used to determine whether current levels of spending in a given country are high or low. For instance, there are many low- and middle-income countries which managed to finance universal access to BSS and improve outcome indicators early on in their development – as we discussed earlier – belying the argument that longer and better lives are a luxury reserved for industrialized countries.[14] This approach requires detailed information on unit costs of providing BSS to determine the financial requirements of universal access.

In the absence of reliable unit-cost estimates, it is difficult to present data about the financial requirements to provide universal BSS by country. An attempt has been made to estimate approximately current expenditures and the requirements to achieve universal access to BSS at the global level (see Chapter 8). The result of those estimates is that a total of $200–250 billion is needed over a fifteen-year period (2000–2015). Although this might seem a staggering figure, it represents less than 1 per cent of global output (Zedillo Report, 2000; WHO Commission on Macroeconomics and Health, 2001; Delamonica et al., 2004).

At the national level, too, if current levels of spending are leaving substantial segments of the population uncovered, the expenditures are obviously inadequate. Of course, current expenditure might be wasteful or inequitable. Consequently, the analysis of the level of spending cannot be done independently from its qualitative aspects. In other words, resources could be sufficient to provide universal access to BSS, but they could be concentrated among some segments of the population (by income group, region, ethnic characteristics, gender), thus failing to guarantee universality. Incidence analysis of government spending, as pioneered by Meerman (1979)

Table 4.3   Basic social service spending as % of national budget

Country	Year	Total BSS	Basic education	Basic health	Water & sanitation	Nutrition	Health exp. as % of GNP*	Education exp. as % of GNP*
South and East Asia								
Bangladesh	1993–4	9.1	7.5	1.6			1.6	2.2
Nepal	1997	13.6	8.3	3.1	2.3		1.3	3.2
Philippines	1992	7.7	6.8	0.6	0.3		1.7	3.4
Sri Lanka	1996	12.7	3.5	4.5	1.0	3.6	1.4	3.4
Thailand	1997	14.6	10.2	4.4			1.7	4.8
Vietnam	1997	9.1						
Sub-Saharan Africa								
Benin	1997	9.5	7.0	2.2	0.3		1.6	3.2
Burkina Faso	1997	19.5	10.6	8.3	0.6		1.2	1.5
Cameroon	1996–7	4.0	2.9	1.0	0.1		1.0	–
Côte d'Ivoire	1994–6	11.4	9.0	1.8	0.6		1.4	5.0
Kenya	1995	12.6	10.6	1.5	0.4		2.2	6.5
Mali	1996	15.9	12.2	3.4	0.3		2.0	2.2
Namibia	1996–7	19.1	11.5	5.7	1.7	0.2	3.8	9.1
Niger	1992	20.4	14.7	4.3	1.4		1.3	2.3
South Africa	1996–7	14.0	10.0	3.5	0.5		3.2	7.9
Uganda	1994–5	21.0	16.0	5.0			1.8	2.6
Zambia	1997	6.7					2.3	2.2
Middle East & North Africa								
Morocco	1997–8	16.6	15.2	1.4			1.3	5.0
Latin America & Caribbean								
Belize	1996	20.3	11.7	8.0	0.7		2.2	5.0
Bolivia	1997	16.7	9.8	4.5	2.3		1.1	4.9
Brazil	1995	8.9	6.0	1.9	0.6	0.4	3.4	5.1
Chile	1996	10.6	9.0	1.0	0.1	0.5	2.4	3.6
Colombia	1997	16.8	7.8	7.6	1.1	0.4	4.9	4.1
Costa Rica	1996	13.1	8.0	3.6	0.1	1.3	6.9	5.4
Dominican Republic	1997	8.7	5.9	2.7			1.6	2.3
El Salvador	1996	13.0	8.9	4.1			2.6	2.5
Honduras	1992	12.5	8.0	4.5			2.7	3.6
Jamaica	1996	10.2	7.3	1.1	1.4	0.5	2.3	7.4
Nicaragua	1996	9.2	4.8	4.1	0.1	0.2	4.4	3.9
Peru[†]	1997	19.3	4.8	5.6	1.4	7.4	2.2	2.9

Notes: * 1993–98   † budgeted figures.

Sources: Country studies; World Bank, World Development Indicators.

and Selowsky (1979), could shed light on these issues. This is taken up in Chapter 5. Issues of wastage and efficiency (i.e. the balance between recurrent and capital costs, wage and non-wage shares of recurrent expenditure)[15] are the subjects of Chapter 6.

In order to assess government performance in financing BSS, both the shares of the national budgets and per capita spending in real terms on BSS (see Table 4.3 for the latter estimates) have been used here. Their trends in local currency can be used to compare the situation over time. Keeping in mind the above problems, absolute figures or shares can also be compared with other countries, but with more than the usual grain of salt. Also, where possible, a comparison of current spending levels with the estimated needs of the country (as manifested in its outcome indicators) is presented.

Findings on the level of public expenditures

This section presents the findings on how much governments are spending on BSS. The number of countries reviewed is 31, with the following regional breakdown: sub-Saharan Africa 12, Asia 6, Latin America 12, and Middle East and North Africa 1. Expenditures are presented in Table 4.3 as a percentage of total government expenditure in order to determine the fiscal priority accorded the basic services by government.

Fiscal adjustment (at least in the 1980s) commonly emphasized the level of public expenditure.[16] This policy bias has had serious consequences for the poor. A review by the World Bank of public spending during adjustment over 1980–93 showed that public spending, excluding debt service, fell as a percentage of GDP – showing how serious the drain debt service became during the period. Most cuts related to economic services (particularly infra-structure). Per capita social spending fell in real terms in almost two-thirds of the countries. Furthermore, the composition of social spending – between primary and tertiary education, and between preventive and curative health – improved in only a few countries, while worsening in many. In fact, 'the Bank's country reports indicate that fiscal adjustments have not resulted in more efficient spending in most countries'. In other words, in most countries where data are available, services that benefit the non-poor received more resources. During adjustment, the bias in favour of tertiary education increased, and the existing imbalances between spending for hospital care and primary health care also remained in the health sector. Non-wage recurrent spending – which determines to a significant degree the efficiency and effectiveness of resource use – was reduced more severely (Jayarajah et al., 1996). Had there been a greater balance between expenditure slashing and

Figure 4.6 Share of basic services in public spending on health and education, selected countries

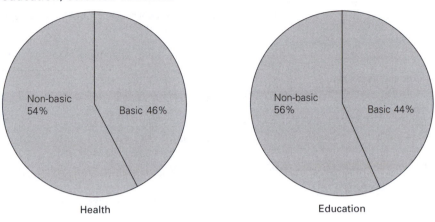

Source: Estimated from country studies.

revenue raising in the deficit reduction strategy, the consequence might not have been the 'lost decade' of the 1980s.

The African countries studied seem to have lower shares of their national budgets allocated to basic health than those in the Latin American countries. The former, on average, allocate less than 3 per cent of their national budgets to basic health, compared to about 4 per cent in Latin America. Moreover, given their lower per capita income, this results in substantially lower real expenditure levels in African countries. This is especially true for Cameroon, Côte d'Ivoire and Kenya.

For the countries on which data were collected, basic services account for less than half of all spending on education and health (Figure 4.6). More is spent on highly specialized hospital care than on basic health care, even though a substantial segment of the population has no access to the most basic health clinic. The same applies to the continuing emphasis on secondary and university spending in countries where most children do not complete even five years of formal schooling (Figure 4.6).

Expenditure on BSS among these countries hovers around 12–14 per cent.[17] This is the case regardless of whether the observations involve the latest ones for each particular country, or all individual observations (i.e. all countries for each year), or the period averages for each country. For any of these possible groupings, the median is also in the 12–14 per cent range.[18] In terms of the composition of BSS expenditures, education absorbs the bulk of resources, almost two-thirds on average (see Table 4.3).

Table 4.4 Education, health and demographic indicators

Country	Illiteracy		Primary gross enrolment		Population growth		U5MR		Reduction in U5MR, av. annual
	1990	1998	1990	1996	1990	1998	1990	1999	1990–99
South and East Asia									
Bangladesh	65.0	59.9	71.6	–	2.0	1.6	144	89	5.3
Nepal	69.4	60.8	107.7	113.0	2.5	2.3	145	104	3.7
Philippines	7.5	5.2	111.3	116.0	2.6	2.2	66	42	5.0
Sri Lanka	11.3	8.9	105.9	109.4	1.1	1.2	23	19	2.1
Thailand	7.6	5.0	99.1	86.9	1.8	1.0	40	30	3.2
Vietnam	9.5	7.1	102.9	115.0	2.2	1.4	50	40	2.5
Sub-Saharan Africa									
Benin	71.9	62.3	58.1	77.6	3.1	2.8	185	156	1.9
Burkina Faso	83.6	77.8	33.3	–	2.3	2.4	210	199	0.6
Cameroon	37.4	26.4	101.1	85.4	2.8	2.7	139	154	–1.1
Côte d'Ivoire	66.2	55.5	67.1	71.3	3.1	2.0	155	171	–1.1
Kenya	29.2	19.5	95.0	–	3.3	2.4	97	118	–2.2
Malawi	48.2	41.8	67.9	–	3.5	2.5	230	211	1.0
Mali	74.4	61.8	26.5	45.1	2.9	2.9	254	235	0.9
Namibia	25.1	19.2	129.3	131.3	2.7	2.4	84	70	2.0
Niger	88.6	85.3	28.8	29.4	3.1	3.4	320	275	1.7
South Africa	18.7	15.4	121.6	–	2.0	1.8	60	69	–1.6
Uganda	43.9	35.0	74.5	–	3.5	2.8	165	131	2.6
Zambia	31.9	23.7	98.7	–	3.1	2.3	192	202	–0.6
Middle East & North Africa									
Morocco	61.3	52.9	66.9	86.0	2.0	1.7	85	53	5.2
Latin America & Caribbean									
Belize	10.9	7.3	111.5	–	2.6	3.8	49	43	1.5
Bolivia	21.6	15.6	94.7	–	2.3	2.3	122	83	4.3
Brazil	19.1	15.5	106.3	119.8	1.7	1.3	60	40	4.5
Chile	5.9	4.6	99.9	101.3	1.7	1.4	20	12	5.7
Colombia	11.4	8.8	102.2	112.5	2.0	1.9	35	31	1.3
Costa Rica	6.1	4.7	100.7	103.3	2.3	1.8	16	14	1.5
Dominican Republic	20.6	17.2	96.6	93.9	2.1	1.8	65	49	3.1
El Salvador	27.5	22.2	81.1	92.9	1.8	2.2	60	42	4.0
Guatemala	38.8	32.7	77.6	88.0	2.4	2.6	82	60	3.5
Honduras	31.5	26.6	107.6*	–	3.0	2.8	61	42	4.1
Jamaica	18.0	14.0	101.3	99.6	1.2	0.9	16	11	4.2
Nicaragua	35.1	32.1	93.5	100.9	2.3	2.6	66	47	3.8
Peru	14.4	10.8	118.5	123.2	1.9	1.7	75	52	4.1

Note: Illiteracy = % of people aged 15 and above; U5MR = under-5 mortality rate per 1,000 live births; Population growth = annual %; * = 1991.

Sources: World Bank, 2000c, UNICEF, 2001.

Table 4.5 Index of real per capita expenditure on BSS (1990 base year)

Countries	1990	1991	1992	1993	1994	1995	1996	1997
South and East Asia								
Thailand*		100.0			134.6		141.8	
Vietnam*		100.0	129.1	162.9	206.2	222.6	223.4	265.2
Sub-Saharan Africa								
Kenya	100.0	106.7	113.3	115.8	146.1	166.7		
Malawi*		100.0	101.6	183.0	144.8	116.9	147.5	121.0
Namibia	100.0	123.8	176.8	159.2	139.1	134.0		
Niger	100.0		144.1					
Latin America & Caribbean								
Belize	100.0		115.2	162.1		138.5	114.1	
Bolivia	100.0	95.2	122.2	142.7	117.3	134.1	131.7	114.3
Chile	100.0	107.4	117.1	128.4	134.8	156.8	173.8	
Colombia	100.0	101.0	115.7	133.0	156.1	202.8	227.8	229.3
Costa Rica	100.0				93.8			
Dominican Republic	100.0	78.7	124.0	158.1	181.5	180.1	205.6	259.4
El Salvador	100.0	99.5	89.0	105.5	119.7	128.1	146.0	
Guatemala	100.0	91.3	128.8	140.0	150.0	138.8	141.3	175.0
Honduras	100.0	110.5	116.8					
Jamaica	100.0	77.4	66.2	106.5	91.7	99.5	105.3	
Nicaragua*		100.0	150.7	164.4	185.4	197.3	210.3	211.8
Peru*		100.0	174.5	271.8	273.0	537.1	454.1	

Note: * 1991 = 100.

Source: Country studies.

Table 4.6 Trends in real per capita expenditure on BSS (in local currency)

Countries	1980	1981	1982	1983	1984	1985	1986	1987	1988	1989	1990	1991	1992	1993	1994	1995	1996	1997
South and East Asia																		
Nepal	–	–	–	–	–	–	–	–	–	–	–	–	70.5	66.9	88.7	91.4	98.0	–
Sri Lanka	–	–	–	–	–	–	–	–	–	–	–	–	–	–	–	–	–	–
Thailand	–	–	–	–	–	–	6.6	–	–	7.7	–	9.3	–	–	12.6	–	13.2	–
Vietnam	–	–	–	–	–	–	–	–	–	–	–	7.6	9.8	12.4	15.7	16.9	17.0	20.2
Sub-Saharan Africa																		
Benin	–	–	–	–	–	–	–	–	–	–	–	–	–	–	–	–	9.3	9.5
Burkina Faso	–	–	–	–	–	–	–	–	–	–	–	–	–	–	–	–	–	–
Cameroon	–	–	–	–	–	–	–	–	–	–	–	–	–	–	–	–	–	–
Côte d'Ivoire	–	–	–	–	–	–	–	–	–	–	–	–	43.0	35.0	19.0	23.0	24.0	–
Kenya	165.0	177.0	173.0	161.0	159.0	145.0	154.0	167.0	155.0	155.0	165.0	176.0	187.0	191.0	241.0	275.0	–	–
Malawi	–	–	–	–	–	–	–	–	20	–	–	20.0	20.0	37.0	29.0	24.0	30.0	24
Namibia	–	–	–	–	–	–	–	–	–	–	263.0	325.0	464.0	418.0	365.0	352.0	–	–
Niger	–	–	–	–	2.7	–	–	–	2.2	2.7	3.4	–	4.9	–	–	–	–	–
Latin America & Caribbean																		
Belize	64.0	–	–	95.8	–	–	112.7	–	–	–	129.1	–	148.7	209.3	–	178.8	147.3	–
Bolivia	–	–	–	–	–	–	–	–	–	–	26.7	25.4	32.6	38.1	31.3	35.8	35.2	30.5
Chile	–	–	–	–	–	–	–	–	–	–	7.6	8.2	8.9	9.8	10.3	12.0	13.3	–
Colombia	58.1	65.5	64.3	65.2	65.0	69.2	64.2	70.2	71.6	72.1	71.4	72.1	82.6	95.0	111.5	144.8	162.7	163.7
Costa Rica	17.6	–	15.7	–	–	15.6	–	–	–	–	16.9	–	–	–	15.8	–	–	–
Dominican Republic	640.8	–	–	–	–	535.5	–	–	422.6	–	425.9	335.1	528.1	673.2	773.1	766.9	875.8	1104.6
El Salvador	–	–	–	–	–	–	–	–	–	–	110.3	109.7	98.2	116.3	132.0	141.2	161.0	–
Guatemala	–	–	–	–	–	–	–	–	–	–	80.0	73.0	103.0	112.0	120.0	111.0	113.0	140.0
Honduras	18.2	18.4	17.0	16.6	16.9	18.0	18.7	20.2	21.2	20.2	19.1	21.1	22.3	–	–	–	–	–
Jamaica	79.8	110.1	122.2	115.9	95.7	81.9	90.1	97.6	115.8	121.1	118.0	91.3	78.1	125.6	108.2	117.3	124.2	–
Nicaragua	–	–	–	–	–	–	–	–	–	–	–	9.0	13.6	14.9	16.8	17.8	19.0	19.2
Peru	–	–	–	–	105.8	76.8	116.9	115.3	44.3	10.6	1.6	10.1	17.7	27.5	27.6	54.3	45.9	–

Note: † budgeted figures.
Source: Estimated from country studies.

Table 4.7 Trend of BSS share in total public spending (BSS as % government spending)

Countries	1980	1981	1982	1983	1984	1985	1986	1987	1988	1989	1990	1991	1992	1993	1994	1995	1996	1997
South and East Asia																		
Nepal	9.2	–	–	–	–	–	–	–	–	–	–	–	11.1	11.1	13.8	12.7	13.6	–
Philippines	–	–	7.0	–	–	–	–	–	–	–	–	–	7.7	–	–	–	–	–
Sri Lanka	–	–	7.7	–	–	–	–	9.2	–	–	13.0	11.5	16.4	14.9	13.0	13.3	12.7	–
Thailand	–	–	–	–	–	–	13.4	–	10.7	12.1	–	14.2	–	–	14.5	–	13.6	–
Sub-Saharan Africa																		
Benin	–	–	–	–	–	–	–	–	–	–	–	–	–	–	–	–	9.3	9.5
Burkina Faso	–	–	–	–	–	–	–	–	–	–	15.1	14.3	19.4	18.5	23.5	17.1	17.5	19.5
Cameroon	–	–	–	–	–	–	–	–	–	–	–	–	–	–	–	–	4.0	–
Côte d'Ivoire	–	–	–	–	–	–	–	–	–	–	–	–	–	13.5	12.4	11.7	11.1	11.3
Kenya	19.9	20.1	18.6	16.3	16.8	17.7	16.9	17.2	16.3	13.5	15.8	12.6	11.0	8.9	12.6	11.0	8.9	12.6
Malawi	–	–	–	–	–	–	–	–	6.0	–	–	6.3	6.8	11.0	8.1	6.4	8.2	7.6
Mali	–	–	–	–	–	–	–	–	–	–	–	–	–	–	–	–	15.9	–
Namibia	–	–	–	–	–	–	–	–	–	–	14.0	15.0	21.0	23.0	22.0	19.0	19.0	–
Niger	–	–	–	–	13.5	–	–	–	11.5	13.5	15.5	–	20.4	–	–	–	–	–
South Africa	–	–	–	–	–	–	–	–	–	–	–	–	–	–	–	–	**	–
Uganda	–	–	–	–	–	–	–	–	–	–	–	–	–	–	21.0	–	–	–
Middle East & North Africa																		
Morocco	–	–	–	–	–	–	–	–	–	–	–	–	–	–	–	–	–	–
Latin America & Caribbean																		
Belize	–	–	–	–	–	–	–	–	–	–	–	–	–	–	–	–	–	–
Bolivia	–	–	–	–	–	–	–	–	–	–	17.2	13.5	15.2	16.2	13.0	15.2	13.7	11.1
Brazil	–	–	–	–	–	–	–	–	–	–	–	–	–	–	–	8.9	–	–
Chile	–	–	–	–	–	–	–	–	–	–	9.4	9.3	9.2	9.5	9.6	10.6	10.9	–
Colombia	11.7	15.0	14.8	15.2	15.1	16.5	12.3	14.6	14.5	12.7	13.2	13.3	13.5	16.3	16.4	19.6	19.9	16.3
Costa Rica	17.6	–	15.7	–	–	15.6	–	–	–	–	16.9	–	–	–	15.8	–	–	–
Dominican Republic	7.2	–	–	–	–	8.4	–	–	10.6	–	5.8	4.6	5.1	5.6	7.4	8.8	9.0	8.7
El Salvador	–	–	–	–	–	–	–	–	–	–	11.2	11.3	9.7	11.8	10.3	12.2	13.0	–
Guatemala	–	–	–	–	–	–	–	–	–	–	8.2	7.8	9.5	10.2	12.6	11.2	11.8	12.5
Honduras	10.7	12.4	9.9	9.1	8.2	8.6	9.4	9.9	10.9	10.7	10.4	14.8	12.5	11.7	8.6	10.1	10.2	–
Jamaica	8.2	11.3	12.8	11.9	12.4	10.7	11.4	13.0	12.2	13.3	13.4	10.1	9.2	8.3	8.6	8.9	9.0	–
Nicaragua	–	–	–	–	–	–	–	–	–	–	–	5.6	7.7	–	–	8.9	9.0	9.2
Peru	–	–	–	–	12.9	11.3	19.9	19.9	26.3	23.9	13.1	5.0	6.1	9.2	7.8	12.9	12.1	–

Source: Estimated from country studies.

In summary, although comparisons across countries of the budget allocation to BSS can be misleading, given the complexities involved in the estimations, it is clear that countries differ substantially in terms of allocation of public spending. When coverage and social outcomes are considered, most of them seem to require additional resources to reach universal coverage of BSS, in particular, given the lack of integration among the sectors. Both the limited overall size of the national budget and the relative size of the social sectors constrain the capacity to increase real spending on BSS. Before we tackle these issues in Chapter 9, it is useful to evaluate the time trend of BSS expenditures in these countries.

Tables 4.5, 4.6 and 4.7 present the trends for the same set of countries in real per capita expenditure on BSS, the share of BSS expenditure in total government expenditure, and the share of public expenditure in GDP. For countries where data on BSS spending per capita is available, the trend is encouraging, even if it means a recovery of the ground lost during the 1980s (Cominetti, 1994). In Latin America almost all countries increased public spending on basic services on a per capita basis over the 1990s (see Table 4.5, which presents per capita expenditures as an index). The Asian countries for which we have BSS per capita expenditure data for several points of time suggest a similar story.

In regard to countries for which we had a long enough time-series on BSS share and BSS per capita expenditure in real terms, there is a fair degree of correlation in their movements over time in the majority of cases. The correlation coefficients were high (and positive) for the majority of countries: Chile (0.93), Colombia (0.77), Costa Rica (0.99), Dominican Republic (0.405), El Salvador (0.747), Guatemala (0.929), Honduras (0.671), Jamaica (0.484), Nicaragua (0.976), Nepal (0.92), Côte d'Ivoire (0.676), Malawi (0.958), Namibia (0.82) and Niger (0.99). This seems to suggest that monitoring the fiscal priority allocated to BSS by governments may be a worthwhile exercise, even though it is the per capita expenditure on BSS that ultimately matters to the recipient.[19]

A few conclusions can be drawn from the discussion of these trends. Some countries increased spending (both in shares and in real per capita terms) and, by and large, their indicators have improved, but quantitative or qualitative deficiencies still remain. Evidently, in the other countries where the allocation or real per capita spending declined, the case for more spending is even stronger. In other words, public spending on BSS is crucial, but looking merely at the BSS/government expenditure ratio without regard to the size of the government or the expenditure trends could be misleading. Casting the issue in terms of 'more or less' percentage points misses the fact that the equity and efficiency of the services delivered are crucial as well (see Chapters 5 and 6) in order to address the deficiencies in coverage. As a result, the attempts to find the 'impact' of these interventions through cross-sectional linear regression analysis need to be evaluated carefully (as we did earlier).

Assessing the impact of (inadequate) spending

The correlation between social outcomes and level of income does not rest on causality running from higher incomes to higher access to BSS. This causal direction would imply a reliance on trickle-down, whereby governments should concentrate their efforts on macroeconomic variables to maximize economic growth and let the markets provide these services (as proposed by Lal and Myint, 1996). This is definitely not the route followed by industrialized nations and the few developing countries that have made substantial progress in terms of life expectancy, literacy and the overall well-being of their populations. The policies that were followed depended on the state as guarantor of access to basic social services. In most cases, the state was not only the major financier but also the main – if not the only – provider of BSS.

We attempted an alternative test including public spending. Evidently, many other factors impinge on the relationship between child mortality and public health expenditures. Two obvious candidates are level of income and female literacy. Consequently, a linear regression was estimated with these two variables as regressors (for 87 countries). A dummy variable for least-developed countries (LDCs) was also included to improve the fit. Visual analysis of the bivariate relationship between income per capita and child mortality indicated a hyperbola. Consequently, the inverse of GNP per capita was used. Other variables such as ethnic fragmentation (used by Filmer and Pritchett, 1997) were not included, as there was no theoretical basis for them. Nevertheless, the inverse of the level of income, female literacy and the LDCs dummy variable accounted for almost 80 per cent of the variation of child mortality around its mean. The coefficients (and t-statistics) were respectively: 4934.33 (2.0); –0.82 (–3.7); and 76.61 (5.3). In other words, increases in the level of income were positively associated with improvements in health outcomes; that is, the larger the inverse of income, the higher the level of child mortality. Hence the positive coefficient, which is statistically significant, for the income variable. For instance, everything being the same, a $100 increase in average GNP per capita from $900 to $1,000 would result in a reduction of the inverse of per capita income which is associated

Figure 4.7 Under-5 mortality (controlling for GNP per capita, female literacy and LDCs) and public spending on health

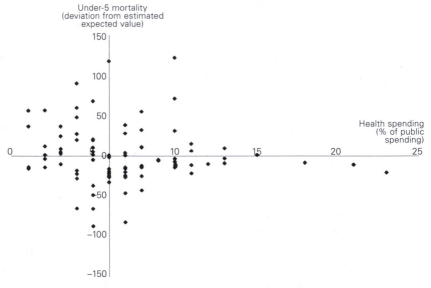

Source: World Bank Development Indicators; UNICEF, 2001: 120.

with a lower (by half a point) U5MR. Evidently, this does not necessarily imply that the lower mortality is caused by the higher income. Similarly, higher levels of female education (proxied by female literacy) are associated with lower mortality, as expressed by the second coefficient, which also is statistically significant. Lastly, the third coefficient means that given a certain level of per capita income, female education, and all other existing factors, infant and child mortality tends to be higher in least-developed countries. Again, the theoretical reasons for this association are not explored here.

The residuals of this regression were then measured against the allocation to health apportioned on the national budget. Because some large countries are federal states (e.g. Argentina, Brazil, India and Nigeria), they were not included in the analysis, as the data only covered central government expenditures.

Although the scatter diagram (Figure 4.7) shows a clear inverse relationship between expenditures and mortality (controlling for GNP per capita, female literacy and LDCs), a linear regression does not capture it. The reason is that there is a wide variability of results. Nevertheless, the absence of a linear relationship is not equivalent to the non-existence of a relationship.[20] Thus, a simple chi-square test was performed to test for independence between the two variables. Residuals show the deviation from expected

U5MR. Residuals were classified as above or below the regression line. When negative, the deviation means lower-than-expected U5MR. Central government health spending was classified as above or below the median – that is, 'high' or 'low' expenditure. This resulted in a two-by-two table. Most of the observations were either in the low expenditure/high mortality (positive residuals) or high expenditure/low mortality quadrants. Although there were some observations in the other two quadrants, they were not numerous enough, so the null hypothesis of independence between the two variables was rejected.

Thus, the analysis shows that there is a relationship between higher public expenditure and lower child mortality (our proxy for health outcomes and well-being), but not a linear one. Two possibilities exist: either the relationship is not linear (which is doubtful given the scatter diagram) or there are still other elements that affect the relationship. This latter is more likely for at least three reasons. First, aggregate public health expenditure rather than expenditure on basic health services was used. This might indicate there is a high degree of allocative inefficiency in the sector. Second, technical efficiency could be a problem – that is, there is scope for achieving higher social outcomes with the same level of resources. Both are discussed in Chapter 6. The textbook definition of efficiency would complement this clause with 'or the same level of social outcomes with less resources'. For the majority of developing countries, however, this is a vacuous definition of efficiency. Obtaining the same low levels of outcomes while spending less will not allow them to narrow the gap between existing social indicators and the goals and targets set for the year 2015 and beyond. Hence, more efficiency needs to be accompanied by higher spending. Finally, the role of the impact of basic social services as a package (i.e. synergy of interventions across the social sectors), discussed above, would also create noise in the relationship between expenditure on all social services and outcomes. However, this reinforces the role of public finance on all BSS expenditure simultaneously.

Others have examined the impact of government spending on education and health in developing and transition countries. Thus, Gupta et al. (2002) use cross-sectional data for fifty countries to show that increased public expenditure on health care and education is associated with improvements in both access to and attainment in schools, and reduces mortality rates for infants and children. They also find that a 5 percentage point increase in the share of outlays for primary and secondary education increases gross secondary enrolment by over 1 percentage point.[21]

For those convinced that, rather than the size of spending, improving the efficiency of public spending, in addition to increasing the plurality of types

Table 4.8 Public expenditure as a percentage of GDP, selected countries

Countries	1980	1981	1982	1983	1984	1985	1986	1987	1988	1989	1990	1991	1992	1993	1994	1995	1996	1997	1998
South and East Asia																			
Bangladesh	7.4	10.3	9.7	8.3	8.1	9.2	9.4	9.1	9.3	11.1	–	–	–	–	–	–	–	–	–
Nepal	14.3	14.5	16.8	20.3	18.4	17.6	16.9	17.4	17.7	19.5	17.2	18.9	16.8	17.0	14.7	16.5	17.5	16.8	17.5
Philippines	13.4	13.8	12.9	12.2	10.1	11.2	13.5	15.9	16.1	18.0	19.6	19.2	19.7	18.5	18.4	17.9	18.5	19.3	–
Sri Lanka	41.4	30.5	34.0	31.1	29.0	33.4	31.9	31.7	31.1	30.8	28.4	29.3	26.9	27.0	27.2	29.3	27.7	25.7	25.0
Thailand	18.8	19.0	20.2	19.6	19.4	20.5	19.5	17.5	15.1	14.3	14.1	14.5	15.0	15.9	16.3	15.8	16.5	19.3	18.6
Vietnam	–	–	–	–	–	–	–	–	–	–	–	–	–	–	26.2	24.5	24.3	22.0	20.1
Sub-Saharan Africa																			
Benin	–	–	–	–	–	–	–	–	–	–	–	–	–	–	–	–	–	–	–
Burkina Faso	12.2	11.7	12.3	9.7	11.4	9.8	12.0	13.2	15.6	14.1	15.0	18.0	17.0	16.8	–	–	–	–	–
Cameroon	15.7	20.7	20.5	20.9	21.9	21.2	21.5	23.2	17.1	20.1	21.2	21.5	18.1	15.9	14.2	12.7	–	–	–
Côte d'Ivoire	31.7	–	–	–	30.2	23.2	26.4	24.5	26.1	22.0	24.5	–	–	–	27.4	26.5	25.3	25.0	24.0
Kenya	25.3	27.0	27.6	25.1	24.7	25.8	24.3	27.9	26.4	30.2	27.5	28.9	24.8	29.9	32.4	28.5	29.0	–	–
Malawi	34.6	35.5	28.9	28.9	27.7	31.3	33.8	32.8	29.4	27.6	26.5	–	–	–	–	–	–	–	–
Mali	19.4	21.4	26.3	26.3	24.9	28.1	27.5	27.2	30.1	–	–	–	–	–	–	–	–	–	–
Namibia	–	–	–	–	–	–	39.0	40.6	35.9	33.4	32.1	39.0	39.6	38.2	–	–	–	–	–
Niger	18.6	–	–	–	–	–	–	–	–	–	–	–	–	–	–	–	–	–	–
South Africa	21.6	23.3	25.5	27.5	27.5	29.1	30.6	30.4	30.6	29.8	30.1	29.5	32.6	34.1	29.8	30.0	30.6	29.3	29.7
Uganda	6.2	4.8	9.6	9.9	13.7	12.9	10.7	–	–	–	–	–	–	–	–	–	–	–	–
Zambia	37.1	36.7	39.2	32.2	29.2	35.1	41.7	31.6	27.8	–	–	–	–	–	–	–	–	–	–

Middle East & North Africa

Morocco	33.1	39.1	37.5	32.3	29.7	30.4	28.9	28.2	28.2	30.5	28.8	27.8	30.1	34.0	32.2	33.3	–	–	–

Latin America & Caribbean

Belize	22.9	26.7	30.0	28.0	24.9	27.2	–	–	–	–	–	–	–	–	–	–	–	–	–
Bolivia	–	–	–	–	–	–	13.3	12.4	14.0	15.2	16.4	16.8	20.3	24.0	23.2	21.1	23.0	22.0	21.9
Brazil	20.2	20.4	21.2	21.2	20.6	25.4	27.9	24.9	31.3	34.7	34.9	24.4	29.2	37.2	33.8	–	–	–	–
Chile	28.0	29.4	34.1	31.9	32.6	30.4	28.3	24.9	23.2	21.4	20.4	21.0	20.8	21.4	20.9	19.9	21.0	20.7	21.6
Colombia	11.5	12.0	13.7	13.1	13.0	12.1	11.7	11.8	11.8	12.3	9.9	9.9	13.0	12.3	12.6	13.4	14.9	15.8	16.0
Costa Rica	25.0	21.0	18.4	23.6	22.8	21.8	26.4	27.2	24.5	26.1	25.6	24.8	23.9	26.2	30.6	29.1	30.1	–	–
Dominican Republic	16.9	16.2	13.5	14.0	13.4	12.6	13.3	14.4	16.3	14.5	11.7	11.1	13.3	17.3	17.1	15.4	15.6	16.7	–
El Salvador	–	–	–	–	–	–	–	–	–	–	–	–	–	–	–	–	–	–	–
Guatemala	14.3	16.1	14.7	12.9	–	–	–	–	–	–	–	–	–	–	–	–	–	–	–
Honduras	–	–	–	–	–	–	–	–	–	–	–	–	–	–	–	–	–	–	–
Jamaica	41.5	39.9	38.6	40.7	33.9	38.5	–	–	–	–	–	–	30.1	30.0	32.3	33.2	–	–	–
Nicaragua	30.4	39.3	49.4	67.7	63.9	59.6	52.3	47.9	31.8	36.0	27.4	30.0	30.1	32.3	33.2	–	–	–	–
Peru	19.5	18.4	17.6	19.5	18.5	17.4	16.7	15.5	13.0	11.7	16.4	13.0	15.9	15.4	16.4	17.3	16.5	15.7	16.0

Source: World Bank, 2000c.

of providers (especially private ones) is the main part of the solution for improving coverage and quality of basic services in developing countries, it is worth examining what share of GDP is allocated to health and education in developed and developing countries. We noted earlier that the historical increase in the size of government (i.e. share of government spending in GDP) in the now-industrialized countries from 1880 onwards is accounted for largely by social spending (Lindert, 2004). Currently, it is quite remarkable that not a single country in the industrialized world spends less than 5 per cent of GDP on government-financed health services (Table 4.8). At the same time, rarely do developing countries have a share of public health spending in GDP of 5 per cent (compare Table 4.3); in most cases it is less than half that proportion. Costa Rica (a country that has no military), viewed as a high-achiever in terms of health and education outcomes, is one of those rare exceptions. Similarly, rarely do developed countries spend less than 4.5 per cent of GDP on publicly provided/financed education. Only a small proportion of developing countries allocate as much as that.[22]

And, as we concluded in our own statistical analysis for developing countries, the health outcomes in developed countries also seem to respond to public health expenditures. Thus, Or (2000) finds that a greater public expenditure share, for given total expenditures, significantly reduces mortality, especially among men, among OECD countries since 1980. She also finds that some familiar factors lower mortality down towards the world-best Japanese standard: higher income, white-collar occupations, cleaner air, abstention from bad consumption habits, and greater total spending on health care. A more public approach to the same health-care expenditures also helps significantly.

Are IMF programmes protecting social expenditures?

If public expenditures have important outcomes for health and educational outcomes, it is clearly necessary to protect those expenditures in times of crisis. What is the experience with IMF programmes in this regard? We saw earlier that a World Bank study had noted that during adjustment over 1980–93 public spending had suffered, as did social spending. The Independent Evaluation Office of the IMF (2003a) investigated what happens to public social spending under IMF-supported programmes using a broad sample of 146 countries over 1985–2000. It compared periods with and without a programme. In the majority of countries for which data are available (about 90–100 for each of health and education), there is no statistically significant difference in health and education spending between these two periods. This is largely true regardless of whether the spending is measured as a percentage of GDP, as a percentage of total spending, in US dollars per capita or in domestic real prices per capita.

This kind of comparison suffers from the limitation that it attributes all the difference in programme years to the fact of having a programme. This is not a suitable counterfactual. Hence the IEO went on to isolate the impact of an IMF-supported programme on social spending, using pooled cross-section time-series data. The results of the regression analysis show that the presence of an IMF programme is associated with increased public spending in health and education measured as either a share of GDP, of total spending, or in real terms compared with a situation without a programme. Public spending in each of the health and education sectors grew by about 0.3 and 0.4 percentage point of GDP. But the positive effects that can be attributed to the programme do not last beyond the programme, and the public health and education expenditure declines geometrically thereafter. Whether this increase in spending protects the most vulnerable groups or basic-level services is a matter on which there is no information in the analysis.

This indifferent outcome in respect of social spending during IMF programmes can be explained by the indifferent nature of the programme content in respect of social spending. Since 1991 there have indeed been guidelines issued to IMF staff directing that they should be explicitly concerned with the effects of economic policies on the poor, and in 1997 new guidelines on social spending were issued to staff to monitor trends in this area and incorporate realistic targets into government budgets in the letters of intent. The executive directors of the Fund/Bank stress, however, that the IMF and the Bank should maintain a clear division of labour between the two institutions, with the IMF taking the lead on the aggregate aspects of macroeconomic policy and their related instruments, and the Bank on issues of public expenditure composition and efficiency. In this situation lack of clarity prevails. Thus the IEO found in fifteen IMF programmes evaluated that in none was social spending clearly defined, and in only 33 per cent were there efforts to identify how social spending could be protected. Although one-third of programmes did explore how to protect social spending, this was typically at a very aggregate level of appropriations such as education spending – not at an intra-sectoral level. 'The use of conditionality to achieve social sector objectives was limited' (IEO, 2003a: 56). Of the fifteen programmes evaluated, only six contained social sector conditionalities in the form of structural benchmarks or performance criteria. In Ecuador, for instance, in the IMF programme, there was clear conditionality on the pricing of fuels, spending control, and raising the VAT, but none of the social measures in the letter of intent of 2000 that could offset these effects was incorporated as a structural benchmark.

In the PRGF-supported programmes (i.e. in low-income countries), collaboration between the World Bank and the IMF is mandated through the PRSP process, which calls for the monitoring of social and other poverty-related expenditures and for an explicit social impact analysis of policy reforms. So in these countries a framework for a coordinated approach to social issues exists – though there is little evidence that it is working. Thus in Zambia in 2004, the government was not able to hire schoolteachers because there was a joint condition by the two organizations that the wage bill should not exceed 8 per cent of the government budget. Similarly, the IEO (2004) notes that although recent PRGF-supported programmes target a smaller and more gradual fiscal consolidation than under ESAFs (the Extended Structural Adjustment Facility of the IMF, since 2000 renamed PRGF), even here the outcomes are not very different between ESAFs and PRGFs.

For middle-income countries (i.e. non-PRGF countries), like Ecuador, there is no framework that can ensure identification of home-grown social-sector programmes that can be the basis of social protection of vulnerable groups in economic crises. Policies to protect social expenditures should be fully domestically owned. Protecting drugs for patients and textbooks for children does not cost much. Given how small public expenditures within health and education are that can save lives and sustain the quality of schooling, protecting them can be both efficient and equitable.

4.4   Concluding remarks

High allocations to health and education in industrialized countries are possible on account of the much higher share of tax revenues in the economy in these countries, compared to developing countries – an issue we take up in Chapter 9. Nor do we deny the need for greater efficiency in the use of resources in most developing countries in the provision of BSS – the whole of Chapter 6 is devoted to this issue. However, those who argue vehemently that public spending makes little difference to social, especially health, outcomes (as the World Bank does in the *World Development Report 2000/2001*), clearly fly in the face of the historical experience of industrialized countries, not to mention the high achievers among the developing countries.

Still, it is the case that many publicly provided services are inefficient. But it is often the case that much inefficiency in public spending stems from resource scarcity. In practice, inadequate resources, inequity and inefficiency are often intertwined. There are minimum requirements on capital, recurrent, wage and non-wage expenditures to provide essential services. Lack of financial resources invariably leads to meagre allocations to one (or more) of these categories, undermining the efficient utilization of other inputs. In other words, insufficiency often creates inefficiency.

Moreover, these insufficiencies reverberate through the structure of social provision. As argued above, when discussing the synergy among interventions, it is not possible to say that one (education, for instance) is more important or should supersede another one (such as access to safe water). What we tried to establish is that neither is 'fully necessary' for achieving positive outcomes, and neither is 'sufficient by itself'. Thus, a minimum level of interventions on each front is required, and these interventions as well as larger interventions ensuring macroeconomic growth need to be integrated. Thus, low expenditure levels in one sector (reproductive health, for instance) have an overall effect on other sectors (e.g. education).

Inequities can also lead to inefficiency; for example, the same level of health spending will have markedly different effects on health outcomes whether or not it is focused on households suffering from easily preventable causes of morbidity and mortality. Thus, the allocation of resources can be both inequitable and inefficient – the subjects of Chapters 5 and 6.

5

The distribution of benefits of health and education spending

The regional averages for social indicators discussed in the previous chapter hide huge intra-country disparities. These disparities would tend to vary not only by gender but also by ethnic groups, regions and different households according to their level of income and wealth.[1] Although this is well known, and some data describing these inequalities are available, this chapter briefly recapitulates data and information on some of these inequalities in outcomes.[2] More importantly, it examines the distribution of benefits of health and education spending for a selection of developing countries in every region.

The source of information for this chapter is mainly the country studies designed and commissioned by UNICEF/UNDP, which provide new information on the incidence of health and education spending by income groups. Section 5.1 provides a sketch of the kinds of disparities in health and education outcomes that are relatively common in developing countries. Section 5.2 examines the evidence on the distribution of benefits of public spending on education as a whole and by level; section 5.3 presents the evidence on the distribution of benefits of public health spending, again overall and by level; both present the implications for education and health outcomes of the inequity in public spending. Section 5.4 attempts to explain the incidence of health and education spending. The final section concludes.

5.1 Disparities in health and education outcomes

The evidence on disparities of outcomes by income available for some of the selected countries is worrisome. For instance, in Nepal almost 60 per cent of the population in the bottom quintile never attended school, while

Table 5.1   Urban and rural enrolment by income group

	Urban	Rural
Benin (GER)		
Poor	45	37
Vulnerable	81	44
Non-poor	114	51
Weighted average	81	44
Côte d'Ivoire (% enrolled)		
Bottom quartile	39	32
Second quartile	40	34
Third quartile	49	36
Top quartile	44	35
Total	44	34

Source: UNICEF country studies.

that share is only 13 per cent in the top quintile (Institute for Sustainable Development, 1998). In Brazil[3] all children in the top three deciles attend school (the vast majority of them private). However, in the second decile 10 per cent of the children never attended school, with the percentage rate increasing to 20 per cent in the bottom decile (Neri et al., 1998).

These disparities, however, give only a partial picture of inequities in a country. There are many other dimensions, often more important, as people do not live in quintiles or deciles. Thus, geographic area or ethnic differences should also be explored. Other social characteristics would be useful too; Pyatt (1999) persuasively argues for a 'social/structural' classification based on source of income or kind of employment.[4] For Honduras, data from the National Demographic Survey for 1983 show that urban-based workers were able to reduce mortality much faster than farmers and agricultural workers.

The location of households impacts on their well-being. This is partly related to the environmental conditions as well as the different types of work done in different regions (e.g. some illnesses are transmitted by animals that live in certain areas; mining towns have their own epidemiological profile). However, one of the main determinants across countries is the insufficient provision of basic social services for rural populations. Thus, for example, in Benin the gross enrolment ratio (GER) at primary level in urban areas is twice as high as in rural ones (Tabélé-Omichessan et al., 1998). A significant, if less dramatic, difference occurs in Côte d'Ivoire (Gbayoro et al., 1997). Interestingly, in both countries, when the geographic classification is combined with income levels, the rural areas seem more equitable (Table 5.1).

Another relevant breakdown for the analysis of inequalities is gender. Gender discrimination is pervasive throughout the world, and especially so in many developing countries. Moreover, many of the most serious aspects of gender discrimination cannot be captured in figures. Nevertheless, just two examples will be presented here to indicate the relevance of gender in accessing education. In Niger, for instance, the male literacy rate is 21 per cent, but for women it is 7 per cent – only a third of men's (Chafani et al., 1997). Similarly, in Nepal 41 per cent of men can read and write, but the literacy rate among women is only 14 per cent. These data can be further disaggregated by income level too. For the bottom quintile, the proportion of women and girls aged 6–24 who never attended school is as high as 85 per cent, against 54 per cent in the top quintile.

Another important classification is the ethnic background of different groups of people. The ethnic background of certain groups has often been used to divide and oppress them; the social indicators for such groups often lag behind. In South Africa life expectancy at birth in 1990 for whites was close to the industrialized country average, while for Africans it was ten years lower. Although this could be partly the result of income differentials between the two groups, there is little doubt that the inequitable distribution of education and health services played a role too.

Given the differences in health and education outcomes within a given country, it is crucial to assess whether different groups in society receive equitable shares of public spending on social services.[5] Although most of the analysis below concentrates on the incidence of public spending by income group, other ways to identify groups within the country are at least as important, as can be seen from the above discussion of disaggregated outcome indicators. In particular, the gender, ethnic and geographic distribution of benefits is analysed too. Both the gender and the geographic distribution of benefits are intrinsically linked to efficiency issues. Gender balance in benefit distribution is efficient because of the important structural role of women in the 'first synergy', which enhances the impact of spending in one sector when good outcomes are present in the other ones (see Chapter 4). Geographic balance in benefit distribution is efficient because of the greater relative impact on outcomes of expenditure where lack of access is most acute. In general, since rural areas are underserved, additional spending in these areas has more impact than in urban ones.

5.2 The distribution of benefits of public spending on education

Data on the usage of education services by different groups have been obtained for nineteen countries. The first observation one can make (see Table 5.2) is that the distribution of total public spending on education is not equally shared. In most countries, the bottom quintile enjoys less than 20 per cent of the benefits of public spending on education (i.e. total subsidy); in some of them, a lot less. On the other hand, the top quintile seems to be able to capture considerably more than 20 per cent of the benefits of these expenditures. This is particularly true in Bangladesh, Guinea and Madagascar. The situation seems to be different in Colombia, in Costa Rica and, particularly, in Chile, which are relative high achievers in primary-school enrolment.

The evidence in Table 5.2 indicates that the benefit incidence of primary-school expenditure is far more equally distributed than the higher level services (secondary schools and, more prominently, universities).[6] In all countries the subsidy to the primary level of education is more equitably shared, except in South Africa (for obvious reasons) and in Guinea. Countries like Chile and Colombia – which have made significant efforts to universalize primary schooling – have a particularly high share of the subsidy at the primary level going to the poorest share of the population. By and large, countries that have been much less successful in universalizing primary schooling also have a higher proportion of the subsidy being absorbed by the richest quintile of the population.

Nevertheless, the high share of benefits from primary education spending that accrue to the bottom quintile in most countries does not take into account the fact that poorer groups tend to have more children. Survey after survey confirms that poor households have more children than non-poor households.[7] Consequently, they *should* receive a larger share of the benefits than their population share because their share in the school population exceeds their share in the total population.

Table 5.3 uses data from Costa Rica, Côte d'Ivoire and Ghana to corroborate this result. In all three countries, the bottom 20 per cent income quintile has more than 20 per cent of primary-school-aged children, while the top 20 per cent income earners have less than 20 per cent of all school-aged children. Yet, the share of benefits of primary-school spending is less than the share of school-aged children for the bottom quintile, except in Costa Rica.

This means that even a progressive distribution of benefits may mask inequities in the education system. Attempts to encourage private education in order to ease the burden of the state, and thus release funds to educate

Table 5.2 Benefit incidence of public spending on education in selected countries

	Total		Primary		Secondary		Tertiary	
	Bottom	Top	Bottom	Top	Bottom	Top	Bottom	Top
Bangladesh (1994)†	14	39	20	21	6	35	2	48
Bolivia (1990)			37	6			12	23
Brazil (1996)†			23	14				
Chile (1996)	34	7	38	5	31	7	6	19
Colombia (1992)*	23	14	39	4	21	10	5	34
Costa Rica (1992)	18	20	34	7	16	16	2	38
Côte d'Ivoire (1995)	13	35	19	14	7	37	12	71
Ghana (1992)	16	21	22	14	15	19	6	45
Guinea (1994)	5	44	11	21	4	39	1	65
Indonesia (1989)	15	29	22	14	5	42	0	92
Jamaica (1993)			31	6	10	20		
Kenya (1992)†	17	21	22	15	7	30	2	44
Madagascar (1993)	8	41	17	14	2	41	0	89
Malawi (1994)	16	25	20	16	9	40	1	59
Peru (1995)	11	24						
South Africa (1994)	14	35	19	28	11	39	6	47
Tanzania (1993/4)	14	37	20	19	8	34	0	100
Uganda (1992)	13	32	19	18	4	49	6	47
Vietnam (1992/3)	11	38	22	18	9	37	0	66

Notes: † Rural only for Bangladesh and Kenya and rural north-east for Brazil.   * Household quintiles.
Sources: UNICEF country studies; Castro-Leal et al., 1998.

only the children of the disadvantaged groups, suffer from problems.[8] This theory generates inequalities, as the children of the wealthier class attend better schools – as observed in Brazil and Chile.[9]

The equity of spending, particularly on primary education, strongly relates to overall outcomes. Figure 5.1 shows the distribution of public spending on education at the primary level in the nineteen countries studied. In each case, countries have been classified in terms of primary net enrolment, a measure of the success of their education policies. Where primary net enrolment rate (NER) is less than 70, it can be observed that the poorest 20 per cent of the population receive less than 20 per cent of the benefits of public spend-

Table 5.3   Benefit incidence and primary education needs
(Ghana, Cote d'Ivoire and Costa Rica)

	Ghana (1992)		Côte d'Ivoire (1995)		Costa Rica (1992)	
	% of subsidy	% of age group	% of subsidy	% of age group	% of subsidy	% of age group
Poorest quintile	22	24	19	24	34	27
Richest quintile	14	14	14	14	7	12

Sources: UNICEF country studies; Castro-Leal et al., 1998.

ing on education. In contrast, countries with enrolment above 70 devote a much larger share of public money to the bottom quintile. Families from the richest quintile can and do send their children to private schools, which is why their 'share' of public spending on education is less than 20 per cent. Nevertheless, the equity of primary spending is more apparent in countries where primary NERs are higher.

Inequalities between urban and rural locations are sharp. In Benin, GER in primary schools in urban areas is almost twice as high as in rural ones. In rural areas the richest groups seem to enjoy a GER of 50 while the poor have a GER of 36. The corresponding ratios in urban centres are 114 and 45. These stark differences are a reflection of the inequities in budget allocations among groups. First, rural areas, where 60 per cent of the population live, receive less than half of the basic education budget.[10] Second, benefit incidence is very dissimilar in urban and rural areas. In rural areas poor families, which constitute around a third of all households, benefit from around a third of the public expenditure on basic education. In urban areas 53 per cent is appropriated by the non-poor, who represent 44 per cent of the urban population.

In sub-Saharan Africa, the benefit incidence of education spending seems to suffer more from gender inequalities than health spending. For the population as a whole, girls received only 37 per cent of the education subsidy in Côte d'Ivoire and 41 per cent in Ghana (Castro-Leal et al., 1998). This applies even at the primary level. In Côte d'Ivoire, girls in the poorest quintile received less than a quarter of the overall education subsidy accruing to the quintile. In contrast, girls in the top quintile fared much better. The gender bias is also observed over time between the poor and non-poor. In Côte d'Ivoire, a series of integrated household surveys revealed that between 1985 and 1988 the gender gap in primary enrolment

Figure 5.1 Distribution of primary education spending and enrolment

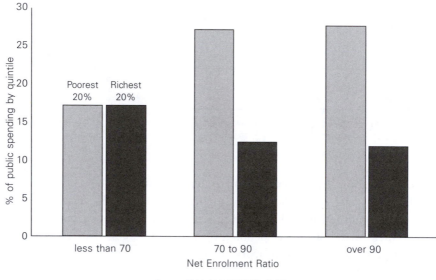

Source: Table 5.2; UNICEF, 2000.

widened by a third for the non-poor and by more than half among the
poor, although the overall enrolment ratio remained unchanged through
this period (Figure 5.2). The primary enrolment ratio actually decreased
for girls from poor households (from 22 in 1985 to 17 in 1988), whereas
it continued to increase for their non-poor counterparts (from 54 to 58
respectively).[11]

Overall, education systems in most developing countries need to improve
the quality of education. What is less well documented is how much the
quality of service varies within countries, and the extent to which the
poor are disadvantaged in this respect. Unit spending in South Africa was
much lower in poor communities, which made a significant difference to
the benefit incidence estimates (Castro-Leal et al., 1998). These variations
in unit subsidies have a massive impact on school quality. For instance, in
Peru the unit cost for primary education was nearly four times higher for
the richest quintile than for the poorest. There is evidence from El Salvador
and Uganda that the unit subsidy actually reaching rural schools is much
less than aggregate data would suggest, pointing to lower education quality
in such areas (Ablo and Reinikka, 1998). There is strong evidence that
school quality has a significant impact on school enrolment decisions of

Figure 5.2 Côte d'Ivoire: primary enrolment by income level and gender (%)

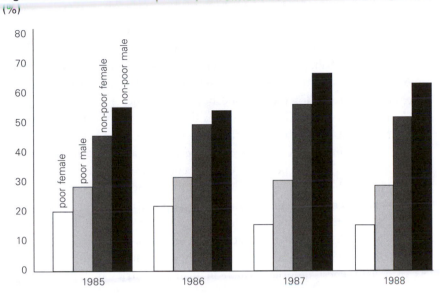

Source: World Bank, Living Standards Measurement Survey.

parents. Leaking and unusable classrooms, inadequate sanitation facilities and the absence of electricity in the school have significant negative effects on decisions to enrol in primary schools. Quality variables (for example, 'no desks') were also found to influence delays in primary enrolment in Ghana (Glewwe and Jacoby, 1992).

As we mentioned above, some of the incidence results depend crucially on the assumption that state expenditure on services used by the relatively poorer groups is the same as the expenditures on the same services for the better off. However, in fact, there is strong evidence that the unit cost – that is, the expenditure per child, of the services received by the bottom quintile is considerably lower than for the top quintile. In South Africa the benefit incidence would seem much more egalitarian when a common unit cost across quintiles is used than when the actual unit costs are used. For instance, when actual unit costs are used, the bottom quintile's share in the benefits of public spending on primary education falls from 26 to 19 per cent. At the same time, the share of the top quintile increases from 13 to 28 per cent. For education as a whole, the results are as dramatic. The share of the bottom quintile drops from 20 to 14 per cent, while the share of the top quintile rises from 20 to 35 per cent.

5.3   Distribution of the benefits of public spending on health

Evidence for seventeen countries on the benefit incidence (by income group) of public expenditure on health is presented in Table 5.4. Although Latin America and sub-Saharan Africa are overrepresented, the pattern in the other regions does not seem to be very different. In order not to overload the table, only the shares for the top and bottom quintiles are reported.

The first observation to be made from this table is that total health spending is not equitably distributed to the poorest groups in society. The bottom quintile (which in many countries does not capture all of the poor) receives significantly less than 20 per cent of the benefits from public spending on health. That is, they do not satisfy the weakest version of equity (that each group receive benefits in proportion to their population size). The poorest 20 per cent of the population get less than 20 per cent of the benefits from public spending on health in all countries surveyed, with the exception of Bangladesh and Costa Rica. Also, and partly as a result of this, they receive less than the richest quintile (which in many countries includes not only the rich but also a great portion of the middle class). The inequality is particularly striking in Côte d'Ivoire, Ghana, Indonesia, Madagascar, Vietnam and, particularly, in Guinea.[12]

A second observation is that there are only two countries where the richest quintiles have appropriated shares lower than 20 per cent. These are South Africa and Costa Rica. It is unlikely that the implication is that in these two countries the benefit incidence of public spending on health is progressive. Rather, it is likely that the richest quintiles do not use the public health service very much in these two countries – relying more on private providers.

The third observation is that spending on basic health services is more equitably shared than total health spending. In some countries, the poor make disproportionate use of primary health facilities. In Kenya, for example, the poorest quintile gained 22 per cent of the government subsidy on primary health, compared with only 14 per cent of the total health subsidy. In Chile – which, as we have seen before, is a high-achiever – the poorest quintile receives 30 per cent of the subsidy on primary health care. In Costa Rica – another high achiever – the bottom quintile receives 43 per cent of that subsidy. For Costa Rica, measurements are available for 1986 as well as for 1992. In both years the bottom quintile received around 30 per cent of public spending in health services. They received 30 per cent of the hospital care expenditures, which shows that the whole of the health-care system in Costa Rica was progressive. Also, it means that the richest group could

Table 5.4 Distribution of public health spending benefits, selected countries (%)

	All health		Quintile shares of Primary facilities		Hospital outpatient	
	Bottom	Top	Bottom	Top	Bottom	Top
Bangladesh (1994)	22	21				
Bolivia (1990)	15	21				
Brazil (1996)	11	23				
Chile (1996)			30	7		
Colombia (1997)	18	27	24	19		
Costa Rica (1992)	30	13	43	7	25	13
Côte d'Ivoire (1995)	11	32	14	22	8	39
Dominican Rep. (1996)			24	12		
Ghana (1992)	12	33	10	31	13	35
Guinea (1994)	4	48	10	36	1	55
Indonesia (1990)	12	29	18	16	7	41
Kenya (1992)	14	24	22	14	13	26
Madagascar (1993)	12	30	10	29	14	30
Peru (1995)	10	27				
South Africa (1994)	16	17	18	10	15	17
Tanzania (1992/3)	17	29	18	21	11	37
Vietnam (1993)	12	29	20	10	9	39

Note: Rural only for Bangladesh and Kenya and rural north-east only for Brazil.

Sources: UNICEF country studies; Castro-Leal et al., 1998.

afford to buy private health-care services, which are seen as being of better quality. The same happened in Chile.

Nevertheless, in many other countries, especially in sub-Saharan Africa (e.g. Côte d'Ivoire, Ghana, Guinea and Madagascar) even spending on primary facilities was not fairly shared. In Ghana and Guinea, for example, of the total visits to a primary health facility, only 10 per cent came from the poorest quintile. Given the costs and benefits involved, household decisions about using publicly subsidized health-care services in these countries result in far fewer visits to primary facilities from poor households than from the wealthier segment of the population. The result is that spending even on

Figure 5.3 Distribution of primary health-care benefits and child mortality (% of public spending by quintile)

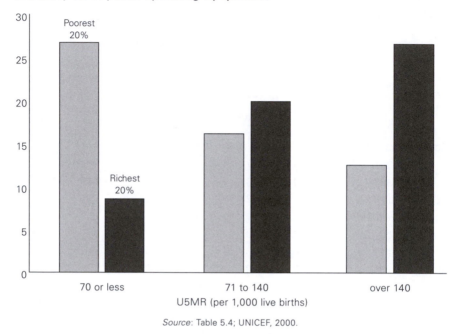

Source: Table 5.4; UNICEF, 2000.

basic health services could be better geared towards providing services to the poor.

However, by and large, the impact of egalitarian spending is strongly reflected in the results. The surveyed countries were divided according to the level of child mortality: very high (above 140 deaths per 1,000 live births), high (between 70 and 140 deaths), and medium (fewer than 70 deaths). The share of primary health-care benefits was calculated for the poorest 20 per cent and the richest 20 per cent of the population in each group of countries. The results are striking (see Figures 5.3 and 5.4).

In countries with under-5 mortality rates below 70, the poorest 20 per cent of the population received more than 25 per cent of the benefits of public spending on primary health care. The same group received less than 15 per cent in countries with child mortality rates above 140 (Figure 5.3). When looking at public spending on hospital care, the results are similar (Fig 5.4). Richer families made more use of hospitals than poor families in countries with medium levels of mortality, but the differences were relatively small – roughly 20 per cent and 15 per cent, respectively. In countries with very high mortality rates, however, the poorest 20 per cent of the population

Figure 5.4 Distribution of public spending on hospitals and child mortality (% of public spending by quintile)

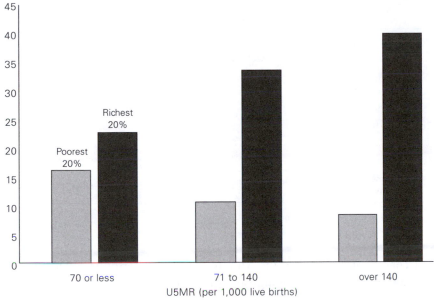

Source: Table 5.4; UNICEF, 2000.

accounted for less than 10 per cent of hospital usage, while the richest 20 per cent accounted for around 40 per cent of usage. This is a far larger proportion than their share of the population would justify, giving them a higher 'share' of the government's spending on hospitals.

Wherever we were able to obtain evidence on the distribution of health spending between rural and urban areas, a strong bias in favour of urban services was observed. In Kenya, for instance, where 70 per cent of the population lives in rural areas, rural health services only receive 13 per cent of the health budget. A similar situation prevails in Namibia, where, at independence in 1990, the health system was characterized not only by gross racial inequities and by an undue focus on tertiary and specialized care, but also by geographical imbalances. The situation has gradually been modified, within a growing budget which has steadily been focused on immunization, control of diarrhoeal diseases, mother–child care, and rural health centres and clinics. Despite these efforts to increase the supply of basic health-care services in the rural areas of the Northwest (efforts which included almost doubling the allocation of the budgeted staff to the region), regional inequities remain. For instance, the state hospital in the capital city

Table 5.5 Distribution by quintile of subsidies for different health services (%)

	Bottom	II	III	IV	Top
Dominican Republic (1996)					
Immunization	21	22	23	20	14
Pap test	27	22	21	18	12
Child check-up	33	21	20	15	11
Pregnancy control	33	22	20	15	10
Colombia (1997)					
Hospitalization (55%)*	25	17	22	15	21
Surgery (31%)*	12	15	9	35	29
Dental (9%)*	0	2	5	23	70
Maternity (2%)*	29	25	19	24	4

Note: * Share in total public health spending.

Source: UNICEF country studies.

still concentrates a third of the Ministry of Health personnel.[13] Despite the increase in per capita spending on basic social services in both Kenya and Namibia in the 1990s (as discussed in the previous chapter), the HIV/AIDS epidemic contributed to an increase in child mortality between 1990 and 1998. Under such circumstances, the inequity of the spending pattern only worsens the plight of the poorest AIDS sufferers.

In Benin, while 60 per cent of the population live in rural areas, public expenditure on health (assuming the same unit costs) is slightly biased, as only 55 per cent are allocated to rural areas. The inequities, however, seem larger within each area. Thus, the rural non-poor account for 42 per cent of the rural population, but receive 51 per cent of the benefits of public expenditure on health in rural areas.[14] Poor rural households represent 34 per cent of the population, but only receive 23 per cent of the benefits of public spending on health. Similarly, the non-poor urban families, which represent 44 per cent of the population, enjoy 58 per cent of the benefits of public spending on health. The urban poor, on the other hand, only appropriate 21 per cent of these benefits although they represent 33 per cent of the urban population.

Table 5.5 provides an interesting perspective on health services affecting women and children. It shows that the benefits of these services, which are an important component of the basic services, are also better distributed than overall expenditures for the sector. In the Dominican Republic, preventive health services (like pregnancy and childcare) are very progressive; within the

Table 5.6 Health services unit costs by quintile

	Bottom	II	III	IV	Top
Côte d'Ivoire (1988, CFAF)	3,347	5,174	7,738	9,419	14,407
Ghana (1992, Cedis)	2,964	4,524	6,314	8,306	12,452
Madagascar (1993/4, FMG)	1,133	2,528	2,573	2,139	4,581
Peru (1997, constant 1996 US$)	0.8	1.0	1.1	1.1	1.2

Sources: UNICEF country studies; Castro-Leal et al., 1998.

education sector, the same holds true for pre-primary and primary public spending. The different benefit incidence even within the basic level of health care is also observed in Colombia, where maternity services (just like pregnancy control in the Dominican Republic) are more progressive than other services. However, for Colombia we also find out that maternity services represent a very small proportion (2 per cent) of total health expenditure.

However, given the qualitative information available for these two countries, it might be incorrect to take solace in these numbers. In both countries, and in particular in the Dominican Republic, there is 'exit' by users in the higher income groups from public facilities and by rural dwellers to facilities located in the cities. This is due to the perceived lower quality of the public facilities, especially in rural areas. Evidently, this perception is partly based on the lack of adequate financing of those facilities (as discussed below).

Unit cost data (by income, and by location or ethnic group) suggest that there may well be large quality differentials in health facilities serving poor and non-poor households. The evidence in Peru, for instance, shows that the unit cost for health services is 50 per cent higher for the top quintile than for the bottom one (Table 5.6), while in the three African countries the unit costs are four times as high for the top quintile relative to unit costs of health services for the bottom quintile.

Although major progress has been achieved in the last few years in South Africa to redress the unfairness of the apartheid system, and to attempt to eliminate 'race' as a category to classify individuals, the information in Table 5.7 is telling. It has also to be pointed out that the efforts of the new authorities are not reflected in these data, which pertain to the early and mid-1990s. In the table, it can be observed that 'race' is associated not only with major differences in terms of infant mortality rates, but also with enormous inequities in the resources allocated per health intervention.[15]

The regional distribution is also interesting because people were forced during the apartheid years to live in so-called 'homelands'. The difference

Table 5.7 Health services expenditures per person by region and race, South Africa

	Unit cost/person (R)	Infant mortality rate
Race		
African	137.8	54.3
Coloured	340.2	36.3
Indian	356.2	9.9
White	597.1	7.3
Region		
Eastern Cape	245.1	44.7
Free State	307.2	45.8
Gauteng	577.1	32.3
KwaZulu-Natal	274.2	44.9
Mpumalanga	158.3	45.1
Northern Cape	265.2	42.9
Northern Province	181.9	52.9
Northwest	203.6	40.1
Western Cape	700.4	24.4

Source: UNICEF country study.

between Western Cape and the rest of the country, in terms of both outcomes (measured by infant mortality rates) and expenditure per capita, again confirms that not only do disadvantaged groups receive less benefit from public spending on health services, but the services they receive are of lower quality. And even if the system looks progressive, as suggested in Table 5.4, it masks the fact that those who can afford to visit private clinics or practitioners (in the upper quintile) would tend to do so if the services are available. It is also worth mentioning that the correlation between expenditure per person and infant mortality when race and province are analysed are −0.86 and −0.91.

5.4 Explaining the incidence of benefits of health and education expenditure

Three main conclusions stand out from the available evidence.[16] First, the distribution of the benefits of public spending (both in education and health[17]) are biased in favour of the richer groups. Evidently, this simple approach implicitly assumes that members of different groups receive the same unit subsidy. This is clearly not true. In most cases, the unit subsidy increases with the income of the recipient, as in Peru, where the state spends 50 per cent more on the health of the top fifth of the population than on the health of the bottom fifth. This, in effect, confirms the Matthew effect: not only do the wealthier groups usually receive a higher share of the benefits of public spending, they receive better-quality services.[18]

Second, the inequity of public spending is much weaker at the basic level of services than at the secondary and tertiary levels. Thus, in a few countries the distribution of the benefits of public spending on elementary education is progressive.

Third, probing beyond the quantitative data, qualitative assessments and indirect data on unit costs often indicate that what looks like a progressive distribution of benefits actually hides a regressive distribution. This emerges from the low quality of the services received by the poorer strata of society.

There are several factors underpinning the inequality in the distribution of public education and health spending in these countries. The first one is that the political process through which budgets are determined usually favour the groups that are most visible, especially those that have a stronger voice in the capital or other important urban centres. Consequently, fiscal resources are channelled to the districts where these groups live and to the services they prefer. This results in the second element (which is clear from the evidence in this and the previous chapter): governments show a tendency to allocate large shares of their budgets to higher-level services, which are not widely used by the poor. In Ghana, for example, two-thirds of the health budget was allocated to hospital services, with a major portion going to one large teaching hospital in Accra. Around nine-tenths of current health spending in South Africa and Vietnam went to hospitals (de Bruyn et al., 1998). And in most of the other countries, over half of the recurrent health budget was devoted to hospital-based care. In Egypt, universities absorb 25 per cent of the total education budget, although they account for only 5 per cent of the student population. Improving the equity and impact of public spending on social services, therefore, would require a shift away from secondary and tertiary levels in favour of basic social services. This is closely related to issues of allocative efficiency, discussed in the next chapter.

Given the current distribution of benefits, it might be very hard to shift allocations without increasing overall expenditure. That is the way found in Namibia in order to arrive at a better balance between rural and urban expenditure. This anticipates the discussion in Chapter 9, where it is argued

Figure 5.5 Enrolment increase in Malawi after elimination of fees and uniforms (million children)

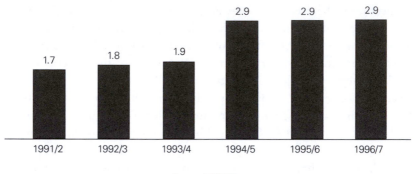

Source: UNICEF.

that more resources would be needed to be able to increase the shares allocated to BSS. In this case, not only will additional resources be needed to facilitate the restructuring in favour of less-privileged groups, but also, because of the low per capita or per unit expenditure that they currently receive, the total expenditure will have to increase quite substantially.

The evidence in Tables 5.1 and 5.6 also shows that for too many countries, the distribution of benefits was regressive even at the basic level of services. Thus, it cannot be ruled out that costs (both direct and indirect) are precluding the lower income groups from accessing BSS. These costs can all be eliminated, or at least mitigated, if more resources are available for BSS.

One kind of direct cost is health charges. They represent a greater burden to the poor compared with the wealthier. There is ample evidence to suggest that health care is much more expensive relative to income for the poor compared with the non-poor. The poor are more likely than the non-poor to reduce their use of health services when prices for health care are higher (Gertler and van der Gaag, 1990; Lavy and Germain, 1994; Reddy and Vandemoortele, 1996). Most of the studies are based on cross-section evidence, and are ambiguous about causation. If government pricing/quality decisions are influenced by utilization, the observed relationship would be difficult to interpret, since utilization would determine price/quality, rather than the other way around. But longitudinal studies incorporating carefully controlled experiments[19] confirm that price increases (without compensating improvements in quality) discourage utilization among the poor.

The evidence also suggests that direct costs discourage school enrolment. When Malawi abolished primary-school fees and uniforms in 1994, the number of pupils increased by nearly half (Figure 5.5).

A significant negative effect of fees on enrolment decisions in Ghana has been reported. The discouraging effect of fees on the transition from primary to secondary schooling was found to be much greater for poor Indonesian children than for the non-poor. Price elasticities of demand for secondary schooling in rural Peru were highest for the poorer groups. If the quality of schooling services available to the poor is inferior, there is every expectation that poor households would be more sensitive to changes in direct costs than those enjoying a better quality of service. Evidently, if governments devoted more resources to BSS, there would be no need to charge user fees.

A very important indirect cost is ease of access – for example, in terms of transportation cost and the opportunity cost of time and effort. In South Africa, for example, the poorest quintile reported travel time of almost two hours on average to obtain medical attention. The richest 20 per cent spent only thirty-four minutes on average (Castro Leal et al., 1998). Though less dramatic, the Ghana Living Standards Survey of 1992 also recorded longer travel and treatment time for poorer households. These costs can dominate the decision as to whether to seek care when an illness or injury occurs. The evidence suggests that the demand for health care is particularly sensitive to the distance to a facility. Distance was found to be a critical factor governing health-care decisions in Colombia, Ghana, Kenya, Côte d'Ivoire and Peru (Gertler and van der Gaag, 1990; Mwabu, et al., 1993; Lavy and Germain, 1994). The easiest way to remedy this problem is to spend more in order to have more and better facilities closer to where people live.

5.5 Conclusion

Ensuring universal coverage of basic social services requires that public expenditure benefits all segments of society in an equitable way to equip the poor with the capabilities to escape from poverty. Evidence from nearly twenty developing countries indicates that health and education spending discriminate against the poor, but that spending on basic health and basic education is less regressive. The data show that, on average, the richest quintile of the population receive about twice as many benefits from education and health subsidies than the bottom 20 per cent of the population.

However, the distribution of benefits depends on the composition of expenditure between basic and non-basic social services. The distribution of benefits from basic social services appears less regressive than that from non-basic social services. The Matthew effect seems particularly strong in higher education. At the primary level, by contrast, the bottom quintile receives more benefits than the top quintile. Caution is counselled when interpreting these results because they critically depend on the measure used. One of the reasons why the poor appear to benefit more from subsidies for primary education is because they tend to have more children than the rich, so that the poorest quintile often account for more than a fifth of the school-age children. Indeed, poor households have more children than non-poor households, so that their relative education needs exceed their population share.

The same point can be made for health, but information on the different health needs between poor and rich is not readily available and quantifiable. Evidence from industrialized countries suggests that factors such as low self-esteem, insecurity and unemployment are associated with higher morbidity and mortality among the poor (Wilkinson, 1994). In short, the evidence above may overstate the progressivity of public spending on primary education and basic heath because of the measure used (i.e. household income quintiles, and not benefits per child or health subsidies per instance of morbidity).

Nevertheless, the above evidence clearly supports the need for broad targeting by increasing the proportion of public spending on basic social services. This will not only lead to a more egalitarian distribution of the benefits, but will also enhance its effectiveness in terms of social outcomes, poverty reduction and future economic growth.

The current education subsidies do not ensure equality of opportunities among socioeconomic groups. Whereas the distribution at the primary level is reasonably equitable, the bias in favour of the wealthier families increases with the level of education. We estimate that over the period of a lifetime, a child from a rich family receives approximately ten times more education subsidies than a child whose family belongs to the bottom quintile, thereby preventing education playing its full potential as the great equalizer in society. The importance of the maldistribution of education subsidies can hardly be overstated because poverty reduction starts, in most cases, with education.

Averages mask important gender gaps in the benefit incidence. For example, it is not uncommon to see females use the publicly funded health and education facilities less, in comparison to males. In Côte d'Ivoire, for instance, the enrolment ratio remained unchanged in the second half of the 1980s, despite a marked decline in the enrolment ratio for poor girls. Figure 5.2 shows that the gender gap in primary enrolment widened by a third for the non-poor and by more than half among the poor between 1985 and 1988. The primary enrolment ratio for girls from poor households actually decreased, whereas it continued to increase for their non-poor counterparts.

The reasons why girls and women in poor households are disadvantaged in public health and education are not totally clear. It may be due to supply-side effects, as facilities available to the poor do not provide relevant or quality services. Or it may arise from demand-side preferences as poor households may decide that females should not use health facilities or attend school because of social values or higher opportunity costs involving time consumption in the daily cycle of a woman's social role. It has been observed that poor households make different health and education choices for males than for females, which may explain, in part, why subsidies are not progressive.

6

Policies to enhance efficiency and improve delivery in the public provision of basic social services

This book is about the role of public spending in promoting human development and poverty reduction – that is, enhancing capabilities (or the alternative combinations of functionings that are feasible for a person to achieve). We have already made the case for public action as critical to the enhancement of capabilities. However, governments have to be equally concerned about the level, equity and efficiency of public spending if public delivery of basic social services is to be universalized. Having examined the first two – the level and equity of spending – in the preceding two chapters, here we focus on technical and allocative efficiency. In practice, when large sections of the population are without access to services, or the services are of poor quality, the reasons lie in resource allocations that are insufficient, inequitable and inefficient. Inequities can lead to inefficiency. For example, the same level of health spending will have markedly different effects on health outcomes depending on whether it focuses on areas or households suffering from preventable causes of morbidity/mortality, or on groups that already have access to a package of minimum health-care services. Thus the allocation of resources can be at the same time both inequitable and inefficient. This is a running theme throughout this chapter.

Allocative inefficiency in spending – or balance in the intra-sectoral allocation by service level within health, education and water sectors – has important implications for spatial (rural–urban) equity. Reallocating resources from urban-based hospital care to accessible primary level preventive services is more equitable and efficient, since it ensures health services for a larger section of the population, including those currently unreached. Given that social indicators tend to be much worse for the poor than for the rest of the population, a reallocation of resources to the basic level expands coverage to the poor and will have more impact on outcomes. In education, public expenditure emphasis on tertiary and specialized services when primary-school-age children are out of school is an inefficient use of public education expenditure.

Technical efficiency – achieving better outcomes with the same resources – would be difficult to achieve in any sector without some balance between capital and recurrent expenditure. In the medium term it is necessary to maintain a balance between the two, so that underfunding of recurrent expenditure does not lead to unwarranted depreciation of capital, while lack of capital spending does not lead to inadequate or ineffective service delivery. The other big issue is that of balance between salary and non-salary inputs in recurrent expenditure by level. This is crucial because teachers without pedagogical materials, or physicians without medicines, are quite inefficient and ineffective. It is usually the case that inadequate funding causes a shortage of critical inputs. At other times, inefficiency is the result of weak policies or poor institutions.

To the extent possible, we shall focus the discussion less on issues of allocative efficiency and equity (i.e. allocation in each social sector), having discussed them earlier, and more on issues of technical efficiency by sector. Inefficiencies that arise from policy failures independent of the size or level of resources allocated is the main area of concern of this chapter – although it is often difficult in practice to separate the effects of the two. While many of the allocative and technical inefficiencies in government delivery derive from inappropriate policies, several problems of state provision derive from the bureaucratic and organizational context of the provision – these are addressed in the following chapter.

Section 6.1 examines issues of allocative efficiency in the education, water/sanitation and health sectors. Section 6.2 goes on to discuss technical efficiency in service delivery in each sector. As an extension of health services, we also examine issues related to reproductive health and nutritional status. The focus of the discourse is on the policies relevant to both low- and middle-income countries. The policy lessons for most developing countries particularly emerge from the contrast in policies between the so-called high achievers (see Chapter 4) and the rest of the developing countries.

6.1   Allocative efficiency

While the state in most low- and middle-income countries has taken a
predominant role in providing public education and public health services,
not all have been equally able to fund the services adequately at all levels.
When choices have to be made in dividing limited resources, the politically
powerful win out; despite the positive externalities from universal provision
of primary level services, it is the relatively poor who have to suffer poorer-
quality public services. Under the circumstances, they have little choice but
either to exit altogether (i.e. drop out in the case of schooling) or to exit to
private providers and incur out-of-pocket expenses. Since the demand of the
poor for health services or water is rather inelastic, out-of-pocket expenses
usually are incurred at the cost of other expenditures (e.g. schooling, if the
household is close to the poverty line). Catastrophic health costs can make
the difference between households being above the poverty line, or falling
below it.

Education

Of the 680 million children in the developing world of primary-school age
(6–11), 115 million are still out of school. In Chapter 4 we briefly argued that
countries that made large improvements in health and education indicators
early in their development process – the so-called high achievers[1] – had
given higher macroeconomic and fiscal priority to health and education than
other countries in their region. However, high levels of public expenditure
on education overall may not be a sufficient condition, and may not even
be a necessary condition, for universalizing primary education – if that
expenditure tends to favour higher education.

   In fact, a significant common feature in these high-achieving countries was
the equity of allocation by level of education – the *sine qua non* of allocative
efficiency in education – or the high priority given to basic education.
This balance may be a prerequisite to ensure essential inputs for schools.
A comparison between high achievers and other countries, where EFA
remains to be achieved, shows interesting contrasts. There was a difference
in the share of public education expenditure allocated to higher education
in 1980 and 1990: the high achievers spent less on it than other countries
in their regions (Figure 6.1). Second, there was a sharp difference in primary
education expenditure as a proportion of per capita income, with the high
achievers normally spending more (Figure 6.2). Third, per pupil expenditures
were also relatively equitable among the high achievers (see Figure 6.3); thus,

Figure 6.1 Selected high achievers by geographic region: higher education as a share of current public expenditure on education (%)

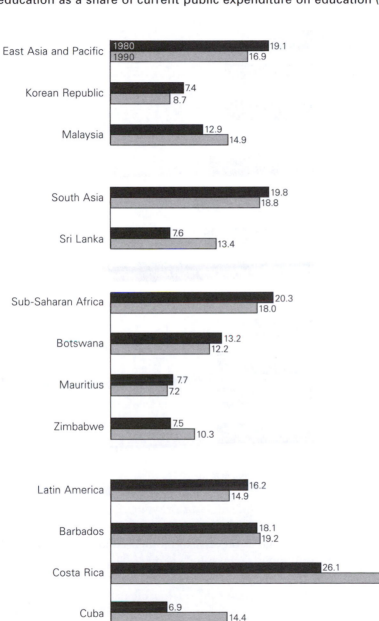

Source: Mehrotra, 1998b.

Figure 6.2 Selected high achievers: % of per capita income spent on each primary (and pre-primary) pupil, *circa* 1980

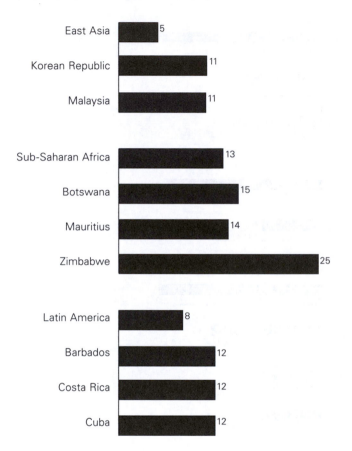

Source: UNESCO, 1993.

Figure 6.3 Selected high achievers by geographic region: per pupil
expenditure as a multiple of primary education, 1980 (%)

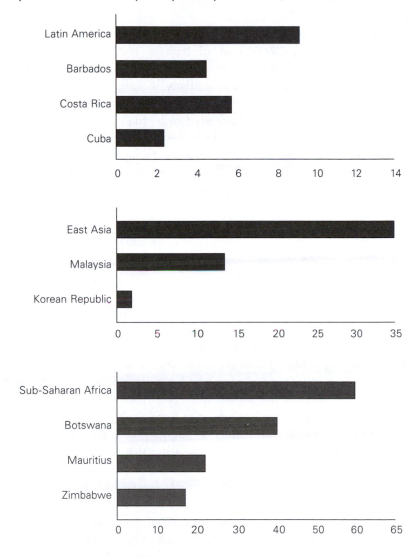

Source: UNESCO, 1993.

per pupil public expenditure on higher education as a multiple of per-pupil primary expenditure is lower in all the high achievers than in other countries in the region.

The inequity of this expenditure pattern within education declined in the 1990s (Mehrotra, 1999) – in all regions. The ratio of per pupil expenditure for higher education compared to primary education declined in sub-Saharan Africa to 25 in 1995. Similarly, in Latin America this ratio had declined to 3 in 1995 (to the level in OECD countries). However, what is still interesting is that it still tended to be highest in regions where the primary school enrolment rates were lowest. In fact, the lower the enrolment rates the greater the difference. In Latin America, where the GER in 1995 on average was 106, the multiple was just 1:3. In South Asia, with a GER of 94, the ratio was 1:8, and in sub-Saharan Africa, with a GER lower than 80, it was 1:25.

When public expenditure on primary education (or health) is either low for structural reasons or tends to fall due to macroeconomic constraints (e.g. to reduce budget deficits), out-of-pocket expenditures by families would tend to rise – assuming that demand for schooling is high. But the demand for schooling by the poor is likely to be highly price-elastic; and the price-elasticity of demand for girls' schooling would be even higher (Mehrotra, 1998b).

Thus, an important cause of dropping out is the cost to parents of sending children to school. There are direct and indirect costs to parents. The former consist of fees and charges, the latter are supplies, uniforms and travel; in addition, there is the opportunity cost of time. Poor households in low-income countries often consider the opportunity costs of schooling as too high; the returns accrue mainly in the long run, are uncertain, and suffer from principal-agent problems (in the sense that the cost is borne by the parent, while the benefits accrue to the child). A considerable body of literature on child labour has emerged in recent years which argues that the effective means of countering school drop-out and labour-market entry by children is to reduce the direct and indirect costs of schooling (Bourguignon, 2002; Rosati and Tzannatos, 2001; Mehrotra and Biggeri, 2003).

UNICEF studies in two African countries (Burkina Faso and Uganda) and three Asian countries (Bhutan, Myanmar and Vietnam) confirm the importance of private costs in discouraging school attendance (Mehrotra and Delamonica, 1998). Private cost is in the range of 10 to 20 per cent of per capita income (Figure 6.4). Uniforms often constitute the single most important cost item for parents. Similar results emerge from surveys in eight states in India – which account for two-thirds of the Indian children out of

Figure 6.4 Education costs and enrolment for primary schools

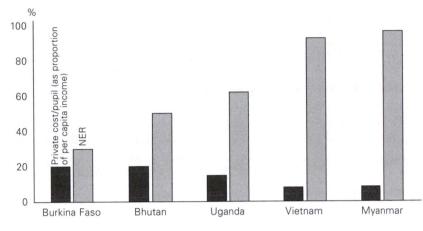

Source: Mehrotra and Delamonica, 1998.

school (Mehrotra et al., 2005). Both usage and equity deteriorate as a result of charges (Tilak, 1997).

For many years in the 1980s and early 1990s there were mixed signals emerging from the IFIs in respect of education (and also the health sector) over user fees. Along with the concern about public-sector spending in the 1980s, World Bank economists developed an economic model illustrating that, where there is excess demand for education, charging user fees at all levels of education would be advantageous from both an efficiency and an equity perspective (Thobani, 1983; Tan et al., 1984; World Bank, 1986; Jimenez, 1986, 1987; Psacharapolous et al., 1986).[2] In fact, the World Bank's policy note argued strongly that governments 'do not tap the willingness of households to contribute resources directly to education'. This policy was most convincing (and actually persuasive in sub-Saharan Africa through the instrument of IMF stabilization and World Bank adjustment loans) for higher education. However, after sharp criticism of the consequences for elementary schooling, by the early to mid-1990s, the Bank distanced itself from user charges at the primary level (Tilak, 1997), but not before doing some damage.

The experience of Malawi is relevant, where enrolment sharply increased in 1994 in the wake of the elimination of school uniforms and school fees. In fact, the irony of the Malawi case is unmistakable (Colclough, 1997). The expansion of enrolment occurred in the very country for which the case for introducing fees – in order to finance more school places, and achieve higher enrolments – was first made by Thobani (1983). Similarly, Uganda and then Tanzania eliminated school fees in the late 1990s, and enrolment jumped as a result.

As we saw above, uniforms are one of the largest elements of out-of-pocket costs. One policy option is for the authorities to indicate that uniforms are not mandatory, and leave it to school administrations and parent-teachers' associations to decide at the local level whether the uniform should be retained or not. Although it is not possible to eliminate all of them completely, some out-of-pocket costs can be substantially reduced. Fees for primary education should be gradually eliminated, as is stipulated by the UN Convention on the Rights of the Child, now ratified by all but two countries in the world: 'State Parties … shall … make primary education compulsory and available free to all' (Article 28).[3]

In the high-achieving countries, which ensured universal primary enrolment and completion early in their development process, primary schooling was largely free of direct tuition fees. Even the indirect costs were kept relatively low. Not all out-of-pocket costs can be eliminated at the same time, because the fiscal burden of such a measure can be considerable. In Sri Lanka, tuition fees were eliminated in 1945; free textbooks and free lunches were introduced in the 1950s; a policy of free school uniform came into effect in 1991. In Botswana, enrolment received a major boost from the decision to cut fees by half in 1973, and was totally eliminated in 1980 (Mehrotra, 1998b). Allocative efficiency implies that public resource allocations to the primary level are such as to progressively reduce, if not eliminate, out-of-pocket costs of sending a child to school. The evidence, in other words, is consistently contrary to the idea that user fees work.

To summarize, allocative efficiency in public expenditure on education consists in allocating public resources to the maximum extent possible in low-income countries to primary education. For example, Korea was allocating over three-quarters of public education spending to primary education in the early 1950s. This is contrary to the evidence from countries with a low Human Development Index (HDI), where no more than 45 per cent of education spending goes to primary education (UNDP HDR, 2002). However, as we argued in Chapter 4, the overall level of education spending is also a determinant of outcomes; it is difficult for governments to shift resources to basic education if the overall education budget is relatively small. Finally, it is difficult for governments to cut out-of-pocket costs for parents unless the level of public spending on basic education rises per capita.

Water and sanitation

Over a sixth of humanity (1.1 billion people) are without access to safe water, and over a third of the world's people (2.4 billion) lack adequate sanitation. Half the world's hospital beds are occupied by patients with water-borne diseases, implying that expensive curative services are being used to treat diseases that could easily have been prevented. Hence, the provision of water and sanitation is critical to triggering the synergies between basic services. Despite some 438 million people gaining access to water supply during the 1990s, the high rates of *urban* population growth in developing countries could not prevent an increase (by 62 million) in the number of urban dwellers lacking access to water supplies in the year 2000. Progress in the provision of urban sanitation was better. An additional 542 million gained access to urban sanitation facilities during the 1990s; the number without such access fell by 41 million. Nevertheless, the total number in the developing world without adequate sanitation is still 2.4 billion (United Nations, 2000a).

Some progress also took place in *rural* areas. Access to water supply in rural areas reached an additional 400 million during the 1990s; thus those lacking safe water fell by 150 million to a total of 915 million in 2000. It is in rural sanitation that the problem is most acute. About 252 million people gained access to adequate sanitation in rural areas during the 1990s; but the numbers of those without access in rural areas did not decline below 2 billion in the 1990s (United Nations, 2000a).

The problem of water for domestic use has to be understood in the context of the global use of fresh water. Two-thirds of the world's water consumption is for irrigation (most of the rest being for industrial use).[4] In terms of allocative efficiency of water use, there is no more important issue than the need to apply more efficient methods of irrigation – and thereby improve its availability for other purposes. More than two-thirds of the additional production needed to sustain the world's growing population must come from irrigated fields. However, an excessive amount of the earth's water is being wasted by defective irrigation systems. Many of the irrigation canals in low-income countries are crude ditches dug out of the fields. Much of the water never reaches the targeted crops. Worse still, it is absorbed into ditches and later leads to salinization which destroys the fertility of the soil, or it lies in stagnant pools that provide breeding grounds for insects. However, if the irrigation canals or ditches are lined with low-cost tile, the water can be directed efficiently to the targeted fields.[5] Even more importantly, as we discuss in Chapter 9, irrigation water is so heavily subsidized by governments – under the influence of rich-landlord-led pressure groups – that the wastage of water would fall if the costs of water provision were at least partially recovered.

Excessive use of groundwater has, in fact, led to serious shortages of water arising in many parts of the world.[6] The Green Revolution, which strikingly increased crop yields across the developing world from the 1960s onwards, was paradoxically a major culprit. The new high-yielding varieties of seeds were not only technology-intensive but also highly water-intensive. As a result sustainable use of water resources, widely practised until then, fell by the wayside (especially, but not only, in South Asia and China). It led to changes in ways in which upper catchments were managed, resulting in a degradation of water resources in tanks, lakes and rivers. Groundwater was now also extracted from greater depths, with shallow hand-dug wells – which until then had provided drinking water – becoming less and less feasible. The situation was worsened by industrial and urban pollution of surface and groundwater resources. In other words, when droughts occurred, they were less natural phenomena than man-made ones. In sub-Saharan Africa, where the Green Revolution was less widespread, destructive deforestation led to massive soil erosion and land degradation. Thus in regions that are traditionally either arid or semi-arid (e.g. large parts of sub-Saharan Africa, peninsular India, and parts of west and northern China), water availability became scarce.

Similarly, in China water problems have reached calamitous proportions. In the late 1990s major rivers north of the Yangtze had dried up. The government hence approved a gigantic project to channel the water of the Yangtze river along a 1,200-kilometre route to drought-stricken northern China.[7] The south-to-north water diversion project is an admission by the administration that the droughts in northern China cannot be blamed on a temporary phase in the weather cycle. Rather, they are a man-made phenomenon caused by such recent events as the massive destruction of forests, marshes and grasslands in the uplands of western China (Becker, 2001). What this clearly implies is that globally, and especially in developing countries, integrated water resources management is essential to ensuring safe drinking water reaches the unserved.

Concerned by this worsening situation and its implications for access to safe drinking water in the late 1970s, the UN proclaimed the period 1981–90 as the International Drinking Water Supply and Sanitation Decade, and the General Assembly has since regularly monitored progress. The reports by the secretary general since then have consistently expressed the view that, in spite of efforts to accelerate the rate of progress in the provision of services, little if any progress is being made in reducing the number of people lacking access to safe water supply and suitable sanitation facilities.[8]

What is extraordinary is that, globally in developing countries, of the population unserved by adequate sanitation 82 per cent are in rural areas, and 85 per cent of that unserved by safe water is also in rural areas. At the same time, WHO estimates that during the 1980s an average of approximately $13 billion was spent annually in developing countries for water supply and sanitation; of this, only one-quarter was spent in rural areas[9] (UNICEF, 1995a).

Allocative inefficiency abounds in the sector. Evidence from Annex Table 6.1 shows what a small share of total government expenditure has been allocated to water and sanitation in most countries (rarely exceeding 2 per cent, and usually absorbing about 1 per cent). The evidence from most of the selected developing countries studied is also that they allocate a much larger share of government spending on water to urban areas than to rural areas – despite the much larger share of rural residents in the total population. Thus in Namibia, although 70 per cent of the population live in rural areas, the share of water resources allocated to rural areas since independence has been as follows: 11 per cent in 1992/3; 13 per cent in 1993/4; 19 per cent in 1994/5; 29 per cent in 1995/6; and 35 per cent in 1996/7 (Radwan, 1997). In Sri Lanka, every year between 1982 and 1996, expenditure on urban water and sanitation was several multiples of expenditure on rural areas (Rannan-Eliya et al., 1998).

This is partly because the cost of services in better-off urban areas can be as high as $550 per capita for water supply and sanitation (UNICEF, 1995). In stark contrast, appropriate technologies in rural and peri-urban areas costing less than $30 per capita can extend rapid coverage to a much larger population. In other words, the problem of low allocation to watsan (which partly accounts for the poor access to safe water and sanitation discussed above) is compounded by rural–urban disparity in allocation, and further made worse by the use of inappropriate technology. The World Summit on Sustainable Development (in Johannesburg in 2002) action plan would suggest that governments believe that the global water crisis can be solved by installing vastly more pipes by 2015. It contains a proposal to build 750 million more piped water connections without actually ensuring there is any water available to make them work (because of water diversion, inefficient water use and degradation of water sources) (Pittock, 2002).

In the light of the slow progress so far, and the huge population that remains uncovered, it is imperative that allocations shift dramatically in favour of rural areas so far as safe water is concerned. However, the need for adequate sanitation is especially acute in urban areas; and in this sector the resources have to be concentrated in the urban areas in the first instance. In terms of sheer numbers, the need for improved sanitation is greatest in rural areas, since 18 per cent of rural residents in developing countries have access, as against 63 per cent in urban areas.

However, the problem is much more severe in urban areas on account of population density, where disease spreads easily without sanitary means of sewage disposal. Allocative efficiency would consist in concentrating resources meant for sanitation in urban areas. Almost half the developing world's population lives in urban areas, and this share will continue to grow. If adequate provision for sanitation in large cities is taken to mean a toilet connected to a sewer, then only 40 per cent of the population in Asian and Latin American large cities, and about 20 per cent of the population in African cities, have adequate sanitation. However, here the emphasis needs to be in providing better services in small and medium-size towns in particular. Such a policy would be consistent with a policy to encourage small and medium industries, and non-farm employment associated with agriculture – a strategy stressed in Chapter 2.

The relevant municipal authorities usually charge for piped water in urban areas. However, there is evidence that by and large water is supplied to towns and municipalities at subsidized rates, thus resulting in an overconsumption of scarce water resources (e.g. Namibia). This is one reason why in recent years there has been a move in favour of privatization and commercialization of state-owned urban water utility companies, with a view to partial or complete cost recovery (World Bank, 1994b) – the experience with which we discuss in Chapter 8. A reason often given for rural areas being ignored is that because most water points are communally owned and operated, the levying of tariffs becomes more problematic, and thus governments and especially private companies have no incentive to provide adequate water supplies to remote locations.

As in health and education, cost sharing and cost recovery are major areas of concern in the water and sanitation sectors – and policymakers need to protect the interests of the poor. Cost recovery in urban water supply in many developing countries is only about 30 per cent of cost (Briscoe and Garn, 1995). Instead of subsidizing those able to pay, there should be cross-subsidization of the poor. However, at the same time, an element of sharing of capital costs of even basic service levels fosters ownership, and recovering recurrent costs helps sustainability (UNICEF, 1995a). But cost recovery from the poor without regard to their ability to pay can only be unjust. Overemphasis on 'ownership' of water supplies through payment undercuts the rights of access of the poor. Cost recovery of piped water supply to individual households rather than basic-level services (e.g. standpipes for communal use) is much more important, as subsidies here typically absorb large resources, and benefit the affluent, who have the ability to pay. Moreover, recovering costs of piped supply in households promotes accountability of the supply institution, and could release funds to improve the coverage of basic services.

In summary, the principles of allocative efficiency – with the objectives of improved health outcomes and affordable access of water and sanitation to all – would require that if faster progress is to be achieved, several conditions have to be met: (1) more efficient use of groundwater for non-domestic purposes (agricultural irrigation and industrial water) has to be encouraged; (2) in public allocation of resources for sanitation, there needs to be much more emphasis than hitherto on densely populated urban areas; (3) cost recovery in water supply in better-off parts of urban areas has to be more seriously pursued.

Health

As in the case of education, the policies of high achievers in health were marked by allocative efficiency of public spending. Allocative inefficiency occurs when resources are devoted to the wrong activities. High public spending on hospital-based care for children with diphtheria is an example of such allocative inefficiency, since the disease can be prevented through immunization. In high-achieving countries policies were marked by a series of specific kinds of health intervention, relevant to about half the existing disease burden from communicable or infectious diseases, poor nutrition, and maternal and peri-natal causes. This requires that resource allocation should establish the right balance between various levels of care: primary, secondary and tertiary.[10]

What is noticeable about most of the high-achieving countries is that they adopted the principles of primary health care long before these had been generally recognized by the world community (in the Alma Ata Declaration, 1978). As regards the health system, these countries emphasized system building and a *comprehensive* approach to basic health care (Halstead et al., 1985; Hill et al., 1993; Mehrotra, 1997). They achieved major reductions in the mortality of mothers and children by focusing the attention of the health system on these population groups. Pregnancy management was supported by good health-referral systems, along with household visits by the first-level health worker. A high proportion of births took place under the supervision of a trained provider. Immunization coverage was found to be particularly high in all these countries. Overall, an effective balance was achieved in supporting first-level health workers while maintaining a well-functioning network of hospitals.

However, in most developing countries, while primary health care was a common area of focus, the approach was more selective. In fact, UNICEF's early start with a comprehensive approach to primary health care (the GOBI–FFF approach, where G = growth monitoring of children; O = oral rehydration therapy; B = breast-feeding; I = immunization; F = female education; F = family spacing; F = food supplements) was transformed into a more selective approach.[11] Through much of the 1980s, what the international agencies (especially WHO and UNICEF, given that the World Bank was still not much into health policy and lending at the time, though that changed) promoted were two simple, life-saving technologies, immunization and oral rehydration therapy, which became the twin engines of UNICEF's Child Survival Revolution.[12] The global campaign from 1985 to 1990 to raise immunization levels to at least 80 per cent in all countries by 1990 did lower child mortality, but did not do much to improve the quality of life of children. Malnutrition continued to be a major contributor to mortality (as we discuss later); if anything, malnutrition remained at a disturbingly high level – in both absolute numbers and incidence (especially in the most populous countries as well as sub-Saharan Africa).

High-achieving countries, on the other hand, not only adopted, in most cases, what could be termed a comprehensive approach, and did so earlier than the selective approach that came to most other developing countries; they also addressed imbalances in human resources, both in terms of recruitment as well as their placement. Thus they adopted supportive human resources policies, like requiring doctors to work with the government health service for a certain period of time. For the vast majority of the population a universally available and affordable system, financed out of government revenues, functional at the lowest level, made effective by allocating resources at the lower end of the health system pyramid, was key to high health status. At the publicly provided services there was little or no evidence of out-of-pocket expenditure by the poor (except in Zimbabwe after adjustment measures were introduced in 1990) (Duncan et al., 1997; Dommen and Dommen, 1997; Loewenson and Chisvo, 1997; Krishnan, 1997; Alailame and Sanderatne, 1997; Mehrotra et al., 1997; Heng and Hoey, 1997; Bishop et al., 1997: Garnier et al., 1997; Mehrotra, 1997).

However, in most developing countries, users of health services make out-of-pocket payment at the time of demanding services – usually formal payments to private providers and often informal payments to public providers

Table 6.1 Expenditure on health globally by households, governments and donors (% of total expenditure)

	Africa	Americas	Middle East	Asia	Global	Poorest 32 countries
Household	39	41	53	62	50	59
Government	28	51	40	36	48	37
Donor	33	8	7	2	2	4

Source: Authors' estimates, based on World Bank, 1993a.

(Narayan et al., 2000). That is a situation that cannot make for fairness – assuming that fairness should be a characteristic of health systems (as WHO rightly suggests, 2000). The household is not only the environment that influences most the health, nutrition and education of children, but is also the principal financier of services. Of all health expenditure in developing countries (or an estimated US$85 billion yearly), half comes from patients' pockets, and in the case of the poorest thirty-two countries in the world nearly 60 per cent (or US$6 per capita) (World Bank, 1993a). The Americas region is the only one where public spending on health exceeds that of direct household payments. In Asia, nearly two-thirds of all expenditure on health comes from household contributions (Table 6.1).

As in other regions, in sub-Saharan Africa the household is the largest contributor to expenditures on health, at 39 per cent, but unlike in other regions donors are second at 33 per cent and governments last at 28 per cent. In India, the role of the government in financing health is even more limited. About 75 per cent of the total expenditure on health care is borne directly by households (Tulsidhar, 1996).

Low-income households, however, have to use proportionately more of their income for treatment. In India, a national survey of expenditure on health showed that as a percentage of family expenditure, low-income families paid 1.1 per cent, middle-income families paid 0.6 per cent, and high-income families paid 0.3 per cent on health care. Considering that low-income families are more likely to have health problems, the overall burden on the poor of covering treatment costs is likely to be even higher than these proportions suggest.

A further setback for health care in the 1980s was the measure of cost recovery and user charges that came with structural adjustment programmes in much of Africa and Latin America. Studies in several countries showed that user fees decrease utilization of medical services. In Ghana, one of the

Bank's high-profile success stories, economic growth was accompanied by user fees in rural clinics that contributed to a doubling of child mortality between 1983 and 1993 (Werner and Sanders, 1997).[13] Creese and Kutzin (1997) find that cost recovery policies have hardly raised revenues, and net revenues are less than gross revenues on account of collection costs. On efficiency, utilization drops after the imposition of charges. One study of thirty-nine developing countries found that the introduction of user fees had increased revenues only slightly, and had reduced the access of low-income people to basic social services.

The most serious impact of user fees on health-seeking behaviour of the poor occurs for the following reason. Since poor households are resource-constrained, they will delay seeking care until an emergency situation arises.[14] Women and children will be the most vulnerable under the circumstances, since the decision to seek medical opinion when sick is not in their hands. For example, half of all women in India are not involved at all in decisions about seeking health care for themselves. For children, the decision is likely to be biased by gender (against girls). Participation in decisions about their own health care tends to increase with education, and if women are working (IIPS, 2000). The delay in seeking medical care, if financial costs are likely to be involved in the first instance, eventually compels the family to seek care at a more expensive level, typically at a hospital (rather than a health centre). The inefficiency and inequity of user fees are obvious, since they lead to worse health outcomes and higher health expenditures. If one factors in the gender-biased decision-making in household allocations of resources, the overall impact on well-being in the household is worse.

Proponents of user fees suggest that they may not necessarily be inequitable, as systems of waiving user fees could be determined, so that those unable to pay are not excluded from public health-care services. However, in practice it has not been easy to establish a well-functioning system of waiver for user fees (as we see below in the discussion of the Bamako Initiative; also see Russell and Gilson, 1997). In addition, public funds are not set aside to compensate local providers for fee reduction for poor patients (Whitehead et al., 2001). In fact, there is a risk that public health providers may start giving priority to patients who can pay. In fact, in Uganda this risk is heightened by the fact that health staff payments and salaries are linked to revenue from fees.

By the early 1990s, however, the Bank may have realized its mistakes, and was advocating that user charges cannot be a source of income for the health (or education) sector at lower levels of service (World Bank, 1994a). However, there is reason to believe that the policy might not be dead, given the widespread support the IFIs have given to expansion of the private sector in health (see Chapter 8 for a discussion of its pernicious effects in poor countries). In fact, the US House of Representatives noted the persistence of the policy, and in July 2000 approved a measure to pressure the World Bank to stop requiring poor countries to charge user fees for basic health services and primary education (Whitehead et al., 2001).

While private expenditure on private providers is widespread, in most developing countries there tend to be four organizational forms of health service provision. One is the ministry of health, with its network of public providers, financed from general taxation. A second is private health insurance based on payment of premiums. The third consists of social security organizations based on salary-related contributions, usually for formal-sector workers. Finally, there are community or provider-based pooling organizations, usually consisting of a small pooling/purchasing organization dependent upon voluntary contributions (e.g. Bamako Initiative-type pooling).

Despite the existence in most countries of the four organizational forms of delivering health services, the second and third forms are more widely applicable in economies with a large formal sector. In most low-income countries, for the poor, who are usually in the rural areas engaged in agriculture, or in informal-sector activities in the urban areas, the realistic options are public finance and public providers, *or* some form of community pooling of household resources to meet the costs of public/private provision, *or* out-of-pocket payment to private providers. Knowing that out-of-pocket payments are neither fair to the poor, nor efficient – given the externalities involved in 'good' health – public provision or community-level pooling are two options that should be widely applicable in all developing countries. Option one – public finance and public provision – has so far proved to be of poor quality in low-income countries, and improvement of quality is crucially dependent upon additional public finance. However, within the limited resources available to health ministries and the system of public provision, we examine later the issues of improving technical efficiency in public provision.

The issue of community pooling, however, deserves further attention here. The Bamako Initiative (BI) is a form of community pooling of resources, and has been implemented to varying degrees in over forty mostly low-income countries (including half the countries in sub-Saharan Africa since the late 1980s). It has shown that organized communities can help sustain local public health services, not only by contributing financial resources but also by having 'voice' in the management of the services. The strategy of the BI is to revitalize public health systems by decentralizing decision-making from the national to the district level, instituting community financing and co-management of a minimum package of essential services at the level of basic health units. The aim is to improve services by generating sufficient income to cover some local operating costs such as essential drug supply, salaries of some support staff, and incentives for health workers. Funds generated by community financing do not revert to the central treasury but remain in the community and are controlled by it through a locally elected health committee. From mere recipients of health care, consumers become active partners whose voices count.

After ten years of implementation of the Initiative, community action in most rural health centres, for instance in Benin and Guinea, enabled nearly half the population to be regular users of the services. It also raised and sustained immunization levels close to Year 2000 Health for All targets (Levy-Bruhl et al., 1997). Charging a modest fee to users is seen in some cases to be the most affordable option for the poorest, who otherwise have to access more expensive alternatives, although it is less clear whether mechanisms exist to protect indigent members of the community. Much of the success has been in ensuring the supply of affordable essential drugs that are readily available in the health centres, under the scrutiny of the committees. Another factor has been the improved attitude of health workers, traditionally one reason for people, especially women, not to use the service.[15]

This experience suggests that pooling of community resources, involving some prepayment by the poor, would be a fair and efficient mechanism for providing health services to the poor. In health systems where individuals have to pay out of pocket for a large part of the cost of health services at the time of seeking treatment, access is restricted to those who can afford to pay, and will most probably exclude the poorest. Fairness of financial risk protection therefore requires the highest possible degree of separation between contributions and utilization. There is a consensus around the central role of public financing in the area of *public health*. For *personal health care*, however, it is not the public–private dichotomy that is most important in determining health system performance but the difference between prepayment and out-of-pocket spending (WHO, 2000).

Prepayment affords protection against having to pay out of pocket and facing a barrier to access; it also makes it possible to spread the financial risk among members of a pool (something that out-of-pocket payment does not allow). General taxation is also a form of prepayment. However, relying on prepaid arrangements, especially general taxation, is institutionally very demanding. General taxation as a main source of health financing is normal with a largely formal economy, where tax collection is easier, whereas in low-income countries the informal sector and small-scale peasant agriculture (household rather than large-scale capitalist farms) are predominant. As we argued in Chapter 9, increasing social expenditures on the basis of tax revenues is indeed a medium- to long-run policy agenda. Similarly, improving the technical efficiency of publicly provided personal (i.e. clinical) health services is called for (see the following section). Meanwhile, other forms of prepayment, especially implemented at the community level, need to be explored and researched – and their replicability examined.

Thus, in order to promote a fair system of health financing, it is necessary to achieve two objectives: one, improve the efficiency and effectiveness of the public health services; and two, promote pooling of resources and spreading of risk, so that the out-of-pocket payments by the poor are minimized. For the latter, it will be important to promote job-based contribution systems (as has happened in many middle-income countries and in low-income countries for the formal sector), and facilitate the creation of community (e.g. BI) or provider-based prepayment schemes (e.g. health cards, as in Thailand). Given that currently the poor end up paying for personal health services in any case, either to private providers or informally to public providers, there is a case for at least ensuring that the poor get value for money for the payment. If prepaid, such payment could well ensure a spreading of risk and pooling of funds. Such fund pools could be directly subsidized by the ministry of health. Such mixed systems have been demonstrated to work in the case of informal-sector workers in India, who have been organized under the banner of SEWA, the Self-employed Women's Association, which has a wide network in many states, in both rural and urban India (see, e.g., Chatterjee and Vyas; 2000; Jajoo, 2000; SEWA, 2000).

6.2 Technical efficiency

Both ministries of finance as well as ministries of education/health should be particularly concerned about getting better outcomes from existing resources, both financial and human. Since ministries of finance often assume that the social sector ministries are engaged in pure consumption, they may have a greater interest than the line ministry (in charge of health, education, water and sanitation) in ensuring that the relevant policy changes are put in place to improve technical efficiency. Unfortunately, however, often donors (especially the World Bank) seem to be the ones driving the efficiency agenda more than the national governments. Notwithstanding, there is a case for improving the cost-effectiveness of donor assistance as well, especially in the social sectors (as we discuss below and again in Chapter 9). As in the preceding section, the education, water/sanitation, and health sectors (including reproductive health) are discussed in turn.

Education

In respect of technical efficiency, there are basically three ways of getting better outcomes from the same envelope of resources in primary education. Two are issues of balance: the balance between capital and recurrent expenditure, and the composition of recurrent expenditure, especially between labour and non-labour costs. The third one is to address inefficiencies that arise from policy failures independent of the allocation of financial resources. We turn to policies later in this section; first we address the balance issues.

There are some fifty-five developing countries where GERs at primary level are less than 100, or where the GER is above 100 for boys but not girls. These countries, we believe, will need additional *capital expenditures* for new buildings and facilities to universalize primary education (Delamonica et al., 2004). In primary education, capital or development expenditures have been historically insufficient in those countries with low enrolment. Nevertheless, high gross enrolment ratios (even higher than 100) can disguise the lack of primary education infrastructure in rural areas. Even in relatively resource-rich countries (e.g. South Africa), development expenditures often account for less than 5 per cent of all primary education expenditure.[16] Contractual obligations of paying salaries mean that this is a first call on any education budget, with capital expenditure being the first to be squeezed.

Several countries experience huge backlogs in building classrooms in line with the growth in the school population. Our estimates suggest that the bulk of extra investment effort needed to reach universal primary education (defined as a net enrolment rate of 100) will be in sub-Saharan Africa, as well as in pockets of South Asia (Delamonica et al., 2004). Countries will need to respond by keeping the unit cost of school construction low in order to meet the demand for school places. One way to do so is to use locally available rather than imported construction materials. In several of the selected countries, for example Cameroon and Niger, the utilization of local construction materials has been encouraged to optimize efficiency (Mehrotra, 1998). Similarly, the use in India of not only local materials but also local construction techniques and local contractors has kept costs down in the expansion under the District Primary Education Programme since 1994. Earlier the use of state construction or large private contractors had tended to inflate costs (World Bank, 1996a). The use of local materials not only reduces cost; it allows local authorities and communities to construct schools, rather than the central government. However, in order to prevent an unhealthy nexus developing between local contractors and local bureaucrats, mechanisms need to be in place to ensure greater local accountability as well (an issue we discuss in the next chapter).

At the primary level the other big issue is that of *balance between salary and non-salary* inputs in recurrent expenditure. This is by far the most daunting challenge in most countries with low NERs and high drop-outs. By and large, the wage bills of teaching and administrative staff often account for 90 per cent or more of recurrent expenditure at the primary level, squeezing out non-salary expenditure.[17] This imbalance gets exaggerated in some developing countries where total allocations for primary education are particularly low. Our evidence is, for example, that emoluments represented 95 per cent of primary recurrent expenditure in Côte d'Ivoire (1994), 97 per cent in Morocco (1991), and 98 per cent in Honduras and Nicaragua (1994 and 1992 respectively) (Gbayoro et al., 1997; Akesbi et al., 1998; Buvinich and Reyes, 1992; Arana et al., 1998). In Indian states, on average, wages and salaries account for 97 per cent of total elementary (grades 1–8) education expenditure (World Bank, 1996a).

The management of the wage bill is of particular importance in sub-Saharan Africa and South Asia, where the need for additional teachers is substantial, if the objective of universal primary education is to be achieved. Additional resources will be required to hire extra teachers. With 26 million primary school teachers in developing countries in 2000, the estimated number of additional teachers required by 2015 ranges between 15 and 35 million – including more than 3 million in sub-Saharan Africa, with more than 1 million in Nigeria alone (UNESCO, 2003). At the same time, in many countries in sub-Saharan Africa and Latin America, teachers' real wages declined over the 1980s and early 1990s (Mehrotra and Buckland, 1998; ILO, 1991). In fact, in many low-income countries teacher salaries declined in the rest of the 1990s as well – Cambodia, the Central African Republic, Kyrgyzstan, Madagasar, Myanmar, Sierra Leone and Zambia (UNDP HDR, 2003). Where teacher salaries decline, teachers habitually take up second jobs in an attempt to maintain their standard of living – with inevitable consequences for teaching time. If teacher morale is not to decline any further, salary increases in those countries where declines have occurred will need to take place if enrolments are to increase, and quality is to be improved.

The combined effect on the total salary bill of the need for increasing the number of teachers while at the same time increasing average teacher salaries can be explosive. This has been an issue particularly in francophone African countries. The average teacher salary as a multiple of per capita income was among the highest in West and Central Africa, at 7.28 (Carnoy and Welmond, 1996). However, simple comparisons of the relationship between average salary and per capita GNP can be misleading. Teachers' salaries relative to GNP per capita tend to fall as per capita income rises, primarily because the education of an average income earner rises relative to teachers' education, as countries become wealthier.[18]

Since this ratio (teachers' salaries relative to income per capita) is misleading, we estimated the deviations of the ratio between the average teachers' salaries and per capita income from a trend line for literacy, on the assumption that where literacy rates rise, the scarcity value of teachers should decline. The countries are presented in Table 6.2 sorted by residual: this residual is the difference between the expected ratio (teacher salary to GDP per capita when adjusted for literacy rates) and the actual ratio. If the residuals are positive it means that the average teacher salary is higher than the literacy trend would predict. Conversely if the residual is negative then the actual salary is lower than expected. Only in sub-Saharan Africa is the ratio strongly positive in many countries (using data for the 1990s). Many francophone countries in Africa belong to the category of those deviating substantially from the trend line (Mali, Burkina Faso, Central African Republic, Rwanda, Mauritania, Burundi), but also Zimbabwe (Mehrotra and Buckland, 1998).

Several strategies (e.g. changing the salary structure and improving teacher utilization) could be adopted for managing teacher costs. Without changing salary levels, a number of instruments can be used to change the salary structure, some of which may reduce cost. One instrument is examining the gap between the minimum and maximum of the scale for teachers, and the other is time taken to fill that gap. In OECD countries, on average, the maximum salary is 1.6 times the minimum on the scale; in developing countries the range is 1.1 to 3.8 (ILO, 1991). As regards the time taken to reach the maximum of the scale, the UNESCO/ILO Committee recommends between ten and fifteen years. Governments need to examine the suitability of the ratio and the time gap that would best suit their fiscal capabilities at a given point of time.

Another instrument is delinking teacher salaries from advanced qualifications. In Togo, for instance, new teachers holding the highest certificate earn 2.78 times more than new teachers in the lowest unqualified entry category (Zymelman and DeStefano, 1993). In twenty of twenty-five countries in sub-Saharan Africa, individuals must teach for fifteen years or more to earn the maximum salary; they need far fewer years of advanced schooling to

Table 6.2 Who may be spending too much on teachers' salaries?

Country	Salary/GDP per capita adjusted for literacy levels
Ethiopia	8.29
Central African Republic	5.97
Mali	5.22
Zimbabwe	5.14
Rwanda	4.97
Burkina Faso	1.78
Mauritania	1.38
Burundi	1.10
Lesotho	0.82
Tanzania	0.63
Madagascar	0.57
Niger	0.50
Kenya	0.30
Togo	0.21
Chad	−0.17
Botswana	−0.88
Côte d'Ivoire	−0.98
Mauritius	−1.22
Benin	−1.25
Malawi	−1.93
Ghana	−3.56
Guinea	−4.51

Source: Mehrotra and Buckland, 1999.

attain that same salary. While few systems would advocate a structure that completely delinks the salary level paid from the qualification level of teachers, governments could contain teacher costs for those teachers with more than the minimum qualifications.

Community-provided housing for teachers in rural areas can help to reduce costs for the state while at the same time bringing the teacher and the rural community together in a sense of partnership. It can also help in reducing teacher absenteeism, while minimizing the time taken by the teacher in transportation to and from school. Where such measures do not resolve the problem of teacher absenteeism, the 'voice' of parents, expressed collectively, can count for a lot. For example, in many countries in sub-Saharan Africa, parent–teacher associations (PTAs) are effective mechanisms for resolving many issues. In India, a constitutional amendment has created the possibility for village elected bodies to constitute Village Education Committees, consisting partly of women and low-caste villagers, to monitor the activities of the school (PROBE, 1999; Mehrotra et al., 2005; Mehrotra, 2006). We discuss improved governance and accountability mechanisms thus created in the following chapter.

To improve teacher performance many countries have adopted merit pay systems. Most of these schemes failed because they 'rewarded individual performance in an organization in which outcomes depended on team or organizational performance' (Kelley, 1997). Where individual merit pay schemes were introduced in Africa they had a negligible impact on teacher effectiveness while adding significantly to teacher costs. Some evidence is now emerging in the USA that rewarding team or institutional performance in the school works.

Improving teacher utilization and effectiveness can also help in containing the cost of the total salary bill in primary education. Improving teacher deployment can help, especially when it redeploys teachers from overcrowded urban schools to rural schools with a small class size. Also, while systems normally have guidelines for workloads in terms of hours of work and sometimes in terms of teacher–pupil ratios, poor teacher deployment often results in utilization well below these levels. Botswana has reported experiments with paying incentives to teachers to teach double sessions, which resulted in doubling of pupils taught with a relatively small increase in salary cost.

Many countries have introduced measures to improve the information management that enables the detection and elimination of 'ghost' teachers and incorrect or double salary payments. While there are initial costs in introducing such management information systems, they can usually be justified in terms of the efficiency gains from better information. The experience of the National Education Statistical Information Systems programme in several sub-Saharan African countries demonstrates both the effectiveness of such programmes, and the time and capacity building required for effective utilization.

A serious problem facing most governments on the question of teacher costs is how to effect dialogue with the teachers' unions. The experience of South Africa is of interest. In 1991/2 teacher salaries constituted 75 per cent of recurrent expenditures, but rose to 83 per cent in 1995/6. This was largely due to the removal of discriminatory practices on grounds of race and gender and then higher-than-inflation salary increases for some classes of educators. Noting that teacher salaries were squeezing out all non-salary inputs, affecting quality, in 1998 the government engaged the unions in dialogue. The teachers' unions accepted the need to reduce the share of teacher salaries in total education expenditure (implying a 1 per cent real decrease in teacher salaries over the next five years). This was done during a medium-term expenditure framework discussion with the unions. The unions accepted, based on the information presented to them on several variables; these included the ratio of teacher salaries to average income in the country, and a comparison of teacher salaries with those of people with the same qualifications in the private sector and other countries. What finally convinced the unions was that any savings made in the reduction of teacher salaries will be channelled back into education for non-personnel expenditure, and that overall education expenditure would not be cut – a critical element in the unions' view.[19]

Apart from reducing the inefficiencies in the pattern of spending, there are also issues of improving the internal efficiency of the primary education system – by addressing *policy failures*. One of the major problems reported in all the countries is repetition. It affects, for instance, 15 per cent of schoolchildren in Peru, 18 per cent in Brazil, 25 per cent in Benin, and 27 per cent in Côte d'Ivoire and Nepal. Repetition is also one of the main determinants of dropping out. In Benin, Nepal and Peru only roughly half of the children who enter primary education complete four years of schooling. In low-income countries, students generally take four additional years to complete the primary cycle, compared with an additional 1.8 years in lower middle-income countries and 1.2 years in upper middle-income ones (Lockheed and Verspoor, 1991). It is paradoxical that countries where the waste of resources is highest are those that can least afford it.

Repetition and drop-out represent important wastage. Even where the cost per pupil is low, the cost per graduate can still be high because of high repetition and drop-out. When a student requires twice the prescribed number of years to finish primary schooling, the cost per graduate is doubled. Lockheed and Verspoor (1991) reported that repeaters occupied more than a quarter of the available school places in seventeen sub-Saharan African countries – an inefficient way of allocating scarce resources.

There are at least three policies that can improve internal efficiency caused by repetition and drop-out. The first is to review the promotion policy. Repetition is usually based on arguments that it helps teachers maintain discipline or helps maintain educational standards. Some of these arguments are unhelpful for achieving universal primary education. In Costa Rica, for instance, repetition was halved by the introduction of automatic promotion in the 1960s. In El Salvador there have been positive experiences with 'guided' promotion. Malaysia and Zimbabwe also adopted automatic promotion (Heng and Hoey, 1997; Loewenson and Chisvo, 1997). Automatic promotion should not be seen as undermining the standard of performance, but as recognition that not all children learn at the same speed so that the education system must be flexible to accommodate different learning needs. A case must be made that automatic promotion should be accompanied by a minimum package of inputs, especially materials and teacher training. Thus, where automatic promotion exists at the primary level (as in many states of India) without adequate instructional time or instructional material, the levels of learning are extremely low (Mehrotra et al., 2005).

The second policy is to ensure the adequate and timely provision of pedagogical materials. One constant element is that teacher and administrative emoluments absorb almost the totality of the financial resources directed towards primary education. This is the case even in countries where teachers' real wages have declined below the minimum living wage. The experience of the high-achieving countries (see Chapter 4 for list of countries) shows that they have managed to contain costs, especially teacher costs, while at the same time maintaining a reasonable allocation for non-salary inputs. Teaching materials accounted for 2.5 per cent of primary recurrent expenditure in Botswana in 1991, 2.5 per cent in Cuba in 1990, and 5.3 per cent in Sri Lanka. The allocations were much lower in other developing countries; for instance, in Honduras in 1994 they barely reached 0.5 per cent of recurrent primary expenditure, and in Nicaragua in 1992 less than 0.3 per cent (Mehrotra, 1998b).

In low-income countries where governments are unlikely to be able to increase resources for paying teachers a living wage, increase teacher numbers, and *at the same time* increase resources for the provision of textbooks and teaching materials and regular in-service training, donor assistance will be of considerable importance. The relative neglect of primary education in the allocation of ODA resources has been explained by 'their preference for supporting investment projects that are capital and foreign exchange intensive, limited in scope and geographical dispersion so as to facilitate supervision, and fairly dependent on donors' expertise in terms of technical assistance and training'. A shift is required away from the earlier emphasis on equipment and other hardware, overseas training, and technical assistance (Bennel and Furlong, 1997; UNDP HDR, 2003).

Donor assistance to primary education could help to develop national capacity for developing education materials. Small countries seldom have the expertise required to write good textbooks, hence the need to contract international experts or import foreign textbooks rather than strengthening national or sub-regional institutions to develop and produce quality textbooks. Donors need to guard against this tendency. In Burkina Faso the local production of schoolbooks since 1987 made it possible to target the course content to the specific needs of the country and to reduce costs, causing prices to drop to a third of their original price.

The third policy is the expansion of early childhood development and pre-primary schooling. Recent scientific findings have confirmed the crucial importance of early childhood development to individuals and societies alike, and are leading to new and innovative approaches to infant and child care (Engle, 1999; UNICEF, 2001). The likelihood of repetition and drop-out is substantially decreased when children attend pre-primary education. Moreover, per pupil costs in early childhood programmes can be kept low because of the many opportunities for mothers and the community to participate in early childhood. In spite of the scientific findings and the low cost of pre-school programmes, the evidence from our country studies shows that coverage remains low. Those countries that have pre-school programmes, such as Brazil, Uruguay and Venezuela, often find that they mostly enrol children of the better-off families.

Another cause of dropping out is the high out-of-pocket costs of schooling (an issue discussed above under allocative inefficiency). Apart from private cost, another family-related factor that should be taken into account is the language of instruction. Where parents are illiterate (and rates of adult illiteracy in both South Asia and sub-Saharan Africa are high), if the medium of instruction is other than the mother tongue, the problems of learning in an environment characterized by poverty are compounded. The chances of drop-out increase correspondingly.

In this context, the experience of the high-achieving countries mentioned earlier has been unequivocal: the mother tongue was used as the medium of instruction at the primary level in all cases. Since multilinguism abounds in developing countries, and is more the norm than the exception, this is a critical issue. There is much research to show that students learn to read more quickly when taught in their mother tongue. Second, students who have learned to read in their mother tongue learn to read in a second language more quickly than do those who are first taught to read in the second language. Third, in terms of academic learning skills as well, students taught to read in their mother tongue acquire such skills more quickly (Mcginn and Borden, 1994).

While multilinguism abounds in most countries, the problem is not beyond resolution. This is because many of these languages are actually quite similar in character, and because these different languages often do not have an independent script of their own, but can be, and are, written in the Latin script. This is precisely the way in which the linguistic problem was resolved in one of the high-achieving countries of the 1980s – Zimbabwe. Even though this country has two dominant indigenous languages, it is divided up into six linguistic regions corresponding to six local languages, and primary-school children start with one of these languages, which is the dominant language of that region, with English introduced simultaneously in the earliest grades. English becomes the language of instruction after grade 3.

In two regions, South Asia and sub-Saharan Africa, gender differentials in enrolment and drop-out are a serious problem. In fact, unless the problem of girls' education is solved, there is little likelihood of primary education being universalized; similarly, as we discussed in Chapter 3, there is little likelihood of a health transition occurring soon or the demographic transition being hastened. The lessons for policy from countries that have eliminated gender differentials in schooling are as follows (Mehrotra, 1998b). First, bringing girls to school and keeping them there requires physical proximity of the school to the home – school mapping to identify least served locations and multi-grade schools in remote areas. Second, low out-of-pocket costs are required, to prevent parents from discriminating between boys and girls when making a decision to send the child, or in times of falls in household income, to keep a child from dropping out. Third, scheduling lessons flexibly helps girls, enabling them to share in household chores and sibling care without forcing them out of school (UNICEF, 1999). Finally, female teachers provide a role model to girls, and also give parents a sense of security about their girl children.[20] Figure 6.5 shows that in the high-achieving countries, all of which eliminated gender differentials in schooling, the proportion of female teachers in all teachers was much higher than the regional average.

However, hiring female teachers assumes that the state has the resources for additional teachers – the very question with which we began this discussion. Unless low-achieving countries are willing to allocate an adequate share of the budget to education, and distribute that equitably to the primary level, there is little likelihood that many of the desirable policies can be put in place.

The responsibility for the provision of basic education rests with the government, but, given the fiscal constraints in the short run, *the role of foreign assistance* can be considerable. Since donors are normally loath to meet recurrent costs of salaries, their contribution can be largely in the area of meeting capital cost requirements, and non-salary inputs on the recurrent side. However, aid to education has not increased significantly in the 1990s. For most donors basic education remains a very small share of declining total ODA (see Chapter 10). The overwhelming conclusion of those writing about ODA to education, since the Jomtien commitments on education for

Figure 6.5 Female teachers as a percentage of all teachers

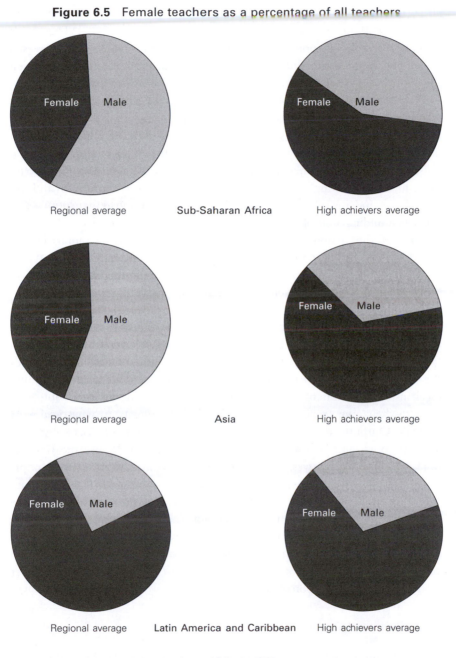

Regional average Sub-Saharan Africa High achievers average

Regional average Asia High achievers average

Regional average Latin America and Caribbean High achievers average

Source: Mehrotra, 2000.

all by the year 2000, is that there is a huge gap between rhetoric and reality (Colclough, 1993; Bennell and Furlong, 1997; UNESCO, 2003). The major exception to this phenomenon was the World Bank, which had increased its lending to education and to basic education in particular. However, even the World Bank's lending to the sector has declined in recent years.

However, it is not the size of aid to education alone that matters; the effectiveness and efficiency of aid to education are as much an issue as the effectiveness of public spending. The effectiveness of education aid is determined by what it is used for. Some 60–80 per cent of all education assistance is spent in recipient countries; the rest is spent in donor countries on education/training courses for developing country nationals and on consultants and instructors from developed countries (Watkins, 2000). The capacity-building role of the latter kind of assistance is unclear.

One of the defining characteristics of the new sectoral approach (in education and health, *inter alia*), being supported by bilaterals and the World Bank, is the minimizing of long-term foreign technical assistance (TA). However, in reality the problems with technical assistance persist. For instance, TA is pursued with little regard to whether the process is strengthening or weakening government capacity and ownership. Authorities are overwhelmed by an influx of technical advisers trying to establish overelaborate systems. It is too often driven by external knowledge, rather than knowledge of the country's circumstances. Parallel systems have been set up, undermining local institutions. Often TA is fragmented, with each donor supplying missions to their own terms of reference, adding complexity to what is already difficult. Outputs are inappropriate, with large amounts of documentation, unread reports and lack of clarity about who will actually use the findings (Development Alternatives, 1998). Of 66 studies on education in Ethiopia documented between 1994 and 1997, half were sponsored by bilateral aid agencies; 17 were sponsored by the government, with a further 9 by the World Bank in combination with the government; 3 were sponsored by multilateral agencies and 4 by NGOs (Watkins, 2000). There is a need for donors involved in sectoral approaches to exercise restraint both in the volume and in the scope of technical assistance (see Chapter 10 for further discussion of sectoral approaches).

Water and sanitation

In water and sanitation, getting improved output/services from the same resources is critically dependent on the use of appropriate technology. For at least two decades now the technology and know-how have been available to expand services of water and sanitation at low cost to rural areas. UNICEF has long promoted the use of these low-cost technologies throughout the developing world – the use of hand-pumps, protected springs and wells, gravity-fed systems, the collection of rainwater, and upgrading of traditional water sources in rural areas. Compared to even mini-piped water systems for rural areas, the costs per capita of these technologies are much lower. These low-cost technologies are the essence of technical efficiency in the water and sanitation sector.

In this sector improved technical efficiency also involves the maintenance of the infrastructure that has been created. Ensuring that wells have been dug and hand-pumps installed – as happened on a massive scale in India through the 1970s and 1980s – is only half the story. A 1994 government of India survey found major problems with the status of hand-pumps: 33 per cent required repair, another 22 per cent needed rehabilitation, and another 12 per cent were completely defunct.[21] Without the participation of users in maintenance, there is little likelihood of this situation being remedied. At least in some countries this is beginning to happen. Thus in India, the Constitution Act (73rd Amendment) gave responsibility in 1993 for drinking water and sanitation (and basic education) to local councils in the villages. The reason is that the public works departments of governments and water boards are centralized monopolies with only a modicum of accountability to users. The local councils (*gram panchayat*) will be responsible for choice of technology, recovering costs and operations, maintenance of rural water supply and sanitation. The community will own the assets. If decentralization takes this form there is a prospect for regular maintenance of installed water-pumps and wells; in fact, this would be the way forward for the expression of 'voice' in this sector.[22]

Involving women helps in the maintenance of these water assets. Women face more problems of workload, privacy, safety and hygiene than boys and men, and hence are interested in sanitation improvements. It is thus often important to convince men that sanitation improvements are worth their inputs. Also women often prove more reliable in maintaining the equipment, such as hand-pumps, in part because they are commonly the ones (with their daughters) who are responsible for fetching water for the family. They should be encouraged to train and get jobs as masons and plumbers. Also, when trained in maintenance they are less likely to move from the community in search of a job elsewhere.

In urban areas, there has been a considerable increase in large-scale private provision of water and sanitation services in developing countries since the early 1990s. The World Bank (2000a) claims that the water supply system in

Côte d'Ivoire, which introduced the first private concession in sub-Saharan Africa, performs better than other urban water systems in West Africa. However, it also states that large-scale private participation may preclude the extension of services to low-income areas and create local monopolies. We agree that water and sanitation utilities – both public and private – would be able to expand access if they covered their operating costs. What needs to end is general government subsidies where operating costs are not covered from the neighbourhoods of the non-poor. Governments can ensure greater access to poor people by subsidizing connections (rather than consumption). There is increasing evidence (from urban water/sanitation projects in thirty-five towns in the Philippines, from Brazil's Watsan Programme for low-income urban populations) of involvement of users in local government decision-making and transparency in service charges to cover operation and maintenance (World Bank, 2000a).

As with water supply, so with sanitation: low-cost technologies are cost-effective, and need to become widespread. Households do not need convincing about the merits of a well or a public standpipe. But they may need to be sold on the merits of on-site sanitation. Hence one requirement is that hygiene education by government and NGOs becomes part of the effort to expand the installation of water and sanitation hardware. Further, the spread of safe sanitation hardware at household and neighbourhood levels requires that products match consumer demand, both in price and in quality. Appropriate technologies include: pour-flush latrine, simple pit latrine, ventilated pit latrine and connections to a septic tank or covered public sewer. Similarly, narrow pipes laid just under the surface cost a fraction of large-width pipes installed deep into the ground (UNICEF, 1995a). In rural areas, waste disposal through composting is sometimes appropriate.

Cost is absolutely central to whether or not a sanitation technology will be adopted in a low-income country. While India has made great progress in the provision of safe drinking water to nearly 85 per cent of its population, in sanitation the situation is very different. Some 800 million people (i.e. 80 per cent of the population), or roughly three times the entire population of the USA – still either defecate in the open or use unsanitary bucket latrines. Even in urban areas, only 20 per cent of the population have access to a water-flush toilet connected to a sewerage system and 14 per cent enjoy water-borne toilets connected to septic tanks or leach pits. Apart from the health consequences of such a system, the social consequences are appalling. The removal of 'night soil' (as human waste is called) led over the centuries to the profession of 'scavenging': men/women from the lowest castes, stigmatized and scorned as 'untouchables', would collect human waste from bucket latrines and the streets. The Indian Constitution bans their segregation, but the scavengers normally live apart from the rest of society, lacking human dignity and human rights.

Two common sanitation technologies known to be ideal for human waste disposal have proved too expensive for widespread installation and maintenance in India, and other developing countries: septic tanks and sewerage. Septic tanks were introduced in India 150 years ago but today less than 20 per cent of houses are equipped with latrines connected to them. In addition to their cost, one disadvantage is that they require a large volume of water for flushing. Another is that they have to be cleaned periodically and sludge disposed of so that it does not cause health hazards or serve as a breeding ground for mosquitoes (and thus the spread of malaria). Similarly, piped sewerage was first tried in India in the late nineteenth century, yet only about 235 of the country's 44,689 towns and cities have been hooked up to the system. Even in these towns, the entire municipal area is not covered, let alone the adjoining suburbs, and not all houses have connections.

However, the pioneering work of an NGO – Sulabh International – has demonstrated an affordable and socially acceptable method of human waste disposal, which is already improving the lives of over 10 million people. It is based on local government–NGO partnership, backed by community participation, and has improved environmental quality in rural and urban slums. Sulabh's solution is a low-cost, pour-flush water-seal toilet with leach pits for on-site disposal of human waste. The technology is affordable by the poor, as there are designs to suit different levels of income. Flushing requires only 2 litres of water, instead of the ten litres needed in other toilets. It is never out of commission, since with two pits, one can always be used while the other one is being cleaned. The latrine can be built with locally available materials and is easy to maintain. Public toilets of this kind have grown; the challenge is now to extend them to households.

The advantages of these technologies is that they are affordable for poor communities, and they can also be easily maintained within communities, thereby generating productive employment. One of the lessons of the past is the inefficiency of the top-down approach: governments moved in to install hand-pumps, tube wells and even ventilated pit latrines, regardless of whether there was a demand for such goods or not.

There are other ways to improve efficiency of resource use. Traditional construction methods – usually encouraged by bidding practices enabling corruption – are the rule in most developing country contexts. There are pecuniary incentives – both legal and illegal – for engineers in the public works departments and private contractors to use large-width piping and installing deep in the ground. These are more expensive than narrow pipes laid just under the surface. The former are appropriate for well-developed areas and those with heavy vehicular traffic, but where traffic is mostly light or on foot and buildings are small (as in slum areas), the latter technology is more suitable.

However, 'voice' again goes to the heart of the matter of fixing public policy and improving effectiveness and efficiency. The poor are invisible to bureaucrats and politicians, and for the latter become useful only for vote gathering at election time. The evidence is that where unrepresented communities act collectively in the form of community-based organizations – and, where necessary, accept the help of NGOs – to demand attention, local governments tend to respond. For example, in the Dharavi slum of Mumbai, pavement dwellers had no alternative but to use the limited public toilets, each of which served 800 people (the alternative was to use the pavements as open toilets). Assisted by local and international NGOs, female construction workers living in the slum were taught how to build latrines. They learned skills that more than doubled their income, and they got modern latrines. The pavement dwellers each get paid 2 to 5 rupees per month for cleaning and maintaining the facilities. The Mumbai Municipal Corporation then promised to assist construction of 2,000 latrine blocks, each with five latrines. Similarly, in Karachi, after years of being ignored by the municipal authorities, slum residents in Orangi organized themselves, with the help of an NGO, and have provided themselves adequate sanitation: each home has a pour-flush toilet connected to an underground sewerage line, all paid for by residents. The NGO provided technical advice and plans for a simplified design, which re-duced the cost by a factor of ten. The NGO did not contribute any funds for construction. Each family invested about a month's income to buy materials and hire labour. Government contractors were avoided, as they inflate costs to include bribes for officials (Khan, 1997).

In the sanitation sector, the biggest unresolved problem is how to improve access to basic sanitation, defined as facilities to address sewerage and sullage disposal at household and neighbourhood levels. But from the perspective of municipal governments, the greater challenge is how to address the drainage and solid waste disposal problems they face. There is a reluctance to invest in basic sanitation alone without attention to the broader issue of disposal. A small fraction of wastewater in cities in developing countries is treated before being returned to the environment. Wastewater treatment is much more expensive than simple access to safe water and household sanitation. There is, hence, a need for research into feasible approaches to the broader range of sanitation services in response.

It may be necessary to accept some increase in environmental pollution external to communities as a first step in improving the sanitation situation. This may reflect the now successful path followed by European and North American countries, which improved household sanitation at the expense of extreme pollution of rivers and waterways.

To summarize, there are a number of policy priorities to ensure technical efficiency in the water and sanitation sector. First, sanitation coverage is much lower than safe water coverage in most developing regions. Hence, policy should focus on sanitation at least as much as safe water. Urban and peri-urban (slum) areas need special emphasis. Second, the problem in the past was lack of integrated approach to safe water, safe sanitation and hygiene within one area. Policy interventions must not ignore any of the three components – safe water, safe sanitation and hygienic practices at household/community level – for desired health effects. Third, the problem is that water systems in rural and peri-urban areas are usually poorly maintained if left to government departments. Hence, local users should be trained in maintenance, reducing reliance on government. Fourth, the problem is that decision-making in the sector has excluded women. What is required is an engendered approach to watsan services, since women are affected most by inappropriate decisions. Fifth, the problem in the past was that many projects in both water and sanitation have adopted a supply-driven, top-down approach. A successful approach should be premised on the idea that once donors/central governments officials leave, the local administrative system can manage on its own. Hence, local capacity building is essential. Also, there is a need to involve the community in decision-making; hence a decentralized approach.

Health

The challenge of improving technical efficiency in the health sector is not insuperable. In the context of limited resources, especially characteristic of all low-income countries, the usual approach to rationing health-care services has been to have strict expenditure controls that do not direct resources to any specific group of diseases but just limit allocations to affordable levels. The result is well known. It usually leads to a decline of overall standards and quality of delivery. The politically strongest providers (e.g. specialists and hospitals) then capture the limited budget, while the needs of the population get bypassed. Health-sector bureaucracies, which were created in the image of the British National Health Service, were useful in expanding services in the first decades after their creation at independence from colonial rule

Table 6.3   Interventions with a large potential impact on health outcomes

	Examples of interventions	Main contents of interventions
1	Maternal health and safe motherhood interventions	Family planning, prenatal and delivery care, clean and safe delivery by trained birth attendant, postpartum care, and essential obstetric care for high-risk pregnancies and complications.
2	Immunization (EPI Plus)	BCG at birth; OPV at birth, 6,10,14 weeks; DPT at 6, 10, 14 weeks; Hep. B at birth, 6 and 9 months (optional); measles at 9 months; TT for women of child-bearing age.
3	Integrated management of childhood illness	Case management of acute respiratory infections, diarrhoea, malaria, measles and malnutrition; immunization, feeding/breastfeeding counselling, micronutrient and iron supplementation, anti-helminthic treatment.
4	School health interventions	Health education and nutrition interventions, including anti-helminthic treatment, micronutrient supplementation and school meals.
5	Family planning	Information and education; availability and correct use of contraceptives.
6	HIV/AIDS prevention	Targeted information for sex workers, mass education awareness, counselling, screening, mass treatment for sexually transmitted diseases, safe blood supply.
7	Treatment of sexually transmitted diseases	Case management using syndrome diagnosis and standard treatment algorithm.
8	Treatment of tuberculosis	Directly observed treatment schedule (DOTS); administration of standardized short-course chemotherapy to all confirmed sputum smear positive cases of TB under supervision in the initial (2–3 months) phase.
9	Malaria	Case management (early assessment and prompt treatment) and selected preventive measures (e.g. impregnated bed nets).
10	Tobacco control	Tobacco tax, information, nicotine replacement, legal action.
11	Non-communicable diseases and injuries	Selected early screening and secondary prevention.

Source: WHO, 2000.

Table 6.4   Access to drinking water and sanitation by rural/urban population and public expenditure on basic water and sanitation as % of total public expenditure, 1995–97

Country	% of population with access to safe water 1990–97			% of population with access to adequate sanitation			basic w&s as % of total exp.
	total	urban	rural	total	urban	rural	
Asia							
1 Bangladesh	95	99	95	43	83	38	
2 Nepal	71	93	68	16	28	14	2.3
3 Philippines	84	93	80	75	89	63	0.3[a]
4 Sri Lanka	57	88	52	63	68	62	1.0
5 Thailand	81	88	73	96	97	94	
6 Malaysia	76	96	66	94	94	94	1.28[b]
7 Vietnam	43	47	42	21	43	15	0.5
Africa							
1 Benin	56	46	71	27	57	8	3.33[c]
2 Burkina Faso	42	66	37	37	41	33	0.62[d]
3 Cameroon	50	57	43	50	64	36	0.1
4 Côte d'Ivoire	42	56	32	39	71		0.6
5 Gabon	67	80	30		72		
6 Kenya	53	67	49	77	69	81	0.4
7 Malawi	47	95	40	3	18	1	1.1
8 Mali	66	87	55	6	12	3	0.3
9 Namibia	83	100	71	62	93	20	1.7
10 Niger	48	76	44	17	79	5	1.6
11 Nigeria	49	58	40	41	50	32	0.0
12 South Africa	87	99	70	87	92	80	0.5
13 Tanzania	66	92	58	86	98	83	0.2
14 Chad	24	48	17	21	73	7	
15 Uganda	46	77	41	57	75	55	
16 Zambia	38	84	10	71	94	57	0.2
17 Morocco	65	98	34	58	94	24	
Latin America & Caribbean							
1 Belize	83	100	69	57	23	87	0.7
2 Bolivia	63	86	32	58	74	37	2.3
3 Brazil	76	88	25	70	80	30	0.6
4 Chile	91	99	41		90		0.1
5 Colombia	85	97	56	85	97	56	1.1
6 Costa Rica	96	100	92	84	95	70	0.1
7 Dominican Republic	65	80		78	76	83	
8 El Salvador	66	84	40	90	98	80	
9 Guatemala	77	76	78	83	95	74	
10 Honduras	76		62	74		57	
11 Jamaica	86			89	100	80	1.4
12 Nicaragua	62	88	32	35	34	35	0.1
13 Peru	67	84	33	72	89	37	1.4

Notes: [a] figure for 1992.   [b] average of five-year plan.   [c] expenditure on W & S sector.   [d] as % of revenue.
Sources: Country studies; UNICEF, 1999.

(WHO, 2000). However, they are the captive of vested interests within them; what was once effective in expanding physical infrastructure and adding services has proved very dysfunctional when it comes to downsizing or shifting priorities.

A different approach would be to ration on the basis of interventions that are 'essential' – as defined in Table 6.4. Mexico has adopted such a package; Bangladesh, Colombia and Zambia have also begun implementation of one (WHO, 2000). Rationing resources – physical and human – according to such essential needs would tend to improve technical efficiency.

One of the main sources of technical inefficiency in the health sector (as we saw in the education sector) is the imbalance of resources between capital and recurrent expenditures. In industrialized countries capital expenditures (buildings and equipment) are usually not more than 5 per cent of total annual health-care expenditures, and are often lower than they were a couple of decades ago (due to cost control through reduced additions to capital). But in low-income countries investment levels tend to be much higher (e.g. 40–50 per cent in Burkina Faso, Cambodia, Kenya, Mali and Mozambique) (WHO, 2000). When such a large proportion of the budget is allocated to capital expenditures, with the rest naturally going to salaries, very little is left over for consumables (especially drugs). More importantly, very little is known about health investments in most low-income countries, including in the public sector.

In all cases, a balance has to be achieved between capital and recurrent expenditures. There are no guidelines or formulas that can apply to every country. Nevertheless, the country studies show several interesting findings. First, the widespread imbalance between rural and urban infrastructure is often compounded by lack of operations budget and qualified staff in rural health centres, while urban health centres are often overstaffed. In the Dominican Republic, for example, it was found that overstaffing in health centres implied that doctors were required to work only three of their regular six hours a day for lack of facilities. Moreover, while up to 40 per cent of rural health centres were estimated to be performing administrative duties, many lacked a doctor (Escuder et al., 1998). Under these circumstances, additional public expenditure on health to maintain the purchasing power of the wages of health staff will not lead to better access to health services. In this case, there is excessive recurrent spending. In other cases, there has been too much capital expenditure. Thus, in Mexico, with too many hospital beds, occupancy rates at Ministry of Health hospitals have been 50 per cent on average, because of inadequate staffing and maintenance, with resulting inefficient use of existing resources (WHO, 2000). Without an appropriate allocation between current and investment spending, an efficient utilization of existing human and physical resources is impossible.

Second, low-income countries, where the incidence of easily preventable diseases is relatively high, tend to depend on donor assistance for investments in health infrastructure. Since donor support seldom covers recurrent expenditure, the national budget has to provide for the staff and materials. Without adequate planning in advance, they are often not budgeted and the new health infrastructure remains idle. Also, the donors' investments often are irregular and not properly incorporated in the countries' regional development plans (Gilson and Mills, 1995).

Third, it seems that countries where the expansion of basic health infrastructure is more pressing, at least judged from their high U5MR levels, capital expenditure tends to be the lowest. For instance, in Nepal and Côte d'Ivoire the share of capital expenditure within basic health spending fluctuates around 5 per cent (Institute for Sustainable Development, 1998; Gbayoro et al., 1997). In contrast, in Sri Lanka, where a health and demographic transition took place many years ago, capital expenditures represented 20 per cent of basic health expenditure (Rannan-Eliya et al., 1998).

Not only is there an imbalance between capital and recurrent expenditure, there is often also a lack of balance within the recurrent budget between wage and non-wage spending. In many countries wages and salaries account for two-thirds or more of the total recurrent budget. Budgetary provisions for medicines, materials, transportation and maintenance are often inadequate. The studies found that the share of non-wage recurrent expenditure has been contracting, leading to shortages of essential drugs and materials. Lack of essential drugs and materials render the health service inoperative, severely affecting efficiency as fixed costs fail to be distributed among large numbers of users.

The contrast between high- and low-achievers is interesting as it shows the need to probe beyond aggregate expenditure data analysis. In Sri Lanka, medicines and supplies represent around a third of recurrent expenditure on the basic health sector, although this figure was higher ten years ago (Rannan-Eliya et al., 1998). The government procures generic drugs, which results in substantial savings. In spite of some evidence that leakages exist, it is widely accepted that health centres are well provided. Nepal, on the other hand, suffers from under-supplied health centres because of a small budget for basic health and a smaller proportion of the funds available to buy medicines and materials (Institute for Sustainable Development, 1998).

The situation is more critical in countries where the allocation to basic health is so small that little is left after paying wages. In an attempt to reverse this situation, Benin, Côte d'Ivoire and Niger have introduced a generic drugs policy that has led to important improvements in the delivery of medicines (Tabélé-Omichessan et al., 1998; Gbayoro, 1997; Chafani et al., 1997). In Niger the cost of generic drugs is a quarter of that of brand names. In Côte d'Ivoire the expansion of the utilization of generic drugs grew out of the recognition that the private sector was unable to supply the population at affordable prices. In Benin, the introduction of the list of generic drugs was accompanied by other policy innovations, such as the integration of the vaccination programme into the primary health-care services. This has led to the inclusion of Benin in the initiative to achieve vaccine independence, which has resulted in substantial increases in immunization coverage from 25 per cent in 1987 to 81 per cent in 1996. Drug lists have been carefully reviewed in Niger and South Africa, where up to 2,000 generic drugs were listed, compared with only 260 in the WHO recommended list. Also, a procurement and distribution system has been developed which does guarantee delivery to every health post.[23]

In countries with high levels of human development (as measured by the Human Development Index, HDI), almost the entire population has access to essential drugs. But contrasts are also striking: within the medium HDI category, in China 80–94 per cent of the population have access, while in India 0–49 per cent do. Most countries with low HDI have low access (defined by the WHO as 50–79 per cent of the population), with Nigeria having very low access (less than 50 per cent).[24]

Within the wage category, care should be given to the internal structure of expenditure. The appropriate ratio of doctors and nurses needs to be based on the specific strategy applied. The experience of the high-achieving countries indicates that many of the outreach and preventive activities are not required to be carried out by physicians.[25] Thus, technical or operational efficiency can be improved by a higher reliance on nurses and other medical staff for specific tasks. The contrast among countries is illuminating: in countries where life expectancy is high, or that managed to raise it quickly, the nurse-per-doctor ratio is considerably higher than in the other countries. That is the case in Zimbabwe (9.5 nurses per doctor in 1990), Thailand (4 in 1990) and Sri Lanka (3.2 in 1996), in contrast to India (1.5 in the late 1980s), Bangladesh (1 in 1990) and Peru (less than 1 in the mid-1990s).[26] In fact, as Table 6.5 shows, countries with relatively low U5MR have a much higher number of nurses per 100,000 persons than doctors; the converse is almost always true with countries with high U5MR.

The World Bank recommended a package of health services for developing countries, including public health and minimum essential clinical

Table 6.5   High achievers versus low achievers: doctors and nurses per 100,000 persons

Countries	High achievers		Low achievers	
	Doctors	Nurses	Doctors	Nurses
Sub-Saharan Africa				
Mauritius	85	241		
Zimbabwe	14	164		
South Asia & Pacific				
Bhutan			20	6
Pakistan			52	32
Sri Lanka	23	112		
Thailand	24	99		
East Asia & Pacific				
Indonesia	12	67		
Rep. of Korea	127	232		
Malaysia	43	160		
Latin America & Caribbean				
Barbados	113	323		
Bolivia			51	25
Brazil			134	41
Colombia			105	49
Costa Rica	126	95		
Cuba	518	752		
Dominican Republic			77	20
Ecuador			111	34
El Salvador			91	38
Haiti			16	13
Honduras			22	17
Nicaragua			82	56
Venezuela			194	77

Source: UNDP, *Human Development Report*, various years.

interventions, which require about 0.1 physician per 1,000 population and between two and four graduate nurses per physician (World Bank, 1993a). But in 1990 the ratio of nurses to physicians was well under 2:1 in India, Latin America and the Middle Eastern crescent. In fact, changing this investment pattern is difficult because of lobby groups (WHO, 2000). The main investment emphasis in the health system over past decades has been on hospitals and specialist care. The emphasis on specialist care required investments in medical schools to staff hospitals. Changes in medical school admissions, geographic distribution of hospitals, financing of private care, and so on, prompt interest groups to complain and resist.[27]

The numerical imbalance is compounded by distribution imbalances in spatial terms. It is almost universally a fact that providers tend to concentrate in urban areas. In Cambodia, 85 per cent of the population live in rural areas, but only 13 per cent of the government health staff are located there. In Nepal, only 20 per cent of rural physician posts are filled, compared to 96 per cent in urban areas. In Angola, 65 per cent live in rural areas, but 85 per cent of health professionals work in urban areas (WHO, 2000).

To correct this situation, service contracts that require a certain number of years in public service, particularly when training is state subsidized, have been implemented in the Philippines and Tanzania, and are common in Latin America.[28] High-achieving countries did succeed in resolving the problem. Malaysia ensured that all doctors trained at public expense were required to serve the public health system for at least three years. This allowed the government to post doctors to the rural areas (Heng and Hoey, 1997). Similarly, Sri Lanka required doctors to work with the government health service; in fact, the medical council of the country would refuse to register physicians trained at public expense without their having served in rural areas (Alailama and Sanderatne, 1997).

In some cases imbalance between capital and recurrent expenditure is the outcome of donor policies. Donors often focus on highly visible investments without adequate consideration of compatibility with other investments or recurrent costs. For instance, Sri Lanka accepted a donor contribution of a 1,000-bed hospital: to operate it took needed resources away from other activities (WHO, 2000). Such short-term thinking and donors' competing agendas are further discussed in Chapter 10. In any case, what is called for is an examination by donors of their past policies.

Public expenditure planning within the health ministry also needs to change. In most developing countries, investment planning is incremental, with last year's budget being the starting point for next year's plan. Ongoing activities are normally not questioned, thus limiting the possibility for changing the resource allocation pattern. Ministries of health (like all other line ministries) call for additional resources, while the ministry of finance prefers maintenance of expenditures at previous year levels. This approach is only feasible if total budgetary resources are growing (see Chapter 9 for this discussion). Especially, but not only, when health ministry resources are declining, prioritizing activities is essential. Instead, faced with an IMF public expenditure cap, in most ministries of health, resources tend to get cut across the board — without regard to the needs of more vulnerable populations or geographical areas or core programme areas.

To what extent is decentralization a means for improving efficiency? In many countries there has been an increased enthusiasm for decentralization as an instrument of improving health-sector performance. The predominant aim is to enhance responsiveness and incentive structures by shifting owner-ship, responsibility and accountability to lower levels of the public sector. Decentralization alone solves few problems. In Uganda, since decentralization the provision of primary health care rests with the district and urban councils, but, because of their weak revenue base, few districts allocate locally gener-ated resources to the service (Ablo and Reinikka, 1998). In Ghana, in the wake of decentralization the unfunded social obligations were passed on to lower levels of government that did not have the financial capacity to absorb this responsibility (WHO, 2000).

Central control is particularly important if balance between capital and recurrent costs is to be observed. Central policy is also necessary on drugs and major technology registration, the development of essential drug lists and treatment guidelines, quality assurance and bulk tendering. But, as WHO (2000) notes, rigid hierarchical approaches to balancing resources result in reactive rather than continuous changes; shortages of essential inputs on the one hand and unspent funds on the other often become problems. Hence after decentralization decision-making among providers must be controlled and guided to meet overall priorities.

Local governments often do not have the institutional capacity to deliver these services effectively. In fact, one of the advantages of decentralized regimes is that they allow for a greater role for 'voice'. For instance, where doctors/nurses do not show up regularly at health facilities, thus leaving the facility underutilized by users, 'voice' has been shown to produce results – an issue we come back to in the next chapter.[29]

A final policy that is often overlooked in the face of donor funding and programmes that are disease-specific is the need for integrating vertical programmes into functional health systems. In far too many health systems that are underfunded from domestic revenues, priorities are often determined

Table 6.6 Decline in total fertility and population growth rate, by region, 1960–99

	Contraceptive prevalence (%) 1995–2000	% of births attended by trained health personnel 1995–2000	Total fertility rate			Population annual growth rate (%)	
			1960	1990	1999	1970–90	1990–99
Sub-Saharan Africa	18	37	6.7	6.2	5.4	2.8	2.6
Middle East & North Africa	49	69	7.1	4.9	3.7	3.1	2.3
South Asia	40	29	6.1	4.1	3.3	2.2	1.9
East Asia & Pacific	81	66	5.8	2.5	2.0	1.8	1.2
Latin America & Caribbean	69	83	6.1	3.2	2.6	2.2	1.7
CEE/CIS & Baltic States	65	94	3.1	2.3	1.7	1.0	0.3
Industrialized countries	72	99	2.8	1.7	1.6	0.7	0.6
Developing countries	59	52	6.1	3.5	2.9	2.2	1.7
Least developed countries	24	28	6.6	5.7	4.9	2.5	2.5
World	61	56	5.1	3.1	2.6	1.8	1.4

Note: Data refer to the most recent year available during the period specified in the column heading.
Source: UNICEF, 2001.

by donor-driven vertical programmes. There is a particular risk that as a result of donor emphasis on the Millennium Development Goals, vertical programmes to reduce tuberculosis, malaria or HIV/AIDS will be introduced, while the goal of health system strengthening that we have emphasized in this chapter will fall by the wayside in the process. There is evidence that where disease-specific programmes are integrated into a functioning health structure, their likelihood of success and sustainability is high, as India's TB programme demonstrates. Using the strategy of directly observed therapy short-course (DOTS), India's programme uses the existing health structure but supplements its activities with additional resources, staff and drugs, with diagnosis and treatment free of charge to patients. Some 436 million people (more than 40 per cent of the population) have access to these services thanks to this integrated approach (Khattri and Frieden, 2002).[30]

Reproductive health

Very few country studies present data on public spending on reproductive health separately. We have obtained data from other sources, which is presented in Table 6.7. The available data indicate that it is seldom a high priority.[31] The table shows the distribution of expenditure for population activities by the following categories: family planning services, basic reproductive health services, sexually transmitted diseases and HIV/AIDs, and basic research and data. For most countries in all regions family planning services account for the highest share of reproductive health activities. In several countries in Africa, however, STD and HIV/AIDS take up the largest share of population activity expenditure – for example, South Africa (90 per cent), Mozambique and Namibia (nearly two-thirds), Central African Republic and Burkina Faso (70 and 82 per cent respectively). In no other Asian or Latin American country is population activity absorbed with HIV/AIDS as in Africa – the only exception being Thailand. Family planning services and basic reproductive health services absorb most of the funds in half the African countries. In most of Asia, Latin America and the Middle East/North Africa family planning and basic reproductive health services account for most of the expenditure on population activities.

Most governments today do not need to be convinced about the need for strong family planning programmes. Nevertheless, there is still very considerable unmet need for modern means of contraception. And the effectiveness of programmes is poor. In too many countries, reproductive health is still dominated by vertical programmes, typically in ministries of health or family welfare, where stand-alone family planning programmes operate vertically alongside other health programmes. In other instances, family planning has been integrated with mother and child health, but often these MCH/FP programmes too are vertically organized within the public health structure. In light of the plan of action adopted at the International Conference on Population and Development (ICPD) in Cairo in 1994, the provision of basic reproductive and sexual health is seen as a necessary component, along with family planning, of a holistic package of basic health interventions.

This approach recognizes that vertical programmes are inherently less efficient than integrated ones that combine all elements of reproductive health into one service package. In South Africa, for instance, the vertical approach to family planning services was discarded in favour of an integrated approach in the late 1980s. Since then, efforts have been renewed to train primary-care nurses in family planning. As a result of these efforts, South Africa enjoys high contraceptive prevalence (unlike most other African countries) and is

Table 6.7 Size and structure of government and NGO expenditure on population activities, 1996

Country	Total expenditure (US$ million)	Family planning (%)	Basic reproductive health services (%)	STD and HIV/AIDS (%)	Basic research, data and pop. & development (%)
Sub-Saharan Africa					
Burkina Faso	5.79	13.58	3.78	81.58	1.05
Burundi	2.13	25.83	20.29	33.40	20.53
Cameroon	0.02	35.29	35.29	23.53	5.88
Central African Republic	2.25	8.62	7.15	70.08	14.17
Ethiopia	8.64	83.45	2.94	1.15	12.47
Ghana	1.77	70.57	7.78	7.05	14.60
Guinea	0.76	49.74	9.63	11.48	29.02
Ivory Cost	4.25	41.29	1.30	5.68	51.74
Kenya	5.70	83.79	2.33	3.65	10.25
Malawi	3.82	54.89	11.98	16.01	17.09
Mali	3.03	47.11	23.54	20.83	8.46
Mauritania	0.34	8.72	8.72	0.00	82.27
Mozambique	8.37	6.60	21.95	65.36	6.10
Namibia	0.63	13.88	12.78	67.19	6.31
Niger	0.06	36.51	34.92	17.46	12.70
Rwanda	0.99	31.28	20.47	14.18	27.54
Senegal	6.88	37.61	20.47	14.18	27.54
South Africa	17.39	0.27	1.51	90.15	8.07
Tanzania	3.35	58.11	9.12	25.31	7.45
Togo	0.58	31.66	2.60	6.06	59.66
Zambia	5.65	5.72	11.03	2.50	80.77
Zimbabwe	21.48	54.51	16.48	25.27	3.74
Total	4.72	36.32	13.00	27.37	23.06
Latin America & Caribbean					
Antigua and Barbuda	0.23	32.90	32.90	34.20	0.00
Barbados	0.37	96.71	2.74	0.00	0.27
Belize	13.16	5.50	75.20	15.10	4.20
Bolivia	1.75	25.83	64.63	1.54	8.06
Ecuador	0.03	55.56	0.00	44.44	0.00
Grenada	0.19	35.11	45.21	14.89	4.79
Guyana	4.14	45.76	20.84	23.74	9.67
Haiti	0.01	0.00	0.00	100.00	0.00

Jamaica	314.05	10.44	70.27	9.09	10.21
Nicaragua	2.37	25.20	3.34	4.74	66.72
Peru	15.77	63.41	18.07	10.15	8.37
St Lucia	0.03	5.88	91.18	0.00	0.00
St Vincent and the Grenadines	0.05	41.30	30.43	21.74	6.52
Suriname	0.01	0.00	33.33	16.67	50.00
Trinidad and Tobago	0.59	42.23	36.82	5.91	15.20
Total	23.52	32.39	35.00	20.15	12.27
Asia & Pacific					
Cambodia	0.90	40.65	14.14	18.71	26.50
India	647.60	48.95	45.50	2.58	2.98
Indonesia	243.98	67.18	25.44	4.02	3.37
Iran, Islamic Republic of	403.89	11.67	78.08	1.12	9.13
Korea, Democratic People's	0.00	50.00	50.00	0.00	0.00
Mongolia	0.16	16.67	19.14	3.09	61.11
Nepal	3.29	76.47	15.93	2.22	5.35
Pakistan	36.34	87.99	8.51	1.40	2.09
Papua New Guinea	2.44	37.42	40.20	4.63	17.75
Philippines	10.60	34.33	28.02	20.82	16.83
Sri Lanka	1.51	58.37	21.91	13.70	5.02
Thailand	58.42	28.54	11.78	58.61	1.06
Vietnam	22.55	98.46	0.34	0.15	1.05
Total	110.13	50.52	27.61	10.08	11.71
Western Asia & North Africa					
Egypt	88.80	56.64	37.02	1.55	4.79
Morocco	22.88	13.15	45.94	4.72	36.20
Sudan	0.93	31.80	36.94	10.60	20.66
Syrian Arab Republic	0.31	62.38	12.54	3.22	21.54
Tunisia	22.56	51.74	46.44	1.82	0.00
Total	27.10	43.14	35.78	4.38	16.64
Countries in transition					
Belarus	0.02	0.00	0.00	0.00	100.00
Moldova, Republic	0.94	37.01	16.38	45.03	1.71
Romania	0.28	19.20	23.91	15.22	41.67
Russian Federation	77.49	12.18	78.54	0.31	8.98
Ukraine	0.08	18.52	74.07	6.17	0.00
Total	15.76	17.38	38.58	13.35	30.47

Source: UNFPA and NIDI, global resource flows population activities, post-IPCD experience.

one of the few areas where racial disparities are the smallest (with prevalence of almost 70 per cent for Africans and 80 per cent for whites being the extremes). However, in many other cases, not enough efforts seem to be made to implement integrated reproductive health programmes.

There has been a debate on whether the supply of family planning services or the demand for such services has more weight in explaining the fertility decline of the past two decades (Bongaarts, 1994, 1995; Pritchett 1994a, 1994b). The crux of the debate involved whether the reductions in fertility in recent decades are the result of expanding family planning services (the supply side) or of decreased fertility desires by couples (the demand side), probably as a result of better education and lower child mortality.

Although there seems to be empirical evidence partially supporting each camp, we believe the debate is miscast. At least since the times of Alfred Marshall economists have known that both blades of the scissors are needed – supply *and* demand. The conditions under which couples can substantially reduce fertility in the absence of modern means of contraception are rare, and of course if they want to have children, no amount of family planning services will reduce fertility.

Other things remaining the same, the demand for children would fall if infant and child mortality were to decline. Children in poor societies are a substitute for missing institutions and markets, especially the institution of social security for old age. Parents make fertility choices based on the recognition that some of their children will die; potential deaths are compensated by a larger number of births. Universal access to basic services holds out the promise that behavioural change over time will induce a lower demand for children, thus breaking the inertia at the micro- or household level, and hence lower the birth rate.[32]

However, as we saw in Chapter 4, the synergy of interventions in basic services works particularly through the mother. Recall the discussion on the life cycle of the educated girl (as opposed to an uneducated girl). Hence, we would argue that achieving gender equality is central to the enterprise of hastening the demographic transition in developing countries. Population growth in the last hundred years has been many times faster than during the first hundred years (1800–1900) after the Industrial Revolution in Europe. In fact, there is a vicious cycle of population growth, poverty and environmental degradation that has been in place for several decades in most developing countries. Population growth is likely to continue until the global population reaches at least 8 billion by the middle of the twenty-first century, and over 95 per cent of this growth is due to occur in the developing world – stretching further the carrying capacity of the earth. In other words, if the demographic transition is to be hastened, enabling individual countries to stabilize their populations quicker, and per capita income growth to occur at a faster rate than would be the case otherwise, then gender equality – and hence the reproductive rights of women – become a priority for policymakers. In other words, gender equality is central not only to the synergy between basic service-related interventions, but also to triggering the second synergy between income-poverty reduction, per capita income growth and health and education advance.

Child under-nutrition and gender discrimination

Nutritional status is the final aspect of health we discuss in this section. We focus especially on the determinants of child under-nutrition, and policies to address it. In sub-Saharan Africa, one in three children is underweight, and in many countries on that continent malnutrition rates of children worsened in the 1990s. The situation in South Asia is much worse. In Latin America and East Asia, there have been large gains in reducing child malnutrition. But overall, the absolute number of malnourished children globally has grown (UNICEF, 1998b). This is despite the so-called 'child survival revolution' of the 1980s and 1990s. In other words, more children are surviving – not dying – but the quality of life of those surviving is worse.

However, the malnutrition problem has no constituency, nor any ministry – unlike health and education, which are full-fledged ministries in most governments, and water/sanitation, which usually has a municipal body in towns and cities. Nutrition is not a 'sector' like the others. Besides, nutritional outcomes are the result of extremely complex society-wide interactions (as we discuss below). As a result, paradoxical phenomena abound. As many as half of South Asia's children are malnourished, a much higher proportion than in sub-Saharan Africa, despite the fact that Africa has a much higher child mortality rate than South Asia (Osmani, 1997; Ramalingaswami et al., 1996).

Malnutrition is an inter-generational problem. Poor nutrition often starts *in utero* and extends, particularly for girls and women, into adolescent and adult life. Low-birthweight (LBW) infants who have suffered intra-uterine growth retardation as fetuses are born undernourished and have a far higher risk of dying in the neonatal period or later infancy. If they survive, they will not catch up on this lost growth later, and are more likely to be stunted or underweight.

This inter-generational aspect of a child's nutritional status compounds the complexity of the nature of interventions required. Nutritional status is mainly the result of: (i) food intake, and (ii) health status. Health status, in turn, is determined by environmental sanitation (discussed above), health services (also discussed above) and caring capacity. Food intake is determined by food availability and caring capacity. Food availability, in turn, is affected by production, distribution (or purchase) and donation of food. Caring capacity (which impacts both the child's food intake and the child's health status) is overwhelmingly influenced by the status of women in the society, since they are the principal caregivers in all societies. The rest of this discussion focuses on these various determinants of nutritional status and the policy options facing decision-makers hoping to improve health outcomes through nutritional interventions. But this discussion is not about the technical efficiency of spending decisions, but merely about which specific nutrition-related interventions can trigger the synergies on which depend health and nutritional outcomes.

As regards food availability for the world as a whole, for developing countries, and even for least developed countries, the per capita supply of calories is above 2,200. Also, there are very few countries where the per capita supply of calories falls below 2,000.[33] This indicates that there are no supply reasons for famines. However, as is well known, averages mask severe intra-country differences. It is not surprising, then, that a high average supply is not a guarantee of famine prevention. For protein-energy malnutrition, much more important than average supply is access to food, which depends on income distribution (entitlement) and other institutional aspects (access to land, role of traders and market structure, government regulations affecting exports, imports and intra-country trade, and so on). Although it is not necessary to produce all food in the country to attain food security, as food can be imported, this is not an appropriate strategy for landlocked countries – which are concentrated in Africa.

Policy advice for sub-Saharan Africa has tended to push in the opposite direction, arguing that free markets should determine how the continent feeds itself. Governments facing fiscal deficits should not provide fertilizer subsidies (although fertilizer consumption in Africa is the lowest in the world), crop price supports or cheap loans. A recent World Bank report suggested that rural African grow cash crops for export (and promote tourism) to generate incomes among poor farmers as well as to earn the foreign exchange they need for imports. This seems to be a mistaken policy goal, especially on a continent where foodgrain productivity has barely grown over the last decade. As we have already introduced a thorough critique of these neoliberal policies in Chapter 2, there is no need to dwell on them again. What is absolutely critical to ensuring adequate food intake, given the unequal income distribution in most low-income countries, is targeted food subsidies for the poor and buffer stocks to smooth volatile prices — without which food entitlements cannot be realized.[34]

In the rest of this section, we turn to child malnutrition, as opposed to hunger (defined as availability of less than 1,900 calories per day per person) in general.[35] In our framework, it is important to highlight the centrality of gender as an underlying cause of child malnutrition (through its caring capacity effects). In particular, the role and tasks of women are crucial in understanding the comparative experience of South Asia and sub-Saharan Africa in respect of the incidence of child malnutrition. In both regions income poverty and availability of food are not very different but malnutrition fates are significantly different – one-half of all under-5s in South Asia versus one-third in sub-Saharan Africa (Ramalingaswami et al., 1996). South Asia also has a much higher incidence of low birthweight (LBW) at term than any developing region. Early textbooks made only tangential reference to LBW as a problem, and it was only in the 1990s that a body of literature emerged which better elucidates the problem. The source of the problem has to be found in the condition of women, especially pregnancy care (Shetty and James, 1994).

Since maternal under-nutrition is a major determinant of LBW, high rates of LBW should be interpreted not only as an indicator of child under-nutrition, but as an urgent public health warning that women of child-bearing age are undernourished as well. The determinants of LBW are indicated by the following maternal nutritional deficiencies: low weight gain during pregnancy leading to intra-uterine growth retardation (IUGR); low pre-pregnancy body mass index (BMI); short maternal stature; and micronutrient deficiencies. LBW is also associated with young maternal age, repeated pregnancies in quick succession, poor access to antenatal care, and a heavy workload in the third trimester. Hence a life-cycle approach to maternal health and childcare is needed. This framework complements the one that was introduced in Chapter 4 concerning the life cycle of the educated girl. There it was shown that interventions in all basic social services had mutually reinforcing interactions with positive effects on the well-being of both mother and child in a closed feedback loop.

Based on this framework we briefly review interventions to prevent LBW, and then those interventions that address malnutrition among the already born. Prevention is critical, as the effects of LBW are largely irreversible. The lessons from a mix of government programmes, which claim to have successfully reduced or prevented LBW, are the following.[36] Since pre-pregnancy weight and pregnancy weight gain are independent and completely additive in their effect on birthweight, interventions need to focus on both. Here successful programmes have demonstrated the success of supplementary feeding. Addressing pre-pregnancy weight for girls would mean a combination of targeted food subsidies for the poor as well as school feeding programmes. Pregnancy weight gain requires food supplementation through an antenatal care programme.

Once a LBW baby is born, apparently there are few well-designed childhood interventions to improve the outcome. Hence the potential interventions are all designed to *prevent* worsening life-chances of such an infant. Nevertheless, after gestation and birth, the benefits of breastfeeding for a child's development have been extensively researched, not only in developing countries but in industrialized ones as well (Jelliffe and Jelliffe, 1978).[37] But the rate of exclusive breastfeeding – its efficient use – is much lower than expected.

In addition to the problem of protein-energy malnutrition, micronutrient deficiencies are widespread in developing countries. Deficiencies with the most obvious and deadly consequences are: vitamin A, iron and iodine.[38] Not surprisingly these are the micronutrients receiving the most attention from the international community, although other vitamins, calcium and zinc are increasingly addressed too. In order to reach vulnerable groups other than school-attending children, three main strategies to address micronutrient deficiencies are available: dietary diversification, food fortification[39] and supplementation.[40] The most cost-effective and sustainable approach is dietary diversification.[41]

Another intervention for LBW babies is growth monitoring. Growth monitoring is the periodic and regular measuring and recording of weight, and sometimes height, of children over time – that is, as they grow up. Obviously, it does not affect nutritional levels directly. However, it is an important tool to help concentrate efforts when and where they are needed. The proper implementation of growth monitoring is itself dependent upon the existence of a public health system functional at the primary level of care.

Finally, school feeding programmes are present in many countries; however, their effectiveness and efficiency has been challenged (World Bank, 1991). The main criticism is that the same level of financial resources would result in better nutritional outcomes if they were targeted and if they were focused on smaller children, because by the time children are in elementary school the effects of malnutrition are irreversible. However, this stance fails to notice that a dietary supplement, even at this age, could stop the growth gap from widening. Also, there are indirect benefits of school feeding programmes, for example indirectly monitoring children who are too young to attend school but need food assistance or micronutrients. In addition, avoiding hunger helps learning, as mentioned above when the synergies among 'sectors/interventions' were discussed. Moreover, many parents who would not send their children to school to learn would send them for the free meal. Witness, for instance, the increases in enrolment that have occurred in the 1990s in many low-achiever states in India after the introduction of the midday meal programme in the mid-1990s (Mehrotra et al., 2005).

A fundamental problem with nutritional interventions is precisely that 'nutrition' is not a 'sector'. In the low-income countries, where the nutrition situation is the most acute, the capacity for intervention is most fragmented and limited.[42] In India, for instance, which is home to the world's largest programme of interventions in early childhood care, the Integrated Child Development Scheme, the focus of the programme has been on the 3–6 years age cohort (NIPCCD, 1992).[43] Bangladesh – with the highest malnutrition rates in the world – initiated an Integrated Nutrition Programme with multiple donor support only in 1995.

Summing up

In respect of health interventions, there are a number of ways to ensure better outcomes from the current envelope of resources and improve technical efficiency. First, vertical structures for disease-specific programmes may be affordable for only those diseases that could be eliminated in a foreseeable time span. Hence, there is a need for integration of vertical programmes into a functional health system. Second, primary health services often overly emphasize family planning and birth control, not overall reproductive health. Integrating family planning and child/maternal services will improve the efficiency of both. Third, there are a number of problems with the way recurrent spending is allocated. A major problem is that human resources are concentrated in urban areas, and many regions have too many doctors, not enough nurses. The policy response should be to enforce the requirement for rural service for graduates of publicly subsidized medical education; and expand training for nurses, with similar requirement for rural posting. Fourth, public health clinics often are not attractive on account of the absence of essential drugs. In the majority of least developed countries, donors and, in other low-income countries, central governments have to find resources for essential drugs to attract patients for curative purposes, so that preventive services can also be delivered. Finally, a number of technical and societal interventions are necessary if malnutrition is to be reduced, so that the life-cycle impact of under-nutrition can be mitigated, if not eliminated.

6.3   Conclusion

Since each of the subsections on health, education and water/sanitation have summarized the main arguments, in these concluding remarks we return to the main thesis of this chapter. We recognize that, although we promote the role of the state in providing basic services for all, state provision often is inefficient. Mostly this is the result of insufficient funding. However, it is difficult to make the case for additional funding, given the problems with sector-specific policies in the current pattern of provisioning. There is much ground for arguing that both the allocative and the technical efficiency of current government spending on social services leave much to be desired.

However, even with additional funding and improved allocative and technical efficiency of government and donor funding, the issue remains of the organizational context in which social services are delivered. If the state had been delivering services effectively in most developing countries, over 10 million children would not be dying from preventable causes, 1 billion people would not be without safe drinking water and 2 billion without safe sanitation, over a 100 million children would not be out of school, and nearly 1 billion people would not be illiterate. If the state has to become a more effective instrument of the delivery of basic services, a deep democratic decentralization of social service delivery is required. This is the subject of the next chapter.

Annex 6.1 Trend of BSS share in total public expenditure, selected countries (%)

	Total BSS	Basic education	Basic health	Water	Nutrition	Reproductive health
Nepal						
1992	11.3	6.70	2.06	2.55		
1993	11.4	7.54	2.37	1.48		
1994	13.8	8.74	2.95	2.11		
1995	12.7	8.15	2.44	2.11		
1996	13.6	8.28	3.05	2.27		
Sri Lanka						
1982	7.7	0.0	2.1	0.6	5.0	
1987	9.2	0.0	5.0	1.1	3.2	
1988	10.7	0.0	4.4	1.0	5.4	
1989	15.2	0.0	5.0	0.7	9.5	
1990	13.0	0.0	4.5	1.0	7.5	
1991	11.5	0.0	4.0	1.1	6.3	
1992	16.4	3.2	4.9	2.1	6.2	
1993	14.9	3.2	4.0	1.4	6.4	
1994	13.0	3.2	4.1	1.5	4.1	
1995	13.3	3.1	4.2	1.7	4.3	
1996	12.7	3.5	4.5	1.0	3.6	
Malawi						
1988	6.0	3.60	0.38	2.02		
1991	6.3	3.80	0.56	1.94		
1992	6.8	3.84	0.51	2.48		
1993	11.0	5.83	0.60	2.48		
1994	8.1	4.39	0.47	3.22		
1995	6.4	4.50	0.62	1.27		
1996	8.2	6.41	0.71	1.08		
1997	7.6	6.67			0.41	
Jamaica						
1980	8.2	6.05	0.67	1.24	0.23	
1981	11.3	8.83	1.29	0.92	0.27	
1982	12.8	9.16	1.42	1.96	0.26	
1983	11.9	8.84	1.26	1.61	0.20	
1984	12.4	9.14	1.40	1.54	0.20	
1985	10.7	7.47	1.26	1.35	0.62	
1986	11.4	7.44	1.36	2.53	0.07	

	Total BSS	Basic education	Basic health	Water	Nutrition	Reproductive health
1987	13.0	8.05	1.55	2.69	0.72	
1988	12.2	8.11	1.20	2.07	0.83	
1989	13.3	8.95	1.60	1.97	0.78	
1990	13.4	8.52	1.74	2.04	1.09	
1991	10.1	7.06	1.09	1.06	0.89	
1992	9.2	5.76	1.44	1.33	0.68	
1993	11.7	8.42	1.09	1.31	0.88	
1994	8.6	5.36	1.28	1.32	0.65	
1995	10.1	6.98	1.00	1.64	0.48	
1996	10.2	7.29	1.06	1.36	0.49	
Kenya						
1980	19.9	15.1	1.9	2.4	0.01	0.5
1981	20.1	15.9	1.9	2.0	0.01	0.2
1982	18.6	14.8	1.3	2.3	0.00	0.2
1983	16.3	13.9	1.1	1.1	0.02	0.2
1984	16.8	13.9	1.2	1.6	0.04	0.2
1985	17.7	14.8	1.6	1.1	0.04	0.2
1986	16.9	14.6	1.7	0.3	0.03	0.3
1987	17.2	14.2	1.5	1.3	0.03	0.2
1988	16.3	14.4	0.9	0.7	0.03	0.9
1989	13.5	11.6	1.4	0.1	0.04	1.4
1990	15.8	12.1	1.4	2.6	0.03	1.4
1991	13.8	10.6	1.4	1.4	0.03	1.4
1992	12.6	10.3	1.3	0.7	0.02	1.3
1993	11.0		1.2	0.6	0.02	8.9
1994	8.9	7.7	0.9	0.3	0.01	0.9
1995	12.6	10.6	1.3	0.4	0.00	1.3
Namibia						
1990	14.0	9.35	4.65	0.00	0.00	
1991	15.0	9.68	4.70	0.62	0.00	
1992	21.0	12.40	5.07	2.07	1.46	
1993	23.0	14.21	5.54	1.40	1.09	
1994	22.0	14.28	5.42	1.14	1.17	
1995	19.0	12.02	5.59	1.16	0.23	
1996	19.0	11.47	5.68	1.66	0.20	

Note: Sri Lanka and Malawi: water and sanitation.

Source: Country studies.

Governance reforms to address the systemic problems of state provision of basic services

While the previous chapter pointed to many of the problems of state provision – poor quality, low performance, limited responsiveness and weak accountability – this chapter is devoted to possible policy responses to these problems of state failure. As stated in the last chapter, the problems of state provision of basic services do not result from resource constraints and allocative inefficiencies alone, but also from the bureaucratic and organizational context of state provision.[1] Non-state provision of basic services is addressed in the following chapter, but here we have concentrated on the state as financier and provider of services, and what kind of systematic reforms are necessary to reduce state failure in service delivery of basic social services.

Section 7.1 examines the organizational context of state provision, and suggests that the nature of the post-colonial state, including its centralized character, is an underlying factor explaining state failure in many respects. Section 7.2 discusses the pros and cons of decentralization, and argues that a certain kind of decentralization alone will enable the state to deliver basic services successfully: deep democratic decentralization. Section 7.3 discusses case studies of deep democratic decentralization, which have demonstrated success in delivery of basic social services. Section 7.4 summarizes the argument.

7.1 The nature of the state as a factor in state failure in service delivery

The state delivers development services in most developing countries in a top-down, bureaucratic manner through sectoral line ministries down to the local level. But this manner of service delivery defeats one of the greatest sources of technical efficiency in the utilization of resources – the synergy of interventions in the various social sectors. Without the state making conscious effort to ensure synergy between interventions in the spheres of health, education, water and sanitation, reproductive health, and nutrition within a geographic location, these latent synergies will not be realized. But the state is incapable of delivering these services effectively as long as it operates vertically. Inter-sectoral action is best triggered through 'voice' at the local level, with village-level planning. If collective voice at the local level puts pressure on local-level functionaries to respond to local needs and demands, instead of delivering services merely based on resource allocation determined at a higher, bureaucratic level of decision-making, two benefits will result: synergy between interventions across sectors and the effective delivery of individual public services.

Reforms within bureaucracy over the years have faced numerous design and implementation problems. Staff at health centres do not turn up regularly, and teacher absenteeism is rampant in many countries. Incentive reforms run up against the civil service norms of guaranteed employment, and salaries which are unrelated to merit. Enhanced monitoring has been difficult to implement, partly on account of political problems and the tendency of hierarchical superiors to prevent punitive action. In fact, if the high-ups in the hierarchy do not protect those lower down – the ones who have the most dealings with the public – the game would be over.

The current post-colonial state structure in most low-income countries is highly centralized, since it was inherited from colonial administrations. The purpose of the colonial administration was its own preservation, and the preservation of its status of distinctness and aloofness from the people it ruled. The function of the colonial administration was to maintain law and order in the country as a whole, and ensure a minimum level of infrastructure services (e.g. water, electricity) in urban areas (where the functionaries usually lived). These functions were to be maintained so that the objective of surplus extraction for the metropole would continue smoothly and unhindered. Meanwhile, the surplus extraction made it possible for the functionaries of the colonial state to enjoy a standard of living in the colony that was roughly commensurate with that in their homeland – and much higher than that of the vast majority of the natives they ruled.

A centralized structure of administration served the purposes of distinctness for its personnel, and the objective of surplus extraction.[2] The post-colonial state inherited the functions of the colonial administration in Asia and Africa – maintenance of law and order, collection of taxes, defence, foreign affairs, and ensuring a minimum level of infrastructure, particularly railways to transport goods to the ports. But it added on developmental ones to the hitherto minimal ones associated with surplus extraction. Very few states in Latin America in the first half of the twentieth century – exceptions included Barbados, Chile, Costa Rica and Uruguay – performed functions that went beyond these minimal ones.

The developmental functions, however, grew systematically everywhere over at least three decades from 1950. The provision of physical infrastructure grew to include the provision of social infrastructure (health, education). It further involved the creation and the acquisition of productive facilities and services (banking, insurance and trade). The monopolies and public-sector enterprises created by this expansion of developmental activities also created a fertile ground for rent-seeking by politicians, bureaucrats and lower-level functionaries. The scope for rent-seeking grew so much as to make it plausible to argue that the state by the late 1970s had turned predatory, while still being developmental.[3] But economic growth – compared to economic stagnation in colonial times – enabled rent-seeking to thrive.

This is hardly surprising given that the structure-in-itself of the post-colonial state was merely superimposed on the existing colonial state structure. The existence of five-yearly elections might have replaced the hitherto unrepresentative, authoritarian state, but the structure's separation from its citizenry survived. In Latin America, the unrepresentative character of the majority of governments (except for a minority of states) was characterized either by direct rule by a military junta, or by civilian politicians heavily dependent upon the military.

What changed dramatically was the nature of personnel in the bureaucratic/political leadership. The colonial bureaucrat had relatively little reason to be a rent-seeker at a personal level; his primary objective was to facilitate surplus extraction for the metropole. The colonial administrators could afford to be morally upright even in the absence of democracy, let alone accountability to the people. The political role of the colonial state was surplus extraction, not personal enrichment. When the most senior administrators were known to be upright, there was less scope for middle- and lower-level state functionaries to be engaged in personal aggrandisement. But the post-colonial state's rapidly expanding developmental role and the growth in the state's fiscal base created the scope for government leaders – both in the legislative and in the executive branches – to engage in personal enrichment. Worse still, sheer indifference to a notion of 'service' by the so-called civil service could be rewarded with political protection or protection by superior bureaucrats. If the village-level public functionary (schoolteacher, doctor or nurse, water engineer) is merely answerable to a distant authority, the former can ignore his clients with impunity, with little to fear in terms of sanctions.

If capability-enhancing basic services for all are to become a reality, what is needed is a state that is genuinely 'embedded' in the larger society (instead of being separate from it), and that has a relationship of reciprocity and mutual interdependence with civil society. That kind of state will not be a structure in-itself and for-itself. It is not as though the state is not currently 'accountable'. To a whole series of networks (the capitalist, the landed, the labour aristocracy) the two key sets of personnel – bureaucrats and politicians – are to some extent already accountable. So the state structure is indeed embedded in networks in society. But the kind of accountability that would interest the poor citizens is that at the community level of the lowest-level functionaries of the state – both elected functionaries (i.e. politicians) and civil servants (e.g. nurse/midwife, schoolteacher, water engineer). Without that accountability, services cannot be delivered effectively. Nor can the synergy of interventions in health, education, nutrition and water, and sanitation be realized without that accountability.

Meanwhile, intermediaries exploit the distance between well-intentioned governmental action from the centre and the village where the school (or health centre) is located, to foil the objectives of the centre. However, hierarchical control of functionaries is rarely effective under such circumstances. In fact, without the state 'enabling' collective voice and action, which emerges as a counterweight to the intermediaries, the delivery of services, and hence the human functionings (in the sense that Sen (2000) discusses them, see Chapter 2), cannot be realized. Since the poor have limited choice of 'exit'[4] (in the Hirschman (1970) sense), 'voice' alone works.

But can decentralization work in improving the effectiveness of the state in all areas under its jurisdiction? The central government is best at tasks with economies of scale, those that rely on its better finance-raising and regulatory powers (capital-intensive facilities, technical expertise, financing, oversight, training). The advantage of decentralization is that better local information (which outsiders lack) can be brought to bear on selection and targeting of government programmes, and a reduction of authority of central bureaucrats that do not face pressures of accountability from citizens directly. It also leaves decision-making in the hands of those who not only have local information, but who can increase the flexibility of public programmes in response to local conditions.

7.2   Capabilities, democracy and decentralization

For Sen, a person's 'capability' refers to the alternative combinations of functionings that are feasible for her to achieve. 'Capability is thus a freedom' (Sen, 2000: 75). Functionings are things that a person may value doing or being – *simple* ones like being able to read and write, being well-nourished and being free from avoidable disease, or *complex* ones like being able to take part in the life of the community and having self-respect.

Our suggestion is that a group of simple functionings – being adequately nourished, being able to read and write, being free of avoidable disease – are synergistically linked to the more complex functionings in real life. For instance, the simple functionings (being educated up to elementary level) are very difficult to achieve without being able to participate in society. In the abstract, they are possible to realize separately, but in practice it is often impossible for the poor to realize even simple functionings without the complex one of participation. The relationship holds in the opposite direction as well: with the functionings of literacy and good health, individuals tend to become more effective 'participants' in society. That, however, is not the subject of this chapter.

In our elaboration on the Capability Approach there is a case for three extensions in order to make the approach operational. First, Sen's distinction between simple and complex functionings is too watertight; in real life, there is mutual interdependence between simple and complex functionings that Sen does not recognize. Second, Sen's formulation of the Capability Approach focuses exclusively on the individual, ignoring the collective capability. Third, Sen's articulation of democracy as a desirable condition for enhancing human capabilities is mistakenly conceived only at the national level, when what matters most for genuine participation is local participation, only realized through deep democratic decentralization. To bring all three points together, the complex functioning of participation the approach postulates needs to be contextualized not at an individual level, but at that of *the community – collective voice and collective action* – to have operational use. Unless thus extended, none of the simple functionings (e.g. the ability to read and write) is likely to be realized, even in democratic states (Mehrotra, 2006a).

The above discussion suggests that decentralization of social services is an appropriate response to the problems of state failure. It is well known that per capita income of a country is highly correlated with quality of government, measured in whatever way, and is also strongly correlated with decentralization. Development is generally accompanied by decentralization. In recent years there has been much academic debate on the advantages and disadvantages of decentralization. But the *type* of decentralization does matter. Decentralization can be fiscal, political and/or administrative. Fiscal decentralization is where revenue collection and expenditure are decentralized to local authorities. Most developing-country governments are not in a position to decentralize much revenue collection, except for limited subjects, to local authorities. Political decentralization implies that local authorities are not appointed, but elected directly by the people. Administrative decentralization (on its own, unaccompanied by political or fiscal decentralization) implies that functions and/or functionaries are transferred to a local authority (which is appointed by a central/provincial government), without necessarily giving the authority much revenue-collecting power. Reasons of space prevent us from discussing these three types of decentralization at any length. However, suffice here to say that since limited revenue-generating capacity in most low- and middle-income countries is likely to prevent much revenue-generation power being devolved to local authorities, much of the discussion below occurs within the context of the need for political and administrative decentralization. It also matters what subjects are decentralized – that is, which functions are transferred to the local authority, and which are retained by the central authority.

By the beginning of the 1990s there was increasing recognition that since hierarchical control is not successful in ensuring delivery of services, decentralization was needed. The 1990s was the decade of the spread of democracy in the developing world. Over a hundred countries now have democratically elected governments, almost twice the number at the end of the 1980s (World Bank, 1999b). It was also the decade of the spread of decentralization. For instance, in Latin America, with the exception of a few small countries, virtually all legislative and executive authorities are now elected in 13,000 units of local government. Similarly, India, Indonesia and the Philippines introduced large-scale decentralization efforts.

Unfortunately, often this effort at decentralization in many countries coincided with an international effort by powerful donors to promote decentralization.[5] The international financial institutions launched their neoliberal 'roll back the state' campaign after the fiscal deficits of overly stretched developmental states grew to unmanageable levels. The IFIs have attempted to cut the state's functions right down to a similar (though not same) level as that of the colonial state. Underlying this neoliberal notion of the minimalist state is a notion of market failure – the state should only intervene where there is likely to be market failure (e.g. basic health, basic education and infrastructure). This notion of the state is keenly informed by the literature on government failure. Government failure, in this view, had characterized the pre-1980 state in most developing societies in two ways: one, it took on many unnecessary roles in the productive/service sectors of the economy; two, it failed to undertake the required regulatory functions in an even-handed manner (which could have enabled capital accumulation to occur in the private sector). However, state structures that were inherited from the colonial state – created for entirely different objectives – were bound to suffer from 'government failure'. The mere imposition of Westminster-style parliaments in new states was not going to transform structures meant for surplus-extraction and law-and-order maintenance into democratic forms of functioning – least of all in largely illiterate societies.

Not surprisingly, decentralization continues to face many problems. While decentralization spread rapidly during the 1990s, the experience with it has not been as notable for successes as one might have expected. Tanzi (1996) argues that local bureaucrats may be poorly trained and thus inefficient in delivering public goods and services. This criticism recognizes a real issue, lack of training, which hinders effective decentralization.

In addition, decentralization may not be appropriate if there are adminis-trative problems of coordinating across jurisdictions. The spillover effects of decisions across jurisdictions could be ignored by each individual community in a decentralized system, but could be internalized by a central govern-ment. This is particularly relevant for investment in highway transport and communication, eradication of communicable diseases, control of pollution, and waste disposal.

Perhaps the most important issue around decentralization arises around distributive conflicts.[6] Most developing countries are characterized by consid-erable social and income inequality, and under the circumstances the problem of 'capture' of the local governing agencies by the local elite can be severe, leaving the poor very vulnerable. Some argue (e.g. Bardhan and Mookerjee, 1999) that the problem of capture might be more serious at the local level. For instance, there are fixed costs of organizing resistance groups or lobbies, and the poor may be more unorganized at the local level than at the national level where they can pool their organizing capacities. Also, collusions at the local level among the elite groups may be easier than at the national level.[7] This is especially the case when the ownership of assets is rather unequal at the local level, or when there is social stratification. For instance, in socially homogeneous Japan or Korea community-level organizations may work better in enforcing co-operative norms. Similarly, Putnam (1993) suggested, on the basis of regional differences in Italy, that 'horizontal' social networks (i.e. among people of similar status and power) are more effective in generat-ing trust and norms of reciprocity than 'vertical' ones.

The relationship between decentralization of government activities and the extent of rent-extraction by private parties is an important element in the recent debate on institutional design. The theoretical literature makes ambiguous predictions about this relationship and it has rarely been studied in the empirical literature. One of the few studies (Fisman and Gatti, 2002) examined the cross-country relationship between fiscal decentralization and corruption and suggested an inverse relationship between them. The evidence in this chapter raises a number of issues for further investigation, including whether particular *types* of decentralization are more effective in combating corruption, and whether there are specific services where decentralized provision has a particularly strong impact on rent-extraction.

This chapter addresses precisely those questions. We provide evidence that certain types of decentralization are more effective than those practised widely so far. There is increasing evidence now that where the *centre* acts to enable the articulation of voice by the local community, the functionaries of the state tend to respond positively to such local-level pressure (Tendler, 1997; Mehrotra, 2006b). There is a three-way dynamic between the state government (central or state government in a federal country), the local authority and civil society that ensures effective service delivery. We call this deep democratic decentralization.

Basic social services closest to the needs of the poorest people – primary health centres, schools, water services – are usually managed by bureaucrats and government employees who report to their superiors within the vertical line ministries. Such government employees rarely feel a strong sense of accountability to the neighbourhoods they administer.

Making states accountable in respect of delivery of basic services, we would argue, requires:

1. A functioning state (not a 'failed' one), and effective state capacity, at both central and local levels.
2. Empowered local authority to which functions, functionaries and finance have been devolved by the central authorities.
3. 'Voice' articulated on a collective basis by civil society, through institutions enabled by the state.

However, the mere existence of the three does not amount to an effective instrument for service delivery. The relationships between these three levels are crucial: local authorities must experience pressure both from above (for accountability to national governments) and from below (for service delivery to local citizens). Hence successful decentralization requires establishing a three-way dynamic among local governments, civil society and an effective central government (Tendler, 1997; Mehrotra, 2002a). The combination of these three elements – a functioning central government, empowered local authority, and voice – will ensure effective delivery of services.

Without effective state authority the central government cannot devolve power to local authority. Decentralization assumes coordination between levels of government and requires more regulation – not less – to guarantee basic transparency, accountability and representation. The state has to oversee, regulate and if necessary sanction local authorities so that poor people really benefit from political reform. The state also has to mobilize sufficient resources to devolve to the local authorities. When a weak state decentralizes, problems arise. In Ukraine, for example, a weak central government has found it difficult to keep local governments functioning with limited resources and little or no civil society engagement at the local level (Blair, 2000).

When a weak state devolves power, it is often because it is accommodating local elites, creating what Mamdani (1996) has called 'decentralized despotism', rather than increasing the democratic space. In sub-Saharan Africa, centralized regimes have tried to control rural areas by appointing their own people at the local level, which is the opposite of sharing political power and increasing local accountability (Turner and Hulme, 1997). Such actions cannot deliver the desired development results. Similarly, decentralization in Papua New Guinea has been more about staving off a break-up of the country under pressure from secessionist movements. The decentralization efforts of the government have been undermined by the difficulties facing the national government attempting to ensure territorial integrity (UNDP HDR, 2003). A military government might be strong, but that does not translate into effective state capacity; a democratic government is more likely to be responsive to voice from the grassroots.

Effective decentralization also needs *local authorities to which finance, functions and functionaries have been devolved*. Responsibilities for delivering social services have to be devolved to local authorities through legislative or constitutional means that transfer control over functions as well as functionaries. But functionaries cannot perform their functions without adequate finance. Local authorities only receive grants from the centre; they should also have local tax-raising authority, which enhances local accountability. The adequacy of finance will determine their success.

Finally, when creating the local authorities, the central government should also create *institutional mechanisms to ensure that the voice of the citizenry can be heard*. Of course, the level of organization of the citizenry will be a crucial determinant of how those mechanisms are actually used, but the mechanisms have to be created.

In Mozambique committed local authorites working in a decentralized system doubled health staff and focused on outreach – improving vaccination coverage and prenatal consultations by 8 per cent. In the state of West Bengal, India, where local authorities (*panchayats*) have been in existence long before they were mandated by a constitutional amendment in every state in 1992, poverty declined sharply in the 1980s (Crook and Sverisson, 2001). Under Operation Barga the panchayats helped improve agricultural technology and reform land tenancy. They also helped register 1.4 million sharecroppers, a near-revolutionary act in a country where in the majority of poor northern states sharecroppers have few written contracts or rights, and are usually at the mercy of powerful landlords.

Similarly, since the late 1980s Mazdoor Kisan Shakti Sangathan (MKSS, the Organization for Workers and Peasants Power) in Rajasthan, India, has been campaigning for the right to information. MKSS organizes public hearings to examine official information – detailed accounts derived from official spending records – and evaluate its validity. It uses these 'social audits' to promote democratic functioning at the level of the village. Such articulation of voice is made effective when the local authority is empowered to remedy the wrongs done by government employees.

There is nothing automatically pro-poor about decentralization, and ensuring that these three actors – the state, local authorities and the citizenry – interact to improve the lives of poor people is a difficult challenge. Dominant groups can capture local authorities. In Bangladesh, Côte d'Ivoire, Ghana, Kenya, Mexico, Nigeria, Papua New Guinea and Uganda decentralization led to neither greater participation nor better social and economic outcomes for poor people.

7.3   Case studies

The following section provides evidence of cases of deep democratic decentralization where there was a remarkable turnaround in social service provision in different regions. On the basis of this evidence some general conclusions are drawn on how governance reforms can significantly impact the effectiveness of basic services, which are the basis of the poor individual's acquisition of functionings and capabilities. Unlike in Chapter 2, where policies of high-achieving *countries* as a whole were discussed, here we will discuss successful examples of *sectors* in other countries where deep democratic decentralization has worked. In fact, while decentralization spread rapidly during the 1990s, as noted earlier, there are not many examples of notable successes. The case studies presented below are instances where deep democratic decentralization has ensured significant improvement in basic services.

Methodologically, one may question whether case study evidence can provide convincing support for demonstrating how service provision is more effectively provided by local governments. However, we are not advocating a spent model, but rather a new model, which has three elements. Evidence on its use is not so widespread that we can cite a large number of studies or cross-country surveys. Hence the argument does indeed have to rely on case studies. Nevertheless, these are not case studies of small projects, but of programmes affecting large cities, or sectors in a small country, or whole provinces in large federal countries where millions of people live, and demonstrate that it is possible to go to scale. The state may have failed in many parts of the world, but there is growing evidence of state success in effective delivery of basic services from a variety of countries.

The cases of deep democratic decentralization are drawn from different parts of the world – from Latin America, from South Asia and from Africa. They are drawn from urban as well as rural areas. They come from low-income countries, as well as middle-income ones. They are also case studies that draw upon experience in different sectors (e.g. health and education). Besides, we are not arguing that all kinds of utilities should be provided in a decentralized manner – only basic services.

Deep democratic decentralization in Ceara state, Brazil

The first example is drawn from the state of Ceara (population 7 million), in poor north-eastern Brazil.[8] A new government took over in 1987 at a time when the state's payroll commitments were consuming 87 per cent of the state's receipts, with little left for non-salary costs, public investment, and servicing of debts; civil servants had not been paid for three months. The state tried to overcome problems in service delivery by forming an alliance with local workers and communities. The initiatives brought pressure on local municipalities from above and below, to improve their performance in public health, agricultural extension, drought relief and building infrastructure such as schools. Here we focus only on public health.

The new government took measures that reduced the share of salaries to 45 per cent in 1991, while federal transfers were decreasing (Tendler, 1997). Only a few years after the rural preventive health programme started, vaccination coverage for measles and polio had tripled from a low of 25 per cent to 90 per cent of the child population, and infant mortality had fallen from 102 to 65 per 1,000 live births. For these achievements, Ceara was awarded (in 1993) the UNICEF Maurice Pate prize for child support programmes, the first Latin American government to win it.

The programme involved the hiring of 7,300 workers (mostly women) as community health agents at the minimum wage, and 235 half-time nurses to supervise them. Before the programme started, only 30 per cent of the state's 178 municipalities had a nurse, and no doctor or health clinic. Before the programme, there was hardly any public health programme. At best, the mayor had an ambulance at his disposal and kept a small stock of prescription medicines at his home, which were given to friends and relatives in return for political loyalty. Four years later, the programme started in almost all of the state's municipalities.

A three-way dynamic between the community, the local government and the central government emerged in each of the programmes.[9] Tendler rightly states that 'the enthusiasm about decentralization in the development community today portrays local government and civil society as locked in a healthy two-way dynamic of pressures for accountability that results in improved government. Central government in this scenario has retreated to the place of an enabling bystander' (Tendler, 1997: 15). Ceara, however, revealed a three-way dynamic that included an activist central government, in addition to the local government and civil society.

A feature of the programme was the use of health agents, who visited households to provide advice and assistance on oral rehydration therapy, vaccination, antenatal care, breastfeeding and growth monitoring. The agents also collected data for health monitoring purposes. Even though the health agents did not earn more than the minimum wage and worked under temporary contracts without job security or fringe benefits, they achieved important health gains.

The presence of an effective central state authority is evident from a number of facts. The state-level authority insisted on hiring people based on merit. Although the jobs paid only the minimum wage and came with no fringe benefits, the position was seen as desirable as it was a year-round rather than a seasonal job. Municipalities that achieved the highest immunization coverage were awarded prizes, that added to the prestige of agents in the communities.

Funds and functionaries were transferred the local authority. The new Brazilian constitution of 1988 increased mayors' access to revenues for health expenditures, as it increased federal transfers to the municipalities in an earmarking of revenues on a per capita basis for health as well as education (as we discuss further in Chapter 9). This demonstrated that the municipality was being empowered with funds. Further, state government's health department took the responsibility for hiring the health agents, and left the hiring of nurses to supervise the health agents for each municipality – thus there was an element of functionaries and functions being transferred to the municipality.

There was other evidence that functions were transferred to the municipal employees. Public health paraprofessionals' primary task is preventative care, but they were also authorized to provide some simple curative care, normally the monopoly of nurses and doctors. The state motivated these grassroots workers by publicizing their work and offering much official recognition for their services (including achievement awards). Workers carried out a larger variety of tasks than usual, and often voluntarily, being able to do this because they had greater autonomy and discretion than usual. The extra tasks of the Ceara cases were not simply slapped onto existing jobs without reason. Second, the greater discretion and responsibilities – which ordinarily are seen to make supervision even more difficult in bureaucracies, and make corruption and bribery easier – did not happen on account of two kinds of pressures. Workers wanted to perform better in order to live up to the new trust placed in them by their clients, itself the product of the more customized arrangements of their work and the public messages of respect from the state.

Voice was also ensured. The public information campaigns by the government about these programmes had provided citizens with new information about their rights to better government and how public services were supposed to work. A message was given to applicants who were not chosen for the job of health agent: they were encouraged to make sure that the health agents followed the rules of the programme. The rules were that the health agents had to live in the area in which they worked, work eight hours a day, and visit each household at least once a month. Thus, the community made sure that health agents performed well.

More recent data suggest that the achievements of the state were sustained. Between 1997 and 2001, IMR fell from 40 to 26 per 1,000 live births. The rate of exclusive breastfeeding for the first four months of life increased from 46 to 61 per cent, and the incidence of child malnutrition was halved from 14 to 7 per cent. The availability of childcare services for 4–6 year olds jumped from 66 to 78 per cent.

Participatory budgeting in Brazilian cities

Our second example of successful decentralization also comes from Latin America: the successes resulting from participatory budgeting in Porto Alegre (capital of the state of Rio Grande de Sul) in Brazil. While earlier chapters have discussed the capture of national-level public spending (especially for social services) by elites, there is rather limited empirical evidence in regard to the degree of capture of governments at lower levels – and this is clearly an area for further research. However, the successful experience with deep democratic decentralization in the city of Porto Alegre, in place since 1989 (i.e. around the same time as the Ceara state innovations began), has spread to many other cities in Brazil and to other Latin American countries – and has indeed been much studied (Baiocchi, 1999; Avritzer, 2000). The constitution of Brazil of 1988 had permitted a great deal of decentralization of resources to the municipalities. The Partido dos Trabalhadores (Workers' Party), after introducing participatory budgeting to Porto Alegre, won elections in 1992 and 1996 in several major cities (São Paulo, Santos, Belo Horizonte, Campinas, Vitoria) and introduced the same participatory budgeting through direct political participation by local citizens.[10] Only a confident state authority can consider encouraging this level of accountability from the executive to the local people. In other words, the accountability runs not vertically, but horizontally out to the people.

It is assumed that the functions that the participatory budgeting process is considering are already in the purview of the municipal authority, and that the functionaries are responsible to the authority. The meetings between the citizens and the functionaries of the executive discuss investment priorities across thematic areas – education, health, transportation, taxation, city organization and urban development – and also review accounts, evaluate past investments, and elect representatives to the Participatory Budget (PB) council.

The most remarkable aspect of the process is the manifestation that 'voice' takes. The process involves two rounds of regional assemblies (since the city is divided into sixteen regions), one round of intermediary meeting and the functioning during the whole year of the PB council. The annual assembly of the sixteen regions in March assesses the previous year's budget and elects representatives to participate in weekly meetings for the next three months to work out the region's spending priorities for the coming year. The three months spent preparing for the second regional assembly involve neighbourhood consultations on issues such as transportation, sewerage, land regulation, daycare centres and health care, and these findings are reported at the second assembly. At the second assembly, two delegates are elected to represent the region in the PB council, to work for five months on formulating the city budget. On 30 September every year, the annual municipal budget is presented to the mayor, which the mayor can accept or remand to the council by his veto.

The council can then amend the budget or override the mayoral veto with a two-thirds vote.

The result is that the technical staff of the executive of the city administration have been subjected to a profound learning process: their technical recommendations must be conveyed in an accessible manner; their case must be demonstrated persuasively, not in an authoritarian fashion; and no alternative solution may be excluded without its infeasibility being demonstrated. A techno-bureaucratic culture has been superseded by a techno-democratic culture (de Sousa Santos, 1998).

The political contract exists between the executive and the community; it does not exist with the legislature. In fact the relationship between the PB and the legislature of the city has been one of constant conflict. According to the constitution, it is the legislature that should approve the municipal budget. Now the PB has pre-empted this responsibility. It does indeed go to the legislature, but since it has already been legitimated by the participation of citizens mobilized by the PB, the legislature's approval is a mere formality. However, the fact is that the legislature had never actually deliberated substantially on the budget. The budget did not indicate the concrete works to be carried out, and hence the executive had considerable leeway in terms of its implementation. This also created the opportunity for legislators to influence the implementation in a clientilist manner. The votes they gathered from their constituency were directly entailed to the works they managed to include in the budget. The PB system ended this clientilist regime, which has put the legislators in a conflictual situation with the PB and the executive.

Another form that 'voice' takes is where several civil society organizations provide political momentum through various meetings and raising awareness, advocating and researching for common community objectives.

The most important outcome of this process of deepening of democratic decentralization, in the form of participatory budgeting, is the output indicators of service delivery. The proportion of the city population with access to water and sanitation increased from 49 per cent in 1989 – when the experiment began – to 98 per cent for water and 85 per cent for sanitation in 1996. The number of students enrolled in elementary or secondary schools also doubled during this period. Presumably the children of the non-poor were already in school, just as the non-poor already had safe water and sanitary means of sewage disposal; hence it is the poor who benefited. One-half of the unpaved streets were paved during this period. Many slums were urbanized. All of this was rendered possible by a 48 per cent increase in local revenue collection.

Schooling: collective voice and state action in Madhya Pradesh and Rajasthan

Like Brazil, India has a federal structure, with two tiers of government, the centre and the states. However, since 1993 India has had a fairly successful decentralization to local governments, which had been moribund since the 1950s. The political commitment with which decentralization has been implemented in the different states has varied enormously. However, two states have enabled the 'voice' of the people to be articulated, Madhya Pradesh and Rajasthan, and in sectors like school education where functions have been effectively transferred to the local authority the results have been remarkable. Madhya Pradesh was the first state to put the newly resurrected system of local government, the *panchayati raj institutions* (PRI) into effect (after the enabling constitutional amendment was passed by the Indian parliament in 1993).[11] A working PRI system was in place in Madhya Pradesh in 1994. It is a facilitating structure for direct community action. The government converted selected programmes, of which primary education was one, into a mission-mode.

Madhya Pradesh and Rajasthan are two of the most populous states in India, and with four other northern states[12] account for two-thirds of the children out of school in the country. However, in the 2001 Census of India (a decennial event), Madhya Pradesh showed an increase of 20 percentage points in its literacy rate (from 44.2 to 64 per cent), the highest increase of any state (along with Rajasthan) during the period 1991–2001. Clearly, the two governments were doing several things right. What were they?

Of the three prerequisites of successful democratic decentralization – an effective state authority; an empowered local body to which functions, functionaries and finance have been transferred by the state authority; and voice of the citizenry – not all were necessarily present in these two states. In the federation of India, education is a state subject, as opposed to a federal (or central) government subject according to the Indian constitution. There is little doubt about the competence of the state authorities, and the first prerequisite probably exists in all the state governments of the country. Despite the fact that the constitutional amendment calls upon state governments to transfer functionaries to the local bodies, most state governments have been loath to do so. Finance, too, has not in most cases been transferred for the school system to the local authority, but, as we shall see below, for the purposes of creating new school funds were indeed transferred to the local body to respond to community demand.[13] However, despite such flawed decentralization, there has been remarkable change because of the three-way dynamic between the state government, transfer of functions to local authorities, and the state creating mechanisms for the articulation of the voice of the citizenry. In other words, even a weak form of deep democratic decentralization can improve governance, and produce tangible results in terms of delivery in basic services.

In *Madhya Pradesh*, instead of academic institutions or the Central Statistical Organization conducting a sample survey, this democratic decentralization opened an opportunity to undertake a door-to-door survey in 1996 by teachers and elected people's representatives to discover the names of children in and out of school. Ironically, this survey was carried out as part of a centrally financed primary education programme (DPEP)[14] – which drives the point home about the difference between taking *enabling action* by the state and *empowering the community*. While most states in India took the enabling action of creating the PRI system, none took as much empowering action as Kerala and Madhya Pradesh.

The village council (panchayat) leadership was seen by the Madhya Pradesh state government as the key player. There were three differences with regard to previous practices. First, instead of using schoolteachers for data collection, the responsibility was widened to a local group including local panchayat representatives and literacy activists. Second, the idea was not just to collect information on which children were in school (from school statistics), but on which children (5–14 year olds) from the village were not in school. Third, the objective in surveying children was not one of statistics collection but to lead the motivational campaign to persuade parents to send their children to school (Gopalakrishnan and Sharma, 1999). It was, in other words, intended to consolidate community management of the primary education system in the state.[15]

A remarkable conclusion – with significant policy implications – emerged from the participatory survey. It is well known that government school-based statistics of enrolment in India are grossly exaggerated, showing inflated enrolment. However, most 'out of school' children contacted through the survey described themselves as 'unenroled' rather than 'dropped out'. The policy implication was that, in addition to the problem of drop-out (which, though not non-existent, may be much smaller than believed hitherto), the major problem is that children have *never* gone to school.

In other words, access to schools is itself a problem – despite past claims hitherto that the norm of provision of one school within a one kilometre distance had been met for 95 per cent of India's children. The policy response of the state government was to introduce a scheme (from January 1997) to guarantee primary schools to all hamlets – not just all villages (given that a village consists of a number of discrete hamlets). Under the scheme (called the Education Guarantee Scheme), if the parents of forty children in a locality (only twenty-five in a tribal area) seek a school for their children, routed through the village panchayat (elected council), the state government is committed to provide, within ninety days, a lower-paid teacher's salary for the purpose.[16] The village panchayat can appoint the teacher from within the community, and it has also to make arrangements for space where the children can be organized into classes. The state government will transfer funds to the village council to enable it to pay the salary of the new teacher recruited from within the community.

The results have been remarkable. While 80,000 schools had opened in the fifty years since independence in Madhya Pradesh as part of the regular government primary school system, 30,000 new schools were created within three years of the scheme's announcement (after January 1997). What is particularly important is that it led to a huge increase in enrolment of tribal children – the very children who had among the lowest enrolment rates among vulnerable groups. It also led to a larger than proportionate increase in girls' enrolment.

The features of the scheme offer profound lessons for other similar situations around the world. The expansion of schools and enrolment was the outcome of a mutually dependent action by the state government, local government and the community. The community's demand for a school ('collective voice') is the initial premiss of government action. Even the provision of a school is a reciprocal action, with the community recommending the teacher from among its local people and the state government remunerating and training her, the community providing space for the centre, the state government providing educational and other contingency materials.

Another state that made remarkable strides during the 1990s is the northwestern state of *Rajasthan*. Literacy rates between Census 1991 and Census 2001 rose by over 22 percentage points (from to 38.5 to 61 per cent), slightly more than Madhya Pradesh. This is again remarkable because, like Madhya Pradesh, Rajasthan is known to be a backward state in respect of every human development indicator.[17]

The processes that led to this achievement in Rajasthan are rather similar to those in Madhya Pradesh. What started as projects – Shiksha Karmi in 1987 and Lok Jumbish in 1992 – became state-wide processes. Both these projects began before the creation of the PRIs down to the village level. In other words, unlike in Madhya Pradesh, where the process began well after the creation of PRIs (constitutional amendment of 1993), in Rajasthan the process began earlier but has been deepened by the PRIs. *All the measures involved an interaction between the state government, the local government and the community.* First, as in Madhya Pradesh, school mapping, carried out with full community participation, is a feature. It was adopted as a means of offsetting the weaknesses of central planning, as manifested by over four decades of failure to universalize schooling. The state has a difficult topography, with large parts of it being a desert. In fact, what school mapping in Rajasthan does is to substitute macro-planning by a central body located in the state capital with micro-planning by the affected community itself. It not only identifies the children out of school – as opposed to counting those in school, as is done in the administrative recording system with highly inaccurate and usually inflated enrolment rates – but it also ensures community mobilization. In other words, it goes beyond the traditional approach to school mapping, which approaches it simply as an exercise in locating schools based on quantitative criteria (Singh, 2000). Instead, it is a means of generating demand for schooling in communities where the vast majority of parents are illiterate, and in such households the child will not necessarily go to school when attaining school-going age (Ramchandran, 1998; Ramachandran and Sethi, 2001).

This is a programme essentially to provide schooling by ensuring the creation of a school in school-less communities or by making an existent but dysfunctional school function again. This requires the hiring of two locally available teachers to substitute for the regular primary school teacher who is frequently absent. It also requires the opening of new schools in school-less habitations.

The Village Education Committees (VECs) are one critical element of voice in the programme. Members of the VEC are selected in the village council (i.e. the local authority). Village-level bodies have been known in the past to be dominated by the power-elite (usually landed, upper-caste, men); hence they are required by the government to give representation to all hamlets, most castes, women and even parents of children not of school-going age. The VEC participates in school mapping, taking decisions in regard to location and schedule of schools; monitoring participation of children in day schools; ensuring availability of textbooks for all children, especially those belonging to poorer sections of society; making regular visits to schools to ensure their regular functioning; obtaining contributions in cash and kind from the community to improve the physical infrastructure and environment of the local school; advising and motivating teachers, also bringing lack of performance to the notice of higher authorities (Singh, 2000).

It is important to emphasize that this programme is not run by an NGO. The transfer of functions is reflected in the fact that it is implemented by a board, an autonomous agency under the control of the state education minister. After the setting up of the elected panchayat structure, links were developed with elected representatives at different levels.

What Rajasthan and Madhya Pradesh demonstrate is that in two of the poorest and most educationally backward states of low-income India, with the worst social indicators in the country, it is possible to transform schooling for the poor – provided the local government functionaries are mobilized in a participatory manner, and government structures, at both state and local levels, are made to respond to collective pressure from the people.

The right to information: the steel frame of deep democratic decentralization

If deep democratic decentralization is to succeed, and the articulation of voice enabled, it will be greatly facilitated by a Right to Information Act – and the abolition of the Official Secrets Act. An Official Secrets Act was operative in almost every country under British colonial rule (and in all anglophone countries). Laws to promote secrecy, instituted by the colonial rulers, were intrinsic to an authoritarian regime, intended for surplus extraction, and have been adopted by post-colonial states. They survive through inertia and create the ambience for graft and corruption under the veil of secrecy.

Sweden was one of the first countries with laws providing freedom of information. Similarly the right to information is also recognized in laws passed in Finland, Norway, Denmark, Canada, Australia and the USA (Sachar, 1999). However, the first problem is that in most low-income countries the right to information has not been recognized in law. In India, Pakistan and Sri Lanka civil society actors have succeeded in the past few years in providing government with a blueprint for right-to-information legislation. In Pakistan, the draft ordinance was passed in a highly watered-down form by the caretaker Leghari government in the mid-1990s and then allowed to lapse by a new government. Nepal has the right to information guaranteed as a fundamental right in the constitution but it has not been used much on account of the ignorance of people about their rights. In India a Right to Information Act was passed in 2005 and is already being used to enforce accountability of corrrupt and indifferent officials throughout the country.

The further problem in a largely illiterate village in a low-income country is how the poor will muster the courage to seek out information – assuming that a right to information was recognized in law. Perhaps the way around the problem is that the village council meetings should be the forum where the documents – once made available – are publicly discussed.[18]

A Right to Information Act can enhance the transparency and efficiency of public services generally, and of basic services delivered by the state in particular. Thus, for example, the school-level allocation of resources in Uganda and in Himachal Pradesh (India) is made public by being posted on the school noticeboard (Govinda, 2002; Reinikka and Svensson, 2002). Deep democratic decentralization, as defined above, coupled with the actual use of the right to information would be a good mechanism for ensuring accountability of government functionaries. In other words, it is not just that government programmes for basic services (health, education, water and sanitation) and poverty alleviation have to be delivered through directly and democratically elected village and local councils. To ensure the accountability of local functionaries, the community needs to have access to all relevant documents pertaining to those projects and programmes.

Health: accountability to the community in sub-Saharan Africa

Mobilizing voice in the health sector has also helped to rejuvenate health services (Mehrotra and Jarrett, 2002). Serious disruption to public health systems occurred during the 1980s in most sub-Saharan countries, when a severe international economic recession and financial indebtedness led to structural adjustment measures in many countries and a marked reduction in the state's role in the provision of services (Chabot et al., 1995). One approach to this crisis lay in the greater mobilization of community resources in the development of local health services, recognizing that patients seeking care were already beginning to pay considerable sums of money for treatment of various kinds. This was the situation in which the Bamako Initiative arose in 1987 – leading in many countries to a reasonably successful example of voice ensuring access to affordable essential health services for an increasing proportion of people (Jarrett and Ofusu-Amaah, 1992).

The Bamako Initiative (BI), implemented to varying degrees in half the countries in sub-Saharan Africa and fewer countries in Latin America and Asia since the late 1980s, has shown that organized communities can help sustain local public health services, not only by contributing financial re-sources but also by having 'voice' in the management of services. The strategy of the BI is to revitalize public health systems by *decentralizing decision-making from the national to the district level*, instituting community financing and co-management of a minimum package of essential services at the level of the basic health units. The aim is to improve services by generating sufficient income to cover some local operating costs such as the essential drug supply (often imported with donor-provided foreign exchange), salaries of some support staff, and incentives for health workers. Funds generated by community financing do not revert to the central treasury but remain in the community or the facility, and are controlled by it through a locally elected health committee. Thus a revolving pool of funds helps to sustain the health service. From mere recipients of health care, consumers become active partners whose voices count.

Like the Madhya Pradesh and Rajasthan cases, the BI, spread across dozens of countries, demonstrates that dysfunctional public service delivery can be revived and rejuvenated when local institutions are strengthened (in this case with some donor support), and the community is directly involved in the decision-making process. The BI has not functioned within an environment of comprehensive decentralization of government – unlike the earlier cases examined in this chapter. However, finance has been transferred to the locally elected health committee. Although functions are still performed by the health provider employed by the ministry of health, the functionary is accountable to the community.

After ten years of implementation of the Initiative, community action in most rural health centres in Benin and Guinea not only enabled nearly half the population to be regular users of the services but also raised and sustained immunization levels close to the Year 2000 Health for All target levels (Levy-Bruhl et al., 1997). Charging a modest fee to users is seen in some cases to be the most affordable option for the poorest segments of the population, who otherwise have to access more expensive alternatives, although it is less clear whether mechanisms exist to protect indigent members of the community. Much of the success was in ensuring the supply of affordable essential drugs that are readily available in the health centres, under the scrutiny of the committees. Another factor was the improved attitude of health workers, traditionally one reason for people, especially women, not to use the service.

Recent assessments have shown that community participation in the Bamako Initiative has actually not been as well defined as originally thought, and that significant community empowerment has not taken place. 'Induced' participation, pushed in many cases by donor demand and often based on political decisions or bureaucratic simplicities, tends to accentuate elite groups in communities, marginalizing women and the spontaneous organizations that are already formed to cope collectively with local problems.

However, even with a relatively weak voice exercised by households and communities, and even in the absence of comprehensive decentralization, significant outcomes have been achieved. It would appear that voice needs to be associated with the retention and use locally of locally generated resources and that these go to improving the health service and achieving sustained outcomes. Greater emphasis, however, needs to be put on working with existing local organizations and motivating their participation in the running of services.

To round off this discussion of local participation: in a classic study of 150 local organizations from developing countries, Esman and Uphoff (1984) gave scores for rural development performance. It was found that local organizations were the most successful, with the highest scores, when the organization was started by local leaders.[19] Yet when outside agencies, either government or NGOs, focused their efforts on building local capacity rather than creating local organizations to implement external programmes, the scores were nearly as high when local organizations were started by local leaders.

7.4 Summing up

1. To have expected accountability from the post-colonial state was to expect the impossible. Despite new constitutions, the post-colonial state was merely superimposed on the structure of the colonial state. The latter was organized along lines intended for surplus extraction; accountability or transparency was not its objective. In fact, it was authoritarian, surplus-extractive, but low on corruption, especially in the top echelons of government. The top bureaucracy lack of corruption had a largely salutary effect on the middle and lower levels. This structure was replaced by a (usually) democratic one, but reliant upon rent-seeking for personal enrichment. The only hope there is for making such a structure accountable is deep democratic decentralization. Within the capability approach, the complex functioning of participation presupposes that needs be contextualized *at the level of the community* – through collective voice and collective action – to have operational use. Unless the capability approach is thus extended conceptually, it is unlikely that the simple functionings (e.g. the ability to read and write) will be realized, even in democratic states.

2. Deep democratic decentralization implies three concepts: (i) democracy at the national level; (ii) decentralization of key functions related to service delivery to local governments; and (iii) institutions and mechanisms to enable the collective voice of the community in the jurisdiction of the local government. Increasingly in the developing world most states now have democracies, especially since the mid-1980s. In the 1990s the number

of states that have adopted some form of decentralization of powers and responsibilities (though much less of taxing authority) has also increased. In the vast majority, the last prerequisite is almost entirely missing. Without all three, states will not finally lose the characteristics they inherited from the colonial state of being a structure-in-itself and accountable to powerful networks at national and local levels.

3. The objective of deep democratic decentralization is to enable the community to participate in a collective manner so that the local-level government functionaries can be made to deliver services as mandated by the central and state governments. In other words, we are not recommending that non-governmental bodies start to deliver services; rather, that voice improves the effectiveness of the delivery of services by the state.

   A significant role for the central government here is: (a) to create local government bodies which can be so influenced, since the effectiveness of programmes or services delivered by central or state governments in a vertical manner is lower than when the same programmes are delivered by local governments; (b) to mandate that local government functionaries, both elected and appointed, are accountable to the local community through mechanisms that are reasonably transparent.

4. Decentralization should involve a substantive role for local governments to be responsible and accountable for the delivery of basic social services (e.g. water and sanitation, basic education, basic health, nutrition supplementation for pregnant mothers and under-5s, midday meals in schools). The evidence presented from a variety of regions of the developing world suggests that deep democratic decentralization does help to improve the delivery of services. Only hierarchical control of functionaries in vertical line ministries is rarely effective in service delivery. Since the poor have little choice of 'exit' (in the Hirschman (1970) sense), 'voice' alone works.

5. The articulation of collective voice can take a variety of forms and use different mechanisms. Whatever forms it takes, where it is successful in achieving the goals it is premised upon a three-way interaction between the central, the local and the community – of a mutually interdependent nature.

6. A critical ingredient of deepening democratic decentralization is the right to information. Legislation is required to place the right to information in the hands of ordinary citizens. But, even more importantly, information about use of funds allocated for various services for each local government needs to be openly placed in the public realm – whether it is for a health centre, a school or a water facility.

8

Promoting complementarity between public and private provision

In the last quarter-century there have been reversals from the policies of universal provision of basic services by the state, which had become dominant since World War II. These reversals have been characterized by efforts in social policies to expand the use of market mechanisms such as insurance, private pensions and user charges. This process has also been accompanied, at least in developing countries, by greater acceptance of the role of civil society and community organizations as elements of a formal system of welfare provision which the state can support and promote.

This welfare pluralism was born of the conservative tide of attacks on the welfare state in industrialized countries, and of the budget deficits and structural adjustment in developing countries. This welfare pluralism takes the clock back to an earlier historical era when social advances and capabilities enhancement proceeded at a much slower pace than during the decades of state-led welfare provision (i.e. the period up to 1980).

In much of Europe, in the first half of the nineteenth century, private providers dominated health, education and water services. But these services were limited. In the second half of the nineteenth century public financing and provision became predominant. Indeed, only when governments intervened did these services, especially health insurance and compulsory schooling, become universal in Western Europe and the northern USA (as discussed in Chapter 2) – in the last quarter of the nineteenth and first half of the twentieth century. The experience of the now-industrialized countries suggests that the sequence for social services should be comprehensive provision by the state early on, followed by more targeted interventions to reach the unreached, and then public–private partnerships to serve different markets – depending upon the nature of services in different sectors.

We have endeavoured to make the case for universalism in the provision of basic services in developing countries. On the one hand, we do not deny the role of multiple actors, but, on the other, we reject state abdication in the presence of pre-existing markets that is typical of neoliberal reforms. Having discussed the level, equity and efficiency of public spending on basic services and the effectiveness of service delivery in the preceding four chapters, the following three chapters are devoted to policies for mobilizing additional resources for basic services – private ones in this chapter, domestic resources for public social services in Chapter 9, and external ones in Chapter 10.

In section 8.1 we discuss why private provision might have increased in developing countries in recent decades. In the following three sections we discuss the role of non–governmental (private and NGO) providers of social services – first in education (section 8.2), then in health (section 8.3) and then in water and sanitation (section 8.4). An appraisal of the current impetus towards privatization in social services from the donor community and the implications of the General Agreement on Trade in Services (GATS) are found in section 8.5. Section 8.6 concludes the chapter.

8.1   Why has private provision increased?

Three factors seem to have driven the private sector's growing role in health and education, and the push to privatize water and hospital services: lack of government resources, low–quality public provision and pressure to liberalize the economy.

One of the reasons why governments have been unable to provide social services effectively or fund large investments in infrastructure is their budget deficits, which grew so large that many governments were forced to adopt structural adjustment programmes, based on IMF and/or World Bank lending. Privatization of public utilities is often pursued with a view towards obtaining revenue, but the biggest returns to government come from eliminating subsidies to loss-making public enterprises.

In some cases, such as domestic water and sanitation (and irrigation funds and energy) the problem of limited government funds has been compounded by distorted tariff structures. State-owned enterprises often charge tariffs that are too low to recoup costs, and user failures to pay tariffs are often overlooked. This approach is the hallmark of inequity, as it subsidizes the non-poor at the expense of the poor, as it is the latter who lack access. As urban populations grow, fiscally constrained local authorities cannot expand services to cover them. Everyone is a loser – as water services decline in quantity and quality in middle-class neighbourhoods, and at the same time fail to reach new poor neighbourhoods.

Second, the lack of resources is linked to a weak record of public provision in many countries. In government schools in India, Bangladesh, Papua New Guinea, Indonesia, Peru, Ecuador, Zambia and Uganda teacher absenteeism is frequent (anywhere from 13 to 26 per cent of teachers absent at any time) (Kremer et al., 2004). Poorly paid public-sector doctors often supplement their incomes by selling drugs intended for free distribution (Van Lerberghe et al., 2002). As a result, poor (and non-poor) people are forced to use private providers, because such providers are more accessible and often dispense drugs as part of their consultations (unlike government facilities, where drugs may not be available (Rohde and Vishwanathan, 1995). To access water, poor people often have to pay exorbitant prices for it from private tankers run by small vendors. Most residents of South Asian cities receive water through the municipal pipes for only a couple of hours at a time, and not every day (Leipziger and Foster, 2003).

The third source of encouragement to private provision and privatization came from the international financial institutions and from donors, as we noted in Chapter 2. The social services are seen as 'frontier areas' in privatization (see section 8.5 of this chapter).

Although we have provided many reasons for government financing and provision in the previous chapters, it is useful to reiterate here that it may be difficult to trigger the synergies among health, family planning, water and sanitation, nutrition and education inputs and outcomes without simultaneous investment in each. If the investment is left to the private sector, there is much greater risk of coordination failure than if the state was to provide the services, instead of merely financing them. This is not to say that private provision (and financing) should not play a complementary role; we are only making the case here for a lead role for the state.

Many bilateral and multilateral agencies are strongly advocating involving the private sector through public–private partnerships (PPPs) as a means of delivering better water and sanitation services, as well as health services. In the health sector, PPPs have multinational R&D-based drug companies as partners in supplying free and discounted drugs. Caines and Lush (2004) examined their involvement in four countries (Sri Lanka, Botswana, Uganda and Zambia) and concluded that these PPPs have facilitated better tropical disease drug availability very substantially, including to the poor – with negligible, if any, side effects.

The private sector's involvement in health, however, takes many forms, which we discuss later (including the domestic private sector). In the water sector, Sohail and Cotton (2001) did case studies of PPP in three South African cities, one Pakistani and one Kenyan city. They concluded that the poor are rarely mentioned at the outset when the PPP framework is drawn up; poor groups exert little pressure, and core issues in PPP development are financial and technical, and not those concerning poverty. We pick up these issues again later.

8.2   Education

This section begins by recalling the role of the public and private sectors in education in the now industrialized countries in a comparable period of development in the nineteenth century. It goes on to consider the role of the private sector in the so-called high-achieving countries. Third, the case for multiple providers in schooling put forward in recent years is examined. Finally, NGO provision in the school sector is assessed.

It was noted in Chapter 2 that there were a number of measures common to the industrialized countries examined (USA, Prussia/Germany, France and the UK):

- First, the state created a public system of schooling that was financed from taxes, and a rising tide of public investment in education was evident in all of them.
- Second, the state worked gradually towards the elimination of tuition fees.
- Third, the state made elementary education compulsory.
- Fourth, varying degrees of centralization emerged, with bureaucracies to run the public school system, including the training of teachers and the creation of an education department.

These measures were in the main taken in the second half of the nineteenth century, except in Prussia, the Netherlands and Switzerland in Europe, and northeastern USA, which were early starters. Countries that developed state-funded systems of public education early on (for instance, Prussia and the northern USA,[1] achieved higher levels of enrolment and literacy. Countries (for instance, England and Wales) with no public system until quite late fared worse in terms of those indicators.

'The history of mass primary and secondary schooling is dominated by the rise of public, not private supply. No high-income OECD country has relied solely on private demand and supply in education, least of all in primary schooling' (Lindert, 2004: 88). The source of some of the private supply was philanthropic or ecclesiastical, but it was the state that subsidized education even in the laggard UK. More important, it was where local government ensured tax-financed public schooling that mass schooling became possible. What is also clear is that there were no crowding-out effects from the increase in public education spending on private schooling. In other words, the rise of tax-based public schooling did not displace private schooling.[2]

Similarly, one can ask the question for high-achieving developing countries: how significant was the private sector in universalizing primary education? It is not as though the industrialized countries were unusual in that the state played a predominant role in universalizing primary education. A similar pattern prevailed in high-achieving developing countries as well, where primary education became universal early in their development process when incomes were still low.

Table 8.1 shows the share of students enrolled in private schools in some developing countries in 1965 and 1975, and also presents adult literacy rates for those countries for 1980, as well as averages for adult literacy for the corresponding regions. Several things stand out from the data.

First, private enrolments tended to be highest in Africa, both East and West, and were lower in Latin America and in Asia. Second, in most countries the private enrolment share declined between the mid-1960s and mid-1970s, presumably as public school systems expanded in the post-colonial period.

Third, and most important, by and large, countries that had literacy rates well above the regional average in 1980 were those where the share of private enrolment was low to begin with and remained low.[3] South Asia, Sri Lanka and, in East Asia, Korea and later Indonesia and Thailand, are seen as being high achievers in mass schooling; in all, the share of private enrolment is relatively low.[4] Similarly, in Africa, Botswana had very few students enrolled in private schools; and it is justifiably seen as a high achiever in schooling, having rapidly raised education indicators in the 1980s prior to the rapid rates of economic growth it experienced thereafter (Duncan et al., 1997). In Latin America, the contrast between the low private enrolment share at primary level in high achievers like Costa Rica and the high share in others like Guatemala and Haiti is worth noting.[5]

Table 8.1　Students enrolled in private schools (1965 and 1975) and adult literacy (1980) in some developing countries

Region/Country	Primary level (%)		Secondary level (%)		Adult literacy rate (%)
	1965	1975	1965	1975	1980
Asia					
Bangladesh	–	8	–	9	29
Indonesia	12	13	–	60	68
Republic of Korea	1	1	48	45	93
Philippines	4	5	66	38	89
Singapore	40	35	3	1	83
Sri Lanka	–	6	9	–	85
Thailand	13	11	50	32	88
Average of South Asia					38
Average of East Asia & Pacific					74
East & Southern Africa					
Botswana	4	5	10	30	58
Burundi	96	92	30	22	29
D.R. Congo	91	–	57	–	60
Ethiopia	25	25	15	–	20
Kenya	4	1	29	49	57
Lesotho	96	100	100	89	71
Madagascar	27	23	66	49	50
Malawi	77	10	5	13	46
Mauritius	34	28	77	6	74
Sudan	2	2	45	13	33
Swaziland	80	80	4	–	60
Tanzania	7	4	–	29	50
Zambia	–	24	4	2	62
West Africa					
Benin	40	5	54	18	18
Burkina Faso	34	7	38	43	11
Cameroon	61	43	73	57	45
Chad	12	10	7	6	33
Equatorial Guinea	–	24	–	3	67
Gabon	53	45	43	32	41
Gambia	–	16	54	46	25
Côte d'Ivoire	28	19	–	28	23

Region/Country	Primary level (%)		Secondary level (%)		Adult literacy rate (%)
	1965	1975	1965	1975	1980
Liberia	25	35	48	43	28
Mali	8	4	10	11	14
Niger	6	5	5	14	9
Nigeria	76	–	–	41	34
Senegal	13	12	22	–	22
Sierra Leone	–	78	–	87	20
Togo	40	29	55	16	33
Average of sub-Saharan Africa					40
Latin America & Caribbean					
Argentina	14	17	41	45	94
Barbados	–	9	26	21	96
Bolivia	26	9	26	24	70
Brazil	11	13	49	25	75
Chile	27	18	38	23	92
Colombia	14	15	58	38	85
Costa Rica	4	4	24	6	92
Dominican Republic	7	12	–	–	74
Ecuador	18	17	38	30	82
El Salvador	4	6	47	47	67
Guatemala	19	14	54	43	54
Haiti	26	42	43	76	31
Honduras	7	5	53	51	61
Jamaica	–	5	–	9	77
Mexico	9	6	29	25	83
Nicaragua	16	15	44	–	61
Panama	5	5	17	14	86
Paraguay	10	13	51	37	86
Peru	14	13	24	17	80
Suriname	–	65	57	52	88
Uruguay	18	17	17	–	95
Venezuela	13	11	23	18	84
Average of Latin America & Caribbean					80

Source: UNESCO, *Statistics Yearbook*, various years.

However, this is not to suggest that there are not exceptions to this general pattern of a high public share in enrolment and the early achievement of high literacy rates.[6] In addition, at the secondary level there are considerable variations among countries (including the high achievers) in respect of the degree to which private provisioning prevails. What is clear, however, is that at primary level most countries with high educational indicators ensured state provisioning early in their development.

This policy of state support in the so-called high achievers was not restricted to basic education but extended to all basic social services; in other words, these states did not rely upon a trickle down of the benefits of growth or a policy of 'unaimed opulence'. These countries, belonging to opposite ends of the political-economic spectrum in terms of macroeconomic policies, made early public investments in basic social services when incomes were still low (Mehrotra and Jolly, 1997) – as we have argued in Chapter 4.[7]

The recent thrust in favour of multiple providers in the area of social provisioning (deriving partly from new institutional economics)[8] has tended to ignore the historical experience of industrialized countries in the nineteenth century, as well as the more recent experience of the high achievers among developing countries.[9] It has relied rather on other kinds of arguments to press the case for a greater role for private providers in education.

A first argument for private expansion, made since the mid-1980s, relies on the scarcity of public funds. As budget deficits got out of hand in many African and Latin American countries in the 1980s, the IFIs in particular started making the case for private-sector expansion in the school system. The argument was that the private sector should be encouraged to substitute for public spending and public provisioning of schooling in developing countries. Teacher salaries, as we saw in the previous chapter, account for 90 per cent or more of primary public expenditure. Most developing-country governments still have budget deficits, and may not be recruiting teachers for government schools, since they have no means of paying for them – when, in fact, universal primary education is impossible without an increase in the number of teachers (Delamonica et al., 2004). Under these circumstances, governments, with their backs to the wall, may have little choice but to accept the expansion of the private school system. However, if this is the dominant reason for the growth of private schools, it seems to derive its legitimacy from a negative logic, rather than from any positive factors favouring the private sector.

However, given the fiscal squeeze on government education budgets, the balance between elementary and secondary education in public expenditure allocation will have to respond to prevailing conditions. If primary schooling has not been universalized (e.g. India), then allocating a high share of public spending to secondary education may be both inefficient and inequitable. But as primary education is universalized, the balance of public education spending is bound to – and in fact must – shift in favour of the secondary level. A study of sixteen developing countries shows that the countries with the highest share of private upper secondary enrolment are also those with the lowest overall enrolment rates (India, Indonesia, Zimbabwe). But in China, Malaysia, Jamaica and Thailand – all with relatively high total secondary enrolment rates – more than 90 per cent of direct expenditure on education reaches the public schools (UNESCO Institute of Statistics/OECD, 2002).

At the same time, a resource-constrained state cannot subsidize elementary education (i.e. grades 1–8) in the private sector, while the public sector is starved of funds. However, as Mehrotra et al. (2005) point out, that was exactly what was happening in India. In India, the private-aided (i.e. managed privately but receiving significant government funding) schools' share in enrolment tends to rise with the level of education: it is lowest at the primary level, rises sharply at the upper primary level, and is the highest at the secondary/higher secondary level. In fact, more than half of children at secondary/higher secondary level are in private (aided and unaided) schools.[10] This kind of subsidy to private schools tends to squeeze the funds available for public elementary schools.

A second argument made in favour of private schooling is that the private sector is a source of competition to public schools and will thus improve efficiency in the public school system. This argument is supposedly based on the empirical evidence from some developing countries suggesting that graduates of private secondary schools perform better in the labour market or that private schools provide better education.[11] The issue is, why do these advantages arise where they do? Hannaway (1991) suggests that private schools perform better because of greater school autonomy and the fact that they are more responsive to student and parent needs. Jimenez and Lockheed (1995) also found differences between private and public schools in management structure, and that private school principals had greater autonomy; greater interaction among teachers was encouraged and monetary rewards were provided for good teaching. In many developing countries, while there are some restrictions on the degree of autonomy that government schools can have, there is a case for greater autonomy being accorded to government schools through the decentralization process we were recommending earlier.

A third argument for greater private provision is based on the better cognitive achievement (as manifested in language and maths tests) of children in private schools compared with that of those in public schools, as indicated in several country studies. A number of papers emerged, largely from the World Bank, reporting a significant private school advantage in terms of cognitive achievement. Cox and Jimenez (1991) and Jimenez et al. (1991a, 1991b) studied Colombia, the Dominican Republic, the Philippines, Tanzania and Thailand, and found that the private school advantage (on maths scores) is in the range of 13 per cent in Colombia to 47 per cent in the Dominican Republic. In the same countries, Jimenez and Lockheed (1995) found that per pupil cost is lower in private schools. In any case this argument has been subjected to some methodological criticism and is not conclusive.

Bashir (1997) notes that these studies using single-level models seemed to show that private schools were more effective. However, studies using hierarchical or multi-level models do not show a clearly positive effect in favour of the private sector in developing countries.[12] In fact, as Bashir (1997) shows, regardless of whether ordinary least squares or multi-level models are used, the inclusion of peer group characteristics and certain school variables (which cannot be manipulated by policy) reduce, if not entirely eliminate, the private school advantage. These models tell us more about the possible variables that influence cognitive test achievement than the public–private comparison. Notwithstanding the range of possible variables influencing achievement that different studies come up with (including those cited above), very few that can be called 'school policy' variables have been shown to explain the variation in school outcomes. Carnoy (1999), Colclough (1997) and Parry (1997) provide similar conclusions.

Thus the case for multiple providers, although it cannot be easily brushed aside, loses much of its force in the light of empirical realities. Besides, the studies above usually relate to the secondary level of education (see, e.g., Jimenez and Lockheed, 1995). In any case, the private sector is likely to grow regardless of whether the government subsidizes it or not, as incomes grow. Therefore, at all levels – elementary, secondary and tertiary – there is a need for much better regulation of the private sector.

Despite its potential drawbacks, public funding of private schools can help in certain circumstances – particularly if governments have trouble paying the full costs (building schools, paying teacher salaries) required to achieve universal primary schooling. To ensure that children from poor families unable to pay school fees are able to attend private schools, governments could finance their education through vouchers. Colombia, for example, introduced a voucher system in response to a shortage of public secondary schools. This approach to public funding of private education can help expand schooling at lower cost for the government, because the only cost the government bears is the voucher. This is slightly different from a voucher system that enables families to enrol their children in the school of choice, public or private. To avoid giving windfall gains to the middle class, who customarily purchase private education, vouchers should be restricted to poor families – as in Bangladesh, Chile, Colombia, Puerto Rico and the UK (West, 1994; Kremer, 2003). Clearly, then, there is scope for promoting complementarity between the public and private sectors.

Moreover, there is a case for the growth of private supply of secondary school and tertiary school places; thus complementarity between the private and public sectors can be encouraged by letting the private sector concentrate on higher secondary and tertiary education, and, if public resources are scarce, the public sector should focus on the primary and junior secondary levels. While public expenditure focuses on primary education, and junior second-ary, in the majority of low income and lower-middle-income countries, even in such countries the private sector should be encouraged to provide access to those willing to pay for higher secondary and tertiary education. This is the path adopted by one of the early high achievers, South Korea. While most of the primary students were and still are enrolled in public schools, the majority of secondary- and tertiary-level students have from the 1950s onward been enrolled in private schools (Mason et al., 1980).

India: a case study

In India (as in other low-income countries) it is mainly the non-poor who are able to make their way past the elementary school barrier (8th grade) to enter secondary school.[13] The fact that a very significant proportion of total enrolment in India at the secondary level is in private schools only serves to confirm this hypothesis, given that out-of-pocket costs in private schools are higher than in public schools. Yet the decision to give a school a grant-in-aid – that is, convert it from private unaided to aided status – is not based on very well defined principles or objective criteria.[14] As Kingdon and Muzammil (2001) rightly note, many aided schools do not even fulfil all the conditions of recognition, and ultimately the decision is taken on political grounds.[15] Initially it is political pressure from the teachers of a particular private school that leads to it becoming part of the grant-in-aid list.

Two consequences for the rest of the Indian education system arise from this phenomenon of conversion of unaided to aided school (Mehrotra, 2006; Tilak and Gounden, 2006). One, it adversely affects the effectiveness of public schools; two, the outcome is inequitable since it increases subsidies to the non-poor. For one, the school stops charging its students fees. In other words, contrary to the principle that a fiscally squeezed state should be targeting its subsidies to the poor, the state actually stops cost recovery from a section of the population that is able to pay, and subsidizes them. For another, teachers are no longer accountable to either the parents or the private management, since their salaries come directly from the state government – a clearly worse outcome for the parents and children in accountability terms.

A second set of outcomes ensues for the state's spending on public education. Teachers begin to be paid government salary scales directly from the state government; that is, the salaries of teachers rise dramatically in most cases, since the majority of teachers in unaided schools receive salaries well below what government school teachers receive. In addition, while all other school recurrent costs were earlier being met from fees paid by parents, now they are met by the state. A significant proportion of government expenditure at the secondary level is devoted to this kind of subsidization of the non-poor.

There is a strong case for elimination of these subsidies for secondary private schools except under very strict conditions. Where grants to secondary schools already exist, they should only be extended provided there are some performance guarantees by the school management as well as teachers. The systems to provide grants-in-aid in other countries need to be studied and applied to suit the Indian context. Unless it can be demonstrated that the cost to the state per school place is lower for subsidizing a private school place rather than a state-school place, and the state has the regulatory capacity to comply with performance guarantees by the private school, it is unclear why such subsidies should be provided in any developing country; particularly if there are demonstrable adverse equity effects, as in the India case.[16]

NGO provision in education

In sub-Saharan Africa there is evidence of involvement of NGOs and religious organizations in the provision of formal school education. However, in Asia and Latin America, NGOs and intermediary organizations have traditionally offered non-formal education and adult literacy work. In Latin America NGOs have adopted a conscientization approach (*à la* Paulo Freire) in such non-formal educational work. In Asia, the exception to the emphasis on non-formal education is the large-scale provision of education in religious institutions (especially Hindu and Islamic ones in India, Bangladesh and Pakistan) and by NGOs (e.g. BRAC).

Another segment of non-governmental schools is that of the mission schools (run by Catholic or Protestant missions), which have a reputation for high educational standards in all South Asian countries and in many African countries. However, such schools are beyond the financial reach of the vast majority of the population in these countries. They tend to cater to the needs of the elite. In other words, equity is not a ground on which one can advocate for such mission-run schools.

In terms of equity and operational efficiency, there is very little evidence in respect of NGO provision of schooling. One of the best-studied examples is that of BRAC schools (Bangladesh Rural Advancement Committee), which are widespread and very successful in Bangladesh (Ryan and Taylor, 1999). Nevertheless, the BRAC schools are part of the non-formal system, catering to only three primary grades, and essentially feed children into the formal school system – a task at which they have been successful and cost-effective. However, it is unclear whether such schools could replace the formal, government school system.

In Africa, there is more evidence about self-help (e.g. harambee schools in Kenya) or so-called community-financed schools. The latter could be defined as private, but not for-profit or financed entirely from fees. In fact, the most salient characteristic of community financing is that at least some resources are gained as contributions from the wider community, and not just from the families of students. Bray (1997) presents evidence from a wide variety of African countries that, although such schools may be filling gaps (arising from lack of state provision), their effects on regional equity are adverse, and the burden of 'community financing' seems to bear heavily upon the poor. When one compares these phenomena with the remarkable success of appropriate policies adopted by the state (e.g. the success of Malawi after 1994 and Uganda after 1995, discussed in earlier chapters), one can only suggest that while the state should encourage NGO efforts which cater to the poor and are complementary to state efforts, such efforts also pose the burden on the state of regulating such schools effectively. In addition, the state also has the responsibility of regulating the for-profit private sector in education. To what extent the state has the regulatory capacity may vary from state to state, but the capacity for effective regulation of both the private for-profit and the not-for-profit sectors needs strengthening in most developing-country states.

8.3 Health

Around the world, clinical services are financed in four ways. Two are private – direct payment and voluntary private insurance; and two are public – compulsory (social) insurance, which is managed or regulated by government, and financing from general government revenues. These forms were discussed in Chapter 5. Moreover, there are three ways of *delivering* clinical services: private for profit, private not-for-profit (e.g. missionary hospitals) and public. It is with the first two forms of delivery that we are mainly concerned in this section.

As in the education sector, the World Bank has been encouraging welfare pluralism, especially in the delivery of health services. We have seen in Chapter 2 that the role of the public sector in the latter half of the nineteenth and early twentieth centuries in Europe in both clinical services as well as areas of public health was predominant, notwithstanding the welfare pluralism. To date, in northern and southern Europe government finance provides access to health services for the majority of the population; in Switzerland and the USA it is mainly private insurance; and in Germany and the Netherlands social insurance prevails (Normand, 1997).

The experience from the high-achieving countries, which managed to improve their health indicators early in their development process relative to other countries in their region, is not dissimilar. They provided universally available health services to all, paid out of government revenues. In many of those countries the relatively well-off opted out by taking private health insurance, or where private insurance services were not available (e.g. Sri Lanka, Kerala) by making direct payment to private providers. But for the vast majority of the population a universally available and affordable system, financed out of government revenues, functional at the lowest level, made effective by allocating resources at the lower end of the health system pyramid – these were the keys to high health status (Mehrotra, 1997).

Nevertheless, since the mid-1980s many countries that had very limited, or that had entirely banned, for-profit practice (e.g. Malawi, Tanzania and Mozambique) have been encouraging private providers by regulatory liberalization and fiscal incentives (not necessarily privatization of public hospitals). Besides, many low- and middle-income countries already have a substantial and thriving private sector – in Latin America, South Asia, Southeast Asia and, to a much lesser degree, sub-Saharan Africa. Correspondingly, a very significant proportion of health expenditure in all regions is private, as we have already seen in Chapter 6.

More than any other region, Latin America experienced in the 1990s an unprecedented transnationalization of its health sector. There has been an increase in the export of managed care from the USA, and its adoption in Latin America. Several multinational corporations (e.g. Aetna, CIGNA, AIG and Prudential) have entered insurance and health services, and they intend to assume administrative responsibilities for state institutions and to secure access to medical social security funds. About 270 million people in Latin America, 60 per cent of the population, receive cash benefits and health-care services paid for by, and often delivered by the employees of, social security funds. The three main ways that these corporations invest in Latin American health systems are through: (a) the purchase of already established companies in Latin America that are dedicated to the sale of indemnity insurance or of prepaid health plans; (b) association with other companies under the framework of a joint venture; and/or (c) agreements to manage social security and public-sector institutions. Penetration by multinational corporations in health of these social security funds is most advanced in Argentina and Chile, has begun in Brazil and is growing, and is in the process of diffusion in Ecuador (Iriart et al., 2001).

This transnationalization of the health sector has been encouraged by the IFIs. World Bank advocacy for the private sector began with its 1987 publication *Financing Health Services in Developing Countries*, which proposed four steps: (a) increase the amount patients pay for their own health care; (b) develop private health insurance mechanisms; (c) expand the participation of the private sector in health care; and (d) decentralize governmental health-care services (World Bank, 1990b). However, while a strategy of this kind ensures that government spending is focused on the most cost-effective interventions, it might still fail to ensure that the sector as a whole will operate in the most efficient manner, given the state's inability and often its unwillingness to perform appropriate regulatory functions. Later the Bank advocated public-sector financing, and possibly provision, for a package of basic preventive and curative services, while more complex services are left to the private sector (as argued in World Bank, 1993a).

The *World Development Report 1993* (on health) similarly states:

> In most circumstances…the primary objective of public policy should be to promote competition among providers – including the public and private sectors…. Competition should increase consumer choice and satisfaction and drive down costs by increasing efficiency. Government supply in a competitive setting may improve quality or control costs, but non-competitive public provision of health services is likely to be inefficient or of low quality.

In Chapter 6 we showed evidence that where appropriate sectoral policies are adopted (e.g. as in the high-achieving countries) problems of quality and efficiency in the public provision of basic services has not proven insuperable. There are plenty of examples of 'highly efficient public health centres and district hospital'. (World Bank, 1993a).[17] Indeed, there is also increasing evidence that efficiency and effectiveness are closely tied to governance issues, and we saw in the previous chapter that deep democratic decentralization has successfully addressed those problems in many locations. What evidence there is in respect of the claims the neoliberals make on behalf of the private sector in health, we examine briefly here.

The evidence on the standards of efficiency and quality in the private sector relative to the public sector is inconclusive (Mills, 1997; Bennett, 1997). First of all, the evidence is that there is very significant market segmentation between public and private sectors, which makes it necessary that case-mix and severity of disease are the same across services before they can be compared. If the public sector is treating rather different types of cases from the private sector, comparisons will be invalidated. Evidence is lacking in developing countries that make these kinds of controls.

Second, there is plenty of evidence of market failure. Bennett and Tang-charoensathien (1994) found that in India, South Africa, Thailand and Zim-babwe private-sector providers rely on relatively untrained staff with limited supervision from physicians. Studies also point out that over-servicing is a major problem in the private sector. A significant proportion of the hospitals and health facilities are in the hands of the private sector in Asia and Latin America, though preventive measures are largely the responsibility of the public sector (Berman and Rose, 1996). In Brazil there was a high rate of Caesarean sections in private maternity patients, explained by the financial pay-off for providers for operating rather than permitting a normal delivery (Barros et al., 1986). Similarly, Uplekar (1989) found that in a slum area of Mumbai drug prescriptions did not match WHO-recommended practices, and a larger number of more costly items was prescribed.

In China following the economic reforms, the collapse of the public health system has meant a near-marketization of the health system. Even public hospitals operate on a fee-for-service basis, since public expenditure on health has fallen drastically since 1980. Simultaneously, there has been a shift in focus from preventive to curative services, which has significantly increased drug sales, since the economic reforms began. Foreign companies have invested in about 1,500 drug-manufacturing ventures across the country. With limited access to professional services and aggressive drug production in an unregulated market, the result is irrational drug use – particularly among poor people.

Third, there is increasing evidence in many countries, both low and middle income, of rising costs and accumulation of technology. In 1993 drugs accounted for 52 per cent of China's health spending, compared with 15–40 per cent in most developing countries – contributing to unnecessarily high medical costs (Tomlinson, 1997). In Korea and Thailand the availability of certain high-technology equipment is the same or greater than that in most European countries, even though the level of per capita income is much lower (Yang, 1993; Nittaramphong and Tangcharoensathien, 1994). Where in Latin America managed care organizations have taken over the administration of public institutions, increased administrative costs have diverted funds from clinical services. To attract patients with private insurance and social security plans, Buenos Aires public hospitals hired management firms that receive a fixed percentage of billings, thereby increasing administrative costs. Similarly, administrative and promotional costs account for 19 per cent of Chilean managed care (ISAPRE) annual expenditures (Iriart et al., 2001).

Fourth, it is often claimed that an expanding private sector will reduce pressure on an overextended public sector, thereby freeing up capacity and resources in the system as a whole. The International Finance Corporation (the arm of the World Bank group promoting private-sector investment in developing countries), outlining its future strategic priorities, considered education and health as targets for the promotion of the private sector on precisely these grounds (IFC, 2002a). In fact, the IFC established a separate Health and Education Department in September 2001 (IFC, 2002b). However, as Bennett (1997) argues, there are no longitudinal studies examining changes in total funding levels in response to increased private-sector funding. Indeed, the IFC itself admits as much: 'By producing extra capacity in the sector as a whole, the public sector will be able to redirect its scarce resources to those most in need.... However, it [this argument] is undermined by a lack of any real evidence.' If anything, private-sector growth may lead to a withdrawal of inputs from the public to the private sector. Thus the growth of the private sector in Thailand in the 1980s and 1990s saw a drain of personnel away from an already stretched public sector (Sitthi-Amorn et al., 2001).

Finally, the effect of privatization of health services and the reliance on out-of-pocket financing is to worsen equity in health care. The most serious effect is that services are refused on account of inability to pay, and illness goes untreated. Thus, the concerns about managed care in Latin America are about restricted access for vulnerable groups, and reduced spending for clinical services as opposed to administration and return to investors. In Chile, about 24 per cent of patients covered under the new managed-care organizations receive services annually in public clinics and hospitals because they cannot afford co-payments (required under the managed care programme). Public hospitals in Argentina that have not yet converted to managed-care principles are facing an influx of patients covered by privatized social security funds. Self-management in Brazil and in Argentina's public hospitals requires competition for capitation payments from social security funds and private insurance, as well as co-payments. To apply for free care at public institutions, poor patients now must undergo lengthy means testing, with rejection rates averaging 30–40 per cent in some hospitals (Iriart et al., 2001). Meanwhile, those public hospitals in Argentina that have not yet converted to managed-care principles face an influx of patients covered by privatized social security funds; they had earlier faced barriers to access due to co-payments and private practitioners' refusal to see them because of non-payment by the social security fund. Also, Latin American managed-care organizations have attracted healthier patients while sicker patients shift to the public sector – undercutting the very notion of pooling of health risk and undermining any possibility of cross-subsidy from the healthier to the more vulnerable.

The results for health equity of privatization of health services and private-sector growth in health care are not dissimilar in the transition economies and in other developing countries. Thus, the impact of the transition to a 'socialist market economy' in China has been that the cost of health care increased rapidly due to health-worker salary increases, growth in drug spending, and an increasing use of expensive technology (at least in richer areas). Meanwhile, government spending on health trailed behind the salary increases, and the public health services started deriving an increasing share of their budgets from sale of drugs and user fees (Bloom, 1997). In household surveys in rural China, 35–40 per cent of people who reported that they had an illness did not seek health care for financial reasons (Hao et al., 1997). In the Kyrgyz Republic, more than half the patients referred to hospital were not admitted, as they could not afford hospital costs (World Bank, 1999a). In Vietnam, the average cost of hospital admission is the same as two months' wages, resulting loans and debts. Thus, in rural North Vietnam, 60 per cent of poor households were in debt, with a third citing payment for health care as the main reason (cited in Whitehead et al., 2001).

An increase in private medical practice and a huge growth in private pharmacies in developing countries are a further source of inequity in health. This arises from the irrational use of drugs, which raises costs and leads to drug resistance. In developing countries, drugs now account for 30 to 50 per cent of total health-care expenditure, while in industrialized countries they account for only 15 per cent (Velasquez et al., 1998). Those who cannot afford professional services are essentially catered to by pharmacies, which often do not follow prescribing regulations. This is especially the case in South Asia, China and parts of Africa. In India, 52 per cent of out-of-pocket health expenditure and 71 per cent of in-patient expenditure go to medicines and fees (Iyer and Sen, 2000). Pharmacies have a financial incentive to overprescribe and sell drugs, which leads to unnecessary drug use and the development of resistance to drugs. Vietnam has a high frequency of antibiotic resistance resulting from irrational drug consumption; two-thirds of those who reported illness in the previous four weeks had obtained medicines without consulting a medical practitioner (Tornqvist et al., 2000). In a poor region of Mexico, three-quarters of health-care visits led to inadequate treatment, particularly from traditional healers or drug retailers. If poor patients have overspent on unnecessary drugs, they may not be able to continue a regimen of drugs (e.g. for malaria or tuberculosis). Then the ingestion of these drugs would become infructuous, and the drug resistance can threaten a whole community. In the developing world there is widespread overprescription of antibiotics for cases of diarrhoea. In six Latin American countries a quarter of drugs bought from pharmacies required a prescription (as they needed medical follow-up), but were sold without one (Whitehead et al., 2001).

This evidence suggests that there is great need for regulation of the private sector in health services (as in education), for reasons both of protecting consumers and of containing costs. However, in most developing countries the government's health ministry normally has an extremely weak information system about the private sector (or, for that matter, about the public sector), underlining their inability (or unwillingness perhaps) to regulate the private sector. Bennett (1997) cites widespread regulatory failure in India in respect of the private sector, with the medical councils 'concerned more with protecting those whom they are supposed to be regulating than with protecting consumers. This problem is well recognized in the literature.' In fact, despite the widespread presence of private providers in South Asia, and the high level of private spending, regulation has failed abysmally in ensuring quality for the majority who access private providers (Rohde and Vishwanathan, 1995).

The evidence on the private sector can thus be summarized, partly following Bennett (1997). On efficiency/quality, the evidence on standards in the private sector relative to the public sector is inconclusive. At the same time, imperfect information on the part of patients may lead to severe market failures in health-care services. On increased resources for health, government commitment to maintaining existing public finance levels is essential if total health resources are to increase with greater private-sector entry. Private provision has also tended to raise costs. Finally, while consumer choice increases as a result of private provision, the implications for consumer welfare are ambiguous.

Case study: India

More than two-thirds of health expenditure in India is incurred in the private sector; this is hardly surprising given that four different studies have demonstrated that the private practitioner is the mainstay of rural medical care, consulted first (and exclusively in most cases) for 60–80 per cent of illness (Rohde and Vishwanathan, 1995). The health system in India is, for all practical purposes, privatized, and the results (except in parts of the country like Kerala) evident in the high child and maternal mortality and the life expectancy of 60.7 years. There are consequences for equity. Deolalikar and Vashishta (1996) found that for three income classes in India, the poorest (below an annual income of Rs 12,500) spent 24 per cent of income on health, while the richest spent 3.4 per cent, and those in the middle 7.6 per cent.

After independence from British rule in 1947, the government decided to abolish a course of study in modern medicine leading to a diploma in medical practice. The licentiates knew that they were meant to serve rural areas, which they did (Ramalingaswami, cited in Rohde and Vishwanathan, 1995). But the policymakers felt they were not good enough and decided that a university degree involving over five years of study, after twelve years of school, should be the minimum professional qualification to practise medicine in India. The result has been that, despite a vast public-health infrastructure, issues of access and equity are extremely serious. In rural India (as in much of rural South Asia), the first port of call of the sick is the uncategorized rural private practitioner, most often unlicensed, and not formally trained. As Ramalingaswami describes them:

> Even those formally trained in the indigenous systems prefer using allopathic medicines. They dispense, rather than prescribe, they are more approachable and responsive than the average government doctor, indulge in detailed conversation with patients in a culturally comforting manner, not lifesavers but alleviators of symptoms. The government health system, on the other hand, is surrounded by problems of physical distance, long waiting times, cursory examinations, no encouragement of dialogue, doctors often unavailable, counting the number of days to return to the urban centre. (Rohde and Vishwanathan, 1995: vi)

This rural private practitioner is helped by the existence of a very large pharmaceuticals industry and the presence of pharmacies at every corner. India is a leader in the world of drug production, with 65,000 licensed products and over 16,000 pharmaceuticals manufacturers licensed in the country. This can be contrasted with only 10 per cent of that number of

licensed drugs in a typical country in Europe and North America. The choice
of drugs by the rural private practitioners is made largely through interaction
with commercial pharmacies in neighbouring towns.

Both the practitioners themselves and their patients consider their practice
limited to minor illnesses, and their treatment is related to rapid relief from
symptoms rather than total cure of the malady. In other words, they are
functioning as primary health-care assistants, who refer the more serious
problems to other professionals, usually located in towns and cities.

An NGO, with government support, should take on the role of identifying, communicating with and improving the practice of rural practitioners.
This would reverse the current situation that neither the government nor
formally licensed practitioners are willing to recognize and improve rural
practice. Such an NGO could become self-financing through fees generated
from membership.

At the same time, a comprehensive list of essential drugs that could be
handled by rural practitioners using standard guidelines for diagnosis and
treatment would be another feature of this system of improved care. For
example, the Indian Rural Medical Association in West Bengal adopted a
WHO list of forty essential drugs for recommended use by its membership.
A simple, clearly written manual guides the practitioner, supplemented
with some training. Raising public expectation of receipt of essential drugs,
together with recognition of practitioners who agree to restrict the practice
to their use, will improve both quality and control. They should be free to
charge as desired, since the practitioners understand better the clientele, and
their ability to pay. Market forces would keep prices down. By discouraging
practices that raise costs to patients and are detrimental to good care, such
as overuse of injections, multiple medications for a given problem, and the
brief duration of treatment offered by most practitioners, health care can be
improved. Equity is not usually associated with these practitioners, but the
widespread distribution of such practitioners, their accessibility to the poor,
their willingness to extend credit to provide services or payment in kind
make an equitable outcome possible even in the private sector.

If the practitioner is a member of this organization that is symbolic of
medical quality, it will help increase the demand among practitioners for
participation in training. It will help the public recognize that the provider
is linked to a higher referral system. It would assure more timely referral of
patients to the level of technology they require, but also reduce overload on
secondary and tertiary facilities (which are often providing primary health
care to many health seekers concurrently).

NGO provision of health services

Apart from for-profit providers, there has been an increase in service provisioning by *civic organizations* in sub-Saharan Africa and parts of South Asia. In India and most of Latin America the non-state sector is not a major actor in direct provision, but plays an advocacy role. The main types of organization are northern and southern NGOs, religious organizations, self-help groups, trade unions, business and professional associations, and non-profit health-maintenance organizations (Green, 1987). Non-state provisioning is most prevalent in sub-Saharan Africa, where churches, NGOs and self-help groups are quite active. NGOs and medical foundations are more prevalent in Asia, in a situation where, as we saw, private provisioning is quite high in curative services. In Latin America, trade unions, business and professional organizations play some role in health-care provision, in a context where state and private for-profit provision are dominant (Zuckerman and de Kadt, 1997).

As with the for-profit private sector, evidence in respect of efficiency, equity and quality of the non-profit private sector in health is anecdotal, and research studies are limited. Comparative assessments of government versus civic provisioning of health and education are almost non-existent (Robinson and White, 2001). However, the poor quality of public health (and education) services in Africa compelled several governments in the early 1990s to reconsider their attitude towards NGOs and church organizations. Controls on voluntary provisioning were abolished and official encouragement was extended to churches and NGOs. External considerations influenced these processes, as bilateral and multilateral aid agencies influenced policymaking and extended assistance to NGOs, and incentives increased for private provision as well. As a result, NGOs have now become an important source of health provisioning in Africa, in many cases with the active support of official donors (Green and Mathias, 1995).

There are few studies assessing the quality of care in the non-profit sector. Bennett (1997) suggests that private non-profit providers may be more efficient relative to the public sector. Gilson et al. (1994) state that a major justification of civic provision of health services is that they are of higher quality than either public- or private-sector providers, but they note that 'available evidence is limited and variable'. Many NGO health projects depend upon expatriate staff, who may have the requisite skills but find it difficult to integrate with local government health services. It is difficult to replicate or sustain health programmes in a situation where an NGO concentrates its efforts in one area, with large external resources and expatriate involvement (Walley et al., 1991).

There are few studies comparing civic providers of health and the public sector on operational efficiency. One of the few that compares costs of NGO and government health services is from India (Berman and Rose, 1996). It found that NGO hospital services were operating at a level comparable to the lower end of the range reported for government facilities, on a similar level to the private for-profit sector.

There is some evidence that management systems in NGO health services tend to be weak. They are often characterized by fragile organizational structures, featuring leadership reliant on personalities, lack of formal accountability and limited client group participation; these often result from the fact they have to maintain links to external funding agencies and local government institutions. If they rely upon external sources of financial support, the funding may be available only for limited periods, and there may be periodic expatriate staff turnover. Where there is limited possibility of cost recovery or getting additional funds from government, this may be a special problem, as in Africa. In India, however, health NGOs are able to mobilize most of their funds domestically from user fees or government grants, and staff are mostly national (Berman and Rose, 1996).

As regards equity, we know that both private providers and government health services are unevenly distributed in rural areas. The NGO sector could indeed fill a gap in rural areas or for the poor in urban areas. It appears that in Africa church missions do locate health services in remote rural areas (Robinson and White, 2001). Similarly, NGOs in India also fill a gap, since they work among poor urban slum communities or remote rural areas with few government health facilities (Pachauri, 1994). NGOs tend to rely on user fees, but no one is excluded. Thus in India the poorest are usually exempt from charges (Berman and Rose, 1996), but that may not normally be the case in Africa.[18]

The evidence thus seems to suggest that NGO provision in health *may* serve a complementary role. However, it is also quite true that NGOs are few and far between, and no comprehensive system of health care is likely to work without a well-functioning public health system.

At the same time, we saw earlier that evidence on the for-profit private sector in health, especially its recent expansion, provides little ground for encouragement without its being subject to much more comprehensive regulation. However, this is not to deny the need for building public–private partnerships for specific purposes. For example, the Rotarians financed a worldwide polio vaccine initiative as part of the Expanded Programme of Immunization. Similarly, the Brazil government successfully financed NGOs to distribute condoms and take hotline calls in the battle against AIDS.

8.4 Water and sanitation

Chapter 6 noted that the water and sanitation sector is quite unique among
the sectors discussed in this book. The proportion of the population of the
world still lacking safe water and sanitary means of sewage disposal by far
exceeds those lacking health or education services. Accordingly, the sector
accounts for the largest share of the resources required to universalize access
to safe water and sanitation. There is little doubt that government provision of
the 'merit good' of water, sanitation and public health has not been achieved
in low- and middle-income countries. However, the trend towards privatization of water/sanitation services in industrial countries began in the 1980s,
long after universal coverage had been achieved through public provision.

This section begins with a review of the growth of public–private partnerships (PPPs) internationally, goes on to examine some specific cases of PPP
in low- and middle-income countries, and concludes with a possible way
forward. The focus of this analysis is, by definition, on ensuring services to
the poor and to those without services – rather than with promoting any
particular form of ownership or management of the watsan sector. This must
take into account the fact that the vast majority of the poor in low-income
countries live in rural areas. In middle-income countries, however, the
majority of the population live in urban areas (e.g. Latin America and the
Caribbean, Central/East Europe and CIS).

It is remarkable that of the 715 reported PPPs between 1989 and 2000
by region in watsan, 60 per cent are located in the most urbanized parts of
the world – Western Europe (16 per cent), North America (12 per cent),
Central/East Europe/CIS (6 per cent) and, most significantly, Latin America
and the Caribbean (26 per cent).[19] The proportion of population urbanized
in these regions is roughly similar: industrialized countries, 79 per cent;
CEE/CIS, 69 per cent; and Latin America and the Caribbean, 77 per cent.

However, this is not to suggest that PPPs have not grown in the rest of
the world. In fact, the distribution of the remaining 40 per cent of PPPs in
the world is as follows: East Asia and the Pacific, 16 per cent (39 per cent
population urbanized); South Asia, 10 per cent (29); sub-Saharan Africa,
10 per cent (38); and the Middle East and North Africa, 4 per cent (62).
This is despite the fact that a much smaller proportion of the population is
urbanized. In any case, worldwide, the present population reported served
by PPPs in middle- and low-income countries probably represents less than
5 per cent of the total urban population in these countries. In fact, in the
433 cities with a population larger than 750,000, ninety cities (20 per cent)
were served by PPPs (Franceys, 2001); however, there are around 40,000

smaller cities and towns.[20] The main concern, hence, remains the estimated 25 per cent of the citizens of developing-country cities that use water vendors, purchasing water at significantly higher prices than piped water (WELL, 1999). The result of this growth in PPPs in watsan in the 1990s has been that many governments now accept that the private sector can share a greater responsibility for the watsan sector than before, and the approach is somewhat different from that for the other utility monopolies, electricity and gas. Since there also seems to be increasing consensus among international donors (especially the World Bank and the IFC) to promote PPPs in urban and peri-urban areas, it is necessary to look at the experience of PPPs in both industrialized and developing countries.

Meanwhile, there is much greater agreement that rural areas will be served through user committees with NGO support. Governments need to focus on promotion, facilitation and coordination of services rather than merely on their provision. In rural areas in particular, sustained service provision would be best achieved through the efforts of local communities and locally based public and private firms, and building this capacity is recognized as an important role for governments. At the same time, the private sector already plays a role in service delivery in the water and sanitation sectors to the poor. At the community level, artisans often construct and maintain water and sanitation systems, performing an important marketing role as well, especially in sanitation. Private-sector involvement is increasing in the design and manufacture of hardware (e.g. pumps, pipes and sanitary wares), in the implementation of schemes (e.g. design and drilling of boreholes), in the delivery of services (e.g. private utilities and co-operatives) and in operation and maintenance (e.g. the increasing number of hand-pump repairers) (UNICEF, 1995a).

Given the growing role of PPPs in the urban areas, what has been the experience with them? Table 8.2 lists PPP contracts with increasing degrees of private participation. They start from co-operatives, moving on to service contracts, management contracts, lease contracts, BOT (build, operate, transfer) contracts and their variations, concession contracts, and finally divestiture implying full private ownership under a regulatory regime.[21] The last has mainly happened in industrialized countries (e.g. England and Wales, though not in Scotland and Northern Ireland), while the rest have been implemented in a variety of low- and middle-income countries. In France, the government owns the fixed assets and one of the three major private companies takes full responsibility for operating the systems, as in a lease contract. In the industrialized countries there is strong evidence that with PPP prices have increased significantly; for example, in France prices are higher in

Table 8.2 Types of PPP contracts in the water and sanitation sector

Contract type	Description	Watsan examples
Co-operatives	Co-operatives can position themselves to be the service providers for certain (often poorer, informal) areas of a city and manage facilities within these areas. This can take many forms.	Port-au-Prince, Haiti
Service contracts	Public authority retains overall responsibility for O&M of the system and contracts out specific system components. Service contracts typically last 1–3 years and contract out services such as meter reading, billing and maintenance.	Mexico City; Santiago, Chile; Madras, India
Management contracts	Public authority transfers responsibility for the management of a full range of activities within a specific discipline such as O&M. Remuneration is based on key performance indicators. Public authority typically finances working and investment capital and determines cost recovery policy. Usually 1–5 years.	Cartagena, Colombia; Gdansk, Poland; Mali; Gabon; Trinidad & Tobago
Lease contracts (or 'affermage')	Private operator rents the facilities from a public authority and is responsible for O&M of the complete system and tariff collection. Lessor effectively buys the right to the revenue stream and thus shares significant commercial risk. Usually 5–15 years but can be extended.	Côte d'Ivoire; Guinea; Czech Republic.
BOT (build, operate, transfer) contracts and their variations	BOT contracts are usually used to procure large, discreet items of infrastructure, e.g. water treatment plants, that require significant finance. The private operator is required to finance, construct, O&M the facility for a certain period of time (usually >20 yrs) before transferring the facility back to the public authority. Variants of BOT are BOOT (build, own, operate, transfer), BOO (build, own, operate).	Mendoza, Argentina (BOOT); Izmit, Turkey (BOT)
Concession contracts	Private operator takes responsibility for O&M and investment; ownership of assets still rests with the public authority. Concessions are substantial in scope (usually a whole city) and tenders are usually bid on the tariff. 25–30 years.	Buenos Aires, Argentina; Manila, Philippines; Cancún, Mexico.
Divestiture	Full private ownership and responsibility under a regulatory regime.	England and Wales.

Source: WELL, 1999. Adapted from Sansom, 1998; Johnstone and Hearne, 1998; Rivera, 1996. Sansom (1998) distinguishes 'complex' PPPs such as concession and lease contracts from service and management contracts. PPP is sometimes done by institutions that have elements of joint public and private involvement. These are two cases in point.

communes with PPP than those without, but there is no information as to what extent standards are correspondingly higher (Franceys, 2001). It is the French pattern that is now being promoted around the world, though the process was started in the UK in the early 1980s (where private company profits have been high).[22]

Service contracts and management contracts together account for 45 per cent of all PPP contracts by number (in operation until November 2000) in low- and middle-income countries. BOT accounts for another 23 per cent, and concession contracts for 18 per cent. The latter tend to be more complex contracts, while service contracts could be seen as an opportunity for developing-country governments to build up expertise in the sector before taking on the more demanding role of managing a concession.[23] Thus the more complex PPPs are mainly found in middle-income countries in regions such as Latin America, Eastern Europe and Southeast Asia. Among the low-income countries, only francophone West Africa has an established record in complex PPP – one reason for which may well be that the international companies most globally active are French. Initiatives are being pursued actively in Southern and East Africa and also South Asia, with support from donors (Webster and Sanson, 1999).

By and large, so far, the term 'PPP' in the watsan sector really implies involvement with a foreign partner. Some 70 per cent of the operating PPPs requiring capital expenditure involving international contractors. Two-thirds of those contractors originate from France – the country with the longest domestic history of PPP (over a hundred years). Contractors' share of the low- and middle-income country market by reported capital expenditure shows that the French Lyonnaise des Eaux[24] (50 per cent) and Vivendi Water[25] (17 per cent) had two-thirds of the market. By number of reported PPPs the same two companies had a 55 per cent share in the overall international market; the British companies[26] had a quarter share, but they have focused on safer markets in Europe and North America. The fact of foreign involvement indicates that privatization also involves about 1 per cent (by staff numbers) of expensive expatriates ($250,000 per annum) to deliver a so-called 'world class' water supply. As Franceys (2001) notes, this clearly puts a limit on the size of the city that can be served by a foreign PPP.

Evidence on whether the PPPs, which have grown from almost nil at the beginning of the 1990s to over 2,350, have been effective is mixed. One of the main claims for privatization was that it delivers the required new capital to the sector; that is the reason why PPPs could be discussed under the heading of mobilizing additional resources for basic services. It is unclear, however, whether any significant new money is coming into the watsan sector, as most PPPs have only a small equity contribution. At the same time, PPP is based on the assumption that in the end the customer pays. PPP has made this fact more obvious, though that is not always government intention.

Sources of conflict in PPPs

There remain a number of sources of tension between the public and private partners in PPPs, some of which will become clearer in the specific cases in Latin America (e.g. Bolivia, Chile) and Africa (e.g. South Africa) discussed below. First, there is usually a sharp difference between what private companies see as the minimal return necessary to sign a contract in a risky country and what governments view as an acceptable level of profit. Consider the following from a World Bank private-sector development specialist on watsan:

> Advisers to developing country governments considering private participation in water will all be familiar with the gasps of disbelief and indignation when they first voice assumptions about expected returns on equity. Governments that have happily (or at least blindly) tolerated high levels of rent seeking and wasteful behaviour by public water company officials can become positively puritanical about relatively modest profit taking by a private company. This is not to say that private companies with a monopoly to supply water services should be allowed to take any level of profit that they choose. But governments should be realistic about the profits that they should allow, recognizing the need of their private partners to earn a reasonable return and to be rewarded for the risks that they shoulder. (Cowen, 1997)

Second, management contracts can be good at improving services for those who already have water connections, but typically do not help those without connections, who are also less politically influential. It remains unclear how next steps can be worked out. The company winning the management contract for a limited period will start with an advantage for later contracts, and in the light of this fact other bidders may not be attracted. Thus, in either case, competition is likely to be limited or absent during the shift to a more complex contract. In other words, despite all the theoretical arguments marshalled by new institutional economics in favour of competition, privatization need not necessarily result in competition, not even in the bidding process.

Third, countries have limited regulatory and administrative capacity to manage such contracts. The political importance of the sector makes bidders nervous about whether governments will maintain a favourable operating environment and a tariff yielding a reasonable rate of return. One advantage of management contracts is that they need not require the kind of regulatory and monitoring infrastructure required by leases, concessions and divestitures. Management contracts, in turn, require clear performance indicators and a monitoring agency with the skills, budget and autonomy to perform the task. However, many of the normal indicators of water utilities' performance may only partially be controlled by the management contractor. For example, as Cowen (1997) rightly notes, water loss reduction in physical terms may depend upon government investment in rehabilitating pipes. Improved revenue collections may depend upon government users paying their own bills and state support for a policy of disconnection for non-payment. Reduction in operating cost may depend on laying off workers.

Fourth, an initial contract in a PPP is often based on incomplete information about many factors – for example, the condition of underground assets, or future investment requirements. Hence provision must be made in contracts to deal with unforeseen events over the life of a contract. International arbitration is often suggested in countries with little history of judicial or regulatory independence. Yet such arbitration is expensive, and for most disputes and for many smaller contracts it may not be realistic.

Case studies of PPPs

Many of these issues have arisen in two cases, discussed here. Since 1984 the Bolivian government has been hailed by the IFIs as an 'early adjuster', and like Argentina had carefully followed the neoliberal policy package. At the insistence of the World Bank, in 1999 the Bolivian government conducted an auction of the water system of the old Andean city of Cochabamba.[27] The auction drew only one bidder: a consortium called Aguas del Tunari, the controlling partner in which was International Water, a British engineering firm then wholly owned by the Bechtel Corporation of the USA. The government, regardless of its weak bargaining position, still proceeded. The terms of the $2.5 billion, forty-year contract reflected the lack of competition for the contract. Aguas would take over the municipal water network and all the smaller systems – industrial, agricultural and residential – in the metropolitan area, and would have exclusive rights to all the water in the district, even in the acquifer. The contract guaranteed the company a minimum 15 per cent annual return on its investment, which would be adjusted annually to the consumer price index in the USA. On co-operative wells Aguas could install meters and begin charging for water. Residents would also be charged for the installation of meters. These expropriations were legal under a new water law that had been rushed through the Bolivian parliament.

The terms of the contract for water privatization were immediately questioned by engineers, environmentalists, a federation of peasant farmers who rely on irrigation, neighbourhood associations, and water co-operatives. In January 2000 surprised business owners and middle-class householders joined the protest, as some bills had doubled, and ordinary workers had water bills that amounted to a quarter of their monthly income. The response of Aguas was simply that if people did not pay their water bills their water would be turned off.

The consortium had agreed in its contract to expand the city's water system, which was going to require large-scale repairs of the deteriorating existing system. The company claimed that it had to reflect in the tariff increase all the increases that had never been implemented before. The consortium had also agreed to finish a stalled dam project, Misicuni, which would pipe water through the mountains. Although plans for the dam had been around for decades, World Bank studies had pronounced Misicuni uneconomic; nevertheless, the dam was included in the contract with Aguas.[28]

The conflict sharpened, protests mounted, the government sent in troops from La Paz. Protests broke out in other parts of the country, and in many rural communities, and national peasant organizations held demonstrations. In April 2000 the national government declared a national state of siege or martial law, and it allowed mass arrests. The company's executives departed. The mayor distanced himself from the company. The government informed the company that because it had abandoned its concession the contract was revoked. A new national water law was passed, 'written from below', as water-rights campaigners say. The management of Cochabamba's water system was returned to the old public utility, SEMAPA. In late 2002, the consortium filed a claim for $50 million against the Bolivian government in the International Centre for Settlement of Investment Disputes, a closed-door mechanism of the World Bank, the same institution at whose insistence Cochabamba's water was privatized as a condition of a loan package in 1997. After a storm of global protests the consortium dropped the claim in 2006.[29]

One can see here several of the latent sources of conflict we mentioned earlier between the three parties involved: the people, the government and the company. First, there was no competition during the bidding stage, and the company obtained terms that were part of the problem. Second, as tariffs did not cover operating costs in the years in the run-up to privatization, the company attempted to raise tariffs suddenly. This brought on massive protests, worsened by attempts to cut off water to those unable to pay. Third, the local and national government could have acted in a more participatory manner, consulting with the affected people, before taking decisions. The dispute finally went to arbitration abroad, rather than within Bolivia, which could have proved rather expensive for the government.[30]

Water privatizations have also caused large-scale protests in many other parts of Latin America. Thus, in Panama popular discontent about an attempted privatization cost the president his bid for re-election. Vivendi, the French water transnational, had its thirty-year water contract with the Argentine province of Tucuman terminated after two years because of alleged poor performance. There was a 100 per cent increase in water rates after Vivendi was granted the concession. Major water privatizations in Lima (Peru) and Rio de Janeiro (Brazil) have had to be cancelled because of popular opposition. Trinidad allowed a management contract with a British water company to expire. Protests against water privatization have also occurred in Indonesia, Pakistan, India, Poland, Hungary and South Africa (Finnegan, 2002).

In South Africa, policy has been characterized by widespread contradictions. Thus, when the post-apartheid government came to power in 1994, the Reconstruction and Development Plan (RDP) announced that, to ensure that every person has an adequate water supply, the national tariff structure must include: (1) a lifeline tariff so that all can afford water services sufficient for health and hygiene requirements; (2) in urban areas, a progressive block tariff to ensure that the long-term costs of supplying large-volume users are met, and that there is a cross-subsidy to promote affordability for the poor; and (3) in rural areas, a tariff that covers operating and maintenance costs of services, and recovery of capital costs from users on the basis of a cross-subsidy from urban areas in cases of limited rural affordability.

However, in 1997, the South African government insisted on enforcing a cost-recovery approach to infrastructure and services offered by municipalities. The 400 or so municipalities were expected to fail and would be amalgamated into large district councils. Yet, the growing municipal fiscal crisis emanated from the Department of Finance, which in real terms cut the crucial inter-governmental grants (which pay for municipal service subsidies) by 85 per cent between 1991 and 1997. This led to massive pressure to cut services, including water, to those who could not pay the unsubsidized bills. At the same time, the government approved in 1997 an International Finance Corporation investment of $25 million in the Standard Bank (the country's largest bank) 'South Africa Investment Fund', with the aim of providing the foreign currency component required for privatization. As the IFC noted:

'The principal objective of SAIF is to invest in infrastructure projects in order to achieve long-term capital appreciation for investors. The Fund will focus on equity investments in the environmental (water, waste, sanitation and sewerage), energy, telecommunications and transport sectors.' SAIF projected a before-tax internal rate of return of 26–27 per cent during the Fund's fifteen-year life in constant dollar terms. The contradiction between the RDP (guaranteeing affordable water to the poor) and the South African government's subsequent policies (cutting grants and then promoting privatization of watsan, guaranteeing high returns to investors) is obvious.[31]

The contradiction is highlighted by the fact that after privatization, cross-subsidies mentioned in the RDP were ruled out. Those whose low income would indicate the need for assistance or differential rates had to pay for these services themselves. Thus, companies like Water and Sanitation South Africa (a Suez/Lyonnaise des Eaux/Group Five joint venture) promised to 'render an affordable, cost effective and optimised service' and ensure that customers are 'willing and able to pay for services, while maximising revenue collection' (Bond, 1998). However, in practice, in the town of Stutterheim, water services were instead characterized by the company's failure to serve any of the 80 per cent of the region's township residents and by mass cut-offs of water by the municipalities of those who could not afford payments. In mid-2000, a cholera epidemic broke out in the province of KwaZulu Natal – affecting nearly 14,000 and taking more than 250 lives. The epidemic started after municipalities cut water supplies to people living in an informal settlement who were unable to afford the user fees.

It is not that there have not been some successes with the privatization of water services (see, e.g., metro Manila).[32] However, the most exhaustive review of the international literature lists the following likely problems with PPPs: 'corruption in the tendering and drawing up of contracts, particularly in the US; monopoly in the privatized service; higher user charges; inflated director's fees, share options, and management salaries; widespread retrenchments; and anti-union policies' (Hemson, 1997).

In fact, the international water companies are themselves recognizing the risks and pulling back.[33] Thames Water had run its Shanghai sewerage plant for four years before China's government ruled in 2002 that the agreed rate of return was illegally high. Thames pulled out in July 2004. Despite this, China is the only country where the international water majors are staying. Veolia added a contract in December 2003 to the seven already there.

A major reason for the major players pulling out is that in most contracts the rate of return is guaranteed in foreign currency, but the national currency often undergoes devaluation. In Jakarta, in Manila, in Argentina – in country after country – there has been devaluation. The companies are happy enough while the national currency is stable, but when, for example, the Argentine peso (long tied to the dollar) collapsed in 2002, the trouble started. Suez's debt was mainly in dollars, but its charges to consumers were in pesos, and it was denied permission to raise them accordingly. Unlike the currencies of other developing countries where the majors have invested, that of China is, if anything, likely to rise – and so in China the water majors are staying for now. Suez eagerly entered Jakarta's water privatization in 1997, and has steadily lost money there: consumer resistance and political unease held up rate rises, which in turn, allied to allegations of poor performance, brought about a court case. Similar problems arose in Manila after the Filipino peso slump.[34]

The way forward

In face of this growing evidence of dissatisfaction with PPPs in the watsan sector, what is the way forward? The structures of the public sector currently provide water services to around 95 per cent of bulk water distribution customers globally. Many are indeed oversized, inefficient, overstaffed and bureaucratic – as normally depicted by the proponents of privatization. Many, however, are organizations which have been delivering reasonable public service, taking both environmental and financial sustainability into account.

Thus, Chile successfully universalized access to safe water to its urban population by 1990 – and, unlike with most other countries in the region, the reforms did not involve the decentralization of the responsibility of the service to other levels of government, such as municipalities, or the direct privatization of the service (Lee, 2002). Traditionally, watsan services in Chile were provided by a variety of central and local government authorities. The large number of organizations, their lack of financial and administrative autonomy, the lack of strategic planning and coordination failures resulted in a poorly operating watsan sector. Reforms began in 1977 with legislation which led to the creation of a centralized service, responsible for water and sanitation in both urban and rural areas throughout Chile. The National Sanitation Works Service (SENDOS) was created within the Ministry of Public Works, to plan, control and regulate. For operational purposes eleven regional agencies were established to cover the country. Thus one crucial aspect of the reform was the separation of the responsibility for the regulation of provision from the responsibility to operate the service.

Second, there was an increase in investment in watsan. In the fifteen years prior to International Water Supply and Sanitation Decade, 1981–90, investment averaged $62 million, but between 1981 and 1990 it averaged

$105 million at 1995 prices. The proportion of population receiving service also increased dramatically to 97 per cent in urban areas enjoying a household connection to water supply and over 80 per cent a connection to a sewerage system. The provision of services to the concentrated rural population was also increased.

Third, private contractors were also involved for some service contracts. However, 41.5 per cent of the population were served by the eleven state-owned regional companies, 50 per cent (in Santiago and Valparaiso) by two other state-owned companies, 4 per cent by a municipal company, and only 3.9 per cent by six private companies. The 1990 legislation (common for all providers, whether public or private) called for a system of concessions for the operation of services. There are separate concessions for the extraction and treatment of drinking water, the distribution of drinking water, and the collection and treatment of sewage. A separate tariff is calculated for each concession held, and exercised, by an operating company. Each regional company and the majority of the private contractors hold all four concessions, but this is not necessary. The concessions are permanent and transferable, but they can be cancelled if the terms are not met by the holder.

Fourth, between 1988 and 1990 there was established a new system for fixing tariffs objectively. The regulator established a maximum tariff on the basis of a model efficient provider and any differences between the actual company holding the concession and the regulator were to be resolved by a tripartite commission of experts. The reform permitted the *gradual adjustment of the existing tariffs to the new, higher levels*. 'This change in the method of establishing the tariffs is the keystone to the new structure of the industry and to the success that has been achieved in the management of the services since 1990' (Lee, 2002).

Although dominated by public enterprises, Chile's water services have been very successful. There were incentives for efficiency: the public enterprises wish to prove that they can be effective and profitable, and the private operators, although small, provide a benchmark for comparison. There was a sharp increase in the contracting out of many operational activities by all companies, including the operation, management and capital investment of whole systems, as well as maintenance of all aspects of the networks, meter reading and billing. Contracting out reduced the number of workers per connection. In 1995 the average level of unaccounted-for water in the water utilities was 30.6 per cent, far less than the Latin American norm of 40 to 60 per cent. There was also an increase in investment, the majority of which comes from operating income, itself made possible by the tariff increases, and the rest from various governmental funds.

Chile is not the only country where watsan services have been delivered efficiently by predominantly public enterprises. In fact, a report by the Public Services International Research Unit (PSIRU) lists case studies of successful public water providers, some of which have themselves fended off attempts at privatization. 'Contrary to common assumptions, there is ample evidence of satisfactory achievement of social and public service objectives through efficient public sector undertakings, in transition and developing countries as well as developed ones' (Lobina and Hall, 1999).

- In *Bolivia*, SAGUAPAC, established in 1979, is a co-operative of 96,000 members (its customers) in Santa Cruz. The co-op invested in large-scale infrastructure, which came in under-budget, allowing the scheme to be extended. The co-op's social credentials are indicated by its maintaining a subsidy on the first 15 cubic metres of water consumed by households per month. It also cancelled an attempt to contract out billing to the private sector, following a decision that disconnecting non-paying customers was contrary to the co-op's social responsibilities.
- In *Hungary*, in 1992, the city of Debrecen's state-run water operation was in need of considerable investment. Attempts were made to contract the service out privately, first to one water transnational then to another, but both attempts were defeated. In 1995 the council decided that water services management themselves had the expertise to carry out the work. The new company, Debreceni Vizmu, made the necessary investment at much lower cost than the bids by the private companies, partly by sourcing supplies locally instead of importing them from France. Prices remained 75 per cent lower than projected by the private companies.
- In *Honduras*, SANAA was similarly faced with privatization in 1994, on account of a history of inefficiency and large debts. Managers instead achieved restructuring with the assistance of trade unions and involving employees in reorganization. Prices rose, but the company retained subsidies on the first 20 litres per household per day, for social reasons, and service quality improved sharply.

In summary, while there is no question that public services in water supply, water treatment, wastewater treatment, and sewerage could not continue in the manner that they have been traditionally run, the evidence does not suggest that wholesale privatization has been very successful at achieving the social and economic objectives. In other words, the experience also suggests that while financial sustainability is important, financial profitability is not necessarily the only or main goal of watsan services.

Where local institutions and the local private sector are weak, public-sector provision of water and sanitation services will remain important. In the role of provider, the government is best able to ensure equity, multisectoral coordination, economies of scale and wide coverage. At the same time, the management role of the community will need to be recognized if sustainable service is to be achieved. Governments can also play a role in decentralization and facilitating the interface between service providers and service users. In addition, the adoption of appropriate technology is vital for programmes to go to scale in a cost-effective manner. Technology transfer is best accomplished through collaboration between government and the private sector.

8.5   The private sector – full speed ahead?

We noted in section 8.1 that there has been international pressure for PPPs and privatization in social services. In fact, recent developments in multilateral bodies – the World Bank, the International Finance Corporation, the WTO – as well as bilateral policies could force the pace of privatization and private-sector development in health, in education and in water and sanitation. We discuss in turn the World Bank–IMF's Poverty Reduction Strategy Papers, the World Bank's Private Sector Development Strategy, the IFC's new strategic priorities, the interest of WTO and GATS in the privatization of basic services, and, finally, regional treaties and their links with the privatization process.

Since 1999 the World Bank and the IMF have required all heavily indebted poor countries (HIPCs) and all countries applying to the Poverty Reduction and Growth Facility (PRGF, or the erstwhile Extended Structural Adjustment Facility, ESAF) to prepare a Poverty Reduction Strategy Paper (PRSP). The PRSP is merely a renamed Policy Framework Paper, and the conditions are the same: 'It is broadly true that the core macroeconomic and structural elements of the early PRSPs have changed little from the programs of the recent past' (IMF and IDA, 2002). In fact, the PRSP Sourcebook of the Bank advocates 'establishing policies that encourage competitive and efficient services sectors, such as allowing entry where possible and encouraging foreign direct investment'.[35] In other words, as a matter of policy, PRSPs will promote private-sector participation in basic services.

Similarly, the World Bank's Private Sector Development Strategy (2002) plans to increase support to the private sector in the provision of basic services. In addition, it will support a series of regular surveys of the investment climate in developing countries, which will form an essential element in the Bank's approval of PRSPs,[36] In fact, the private-sector strategy paper calls for more effective coordination between its private-sector window, the IFC, and its soft-loan window, the International Development Agency (IDA), which only lends to seventy-eight low-income countries. The aim of the coordination is to involve private-sector participation in up to 40 per cent of IDA operations. In other words, both through HIPC debt relief conditionality (via PRSP approval), and through regular IDA conditionality for non-HIPCs – rather than through any national ownership of policies – private-sector participation is to be encouraged in low-income countries.

That there is an interlocking set of conditionalities – between IDA, IFC and the IMF – in respect of private-sector participation in basic services is clear from the above, as well as from IFC's own paper setting out new strategic priorities (IFC, 2002a). The IFC, according to this strategy, will now focus on frontier areas where there is at present little available capital, and on frontier countries that receive limited private capital from abroad. With this in view, in September 2001 the IFC established a separate Health and Education Department. The IFC will promote private-sector health involvement in India and Pakistan in South Asia; in the Philippines and China in East Asia; in Kazakhstan, Poland, Romania and Russia in the CEE/CIS; in Côte d'Ivoire, Kenya, Nigeria, South Africa in sub-Saharan Africa; in Egypt and Turkey in the Middle East; and in Brazil, Colombia and Mexico in Latin America. This is despite the common knowledge that IFC investments in the past have responded to existing patterns of demand from the affluent sections of the population in any country.[37]

Finally, the emerging body of international investment law coming out of the dispute settlement tribunals of the World Bank's International Centre for the Settlement of Investment Disputes tilts strongly in favour of the rights of multinational companies and against the rights of national governments.

8.6 Conclusions

In summary, despite the mixed experience with the private sector in school education, the definitely harmful experience with privatization and with private-sector growth in health services, and the controversial developments in public–private partnerships in the water and sanitation sectors in low- and middle-income countries, there is pressure from all international agencies – through interlocking conditionalities and other means – to promote the growth of the private sector in basic social services, and where possible privatization of public services.

Table 8.3 Two alternative systems of social service delivery

State-led provision		Market-led provision	
Distortion	Benefits	Benefits	Distortion
• Co-opted and abused by elites • Inertia • Indifference	• Equity • Social integration • Lower unit cost	• Pluralism • Minority sensitivity • Innovation	• Inequality • Social exclusion • Survival of the fittest

The jury is still out on the comparative cost, quality and operational efficiency of voluntary versus state provision. Where NGO financing and provision have filled gaps in state provision, and tried to reach the unreached in remote rural areas, the sector is to be encouraged. However, what needs to be encouraged is complementarity between state and civic organizations, since the NGO sector cannot be a substitute for the state. The role of the state is to ensure this complementarity.[38] The state has to create the enabling conditions for local institutions to emerge which serve both to express the 'voice' of the community and, where necessary, to provide services to the unreached and their most vulnerable, thus filling the gaps left by the state.

Table 8.3 tries to capture our exposition on the roles of state and private provision. The basic premiss is that they belong in two different conceptual categories, with contrasting or opposing values, but constituting a continuum in their actual implementation in the real world. Moreover, both of them are liable to be abused and misapplied.

The basic premiss of state-led provision of basic social services, besides the practical ones (e.g. lower unit costs, mentioned at the beginning of this chapter), is that society, through its political representatives, channels collective action (taxing itself to obtain resources and hire people) to deliver the goods that should be provided to everybody. Thus, the historical experience of now-industrialized countries and the 'high-achieving' countries suggests that basic education and primary health were early on recognized as particular services to be provided free. Thus, no distinctions are made among recipients, everybody is equal. This promotes social integration, as enjoying the services does not depend on political favours or the ability to pay, but is based only on citizenship. Political cohesion and nation building are also enhanced this way.

When these services can be bought in a market, as if they were candy or cigarettes, a very important shared value is lost. Nevertheless, there might be some reasons for loosening the reins of state provision. This is clearest in education. Some groups (say, for religious reasons) might want to have the freedom to teach their children in a certain way. So long as this is not disruptive of the social fabric (e.g. preaching hate-mongering or violence), this could be allowed to promote pluralism and protect minorities. Also, as education is complex, at any given time parents might prefer certain pedagogical tools. State schools cannot be changing rules and curricula all the time, but outlets for innovation in private schools, again within the general guidelines mentioned above, could be allowed.

However, two further points need to be recognized. First, states can accommodate some of these concerns. For instance, flexibility in terms of curriculum can be achieved within the state system. Also, this flexibility could include the concerns of minorities in special, state-run schools.

Second, the advantages of the state-led and market-led approaches can be trumped if distortions occur. The one most commonly mentioned in the literature in recent years is the inequity that emerges as public spending is concentrated in well-to-do areas, creating or reinforcing inequities. Also, lack of innovation deriving from bureaucratic inertia can lead to sclerosis and declining quality. Finally, state monopolies can result in authoritarian tendencies and indifference to citizens' concerns. Obviously, the solution for these problems is not privatization but an engaged civil society which participates in the political decision process (see Chapter 6). Moreover, unfettered markets also have their pitfalls and distortions. When the services are offered only to those who can pay or are willing to pay more, inequality increases. Markets, by their very nature, are a rationing mechanism, which means that applying commercial values in the provision of basic social services will necessarily result in social exclusion. This, in turn, can generate resentment and social conflict.

In practice, in most countries, there are no complete state monopolies in the provision of social services. The important point is that even if some room is allowed to private providers, they, or their practices,[39] should not be dominant. When state provision is not feasible or pluralism is considered an important value, state guidelines and regulations are vital to ensure universality and equality in access to basic social services, which in turn promote social cohesion and individual capability enhancement.

Countries, their leaders and, most importantly, their citizens need to keep these differences in mind when evaluating the role of the private sector in the provision of basic social services.

Part III

Mobilizing domestic and external resources

9

Taxation and mobilization of additional resources for public social services

The previous chapter raised some questions about the wisdom of privatization in health, education, and water and sanitation on the basis of the available empirical evidence. From a theoretical point of view, moreover, basic health and basic education are quite unlike normal private goods. We have established (in Chapters 2 and 4) that there are not merely externalities flowing from their provision not captured in private calculations of costs and benefits, but there are synergies between these goods/services (not quite captured in the notion of externalities). Hence, market prices are not an effective mechanism for allocating water/sanitation services, or basic health and education. Clearly, government alone is able to offer a credible guarantee of universal access to water and sanitation, basic health and basic education.

As market efficiency does not conform to any notion of justice from a distributional perspective, taxes and transfers have historically been used to redistribute income and welfare (e.g. by providing services directly). However, in reality progressive transfers and taxes are difficult to implement, due to the power of the rich to evade or avoid taxes (we address this issue later). Aside from the dictates of traditional welfare economics, any theory of justice would suggest that in the absence of other realistic means of enhancing the capabilities (or choices) of poor individuals – like redistribution of assets, especially land – basic service provision can enable the poor to acquire simple human functionings (e.g. the ability to read and write, or to escape avoidable disease). Hence the role of the state is critical, especially in developing countries. However, given the scale of the unmet need in basic services in most low- and middle-income countries, it follows that the state will need to

Table 9.1 Resource requirements to universalize access to BSS

Type of service	Estimated cost of universal access to health, water and sanitation, and education (orders of magnitude, 1995 US$ billion/year)		
	Current	Additional	Total
Basic public health package (including nutrition)	6	14	20
Essential clinical services	29	26–31	55–60
Reproductive health and family planning	10	8–10	18–20
Low-cost water and sanitation (rural and urban)	8	11	23–25
Universal primary education	83	9	90–91
Total	136	70–80	206–16

Sources: For the public health package and essential clinical services, see World Bank, 1993a; for reproductive health, and for water and sanitation, see Water Supply and Sanitation Collaborative Council, Geneva; and for primary education, see Delamonica et al., 2004.

mobilize additional resources to enhance its citizens' capabilities – especially if the Millennium Development Goals are to be met.

We have estimated that in developing countries between $206 and $216 billion (in 1995 prices) is needed to provide basic social services to all, and that an estimated $136 is spent on these services (see Table 9.1) (Annex 9.1 gives the basis of the estimates).[1] This results in a $70 to $80 billion shortfall,[2] which is about twice as high as an earlier estimate at the time of the World Summit for Social Development (March 1995) of between $30 and $40 billion calculated in 1994, based on available data from the early 1990s. The approximate doubling of the estimated additional resources required for universal access to basic social services indicates that significant progress still needs to be made in achieving many of the social development goals of the 1990s. It also reflects an increase in population and prices, as well as better estimates of costs. Note also that these are estimates that focus on basic health, water and sanitation, and basic education goals, and do not include the costs of reaching the hunger, poverty or other targets.

The significant difference between current spending and the resources required to reach universal access to basic social services implies a need for increased allocations to basic services in most developing countries. But the question is how best to achieve this – and the dominance of the policy advice of the international financial institutions, and the theoretical models that influence them, acquire practical significance here. From a pure and simple algebraic approach, there are four possible ways (and, of course, any combination of the four):

1. Increasing the share of total public health or education or water/sanitation expenditures for *basic services*, while leaving all other expenditures (including the non-basic expenditures in the social sectors) the same.
2. Increasing the *share of sectoral allocation for health or education* as a whole in total public spending, while leaving the intra-sectoral allocation for basic services the same.
3. Increasing the public spending share in the GDP, while leaving the inter-sectoral allocation across sectors of the national budget and intra-sectoral allocation within the health and education budget the same. This would mean enhancing the revenue base of the state (in order to contain the budget deficit) through improving tax collection, expanding the tax base, or increasing taxation levels, to *increase the revenue-to-GDP ratio*.[3]
4. Increasing *public expenditure per capita* (as revenues increase with growing GDP), without altering the inter- or intra-sectoral allocation or the public spending to GDP ratio. This would be dependent on an enhancement of the revenue base of the state as a result of output expansion and income growth. Since such increases in public spending are dependent on economic growth, we would refer the reader to our discussion in Chapter 2 and where the determinants of growth are discussed.

The remainder of this chapter explores the prospects for mobilizing additional resources for BSS through the first three means.

Countries with higher incomes spend a larger proportion of that income (GDP) on tax-based social programmes – that is well established.[4] But the social spending share in turn affects income growth (Lindert, 1994), as we also argued – through the second synergy in Chapter 2.[5] In other words, if the experience of industrialized countries offers any lesson, it is that while social spending may be an endogenous variable, governments also need to treat it as an exogenous one.[6] With this conviction, we turn to the means available to developing countries (other than ODA) for mobilizing resources for basic services.

Section 9.1 examines the scope for intra-sectoral restructuring of expenditures within health and education. Section 9.2 discusses the prospects for reallocating in favour of health and education, away from defence, external debt amortization and unproductive subsidies, but also by changing the composition of the civil service. Section 9.3 examines the prospects for mobilizing additional revenues from taxation, both domestic and international sources. Section 9.4 discusses the earmarking of funds (or hypothecated taxes) for basic services. The chapter closes with an examination of public expenditure in a historical context, especially by comparing the growth and pattern of public expenditure in industrialized and developing countries.

9.1   Intra-sectoral reallocation of public spending

We have already seen that in a majority of developing countries the intra-sectoral allocation of public spending within health and education is biased in favour of higher-level services. In general, it is primary education, preventive primary health-care services in rural areas, and low-cost rural water and sanitation services that have been bypassed.

However, intra-sectoral restructuring of expenditures is likely to be resisted by the non-poor, who benefit from the current pattern of spending. Political economy considerations are of paramount importance to governments. While they may persistently test the patience of the poor, they must beware the wrath of the rich even in the short-run. Intra-sectoral reallocation in favour of basic services is much easier if carried out when the funding envelope for the sector as a whole is increasing. In other words, if governments can shift resources in favour of health or education from other uses, such as economic services, defence or debt payments, the politically difficult task of reallocating resources within the health and education sectors becomes that much easier. In other words, for inter-sectoral reallocation in the short run, we have a non-Paretian allocation in mind – that is, unproductive subsidies in economic services/defence/debt servicing would receive *less* resources, and the released resources would be transferred to health and education. The realism of such a proposal can be legitimately questioned in the medium run; if the total revenue base of the government is increasing, then non-discretionary (i.e. non-debt amortization related) expenditure on all budget heads can increase. However, within the health (or education) sector, we have a Paretian solution in mind; the higher levels of service will not be made worse off, while the primary level of service will benefit from increased expenditure. Within health and education, there will be less political resistance if higher-level services do not suffer from budget cuts.

In addition to this 'political' rationale for creating the right conditions for intra-sectoral reallocation, our studies suggest sound technical reasons for maintaining or increasing overall health or education expenditures while increasing basic-level service provision. Urban areas are particularly vulnerable to infectious diseases, for example cholera, which spreads easily in overcrowded locations. From this logic we derived the importance of safe water and proper sanitation in towns and cities in Chapter 6. University libraries that lack relevant textbooks do need adequate funding. Within the health sector, hospital and clinical services may be stretched to breaking point by HIV/AIDS patients, making it difficult for clinical services to cope with other patients. In Zambia, for example, health systems are being overwhelmed by cases of secondary infections such as tuberculosis, pneumonia and measles, to which those living with HIV are vulnerable. And HIV/AIDS claims the lives of over 600 teachers a year – equivalent to half of the graduates from teaching colleges. There can be little argument about the need to maintain overall health, water and education budgets in the face of such challenges.

In the *education* sector, there are many reasons for a dominant public-sector role at lower levels of schooling. Parents are not in a position to finance education by borrowing; a purely private system can only function efficiently with perfect capital markets, and imperfections in capital markets abound in all countries, whether they are middle income or low income. Also, in addition to the synergies we have discussed in Chapter 2, universal schooling has an equalizing effect on income distribution and thus may compensate for differences in family background. If education is a normal good, richer parents will buy more education for their children. Thus inequality may be passed on from generation to generation, without state intervention.

We have already established that there is no scope for cost recovery at the primary and junior secondary levels of education (see Chapter 6 for discussion on allocative efficiency). If anything, the experience of Malawi since 1994, of Uganda since 1996, of Kenya since 2003, and of Tanzania and Lesotho this decade has been that the elimination of fees has raised enrolments at the primary level dramatically.

Meanwhile, within the education sector, alternative means for *additional* financing for higher education have to be found.[7] In the context that illiteracy rates in Tanzania had risen from 10 per cent in 1986 to 16 per cent in 1992, a World Bank study (1994b) noted that in Tanzania the opportunity cost of sending one student to university was not sending 238 students to primary school. Similarly, much more is spent by the state per pupil in higher education than at the primary level (see Figure 9.1) in most developing countries. However, that is not the case in the high-achieving countries (see Chapter 2 for definition and list of countries). Thus, reallocation of resources from university to primary education could prevent a further increase in illiteracy and can be defended on the grounds of equity.

Thus, India has a larger population of illiterates than its total population was in 1947, at the time of independence from British rule. Yet, in India,

Figure 9.1 Per-pupil expenditure ratios by region, 1995

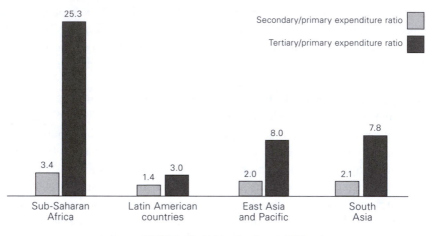

Source: UNESCO, World Education Report, 1997.

publicly funded, high-quality, professional institutions of higher learning (e.g. medical colleges, the institutes of technology and other engineering colleges, and the institutes of management), which churn out world-class professionals, barely cover a fraction of their costs from fees (see Mehrotra et al., 2005, for details).[8] Given the high private returns to higher education and other non-basic social services, the well-off can and will finance their higher education. In India and other parts of Asia there has been an increase in cost recovery (Tilak, 2002; Bray, 2002). Tilak (2004) has argued that too much cost recovery is taking place in Indian universities; however, his own data suggest otherwise. He presents data for the 1990s for 35 universities for their income from various sources (government subsidy, cost recovery, internal sources, and others). For 16 universities, more than 75 per cent of income, and for 15 universities 50–74 per cent of income is from government subsidies. Only for 4 universities is less than 50 per cent from government subsidy. And only for 15 universities does cost recovery exceed 20 per cent of income.

However, it is critical that cost recovery should lead to improvement in facilities in public education at these higher levels. Enhanced recovery is likely to meet parental and student resistance unless the resources are directly ploughed back to items like improved library facilities and student loans and bursaries for poor students. In other words, enhanced cost recovery does not imply that the additional resources flow back to the government treasury. Enhanced cost recovery at these higher levels of education can actually be an instrument for improving both the efficiency and the equity of the higher education system. We saw in Chapter 5 that the incidence of higher education spending was particularly skewed in favour of the rich, and, at the same time, that the enrolment ratio at tertiary level is still low in South Asia and sub-Saharan Africa, though not in Latin America. In Latin America, higher education (with an enrolment ratio of 20 per cent in 1994) has more than reached the 15 per cent cohort enrolment threshold internationally recognized to represent 'mass higher education'.

Defence of total public subsidization of higher education in developing countries[9] based on comparisons to higher education rates or public expenditures in developed countries ignore the fact of limited access to even elementary (let alone secondary) education in many developing regions, and the questionable quality of school education in most developing regions. It also ignores the fact of the overall wealth of developed societies and their governments – public spending as a share of GDP exceeds 40 per cent in most developed countries (a share well above that for developing countries). It is not without reason that the median for total public expenditure to GDP in high HDI countries was 35 per cent in 1999, while in medium HDI countries it was 25 per cent, and in low HDI countries it was 21 per cent.[10] In fact, among OECD countries, the share of public expenditure in GDP in the Scandinavian countries tends to be around 50 per cent, in the rest of the Europe around 40 per cent, and only in countries like the USA and Japan does it drop to around 30 per cent.

If industrial countries spend one-sixth of their education budgets on tertiary education, they can afford to, given that they universalized elementary schooling at least a century ago in most cases. Moreover, even in industrialized countries, higher education institutions mobilize a significant proportion of resources from non-government sources. Tuition covers 15–35 per cent of the costs of higher education in the UK, the USA, Spain and Japan, and receives the highest share of revenues from other incomes, such as industry or alumni funding (Tanzi and Schuknecht, 2000). That is the route that higher education institutions in emerging market economies will have to follow. In addition, as we noted in Chapter 6, they will need to encourage higher education to be provided at competitive prices by the private sector – as South Korea has successfully managed to do since the 1950s. A system of student loans for higher education and scholarships for meritorious poor students has to be in place to ensure equity considerations are not overlooked.

Historically, the industrialized countries were allocating a much larger share of public education expenditure to elementary and secondary education a hundred years ago than developing countries do even today (see Table 9.2)

Table 9.2 The now-industrialized countries: share of public education
expenditures by level, *circa* 1900 (%)

Country	Elementary	Elementary and secondary
Australia	–	95.9
Belgium	94.2	96.7
Canada	–	94.2
France	72.5	90.3
Germany	77.8	88.7
Japan	85.2	88.7
Netherlands	77.1	92.5
New Zealand	–	95.3
Norway	83.7	90.7
UK	80.4	–
USA	–	93.6

Source: Lindert, 2004.

– even though for the majority of low-income countries even elementary education enrolments are lower, and for lower-middle income countries secondary school enrolments are lower, than for the now-industrialized countries a century ago. If publicly funded higher education became the norm in industrialized countries in the latter half of the twentieth century, it has been premissed upon first universalizing school education at least half a century before the norm, in respect of higher education, became universal.

The case for increasing cost recovery in higher education in some developing countries does not imply that tuition fees should be the only component, nor that there is no role for free, publicly provided universities. To counteract the risks of increased social elitism, if tuition fees are introduced, they should be phased in and complemented with loans for higher education. Most tertiary-level students in public educational institutions are from a middle class ranging from substantial privilege to modest background, while the very rich, like the very poor, are only a minority. This is particularly true in Latin America and South Asia (though perhaps less so in sub-Saharan Africa). Hence, reduced subsidies risk creating a less diverse student body in higher education. In fact, one of the main reasons the poor tend not to pursue higher education lies more with the weaknesses of the lower educational levels of schooling (in that it does not prepare them for formal-sector employment), and the limited employment opportunities in the formal sector of the economy, than with financial policies affecting higher education. Moreover, in the context of mass primary education and substantial secondary education enrolment typical of many middle-income countries (especially Latin American ones), free universities provide a major stimulus for children of poorer households to finish their secondary schooling (as they have the possibility of continuing their future studies) and an unparalleled route towards joining the middle class. This 'social development' aspect of public universities is often overlooked by the orthodox writers who propose a one-size-fits-all approach to higher-level education financing (i.e. increasing tuition fees). In our view, the context, in particular enrolment trends and achievement at the elementary and secondary level, should guide the provision and financing of public higher education, as well as subsidizing students to attend private universities, with a bias towards lowering barriers to access to higher education and using progressive general taxation (see below) to finance public universities.

In the *health* sector, the situation is much more complicated. We have seen in earlier chapters that the bias of health expenditures in favour of tertiary-level services is pronounced. However, we have also seen that the effects of cost recovery in the health sector can be grave, which raises the issue as to how intra-sectoral reallocation of public health spending can be feasible in a resource-constrained environment at the sectoral level. In most industrialized countries, user charges are not part of the reform agenda; in fact, performance improvement in the health sector is seen to depend more upon changing the behaviour of providers than that of consumers.

The case for cost recovery in health was strongly voiced in a policy paper in 1987 by the World Bank (see Akin et al., 1987), which called for user charges, insurance, decentralization, and a greater role for the private sector. It assumed that user charges offered the possibility of reducing excess and unnecessary demand for free services, and that a graduated fee system would encourage citizens to use lower-level health services first. The 1993 *World Development Report* (World Bank, 1993a) presented a more refined position. Market-failure arguments were used to advocate public financing of public health services and some essential clinical services. In countries where the cost of the basic package of essential clinical services was financially infeasible for government, selective user charges and targeting mechanisms were suggested. The argument in favour of user charges was that charging fees can improve equity if fees are used to improve quality (an argument not dissimilar to the one we used above, though only in respect of higher education).[11]

However, there is a qualitative difference between education and health in the nature of demand for them. For education, parents can anticipate and plan for the costs of schooling up to the age that they are able to finance and the child is willing to study. However, costs in health are unpredictable – both in incidence and magnitude (Colclough, 1997a). Catastrophic health costs can wipe out a family's savings, and a vulnerable family is likely to fall below the poverty line under such circumstances. For instance, in India medical costs are said to be the second most important reason (after dowry for a girl's marriage) for vulnerable families being pushed down below the poverty line. Hence, while user fees at higher levels might be justified as a short-term, temporary measure if a government faces a particularly resource-constrained environment (as in all low-income and most middle-income countries), the case is rather different in respect of health services. On account of the unpredictability of health cost, insurance mechanisms or public finance – advocated in Chapter 6 – are the appropriate means for financing health services for the majority of the population, and especially for the poor.

Nevertheless, cost recovery in some form or other characterizes the health systems of most African countries now. Korea, Thailand, Malaysia, Singapore and Indonesia also have some user charge policy in place for health; these coexist as cost-sharing provisions with national or partial social insurance. In Latin America as well, cost-sharing is an important component of health insurance systems. However, as Creese and Kutzin (1997) rightly point out, establishing or raising fees is not the same thing as getting a user charge system to operate as a means of improving efficiency; nor is it a basis for ensuring equity in the provision of services. We saw in Chapter 6 that out-of-pocket costs (or private expenditures) account for most of health spending in most developing countries. In India, the majority of contacts between the sick and a health provider are with private providers – a majority of them poorly qualified – at considerable cost, both in financial and health terms, for the population (Rohde and Viswanathan, 1995).

The arguments in favour of user fees made by its proponents are the following: they may raise revenue, improve efficiency and quality, and improve access and equity. The evidence, however, suggests that increased use of user fees since the World Bank advocated them has not contributed any of these potential benefits (Barnum and Kutzin, 1993; Creese and Kutzin, 1997; Arhin-Tenkorang, 2000). While the Bank expected that revenues of the order of 10–20 per cent of recurrent expenditure would be raised, net revenues have been much lower than gross revenues on account of collection costs. Second, increased use of user fees does not promote efficiency, since there is little evidence of moral hazard in the form of excess of free facilities; users, particularly poor ones, already have to take account of the cost of time and transportation when visiting a health facility, which minimizes excess use. In fact, after the imposition of user fees utilization actually drops, with adverse equity effects. Nor does the evidence suggest that differential pricing of lower and tertiary facilities has resulted in more effective utilization of primary, as opposed to tertiary, facilities, as was expected.

As argued in Chapter 6 (in the light of the success with the Bamako Initiative experience with cost sharing), several conditions must coexist if increased user charges at government health facilities are to lead to an *increase* in access to the poor. Local revenue retention is one. There is evidence that this has led to improved quality in service, and hence greater utilization of services. Second, appropriate management skills and financial institutions need to be in place for local fee retention to lead to improved quality of service. This involves having staff trained in basic financial management, the existence of banks to deposit the funds, use of simple audit procedures, and community committees for oversight of the use of funds (WHO, 1994). Finally, if the increased revenues (from user fees) and improved quality actually *reduce* the cost to the poor of accessing effective care, there would be a basis for levying such fees (Creese and Kutzin, 1997). This last condition may be met if the 'exit' option for the poor involves higher payment to a private provider (e.g. as is common in much of South Asia, where private providers are abundant), or if the community in question is relatively isolated (e.g. as in many parts of low-density parts of Africa or even certain parts of South Asia).

Public spending on health and education increased between the mid-1980s and the mid-1990s in a large number of low-income countries. For 118 developing (and transitional) economies, real per capita spending increased on average by 0.7 per cent a year for education (and 1.3 per cent a year for health). Such spending also rose as a share of total spending and national income (World Bank, 2000a). But it has also been observed in a review of World Bank experience of structural adjustment over the 1980–93 period that increasing health and education did not translate in adjusting countries into increased allocations for basic health and basic education (Jayarajah et al., 1996). Clearly, despite all the Public Expenditure Reviews that have been conducted by Bank staff, the emphasis on basic services is not being implemented into policy. Later evidence for the 1990s, cited in Chapter 4, showed the same result.

9.2 Inter-sectoral restructuring of public spending

What is the scope for increasing public resources for basic services through inter-sectoral resource shifting? It is not possible to prejudge what shares should go to different government services such as administration, justice,

Figure 9.2 Basic services versus defence in public expenditure

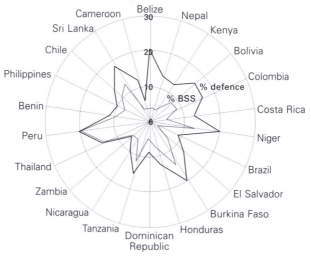

Source: Table 9.2. All years as table.

defence or economic services. Nevertheless, our studies suggest that, predictably, there are three factors that are unduly burdening many budgets: defence spending, debt payments and unproductive subsidies.

Table 9.3 presents the share of BSS, defence and debt service in public expenditure in the countries studied. In many countries examined, including Benin, Cameroon, Chile, the Philippines and Sri Lanka, defence spending absorbs more resources than basic social services (Figure 9.2). Several of these countries face 'internal' wars.

Defence spending

In respect of defence, South Asia, with the largest number of poor in the world, is the only region where military spending increased while global military expenditures were falling in the 1990s (SIPRI, 2001). In fact, globally standing armies had been reduced by 16 per cent over 1987–94, by 24 per cent in industrialized countries and by 10 per cent in developing countries. However, in South Asia the size of these armies increased by 7.5 per cent.[12]

After the end of the cold war, military spending in developing countries has declined from an average of 4.9 per cent of GDP in 1990 to about 2.4 per cent of GDP in 1995 (Gupta et al., 1996).[13] Yet, despite this peace dividend after the end of the cold war, in an average year more than one-

Table 9.3 Share of basic social services, defence and debt service in public expenditure in selected countries

Country	Year	Total BSS	Defence	Debt service
Asia				
Nepal	1997	13.6	4.7	14.9
Philippines	1992	7.7	9.9*	30.7*
Sri Lanka	1996	12.7	18.5	21.5
Thailand	1997	14.6	14.2*	1.3*
Africa				
Benin	1997	9.5	11.0	10.8
Burkina Faso	1997	19.5	13.9*	10.2
Cameroon	1996–7	4.0	12.2*	36.0
Côte d'Ivoire	1994–6	11.4		35.0
Kenya	1995	12.6	4.0	40.0
Namibia	1996–7	19.1		3.0
Niger	1995	20.4	13.0	33.0
South Africa	1996–7	14.0		8.0
Tanzania	1994–5	15.0	11.5	46.0
Uganda	1994–5	21.0		9.4
Zambia	1997	6.7	6.0	40.0
Latin America & Caribbean				
Belize	1996	20.3	4.4*	5.7*
Bolivia	1997	16.7	8.2*	9.8*
Brazil	1995	8.9	2.7*	20.0
Chile	1996	10.6	13.3	2.7
Colombia	1997	16.8	8.7*	7.9*
Costa Rica	1996	13.1	5.5	13.0
Dominican Republic	1997	8.7	4.8*	10.0
El Salvador	1996	13.0	7.0	27.0
Honduras	1992	12.5	7.5	21.0
Jamaica	1996	10.2		31.2
Nicaragua	1996	9.2	5.8*	14.1*
Peru†	1997	19.3	19.0	30.0

* From IMF, *Government Finance Statistics Yearbook*. Information may be for latest available year.
† Budgeted figures.

Source: UNICEF country studies.

third of the world's population lives in a country at war (Drèze, 1999). Most of these conflicts are 'internal' wars, rather than inter-state disputes.[14]

Since so much of the discussion here has been over health and education as public goods, it is worth noting that, paradoxically, national security is a public good as well. Military spending is claimed to be positive for the economy – encouraging modernization, supplying technological innovations to civilian industries, contributing to the building of physical infrastructure (e.g. roads), providing modern education and health services to at least defence personnel. But the real issue is whether these positive gains are being purchased at the cost of human development for the majority of the population. Moreover, several authors have argued that the positive externalities of military expenditure are grossly exaggerated (e.g. Smith, 1977, 1978; Scheetz, 1985). Apart from causing widespread civilian deaths and injuries, there are many ways in which armed conflict disrupts the quality of life: entitlement crises – profiteering on the one hand and famines on the other (as in Sudan, Cambodia, Iraq and Mozambique); collapse of public services (as in El Salvador, Guatemala, Nicaragua, Nigeria, Uganda); environmental degradation (as in Vietnam, Kuwait, Iraq); forced displacement (as in Angola, Liberia); breakdown of the social fabric, political repression and personal trauma (Drèze, 1999). Then there are the opportunity costs of human development forgone, the current financial cost, plus the burden on future generations since most arms purchases from abroad are made against suppliers' credit. Since arms purchases are normally made internationally, there is also the burden of foreign exchange costs.

It should be stressed that many of the conflicts mentioned in the previous paragraph were fuelled by the cold war. Once it was over, many of them were resolved. Nevertheless, new conflicts emerged afterwards, most prominently global terrorism, which is partly a response to the despair of the excluded population. Providing BSS and launching the positive synergies and virtuous circles described in this book could contribute to reducing some of the sources of global terrorism. Here, too, ODA ought to play a fundamental role (if anything due to self-interest). However, it is important, in order to enhance both the effectiveness of the interventions and the self-respect of the countries themselves, that the policies and programmes be home-grown, and not perceived as *quid pro quo* for external aid.

External debt service

In the countries examined, external debt service is a more serious drain on the government's budget than defence expenditure (Figure 9.3). In many

Figure 9.3   Basic services versus debt service in public expenditure

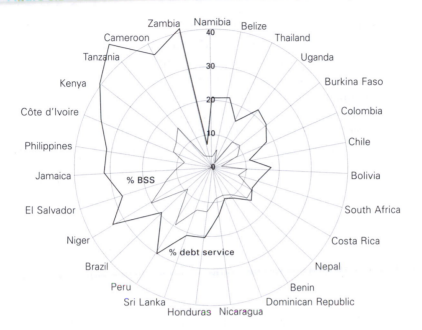

Source: Table 9.2. All years as table.

cases, debt service alone surpasses, often by a wide margin, the allocation to these services. This was true in Brazil, Cameroon, Côte d'Ivoire, El Salvador, Jamaica, Kenya, Nepal, Niger, Peru, the Philippines, Sri Lanka, Tanzania and Zambia. Of the twenty-seven countries for which data are available, only ten spent more on basic social services than on debt servicing.

International action is vital on debt relief. Bilateral and multilateral donors, particularly the IMF and the World Bank (which together account for most of the multilateral debt), launched an initiative in 1996 to address the debt crisis of the poorest countries.[15] This Highly Indebted Poor Countries (HIPC) Initiative identified two thresholds to determine whether a low-income country can repay its debt on a sustainable basis. Under the original initiative of 1996 the debt-to-exports ratio was to be below the 200–250 per cent range, and the debt-service-to-exports ratio had to be below the 20–25 per cent range. For countries that exceed these thresholds, a programme involving strict macroeconomic management for several years could eventually lead to some form of debt relief.

The inability of the first-generation HIPC to address the problem resulted in another initiative. An enhanced initiative was announced in mid-1997 by the G7 countries. To be eligible for debt relief under the revised HIPC, a country must be very poor – that is, IDA eligible, and eligible for support under the IMF's Poverty Reduction and Growth Facility (the reformed and renamed Enhanced Structural Adjustment Facility); have an unsustainable debt burden; and pursue good policies.[16] Under the new framework, an unsustainable debt burden is defined as a stock of debt that is more than 150 per cent of exports (not 200–250 per cent as under the previous arrangement) on net present value basis. For very open economies, the exclusive reliance on external indicators may not adequately reflect the fiscal burden of external debt. A net present value (NPV) debt-to-export target *below* 150 per cent can be recommended if the country concerned meets two criteria at the decision point: an export-to-GDP ratio of at least 30 per cent and a minimum threshold of fiscal revenue in relation to GDP of 15 per cent. For countries meeting these thresholds, an unsustainable debt burden is defined as a NPV debt-to-revenue ratio of more than 250 per cent at the completion point (World Bank, 2000b). In other words, sustainability is still largely defined in terms of debt-to-export ratios.

However, debt-sustainability should also be considered from the perspective of fiscal balance and the capacity of governments to carry out their core responsibilities. Take one example: Zambia. About 40 per cent of government revenues have been allocated to servicing external debt (Figure 9.2). This is actually more than the budgets of the entire health and education ministries combined. At the same time, child mortality rates are rising, and only about one-third of children are fully vaccinated. The numbers of children out of school are actually increasing. This is an unsustainable situation in terms of human development outcomes, whether or not it is unsustainable in HIPC terms.

In other words, a fundamental problem with debt-relief initiatives, including the HIPC Initiative, is that they define debt sustainability on the basis of debt-to-export ratios. It is governments, however, that must service debts, not exporters (even though the servicing has to be done in foreign exchange). Most HIPCs have liberalized their trade policies and capital-account regulations, with the private sector now accounting for 80–100 per cent of export earnings. But governments have only limited access to this revenue through taxation. The fiscal burden on governments, using budget revenue as the denominator, would be a more accurate indicator of a country's ability to repay its debts and would also highlight the true cost of debt servicing in terms of human development.

Therefore, perhaps no more than 10 per cent of the revenue of HIPCs should be spent on debt servicing. Countries spending more than 10 per cent of their revenue on debt service cannot be expected to meet poverty-related expenditure requirements. This should be one measurement for determining eligibility for HIPC debt relief. Such a proposal is similar to a US Congress recommendation that debt servicing should not exceed 10 per cent in the case of HIPCs.

In early 2003 seven countries had reached their completion point, meaning that some of the *debt stock* had been forgiven. By December 2005 a total of eighteen countries had reached completion point – a full ten years after the HIPC began. Another ten countries had reached decision point, implying that they can benefit from *debt service* relief. The remaining pre-decision point countries that are potentially eligible for the Initiative have been beset by persistent social difficulties such as continual internal civil strife, cross-border armed conflict, governance challenges, and substantial arrears problems. A few of them, however, have made progress towards establishing a track record of macroeconomic performance that is a requirement for qualifying for debt relief. It is not designed to cancel 100 per cent of debts but to reduce debts to a level which the creditors claim is 'sustainable'. But even countries which have completed the process struggle to meet their debt repayments, and have to divert money from vital public services.

In summary, only thirty-eight countries are 'eligible' – and only twenty-eight of these have even qualified to enter the scheme. Many countries, such as Kenya, Haiti and Sri Lanka are extremely poor and severely indebted, but are not eligible for HIPC. There should be cancellation of all unpayable debts – not just those of countries on this limited list.

The evidence shows that governments in the debt-relief recipients are using their additional resources to increase spending in health and education. Under the HIPC Initiative, a viable and comprehensive poverty reduction strategy is to be put in place prior to the decision point. Poverty Reduction Strategy Papers (PRSPs) are to be prepared by countries for the purpose, which have to be approved by the IMF and the World Bank.

However, the debt relief has not been either fast or deep, and fewer countries have benefited than anticipated. Based on the original schedule, nineteen countries should have reached completion point by early 2003, not the seven that did. Moreover, it is not certain that the debt relief will be enough to escape the debt trap. The IMF/World Bank projections of debt sustainability were dependent on assumptions that were overly optimistic. First, an assumption was that exports would increase. The initial HIPC analysis was conducted when there was a global economic boom. In the coming decade, exports will need to be at almost twice the rate of the 1990s if HIPC countries are to be able to service their debts. A second assumption was that new borrowings would decline from 9.5 per cent of GNP to 5.5 per cent, and grants were expected to double (UNDP HDR, 2003). However, a few HIPCs are borrowing at higher than expected interest rates.

Even the World Bank admits:

> Despite the significant progress in implementing the enhanced HIPC Initiative, challenges remain. In terms of countries reaching decision and completion points, progress has been slower than originally foreseen by the international community and country authorities. Performance under IMF-supported programs has not been even across decision point HIPCs due to problems in program implementation. Some countries have either experienced problems in program implementation or do not have an IMF-supported program in place after having had protracted delays in establishing a satisfactory record of performance. The sunset clause has been extended for another two years to allow these pre-decision point countries an opportunity to qualify for HIPC debt relief.

HIPC, which was meant to conclude in 2004, has thus been extended for another two years.

But these are not the only problems. Even after such countries had reached completion point and were receiving debt relief, their stock of debt was higher than the limit of 150 per cent of exports, and thus they are receiving top-ups (e.g. Burkina Faso, Niger). Their exports have not risen as projected, confirming that the projections were over-optimistic. The projections for actual debt servicing over 2004–06 are higher than what they had paid over 2001–03. For these reasons, there is widespread resentment building up among the HIPCs that the international community is being asked to write off Iraq's debt when 100 per cent of the HIPC debt has not been written off. The international NGOs are calling for the revaluing of the gold reserves of the IMF (currently valued at around $40 an ounce, when the world market price is over $500) to enable the multilateral institutions to write off their debt to the HIPCs.

Subsidies

Other than defence and external debt, the third major source of haemorrhaging of public finance is through indiscriminate subsidies. Most governments are guilty of permitting such haemorrhage. In five countries in Latin America the ratios of public subsidies in water and sewerage of the richest to the poorest quintiles range from 2.8 to 1.3 (World Bank, 1994a).

However, considering the colossal waste of human potential in South Asia, we need merely exemplify this vicious cycle with the cases from there. In Bangladesh, subsidies on infrastructure services are about six times larger for the better off than for the poor (World Bank, 1994a). Power price subsidies disproportionately benefit higher-income households, which use more energy than poorer households. In Nepal, fertilizer subsidies – which absorb between a quarter and a fifth of total budgetary outlays for agriculture – benefit the poorer farmers the least (Prennushi, 1999).

Subsidies could be on merit goods, or non-merit subsidies. The government often provides excludable public services on which it can recover costs, but may actually provide them at lower than average cost because they are merit goods. Such subsidies for merit goods are legitimate, but too often subsidizing goods that have very little merit-good element is the norm. The latter can be justified only on redistributive grounds; but most of the latter are actually available only to the non-poor. For instance, Rao (2005) has shown that for the central government of India, total explicit subsidies (e.g. on food, fertilizer and exports) and implicit ones (for social and economic services on which costs are not recovered) for 2002/3 amounted to 4.3 per cent of GDP. Of these, 2.8 per cent of GDP consisted of non-merit subsidies accrued in economic services. The problem does not stop there. Srivastava and Amor Nath (2002) estimated the merit/non-merit subsidies provided by state governments of India. They found that state governments provide few explicit subsidies, but implicit subsidies through unrecovered costs on social and economic services were 11 per cent of GDP, of which non-merit subsidies were 5.2 per cent of GDP. The public services with a significant element of non-merit subsidies included electric power to consumers (industrial, agricultural and household), irrigation, urban water supply and sanitation (to those able to pay), industry, higher education and housing. In addition to these unrecovered costs from non-merit subsidies there are implicit subsidies from tax incentives, which are not easily quantifiable.

These are the areas where user charges need to be imposed which at least cover costs. In India this would eliminate the major cause of the state governments' bankruptcy – which are the governments that account for 85 per cent of health and education expenditures. Subsidies of 15 per cent of GDP have to be compared to the 3.8 per cent of GDP that goes to the entire education sector. Cutting such subsidies would also discourage rich farmers from using nearly free power to pump cheap but scarce water to overirrigate crops. Such subsidies reduce the efficiency of the productive system.

Cutting such subsidies would also eliminate the source of budget deficits – which for the central and state governments in India taken together have amounted to around 10 per cent of GDP over 1998–2003, up from around 7 per cent over the preceding five-year period. Economic growth comparable to that experienced by the East Asian high-performing economies is only possible through state investment in physical (especially power generation) and social infrastructure, but bankrupt governments cannot invest.[17]

A clear principle could be that subsidies should not be given on the use of agricultural or industrial inputs for production, except in compensation for specific positive externalities of their use. Similarly, subsidies should not be given on private consumption of any kind of good unless they are targeted to poor groups (e.g. a targeted food subsidy for the poor), or compensate for specific positive externalities in consumption (e.g. nutritional supplementation for poor pregnant women or poor school-going children), or are necessary to ensure that all have access to certain goods regarded as merit goods, such as health and education.

The composition of expenditures by economic classification

The preceding discussion has discussed the scope for inter-sectoral reallocation in favour of BSS by examining the expenditure categories by functional classification. But one of the most serious criticisms that have been levied against government waste is that the wastage arises from overmanning in government offices. The problem has been, however, that the health and education sectors are often unable to hire additional doctors, nurses and teachers on account of budget constraints. In other words, from the viewpoint of the poor, there is often a mismatch between the manpower requirements of public service delivery (which are usually undermanned) and the overmanning that often characterizes other parts of the bureaucracy.

One such example comes from India. There are four classes of government employees, class 1 comprising the senior national civil service, class 2 the provincial civil services, class 3 the clerks, and class 4 the messengers, drivers and so on. What is remarkable is that some 88 per cent of the Indian civil service consists of class 3 and 4 employees.[18] There is a need to examine the composition of the civil service in most developing countries to determine to what extent it is geared to meet the requirements of basic social-service delivery for all. For instance, it may be possible to retrain at least class 3 employees to become schoolteachers, and class 4 employees could be trained to perform more development-oriented tasks, as government administration becomes more dependent on information technology.

Containing budget deficits and medium-term expenditure frameworks

Excessive defence expenditure, inappropriate subsidies, external debt payments, combined with weak capacity to raise genuine and sustainable tax revenues, are the main causes of budget deficits in developing countries. High budget deficits have to be funded with domestic (or foreign) debt – which completes the vicious cycle. High government borrowing pushes up the interest rate for all borrowers – raising the costs for private (and public) investment. Higher economic growth can only be expected if such subsidies can be cut and investment increased.

Large budget deficits constrain macroeconomic policy in general and the prospects for increasing social expenditure in particular. For instance, in Niger the budget deficit averaged close to 10 per cent of GDP since the mid-1980s. In Nepal it amounted to 10 per cent of GDP in 1992 and has remained at that level for an extended period. For Tanzania, it was 14 per cent in 1993 and 13 per cent in 1994. In India the combined central and state government fiscal deficit to GDP ratio was around 10 per cent. This means that not all the resources generated from additional taxation or budget restructuring will be available for social spending.

A second point is the sustainability of public expenditure on social service in the long run. As fiscal deficits are incurred, the national debt accumulates. This debt constrains discretionary allocations in the future as interest payments and amortization increase, and imposes a serious burden on future generations in many countries. When governments are not able to raise sufficient revenues, overall expenditures are restrained both in the short run and in the longer term.

While discussing intra-sectoral reallocation (within the health and education sectors), we argued the case for such reallocation if resources for the sector as a whole were increasing. The latter can be achieved through inter-sectoral reallocation, but only if two requirements are met. One requirement is technical, the other is more challenging to the extent that issues of political economy are involved.

The technical issue involves the need for budget reform. Reformers in OECD countries and, in increasing numbers, in developing and transition economies are stressing the need for changes in budget systems, emphasizing the three levels of overall fiscal discipline, strategic prioritization and efficient and effective service delivery (or value for money) (World Bank, 1998). The stress on better public expenditure management had led to the World Bank working with governments – starting in the late 1980s – to prepare public expenditure reviews. A two-pronged approach is now developing. One is that central agencies focus on reforming the policy, planning and budgeting systems so that they are more demanding of a performance orientation. In an increasing number of countries – not only those HIPCs which are implementing a Poverty Reduction Strategy Paper – there is gradual introduction of a Medium Term Expenditure Framework (MTEF) (e.g. South Africa). The MTEF consists of a top-down resource envelope, a bottom-up estimation of the current and medium-term (usually three years) costs of existing policy, and, finally, the matching of these costs with available resources (World Bank, 1998). Within the MTEF, the second prong is the sectoral MTEF, or the sector-wide approach or sector investment programme (SWAP/SIP) – which we discuss in the next chapter.

These reforms are a response to the problems accumulating from the early post-independence decades.[19] Driven by the needs of physical and social infrastructure ('social overhead capital' in the terms of Hirschman (1958)), *the capital side of the government budget had led the recurrent*, giving an expansionary bias to government expenditure.[20] In at least aid-dependent countries of the world, the capital budget is driven by donor assistance. However, very little attention is paid to the financial costs the government will have to bear once donor support has ended and to estimates of recurrent costs. This leads in future years to the finance ministry stressing availability of resources while the line ministries stress needs at the time of budget planning. There is greater recognition now that *the recurrent budget should be the starting point*, and the development budget and the recurrent budget should be integrated into some sort of medium-term expenditure framework. Such a framework could ease the task of simultaneously addressing the three sources of budget deficits – defence spending, debt service and subsidies – that have strangulated government spending.

However, while the MTEF can improve planning once the essentially 'political' decisions regarding allocations have been made, it does not resolve the political economy issue of how to cut unproductive subsidies (both for production and consumption) or military expenditures. The underlying problem is the interest groups lobbying for such expenditures. What is needed is political 'voice' that can offset the pressure groups, whose voices are embedded in the governing elite. Of course a prerequisite is democracy, without which participation in civil and political life is limited. However, having the 'capability' or freedom to participate and possessing the 'functioning' of actual participation do not necessarily translate into influence, even in a democracy; in an authoritarian state such functioning is out of the question. In other words, in addition to democracy, collective voice and collective action would be necessary; just as the trade unions or the confederations of industry or the military establishment or the wealthy farmers have collective institutions to voice their positions – and lobby with the cabinet. The experience of the high-achieving countries (see Chapter 2) suggests that voice does work, as does the evidence we discussed in Chapter 7.[21]

9.3   Enhancing revenues

This brings us to the third method available to governments wishing to increase the resources for basic social services: revenue generation, and thereby an increase in total public spending to GDP across the board, while leaving the inter-sectoral and intra-sectoral allocation untouched. The existence of large budget deficits, however, has forced governments to undertake macroeconomic stabilization and adjustment aiming at cuts in budget deficits and public expenditure. Since the early 1980s, these adjustment policies have been characterized by an almost exclusive emphasis on public expenditure reduction in the quest for budget deficit reduction. In an external review of Extended Structural Adjustment Facility (ESAF) programmes, a group of independent experts noted that public spending limits have often been set too tight, with detrimental effects on human capital and growth. This was again the case in the policy conditions laid down in the IMF's response to the Asian economic crisis (Stiglitz, 2002). Our studies show (see Chapter 4) that, for all cases, real per capita BSS expenditure only declined when the public expenditure share in total output declined.

Size of total revenues

The IMF's *Government Finance Statistics* reveal that over 1990–2001, total tax revenue to GDP ratio in low-income countries was 14.1 per cent, 18.5 per cent in lower-middle income countries, 23.1 per cent in upper-middle-income countries (IMF, 2004);[22] non-tax revenues could add an additional 4–5 per cent of GDP to total revenues in each country. For the tax ratio, while these are unweighted averages for low-income and middle-income countries, there is a great dispersion around these means. Thus, India's tax revenue to GDP ratio (combined for the central and state governments) was 14.1 in 2001/2.[23] Given India's social needs – it has the world's largest number of malnourished children (and one of the highest rates of malnutrition) as well as the largest number of children still out of school – this revenue effort, which is no lower nor any higher than that for low-income countries generally is clearly not good enough.

In Africa, in CFA zone countries (all low-income countries), the tax revenue to GDP ratio was stable through the 1980s at 16 per cent (comparable to the sub-Saharan average of 16.6 per cent over 1990–99), although it fell to 8.5 per cent over 1991–93, rising again to 18.3 per cent over 1994–96 – averaging 15.7 per cent over 1980–96. The fact remains that in CFA countries the tax revenue to GDP ratio has not risen over the entire period of structural adjustment of the 1980s and 1990s, and nor have non-tax revenues.[24] In non-CFA countries, the tax revenues have hovered around a lower level than in CFA countries, averaging 14.7 per cent over 1980–96 (15.1 per cent over 1980–85, 14.5 per cent over 1986–90, 15.6 per cent over 1991–93, and 16.4 per cent over 1994–96). In addition, the real problem in sub-Saharan Africa has simply been the stagnant or declining GDP, and thus the absolute size of revenues have shrunk in size. Worse still, the external indebtedness of the governments has grown, preventing them from increasing social expenditures. It is for these reasons that debt relief and additional ODA are so critical to financing social services in Africa.

There are a number of countries in Africa that are performing much better than their peers in terms of generating tax revenues – judging by the mean for low income (LIC), low-middle (LMC) and upper-middle income (UMC) countries (based on data for 2000). Thus, Namibia (29.9 per cent), South Africa (25.4 per cent) and Swaziland (26.8 per cent) have a higher tax-to-GDP ratio than LMCs (18.5 per cent) – and also a higher ratio than the sub-Saharan unweighted average of 16.6 per cent (based though on only twelve countries). Senegal (17.2 per cent) is generating more revenues than LICs on average (14.1 per cent), but Madagascar (11.3 per cent) is not, and nor is Uganda (10.9 per cent).[25]

There are a number of countries in Latin America too that could increase their tax-to-GDP ratio. Thus Argentina's tax ratio at 12.9 is well below the UMC ratio of 23.1 (over 1990–2001), as is Chile's at 17.8. Mexico's tax ratio is even lower (13.2 per cent), although Mexico too is a UMC. Dominican Republic (15.6 per cent) is also well below the LMC mean of 18.5 per cent of GDP; El Salvador even more so (13.2 per cent). All these countries also seem to be below the unweighted regional average for Latin America of 17 per cent of GDP.[26]

One can see that the oil-rich countries tend to have much lower tax ratios relative to other countries in their grouping, because their non-tax revenues (i.e. oil revenues) generate enough resources for the state. Venezuela, Bahrain and Iran fall into this category.

The ability to undertake public expenditure on social services can be affected by the stability of revenues. At 18 per cent of GDP, India's total revenue base is below the developing economy average of 26 per cent of GDP, but it is far more stable. The volatility in India's revenue base is one-third of that of other developing countries, owing to the low volatility of GDP growth (Hausmann and Purfield, 2004). The volatility in total revenue growth was 11.8 per cent over 1990–99 in Latin America, and 12.6 per cent in developing countries generally, but only 4.5 per cent in India. Such volatility impacts adversely on the Latin American countries' ability to finance social services on a stable basis. Besides, tax effort is supposed to increase, and tax revenue to GDP grow, with the level of per capita income. However, although per capita income in Latin America is much higher than in sub-Saharan Africa, there is hardly any difference between the tax revenue to GDP ratio in the two regions over 1990–2001: 17 per cent as against 16.6 per cent.

On the tax side, the general approach in structural adjustment was that an increase in tax rates was recommended only if unavoidable. On the assumption that lower rates would ensure better compliance with tax laws, they were likely to raise revenues (Williamson, 1990). When combined with a broadening tax base, the tax-to-GDP ratio was supposed to rise. However, in the vast majority of countries in sub-Saharan Africa and Latin America the tax-to-GDP ratio has stagnated or declined (Mehrotra, 1996). This is not surprising, given that trade taxes account for the largest share of tax revenue in developing countries; and with tariffs declining under the WTO regime, the share of trade taxes was bound to fall.[27] Unfortunately, other taxes have not grown to compensate for the fall in the contribution of trade taxes. Even India experienced a decline in the central government's tax-to-GDP ratio by two percentage points in the 1990s after the economic reforms – on account of declines in the contribution of trade taxes (Rao, 2005).

We recognize that substantively what has changed with fiscal stabilization policies is that, on average, for the low-income countries PRGF-supported programmes target a smaller and more gradual fiscal consolidation than programmes under the erstwhile Extended Structural Adjustment Facility (ESAF), and give more weight to revenue increases than expenditure contraction (IEO, 2004). However, even here the Internal Evaluation Office of the IMF finds that the outcomes are not very different between ESAF loans and its renamed successor, the Poverty Reduction and Growth Facility (PRGF).

Many countries, particularly in Latin America, undertook reforms in taxes during the 1980s. The initial efforts, consistent with the requirements of the Washington Consensus, emphasized lower tax rates, indexing for inflation, and broadening the tax base. These reforms were typically unsuccessful in substantially increasing revenues (Dasgupta and Mookerjee, 1998).[28] As a result, later in the 1980s and 1990s significant changes in tax administration were introduced in a handful of Latin American countries, and also in Indonesia and the Philippines.

There is an urgent need to reverse this phenomenon of fiscal inertia through a greater focus on revenue generation as a means of increasing social spending. Low revenue collection is the combined outcome of institutional weaknesses, dependence on trade taxes for many developing countries, and low incomes. We recognize that none of these factors can be altered in the short run. Domestic revenues can only be increased over a longer time horizon. In fact one has to acknowledge that, over the short to medium term, budgets cannot be balanced via increased taxes.[29]

However, there needs to be more explicit recognition internationally of the fact that adjustment has focused much more on expenditure reduction than on revenue generation. Much more could be done to strengthen tax collection to prevent tax evasion and tax avoidance. Moreover, much more could be done to enhance the tax base, by enlarging the tax net to catch those who are currently escaping it. The international financial institutions need to take much more seriously the technical support requirements of most developing countries, but especially those in sub-Saharan Africa and Latin America, in the area of tax administration and collection.

Which sources of revenue should finance basic services?

For developing countries, the total tax revenues are derived almost equally from three sources: domestic taxes on goods and services (general sales tax, excises); foreign trade taxes (mostly import duties); and direct taxes (mostly from corporations, rather than individuals).[30] Wealth/property taxes and social security contributions make a marginal contribution. However, for industrialized countries, income taxes (mostly from individuals) make the largest contribution (36 per cent, *circa* 1987), with domestic taxes on goods and services and social security contributions accounting for slightly over a quarter each of total tax revenue, with trade taxes quite insignificant (Burgess, 1997). The question relevant to our purposes is: which kinds of taxes are likely to meet the requirements of implementability, buoyancy and stability for meeting the resource requirements of basic services?

Governments of developing countries collect, on average, about 20 per cent of national income as government revenue,[31] which is considerably less than the proportion collected by governments of industrialized countries (at least 40 per cent in all European Union countries, except the UK, Ireland

and Spain, where it is just under 40 per cent). The revenue-to-GDP ratio can rise in the following ways, *inter alia*: the tax base is widened; tax avoidance and tax evasion are reduced; and new sources of international taxation are found. We will examine each in turn.

Domestic taxes: direct or indirect taxes?

Atkinson (1989) has argued that in industrialized countries, personal income and social security taxes are normally seen as key instruments for the redistribution of income. However, as we have seen above, in developing countries these account for a small proportion of revenues; hence their use as instruments for redistribution of income is likely to be restricted (Burgess, 1997). The IMF (2004) subscribes to this point of view: 'In view of the high share of agriculture and informal economic activity in many countries, corporate and personal income taxes are unlikely to be a major source of domestic revenues in the short- to medium-term.' However, a growing literature suggests that while social security taxes will remain marginal to the redistribution objective in developing countries, this may not necessarily be the case for income taxes. Thus, we do not subscribe to the pessimism about redistributive income taxes to finance basic health and education.[32] Burgess and Stern (1993) find that in some countries tax reform has led to significant improvements in the contribution of direct taxes to overall revenue. Moreover, the point is not to improve income distribution for its own sake, but because greater equality is important in order to reduce poverty and promote capabilities, as discussed in Chapter 2. Hence the scope for improving revenues based on direct taxes is examined first.

Optimal tax theory (associated with the work of Ramsey, Mirlees and Diamond[33]) is traditionally concerned with the tax structure, and its efficiency and incidence. The traditional approach uses a general equilibrium framework, and is primarily concerned with 'getting prices right'. While this approach is important, there is almost total neglect of administrative feasibility (Dasgupta and Mookerjee, 1998). An alternative, though complementary, approach is to focus on taxpayer incentives and the design of tax administration, where the principal concern is to 'get incentives and institutional arrangements right'. Issues of administrative feasibility acquire particular significance in developing countries, where corruption in the tax departments of governments is known to be rife. It is useful, therefore, to examine the literature on tax compliance and issues of enforcement of existing tax law.

For instance, the performance of Indian income tax collections is particularly poor. Economic development is normally associated with growth in the relative contribution in personal income taxes to revenue. This is caused by factors such as the widening of the taxpayer population, personal income rises, and improvements in enforcement technology and administration. However, the experience in India (and in many other countries, especially Latin America) has bucked this normal trend. In India the share of income taxes in total central tax revenue over the period 1970–90 actually fell from 14.7 per cent to 9.7 per cent, as did the proportion of personal income tax in non-agricultural GDP.[34] Evidence suggests that the proximate cause for the poor and deteriorating performance of Indian income tax revenues is tax evasion (Dasgupta and Mookerjee, 2000). It was poor revenue performance and a fiscal crisis that had forced Latin American countries to undertake large-scale tax administration reforms in the late 1980s and 1990s. Countries such as Colombia, Costa Rica, Ecuador, Peru[35] and Jamaica achieved significant gains from comprehensive reforms, which included administrative reforms.

Meanwhile, the implications of low (and, in certain countries, like India, falling) income tax collection is that the government is compelled to rely on indirect domestic taxes and trade taxes, as well as administered price increases for products of public enterprises. These taxes are regressive and inflationary, hindering the synergies described in Chapter 2. Moreover, in large federal countries they create problems of coordination of indirect taxes between central and provincial governments. The resulting cascading effects distort relative prices, besides encouraging excessive vertical integration. Imports are discouraged by the high levels of tariffs (that must compensate for poor income tax collections) and, correspondingly, expenditure on essential infrastructure and basic social services is restricted.

While it is clear we are advocating for a much larger share of direct taxation of wealthy groups substantially through more progressive income taxes, it has to be acknowledged that in developing countries it would be possible to increase government revenue through better compliance with, and a higher collection rate of, currently existing taxes. For instance, as part of a comprehensive reform of its tax administration during 1988–92, the Mexican system awarded a bonus to the collectors. It represented about 60 per cent of additional collections. As a result of the bonuses the number and yield of audits increased almost overnight. The share of audits generating additional revenue increased from 38 per cent in 1988 to 90 per cent in 1990. Limiting the discretionary authority of tax officials would also help improve compliance and reduce evasion. Computerization of tax administration can help control corruption, as it makes it harder to tamper with records.[36]

Improved tax administration has also resulted in an increase in the 1990s in the share of personal income taxes in total tax revenues even in India.

A number of innovations account for this shift. Expansion of the scope of tax deduction at source has been very effective in reaching the hard-to-tax group (Rao, 2005). Moreover, every individual living in large cities covered under any one of the six conditions (ownership of house, cars, membership of a club, ownership of credit card, undertaken foreign travel, and subscriber to a telephone connection) is necessarily required to file a tax return.

Thus, as we mentioned above, the international financial institutions (IFIs) must seriously focus technical support for tax administration and collection requirements in most developing countries, but especially those in sub-Saharan Africa and Latin America, rather than meddling with their expenditure levels, if they intend to help the poor.

Trade and international taxes

There are many a priori reasons for believing that there may be revenue losses due to globalization – and these need to be addressed, if new resources are to be found for social purposes. There are three grounds for this fear. First, capital movements increase opportunities for evasion – because of the limited capacity that any tax authority has to check the overseas income of its residents; evasion is also encouraged since some governments and other institutions systematically act to conceal relevant information. Where dividends, interest, royalties, management fees are not taxed in the country in which they are paid out, they may easily escape being noticed in countries where the recipients of such income live. There have been large non-resident aliens' bank deposits in countries like the USA that charge no taxes on the interest from such deposits.[37]

Second, avoidance (as opposed to evasion) may increase, given the differences internationally in tax rules and rates, because of the element of effective choice of tax regime that international tax treatment of enterprise income commonly offers (Clunies-Ross, 1999). This is likely for taxation of the profits of corporations and other enterprises that have international operations. Transfer prices for goods, services and resources, moving between branches of a company, provide opportunities for shifting income for tax reasons to minimize the revenue due.[38]

Third, the competition for international inward investment may lead governments to reduce the income-tax rates, and increase the income-tax concessions, that fall on international investors (Clunies-Ross, 1999). Income tax rates have fallen sharply since the late 1970s (though globalization may not be the only factor here). Tanzi (1996) notes evidence that there have been sudden outflows of capital in response to certain changes in tax policy.

This suggests that governments find themselves constrained by international competition in the rates that they can apply; that there has been a decreasing readiness of countries to raise rates or to tax dividend and interest income on the ground that to do that would encourage capital flight. Yet it has been well known for a long time that granting of direct-tax concessions has little or no effect even in diverting investment internationally, let alone increasing its global amount. Hence, concessions are an unnecessary loss of revenue. Beggar-thy-neighbour policies will lead to losses of revenue for all developing countries, in a mirror image of the race to the bottom of labour and environmental standards, which also negatively affect the possibility of pursuing inclusive, sustainable human development.

Domestic indirect taxes

While sales and excise taxes have accounted for most of the indirect domestic taxes, there is greater scope emerging in developing countries for introducing value-added tax (VAT) as a means of raising revenue.[39] Burgess (1997) argues that since VAT covers a large share of the value added in an economy, revenue from VAT is buoyant – that is, tends to rise with (or faster than) economic growth. VAT systems have been introduced in over thirty developing countries, and more are being established. China introduced one in 1994, and India did so in 2005. To maximize revenues from VAT, countries need to ensure that the tax base is as broad as possible and the rate structure simple.

It is notable that there is little variation in the role of indirect domestic taxes across different low-income countries, but these taxes are substantially more important for middle- and high-income countries (Dasgupta and Mookerjee, 1997). They have been found to be implementable in countries with low administrative capacity, buoyant and stable.

The buoyancy of VAT can be contrasted with foreign trade taxes, which are known to be sensitive to fluctuations in world prices. Given that for a large number of low-income and even middle-income countries, the export structure is characterized by a high commodity concentration of exports, excessive reliance on trade taxes can destabilize the revenues and spending of such countries. In Latin America, for instance, the contribution of VAT has been increasing over time, and by the mid-1990s accounted for between 1 and 5 per cent of GDP for Uruguay, Peru, Mexico, Guatemala and Colombia, and for 9 per cent of GDP in Chile. In nearly all developing countries where it has been introduced, its contribution to tax revenues has been increasing (Burgess, 1997).

Excise taxes are another important source of revenues in developing countries. They are levied particularly on a few products – alcohol, tobacco, petroleum, vehicles and spare parts. They exhibit several positive features from a revenue perspective: few producers, large sales volume, relatively inelastic demand, and easy observability. Excises may be levied on the basis of quantities leaving the factory or at the import stage, thus simplifying measurement and collection, enabling extensive coverage, and limiting evasion and better physical monitoring. Currently, excise taxes amount to less than 2 per cent of GDP in low-income countries, compared to about 3 per cent in high-income countries. They have a buoyant base and can be administered at a low cost.

9.4   Earmarking of funds (or hypothecated taxes)

Having discussed a menu of options in both expenditure reallocation (inter- and intra-sectoral), as well as revenue mobilization, there is a need to bring the revenue/expenditure discussion together in order to ensure that additional revenues actually benefit basic social services. Earmarking of funds (or hypothecated taxes) are one way forward. Here we discuss the case for and against earmarking.

The case for earmarking of funds for basic services: the international experience

Normally when a new tax is imposed, there is much public resistance. However, when a source of revenue is identified for specific programmes that are known or seen to have a high social benefit, the normal resistance of taxpayers to new taxation can be overcome. This is one major factor in favour of hypothecated taxes. Such earmarked taxes have been used in many countries at different times in their history. They have taken a variety of forms :

- taxes on property;
- taxes on business;
- taxes on certain commodities, especially intoxicants or cigarettes;
- taxes on imports;
- taxes on interest or dividends.

They can be national taxes, or levied at other levels of government – an issue to which we shall return.

An argument against earmarked taxes has been that they might not add to resources for the particular purpose they are meant, as the government may simply divert resources hitherto devoted to, say, education to other purposes. Government resources are fungible, and the possibility of diversion has also been the argument made against project aid from external sources (see next chapter). It may simply help the government to divert its own resources, for instance for military purposes. Clearly, if earmarking is to be used for elementary education, specific safeguards have to be built into the spending mechanism.

Despite the risks associated with it, earmarking of revenues has been implemented in industrialized countries for education. Earmarked taxes have been used for education in the USA at the state level (Lockheed et al., 1991). There are also examples of earmarking from the developing world – in every developing region. The Republic of Korea – which was a high achiever in terms of mass schooling very early in its development process – has used earmarking to good effect. In 1982 the government was finding that the general budget was unable to meet the costs of the education system. It introduced a five-year education tax on spirits (liquor), tobacco, interest and dividend income, and the banking and insurance industry. Five years later the tax accounted for 15 per cent of the education ministry's budget. Other Asian countries – China, Nepal and Philippines – have implemented earmarking for education. India introduced a surcharge on income taxes of 2 per cent in 2004 to be earmarked for elementary education – the surcharge came after the Indian government committed itself (through a constitutional amendment) to making elementary education a fundamental right of every citizen (Mehrotra et al., 2005).

Earmarked taxes for education have also been used in Latin American and African countries. Brazil imposed a 2.5 per cent salary tax on the wages of employees in the private sector, and the funds are used exclusively for primary education. The federal government collects the tax, two-thirds of which go to the states. Alfonso and de Mello (2000) argue that earmarking of revenues in both education and health have yielded good results in Brazil. This experience from a wide variety of countries seems to suggest that, designed appropriately, earmarked funds for specific purposes for a sector, from dedicated revenues, can play a useful supplementary role in general budgetary allocations to the sector.

The case against earmarking extra-budgetary funds

The international experience does point to certain pitfalls that should be avoided if earmarking is resorted to. Potter and Diamond (1999) point out that in most OECD countries, comprehensiveness and transparency are achieved by designing a budget system with three key characteristics: annuality,[40] unity[41] and universality. The last principle – universality – states that all resources should be directed to a common pool or fund. In general, in other words, earmarking of resources for specific purposes is to be discouraged. The three characteristics are needed to ensure that all proposals for government expenditure will be forced to compete for resources, and that priorities will be established across the whole range of government operations. It will be immediately obvious from these principles that they are derived mainly from the macroeconomist's concern for budgetary control, and the fear that extra-budgetary funds (into which earmarked resources are placed) might diminish the finance ministry's ability to determine resource allocation. Given the experience of runaway budget deficits since the early to mid-1980s in many developing countries, this concern is by no means illegitimate.

In summary, however, if adherence to these principles ignores the institutional development needs of certain sectors – which have tended to get traditionally ignored in many developing countries – then, in limited cases, the case for earmarking of resources is a legitimate one. The case for earmarking gains strength also from the proposal that it is not existing financial resources that would be earmarked, but new resources that would be mobilized and then dedicated to primary education, basic health, or water and sanitation.

Too many extra-budgetary funds should indeed be discouraged.[42] In other words, one cannot make the case that earmarking can be resorted to for ensuring the delivery of *all* basic social services. A lot of the IMF critique of extra-budgetary funds derives from the indiscriminate use of funds that was rampant in many African countries as well as countries of the former Soviet Union (after 1991). Nevertheless, selective use of funds is more appropriate. Thus, it will be appropriate to use, for instance, part of the proceeds from the disinvestment of state-owned enterprises for creating a fund for some social service, say meeting maternal or child nutritional needs. Similarly, social security funds are a feature of many countries. Second, we have given many examples above of earmarking of funds for education and health services. Third, earmarking of funds for infrastructure, especially road maintenance, is good if it prevents the diversion of resources needed for road maintenance (often seen as not politically attractive) to other purposes; poor road maintenance can lead to higher capital expenditures in the long term. The World Bank has encouraged, as part of its Roads Management Initiative (launched in 1988), a 'second-generation road fund', emphasizing transparency, accountability and financing by user charges. Gwilliams and Shalizi

(1997) note that these funds 'compensate for political and administrative myopia and ensure the allocation of resources to a low profile economic activity with particularly high returns', especially when they go hand in hand with some form of user-charge financing.

9.5 Public expenditure effectiveness and performance budgeting

Industrial countries currently have much higher levels of public expenditure to GDP ratios than developing countries do. Wagner's Law[43] has been one of the best-known explanations for the growth of government: that a rise in public spending was a natural development that would accompany the growth of per capita income. While cross-section analysis today would naturally confirm this phenomenon, historically there have been other factors which influenced public spending (see Lindert, 2000; Holsey and Borcherding, 1997). As we saw in Chapter 4, the average share of public expenditure in GDP increased slowly between 1870 and World War I, growing from 10.7 per cent in 1870 to 11.9 per cent in 1913. The First World War increased public spending (due to war-related expenditures) to 18.7 per cent on average (with the war-affected countries exceeding that share). Before World War II, the Great Depression caused the erosion of legal-institutional constraints on fiscal deficits. Also, the acceptance of welfare rights led to average unweighted public spending growing from about 22 per cent in 1937 to 28 per cent of GDP in 1960 (Tanzi and Schuknecht, 2000).

The 1960s and 1970s were the heyday of Keynesianism, and public expenditure increased from 28 per cent in 1960 to 43 per cent of GDP in 1980 (after which a decline set in). Nevertheless, no industrial country kept public expenditure below 30 per cent of GDP – only Japan and the USA among major industrial countries remained around that level, while in Sweden and the Netherlands it rose above 50 per cent. It was in the wake of this growth that the rent-seeking of policymakers began to be emphasized in the public choice and new institutional economics literature – which slowly became influential.

However, even those advocating cutting the role of the state in industrialized countries (see, e.g., Tanzi and Schuknecht, 2000) say that even after allowing for the cuts, the size of the state in these countries is likely to remain around 30 per cent of GDP.[44] Compare this figure to the size of the state in the countries we have been discussing in this study (Table 9.4). Only a handful of countries are anywhere close to that figure – Sri Lanka (a relative high achiever), Namibia, South Africa (both middle-income

Table 9.4 Public expenditure as a percentage of GDP, selected countries

Countries	1980	1981	1982	1983	1984	1985	1986	1987	1988	1989	1990	1991	1992	1993	1994	1995	1996	1997	1998
South & East Asia																			
Bangladesh	7.4	10.3	9.7	8.3	8.1	9.2	9.4	9.1	9.3	11.1	–	–	–	–	–	–	–	–	–
Nepal	14.3	14.5	16.8	20.3	18.4	17.6	16.9	17.4	17.7	19.5	17.2	18.9	16.8	17.0	14.7	16.5	17.5	16.8	17.5
Philippines	13.4	13.8	12.9	12.2	10.1	11.2	13.5	15.9	16.1	18.0	19.6	19.2	19.7	18.5	18.4	17.9	18.5	19.3	19.3
Sri Lanka	41.4	30.5	34.0	31.1	29.0	33.4	31.9	31.7	31.1	30.8	28.4	29.3	26.9	27.0	27.2	29.3	27.7	25.7	25.0
Thailand	18.8	19.0	20.2	19.6	19.4	20.5	19.5	17.5	15.1	14.3	14.1	14.5	15.0	15.9	16.3	15.8	16.5	19.3	18.6
Vietnam	–	–	–	–	–	–	–	–	–	–	–	–	–	–	26.2	24.5	24.3	22.0	20.1
Sub-Saharan Africa																			
Burkina Faso	12.2	11.7	12.3	9.7	11.4	9.8	12.0	13.2	15.6	14.1	15.0	18.0	17.0	16.8	–	–	–	–	–
Cameroon	15.7	20.7	20.5	20.9	21.9	21.2	21.5	23.2	17.1	20.1	21.2	21.5	18.1	15.9	14.2	12.7	–	–	–
Côte d'Ivoire	31.7	–	–	–	30.2	23.2	26.4	24.5	26.1	22.0	24.5	–	–	–	27.4	26.5	25.3	25.0	24.0
Kenya	25.3	27.0	27.6	25.1	24.7	25.8	24.3	27.9	26.4	30.2	27.5	28.9	24.8	29.9	32.4	28.5	29.0	–	–
Malawi	34.6	35.5	28.9	28.9	27.7	31.3	33.8	32.8	29.4	27.6	26.5	–	–	–	–	–	–	–	–
Mali	19.4	21.4	26.3	26.3	24.9	28.1	27.5	27.2	30.1	–	–	–	–	–	–	–	–	–	–
Namibia	18.6	–	–	–	–	–	–	–	–	–	–	–	–	–	–	–	–	–	–
Niger	–	–	–	–	–	–	39.0	40.6	35.9	33.4	32.1	39.0	39.6	38.2	–	–	–	–	–
South Africa	21.6	23.3	25.5	27.5	27.5	29.1	30.6	30.4	30.6	29.8	30.1	29.5	32.6	34.1	29.8	30.0	30.6	29.3	29.7
Uganda	6.2	4.8	9.6	9.9	13.7	12.9	10.7	–	–	–	–	–	–	–	–	–	–	–	–
Zambia	37.1	36.7	39.2	32.2	29.2	35.1	41.7	31.6	27.8	–	–	–	–	–	–	–	–	–	–
Middle East & North Africa																			
Morocco	33.1	39.1	37.5	32.3	29.7	30.4	28.9	28.2	28.2	30.5	28.8	27.8	30.1	34.0	32.2	33.3	–	–	–
Latin America & Caribbean																			
Belize	22.9	26.7	30.0	28.0	24.9	27.2	–	–	14.0	15.2	16.4	16.8	20.3	24.0	23.2	21.1	23.0	22.0	21.9
Bolivia	–	20.4	21.2	21.2	20.6	25.4	27.9	24.9	31.3	34.7	34.9	24.4	29.2	37.2	33.8	–	–	–	–
Brazil	20.2	20.4	21.2	31.9	32.6	30.4	28.3	24.9	23.2	21.4	20.4	21.0	20.8	21.4	20.9	19.9	21.0	20.7	21.6
Chile	28.0	29.4	34.1	31.9	32.6	30.4	28.3	24.9	23.2	21.4	20.4	21.0	20.8	21.4	20.9	19.9	21.0	20.7	16.0
Colombia	11.5	12.0	13.7	13.1	13.0	12.1	11.7	11.8	11.8	12.3	9.9	9.9	13.0	12.3	12.6	13.4	14.9	15.8	–
Costa Rica	25.0	21.0	18.4	23.6	22.8	21.8	26.4	27.2	24.5	26.1	25.6	24.8	23.9	26.2	30.6	29.1	30.1	16.7	–
Dominican Republic	16.9	16.2	13.5	14.0	13.4	12.6	13.3	14.4	16.3	14.5	11.7	11.1	13.3	17.3	17.1	15.4	15.6	16.7	–
Guatemala	14.3	16.1	14.7	12.9	–	–	–	–	–	–	–	–	–	–	–	–	–	–	–
Jamaica	41.5	39.9	38.6	40.7	33.9	38.5	–	–	–	–	–	–	–	–	–	–	–	–	–
Nicaragua	30.4	39.3	49.4	67.7	63.9	59.6	52.3	–	47.9	31.8	36.0	27.4	30.0	30.1	32.3	33.2	–	–	–
Peru	19.5	18.4	17.6	19.5	18.5	17.4	16.7	15.5	13.0	11.7	16.4	13.0	15.9	15.4	16.4	17.3	16.5	15.7	16.4

Source: World Bank, World Development Indicators, 2000.

countries with growing social provisioning) and Costa Rica (another high achiever). In fact, two other high achievers, Malaysia and Mauritius, also had increased public spending to unprecedented levels by the early 1980s (44 and 36 per cent respectively), which enabled them to ensure much higher social provisioning than was prevalent in other countries at the same level of per capita income.

The growing role of the state will have to be premissed upon a more effective state as well. If in the preceding two sections we have argued the case for much greater revenue mobilization to reinforce the role of the state in public investment in physical and social infrastructure, there is also a case for much *better management of resources* in order to ensure that spending is pro-poor. Chapter 7 made the case for voice from below if service delivery is to improve. However, accountability *within* the bureaucracy would need to improve as well.

Better management of resources involves, as we noted earlier, a medium-term expenditure framework (MTEF), especially if better balance between capital and recurrent expenditures is to be ensured. Thus, in South Africa, for example, the ability of the executive to spread the pain of lower than expected economic growth between 1998 and 2000 over the medium term, rather than imposing severe spending disruptions in one year, also built support for the system.

Better management of resources would also imply a move in the direction of performance budgeting. Many developing-country governments hold implementing agencies responsible for keeping expenditure in line with budgets, instead of overspending or diverting spending to other uses.[45] But public-sector managers should also be able to justify their budgets, and be evaluated, in terms of the results to be achieved. Without such a link, it is impossible for civil society or the legislature to hold the government to account for the quality of government services. Performance budgeting links budget allocations to intended outputs (e.g. delivery of a defined package of health interventions to a specified population) and outcomes (e.g. the extent to which spending contributes to reduction of infant mortality targets). The implication is that instead of merely measuring inputs we also examine outputs and outcomes.

Performance budgeting also involves giving greater discretion to managers in the use of inputs; otherwise it is difficult to hold them accountable for results. However, there are questions over how appropriate performance budgeting is for developing and transitional economies (DFID, 2001). Some have argued that these countries should first establish reliable external controls, then set up internal control systems, before moving to performance

Table 9.5 Types of accountability

Type of accountability	Exercised by	What is controlled	Mode of accountability
Financial: external	*Central agencies*: provide approval for each discrete transaction or group of expenditures.	*Inputs*: specific items of expenditure.	Compliance with itemized budget and government-wide rules. Pre-audit of transactions: control is imposed before any expenditure of funds.
Financial: internal	*Spending departments*: those who spend the funds have first-instance responsibility for ensuring the legality and propriety of their actions.	*Inputs*: classes of expenditure.	Department systems comply with government-wide standards. Post-audit of transactions: managers do not have to obtain outside approval before they act.
Managerial	*Spending managers*: given discretion to spend appropriated resources in exchange for being held accountable for performance.	*Outputs and total running costs*: focus on what managers are producing rather than what they are buying.	Accountability for performance. *Ex ante* specification of performance targets. *Ex post* audit of results.

Source: Schick, 1998, cited in Guidelines for DFID – Understanding and Reforming Public Expenditure Management, Version 1, March 2001.

accountability (see Table 9.5) (Schick, 1998). In fact, the data requirements of performance budgeting are quite heavy. Many countries have tried to implement them with the enthusiastic support of donors. In South Asia, India and Sri Lanka, and in Southeast Asia, Malaysia, the Philippines and Singapore have adopted types of performance budgeting with uneven results. Many Latin American countries have also done the same. However, by and large, where it has been introduced it has been scaled down. Nevertheless, moves towards performance budgeting would be a welcome transition.

Meanwhile, in respect of basic services, we have already argued in Chapter 7 that deep democratic decentralization is critical for improving service delivery. Pressure from the bottom up will need to combine with improved management within the hierarchical set-up if delivery of basic services is to improve.

9.6   Concluding remarks

We identified three main ways in which additional resources can be generated to underpin public provision of basic services. If public expenditure restructuring in favour of BSS is perceived as a zero-sum game in which the non-poor will be the losers, there is little likelihood of success in such restructuring. If the non-poor are to acquiesce politically to the restructuring of expenditure to favour the poor, increased revenues will be needed to provide room for manoeuvre to decision-makers. In other words, in principle, within the constraints imposed by the political economy of decision-making, it may be possible to devise a set of tax measures (combining progressive direct taxes and neutral or progressive indirect taxes) with a consequent increase in revenues, which would enable restructuring of expenditure – both intra- and inter-sectorally – to occur.

At one level, 'finding' financing for BSS is easy. As the discussion above shows, there are many budget lines that could be considered unproductive or less meritorious than spending on BSS for children. However, they all imply important redistribution of public benefits. Thus, for reasons of political economy and for technical reasons, the evidence reviewed in this chapter indicates that intra-sectoral restructuring is easier during periods of increasing resources for the health and education sector as a whole. Consequently, more resources can be generated for basic services through inter-sectoral restructuring than merely through intra-sectoral reallocation. In some countries inter-sectoral reallocation has enabled increasing resources for basic services in the short term. In recent years, for example, Uganda and Malawi have shown that it is possible to undertake intra-sectoral reallocations under conditions of increasing overall resources for the education sector – with remarkable results for outcome indicators in primary education.

However, as both basic and non-basic levels of services are needed (e.g. both primary schools and universities, and both community health centres and hospitals, are needed) a balance needs to be struck. In other words, providing university education to a few when most children cannot finish the few grades needed to ensure literacy and numeracy clearly points to the imperative of intra-sectoral restructuring. Nevertheless, this rebalancing will not be sufficient to generate, in the long run, the required resources to achieve universal access to basic social services of good quality.

Thus, the emphasis must be on enhanced resource generation, and new ways of financing social services. The emphasis of the last two decades on expenditure reduction as a means of budget deficit reduction has to change. We noted in Chapter 4 that in states where the public-expenditure-to-GDP ratio was found to be rising, BSS per capita had also been rising. In the long run, international financial institutions must provide more technical support for improving tax collection and new sources of revenue generation. Gradual increments in the revenue base will also ease the pain of inter- and intra-sectoral restructuring. And hypothecating taxes for specific high-return activities in health and education (as, e.g., Brazil has done) can substantially increase resources as well as make them stable. Stability of recurrent expenditures is essential since additional nurses and teachers cannot be hired today and fired tomorrow. In the long term, economic growth can also enhance the revenue base – though for the government of the day that is often of theoretical significance unless growth is very rapid. Moreover, the investment in education, health, water and sanitation, nutrition – in short, in the capabilities of the population – will be the foundation for future economic growth (see Chapters 1 and 2).

Annex 9.1 International taxation and other potential international sources of development finance

This chapter has concentrated on domestic sources of finance within developing countries. This annex complements the discussion in this chapter and the next by summarizing a series of proposals regarding international sources of finance to meet the financing requirements of the Millennium Development Goals. Clearly, one such source is simply increasing ODA – a subject we discuss in the next chapter. However, there are other potential sources of external development finance, and that is the subject of this very brief note (which draws upon Atkinson, 2004).

1. *Global environment taxes* These could be taxes on goods generating environmental externalities, specifically a tax on use of hydrocarbon fuels according to their carbon content. A tax in high-income countries alone could raise the $50 billion additional ODA. To generate such revenue from a carbon tax, the tax rate required is much smaller than that considered in proposals to reduce global warming. Its disadvantages are that the distributional effect on households within high-income countries would need to be offset, and there would be administrative costs of operating such a global tax. An obstacle is that it requires the general agreement of high-income countries, and account has also to be taken of existing national taxes (New Zealand introduced a carbon tax in 2004) (Sandmo, 2004).

2. *Currency transactions tax (Tobin tax)*   A tax on foreign currency transactions, covering a range of transactions (spot, forward, future, swaps and other derivatives). Based on a tax rate much smaller than those considered in proposals to reduce exchange rate volatility (which was the original rationale given by Tobin), the tax could generate $15–28 billion for global public use. The tax would have to be passed on to final users. Its disadvantages are that the final distributional effect and impact on real transactions is hard to predict, and the administrative cost of operating a global tax would have to be determined. The main obstacle, again, is that it requires general agreement.

These transactions in 1995 amounted to around US$300 trillion a year (BIS, 1995–6). Hence a 0.1 per cent tax, even if it caused the level of foreign exchange transactions to halve, would lead to roughly $150 billion being collected, or 2.5 times the current level of ODA to all developing countries. A smaller tax would accordingly reduce the tax revenues. Those who have examined the practicalities of such a 'Tobin tax' argue that it is technically feasible, provided it is adopted uniformly by the countries which have all the main foreign exchange markets (eight countries, including Hong Kong, and counting the whole European Union as one). The collection of such a tax would necessarily be through the banks in these industrialized countries and therefore the revenue would go to those governments; however, that does not imply that that same government should receive the revenue.

A civil society movement has prompted resolutions in support of such taxes in dozens of cities across the world (including more than fifty in France). Many labour unions throughout the world have also called for such taxes, including the AFL–CIO in the USA. Legislation in support of such taxes has been introduced in the French Parliament, the European Parliament, the US Congress, and was approved in 1998 by the Canadian Parliament.

Carbon taxes and currency transaction taxes are not the only taxes proposed. Other proposed global taxes include a 'brain drain' tax, an international air transport tax (introduced in 2005 by France to fund HIV/AIDS programmes, mainly in sub-Saharan countries), taxation of ocean fishing, taxation of arms exports, and a luxury goods tax (Clunies Ross, 1999; Nissanke, 2004).

3. *Creation of new Special Drawing Rights (SDRs)*   The original purpose of SDRs was to create international liquidity. But this is a proposal to create SDRs for development purposes, with donor countries making their SDR allocation available to fund development. An allocation of $25–30 billion

could make significant contribution, but their usefulness may depend upon the frequency of SDR creation. The main obstacle would be that it has to be ratified by one hundred members of the IMF with 85 per cent of voting power (Areyeetey, 2004).

4. *International Finance Facility* This is a long-term, but conditional, funding guaranteed to the poorest countries by donor countries (a proposal of the UK government, already initiated in some form for funding vaccines for poor countries). The idea is that long-term pledges of a flow of annual payments to the IFF would leverage additional money from the international capital markets. Its advantage, if introduced as planned, could be to achieve a flow of $50 billion for 2010–15, building up from 2006 and falling to zero by 2020. It would provide predictable and stable flows with an agreed disbursement mechanism. Its main disadvantage is the cost of negotiation and administration of a new organization. It is also difficult to ensure additionality. It also requires sufficient donor countries to sign up, and to continue to make commitments. The good news is that the involvement of all high-income countries is not required, but it does require sufficient donor countries to sign up, and to continue to make commitments (Mavrotas, 2004).

5. *Increased private donations for development* The proposal is that measures should be put in place by governments to encourage private funding of development: tax incentives, global funds, corporate giving, and the Internet. The double dividend here is that giving benefits both donors and recipients. Advocates argue that total charitable giving is sizeable (in the USA 1.5 per cent of GNP) and there is potential for development to attract a larger share (Micklewright and Wright, 2004).

6. *Increased remittances from emigrants* Remittances are a large, growing and stable source of funds. They can contribute to infrastructure projects. Advocates argue that a reduction in transfer costs could increase remittances, and the advantage is that the transfers benefit both donors and recipients. The downside may be that it could run into money laundering and counter-terrorism legislation (Solimano, 2004).

7. *Global lottery* A global lottery could be operated through national state-operated and state-licensed lotteries, with proceeds shared between national participants and an independent foundation in conjunction with the UN (Addison and Chowdhry, 2004). One obstacle with such a scheme could be competition with national lotteries.

Atkinson (2004) summarizes the various proposals. If rich countries were to generate the additional ODA needed for the MDGs, none of the innovative proposals would be required. However, they would be required if the ODA was not forthcoming. As regards the global taxes, he notes that if levied at low rates, these taxes (on carbons and currency transactions) may not discourage pollution and speculation (as they were intended to do in their original form), but could generate significant resources for development. Second, he concludes that, given that there will be opposition to global taxes, there are alternatives to them: the IFF and creation of SDRs. Third, the issue of additionality will always remain: if other sources of finance discussed here become operational, high-income-country governments may reduce ODA – a risk of crowding out. Fourth, he notes that only the carbon tax is sufficient on its own to meet the requirement of the additional $50 billion ODA needed (according to the Zedillo Report to meet the MDG external resource requirements). Hence, a package of measures will be required. Finally, he finds that there is only limited understanding of the economic impact of the different proposals, which may remain a deterrent to their implementation.

10

The consistency between aid and trade policies and the Millennium Goals

There are various, conflicting estimates of the cost of universalizing access to basic social services, many carried out in the context of assessing the financial needs of achieving the MDGs (e.g. the Zedillo Report of 2002, OECD/DAC, 2002; World Bank, 2002). In spite of different assumptions, models, data shortages, and other difficulties, most indicate an additional $50–80 billion per annum for all developing countries, with the largest needs for additional external resources to be found in sub-Saharan Africa and South Asia. Within the last decade, governments of donors and developing countries have committed themselves to universalizing access to basic social services: basic health, basic education, water and sanitation, and reproductive health. These commitments were first called the International Development Targets by the donor community (OECD, 1996a). Later most of the same targets were agreed in the UN by all countries as the Millennium Development Goals (MDGs).[1]

The bulk of the resources for this task will come from the national budgets of developing countries. However, the scale of the resources makes the task daunting for most low-income countries without additional official development assistance (ODA) for basic services. The role of ODA will be to create the fiscal space in low-income countries to enable the goals to be realized – in our view, an essentially transitional role. This should be a short- to-medium run transitional role since one of the most serious problems in a group of low-income countries – mainly African ones – is that of aid dependence. Having played this transitional role – especially at a time when the burden of external debt servicing is unsustainably high for around forty Heavily Indebted Poor Countries (HIPCs) – the role of ODA can diminish in the future.

Since basic social services are heavily labour-intensive, the local cost component in each of the subsectors comprising what we call BSS is rather high. This is perhaps a major explanation for the relatively low priority accorded to such services in ODA in the past. Some have argued that aid for BSS is not a very good method of financing basic health and basic education. Several reasons have been given (Burgess, 1997). It is not a stable source of finance, as the flow may fluctuate wildly depending upon the political vagaries of Western donors. Also, resources will not increase in line with economic and population growth. In other words, ODA for BSS fails to satisfy the criteria of stability and buoyancy, which is not helpful for sectors where the costs are mostly recurrent.[2] However, the forty or so HIPCs are so squeezed fiscally that there is little likelihood of an improvement in the access to basic services without additional ODA. In addition, the needs of the low-income non-HIPC countries with large gaps in access will also require additional ODA.

In recent years donors themselves have been keen to allocate resources to objectives that alleviate poverty. All donors agree that universal provision of basic social services is an integral part of a strategy of donor support for poverty alleviation (OECD, 1996a). However, so far there has been almost no external analysis of the relationship between ODA trends and the International Development Targets (IDTs) agreed by the donors in 1996 (most of these same IDTs were renamed the Millennium Development Goals by a summit meeting in 2000 at the UN). This chapter addresses the degree to which the objective of poverty alleviation through financing of BSS has become an integral part of the development assistance strategy of major bilateral and multilateral donors. Our conclusion is that the size, composition and quality of aid still does not suggest that eliminating human poverty has become the overriding objective of aid.

In Section 10.1, we spell out the donor governments' institutional response to the MDGs. Section 10.2 examines the statistical information from donor sources, on ODA to BSS, looking at trends in total ODA and ODA to BSS – both bilateral as well as multilateral. It also examines the sectoral composition of ODA to basic services. Section 10.3 examines issues of a more qualitative nature in relation to the main social basic services: education (including basic education), health (including basic and reproductive health), water and sanitation, and new developments in aid policy in relation to these sectors. Sections 10.2 and 10.3 draw primarily on data from OECD's Development Assistance Committee since 1994 in relation to basic health

and basic education – which were the two missing areas of data relevant to
the international development targets. Section 10.4 addresses the modality of
aid to social services – project aid versus the more recent sectoral approach
– and examines some evidence on the latter. In Section 10.5 the chapter
briefly addresses the industrialized–country policies that can have a significant
impact on prospects for achieving the MDGs and poverty reduction in
developing countries. Agricultural, trade, investment and other policies of
OECD countries can affect the ability of developing countries to capitalize on the opportunities afforded by globalization, and increase the risks
associated with increasing international economic integration. However, as
we shall see, despite some positive steps taken at OECD level, only a small
minority of donor development agencies and their governments have taken
concrete steps to ensure that their domestic policies and their positions on
international policies are consistent with poverty reduction.

10.1   Aid policies and poverty reduction

OECD's Development Assistance Committee (DAC) committed itself in
1996 to the development goals – International Development Targets (or
IDTs) – outlined at earlier United Nations conferences.[3] The goals are:

- halving the proportion of people living in extreme poverty by 2015;
- universal primary education in all countries by 2015;
- elimination of gender disparities in primary and secondary education by
  2005;
- reduction in under-5 mortality by two-thirds of the 1990 level by
  2015;
- reduction of maternal mortality by three-quarters during the same
  period;
- access through the primary health care (PHC) system to reproductive
  health services by 2015;
- national strategies to reverse current trends in the loss of environmental
  resources by 2005 and a reversal of these trends by 2015.

These goals are similar to the Millennium Development Goals (MDGs)
agreed in 2000 by *all* countries (see Annex 1.2 for list of MDGs and
associated targets). There are differences: first, access to reproductive health
services were eliminated from the UN General Assembly's MDGs, at the instance of the US government; second, 'combat HIV/AIDS, malaria and other
diseases' was added; and third, 'develop a global partnership for development'

between rich and poor countries has been added as an eighth goal. In fact, it is in the light of this last goal (goal 8 of the MDGs) that this chapter is written.

Clearly all of these MDGs (with the exception of the first and last), relate to the provision of basic social services. Ever since the *World Development Report* of 1990 emphasized the role of the social sectors as a means of alleviating poverty, bilateral donors have included investment in the social sectors – particularly basic social services – as an important element in their strategy for poverty reduction. For several agencies, this implied a commitment to the target of the 20/20 Initiative, which proposed that 20 per cent of ODA, and 20 per cent of developing countries' public spending, be allocated to BSS.[4] In reality, however, while agencies may be unsure about issues of redistribution of income and assets, an improved distribution of human capital is an area that they tend to support (OECD/DAC, 1999).

More than statements of goals and targets, and policy pronouncements regarding the need for building partnerships with recipients, the real issue is to what extent ODA has responded to these policy pronouncements. This issue is examined in the following two sections.

However, should we have high expectations of a poverty focus of aid, when the past history of aid tells a different story? Browne (2006) – as a long-time observer of aid (see Browne, 1990, 1997) as well as a practitioner – summarizes several decades of practice as follows. First, aid is not correlated with human development levels of countries. For 1980, 1990 and 2000, the relationship is entirely random. Second, aid is not correlated with country income levels. The low-income countries (income per capita below $735 per annum) account for three-quarters of people living in poverty, but receive only 40 per cent of aid. Third, aid is volatile. After rising for three decades until 1992, it fell sharply after the cold war ended. Fourth, the size of aid also depends on donor concerns of affordability – aid gets cut when donors face fiscal strains. Finally, aid is usually related to the non-developmental objectives of donors – commercial, geopolitical or strategic/security ones.

10.2   ODA for basic social services: the quantitative evidence

For most low-income countries, external resources will be critical to the achievement of the MDGs. However, what is the record on total ODA, especially since the announcement of the IDTs (1996)? It fell from a high of 0.61 per cent of GNP in 1961 to 0.37 in 1980, further to 0.31 over 1988–89 and to a low of 0.24 in 1999 and 0.23 in 2003. Only a small

Table 10.1   Net flows of ODA to direct recipients and intermediaries, 1990–98 (US$ billion)

	1990	1991	1992	1993	1994	1995	1996	1997	1998	1999	2000
DAC	54.5	58.6	62.7	56.5	59.2	58.9	55.4	48.3	51.9	52.1	49.5
Bilateral recipients	37.7	42.2	42.2	38.4	40.3	39.5	38.1	31.3	34.1	37.9	49.5
Intermediaries	16.8	16.4	20.5	18.1	18.9	19.4	17.3	17.0	17.8		
Multilateral institutions	15.8	15.4	19.6	17.2	17.9	18.3	16.3	16.0	16.8	14.2	13.5
NGOs	1.0	1.0	0.9	0.9	1.0	1.1	1.0	1.0	1.0		
Non-DAC	6.0	1.4	1.7	1.5	1.4	1.1	1.3	1.0	–		
Bilateral recipients + NGOs	0.2	1.2	1.2	1.1	1.0	0.8	0.8	0.6	–		
Multilateral institutions	5.8	0.2	0.5	0.4	0.4	0.3	0.5	0.4	–		
Total	60.5	60.0	64.4	58.0	60.6	60.0	56.7	49.3	–		

Note: From 1993, forgiveness of debt for military purposes was not reported as ODA, but as 'Other Official Flows'.

Source: OECD, Development Cooperation Report of the Chairman of the Development Assistance Committee (DAC), Paris, various issues.

number of countries have ever exceeded the UN target of 0.7 of GNP for aid (set in 1970). Table 10.1 shows that ODA declined not only as a share of donor GNP, but also in absolute terms. Net ODA (DAC and non-DAC) rose to $62.7 billion in 1992, and since then declined to an average of $50 billion annually over 1999 and 2000 (in 2000 dollars it was $58 billion in 1990 and $54 billion in 2001).

Denmark, the Netherlands, Sweden and Luxembourg are the only European Union member states that meet the ODA standard (which is accepted by all UN members, except the USA). Norway, a non-EU member, is also part of this club. Luxembourg, the newest member of this group, has proved that it is possible to raise ODA to 0.7 per cent of GNP in a short time. None of the G7 countries are members of this group, which on average allocated 0.21 of their GNP to ODA (1999) (See Figure 10.1). These five countries also have the highest grant equivalent of total ODA as a percentage of GNP. These five also provide the highest ODA per capita of donor country – in the range of $184 and $326, compared to a range of $33 (USA) to $98 (France) for the G7 countries (1998–99) (OECD, 2001).[5]

Figure 10.1 Official development assistance (% of combined GNP)

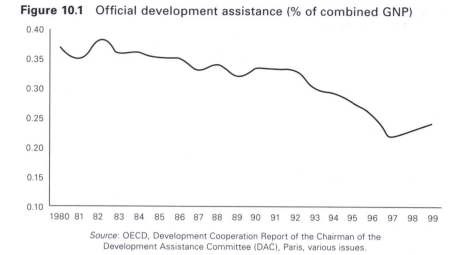

Source: OECD, Development Cooperation Report of the Chairman of the
Development Assistance Committee (DAC), Paris, various issues.

As ODA fell from 0.35 per cent of OECD countries' GNP in 1990
to 0.22 per cent of GNP in 2000, the magnitude of BWI, especially IMF
funding, increased (as we noted in Chapter 2). The number of prolonged
users of IMF funds rose: 44 countries (29 eligible for the PRGF) were
prolonged users at some point during 1971–2000. It is ironic that the IMF
was always intended, in its core operational approach, to focus on achieving
a restoration of external and domestic balance and sustainability *within a short
period of time.* It was the World Bank that was meant to be the development
institution, lending for long periods. However, the IMF has become involved
in prolonged lending to the same group of countries. Thus, over time, the
IMF has become embedded in local policymaking.[6] As we noted earlier, it is
not entirely clear that its policy prescriptions are leading to economic growth,
and could thus be undermining the prospects for achieving the MDGs.

Aid levels continued to fall through till 2001. Since then, total aid
from Development Assistance Committee (DAC) members of OECD have
raised their ODA to $78.4 billion in 2004 – its highest level ever. Yet the
ODA/GNI ratio at 0.25 per cent remains short of previous averages, as we
saw above, and of course the UN ODA target. In fact, ODA growth has
not matched donors' economic growth over the past decade. The ODA/GNI
ratio rose to 0.25 per cent in 2003 and 2004, up from 0.23 per cent in
2002 and 0.22 per cent in 2001, but even then well below the average of
0.33 per cent reached in 1970–92. What is equally important is that while
a significant share of the ODA increase over the four years 2001–04 went
to the LDCs, most was actually in the form of debt relief and emergency
and reconstruction aid (OECD, 2005).

It is expected that there may be further substantial increase in real ODA in line with the Monterrey Consensus (a financing-for-development conference that took place in the run-up the Millennium Summit). Other than five donors (listed above) that have met the 0.7 per cent of GNI target, seven others have committed to reach it before 2014: Belgium, Finland, France, Germany, Ireland, Spain and the UK. The European Union has launched proposals for all EU DAC members to reach 0.51 per cent by 2010 as an interim step towards 0.7 per cent by 2015 (the target date for achieving the Millennium Goals). Canada and Switzerland have also made commitments to reach higher ODA targets, and the USA has already increased its aid by more than the 50 per cent it pledged at Monterrey. OECD (2005) notes that if these existing commitments are met, ODA will reach $115 billion (at 2004 prices and exchange rates) by 2010 – still below the estimates of the amounts required to help many more countries attain the Millennium Goals by 2015 than those presently expected to do so.[7]

While for all low-income countries ODA as a share of GNI was 2.8 per cent over 1990–94, it fell slightly to 2.6 per cent over 2000–03; ODA fell also as a share of gross fixed capital formation from 13.9 per cent to 11.9 per cent over the same period. In sub-Saharan Africa the declines were even sharper: from 6.6 per cent of GNI to 5.3 per cent, and from 40.7 per cent of GCFC to 27 per cent (World Bank, 2004, 2005). Given that we have seen in the preceding paragraphs that aid has been rising in absolute terms quite significantly, it is remarkable that its share in GCFC has fallen rather sharply in early 2000s compared to the early 1990s, especially in sub-Saharan Africa – which, of all regions, is in desperate need of increased investment. The answer lies in the fact that additional ODA has been absorbed into increasing foreign exchange reserves. In sub-Saharan Africa, foreign exchange reserves rose from $21 billion in 1996 to $34 billion in 2000, and further to $58 billion in 2004 (World Bank, 2005). (Reserves have risen in East Asia and South Asia as well, but the reasons for that phenomenon is increasing exports and remittances, rather than ODA.) Part of the explanation for falling share of aid in GCFC despite increasing ODA is low absorptive capacity; but part of it has to do with the monetary and low inflation targets that IMF programmes have prescribed. For countries in Africa, there is a real opportunity cost in terms of public investment foregone if ODA is not being spent for that purpose.

A final concern is the predictability of ODA flows. Fiscal planning in recipient countries is dependent upon the predictability of aid, especially when it is programme assistance. Donors should be giving some indicative projections even when donors' budget cycles may prevent them from

Table 10.2　Share of BSS in total (bilateral) ODA commitments (%)

	1994	1995	1996	1997	1998	1999	2000	1994–96	1997–98	1997–98*
Australia	9.7	8.4	10.9	10.3	10.9	21.6	17.1	9.5	10.5	11.9
Austria	0.6	5.4	6.5	3.6	9.4	40.6	20.7	4.0	6.8	8.5
Belgium	5.2	3.0	3.9	5.2	4.2	13.9	17.0	3.9	4.7	6.7
Canada	0.7	4.7	3.7	1.7	1.4	6.2	10.9	3.1	1.5	5.1
Denmark	2.2	1.4	7.7	6.2	4.9	53.1	15.5	4.2	5.6	11.7
Finland	8.6	5.3	7.0	6.1	6.2	15.0	12.0	6.8	6.1	12.5
France	2.6	2.8	4.8	2.6	1.9	0.0	7.6	3.3	2.2	3.6
Germany	9.0	9.2	7.6	9.4	9.4	23.2	21.9	8.6	9.4	11.3
Ireland	3.4	4.7	4.0	0.0	2.3	0.0	6.2	4.1	1.2	3.1
Italy	1.4	2.0	2.3	4.5	1.2	18.5	16.4	1.9	2.5	5.3
Japan	8.2	9.0	12.6	10.4	9.4	21.7	37.0	9.8	9.9	11.4
Luxembourg	0.0	1.0	0.8	18.7	18.1	26.2	33.7	0.6	18.4	21.3
Netherlands	4.1	4.4	10.1	5.0	8.8	15.2	9.3	5.7	7.0	11.2
New Zealand	1.3	1.1	0.0	0.0	5.5	9.7	7.4	0.8	2.5	3.5
Norway	1.7	7.1	6.1	5.6	5.7	18.3	9.0	5.2	5.7	13.3
Portugal	0.1	0.6	7.5	2.2	0.7	0.5	1.5	1.6	1.6	3.4
Spain	1.0	5.8	5.3	5.2	5.9	18.0	12.9	4.4	5.6	6.2
Sweden	11.4	6.9	10.1	9.8	5.1	13.1	10.6	9.4	7.2	11.1
Switzerland	1.4	2.0	4.9	0.0	8.4	16.6	9.9	2.6	3.1	6.6
United Kingdom	2.1	2.2	5.5	3.3	5.9	18.5	18.1	3.3	4.7	7.8
United States	5.0	12.4	8.9	8.2	9.4	15.5	15.2	8.6	8.8	11.6
Total	5.5	7.2	8.3	7.2	7.2	16.0	16.5	7.0	7.2	9.6

Notes: Basic services include basic education, basic health, population and reproductive health, nutrition and water supply. *Including multilaterals.

Source: OECD, Development Assistance Committee database; OECD, DAC, Development Cooperation Report, various issues.

giving firm commitments for several years. Without such indications or commitments, there is little meaning in donors expecting governments to prepare Medium Term Expenditure Frameworks, which is increasingly seen as central to the PRSPs. OECD (2005) notes that, for African recipients, ODA volatility is lower in more stable countries and higher in more unstable ones. A large number of recipients face year-to-year variations in ODA averaging 10–20 per cent, but in conflict countries it can go up to 50 per cent.

Table 10.3 Share of BSS in ODA of selected multilateral agencies, 1996

Multilateral agency	Share of BSS (%)
UNDP	17.0[a]
UNFPA	83.0[b]
UNICEF	76.0[c]

[a] *sample* review of 60 per cent of ongoing projects – covering indicative planning figures and cost-sharing.
[b] All of UNFPA's mandate lies completely within the 20/20 Initiative perspective; therefore the percentage is calculated by showing income net of administrative budget as a share of total income.
[c] Share of general resources programme expenditure allocated to BSS as defined in the Oslo Consensus, excluding emergency expenditure.

Source: Estimates provided by UNICEF, UNDP and UNFPA.

The composition of ODA and basic services

The MDGs are unlikely to be achieved in the least developed countries without additional resources for universal access to basic services. However, under 10 per cent of the bilateral ODA is allocated to basic health, basic education, and water and sanitation (Table 10.2). Moreover, watsan – which accounts for 5 per cent of ODA – is not only drinking water and sanitation.[8] The ODA for BSS showed little change in the period since 1996 on aggregate.

The multilaterals – the World Bank's IDA, the soft-loan windows of the regional development banks, and the UN agencies – are the other sources of ODA. The multilaterals account for a third of all ODA (including about a third of total ODA globally to basic social services) (see Table 10.5 below). Over 1995–96 and 1997–98, on average, about 11 per cent of the International Development Agency's (IDA) lending went to basic services – not much different before and after the IDTs were announced.

The multilaterals of the UN system allocate a varying proportion of their assistance to BSS (see Table 10.3). UNDP's support to governments has always tended to cover a large number of areas, cutting across the whole economy. Its broader mandate explains the fact that, according to its own estimate, less than one-fifth of its assistance goes to BSS. On the other hand, the UNFPA devotes over three-fifths of its assistance to reproductive health, and UNICEF's own estimate includes the allocation of 76 per cent of assistance to cover basic health, basic education, nutrition, water and sanitation, excluding the emergency operations expenditure for humanitarian relief.

Next we examine the sectoral composition of ODA for the social sectors. For each of the major social services relevant for the achievement of the IDTs (education, health, watsan), we examine the allocations of ODA before and after the announcement of the IDTs in 1996.

Education

Given the commitments made to Education for All at the Jomtien Conference in 1990, one would expect that ODA earmarked for education – not just basic education, but overall – would have increased. However, between 1990 and 1995, it rose very slightly, from $5.5 billion to $6 billion, and tended to decline until 1998. There was an important increase during 1999 to $7.2 billion. However, by 2000 it had declined considerably to $3.5 billion in 2000 (see Table 10.1). Nonetheless, since the announcement of IDTs, it has averaged $5.6 billion. As a share of total commitments ODA for education hovered around 10 per cent throughout the 1990s. However, its share fell over 2000–01 to 8 per cent.[9]

ODA to basic education – most relevant for universalizing primary education and eliminating gender disparities in schooling – has not risen much either. Indeed, the share of basic education in comparison with total/bilateral education ODA is small. Despite the fact that more and more donors have been reporting their ODA to basic education, the absolute value of DAC bilateral assistance to basic education was $644 million over 1995–96, on an average annual basis, and $678 million over 1997–2000 – higher, but not significantly, after the IDTs were announced (see Table 10.2). Nevertheless, as Table 10.2 shows, bilateral ODA commitments to basic education did indeed rise in 1999 and 2000. However, 'increase' corresponds with a decline in the 'unspecified' part of ODA from 30 per cent in 1998–9 to 21 per cent in 2000–01, and the increase 'may partly arise from a reclassification of aid flows from the 'unspecified' category' (UNESCO, 2003: 236).

At the same time, schooling indicators in developing countries barely changed over the 1990s. In the regions with the lowest net enrolment rates at primary level, there was only a marginal increase over the decade. The share of basic education in total education aid was 13 per cent over 1998–99, and rose to 24 per cent over 2000–01.

Multilateral institutions (African Development Fund of the AfDB, Asian Development Fund of the ADB, the IDB Special Fund, the European Development Fund of the EC, IDA, UNDP and UNICEF) together provided an average of $954 million a year in education ODA. The amount fell to $799 in 1999–2001 (DAC Online database). Education's share of total multilateral commitments fell as well. IDA lending to education has declined in the 2000s as a proportion of total lending, and IDA lending to education now constitutes only half of its level in the mid-1990s; IDA lending to basic education also seems to have declined in 2000–01 compared to 1998–99

(UNESCO, 2003). The EFA Fast-Track Initiative, a good example of inter-agency work, could increase the funding for some countries. However, UNESCO (2003) reports that the Initiative has yet to receive substantial and concrete international support for its activities.

In summary, total ODA to education has been declining. Even though the share of basic education in total education aid increased in the most recent years, it is likely that some of the increase is due to reclassification to the basic education subsector from the 'unspecified' aid to education. We had estimated that the total additional resources required for EFA was $9.1 billion per annum of total resources (domestic and foreign) (Delamonica et al., 2004), and UNESCO (2002) estimated that additional aid of US$5.6 billion per year was required. The additional $1.5 billion currently flowing in is insufficient to meet the requirements of EFA.

Health

The value of bilateral donor assistance to the health sector as a whole (as opposed to basic health) grew from $2 billion in 1990 to $4 billion in 1999 (Table 10.3). By 1995–96, most DAC donors were reporting their ODA to basic health: over 1995–96 ODA to basic health averaged about $990 million; over 1997–2000 it averaged $953 million (see Table 10.4). Overall, just 2 per cent of total ODA was allocated to basic health over the 1990s.

Multilateral institutions provided an average of $872 million a year over 1996–98 to health services, though in 1999–2001 that fell to $673 million a year. But commitments to basic health care (including infrastructure and infectious disease control) were $264 million a year in 1996–98 and stayed at much the same level ($249 million a year) in 1999–2001.

The health, basic health and water/sanitation ODA is naturally of some concern since health outcome indicators barely improved over the 1990s. There was least improvement in under-5 mortality (an IDT goal) over 1990–2000 in the region with the highest U5MR – sub-Saharan Africa.

Assistance to population/reproductive health services tended to increase over the 1990s; it averaged $572 million annually over 1990–96, and $897 million over 1997–2000 – but here, too, the outcomes relevant to the IDTs remain dismal (see Table 10.5 below). The proportion of births attended by skilled health personnel has been recommended as a measure of progress for maternal mortality – reduction of which is an IDT. In SSA, where maternal mortality is highest, delivery care did not improve over the 1990s, with barely 42 per cent of mothers covered during delivery, as against 40 per cent in 1990.

Water and sanitation

The water challenge is greatest among all the basic social services, since many more millions are without improved water sources than without access to schooling or basic health services. ODA for water and sanitation accounts for the largest share of all BSS-related ODA. It amounted to $1.8 billion in 1990, rising to $3.1 billion a year in 1999–2001. The share of water and sanitation in total ODA remained relatively stable in the 1990s, at 6 per cent of bilateral and 4–5 per cent of multilateral aid.

Multilateral ODA to water and sanitation was $575 million (annual average commitment) over 1996–98, with IDA accounting for over half ($323). The entry of the EC increased the amount to $730 over 1999–2001. OECD (2005) also notes two other features, which need some attention: first, half of donor commitments were allocated to just ten countries; and second, a significant share of resources went to countries with already high access to water services, although it was not clear whether they were used to improve access.

However, until earlier in this decade, OECD/DAC did not disaggregate this data for drinking water and for other uses. In fact, if water supply is excluded from the calculation of ODA for BSS, the share of DAC bilateral ODA allocated to basic social services falls from around 10 per cent of ODA to 5 per cent. We now know that water supply and sanitation accounted for three-quarters of aid to the water sector in 1997–2001. However, most aid to water supply and sanitation goes to large systems.[10] The number of projects drawing on low-cost technologies offering the best prospects of increased coverage for poor people (see Chapter 6) – hand-pumps, gravity-fed systems, rainwater collection, latrines – is very small (OECD, 2003). Thus the composition of aid to water and sanitation has to change.

ODA to water and sanitation in 1994–96 also hovered around the same share of total received in 1990–91. Table 10.4 compares ODA to rural projects for water/sanitation with the share of rural population in total population in a set of countries for which data is available in Development Cooperation Reports prepared by UNDP recipient country offices. We find that for the majority of countries where data enable us to distinguish allocation patterns, ODA allocations have gone predominantly to urban sector or sector policy/others despite a much higher share of the population living in rural areas – confirming what we noted above. Further, OECD DAC data indicate that only 12 per cent of ODA for water went to countries where less than 60 per cent of the population has access to safe water (OECD DAC, 2003).

Table 10.4   ODA to drinking water and sanitation sector by recipient: project-wise distribution, mid-1990s

	Year	ODA (US$ million)	Rural (%)	Urban (%)	Policy (%)	Rural pop. (%)
Latin America						
Paraguay	1995	11,484	1.5	28.4	70.1	46.0
Peru	1994	22,498	8.4	50.6	41.0	28.0
South Asia						
Bhutan	1996	2,983	0.0	78.2	21.8	93.0
India	1994	19,762	30.8	40.6	28.6	73.0
Nepal	1996	39,085	0.0	2.0	98.0	89.0
Bangladesh	1993	20,623	25.7	30.1	44.2	80.0
East Asia & Pacific						
Vietnam	1996	40,122	61.0	32.9	6.0	80.0
Philippines	1996	38,238	0.4	95.8	3.8	44.0
Middle East & North Africa						
Lebanon[a]	1997	7,782	0.0	100.0	0.0	12.0
Morocco	1996	26,371	29.6	46.6	23.8	47.0
Yemen	1996	9,469	1.3	98.7	0.0	65.0
West Africa						
Madagascar	1995	9,443	15.6	71.1	13.3	72.0
Swaziland	1996	357	50.7	0.0	49.3	67.0
East Africa						
Benin	1996	8,353	40.2	29.5	30.3	60.0
Côte d'Ivoire	1995	4,945	31.9	29.1	39.0	55.0
Cameroon	1996	14,353	81.7	2.3	16.0	53.0
Ghana	1995	26,466	27.9	42.1	30.0	63.0
D.R. Congo[b]	1996	3,139	0.0	88.7	11.3	71.0
By region						
Latin America	1994–95	16,991	5.0	39.5	55.6	37.0
South Asia	1993–96	20,613	14.1	37.7	48.2	83.8
East Asia and Pacific	1996	39,180	30.7	64.4	4.9	62.0
Middle East and North Africa	1996–97	14,541	10.3	81.8	7.9	41.3
West Africa	1995–96	4,900	33.2	35.6	31.3	69.5
East and Central Africa	1995–96	11,451	36.3	38.3	25.3	60.4

Note: In some projects there were not enough details available; hence it was difficult to categorize them precisely.
[a] ODA figures represent total commitments and not the disbursement during the year.
[b] No details are available.

Source: UNDP, DCRs, various years.

Table 10.5 ODA to BSS by IDA and regional development banks, 1995–98 (average, US$ million)

	IDA		AfDF2		AsDF3		IDB SF		Total banks	
	95/6	97/8	95/6	97/8	95/6	97/8	95/6	97/8	95/6	97/8
Basic education	4,131	154		22	25	142			438	319
Basic health	130	239	3	31	21	41			154	311
Population/reproductive health	109	302		1	42				151	302
Water supply	146	163	29	30	129	93	35	34	339	320
Total BSS	798	858	33	84	217	276	35	34	1,083	1,253
as % of concessional lending	13.8	13.4	18.2	9.3	19.2	20.4	6.4	6.3	14.2	13.6
Total BSS excl. water supply	652	695	3	54	88	183	0	0	743	933
as % of concessional lending	11.3	10.8	1.9	6.0	7.8	13.5	0	0	9.7	10.1
Total concessional lending	5,794	6,411	181	904	1,127	1,354	549	541	7,651	9,211

a   Includes a large district education project in India.
b   The data for AfDF in 1995–96 reflect the low point in their activities prior to the recent capital replenishment.
c   Data for 1998 not yet available, data for 1997 taken instead.

Source: OECD, DAC, 1999.

For aid, an abiding issue has been fungibility. In fact, as McGillivray and Morrissey (2001) argue, fungibility studies have been granted too much attention.[11] It is more important to examine the fiscal response of the aid recipient in order to determine the effects of aid on behaviour regarding total spending, tax revenue and borrowing. The evidence, they find, suggests that aid tends to increase total spending by more than the amount of the aid. Hence the risk of fungibility is no argument for not increasing ODA for basic services.

10.3   Aid to basic education, basic health and water and sanitation: some qualitative issues

The MDGs are unlikely to be achieved without developing-country action to increase the level and improve the efficiency and equity of public spending on BSS – this argument has run right through this book. However, the same applies to ODA. In this section, we examine the quality and composition of current ODA to three key areas related to the MDGs: basic education, basic health, and water and sanitation.

Education

In the education sector, the World Bank is now the largest source of external assistance. In absolute terms, Bank funding for basic education doubled from 1989–90 to 1995–96. Funding for basic education in sub-Saharan Africa doubled between 1989–90 and 1993–94, and then fell to a level only slightly higher than in 1989–90. Some very significant increases in absolute terms in World Bank lending to education took place in the South Asia region, as well as in East Asia and Latin America. However, middle-income countries are not interested in borrowing from the World Bank for primary education. IDA (the World Bank's soft-loan window) projects tend to focus more on primary or basic education than do non-IDA loans.[12] IDA lending, which accounts for most of multilateral ODA for basic education, remained stable through the 1990s, but has tended to fall since the late 1990s.[13]

The decline of IDA resource flow to primary education in sub-Saharan Africa may be explained partly by the competition for resources from South Asia, and partly by the fact that other sectors are absorbing more resources from IDA in Africa, such as public-sector reforms. This emphasis on public-sector reforms is in line with the recent World Bank (1998) study on aid.[14] Combined with this has come a new emphasis on sector-wide approaches (SWAPs) and sector investment programmes (SIPs) (which we discuss in the next section).

However, certain aspects of Bank analytical and lending work have raised questions. In order to ensure better learning outcomes, the Bank's knowledge dictated a predominant role for textbooks in the policy package from the mid-1970s on. It is not that the emphasis on textbooks per se was wrong, but the emphasis was misplaced relative to the neglect of the role of the teacher. For much of the 1960s – when Bank lending to education began – to the early 1970s, lending to education was a bricks-and-mortar affair, with most lending going to building school infrastructure. In fact, most of the staff in the Bank's education department were architects (Jones, 1992). Bank loans mainly provide the foreign exchange cost of projects, and hence were limited in their applications early on, as foreign exchange costs of primary education projects are normally low. Once construction activities in borrowers declined, and the Bank developed a greater interest in school-wide quality, it was a challenge to find new areas within education to loan monies to. One aspect of pedagogy, textbooks, helped serve the need for new, tangible areas of lending from the mid-1970s. Such bankable avenues of loaning money and the Bank's emphasis on them can mask dangers to borrowers, who may mistakenly look to the Bank for a comprehensive and balanced view of educational development. One outcome was that in many countries the issue of teacher remuneration, incentives and teacher development was ignored – with serious adverse consequences for school effectiveness. About five years ago this imbalance in emphasis in Bank sectoral analysis was corrected – too late in the day. The 'knowledge bank' has taken rather long to acquire that knowledge, and has repeatedly demonstrated the characteristics of a 'slow learner'.

The issue is not just the inadequate level of external resources for basic education, but also its composition. We highlight two problematic aspects of education assistance in the past. First, technical assistance or cooperation (TC) takes up a significant share of total aid, which is largely absorbed by expatriate personnel. A World Bank study indicates that TC represents between one-quarter and one-third of all external economic assistance to African countries (World Bank, 1996b, cited in Habte, 1999). In fact, UNESCO analysed the contents, procedures and manning of about 240 leading education-sector studies on Africa undertaken during 1990–94. It found that all of the studies had been undertaken by expatriate-led teams with only nominal representation or inclusion of local researchers, who were never included as senior consultants or document authors. It also noted that the issue of institutional capacity had been raised since independence days and that a large number of courses, training, short- and longer-term scholarships have been provided. 'Yet still those who study African education point to a deficiency of managerial and administrative skills' (Samoff, 1996).

Second, although in principle the software of education (strengthening educational administration, development of teaching materials, training of teachers) is emphasized, in practice the construction of classrooms is the most common cooperation activity, particularly in Africa (Colclough, 1993; Yokozeki and Sawamura, 1999).

Health

In the last half-century, donor policies to improve health have evolved through a number of somewhat overlapping stages.[15] In the early years, there was a disease-specific approach, focusing on particular diseases: for example, malaria, tuberculosis and smallpox, and the international response concentrated on technical solutions such as DDT (for malaria control), penicillin and vaccines. In the 1970s came the primary health care approach, culminating in the 1978 international conference in Alma Ata. This approach arose at the same time as the 'basic needs' approach in development policy was being formulated. WHO was a major player, along with UNICEF, in this push for 'Health for All'.[16]

From the early 1980s on, as economies declined and debt burdens climbed, the World Bank became a lead player in health – as in education. However, despite the declining output and increasing debt burdens, the Health for All efforts had taken root, and, despite the economic decline in Africa and Latin America, the Universal Campaign for Immunization, started jointly by WHO and UNICEF in 1985, achieved its goal of immunizing 80 per cent of all children by the year 1990. Even in the lost decade of the 1980s, the child survival and development revolution had begun to have its effects – with child mortality continuing to decline even in countries that suffered significant economic declines. So, while the role of WHO and UNICEF may have been overshadowed by that of the Bank (Jolly, 1997), the financial and technical support and advocacy role of these agencies helped to sustain the trend in mortality decline set earlier.

Meanwhile, the Bank increased its role in health policy dialogue as well as in international lending for health. The focus shifted to systems and finance: privatization, contracting out, decentralization, and shifts in the role of the state and health ministries. However, in the 1990s, there was an increasing concern that health system reforms were not helping the poor – and were possibly even making them poorer. Health emerged as an integral element in investment in human capital and the fight against poverty (WHO, 1999).

Several issues remain in relation to external assistance for the health sector. First, there have been large variations in the amounts devoted to specific health problems. Leprosy, river blindness and sexually transmitted diseases are well funded, while a number of other problems – such as acute respiratory infections, maternal mortality, and nearly all non-communicable diseases – are comparatively under-resourced (WHO, 1999).[17]

Second, there has been a significant increase in the number of actors in the arena of external assistance for the health sector: WHO, UNICEF, UN Population Fund, UN Development Programme, and UNAIDS were already operational within the UN family. The regional development banks, international non-governmental organizations and many public–private partnerships have now joined them.[18] This creates its own problems of coordination within the health system, especially in aid-dependent poor countries.

Finally, with the MDGs and their emphasis on specific diseases – tuberculosis, malaria and HIV/AIDS – there is a serious risk that the endemic problems of health systems (discussed mainly in Chapter 6) will remain under-resourced, and that disease-specific vertical programmes (e.g. the Global Fund for Malaria, TB and HIV/AIDS) will overtake the incipient effort to improve health systems. Unless vertical programmes are integrated into functional health systems, there is little likelihood of a health transition occurring in poor countries and the MDGs being achieved. Unlike the simple goal of universal immunization, the MDGs cover the whole gamut of diseases characteristic of a poor country's disease burden, and require a systemic response.

Water and sanitation

As regards the water and sanitation sector, in every developing region we compared the share of ODA committed to rural projects with the share of rural population in total population. As noted earlier, in the vast majority of countries the share of ODA allocated to rural projects is much lower than the population resident in rural areas (except in Paraguay, Peru and Bangladesh).

Based on questionnaires sent to DAC donors for a UNICEF-funded study of ODA for water and sanitation (Alur and Jobes, 1995) in 1994, the distribution of all ODA for water and sanitation was as follows for the period 1990–94: 13 per cent for rural water and sanitation; 38 per cent for urban water and sanitation; and 49 per cent for water resources. With such a small share of ODA for water and sanitation allocated to rural areas, there was little likelihood of the problem being seriously resolved.

External assistance for water and sanitation has undergone some evolution. UNICEF has been an important player, along with a small number of bilateral donors who are active in the area of drinking water and sanitation. Since the late 1960s, UNICEF has supported government programmes for provision of a minimum level of water supply and sanitation for those in the greatest need. This began as a response to drought emergencies and the initial support focused on the rapid drilling and installation of bore-holes with hand-pumps in rural areas. In the 1970s UNICEF and donor assistance diversified into relatively large-scale national water programmes, including the provision of sophisticated drilling rigs and equipment, but also low-cost technologies like gravity-fed systems, protected springs and wells, and upgrading of traditional water sources in rural areas. However, UNICEF and a few bilateral donors (e.g. Denmark) cannot bear the burden of the external resource requirements alone.

10.4 Modality of aid to basic services
– whither the sectoral approach?

The form of assistance is an important issue in improving the effectiveness of external support for BSS. Since the 1960s, the project has been the normal mode for the provision of donor support, and continues to be so. The project has been justifiably criticized for the creation of enclaves with limited spread effects and poor linkages to other sectors or geographical areas. It has also been criticized for the limited scope of local ownership; for being donor-driven in design and management; and for bypassing the budget prepared by the ministry of finance in the recipient country and, therefore, distorting national planning.[19] Little attention may be paid to the integration of the project into the main activities of the relevant line ministry.

Under the circumstances, it is not surprising that, since the mid-1990s, other modes of donor intervention like programme support and sectoral programmes are increasingly used in several sectors – particularly in health and education. The larger donors have, in particular, espoused the sectoral approach, even though projects are still a major part of their portfolio. However, more often than not, since the bilateral agencies have few staff with experience or the relevant skills in institution-building and governance, or macro-level social development expertise and experts in health and education, it is usually the World Bank that ends up in the driver's seat.[20]

Sectoral programmes require domestic capacity building

Related to the question about who is in the driver's seat (national ownership) is the question of national sustainability – the latter being dependent upon national capacity. Many sector-wide approaches use conventional technical assistance to address the shallowness of national capacity. The World Bank reports that in fourteen of nineteen Sector Investment Programmes (SIPs) with relevant information, technical assistance absorbs more than 5 per cent of the SIP budget – in three cases the proportion is in excess of 20 per cent (see Table 10.6). Moreover, donor attempts to lead the policy process with short-term TA often fails (Foster et al., 2000).

Technical cooperation (normally involving locating an expatriate adviser, who is paid a salary that is several multiples of local staff salaries) meets not so subtle, but real, donor needs. Such personnel are the eyes and ears of donors within local administration, and provide donors with some reassurance that project money is not being misspent or misappropriated. For the period 1970–95, technical cooperation grants comprised on average 25 per

Table 10.6 Technical assistance in SIPs

Programme	Description	% of SIP
Mozambique Health	Improve capacity of MOH to train staff by refurbishing institutions and improving training; in-service trainings; general training operations.	10.0
Zambia Health	Large amount primarily covers foreign doctors employed in Zambia to implement programme. Due to 'brain drain', local capacity is inadequate.	10.0
Malawi Water*	Institutional restructuring, commercial financial management and accounting, operations and maintenance, and central services. Funding for up to 13 person years of TA.	13.0
Uganda Health	Training to district health teams, focusing on development of skills in management, planning, accounting, monitoring and evaluation, research and studies. Will use international and local consultant services.	21.0
Ghana Education	In-service and pre-service training for teachers; develop tests to assess student performance, curriculum review, develop strategy for girls participation, design and implement information system.	9.2
Benin Health*	85 person months of external specialists support for implementation and 199 person months of local consulting services.	12.0
Niger Health	Consulting services, research and studies: Project supervision, implementation and monitoring support, institutional development, research, studies, surveys; training for district health teams. Concerted effort will be made to recruit national consultants. Will use University of Niamey for training programmes when possible.	11.0
Sierra Leone Health	Management training programme to develop skills for managers at District Health Management teams; most training conducted in country using local institutions.	3.7

* Classified as 'not full-fledged SIPs' in a recent report, *Sector Investment Programs in Africa: A Review of Implementation Experience*, June 1996.

Source: Staff appraisal reports of various IDA credits, World Bank.

cent of annual total ODA (Arndt, 2000). The data do not suggest that there was any decline over the period, since the average over 1993–95 (30 per cent of total ODA) is actually higher than the average over 1970–95. Over the quarter century, in the Americas TC has the highest share in total ODA received by the region (34 per cent), followed by sub-Saharan Africa (30 per cent), North Africa (24 per cent) and Asia (17 per cent).

Budget support by donors and the government budget

The experience with the project approach over several decades had shown that as long as agencies channel funding outside the developing-country government's budget process they will remain 'part of the problem rather than part of the solution' (Foster and Merotto, 1997). At the same time, there remain serious weaknesses in the sectoral approaches that have been adopted to date. The need to improve coordination, increase ownership and reduce aid dependence is increasingly recognized by the donor community, and the resulting answer is a new emphasis on partnership. But, as the chairman of the OECD DAC stated: 'The principles of self-reliance, local ownership and participation which underlie the partnership approach are inconsistent with the idea of conditions imposed by donors to coerce poor countries to do things they don't want to do in order to obtain resources they need' (OECD, 1996a).[21]

Budget support – not merely for a sector, but for inclusion in the government's budget – would leave more leeway for government policy-making. If donors do hand over control to the recipient-country government, pooled resources could be disbursed by the recipient according to a general development strategy, including a human poverty reduction plan, discussed in advance by donors and the country – rather than through specific programmes and projects in a particular sector (Kanbur et al., 1999). This is the direction in which we need to move, with the exception that in the short run, more donor resources need to be allocated to basic services. If the developing-country government has a poverty-reduction plan in place, then budget support should be able to support such a plan under the direction of the recipient government.[22]

Right now, we are far from the pooling of resources, since differences exist among donors regarding the degree of harmonization possible. Some donors have shown a willingness to move together on harmonization, while others have not (Weissman and Foster, 2000). Some donors are restricted by a legal prohibition on financing recurrent expenditures; others are required to report details of their expenditure to parliament. The World Bank's own procedures are rigid and prevent full pooling. In any case, there is a conflict with the Bank requirement that all procurement be open to all its members, while donors have tying requirements.

If the language of partnership is to be taken seriously, then it should mean giving one the right to make demands on the other. Helleiner (2000) makes a number of excellent suggestions towards restoring the balance in aid relationships – just as there are performance requirements for recipients, there should be donor performance monitoring in respect of ODA.[23] First, we know that it is typically not the case that ODA passes through a recipient-government system, let alone through its budget. Large shares of ODA expenditures are made directly to the suppliers of goods and services to aid agencies (including private firms, NGOs and individuals) – more often to the donor-country nationals than to those of the recipient country. Tanzania is a country where major efforts have been made to transfer 'ownership' of development programmes from aid donors to the government, but only 30 per cent of ODA was estimated to flow through the government budget in 1999. Just as there are recipient performance indicators, each donor's ODA expenditure that finds its way into the national budget system should be a performance indicator for donors. Second, there should be some attempt to assess donor coordination and willingness to accept local priorities; a quantitative indicator of this would be the percentage of ODA commitments that stand outside agreed priorities or coordination systems. Third, donors could agree to untie all aid to the least developed countries. The OECD (2005) itself notes that tying raises the cost of many goods, services and projects by 15–30 per cent on average. This implies that tied aid reduced the value of bilateral aid by $5 billion to $7 billion in 2002, a conservative estimate that ignores the indirect costs. In fact, the OECD notes that 'tied aid often results in higher transaction costs for recipients and is a serious barrier to harmonizing donor procedures. It is incompatible with country owned procurement systems and their integrity, a basic component of the Paris Declaration process' (OECD, 2005: 22).[24]

Fourth, technical assistance still accounts for $4 billion per year and about 25 per cent of all bilateral assistance to sub-Saharan Africa (going up to 40 per cent of total ODA in some countries). Therefore the percentage devoted to technical assistance should be monitored.[25] In fact, Browne (2006) makes an excellent suggestion that TA must not be prepaid, which it always has been from the beginning of aid. Instead of being prepaid, if TA was purchased as and when needed by recipients – rather than accepting what skills 'packaged and purveyed in definable units ("projects")' donors are willing or interested in providing – the supply-driven mismatches with actual need would not arise.

Fifth, to discourage corruption fed by aid, donors should provide, on a public basis, access to specific fgures on aid flows, mechanisms and intended target recipients so that independent monitors within or outside recipient countries can provide effective scrutiny. Also, donors have to ensure that corruption is not aided and abetted by their own private sector, and that the earnings from corruption are not laundered through their own financial markets. Naturally, on the recipient side, minimizing corruption fed by aid would mean public financial accountability through national audit institutions and parliaments – which is usually five years too late and poorly funded. For expenditure, public accounts should include itemized statement of all public spending (especially military and police). For revenues, itemized information should be available on royalties and taxes on turnover paid by all corporate bodies and aid flows, which should be debated in parliaments (as rarely happens). A right-to-information Act should enable this information to be made available on a mandatory basis. Such action would supplement the civil society watchdog function we discussed in Chapter 7.

Reducing aid dependence

These issues cannot be separated from the question of conditionality and aid dependence. Kanbur (2000) rightly argues that conditionality is not adhered to by recipient governments, in fact, and the institutional dimension of the donor–recipient relationship is the key to this failure.[26] The institution of aid dependence is linked closely to the need of donor agencies to disburse large amounts of funds while apparently keeping accountability for these funds to donor-country taxpayers.

This complex game that donors and recipients constantly play is consistent with the aid dependency syndrome,[27] and with the finding that most of African countries' public investment (and more than 10 per cent of their GNP) is financed with aid. A particularly important example of this is taxation, which is negatively correlated with aid inflows (Moore, 1998). In other words, in the light of our argument in the previous chapter on the criticality of tax revenue mobilization for investment in BSS, aid dependence is particularly pernicious in the medium to long run. In fact, we began this chapter by stating that the need for additional ODA is essentially transitional, to create the fiscal space to enable African countries (and especially HIPCs) to move to a self-sustained pattern of public investment and growth. Hence, we would strongly endorse Kanbur's suggestion that the donor–recipient relationship, in the short run, has to become of a more arms' length nature; cancelling the debt burden is the basis for starting again with a clean slate. Only an arm's-length relationship will ensure the space that countries need to arrive at a domestic consensus on national policies where distributional conflicts are involved (as we saw in Chapter 3); conditionality alone will not lead to the commitment that donors are looking for. This suggestion is consistent with the IMF Internal Evaluation Office (2003) proposal (see Chapter 3) that the IMF should let 'authorities have the initial responsibility for proposing a reform program, which should be the starting point for negotiations'.

Other means of reducing aid dependence are discussed in the next section. We have seen that aid policies could be improved in terms of the allocation to BSS, its composition, modality and the conditions that are attached to it. However, there are other ways to improve the poverty focus of international policies, which can be compromised by policies outside the sphere of development cooperation.

10.5   Improving the consistency of donor government policies

Many factors limit the ability of developing countries to capitalize on the opportunities provided by globalization, including international and developed-country policies. As a DAC study (1999) notes, global summits call for the halving of the numbers of the world's food insecure, while agriculture and natural resource skills are cut within aid agencies; or ministries of trade promote trade liberalization, while the aid agencies are unable to build developing-country capacity for trade negotiation. Only a minority of development agencies have taken tangible steps to ensure that their domestic policies, and their position in negotiations on internationally agreed policies, are formulated with poverty reduction in view. One example of this is the UK, which in White Papers on International Development (DFID 1997, 2000) has committed to work for sustainable development in four areas: the environment; trade, agriculture and investment; political stability, social cohesion and conflict prevention; and economic and financial stability.[28]

To achieve consistency, at least four issues need discussion:

• market access;
• commodity prices;
• the link between trade-related intellectual property rights (TRIPS) under the WTO and availability of essential drugs;
• the General Agreement on Trade in Services (GATS) and liberalization in social services.

We should emphasize that the following discussion is not intended to be a comprehensive analysis of these issues, but only illustrative of the nature of the inconsistency between the international rhetoric of poverty reduction and the reality of actual industrialized-country policies that might undermine the achievement of that goal.

Market access

One of the starker inconsistencies in industrialized-country policies is the fact that their ministries of finance promote investment liberalization by developing countries, while ministries of trade impose import quotas when investments in recently liberalized partner countries increase their exports to industrialized countries. There are sound reasons why trade liberalization often leads to negative results. For instance, rapid liberalization of trade may have contributed to a widening of the trade deficit in developing countries in general. Liberalization led to a sharp increase in imports, but exports failed to increase. For developing countries, excluding China, the average trade deficit in the 1990s was higher than in the 1970s by 3 percentage points of GDP, while the average economic growth rate was 2 percentage points lower (UNCTAD, 1999). Clearly, while a country can control how fast to liberalize its imports, it is unable to force the pace of export growth on its own.[29] Export growth partly depends on the infrastructure, human and enterprise capacity for new exports, which takes time to achieve. Low-income countries need technical support in building up this export capacity.

Second, although industrial countries apply very low average tariffs in their trade with each other, they have some of their highest tariffs against the poor countries – three to four times higher (UNDP HDR, 2003). Developing countries account for less than one-third of developed-country imports but for two-thirds of tariff revenues collected.

Third, while the constant exhortation to developing countries is to support free trade, developed countries normally apply low tariffs to raw commodities but those rates rise sharply for intermediate or final products. Thus such tariffs help to keep Ghana and Côte d'Ivoire locked into a volatile, low value-added raw cocoa market, while Germany is the largest exporter in the world of processed cocoa (UNDP HDR, 2005). Thus, while we may have been making a strong case for industrial policy and its successes in Chapter 3, market access for processed product exports from developing countries remains limited.

Fourth, while we have shown that the Millennium Goals are unlikely to be achieved without increased agricultural output and incomes in developing countries, the prospects of that happening are seriously undermined by EU, US and Japanese agricultural subsidies and protectionism. Developing countries lose about $24 billion a year – which is one-third of the 2004 level of (increased) ODA – in agricultural incomes from such protectionism and subsidies in rich countries, not counting the spillover and dynamic effects. The US Department of Agriculture estimates that the country's 20,000 cotton farmers will receive government payments of $4.7 billion in 2005 – an amount greater than the US aid to sub-Saharan Africa (UNDP HDR, 2005). Thanks to the Common Agricultural Policy, the EU is the world's second largest exporter of sugar, a commodity in which it has no comparative advantage. EU sugar farmers and processors are paid four times the world market price for sugar, creating a 4 million tonne surplus. The surplus is then dumped on world markets relying on $1 billion in export subsidies paid to a small group of sugar processors. Developing-country exporters bear the consequences. More efficient producers and exporters of sugar take foreign exchange losses of about $494 million for Brazil, $151 million for South Africa, and $60 million for Thailand.

Fifth, we argued in the previous chapter for additional tax revenue mobilization in developing countries if the Millennium Goals are to be financed, and the Monterrey Consensus recognizes that need as well. Yet, under WTO rules regional trade agreements are required to extend tariff liberalization to 'substantially all trade'. The European Union has put this commitment at the centre of its negotiating position. While for rich countries tariff revenues account for a miniscule proportion of total government revenues, in most low-income developing countries, tariffs are very important to total revenues; in sub-Saharan Africa they are a third of government revenues. UNDP (2005) notes that 76 African, Caribbean and Pacific group of countries could stand to lose 40 per cent of their tax revenues as a result of a new set of Economic Partnership Agreements.

The relationship between commodity prices and debt

Declining commodity prices drain significant resources from developing countries. There has been a net flow of resources from, rather than to, the developing world on account of the decline in commodity prices. The main reason for the crisis of debt facing the HIPCs in particular is the long-run secular decline in their net barter terms of trade since the 1970s. The decline in commodity prices has affected not only the HIPCs, but the balance of payments of other developing countries as well. As noted above, the balance of trade deficit of developing countries was a full two percentage points greater in the 1990s than it was in the 1970s. Debt relief is not charity – it is merely a means of compensating (only in part) for the net resource flow out of the poorest countries due to falling commodity prices. In other words, the cancellation cannot be a substitute for fresh additional ODA. If there is an element of 'moral hazard' in HIPC country debt cancellation, it is not any more so than the moral hazard inherent in the huge bail-out of international banks implicit in the IMF deal in post-crisis East Asia in 1997. But the cancellation of debt alone will not suffice so long as the long-run deterioration in the terms of trade of the least developed countries continues. In fact, there is a risk of the current situation of the debt trap repeating itself in the future. Even the World Bank (2000a) argues for the provision of such global public goods as global commodity price insurance instruments to address key price volatility problems of developing countries.

The objective of foreign aid is to be able to shed it – but as we showed in Chapter 3, the share of aid in recipient GNI and gross fixed capital formation has only increasead. Countries with a high commodity concentration of exports cannot expect to shed their aid dependence unless they can diversify their exports – but that requires market access, and more consistency between the trade and ODA ministries of industrialized countries.

The least developed countries are especially vulnerable to external shocks – whether it is from terms-of-trade losses or weather changes – that can make a nonsense of budget planning for health and education investment in any given year. As a result, they have special needs for compensatory and contingency financing.[31] It is well known that although there is a facility offered by the IMF (Compensatory and Contingency Finance Facility), it is never available without new conditions and heavy transaction costs. Bilateral donors usually give larger amounts than the Bank and the Fund, and could increase their flows of ODA at times of external shocks – and thus help to stabilize the availability of foreign exchange for the poorest countries (Helleiner, 2000).

TRIPS and essential drug availability

The third issue relates to TRIPS and the availability of drugs in developing countries – and there is wide scope here for greater consistency between industrialized-country commitment to the poverty-alleviation goal and industrialized-country policies. Under the TRIPS agreement, inventors are rewarded for the commercial risk they take in investing in research for new drugs with a temporary monopoly, lasting twenty years under the WTO rules, during which they have the right to sell their inventions at the price they choose. Governments of developing countries, on the other hand, have to balance between the public good and private monopoly. In respect of several drugs a serious conflict exists. For instance, in Brazil and Thailand, domestic companies are able to market a version of the drug fluconazole, used in the treatment of meningitis, at annual treatment prices of $100, compared to $3,000 for the patented product price. In

India, companies market ciprofloxacin, an anti-infective drug used in the treatment of bloody diarrhoea, at one-eighth of the price charged in Pakistan, where only the patented version is available (UNDP HDR, 1999b). In Brazil and South Africa, the governments waived patent rights on HIV/AIDS drugs, allowing local companies to produce cheap versions. Prices fell by 80 per cent (Koivusalo, 1999). In 2001, almost every Brazilian AIDS patient received free of charge the same triple therapy cocktail of anti-retroviral drugs that has improved survival prospects in the USA. The HIV/AIDS death rate has been halved, and the savings to the health budget are estimated at $400 million.

Unless industrialized-country governments support developing-country government action in this sphere, multinational drug companies will use the TRIPS to prevent access to life-saving drugs to the poor in developing countries. The US government has not resorted to the WTO disputes mechanism on actions taken by developing countries, but, backed by the pharmaceuticals research and manufacturers of the USA, has been threatening trade sanctions under US domestic law (Special 301 trade law) against sixteen countries (including India, Egypt and Thailand), inviting them to strengthen their patent protection. Some forty drug companies took the South African government to court in South Africa, contesting a law that allows the government to import cheap drugs for AIDS patients, thus bypassing the monopoly granted to patent holders. Clearly, what is needed is a thorough reform of the WTO intellectual property rules, including a reduction in the period of patent protection, stronger health safeguards, and a total ban on threatened use of trade sanctions.[32]

Trade in Services

In 1994, the General Agreement on Trade in Services (GATS) became part of the final document emerging from the Uruguay Round of trade negotiations. GATS sets the framework for legally binding rules in the WTO. It covers four 'modes of supply': cross-border (e.g. e-commerce and telecommunications); consumption overseas (tourism or health provision); commercial presence (by establishing banks, insurance companies or financial institutions); and temporary movements of people. The developed countries are most interested in the third mode, the developing ones in the last.

It is not just that the international financial system is gearing itself for promoting greater private participation in basic services; the international trading system is already set up to perform that role. Thus the World Trade Organization (WTO), created after the 1994 round was completed, became a forum for promoting privatization of public services, in those countries which have not been subject to the conditionalities of IDA–IFC–IMF. GATS requires all WTO members to introduce '*progressive* liberalization' of their service sectors through successive rounds of market access negotiations. Industrialized countries have said that *basic* public services are exempt from the GATS liberalization programme. However, the WTO recognizes that the precise extent of the exemption is unclear. In any case, WTO member states of the EU are already using market access negotiations to request others to open public services.[33] In fact, the WTO has stated that all countries joining the WTO since 1995 have scheduled more GATS commitments than existing members at similar income levels (WTO, 2001).

GATS establishes a legal framework for international trade in services through both general trade rules and specific national commitments governing access to domestic markets by foreign suppliers. These commitments are subject to rounds of negotiations, with the first round (GATS 2000) having got under way in January 2000. GATS applies to all government measures (at all government levels) affecting 'services trade' including laws, regulations, administrative decisions and even unwritten practices.[34]

For the past two decades services trade has grown faster than merchandise trade. Indeed, it is the largest and the fastest growing sector of the world economy. In 1999, the value of cross-border trade in services amounted to US$1,350 billion – about 20 per cent of total cross-border trade. Of this sector, trade in social services – health, education and water/sanitation – are potentially the most profitable. Annual global expenditure on water services exceeds US$1 trillion; on education it exceeds US$2 trillion; and on health care it exceeds US$3.5 trillion.

Given such lucrative business prospects in social service trade, many critics have asked, 'Does GATS go far enough to protect the ability of national authorities to decide how best to deliver basic social services, including the determination of the extent to which foreign suppliers should engage in its delivery?'

On the one hand, the agreement allows governments much discretion in deciding how, when and whether to open service sectors to international trade. First, no member country is required to open any specific sector to foreign competition. Second, countries may set conditions on the nature and pace of such liberalization. Third, governments may, with adequate compensation, suspend or modify existing commitments. Additionally, Article 1:3b of the agreement explicitly issues a 'governmental authority' exclusion, which defines services covered by GATS as 'any service in any sector except services in the exercise of government authority'. Finally, countries may invoke general exceptions in Article XIV to protect major public interests, including safety, national security and human, plant or animal health.

On the other hand, Article XIX commits members to 'successive rounds of negotiations ... with a view to achieving progressively higher levels of liberalization', and countries will come under increased pressure to liberalize new areas of service delivery, likely including basic social services. More worrying, *unwritten practices* during negotiations and *undefined terms* left hanging in the agreement could strip governments (or cause governments to strip themselves) of the above safeguards.

Unwritten practices

During negotiations there is often enormous pressure on countries, especially developing countries, to open their markets to competition from foreign companies. Russia's bid for WTO membership, for example, was set back as the European Union continued to pressure Russian officials to open more services to foreign competition. Vietnam, also hoping to join the WTO, has faced great pressure to liberalize a number of services, including health and education, in the negotiations leading to a bilateral trade agreement with the United States. China was similarly required to liberalize key service sectors (e.g. insurance, retail distribution) before gaining admission to the WTO in 2001 (Save the Children, 2002). Additionally, these high-pressured negotiations often take place behind closed doors, leaving critics worried that negotiators may place great pressure on some countries to open their markets and that such practices are not adequately reported to watchdog groups and the press.

And only the savvy delegate – often representing an industrialized country – will be able to successfully steer himself through such complex and cumbersome trade negotiations and procedures. Delegates from developing countries – often disadvantaged by poor training in trade negotiations or a lack of adequate staff support – may inadvertently undertake actions that breach the agreement. For example, the Code of Marketing Breast-Milk Substitutes, adopted as national legislation in many countries, restricts advertising of breast-milk substitutes on public health grounds. The code would be considered a market access limitation, which is prohibited under GATS if a sector has been committed to and no such limitation had been officially registered. Three developing countries have committed their advertising sectors to liberalization – Burundi, Jamaica and the Gambia – but have not registered this limitation, thus breaching Article XVI of GATS. Other member countries could challenge this breach, leaving a distinct possibility that they would ask for the Code to be repealed.

Undefined terms

Much controversy surrounds the 'governmental authority' exclusion from negotiations under GATS. As stated above, the exclusion appearing in Article 1:3b defines services covered by GATS as 'any service in any sector except services in the exercise of government authority'. But the exclusion is qualified in Article 1:3c, specifying that it only applies to those services provided *neither on a commercial nor on a competitive basis.* Governments, however, rarely deliver basic social services exclusively, and instead deliver these services through an ever-changing public–private mix of actors that compete for clients. The precise scope of services excluded, therefore, remains undefined and ambiguous. If basic social service delivery does not meet exclusion criteria, it is likely that national legislation and other directives used by governments to ensure equitable and efficient delivery of these services will conflict with GATS. For example, state aid to NGOs operating schools and clinics in underserved areas could violate GATS if a government liberalized its health and education sectors and these market conditions were not registered at that time.

We saw in Chapter 8 that the international financial institutions have promoted the private sector in basic services. We have seen above that this remains an issue in GATS within the WTO. There is some evidence that in the regional and bilateral treaty system there is active promotion of privatization in the same areas. For seventy-six ACP countries the renegotiation of their trade relationship with the EU proposes increased liberalization of service sectors above and beyond the level required by multilateral agreements. It asks for a 'reciprocal liberalization of trade in services' to match that of the EU, in contrast with the explicit guarantee in GATS that developing countries must be allowed to liberalize their own services on a non-reciprocal basis and at their own pace. Similarly, the proposed agreement to establish a Free Trade Area of the Americas offers a framework for the USA to promote its services liberalization programme throughout the Americas in sectors including health, education, water and environmental services (Hillary, 2002).

10.6   Concluding remarks

The primary responsibility for the achievement of the Millennium Development Goals lies with developing-country governments. However, for over fifty countries in the developing world – not just the least developed and the HIPCs – the achievement of the MDGs will require international action from bilaterals as well as multilaterals. Several of the smaller donors are allocating over 0.7 per cent of GNP to ODA, and also increasing allocations to basic services (though Germany, Japan and the UK also belong to the latter category, giving priority to BSS). In an ideal world, the larger donors would follow the example of the smaller donors in terms of size of ODA and the latter category of donors in respect of priority to BSS.[35]

While overall ODA has increased significantly in recent years, if the experience of the 1990s is any indicator, ODA for basic services remains seriously deficient in several ways:

- its level is low;
- its composition needs sharp modification in education and water/sanitation, and, to a lesser extent, in health;
- its modality – especially the shift from the project to the sectoral approach – requires much greater modification in respect of current donor methods;
- the approach has to be profoundly modified to give real meaning to the language of partnership. In fact, once past debts are rapidly cancelled, the yardstick for evaluating aid needs to return to reduction in aid dependence.

Finally, there is an urgent need for consistency between aid policy and other international policies of the industrialized countries. In the early chapters of this book we argued that there are risks of the Millennium Development Goals not being realized because of the macroeconomic policies that countries are expected by the orthodoxy to follow. But here we have argued that consistency is also required between the social goals embodied in the MDGs and a whole range of trade policies pursued by industrialized countries. The goal of consistency may not benefit from the domestic political weakness of development cooperation agencies, which limits their ability to lobby other domestic ministries, especially trade and finance ministries. However, without ensuring coherence between industrialized–country domestic policies and aid policy, poverty reduction may remain a mirage.[36]

Annex 10.1a   Bilateral ODA commitments (grants and loans) to education (US$ million)

	1991	1992	1993	1994	1995	1996	1997	1998	1999	2000	2001	2002	2003
Australia	144.0	161.6	121.7	237.6	201.2	299.2	194.4	248.6	154.5	131.5	106.2	77.1	57.6
Austria	91.6	104.8	103.7	98.1	98.9	87.8	115.6	124.5	92.8	112.0	62.3	64.4	75.5
Belgium	92.1	73.8	70.6	73.4	51.3	60.4	53.6	74.0	61.5	87.0	64.3	87.8	123.5
Canada	160.8	93.3	125.0	101.7	121.5	148.6	102.2	249.5	115.6	231.4	176.5	217.8	219.6
Denmark	31.1	68.5	38.9	58.0	31.6	59.1	31.3	46.8	49.1	17.7	75.6	28.3	96.3
Finland	10.2	23.5	8.5	12.1	7.0	15.7	12.6	24.4	18.0	28.3	25.9	32.8	16.8
France	1590.9	1628.8	1568.4	1677.4	1681.2	1594.9	1712.2	1800.8	1222.8	1331.5	839.3	1021.5	1225.3
Germany	847.5	787.0	969.8	1045.4	1106.9	1041.7	992.2	1007.3	698.7	898.3	623.1	777.8	897.4
Greece	12.2	5.7	10.2	7.0	44.3	45.8							
Ireland	0.0	3.2	4.9	7.9	15.1	15.8	21.6	39.0	26.3	38.1	40.9	43.9	51.9
Italy	119.6	145.9	65.9	81.6	38.4	48.3	32.2	71.6	23.2	87.3	41.8	174.4	70.4
Japan	720.0	853.4	975.0	1239.8	1062.6	1226.6	852.5	1134.8	765.1	1104.2	834.6	888.7	1104.0
Luxembourg	1.3	1.3	5.6	6.6	9.9	12.0	123.7	19.7	116.6	11.0	0.0	12.3	
Netherlands	197.8	136.3	131.4	91.7	148.1	129.8	170.1	187.1	175.7	220.9	240.4	180.1	351.8
New Zealand	11.3	32.0	25.2	28.9	31.9	33.4	35.9	45.6	33.1	36.6	28.6	30.9	35.4
Norway	27.5	25.3	22.1	20.8	38.0	42.5	47.4	107.6	42.5	116.8	86.5	103.4	133.6
Portugal	13.6	22.5	29.3	20.6	33.1	17.0	21.2	20.5	25.6	28.4	30.8	47.2	45.2
Spain	54.5	71.7	51.4	78.6	67.4	81.0	103.2	125.8	132.1	153.1	147.4	147.6	137.0
Sweden	74.3	110.9	77.7	102.5	94.8	109.9	95.0	113.4	63.6	82.7	61.6	66.8	96.3
Switzerland	53.9	45.8	44.9	31.0	35.0	23.4	27.9	59.7	27.5	45.8	32.8	34.4	39.8
United Kingdom	219.3	251.9	200.2	189.7	183.9	172.2	177.7	249.6	175.3	260.8	148.3	270.6	286.2
United States	348.8	431.2	324.1	385.6	386.4	265.6	246.2	284.1	185.3	357.7	264.8	294.5	433.5
Total	4814.2	4936.4	4800.9	5448.2	5522.8	5465.4	5113.6	6053.5	4077.6	5443.1	3930.4	4511.3	5546.8

Sources: OECD, Development Assistance Committee database; OECD, *The DAC Development Cooperation Report*, various issues.

Annex 10.1b Share of education in total bilateral ODA commitments (grants and loans) (%)

	1991	1992	1993	1994	1995	1996	1997	1998	1999	2000	2001	2002	2003
Australia	24.9	26.3	13.9	23.0	21.6	31.1	25.4	27.2	19.8	12.4	11.0	8.4	5.6
Austria	14.9	19.7	10.6	17.6	15.8	20.2	21.3	21.0	19.3	16.4	14.9	20.1	18.2
Belgium	16.1	14.9	13.4	14.3	10.1	11.6	9.5	11.2	11.7	12.8	12.6	9.7	13.1
Canada	8.8	5.4	8.0	6.3	8.5	10.4	7.3	10.0	8.6	8.9	11.1	13.3	10.9
Denmark	4.1	8.5	5.0	6.4	3.0	7.5	3.6	5.5	6.2	1.7	8.5	3.3	8.1
Finland	1.9	4.4	3.0	5.3	3.6	7.3	5.1	7.7	8.0	8.1	10.0	9.7	10.7
France	26.5	25.2	23.0	24.8	26.5	26.1	31.2	29.0	26.3	25.7	20.8	20.8	20.7
Germany	13.6	13.2	15.1	15.6	16.3	16.6	17.5	16.1	19.0	16.6	16.9	16.9	16.6
Greece	6.3	5.8	8.1	6.8	22.6	17.6							
Ireland	27.9	24.6	22.6	23.0	17.7	18.0	18.2	15.9	18.8	18.1	19.4	17.3	16.1
Italy	5.3	6.2	3.0	5.8	3.4	5.8	4.1	5.8	3.3	7.7	4.0	5.7	6.7
Japan	6.6	6.1	7.4	7.4	7.0	7.4	5.7	7.3	5.6	7.8	7.7	6.7	9.9
Luxembourg	5.7	5.7	12.2	12.2	18.1	18.0	21.4	23.7	13.8	23.5	8.8	14.4	
Netherlands	9.4	7.7	6.2	4.3	6.6	6.4	8.0	7.8	7.4	20.8	6.5	20.2	10.5
New Zealand	16.0	37.6	32.4	34.1	34.4	34.4	35.7	35.1	34.6	21.1	30.4	15.4	26.0
Norway	4.6	3.7	3.6	2.7	4.7	5.7	6.0	9.4	5.7	13.7	8.7	13.1	10.6
Portugal	16.4	16.4	18.6	17.0	22.6	15.8	24.4	10.6	7.9	9.2	13.6	22.7	12.8
Spain	4.8	6.6	7.0	8.3	9.2	9.9	10.0	11.8	13.4	8.0	14.4	7.5	10.3
Sweden	4.9	8.0	5.4	7.7	7.1	8.9	6.7	7.6	4.9	5.0	5.2	4.5	5.9
Switzerland	9.1	7.2	6.6	5.5	4.3	3.0	5.0	3.6	5.0	5.4	4.5	5.6	4.0
United Kingdom	12.1	12.7	11.4	11.5	9.8	9.3	8.3	9.0	6.7	6.5	4.9	6.0	5.7
United States	2.5	3.6	3.8	4.6	4.7	3.8	3.2	3.0	2.1	5.9	2.4	5.0	2.4
Total	9.1	9.1	9.6	10.4	10.8	11.2	10.7	11.0	9.2	8.3	8.9		

Sources: OECD, Development Assistance Committee database; OECD, The DAC Development Cooperation Report, various issues; OECD, 2001: 2/1.

Annex 10.2 Bilateral ODA commitments to basic education (US$ million)

	1995	1996	1997	1998	1999	2000	2001	2002	2003
Australia	11.0	38.4	15.0	46.3	37.4	40.3	28.3	34.7	23.4
Austria	1.1	1.4	1.5	3.5	2.4	2.4	2.1	1.9	2.2
Belgium	1.5	2.2	2.2	3.2	4.6	5.9	6.0	7.1	16.4
Canada	18.1	3.4	9.1	10.4	11.0	29.8	45.7	86.9	96.0
Denmark	8.1	1.3	3.6	1.3	39.7	3.9	49.2	9.1	36.8
Finland	3.5	6.2	7.8	3.6	5.9	3.1	3.8	4.2	3.4
France	0.0	187.3	115.8	198.1	213.6				
Germany	222.9	199.6	187.3	123.7	115.4	90.2	96.8	63.3	88.8
Greece	0.0	0.0	0.0	16.3	18.1				
Ireland	0.0	0.0	0.0	0.0	15.4				
Italy	1.7	0.3	1.5	0.2	0.1	0.0	0.0	0.0	9.4
Japan	34.1	118.9	34.5	106.8	43.1	73.3	77.1	71.0	70.9
Luxembourg	5.5	6.3	4.8	8.3	2.0	5.2	0.0	2.2	
Netherlands	53.6	21.9	81.5	63.0	103.5	138.1	165.5	134.3	231.8
New Zealand	0.1	0.1	5.6	2.3	3.8	2.2	2.3	3.0	8.0
Norway	25.5	17.6	19.1	62.0	16.5	56.8	40.5	42.1	65.6
Portugal	3.1	0.7	3.1	0.6	4.2	1.8	4.4	3.9	3.6
Spain	7.3	9.0	7.5	20.3	12.7	22.8	21.1	22.4	27.6
Sweden	58.1	49.0	52.1	62.1	35.8	33.9	26.1	17.5	26.5
Switzerland	4.1	3.1	8.7	19.9	10.6	14.9	11.7	11.2	14.5
United Kingdom	25.4	23.9	30.2	63.1	76.7	85.4	93.5	151.2	194.5
United States	109.5	105.9	73.5	109.7	138.5	175.5	228.9	215.9	356.1
Total	476.0	587.9	540.3	671.7	683.7	852.7	1013.7	1108.5	1550.9

Sources: OECD, Development Assistance Committee database; OECD, *The DAC Development Cooperation Report*, various issues; OECD, 2001: 2/1.

Annex 10.3 Share of health and population in total bilateral ODA commitments (grants and loans) (%)

	1991	1992	1993	1994	1995	1996	1997	1998	1999	2000	2001	2002	2003
Australia	3.7	3.5	6.8	6.8	10.3	7.8	11.9	8.7	9.6	9.5	7.4	8.8	6.8
Austria	4.2	2.5	1.5	3.4	2.1	8.3	1.9	13.8	4.8	12.2	4.7	7.8	3.9
Belgium	12.0	13.4	12.0	11.5	10.9	10.5	10.4	12.6	11.4	11.7	9.6	7.6	6.8
Canada	1.8	1.7	2.8	3.9	3.7	4.1	2.9	1.9	2.4	2.9	2.9	6.4	4.3
Denmark	10.2	9.8	10.4	8.9	11.3	7.1	8.9	9.0	1.7	8.6	4.3	6.3	7.1
Finland	4.5	1.6	5.9	3.7	7.0	4.4	7.6	4.9	7.7	5.7	8.5	6.6	10.0
France	4.5	2.9	2.8	3.4	3.5	3.7	3.7	3.5	3.2	4.3	3.6	3.7	4.2
Germany	1.6	2.0	2.8	3.4	3.3	4.4	3.3	3.6	2.7	2.5	2.5	2.3	2.7
Ireland	8.1	7.5	9.0	11.7	11.9	14.5	13.9	10.1	13.7				
Italy	4.4	4.3	2.8	4.0	4.2	4.0	3.9	4.7	3.5	10.3	15.3	10.2	14.9
Japan	2.0	2.1	2.0	2.3	2.5	2.3	2.7	2.5	2.4	2.5	2.0	2.3	3.1
Luxembourg	20.3	20.3	16.3	16.3	20.7	20.7	19.8	22.1	8.5	11.2	2.5	10.5	
Netherlands	6.2	2.7	6.0	4.8	5.4	5.2	5.8	4.6	3.7	5.0	3.1	3.4	4.5
New Zealand	2.5	2.3	2.5	2.3	2.5	2.5	3.6	4.5	4.2	4.4	3.6	4.9	4.2
Norway	6.8	1.6	7.8	3.8	5.4	6.2	5.6	5.8	4.1	5.0	4.7	5.4	5.9
Portugal	0.9	0.9	1.5	2.4	4.4	5.2	3.9	4.8	1.5	3.5	3.1	4.2	2.7
Spain	7.4	6.2	7.2	10.9	13.5	11.0	14.6	8.5	6.6	6.4	5.7	6.7	6.8
Sweden	8.7	9.3	9.1	10.0	8.9	9.0	7.6	6.0	5.9	3.2	5.3	3.2	3.3
Switzerland	5.2	3.3	3.0	2.4	3.1	1.8	3.3	5.1	3.9	5.2	4.4	4.1	3.4
United Kingdom	3.7	4.6	4.3	7.2	6.9	8.7	8.4	7.7	8.6	5.3	8.5	6.4	5.2
United States	4.0	5.6	63.6	10.4	68.1	11.5	12.9	6.6	8.0	4.3	4.6	3.9	5.0
Total	3.7	3.7	4.3	4.9	5.5	5.3	5.8	4.6	4.5	4.2	4.2	4.0	4.7

Sources: OECD, Development Assistance Committee database; OECD, *The DAC Development Cooperation Report*, various issues.

Annex 10.4 Bilateral ODA commitments to basic health (US$ million)

	1995	1996	1997	1998	1999	2000	2001	2002	2003
Australia	63.5	42.2	52.4	67.3	43.5	64.7	43.1	43.8	42.0
Austria	8.0	2.8	8.6	56.0	24.6	76.6	23.3	24.1	13.4
Belgium	15.5	23.1	24.9	31.5	40.4	37.6	39.2	38.9	40.0
Canada	4.5	29.9	6.4	12.7	21.0	19.3	44.8	70.8	61.7
Denmark	1.5	10.9	5.0	75.3	14.4	74.0	14.0	36.7	66.1
Finland	6.7	1.3	3.2	7.9	4.6	11.0	11.9	7.3	8.6
France	8.6	13.8	16.0	24.7	42.5	25.0	48.3		
Germany	90.5	95.5	81.7	115.3	66.1	95.4	64.8	57.3	81.9
Greece	1.7	5.2	3.1	3.3	11.4	6.1			
Ireland	0.0	0.0	0.0	0.0	17.8	24.8			
Italy	15.4	10.0	10.4	22.9	17.4	23.1	15.8	39.7	14.5
Japan	212.2	88.8	152.4	93.5	89.1	109.3	80.2	97.8	89.4
Luxembourg	8.9	10.0	8.6	10.7	4.1	5.7	0.0	4.8	
Netherlands	37.6	46.6	45.1	31.6	45.2	56.0	58.2	54.4	41.6
New Zealand	0.6	0.6	4.3	2.9	3.3	2.3	4.2	3.1	
Norway	17.8	23.8	12.9	25.0	13.0	25.5	31.6	33.3	39.9
Portugal	5.4	1.3	3.0	1.3	0.5	0.5	0.5	0.4	1.2
Spain	37.0	31.4	46.6	46.9	48.9	63.1	55.0	72.1	72.0
Sweden	83.9	61.2	54.5	44.2	26.7	18.8	21.0	25.7	22.5
Switzerland	0.4	3.6	10.3	49.7	17.4	35.5	23.6	22.8	27.8
United Kingdom	80.5	19.4	77.3	48.9	146.3	61.1	165.2	70.3	103.8
United States	317.9	308.5	214.7	296.4	276.4	404.3	554.1	546.2	803.9
Total	657.9	787.5	810.5	994.6	911.3	1186.5	1293.6	1276.8	1638.1

Sources: OECD, Development Assistance Committee database; OECD, *The DAC Development Cooperation Report*, various issues; OECD, 2001: 2/1.

Annex 10.5 Bilateral ODA Commitments (grants and loans) to population/reproductive health (US$ million)

	1991	1992	1993	1994	1995	1996	1997	1998	1999	2000	2001	2002	2003
Australia	23.5	8.0	21.9	19.9	17.0	16.1	13.6	19.5	22.3	30.3	23.4	30.5	26.4
Austria	0.4	0.0	0.1	0.0	0.1	0.1	0.0	0.1	0.0	0.2	0.6	1.0	
Belgium	24.2	26.4	25.1	13.8	11.1	1.3	1.2	3.2	5.3	6.4	10.8	12.3	17.8
Canada	1.1	1.4	0.7	19.2	11.1	24.4	12.3	9.3	28.8	22.9	42.3	32.3	90.5
Denmark	0.3	0.3	2.3	1.8	2.8	3.0	9.8	7.4	13.4				
Finland	2.8	0.7	4.1	2.4	0.3	2.5	0.6	1.9	1.0	4.8	2.0	6.2	1.4
France	207.8	0.0	0.0	6.8	4.8	11.5	8.4	11.7					
Germany	278.0	15.7	313.8	73.8	76.1	111.8	67.6	75.4	59.4	52.6	52.0	69.6	86.4
Greece	0.0	0.0	0.0	0.2	0.5	0.5							
Ireland	0.0	0.0	0.3	0.3	0.3	0.3	0.0	0.0	0.0	1.1	4.1	4.3	
Italy	1.1	33.1	0.3	0.0	1.5	0.9	1.0	1.9	3.9	2.0	6.8	1.7	5.0
Japan	9.4	13.0	13.0	27.0	25.1	26.4	31.8	16.7	28.2	14.0	23.2	13.4	15.8
Luxembourg	2.2	0.0	1.1	0.0	0.0	2.3	0.0						
Netherlands	35.6	2.8	32.5	3.8	1.4	3.3	14.9	26.2	38.5	43.0	57.5	33.8	85.3
New Zealand	0.0	0.1	0.2	0.3	0.3	0.3	0.9	0.7	0.8	0.5	0.8	1.7	
Norway	16.6	0.4	17.8	9.5	14.1	13.2	19.0	20.0	13.7	31.6	32.9	33.0	42.6
Portugal	0.3	0.2	0.0	0.0	0.0	0.0	0.0						
Spain	0.2	0.1	3.6	0.8	4.4	1.9	3.0	3.9	5.2	8.0	8.8	11.8	
Sweden	13.4	9.8	14.1	8.4	1.8	5.6	10.6	34.2	21.1	37.6	31.8	32.3	55.1
Switzerland	1.2	0.9	4.7	0.8	4.7	1.0	5.0	3.4	3.6	2.9	2.0	1.8	
UK	11.7	15.1	23.7	28.1	27.8	30.8	56.7	72.7	83.2	88.1	91.9	98.7	148.9
USA	293.1	284.7	381.1	401.2	444.7	403.8	490.7	510.9	635.1	781.7	993.7	1151.2	1418.8
Total	557.6	394.8	601.3	613.2	632.8	648.2	722.2	837.8	957.2	1183.0	1414.0	1549.3	2060.1

Sources: OECD, Development Assistance Committee database; OECD, *The DAC Development Cooperation Report*, various issues; OECD, 2001: 2/1.

Annex 10.6 Bilateral ODA Commitments (grants and loans) to water supply (all water supply, not only low-cost) (US$ million)

	1991	1992	1993	1994	1995	1996	1997	1998	1999	2000	2001	2002	2003
Australia	23.8	32.5	35.7	30.8	28.9	26.7	23.5	26.9	27.8	28.2	18.6	26.2	17.4
Austria	27.1	17.9	10.9	31.0	22.0	28.3	49.1	38.7	42.5	55.4	19.3	34.6	16.7
Belgium	13.2	7.3	15.3	9.9	10.0	10.8	9.4	14.5	9.3	13.4	9.8	17.6	21.1
Canada	45.9	23.8	38.3	11.9	23.6	13.4	26.3	21.6	29.2	27.0	35.2	48.3	54.4
Denmark	97.5	59.1	135.5	68.1	188.7	51.3	112.6	174.9	51.1	144.2	36.8	37.5	137.5
Finland	24.8	48.8	24.0	17.5	19.2	15.8	17.7	17.6	12.9	15.3	17.3	13.9	10.6
France	95.4	149.6	166.0	176.6	300.9	214.3	240.3	171.5	122.7	126.1	154.6	133.3	182.3
Germany	263.4	261.7	396.3	396.1	436.1	492.9	412.9	436.6	385.3	405.3	284.0	382.4	327.4
Greece	0.8	0.6	0.6	0.7	0.7	1.1							
Ireland	1.2	0.7	2.7	6.8	5.3	6.8	5.7	7.6	7.1	7.8	11.6	14.0	16.4
Italy	139.2	182.4	101.3	45.5	32.9	43.5	28.8	54.6	33.9	37.7	28.4	11.2	5.3
Japan	609.0	869.5	1050.0	1589.0	1617.9	1638.7	1541.8	1236.8	1581.8	786.4	1129.0	830.3	544.2
Luxembourg	1.1	0.9	0.7	1.4	2.1	6.1	6.6	5.0	4.9	0.0	7.2		
Netherlands	57.8	85.0	60.1	110.1	78.5	82.0	103.0	86.5	76.2	103.2	82.2	88.1	135.3
New Zealand	0.9	0.8	0.7	0.4	0.4	0.4	1.4	2.0	1.3	1.7	1.2	1.4	1.6
Norway	19.4	5.3	10.3	19.4	10.7	21.4	17.7	28.8	22.6	45.5	20.6	32.8	27.8
Portugal	0.4	0.3	0.3	0.2	0.2	0.4	0.3	1.0	0.3	0.7	1.1		
Spain	37.1	26.6	19.1	48.2	13.2	29.2	27.2	19.9	21.4	31.4	32.9	52.0	65.6
Sweden	44.0	33.7	55.7	38.6	52.5	27.4	33.0	48.2	22.4	64.9	24.1	47.0	34.5
Switzerland	29.6	12.7	20.2	10.0	28.1	9.8	33.1	61.3	25.5	43.2	23.4	29.2	27.1
UK	57.1	58.4	48.1	45.2	45.3	40.8	52.3	63.8	50.9	63.2	31.1	36.7	23.1
USA	417.2	405.2	242.8	227.9	87.6	100.8	152.7	195.1	159.6	356.4	97.6	277.9	524.6
Total	1984.3	2280.7	2337.9	2880.2	2906.8	2847.2	2889.7	2713.1	2685.5	2406.6	2048.6	2136.3	2183.1

Source: OECD, Development Assistance Committee database; OACD, *The DAC Development Cooperation Report*, various issues; Development Assistance.

11

Conclusion

Since the 1980s businesses, governments and financial leaders have extolled the virtues of markets and argued that market-friendly policies are the only way to forge a new, better world. Governments have become more interested in the health of markets than in the health of their own people, debasing democratic governance. In spite of the case made in the North and the South that market-friendly policies were growth-oriented, and that economic growth should be the dominant objective of macroeconomic policy in order to achieve greater welfare for all, economic growth in the 1990s was slower and more volatile than in the 1960s and 1970s. The economic growth that was actually achieved did very little to reduce income poverty (except in China and India, which followed rather unorthodox policies in any case, even after their economic reforms began).[1]

Belatedly, there has been some shift in thinking, and there is recognition that there are many important 'factors underlying changes ... that make growth more or less pro-poor. Careful country-specific analyses paint a more nuanced picture.'[2] The *World Development Report 2006* focus on equity and development is a welcome development, especially its recognition of the need for greater equity in access to land. The real issue is whether, to what extent and when this 'nuanced' analysis becomes part of the IFIs' and developing countries' policymaking toolkit on a daily basis. Even more, policymakers in developing countries need to acknowledge that economic growth can increase the gap between rich and poor, hence the quality of growth matters. There is ample evidence that in about a third of seventy-eight countries for which a long enough time series exists on trends in within-country income distribution over the last two decades, inequality has increased.

This book has attempted to show at various levels that an alternative exists to the market-based theoretical models and policy recommendations that dominated the 1990s. In particular the earlier chapters of the book tried to show that the empirical record in terms of stabilization and economic growth of these policies has been poor. Not surprisingly, income poverty has not declined during the last ten years, except in a small number of key countries (e.g. India, China, Vietnam). More importantly, human development is not achieving its potential.

However, this book is more than an empirical critique. It presents the case for a different theoretical vision, by linking in a novel way different strands of literature, which usually do not overlap, such as: the capabilities and women's agency approach (which is different from the human capital perspective, while incorporating it); the neo-structuralist ideas on open economy macroeconomics; evolutionary and complex systems thinking on economic growth; post-Keynesian views on fiscal policies; the surplus approach to understanding the sources of investment and the distributive conflict; and institutional models on participation and incentive structures.

These theoretical ideas can be contrasted with those that usually underpin traditional policy advice: abstract separation of economics from its institutional foundations in politics and society or a narrow economic view of institutions of the so-called neo-institutional literature; super-rational individuals who maximize their own (and only their own) utility over an infinite time span; money-metric and profit measures as main indicators of efficiency, or well-being; reliance on 'imperfections' to explain real world market behaviour; and simplistic causal mechanisms. These assumptions are usually found wanting on the fact that they provide an inaccurate assessment of the actual conditions of countries, and thus lead to misguided policy conclusions.

It has long been known that separate interventions in health, nutrition, water and sanitation, fertility control, and education complement each other, and thus increase the impact of any one from interventions in any other. We noted that gender equality and women's capabilities are central to the triggering of this first set of synergies (or feedback loops among the interventions in health, education, nutrition, water and sanitation). But we identified another set of synergies (of which the first set is a subset). This is between health/education status, income poverty-reduction and economic growth. In recent years there has been a spate of literature showing the links from lower inequality to higher growth. We focused on income-poverty reduction, rather than income inequality reduction, since the latter may or may not always lead to the former.

This synergy can be succinctly expressed as the enhanced impact the rate of change of an independent variable has on the rate of change of a dependent variable, given the presence of a third variable. This led to two interrelated implications. First, the impact of a policy (e.g. to promote economic growth) on another one (say poverty reduction) crucially depends on the level of a third variable (e.g. expansion of functionings). In other words, economic growth will be more successful in reducing income-poverty – the elasticity of poverty-reduction will be higher – the more equitably distributed human capital is. Second, standard tools of marginal analysis, rates of return or linear regressions are inadequate to establish the importance, relative weight or priority of these interventions because the presence of these synergies (or feedback loops) creates non-linearities. For instance, trade liberalization in a context of low levels of human capital will have a very different impact than the same policy (and other elements being equal) in a situation where the citizens are healthy and highly trained.

As a theoretical construct, this notion of the dual synergies needs to be distinguished from some antecedents along similar lines in the development economics literature. First, the synergy notion has to be distinguished from the concept of linear stages of development that was characteristic of the writings of Rostow (1959, 1960). Instead, development proceeds in a non-linear path where different interventions and outcomes are enmeshed in virtuous or vicious cycles (Taylor et al., 1997).[3] Second, following the classical development theorists who recognized that long-run economic growth is a highly non-linear process, our dual synergy model is similar to the Rosenstein-Rodan (1943) idea that posited the need for a government-financed series of interdependent investments, to take advantage of external economies and economies of scale and propel developing countries from a low-level equilibrium trap, with limited growth of per capita income, to a high-level equilibrium path, characterized by self-sustaining growth. In the view of the classical development economists, endorsed here, development could not be induced by a minimalist state.[4] Third, our theoretical construct also draws strongly upon the literature of the last two decades which emphasizes the positive externalities in interventions in health, education and family planning. Our main criticism of the notion of externalities is that it does not capture fully the feedback effects from human development outcomes back to social service inputs, and the virtuous cycle from inputs to outcomes in an upward (or downward) spiral. Finally, our dual synergy construct is grounded in the capability approach, especially its emphasis on women's agency – particularly in the version now associated with the work of Amartya Sen and Martha Nussbaum. We strongly agree that women's agency is critical to triggering the first set of synergies.[5]

One policy implication of the dual synergy theoretical framework is that if economic growth remains, as it has in the past, as the dominant objective with macroeconomic policy determined first – while 'social policy' is expected to address the social consequences of economic policy – this synergy will not be realized. This is one of the major respects in which our argument differs from that based on orthodox economics – that has remained bound up within a utilitarian approach, with a command over commodities as the basis of human satisfaction. Our dissatisfaction with a utilitarian approach is a major reason why we espouse the capabilities approach, since within the latter the distinction between the 'economic' and the 'social' discourse disappears. The capabilities of humans have intrinsic value; they also have instrumental value in enabling social and economic change (Sen, 2000). The dual synergy theoretical framework is an attempt to use the capability approach to provide a conceptual basis for development policy – in other words, to operationalize the capability approach.

This is not the only way our theoretical framework differs from the approach of mainstream thinking in development. A second respect in which it differs is the degree to which it places emphasis on gender equality, as the cornerstone of development strategy and policy, and as a guide for evaluating 'good' government. The issue of women's capabilities and their agency are not merely additional variables to take into account in our alternative framework; they are among *the most critical variables*. This is because, unlike in a comparable historical period in the now industrialized countries, contemporary developing countries will be unable to structurally transform their economies and society without much greater gender equality. Hastening the demographic transition and reducing the fertility rate is the flip side of increasing per capita income; and greater gender equality is an instrument of reduced fertility (Mehrotra, 2002c).

A dual synergy framework is a framework for analysis, to understand the economic and social circumstances of different countries. It is a conceptual toolkit for explaining failure in human development outcomes, and also for explaining success. We attempted to understand the positive experiences of the now industrialized countries or that of high achieving among the developing countries within this dual synergy framework.

We also used the framework to devise macroeconomic policies which can promote pro-poor economic growth – pro-poor defined as that growth which raises the incomes of the poor by more than that of the non-poor. With this objective, we emphasized a few institutional issues that have been underplayed in development discourse in the last two decades. Land ownership/tenancy issues are one of them; and growing landlessness in rural areas in countries with surplus labour and very significant agriculturally dependent populations is another. Managing distributional conflict during the structural adjustments required by external shocks is centrally important in explaining the variation in country experiences in the sustainability of economic growth. Managing distributional conflict requires redistribution before, as well as with, growth.

In addition, pro-poor industrial growth will require industrial policies. Industrial policies may appear passé in the twenty-first century, but there is still no alternative to them. Even the orthodox paradigm has relied on them; the only difference is that they have emphasized export-orientation in manufacturing and attracting foreign direct investment. Both are worthy elements of any industrial policy, but both can lead to enclave-type development, and there is more to industrial policy than these two elements. WTO restrictions still allow considerable leeway for selective industrial and technology policies. Unlike the World Bank and the IMF, where the G7 countries control 48 per cent of the vote, the WTO is supposedly run on the 'one country, one vote' principle, and despite the use of consensus decision-making (where green room discussions are dominated by a limited number of countries) there is some room for manoeuvre (Chang, 2003). First, to protect domestic industry, many developing countries have decided on tariff ceilings that are still considerable. The least developed countries have until 2006 to reduce tariffs. Second, infant industry protection is still permitted (up to eight years). Third, there is still provision for 'emergency' tariff increase on two grounds: one, a sudden increase in sectoral imports, already used by many countries; two, an overall balance-of-payments problem, for which almost all developing countries qualify, and which many countries have also used. Fourth, subsidies for agriculture, regional development, basic R&D, environment-related technology upgrading are still allowed. Also, the subsidy restrictions only impact 'trade-related' policies, while many domestic policies are still allowed, including subsidies to new enterprises, for investment in particular skills, for equipment investments, and so on. Fifth, several countries can use compulsory licencing provision in respect of trade-related intellectual property rights to produce drugs, especially for treating the HIV/AIDS virus, and generic drug manufacturers in India, China, Brazil are challenging the monopoly of the drug transnationals. Finally, despite the trade-related investment measures agreed under the WTO, governments can maintain or even strengthen local-content requirements, which is essential for technological upgrading. Countries are still allowed to adopt export promotion measures, so that transnationals are required to export final products equal to the value of imported components, or adopt export requirements for transnationals in export processing zones.

Industrial policy in the twenty-first century will also need to support micro- and small enterprises in a way that was underemphasized in the last half-century. Slow growth in manufacturing employment in the last half-century has led to an increase in the informalization of employment in urban areas in most developing countries (outside the 'tigers' like Korea and Taiwan). While all the tigers had some policies for small enterprises (normally defined as enterprises employing 10–50 people), a significant share of employment today in developing countries is in micro-enterprises (under 10 employees), and even more commonplace is employment (especially of women) which tries to avoid the employer–employee relationship deliberately, to avoid any legal obligations (especially of social protection) that come from registration of firms and such a formal relationship. That is the reason we argued strongly for policies that support micro-enterprises and some form of social insurance for the growing class of informal-sector workers.

We also noted the need for alternative macroeconomic policies – which are more home-grown than we have seen in most developing countries in recent decades. In fact, the historical significance of more home-grown macroeconomic policies cannot be over-emphasized. Orthodox policies have not led to economic growth in the majority of countries that adopted them – and it is rather unhelpful to argue, as some do, that they were not fully owned, and implemented half-heartedly, and hence were not effective. For the comprehensive conditionality that both low- and middle-income borrowers from the international financial institutions are subjected to be acceptable, the governance of the international institutions would need to be seen as more legitimate.

Besides, we argued that high levels of external indebtedness in both least developed (now 49 of them) and 21 emerging market economies – which together account for the overwhelming majority of the world's poor – have periodically disabled fiscal policy. Without enabling fiscal policy, the likelihood of the Millennium Goals being achieved is minimal.

The doctrines of 'small' government and fiscal austerity (see, e.g., Tanzi and Schuknecht, 2000 for such a position) followed in many developing countries in the past two decades contradict the historical experience of most industrialized countries and many developing ones that enhanced the capabilities of their people. There, the role and size of the state consistently increased, and with it the revenue base, throughout the twentieth century; and most of this growth was accounted for by social spending. Social spending grew from 1880 on through much of the twentieth century in industrialized countries. This growth was not of the bureaucracy or the military and undemocratic in nature, as has been common in developing countries, and as was pervasive under the old regime in transition economies. Democratic participation guided policies in these countries in a way that allowed states to gather surplus through taxes to implement policies to enhance citizens' capabilities. Through much of the twentieth century, this was done not only based on and respecting the civil and political rights of citizens, but also strengthening and expanding their economic and social rights – relying on a growing tax base. In fact, there are strong, direct connections between ways in which governments raise revenue and the quality of governance that they practice.

> In OECD countries, the tax relationship underpinned formal mechanisms of political accountability and public financial management ... governments (notably in Britain and the Netherlands) negotiated with taxpayers, including holders of mobile capital, in ways that created joint gains to both rulers and taxpayers ... there was a process and a forum (parliament) in which taxes were negotiated, which encouraged taxpayers to get involved in policymaking, and rulers to adopt policies that were mutually beneficial. (Moore et al., 2005)

In spite of the imperfections and shortcomings of these experiences, they show that state policies can be used to increase universal well-being in ways that cannot be done on an individual basis through markets. Public expenditure as a percentage of GDP in these countries now stands at an average of more than twice that for most developing countries. In order for developing countries to grow, their governments will have to grow (yet another area where our approach differs from the orthodox approach) – but along the lines just described.

A few simple elements, discussed in the second part of the book, can help in this task. The first is increasing government expenditures on basic services. Developing-country governments are allocating 12–14 per cent of total government expenditure on basic social services. In sub-Saharan Africa and South Asia, basic education receives a meagre 10 per cent or less of total public spending, which leaves millions of boys and girls out of school and adult illiteracy on the rise. Similarly, primary health-care spending accounts for even less in countries where U5MR has been relatively stagnant for a decade and life expectancy has declined (in some countries particularly affected by the HIV/AIDS pandemic).

This pattern of public spending – or rather neglect of basic services – is in stark contrast to the experience of high-achieving developing countries and industrialized ones. There the state has taken a pre-eminent role in the investment and promotion of health and education services. However, the new orthodoxy has favoured the resort to multiple providers (and the state as one among many), market forces, privatization and cost recovery for state-provided services. In the industrialized countries the state was responsible for promoting public education and a public health system on a mass scale, for a majority of the population – not for a narrow elite. Early in their development process, industrialized countries not only experienced an agricultural revolution prior to the Industrial Revolution, but elementary education expanded rapidly and through the nineteenth century as the Industrial Revolution gathered momentum. Most industrialized countries also provided full coverage of the population with publicly funded health systems long before privatization of the health or education system was attempted in the last decade.

Second, the experience of the fifteen or so high-achieving developing countries was also quite different in another respect. What marked their spending pattern in terms of health and education was its equity across levels of service (favouring the lower and basic levels within health and education). In contrast, we found grossly inequitable patterns of spending within these sectors in our studies. Policymakers need to study and absorb the experiences of these high-achieving countries – countries with better social indicators than expected given their levels of national income.

Third, the evidence regarding the distribution of health and education spending between the poor and non-poor shows that it matters. The distribution of public spending benefits in education and health are usually biased in favour of the richer groups. In addition, expenditure per recipient increases with the income of the recipient. Not only do the better-off groups usually receive a higher share of the benefits of public spending; they receive better-quality services. A more detailed probing of the information on unit costs often finds that the poorest receive lower-quality services despite their greater needs. However, the distribution of benefits at the basic level of services is more egalitarian than at the secondary and tertiary levels.

Fourth, the contrasts between the policies of high achievers and the rest extend to other aspects of policy. They offer many principles of good practice which help improve efficiency of spending: basic education and health care are provided free of charge; schoolchildren learn in their own language and progress automatically through grades; there are more female teachers, and so on. There are functional health services in rural areas; there are adequate budgets for essential and generic drugs; there is greater reliance on nurses and other medical staff than on physicians; and there is compulsory rural service for personnel trained at public expense.

There are economies of scale in the state providing the basic services (as opposed to merely financing them). The coordination in investment that is necessary for the synergies in interventions in basic services to be realized is best achieved if the state is the main provider. However, state functionaries in many developing countries have indeed been characterized by rent-seeking behaviour. Ensuring greater accountability and transparency of the state providers of basic services crucially hinges now on the spread of deep democratic decentralization. At least in respect of basic services, the formal institutions of democracy alone do not work. Democracy at the macro-level rarely translates into power for the poor.[6] If it did, we would have more evidence of pro-poor economic growth and dramatic improvements in human development indicators in those Latin American, African and East European countries that went democratic over the 1980s and 1990s. For accountability of state service providers to improve, democracy has to be deepened, with decentralization reinforced by the collective voice of the people – or deep democratic decentralization. We have provided evidence from different developing countries where it has been shown to work – in parts of Brazil and India in particular.

Fifth, in basic education and in clinical health services, the private sector will remain a means for meeting differentiated demand, but technical capacity to regulate the private sector has to be built up; there is a role here for the UN and for other international agencies. By and large, in low-income countries, public resources will need to be concentrated at the primary level – as poor children barely get beyond the primary level, if they even complete it; girls tend to drop out more. In middle-income countries, quality improvements throughout the school system (including colleges and universities) are a prerequisite for human capital levels commensurate with labour demands of an industrial structure that is moving up the product–cycle ladder.

In the health sector we found that the private sector's role in most low-income and middle-income countries was not consistent with either equity or efficiency objectives. Similarly, while cost recovery has grown in the health sector in most developing countries, the evidence here was that it has not raised significant resources, while curtailing demand. Thus, there is little clear evidence in favour of greater cost recovery in publicly provided/financed clinical services. On account of the uncertain and unpredictable nature of demand for health services, growing government financing is essential alongside pooling of community resources so that there is pooling of health risk.

In water and sanitation, the private sector's role as a provider grew in the 1990s – though at most it only covers about 5 per cent of the urban population in the world. The evidence does not bear out that it has begun to serve the poor population. We presented evidence that the state has shown itself capable of serving the majority of its population with safe water and sanitation, provided tariffs for water and sanitation services are raised to cover costs from the wealthier areas to enable cross-subsidization to occur. But the very large body of the unserved population in the world and the concomitant resources requirements imply that public–private partnerships will grow, and need to grow, provided that the state becomes a better regulator than it has so far proved to be. What is clear is that water and sanitation are too basic to life for profit-oriented foreign investment to be encouraged, and it may be preferable for governments to encourage domestic enterprise to engage in public–private partnerships. In the area of social services, the watsan sector is by far the greatest challenge in the coming decade.

Sixth, we made a strong case for mobilizing additional resources. In the short term, only limited additional resources can be mobilized by intra-sectoral reallocation within the social sectors. Cost recovery at higher levels of service is necessary in certain sectors (as we saw above) to enable additional public resources to be directed to basic services in education, and to rural areas in watsan sectors. But, for reasons of political economy, intra-sectoral restructuring is easier during periods of increasing resources for the health and education sector as a whole. Long-term progress on basic services requires inter-sectoral reallocation – especially away from defence (in some countries only), external debt (in most least-developed countries) and both external and domestic debt (in other low-income and in most middle-income countries), and subsidies to production or consumption that have no positive impact on the well-being of the poor (that characterize most developing countries).

Even more importantly, macroeconomic policies will need to place more emphasis on revenue mobilization. Measures could include new types of taxes – including international ones. International financial institutions need to recognize that public expenditure cuts as a means of budget deficit reduction have negative effects and must be balanced and tempered by revenue-raising measures, but this is not possible if governments do not seek their assistance. However, income taxes as a source of revenue in developing countries remain low, despite growing per capita incomes. Administrative reforms in a number of middle-income countries in the 1990s have enabled income taxes to rise. Institutional reforms targeting the incentives of taxpayers and tax-collectors have shown to yield significant revenue gains, and will have to be adopted in other low- and middle-income countries. Increasing use of such indirect taxes as value-added taxes has also been demonstrated to generate increasing resources.

Additional revenue may not benefit social services unless a certain amount of earmarking for basic services – for basic education, public health and basic clinical services, and for drinking water and sanitation – is introduced. This may require legislative, maybe even constitutional, measures to protect existing funding for these services; in other words, given that resources are fungible, earmarking would be unjustifiable unless it resulted in additional resources for basic services, beyond what is currently allocated to it in the budget.

Finally, the rhetoric of the Millennium Development Goals from the donor community – about which developing-country governments show increasing scepticism – has not been matched by the reality of official development assistance. If the experience of the 1990s is any indicator, ODA for basic services remains seriously deficient in several ways: while overall ODA has increased since 2001 after falling over the decade of the 1990s, it still stands at a level relative to donor-country GNP well below levels achieved earlier. In other words, while the rich countries have grown richer, they have not become more generous. Even more, the share of basic services within it has remained low at around 10 per cent; its composition needs sharp modification in education and water/sanitation, and to a lesser extent in health; its modality – especially the shift from the project to the sectoral approach – requires modification in respect of current donor methods and procedures; and the conditionality approach has to be altered fundamentally to give real meaning to the rhetoric of partnership.

At the same time, there is an urgent need for consistency between aid policy and the other (mainly trade- and domestic-subsidy-related, technological transfers, GATS, TRIPS) policies of industrialized countries. We found that in many basic services (health, watsan) privatization has not benefited the poor, yet every international forum is used by multilateral and bilateral donors, including the WTO, to encourage privatization of services. Without ensuring coherence between industrialized-country domestic policies and aid policy, developing-country governments' scepticism about the rhetoric of international development goals and targets will survive well beyond the 2015 target deadline. Worse still, enhancing the capabilities of the poor will remain a mirage.

Notes

chapter 1

1. Currently government policies and institutions are evaluated, and the determination made by Bank staff whether countries are worthy of receiving World Bank funding, on the basis of a Country Policy and Institutional Assessment (CPIA). There are twenty items to be assessed, each with a 5 per cent weight in the overall rating. They are grouped into four categories: (A) Economic Management: 1. Management of inflation and macreconomic imbalances; 2. Fiscal policy; 3. Management of public debt (external and domestic); 4. Management and sustainability of development programme. (B) Structural Policies: 5. Trade policy and foreign exchange regime; 6. Financial stability; 7. Financial sector depth, efficiency and resource mobilization; 8. Competitive environment for the private sector; 9. Goods and factor markets; 10. Policies and institutions for environmental sustainability. (C) Policies for Social Inclusion: 11. Gender; 12. Equity; 13. Building human resources; 14. Social protection and labour; 15. Monitoring and analysis of poverty outcomes and impacts. (D) Public Sector Management and Institutions: 16. Property Rights and rule-based governance; 17. Quality of budgetary and financial management; 18. Efficiency of revenue mobilization; 19. Quality of public administration; 20. Transparency, accountability and corruption in the public sector. For indicator, the rating scale goes from 1 (low) to 6 (high); with 1 being unsatisfactory for an extended period and 6 being good for an extended period. http://siteresources.worldbank.org/IDA/Resources/CPIA2003.pdf.
2. For such a critique among many others, see Robinson, 1956; Sraffa, 1960; Shaikh, 1974; Garegnani, 1970; Robinson, 1964; Nelson and Winter, 1982; Marglin, 1984; Nell, 1992; Taylor, 1991; Dutt, 1990; Simon, 1991; Hirschman, 1981.
3. Imports can only be purchased with local production or by borrowing. Most developing countries know all too well the unsustainable implications of borrowing.
4. This, by no means, should be interpreted as implying that workers are not poor or enjoy an adequate standard of living.
5. In recent years, there has been a spate of literature showing the links from lower inequality to higher growth (Birdsall et al., 1995; Li and Zou, 1998; Forbes, forthcoming). We focus on income-poverty reduction, rather than income inequality reduction, since the latter may or may not always lead to the former. Also, the empirical strength of the linkage between lower inequality and higher growth is still questionable.
6. Sri Lanka is a good example (see, e.g., Taylor et al., 1997 for a discussion).
7. Botswana is an example (see, e.g., Duncan et al., 1997 for a discussion).
8. Needless to say, they implemented policies and strategies without reference to the

synergies we described *ex-post*, as they represent an interesting case of what Lindblom calls 'muddle-through'.

9. This hierarchy of policy is reflected in the hierarchy of government service, where a career in the Finance Ministry is typically preferred over one in Social Affairs/Education/Health. When the Ministry of Finance fully grasps the case for human development, this hierarchy will melt away.

10. All data in this subsection are drawn from UNDP, *Human Development Report 2002* and *2003*.

11. The $1 a day poverty line measure of poverty has itself been subjected to trenchant criticism on philosophical and methodological grounds. For such a criticism, see Reddy and Pogge, 2002.

chapter 2

1. See also Mkandawire, 2004.

2. This has been partly recognized by the moves of the World Bank into the social field, but that has its own problems, as we discuss below in this chapter.

3. Needless to say, they implemented policies and strategies without reference to the synergies we described *ex-post*, and they represent an interesting case of what Lindblom (1959) calls 'muddle-through'.

4. Interestingly, Lal and Myint (1996) criticize this neoclassical theoretical basis but retain most of the policy recommendations.

5. This was particularly the case in Latin America, from Mexico to Argentina. As this books goes to press, however, it seems that a new set of alliances are emerging in many countries, especially in the Southern Cone/MERCOSUR.

6. The emerging market economies we have in mind are mostly, but not only, middle income countries; they also exclude the oil-rich countries of the Middle East. They are, in alphabetical order: Argentina, Brazil, Bulgaria, Chile, China, Colombia, Costa Rica, Ecuador, Egypt, India, Indonesia, Jordan, Korean Republic, Lebanon, Malaysia, Mexico, Morocco, Nigeria, Pakistan, Panama, Peru, Philippines, Poland, Russia, South Africa, Thailand, Turkey, Ukraine and Uruguay (Dervis, 2005).

7. This is reminiscent of Keynes's aphorism on beauty contests.

8. For elaborations, and criticisms, of this view see Sen, 1982, and the sources cited therein. Taylor (1984) and Uvin (2002) also present interesting criticisms and limitations of Sen's approach. A particularly nagging one is to specify concretely what should be included in the list of capabilities. In practice, they have been measured by the traditional basic needs (such as health, education, etc.), especially by the *Human Development Reports*. Moreover, the term 'capability' is often given another meaning, akin to 'good things or characteristics to enjoy', such as a good education or health status. Sen says that capabilities allow people to achieve 'functionings', which are the ones people value (e.g. a healthy and long life, being educated, participating in society). It should be noticed that his is not a 'space of valuation', such as capabilities in the sense described in the text, but actual objectives (similar to universal education or universal health care, with the twist that emphasis is on actually achieving what those services intend to provide rather than staying at the level of provision without regard to their effect on people's lives). As we want to maintain the distinction made by Sen between capabilities and functioning, we retain the former term for the space between commodities and utility and the latter for the objectives and attainment of social policy in a broad sense.

9. After many years of criticisms levelled against the IMF that reduction of fiscal deficits was made overly dependent upon expenditure reduction, rather than tax revenue generation, there has been a change in practice in recent years. See, e.g., Internal

Evaluation Office's report evaluating the PRSP and Poverty Reduction and Growth Facility loan agreements (IEO, 2004).

10. For instance, no one can legitimately claim that fiscal deficits of 10 per cent of GDP are inherently good, especially when accompanied by inflation rates of over 15 per cent per annum.

11. IEO, 2004 notes that PRGFs do attempt to drive down inflation rates if they are at 10 per cent or above, but not if they are at 5–10 per cent.

12. See, inter alia, Benería, 1992; Ferber and Nelson, 1993; Nelson, 1996; Budlender et al., 1998; Elson and Catagay, 2000; and Fundacão F. Ebert, 2003. For an analysis of why women's capability-enhancement is a necessary condition for triggering the second synergy as well, see Mehrotra, 2002b.

13. Rather, an increased flexibility of labour laws is promoted only to weaken the bargaining power of workers vis-à-vis employers, to permit the latter to obtain a larger surplus.

14. It must be remembered that neoclassical economics deals with a very particular type of rationality, but there are multiple rationalities.

15. The complementarity between state and non-state providers (especially through charity-like INGOs or religious groups as well as for-profit providers) is explored in Chapter 8.

16. See also Sader et al., 1995; Tavares Soares, 2003.

17. See Reddy and Pogge, 2002; and Vandemoortele, 2000 for criticism of this measurement.

18. For a full debate on the merits and demerits on conceptual and empirical grounds of using $1 a day as a poverty measure, see www.socialanalysis.org. What is most remarkable just in Asia is that for 13 countries for which income poverty estimates are available for two points of time based on the $1 a day poverty line, in six of those 13 countries the estimates for poverty based on the national poverty line indicate that time trends for poverty are going in the opposite direction to those based on the dollar-a-day line.

19. The experience of the largest Latin American countries can be found in Cordera and Ziccardi, 2000; Heymann and Kosacoff, 2000; Jaguaribe, 2002; and Tavares Soares, 2004.

20. See Reddy and Pogge, 2002; and Vandemoortele, 2000 for criticism.

21. In this context, his unveiling of the hypocrisy and power-wielding by some groups (especially financial interests) in industrialized countries is welcome, albeit of anecdotal value.

22. See Kanbur, 2000 for a similar point of view for low-income, aid-dependent countries. See Dervis, 2005 on emerging market economies.

23. In fact, Rodrik states:

> None of this is to suggest that the specific institutional reforms that dominate the agendas of the Bretton Woods institutions are without merit. No one can be seriously against the introduction of proper accounting standards or against improved prudential supervision of financial intermediaries. While some of the standards are likely to backfire in practice, the more serious concerns are twofold. First, these standards are the wedge with which a broader set of policy and institutional preferences – in favour of open capital accounts, deregulated labour markets, arms-length finance, American-style corporate governance, and hostile to industrial policies – are imparted on [sic] the recipient countries. Second, the agenda focuses too much on institutional reforms needed to make the world safe for capital flows, and therefore necessarily diverts political capital and attention from institutional reforms in other areas. The risk is that such an approach privileges freedom of international trade and capital mobility in the name of 'sound' economic policy, and that it does so at the cost of neglecting other goals of development policy that may potentially clash with it. (2000: 27)

24. A counter-argument to this definition is proposed by Ravallion (2005). He claims that if the rate of growth in a country is very strong, the incidence of income poverty could decline faster (even if their share of total income declines) than in the case of slower 'pro-poor' growth as defined in the text. While this is a theoretical possibility, it misses an important conceptual problem. It assumes that in a process of rapid growth, the income-poverty line will be fixed in the medium term. This is not correct, as the growth elasticity of the poverty line is positive, and usually close to one.

25. Although it is widely agreed that poverty is a multidimensional concept which involves more than income, in this section the focus is in the traditional definition based on an income-poverty line (Orshansky, 1965; Ravallion, 1997; and Lipton and Ravallion, 1994 present the traditional poverty line method). Criticisms and extensions can be found in Streeten et al., 1981; Sen, 1985; Gore and Figueiredo, 1997; and Wratten, 1995. Thus, in what follows the expression 'income-poverty' will be used.

26. The reference here is specifically to the instruments of fiscal policies (tax, expenditure and borrowing), monetary policies (the management of the demand for, and supply of, money by the central bank through interest and exchange rate policies) and trade policies – with the objective of maintaining sustainable fiscal and current account balances in the economy.

27. Monetary and fiscal policies suggested by the Washington Consensus were trenchantly criticized during the East Asian economic crisis of the late 1990s – especially its 'cookie-cutter' or 'one size fits all' approach. When the financial crisis in mid-1997 turned into an economic crisis, the IMF imposed austerity measures – balanced budgets and tighter monetary policies. However, the effects of its measures likely turned a slowdown into a recession (Stiglitz, 2000). Seemingly without learning anything from this experience, the IMF advocated similar policies in Latin America in the current decade, with similarly disastrous results.

28. This is not surprising, given that governments committed to reducing income poverty will find it difficult without investing in human capital. On the other hand, the reverse is not necessarily true, i.e. governments investing in human capital need take no direct action to reduce income poverty, and may rely largely upon the trickle-down of growth.

29. The answer is obvious too: because other growth-oriented policies (technological change to induce productivity increase, macroeconomic stability, etc.) are not present.

30. In UNDP, UNESCO, UNFPA at al., 1998 a similar exercise, with different countries, and for a different time period was carried out. The results are completely consistent, pointing to their robustness.

31. See Sen, 1995 for an explanation.

32. In what follows, we are expanding Sen's classification as we add a third variable (income poverty reduction) to his analysis. As we have three bimodal variables and their order is not important, we have 8 (i.e. 23) combinations in Table 2.2.

33. Similar arguments can be heard from the middle classes in developing countries (e.g. India), on the ground that if child workers attended school, who would do work as domestics, or in other urban services (Wiener, 1995).

34. Similarly, it is noticeable that where public systems were slow to develop (England and Wales, the American South), educational levels were noticeably low (Green, 1990).

35. The similarity with the defence/control of the uneducated is striking.

36. Vaccination, which has been compulsory for infants since 1853, closely associated with the Poor Law, and often poorly administered, had bred popular resistance from its inception.

37. See below.

38. The elimination of fees is critical to the increase of enrolments, since parents are incurring both the direct costs of schooling and the opportunity cost. For 1900, Theodore Schultz (1961) has estimated such opportunity cost at about two-fifths of direct expenditures,

a proportion that rises to almost unity in 1956, as enrolment rates in secondary and higher education greatly increased. Fishlow (1966) estimated opportunity costs for 1860, 1880 and 1900 and found they were about the equivalent of the total public contribution to all levels of the educational system.

39. McKeown (1976) argued that, historically, both therapeutic and preventive medicine had been ineffective, and that the reduction of infant mortality was primarily an economic issue. Thus, instead of investing money in sophisticated medical technology, perhaps even in public health measures, it seemed preferable to promote programmes capable of increasing the nutritional level of the whole population and enhancing the resistance of its younger members to the aggression of germs and parasites. Preston and Haines (1991), however, suggested, on the basis of the lack of social-class differentials in child mortality in the USA around 1900, that 'lack of know-how rather than lack of resources was principally responsible for foreshortening life'.

40. It is noticeable that per capita GDP grew from $535 in Germany in 1870 to $1,374 in 1950; on the other hand, in the UK it rose from $972 to $2,094.

41. Green (1990) notes the absence of scientific and technical education until the mid-nineteenth century in Oxford and Cambridge. In the rise of British industry, apparently, universities played no part whatever; indeed formal education of any sort was a negligible factor in its success.

chapter 3

1. Japan and Korea had highly restrictive policies against foreign direct investment, though Taiwan less so, as part of industrial policy. Several studies conclude that foreign direct investment has an adverse effect on income distribution (Bornschier and Chase-Dunn, 1985).

2. See Nolan, 1995 for the corruption associated with FDI in China. Chudnovsky and Lopez, 2002 report on the connection between integration and FDI in South America.

3. This is not a purely technology-driven argument. Many concomitant changes in institutions, policies and market behaviour also took place in now industrialized countries, which are not present in developing ones.

4. Like Breman (1996) and Chen et al. (2002), we prefer to use the term 'informal economy' for the informal sector. First, the informal and formal parts of the economy are interlinked, and referring to them as two sectors is misleading. Second, it is unhelpful to use the term 'sector' as a classificatory device for both the formality/informality of work status and for industry groups or commodity chains – and 'sector' is better reserved for use with the latter. For work status, workers all over the world increasingly face degrees of informality.

5. From 62 million in 1900 in Latin America to 480 million in 1995; from 118 million in Africa to 732 million; and from 937 million in Asia to 3,458 million.

6. In fact, Wal-Mart is a very large part of the export success of China, accounting for a signficant share of its foreign-enterprise driven export boom within this first decade of the twenty-first century.

7. As Lewis argues, 'If 70 per cent of the labour force consists of low productivity food farmers, with only a tiny surplus, the market for domestic manufactures is strictly limited. As the limits are approached, the pace of industrialization can be maintained only by exporting manufactures' (Lewis, 1978: 31–2). However, in this case – although the GDP may increase substantially – it can be very difficult to diffuse the welfare and technology, and most of the population would receive few benefits. Most of the population working in the informal sector would remain poor or stagnating with

low productivity and disguised unemployment or would be exploited by globalized production chains without getting any benefit from growth. Here, we argue that in the process of clustering, local demand can increase if workers receive the benefits of growth in terms of social protection and higher wage.

8. In 1890 Marshall affirmed the relevance of clusters of micro-, small and medium-size enterprises in the industrialization process of a country (Marshall, 1920).

9. In essence her argument is that informal activities which do not protect workers, promote innovations or respect the environment in order to maintain or increase profits are detrimental even to the capitalists. Thus, by not enforcing regulations and protections, governments (both national and local) undermine their possibility of success. Thus, the trade-off between short-term profits and lack of regulation is a 'devil's deal'. Tendler (2004) provides examples of cases where public policies assisted producers to overcome their fears of regulations, with positive results for workers, capitalists, productivity and environmental protection.

10. Even in services, such funds are not entirely inconceivable. They are already in place for film and cinema industry workers in India.

11. For an extensive discussion of Millennium Development Goals (MDGs), see UNDP HDR, 2003.

12. As evidenced by the contrast of the performance of Malaysia and Chile as opposed to Argentina, Brazil or Russia.

13. Even the now-industrialized countries did not, in the nineteenth century, follow the free-trade policies that they have preached to the developing countries. For an excellent elaboration of this point, see Chang, 2003.

14. See Mehrotra and Biggeri, 2002b; and for a more detailed discussion, Mehrotra and Biggeri, 2006 for a discussion of how this might be achieved, without putting an inordinate burden on the government budget.

15. Just as many countries tried to 'import' many policies and programmes that were inappropriate to their context and problems early in their development (what Pritchett and Woolcock (2002) call 'skipping straight to Weber'), now (fifty years later) a similar mistake is being made by those who prescribe these liberalization policies.

16. Ranis and Stewart (2000) have empirically tested the relationship between economic growth and human development (HD) (the latter defined simply as health and education status), by cross-country regressions for 1960–92 using data for 35 to 76 developing countries. They found a significant relationship in both directions, with public expenditures on health and education, notably female, especially important in the chain from growth to HD, and the investment rate and income distribution significant in the HD to growth chain. This gives rise to virtuous or vicious cycles, with good or bad performance on HD and growth reinforcing each other.

17. OECD (2005) notes that the PRSPs are being reviewed by the World Bank, the IMF and the UN Economic Commission for Africa's PRSP Learning Group, following an evaluation by independent evaluators, to improve their usefulness as a basis for donor alignment.

18. Dervis (2005) goes on to make a series of very detailed suggestions about the need for the creation of a UN Economic Security Council, with wider representation than is currently the case with the Executive Boards of the IMF and the World Bank. For similar suggestions, see Nayyar, 2002.

19. Nevertheless, given that capital accumulation has been falling, the impact on growth will be inevitable. In all developing countries, the average annual rate of growth of gross capital formation (which includes both public and private investment) slowed from 2.1 per cent during 1980–90 to 1.7 per cent during 1990–2002. In low-income countries, where investment growth is critical to reaching the MDGs, the growth rate slowed over the same period from 4.7 per cent to 4.2 per cent. In lower middle-income countries,

the rate dropped precipitously from 3.4 per cent to 0.3 per cent (World Bank, 2004). This happened when gross foreign exchange reserves rose, not only in East Asia (which is well known) but also in South Asia, and even in sub-Saharan Africa (in the latter from $21 bn in 1996 to $58 bn in 2004, primarily because of rising ODA) – all of which has an opportunity cost in terms of investment.

20. These are: Argentina, Brazil, Chile, Colombia, Costa Rica, Ecuador, Mexico, Panama, Peru and Uruguay in Latin America; Bulgaria, Poland, Russia and Ukraine among the European transition economies; Egypt, Jordan, Lebanon and Turkey in the Middle East; Nigeria and South Africa in sub-Saharan Africa; and Indonesia, Korea, Malaysia, Pakistan, Philippines, Thailand in Asia, and also China and India.

21. The IMF also determined that the warranted ratio for 14 industrialized countries was as high as 75 per cent, but only because the latter's debt had longer maturities, they had higher fiscal revenue to GDP ratio, less variability of that revenue, lower real interest rates, lower exchange rate risk, and a track record of higher primary surpluses than emerging market economies (Dervis, 2005).

22. The Fund was not a significant player in either the Plaza Agreement or the Louvre Accord, both crucial examples of policy coordination among industrialized countries, Ahluwalia (1999) points out.

23. It was Montek Singh Ahluwalia who headed the IMF's new Internal Evaluation Office in 2000–03 (before he became the Deputy Chairman of India's Planning Commission).

chapter 4

1. Positive externalities occur when the consumption of a good or a service has positive effects on people who do not use them directly. For example, immunization not only protects the individual who gets the vaccine, but also prevents the spreading of the disease, thereby protecting everybody else in society.

2. Before 1880, most social spending was on basic assistance to poor families (or family assistance, then called 'poor relief') and public education. Since then it has included public non-contributory pensions, public health expenditures, housing subsidies, and the last to be introduced, unemployment compensation (Lindert, 2004).

3. Using their notation and giving examples of the elements which could be included in the 'health production function': Y = exogenously determined level of household income; H_1 = Food; P_1 = price of food; H_2 = a medicine; P_2 = price of the medicine. Assume that $H_1^\star$ is the minimum food requirement for two children to survive and $H_2^\star$ is the minimum of the medicine to avoid one death. If $Y < P_1 H_1^\star + P_2 H_2^\star$, then the optimum choice of the 'empowered' consumer is to decide which child to let die!

4. Two final points about the theoretical arguments. They assert that the case of countries where PHC activities have demonstrably contributed to U5MR reduction and other positive health outcomes are non-replicable exceptions. This is not true as there is ample evidence that societies of many different regions, cultures, population sizes, ethnic composition and political ideology have been able to apply these principles while adapting them to their specific circumstances (Mehrotra and Jolly, 1997). In addition, they completely confuse the relationship between the symptoms of an illness and 'willingness to pay' (Mehrotra and Jolly, 1997: 32, 33). They do not say (this might come from a lack of knowledge about the health production function) what a 'serious' condition is: a cough (a cold or pneumonia?), cancer (which might grow for several months without symptoms), diarrhoea (which could be considered normal for some seasons or after eating certain fruits, but which could lead to serious dehydration causing death, especially among children).

5. What is ignored is that in most of their examples the reason public provision is of low quality is precisely because of lack of funds. In other words, one of the main reasons (though not the only one) why PHC centres are understaffed and lack supplies is due to insufficient spending.

6. Following their argument (because public expenditure turned out to be rather insignificant) countries should not attempt (publicly or privately) to provide water, because access to safe water does not seem to be statistically related to health outcomes. Also, we should try to (a) convert Muslims (b) break up multi-ethnic countries because those two variables affect negatively on health. See McCloskey and Ziliak, 1996 for an illuminating discussion of the generalized misunderstanding and misuse of statistical significance tests.

7. However, they do not point this out. They also fail to mention whether or not the reported R squares have been adjusted for the number of independent variables. It gets worse as they consider income inequality, which is not significant even at 10 per cent in any of the six regressions, yet they do not consider public spending as important.

8. There are at least four other benefits of schooling, which extend beyond the conceptual framework outlined in the text. First, it raises the prospect for gainful employment outside the home. Second, it enables people to invoke their legal rights. Third, illiteracy can limit the political voice of people. Fourth, education, especially of women, helps to enhance the autonomy women have in household decision-making.

9. Other problems, including some conceptual confusion, with public–private cooperation are discussed by Mitchell-Weaver and Manning, 1991.

10. The policy lessons from these high achievers can also be found summarized in Mehrotra, 2000 and in Mehrotra, 2004a – both policy papers downloadable from the Internet.

11. The relationship between infant mortality and primary enrolment is, of course, a complex one, influenced by lagged effects and various other factors.

12. The 1995 *Human Development Report* for UNDP also provides a set of measures on social and political elements of women's status.

13. For instance, for the health sector, the World Bank recommended expenditure of US$12 per capita per year for basic health services in low-income countries. This figure, in 1990 dollars, represents an average of the expenditure required in those countries to provide essential clinical and health services (World Bank, 1993b).

14. A detailed analysis of these experiences can be found in Mehrotra and Jolly, 1997.

15. More important than these shares, nevertheless, is to know if the expenditures correspond to inputs which enhance the quality of the services. Estimating aggregate expenditures are, then, only the first step in the analysis of the content of the policies and their adequacy in a given country.

16. It is true that since the late 1980s the World Bank's poverty assessments and public expenditure reviews have paid increasing attention to the composition of expenditure.

17. This is an unweighted average, as it should be, as we are trying to describe the behaviour of a 'typical' country, not of the whole group, which is composed of very heterogeneous countries.

18. Only two of the thirty countries are an exception: Sri Lanka and Peru. In Sri Lanka the relatively low allocation to basic education could be explained by the fact that universal access to primary education was achieved several decades ago and adult illiteracy is almost non-existent. In Peru, the composition of the BSS budget allocations is dominated by nutrition. In both cases, the share of basic education in BSS is about 20 per cent. At the other end of the spectrum, Chile, the Philippines and South Africa allocate over 80 per cent of their BSS budgets to basic education.

19. We also estimated the correlation coefficient over time between BSS per capita expenditure in real terms and the public expenditure to GDP ratio; the coefficient was (positive) reasonably high in half the cases, but the relation did not hold in the remaining half.

20. Also, given the measurement problems, as discussed for instance in Srinivasan, 1994, more sophisticated techniques would not have been warranted.

21. Similarly, Reddy and Miniou (2002) analysed 118 countries, and, after identifying stagnators (measured as level of per capita income), explored the impact of stagnation on human well-being. They found that the impact of higher health expenditures on the rate of improvement in well-being indicators is notable. Thus an increase of health expenditure by 1 per cent of GDP is associated with a 2.5 percentage point increase in the rate of improvement of life expectancy, a 4.6 percentage point reduction in U5MR, and a 2.1 percentage point reduction in IMR over 1960–2000. This suggests that the role of public action in supporting an adequate health infrastructure can be critical in counteracting the results of stagnation.

22. In sub-Saharan Africa the share of public education spending in GDP does reach 5 per cent. However, as Colclough (Colclough and Al-Samarrai, 2000) shows, low enrolments in Africa are a function of several factors. African countries have one of the highest unit costs of primary schooling. Second, on account of high fertility rates over the past four decades, the number of children of school age has continued to increase, compelling that a large share of GNP be allocated to education. When high unit costs are combined with a large school cohort, the expenditure on public schooling is bound to be high. What this requires are policy measures to lower unit costs and control fertility – as we discuss in Chapter 5 – and higher expenditures in many of the African countries. In many high-achieving developing countries, those unit costs have been kept low, and a timely provision of universal schooling and health services has ensured a fertility decline – thus reducing the school-age population by the 1980s (Mehrotra, 1997).

chapter 5

1. Gender differences are usually reported for education data (enrolments and literacy); access to water and sanitation is usually reported for urban and rural areas. Although there are other indicators for which some of these differences are not important (e.g. there seems to be no gender differences in child malnutrition, see UNICEF, 1995b, most social indicators are usually presented without disaggregation. The National Human Development Reports prepared by UNDP and the Multiple Indicator Cluster Surveys prepared by UNICEF are good sources of data with gender and geographic differentiation. They seldom, however, provide information by level of income. Demographic and Health Survey (conducted in many countries by Macro-International) data sets are useful for this purpose, but wealth, rather than income, indices need to be constructed out of some of the indicators reported in these surveys.

2. At least since the beginning of this century, it has been known that poorer families suffer from higher child mortality. The Children's Bureau in the United States, already in 1918, established that Infant Mortality Rate was 170 per 1,000 for poor families, but was a third of this for top income earners (Skocpol, 1992).

3. The data correspond to the metropolitan area of Rio de Janeiro.

4. He shows that this approach can be traced to Petty's pre-Smithian descriptions of seventeenth-century England.

5. Benefit incidence analysis allows us to determine the share of the budget benefiting different groups of people. Standard references for benefit incidence analysis include: Aaron and McGuire, 1970; Meerman, 1979; Selowsky, 1979; van de Walle and Nead, 1995. In undertaking the benefit incidence, we required the country teams to adopt the following steps. First, the monetary value of the unit cost of the service needs to be estimated. Although this information may usually be gathered from officially

reported recurrent public spending on the service being analysed, it usually has to be estimated by dividing the expenditure by the number of users. This implicitly assumes unit costs are the same for all beneficiaries, although, as it is reported below, this is usually not the case. Second, the population has to be divided into different groups. The most common grouping is by income (often by quartiles or quintiles, rarely by deciles, and sometimes just poor versus non-poor); alternatively, gender ethnicity, location (urban or rural) or other characteristics can be used. The third step is to estimate usage of the service by individuals (or households) from each of the different groups. For example, enrolment rates for children living in households from different income levels, or number of individuals from each income group visiting primary health-care centres and hospitals. The fourth step is to multiply the unit cost by the numbers of individuals in each group in order to estimate how much spending accrues to each group. Fifth, express, for each group, the above-estimated number as a percentage of the total spending for the sector or subsector.

6. In the Dominican Republic – one country for which incidence data exist over time – the progressivity in the education sector has increased in the last few years (Escuder et al., 1998). Thus, while the share of public spending for pre-primary schooling appropriated by the richest quintile was constant between 1991 and 1996, that of the lowest quintile increased from 28 to 36 per cent. A similar pattern was observed at the primary level. However, at the secondary and tertiary levels, the middle and top quintiles receive higher shares than the bottom quintile. In both years, the bottom quintile received around 30 per cent of public spending in the education sector. The main differences occur at the university level. In 1992, the bottom 20 per cent of the population received less than 2 per cent of university public spending.

7. In Jamaica, for instance, households in the bottom quintile had, on average, 2.6 children under the age of 15, while households in the top quintile had only 0.6 children on average. In Pakistan, the poorest decile had an average of 3.3 children under the age of 9, compared with a national average of 2 children. In Indonesia, the poor had an average of 1.7 children, compared with a national average of 1.2. In Nepal, the poor had an average of 3.5 children, against an average of 2.5 for the non-poor. In Guyana, poor households had, on average, nearly twice as many children (2.6) than the non-poor (1.4). In Benin, poor households represented 32 per cent of the population but accounted for 38 of the school-age children.

8. Notice also the risk of repeating the arguments of the early Victorian educators, who were interested in education as a means to exert control and authority over the 'lower classes' (see Chapter 2) instead of using education to promote human capital and generating knowledge capabilities.

9. Colclough (1993) stresses that, generally, private schools are not better because they are more efficient. Rather, they are better because they provide a different kind of education, better suited to the needs of the wealthy.

10. Indirect evidence seems to suggest that these inequalities are amplified at higher levels of education.

11. Data derived from the Côte d'Ivoire Living Standards Measurement Surveys.

12. A USAID-sponsored comparative study found a similar disturbing equity problem with health expenditure in Guinea.

13. Investment in safe water supply in rural areas also increased from 11 per cent of the total water investment expenditure in 1992 to 35 per cent in 1996. Nevertheless, these efforts need to be further increased in order to redress the previous biased legacy. The urban bias in the water and sanitation sector can also be observed in Niger where only 20 per cent of the population live in urban areas. Nevertheless, half of the allocation to the water and sanitation sector is invested in urban water supply. As a result, the access to safe water is twice as high as in rural areas.

14. These intra-area estimates are probably less affected by the assumption of equal unit costs than the comparisons between rural and urban expenditures.

15. As in the case of the benefit incidence by income group, where the benefits from public spending on health are less regressive than the primary income distribution, the primary income distribution in South Africa by 'race' is even more unequal than the per capita public health spending (de Bryun et al., 1998).

16. In most of the countries for which we found information, individuals have been grouped according to the total expenditure per capita of the households to which they belong. For most countries the data come from the UNICEF and UNDP country studies. As collecting this information requires a detailed consumption and/or income survey, which was not available in many countries, additional evidence was used from other countries. In particular, in order to be able to include more examples, some results from studies conducted by the World Bank have been included.

17. There is not enough information available on the benefit incidence of public expenditures on nutrition, reproductive health, and water and sanitation to draw any conclusion for these sectors. The likelihood that they would be any different, however, is almost nil.

18. This does not mean that the poorer groups receive no benefits at all. See Van de Walle and Nead, 1995; and Lipton and Ravallion, 1994.

19. Such as Litvack and Bodart, 1993 in Cameroon; Gertler and Molyneaux, et al., 1997 in Indonesia.

chapter 6

1. The countries were: Sri Lanka and Kerala state (India) in South Asia; the Republic of Korea and Malaysia in East Asia; Cuba, Costa Rica and Barbados in Latin America and the Caribbean; and Mauritius, Botswana and Zimbabwe in sub-Saharan Africa (Mehrotra and Jolly, 1997). For Botswana and Zimbabwe, the analysis refers to the period up until the early 1990s, before the HIV/AIDS epidemic ravaged these two societies.

2. In fact, the World Bank (1986) strongly advocated user charges in Malawi at the secondary level, arguing that with user charges education can expand with no loss of equity. Remarkably, in 1994, when Malawi eliminated fees and uniforms enrolments increased dramatically throughout the school system. See UNICEF, 1998a.

3. See also the Addis Ababa Consensus on principles of cost sharing in education and health: prepared by the ECA, UNICEF and the World Bank, 1998.

4. For example, India is heavily dependent upon groundwater sources (the other sources of freshwater being rain and surface water – lakes, tanks, rivers). Groundwater provides 80–90 per cent of domestic water supply in rural areas in India; but domestic water use accounts for only about 5 per cent of the total water extracted from the ground (Nigam et al., 1997).

5. Similarly, the water run-off from irrigated fields, now largely wasted, can be trapped and held in tanks or reservoirs for other uses.

6. Water issues could lead to serious inter-country conflicts. US intelligence experts have identified over a dozen flashpoints where war could result from disputes over control over water where rivers flow through several countries before emptying into the sea. In the past countries have gone to war over land or oil. In the future, another danger would be war over water.

7. The Yellow, Huai, Hai, Fen and Luan rivers, as well as the Bayang marshes, all of which helped to sustain Chinese civilization for 5,000 years, are under threat of extinction.

8. At least in India, very significant investments were made to ensure safe water, especially in rural areas in the 1980s In total, during the five-year planning periods 1951–56 (First Plan) to 1992–97 (Eighth Plan) Rs 336 billion, or 3.3 per cent of the total government

budget, was allocated to water and sanitation, of which 60 per cent (Rs 202 billion) was for rural areas. From 1991 to 1995, total external assistance for water supply and sanitation was US$339 million, or 2 per cent of total external disbursements in India over the period (World Bank/Government of India, 1997).

9. On average, governments contributed about 65 per cent of the total, with external agencies providing the remaining 35 per cent.

10. Primary care refers to the first point of contact between patient and health-care system; secondary refers to a referral level (usually a hospital); and tertiary care refers to a specialist referral hospital. However, balance between them in actual delivery of health services is often not present. A study in Kenya showed that of the outpatients treated at the provincial hospital level, only 20 were referred there. The other 80 per cent were 'self-referred', although up to 80 per cent of them could have reached a health centre in less time than needed to arrive at the provincial hospital (Mehrotra, 2006a). The conclusion of the study was not that people necessarily prefer provincial hospitals over health centres but that the comparison of the cost and effectiveness of the two services came out in favour of the health centres. Not only was the cost per consultation at the provincial hospital much higher than at the health centre, the percentage of correctly identified symptoms was considerably lower than at the health centres. An integrated referral system avoids substantial wastage and increases efficiency under these conditions.

11. Werner and Sanders (1997) argue that UNICEF caved in to US State Department suggestions that the comprehensive PHC approach was 'too political', and criticisms from the Johns Hopkins School of Public Health that comprehensive PHC was too all-encompassing and a more limited selection of priority health problems affecting high-risk groups was needed. Rohde et al. (1993) argue for a more comprehensive approach. Authors (e.g. Hill et al., 1993) in that book, published for UNICEF, suggest that the dichotomy was an unhelpful one. Nevertheless, in practice the selective approach was what WHO/UNICEF focused on through much of the 1980s, though less so in the 1990s.

12. ORT, or oral rehydration therapy, involves giving lots of fluids to children with diarrhoea, to prevent death from dehydration.

13. The most unfortunate example of 'cost recovery' relates to ORT. Second to pneumonia, diarrhoea is the world's biggest killer of children (over 3 million a year). All children who die from diarrhoea are malnourished; well-fed children tend to recover. To minimize death from diarrhoea, the international agencies promoted wide distribution of ORS – factory-produced aluminium envelopes of oral rehydration salts to be mixed with a litre of clean water. These packets were relatively costly and created a dependency. However, it was considered safer than teaching mothers to prepare simple and cheap home-made drinks. At first the ORS packets were distributed free. But when cost recovery began, health ministries were forced to charge families. While 10 US cents a packet is not much, for a poor family living below the poverty line (even the Bank's $1-a-day poverty line), 10 cents may cut into the food budget. Today ORS has been commercialized and become big business (Werner and Sanders, 1997).

14. For evidence for this phenomenon for Vietnam, see Segall et al., 2000.

15. It is not suggested here that problems have not arisen with the implementation of the Bamako Initiative. In many countries the BI is another name for revolving drug funds. There is also evidence on the lack of local voice in the implementation of the BI, and its exclusionary effects on the poor.

16. This problem intensified in South Africa in recent years on account of the sharp rise in teachers' salaries after the end of apartheid – with a view to removing the discrimination in teacher salaries which had existed (de Bruyn et al., 1998).

17. At the secondary level in developing countries the share of teacher costs is about 80 per cent; at the higher level it is about 60 per cent (Mehrotra and Buckland, 1998).

18. Carnoy and Welmond (1996) estimate the deviations of the above ratio (average teachers' salaries relative to GNP per capita) from a GNP per capita trend line. This deviation offers a more accurate measure of the relative value countries put on their teachers at different stages of development. Unlike the previous index, some African countries (e.g. Tanzania, Malawi, Madagascar, Kenya and Guinea) that appeared to pay rather well, relative to their GNP per capita, pay poorly when their salaries are adjusted for the GNP trend line. However, a very large number of African countries (Rwanda, Mali, Ethiopia, Burkina Faso, Niger, Mauritania, Zimbabwe, Côte d'Ivoire, Burundi, Benin and Togo) still pay comparatively well, even when adjustment is made for the trend line.

19. Based on a personal communication with Julia de Bruyn.

20. In many African countries in the early years of secondary level and beyond, the phenomenon of teachers who become 'sugar daddies' is seen as a disincentive to send post-puberty girls to school.

21. The urban situation was less serious with about 26 per cent requiring repair or rehabilitation (World Bank/Government of India, 1997).

22. Nigam et al. (1997) suggested that this process in India was at a very early stage in most states. As the state governments control the grants to the panchayats, they still have control of their day-to-day functioning.

23. For further analysis of generic drugs lists, see World Bank, 1994a; and Kanji et al., 1992.

24. Data from UNDP HDR, 2002.

25. Physicians themselves could be excessively trained in specialized care, as Sahn and Bernier (1995) find to be the case in many countries.

26. Griffin (1992) presents further evidence along these lines for Asia.

27. Sometimes actors, for a range of motives, may be right to criticize and stop ill-conceived reforms which may result in lower, costlier or more unequal service provision.

28. WHO (2000) notes that there have been problems with these arrangements: the staff concerned are usually junior, placements are short-term and unpopular, mentoring arrangements are inadequate, and overall geographical imbalance is little affected. However, to us these do not appear to be problems so serious as to offset the huge advantages accruing to the population. If the geographical imbalance remains unaffected by the policy, there are probably design problems with the schemes in place.

29. In Kerala state, if a doctor does not show up in a facility, the users are organized enough to make that known to the authorities (Krishnan, 1997). However, in other states of India, absenteeism by doctors at health facilities and by teachers in schools is a perennial problem.

30. Once a decision is made to start a programme in a district, the health administration forms a society, which hires staff for a TB unit, covering 500,000 people. The state government trains the doctors in DOTS and hires the lab technicians. Policy direction, drugs and microscopes are provided by the central government, with financial assistance from the World Bank and bilateral donors.

31. The country studies corroborate this thesis. In Kenya, for example, reproductive health services have declined dramatically since 1980. As a share of government spending, they were reduced by more than half from 0.5 per cent in 1980 to 0.2 in 1996. In real per capita terms, they have also fluctuated. The unreliability of funds had negative impact – though it is difficult to say how much was due to funding uncertainties.

32. There is, moreover, a macro-inertia that prevents birth rates in developing countries from following death rates downward; their populations are quite young, on average, and this characteristic will keep overall birth rates high even if fertility rates are reduced in different age groups.

33. For example, Drèze (2001) states that there was no greater scam in India at the beginning of the decade than the so-called food subsidy. The farm price support is 'nothing short of mass murder'. The government in 2001–01 spent over $2 billion on the food subsidy. Rich

farmers are the beneficiaries of support prices, which keep food prices up while more than half of Indian children are chronically malnourished. The support prices doubled over the 1990s. The rich farmers also benefit from huge subsidies in free electricity and irrigation water, and the three subsidies together leach away an estimated 14 per cent of GDP. While state granaries are bursting with rotting stocks, under-nutrition takes an acute form in drought-affected areas and is chronic in most of the country.

34. Thus, for example, the northern states of India have rates of severe malnutrition which are the same as the rates of moderate malnutrition on average in sub-Saharan Africa. However, southern states in India, especially Kerala, have much lower malnutrition rates than in the rest of the country. One of the determinants is the per capita availability of foodgrains through the public distribution system and the percentage of rural population receiving subsidized cereals through the public distribution system – which are much higher in the latter (Drèze and Sen, 1998).

35. Child malnutrition (underweight) is defined as body weight lower by >2 standard deviations as compared to the reference population. Stunting is defined as height-for-age lower by >2 standard deviations as compared to the reference population. Wasting is defined as weight-for-height lower by >2 standard deviations as compared to the reference population. Malnutrition data, where they are collected, is far more reliable than hunger data; the latter is usually derived by FAO from a combination of production, export and import data in respect of food items.

36. Given the recent history of the science of LBW reduction programmes, little has been implemented which translates existing information into effective programmes to improve maternal nutrition and prevent LBW. The first meeting of the UN ACC/SCN Working Group on the Prevention of Foetal and Infant Malnutrition (April 1999) identified the need to document best practices for LBW treatment. That has since been done.

37. Also, it is well known that breastfeeding benefits the mother (Dermer, 2001), highlighting yet another element where there are synergies among the various interventions.

38. Vitamin A deficiency leads to blindness, iodine deficiency leads to goitre and cretinism, and iron deficiency leads to anaemia and maternal mortality (UNICEF, 1998b).

39. Three of the most important practical restrictions in establishing food fortification programmes are that the chosen food be consumed by the target (or whole) population, be available in most meals independently of socioeconomic status and bioavailability. Consequently, it is not easy to find the appropriate food to be fortified. In the case of iodine, the most widely used and successful has historically been salt, which has been used for over seventy years. For iron, cereals, cereal flours, sugar and salt have been tried (Seshadri, 1997); and for Vitamin A, fats and oils, sugar and cereals.

40. As fortified food might not reach the whole population, or because of the special needs of some groups or regions, supplements need to be introduced. These can be provided with tablets, capsules or injections. Consequently, they are relatively costlier per recipient. Nevertheless, the yearly cost per person is usually less than 0.05 per cent of per capita income. Supplements are particularly important for children and pregnant women.

41. There are two main reasons for this. First, under most circumstances substituting one element in a diet for another has little financial implication. Second, eating the food in which the micronutrient is naturally present is the easiest way to address the issue of bioavailability – that in order for the body to acquire the micronutrients, they have to be ingested with other elements which allow its absorption. Nevertheless, sometimes, because of the cost, availability or cultural patterns, this approach is not possible. Moreover, it takes time. Then food fortification is required.

42. Regarding Africa, our studies found several problems with the nutrition-related programmes. For example, the problem was not only the low level of funding but also the duplication of programmes. Expenditure on nutrition programmes in Kenya, which are run by several agencies, most notably the health and education ministries, is insignificant

and fluctuates wildly without a particular pattern (Nganda and Ong'ala, 1998). In Benin, the most important problem was found to be the irregular level of funding and the concomitant difficulties in planning (Tabélé-Omichessan et al., 1998).

In South Africa, several inefficiencies were found in the nutrition programme. First, parasite control, micronutrient supplementation, and nutrition education had not been included in the programme – some of the least expensive and most effective nutrition interventions. Second, it has been found that the quality of the food distributed through the programme was of substandard quality. Third, pre-school children, where malnutrition impacts the most, were not properly targeted (de Bruyn et al., 1998).

43. It is only recently that the 0–3 age group – the relevant age group to prevent the worsening of nutritional problems associated with life-cycle causes – is beginning to be addressed through the programme, a quarter-century after it began in 1975.

chapter 7

1. There is a considerable literature related to state failure, under the rubric of 'new political economy', also referred to as the literature on rational choice and rent-seeking. See Bates, 1988; for a critique see Grindle and Thomas, 1991; Fishlow, 1991; and Streeten, 1993.

2. Dutt wondered about the inability of the British colonial government to devolve power to local communities: 'It is somewhat remarkable that no British administrator of this period seriously endeavoured to improve the police and general administration of the country by accepting the cooperation of the people themselves and their Village Communities' (Dutt, 1903: 196). He went on:

> India had been the earliest home of Village Communities, and for centuries and thousands of years these self-governing Communities had maintained order and peace, and settled disputes in villages, even when there was anarchy in the realm.... And in Northern India, Sir Charles Metcalfe had stated in 1830 that ... 'they seem to last where nothing else lasts. Dynasty after dynasty tumbles down, revolution succeeds to revolution, Hindu, Pathan, Moghal, Mahratta, Sikh, English, are masters in turn, but the Village Communities remain the same.'... It is a lamentable fact that these ancient and self-governing institutions have declined, and virtually disappeared, under the too centralized administration of British rule.... No system of successful self-government has been introduced after the old forms were effaced; no representatives of the village population help the administration of the present day; and an alien Government lacks that popular basis, that touch with the people, which Hindu and Mahommedan Governments wisely maintained through centuries. (Dutt, 1903: 196–7)

3. This story largely applies to much of South Asia as well as to sub-Saharan Africa, naturally with certain variations on this broad theme. On South Asia, see Bardhan, 1984; Wade, 1985, 1989. The story is more complicated in much of East Asia (see Khan, 2001), and in Latin America (for an example, see Ames, 1977).

4. The degree of choice is discussed further in different contexts in the following chapter.

5. Sometimes these were coupled with internal political actors with their own agendas. For instance, during the military dictatorship in Chile, decentralization of education was one of the tools used to subdue opposition to the regime, reduce wages, and worsen working conditions (Parry, 1997).

6. See Bardhan and Mookerjee, 1999, 2000, for a theoretical framework for appraising the trade-offs involved in delegating authority to a central bureaucracy as opposed to an elected local government, for delivery of public services from the viewpoint of targeting and cost-effectiveness of public spending programmes in developing countries.

7. Thus, policymaking at the national level may represent greater compromise among the policy platforms of different parties.

8. Ceara is about the size of Portugal, Belgium and the Netherlands combined.

9. In this case, the 'central' government is being used in the sense not of the federal government, but of the state (i.e. provincial) government, which in this case would share the characteristics of the central government.

10. The president of Brazil, Lula da Silva, leads the Workers' Party that was responsible in the 1990s for introducing this form of deep democratic decentralization.

11. In contrast, Bihar (which has had the worst educational and social indicators in the country, comparable to those in much of sub-Saharan Africa) was the only state which did not have PRI elections until 2001.

12. Bihar, Uttar Pradesh, West Bengal and Andhra Pradesh are the other four. These states (plus Assam and Tamil Nadu) are the subject of two books on the financing of elementary education: Mehrotra et al., 2005; Mehrotra, 2006a.

13. For instance, as Rao and Singh (2005) note, barely 4 per cent of total government expenditure by central, state and local governments is undertaken in India by local governments.

14. The District Primary Education Programme (DPEP) has been run on a decentralized and participatory basis by state-level bodies, but with many of the top-down elements being retained (see Bashir and Ayyar, 2001). Madhya Pradesh also had the largest number of districts covered by DPEP of all Indian states, and hence received a considerable proportion of total DPEP funds disbursed by the central government.

15. One outcome of the survey was the development of a Village Education Register as a basic record of educational statistics of each village, to be maintained in two copies at the village panchayat and the school. The survey was also used as a basis of cohort monitoring for completion of primary schooling.

16. One of the main reasons for the success of the EGS is its cost-effectiveness. In regular (non-EGS) schools, teacher salaries account for over 90 per cent of costs at the primary level. Schoolteachers in regular schools are strongly unionized and an important political force, and receive salaries that are high relative to per capita income (Kingdon, 1994). However, EGS schoolteachers are paid only a third or less of what regular schoolteachers are paid.

17. Now the only two states that continue to live up to their BIMARU status in respect of schooling are Uttar Pradesh (with a population the size of Russia or Brazil) and Bihar. The English acronym BIMARU comes from the names of the four states with the worst human development indicators: Bihar, Rajasthan, Madhya Pradesh and Uttar Pradesh. As it happens, the word *bimaru* in Hindi means sick.

18. As a local NGO in Rajasthan, the MKSS, has done (Roy, 1999).

19. Some similar arguments emerge if the co-operative movement is examined. In India, co-operatives have become parastatals. They have had an overdose of state patronage and nearly absolute control by the Registrar. A co-operative is supposed to have voluntary membership; all its members should be its user–owners; a co-operative should be democratically managed by those who derive their authority from members and are fully accountable to their members. But in fact none of these conditions is met in reality (Saxena, 1997).

chapter 8

1. Also Switzerland and the Netherlands.

2. The estimates of spending in Germany, France and the USA suggest that the share of income spent on private education did not change, despite the sharp rise in the share

spent on public education (Lindert, 2001). This is an interesting finding, in the light of the possible argument that the private sector may well be a source of the crowding out of the public-sector schools in many parts of India (see Tilak and Sudarshan, 2000).

3. In each region there are some exceptions to this broad pattern. For instance, Zimbabwe is one. However, this country became independent only in 1980 after a long liberation struggle; in 1979 nearly all schools were in the private sector, since the white racist regime had not made investments for schooling for black children, and hardly any public schools existed. After independence, Zimbabwe rapidly expanded its public school system and universalized primary education in a few years, thus ensuring a very high literacy rate (Loewenson and Chisvo, 1997). Mauritius is another such exception; its relatively high share of private schools in the 1960s and 1970s is explained by the large number of ethnic minorities in the country, which were permitted to run their own schools. However, the public school system soon expanded, and Mauritius is seen as a high achiever in the region (Dommen and Dommen, 1997).

4. On Sri Lanka, see Alailama and Sanderatne, 1997; on Korea, see Mehrotra et al., 1997; on Indonesia, see Stalker, 2000, and Betke, 2001; on Thailand, see UNICEF, 2001.

5. On Costa Rica, see Garnier et al., 1997.

6. Lesotho and Swaziland had high private shares in enrolment in the 1960s and 1970s and also achieved high literacy rates, but these are rather special cases, bounded completely by apartheid South Africa, which subsidized a client regime there. Besides, these are small, resource-rich countries with miniscule populations and a large church-supported missionary school system.

7. For a detailed examination of the adequacy, efficiency and equity of the public spending pattern in relation to education for the high-achiever countries, see Mehrotra, 1998b.

8. See the World Bank's *World Development Reports*, 1997 (on the role of the state), and 2000/01 (on attacking poverty).

9. While the international financial institutions (IFIs) engage in a considerable body of research, very little is ever done by way of historical analysis. In fact, it is remarkable that a certain brand of theory (neoclassical increasingly being superseded by new institutional economics) informs the research most of the time, while for the rest there is a contemporaneous, short-term and empiricist bias to the research produced by IFIs. Often the research is characterized by pooling cross-country data and running regressions on them, and then usually drawing some market-friendly policy implication. On this methodological bias and the tendency to ignore rigorous research into economic or social history with contemporary implications, see Mehrotra, 2002.

10. Given the requirement for government schools to be located within 1 kilometre of every habitation, such schools have resulted in a large number of very small schools, a shortage of teachers, and multi-grade teaching. Most government schools offer only classes 1 to 5. However, aided and unaided schools tend to serve larger populations, and hence offer classes 1 to 12 (Bashir, 1997).

11. Bedi and Garg (2000) compared, for example, earnings differentials in Indonesia between public and private secondary school graduates after correcting for selection bias. They found that (contrary to conventional wisdom in Indonesia) selection-corrected earnings differentials revealed that private non-religious schools were more effective. The observed earnings advantage enjoyed by private school graduates was explained by their characteristics and the selective nature of their student intake.

12. As Bashir rightly points out, a major weakness of single-level models (OLS) is that the within-school variation (within the government and private schools) is entirely ignored, and the effect of pupil-level variables on individual outcomes cannot be ascertained. Models using schools means alone cannot take account of situations where a pupil's outcome is influenced both by her socioeconomic status and by the average socioeconomic status of those children in the school. In the multi-level model (a slight

misnomer since most used are two-level models), the pupil-level model consists of the regression of the pupil's test score on pupil characteristics. The school-level (second level) model then enables the regression to separate out the within-school factors from the between-school factors influencing achievement.

13. There is overwhelming statistical evidence that enrolment rises with income – that is, the higher the level of family income, the higher the share of children enrolled in school, and the higher the number of years of education completed before they drop out. For evidence in India, see Srivastava, 2005.

14. To be eligible for aid, a private unaided school must be recognized; and to be eligible for recognition, a private unaided school must be a registered society, have an owned rather than a rented building, employ only trained teachers, pay salaries according to government prescribed norms, have classrooms of a specified minimum size and charge only government-set fee rates. It must also instruct in the official language of the state and deposit a sum of money in the endowment and reserve funds of the government's education department.

15. While Kingdon and Muzammil (2001) analyse the situation in Uttar Pradesh, the process is not dissimilar in other states.

16. Tooley's (1999) analysis (for the International Finance Corporation, and widely publicized by them) about the equity effects of the expansion of the private sector (including in India) is rather simplistic. He believes that the expansion of the private sector can improve equity; but the argument is made without any clear reference to whether one is talking about the elementary system, the secondary level, or tertiary education.

17. Although studies of satisfaction levels with public-sector health services are limited, Iriart et al. (2001) report ten citations concerning satisfaction in Latin America. Five studies about users' satisfaction with public-sector primary-care clinics showed high levels of satisfaction; another study about a public-sector home-care programme also showed satisfaction was high; three articles provided data that show high levels of satisfaction with public hospitals; of two studies on satisfaction with nursing services, one found high satisfaction and the other low satisfaction on several indicators.

18. See references cited in Robinson and White, 2001.

19. Data drawn from Franceys, 2001.

20. Many of these (2,350 of them) have operating PPPs, according to Franceys, 2001.

21. For a detailed analysis of the various types of private participation in the provision of water services, see Lee and Jouravlev, 1998.

22. PPPs have led to impressive profits in the UK for companies (12 per cent return on capital when borrowing at perhaps 7 per cent with 20–40 per cent gearing), a level much higher than in France and the Netherlands. To limit the possibility of abuse of the monopoly position in meeting a basic need, England and Wales introduced three regulators.

23. In high-income countries, BOT, concession contracts, divestiture (i.e. purchase at a discount) and partial divestiture, and outright purchase account for nearly 70 per cent of all PPP contracts (Franceys, 2001).

24. Now owned by French Suez.

25. Now called Veolia Environnement.

26. Mainly Thames Water, which handles London's water and sewerage, was privatized in 1989 by Mrs Thatcher's government.

27. This account draws upon Finnegan, 2002.

28. Finnegan (2002) notes that the Mayor of Cochabamba insisted with the central government that Misicuni be included, otherwise the leasing of the water system to foreign bidders would be stopped, as it had been in 1997.

29. The US government has not decided whether to formally call the breaking of the contract in Cochabamba an expropriation, which would affect future foreign investment in Bolivia.

30. The Bolivian government had awarded another concession for water and sewerage services in La Paz in 1997. In its first years of operation the concessionaire, the French transnational Suez Lyonnaise des Eaux, met its first expansion mandate and took many steps to expand in-house water connections in low-income areas (Komives, 1998). The area, known as El Alto, is home to nearly three-quarters of a million people, virtually all of them Indians arrived from the countryside. Accustomed to extremely careful use of water, without wasting a drop, they continued to limit use of water even after taps were installed in their home. Suez, disappointed by its return on investment, raised its rates. The rates were pegged to the dollar, and when the local currency was devalued residents' concerns about the service rose sharply. Finnegan (2002) reports that when a World Bank official was asked, she said that there was a basic problem: 'Those Indians needed to learn to use more water.' Since writing these paragraphs, the situation in Bolivia has deteriorated partly due to what we describe in the text and partly due to similar attitudes by the government in other areas, related both to privatized services and other issues. Eventually the government collapsed in the face of mounting strikes and civil unrest throughout the country.

31. Bond (1998) notes that the South African government policies were strongly encouraged by the World Bank, and were of course consistent with the IFC's investment objectives.

32. For evidence, see a series of reports, examining the pros and cons of various privatizations from around the world in the water sector, at www.icij.org.

33. *The Economist*, 28 August–3 September 2004.

34. *The Economist* reports: 'The water barons' trouble has sprung not just, or even mainly, from the poor countries' consumers, officials or currency risks, but from their own fast growth, and resultant debt, in rich ones. And that, indeed, is where the biggest recent retreats have been' (28 August–3 September 2004: 58).

35. A number of PRSP already announce government plans for promoting private-sector involvement in public service provision in Honduras, Mozambique, Nicaragua and Uganda. The PRSP in Burkina Faso is committed to eliminating monopolies in public utilities, and Nicaragua and Kenya have agreed to increase private-sector involvement in water delivery (Marcus and Wilkinson, 2002).

36. The investment climate will be given attention when there is a possibility of a country receiving finance from the International Development Agency (IDA), the soft-loan window of the Bank.

37. For example, in Malawi, IFC has an 18 per cent share in a 64-bed hospital, Blantyre, which has been a failure in both financial and health-care terms. Thus, as Save the Children (2002) states: 'the private hospital has been unable to achieve even a 20 per cent utilisation rate'.

38. On the basis of a study of sixteen countries in Asia, for instance, Uphoff (1993) concludes that 'countries which had the best linkage between central government and rural communities through a network of local institutions had the best performance in agriculture and in social indicators.'

39. In other words, state providers that behave like for-profit companies will cause the same problems that arise from the market approach.

chapter 9

1. For an explanation of these estimates, see Annex 9.1.

2. This shortfall is consistent with the various estimates that were prepared by different agencies and researchers in the light of the MDGs and the Monterrey Conference (see e.g. the Zedillo Report, World Bank, WHO and UNICEF). These estimates often are

higher than ours because the MDGs include income-poverty reduction, which ought not to be included in the cost estimates of basic social services.

3. We would exclude two other possibilities of raising the public expenditure to GDP ratio: (a) public borrowing, and (b) deficit financing (through printing money) for well-known reasons, discussed elsewhere (see e.g. Burgess, 1997).

4. For industrialized countries, Lindert has argued that after 1880 social spending got an earlier start not only in countries with more universal suffrage, with votes for women, but also with higher income.

5. Lindert (1994) demonstrates this using a simultaneous equation model, using pooled data from twenty-one countries over six pre-war benchmark dates – with enough separate influences on the two kinds of endogeneous variables to allow their sources to be identified statistically.

6. The deadweight costs of social programmes are close to zero – unlike what a lot of the Anglo-American neoliberal literature has argued. Thus, there is little evidence that a large welfare-state establishment drags down growth (Lindert, 2000). The period with fastest-growing welfare states in industrialized countries (post-war to 1980) was historically the best era for economic growth.

7. However, full cost recovery for higher education cannot be implemented without some exemptions for poor students and student loans at positive real rates of interest.

8. A significant proportion of the graduates of these publicly subsidized institutions – demand for whom is high in most industrialized countries and increasingly in other emerging economies – migrate abroad in significant numbers. For instance, as many as a third of firms in Silicon Valley, California, are firms started by Indian graduates of these institutes – all trained at public expense. By contrast 4 billion of India's population are illiterate, partly on account of the underfunding of elementary education.

9. For an example, see Tilak, 2002, who bemoans the fact that cost recovery is increasing in Indian higher education. He suggests that cost recovery through student fees in India is not significantly different from corresponding rates in other developing and developed countries. 'Even in many advanced countries higher education was supported by the state to the extent of 55–93 per cent of total expenditures in the late 1980s.'

10. Estimated from data drawn from World Bank, *World Development Indicators 2001*, which in fact do not have data for high-HDI countries like France, Germany, Luxembourg and many other OECD countries that have a high public expenditure ratio.

11. For the health sector, we made a similar argument in Chapter 5 in relation to the WHO–UNICEF initiative called the Bamako Initiative. However, recall that that argument was made in the context of community pooling of resources to meet a variety of costs, and involved, among other things, improvements in quality of service and local retention of funds. User charges in health, when they flow to the treasury, barely account for a miniscule proportion of total funds available to the health ministry; thus, without contributing much to resource mobilization, they end up denying services to the poor.

12. India with a billion people has a standing army of 1.3 million; Pakistan (with 135 million) has nearly 600,000 armed forces personnel. After the Kargil war in the summer of 1999, triggered by Pakistani infiltration across the line of control in Kashmir, India increased its defence expenditure sharply; Pakistan followed suit.

13. In fact, in a group of Highly Indebted Poor Countries (HIPC), the share of military spending in GDP fell by the same amount (0.6 per cent) as the increase in the share of education and health spending (IMF, 1999).

14. There is a possibility that haphazard reduction of military expenditure has contributed to a increase in internal violence, as underpaid or demobilized soldiers turned to looting, crime and other violence.

15. A paper prepared by the staff of the IMF and the World Bank (IMF, 1999) presents numbers similar to ours for debt service and social spending (though, of course,

emphasizing that net external resource inflows are many times larger than the total of education and health spending). They note that for the seven countries which had reached their Decision Point under HIPC in 1999 expenditure on health and education combined (not BSS) averaged about 6 per cent of GDP, while debt service paid (not just due) was 7 per cent (over 1993–97). Aggregate data reveal a similar picture for the broader group of twenty-eight HIPCs for which data was available.

16. In contrast to the original framework, where debt reduction was calculated on projections of debt stock at the completion point (i.e. completion of full ESAF programmes – six years), relief under the new framework will be committed based on actual data at the decision point – that is, earlier. Now the completion point can be moved up if the country's performance on macroeconomic, structural and social policies is good.

17. Private – both domestic and foreign – investment will 'crowd in' if this investment in physical and social infrastructure were to occur, not crowd out (as some neoliberals have argued). The need for investment in the power sector and infrastructure in India is vast – $30–40 billion a year for the next decade, as estimated by the National Council of Applied Economic Research.

18. *India Today*, 7 August 2006, quoting Ministry of Finance, Government of India, data.

19. Earlier reforms had attempted, in the 1970s, zero-based budgeting, but without much success; those efforts were abandoned.

20. Most countries operated a dual budget system, constituted by a recurrent budget, and a capital or development budget. Development budgets were largely about public capital investments such as power supplies, roads and bridges, schools and universities, and hospitals and clinics. Even then they contained activities that were recurrent and capital projects. Donors financed this expansion. (For example, the Indian budgets are divided into plan and non-plan expenditures: plan expenditures are for new projects included in each five-year plan; in the following plan period, any expenditure on the preceding Plan's projects would be called Non-Plan expenditure. Thus Plan was mostly capital expenditure, but also included recurrent expenditure; Non-Plan expenditure can be both capital and recurrent expenditure.)

21. Similarly, Tendler and Freedheim (1994), based on their study of a public health programme in Brazil, conclude that members of a state institution can be motivated by public service, that notions of self-interest and 'public calling' can be combined, and these motives can be created and reinforced by a combination of *measures and pressures from above and below.*

22. Based on data for 21 low-income, 26 low-middle income, and 20 upper-middle-income countries.

23. But its total revenue (including non-tax revenue) was 18.5 per cent (Planning Commission, 2002a).

24. Thus non-tax revenues were 1.9 per cent of GDP over 1980–85, 2.6 per cent over 1986–90, 2.8 per cent over 1990–93, and 0.8 per cent over 1994–96 (Agbeyegbe et al., 2004). In non-CFA countries, they have not risen; they were 1.6, 1.6, 1.7 and 1.8 per cent of GDP over the same periods.

25. Country data for tax revenue to GDP from World Bank, *World Development Indicators 2004.*

26. The regional average is for 16 Latin American and Caribbean countries. See IMF, 2004: 5, Table 3, for regional averages and LIC, LMC and UMC averages.

27. Agbeyegbe et al. (2004) in a IMF working paper, however, support the notion that trade liberalization accompanied by appropriate macroeconomic policies can be undertaken in a way that preserves overall revenue yield.

28. Also, see Carciofi and Cetrangolo (1994), where evidence is cited that at the end of the 1980s, Latin American countries still had tax-to-GDP ratios which were well below what might have been anticipated from their level of per capita income.

29. For the least developed countries, it should be possible for donors to alter their disbursement profiles over time so as to accommodate shocks and create bigger and better compensatory financing mechanisms. For further discussion, see Chapter 10.

30. IMF, 2004 notes that for LICs, their 14 per cent tax revenue to GDP is accounted for by foreign trade taxes (4.2 per cent), excises (1.8), general sales tax (3.1), and social security (1.8). For LMICs, their 18.5 per cent tax revenue/GDP ratio is accounted for by a lower share for foreign trade (3.4 per cent), and a higher share of excises (2.3), general sales tax (4.9), and social security (3.7). For UMICs, their 23 per cent tax/GDP ratio has even lower shares for foreign trade taxes (3.1 per cent), and even higher shares for excise (2.5), general sales tax (5.9) and social security (6.4) (IMF, 2004).

31. For low-income countries this share averaged about 17.5 per cent of GDP (excluding China and India) in 1997.

32. Burgess and Stern (1993) find that in some countries tax reform has led to significant improvements in the contribution of direct taxes to overall revenue.

33. See Ramsey, 1927; Mirlees, 1976; and Diamond and Mirlees, 1971.

34. Thus in 1989–90 personal income tax generated less income than the entire amount spent on the fertilizer subsidy that year (Dasgupta and Mookerjee, 2000).

35. Peru managed to increase tax revenues as a whole from 5.4 per cent of GDP in 1990 to 9 per cent of GDP in 1991. Mookerjee (1997) notes that it is difficult to say whether these changes were caused entirely by the tax reform, since other administrative reforms were implemented at the same time.

36. In developing countries, outside of agriculture, a large proportion of those not in formal, organized manufacturing activities are in the so-called informal sector. However, the tax administration in many countries is either unable to cope with this sector of largely untaxed incomes, or is unwilling, having been co-opted in a web of corruption. Dasgupta and Mookerjee (1997, 1998) spell out other reforms on the basis of the international experience. They mention the need for motivating high-level officials to evaluate the performance of their subordinates. This is encouraged by autonomy over budgets, personnel and control, which were increased in tax administration reforms in Argentina, Colombia, Ghana, Jamaica and Peru. In some cases budgets were linked to revenues collected. Some countries liberalized the rules for contracting out operations to the private sector.

37. Some suggestions have been made to deal with these problems, based on the following principles. First, withholding taxes on interest, dividends, royalties and management fees, if these payments are to cross borders, would be collected universally, at a set of uniform rates which are agreed internationally. Second, there should be a single international code system for identifying payers of individual payers of individual and corporate income tax, so that tax authorities can share information about taxpayers without revealing it to others. Third, a tax return to any tax authority of the income of a corporation or other enterprise would be required to give information relating to the total world income of the firm (Clunies-Ross, 1999).

38. Tax havens provide the possibility of avoidance by forming holding companies and shifting ostensible residence (Tanzi, 1995).

39. By the late 1990s VAT had been introduced in over thirty developing countries in Asia, Africa, Latin America and Eastern Europe.

40. Annuality means the budget is prepared every year, covering only one year; voted and executed every year – even though most OECD and some developing countries now develop the annual budget within a multi-year perspective, through the preparation of medium-term revenue and expenditure framework.

41. Unity means that revenue and expenditure (and borrowing constraints) are considered together to determine annual budget targets.

42. Curiously, the IMF does not seem to indicate how 'too many' might be defined. We

found little in the literature which might suggest that a certain percentage of public
expenditure would be deemed too high for allocation to extra-budgetary funds.

43. Named after a publication by Adolf Wagner in 1876.

44. Thus, they argue that many so-called redistributive policies in industrial countries do
not benefit those in real need but, rather, benefit politically important groups or tax and
subsidize the same families at the same time (tax churning). If all churning were eliminated,
public spending would not have to be more than about 30 per cent of GDP.

45. For an example of diversion in Uganda, see Reinikka and Svensson, 2002.

chapter 10

1. Significantly, the reproductive health goal, agreed at the International Conference on Population and Development in 1994, was dropped on the insistence of the US delegation.

2. For instance, one could argue that aid may be more effective in financing large capital
(and foreign exchange)-intensive projects at the tertiary level (e.g. universities, hospitals),
where initial costs and technical requirements are higher and professional lessons similar
(Burgess, 1997).

3. The goals were stated in OECD, 1996a.

4. The 20/20 Initiative found a place in the Programme of Action of the World Summit
for Social Development (Copenhagen, March 1995).

5. These five were called the G0.7 by the ministers of development cooperation of the
five countries (*Financial Times*, 19 November 2001).

6. See IEO, 2003a.

7. OECD, 2005 also notes that non-DAC/OECD donor's aid is also growing.

8. OECD DAC's Creditor Reporting System includes the following categories under
water and sanitation: water resources; rural and urban water and sanitation (including
drinking water); water resources protection; and emergency distress relief. In other
words, the share of basic services in total ODA is an overestimate.

9. Similarly, in absolute terms, 'although there was some improvement in 2001, as compared
with the previous year, taking the two years together, bilateral aid to education fell by
16 per cent between 1998–99 and 2000–01' (UNESCO, 2003).

10. This includes aid to water resources policy, planning and programmes, water legislation
and management, water resources development, water resources protection, water supply
and use, sanitation (including solid waste management), and education and training in
water supply and sanitation. Dams and reservoirs primarily for irrigation and hydropower
and activities related to water transport are excluded.

11. Pronk (2001) agrees: 'on balance and in the long run, catalytic crowding-in effects [of
aid] will outweigh fungibility or crowding-out effects.'

12. The IDA loans are meant for low-income countries. However, the main window for
loans to middle-income countries is the International Bank for Reconstruction and
Development, which lends at higher than IDA rates.

13. It averaged $93 million annually over 1990–92, $300 million over 1993–95, $311 over
1996–98, and $246 million over 1999–2001, according to OECD DAC's online data-
base.

14. As the World Bank (1998) noted: 'In countries with basically sound policies but weak
capacity for delivering services, project aid should be a catalyst for improving the efficacy
of public expenditures. Countries without good policies, efficient public services, or
properly allocated expenditures will benefit little from financing, and aid should focus
on improvements in all three areas.'

15. The World Bank (1993a) reported a rapid increase in health-sector ODA during the
1970s. However, that was not sustained and during the 1980s the amount of aid to

health and population stagnated. Its share in total ODA declined from 7 to 6 per cent between 1981–85 and 1986–90 on an average annual basis.

16. Debate at this time centred on whether an integrated or a selective approach to primary health care was the way forward. See Rohde et al., 1993 for a discussion.

17. To enable treatment of Aids patients in sub-Saharan Africa, a study by the Harvard Centre for International Development (under Jeffrey Sachs) has called on industrialized countries in 2001 to increase dramatically their current expenditures for international Aids programmes and to pool their aid into a global trust fund jointly administered by UNAIDS and the WHO. The study proposes that $1,100 per patient could cover prevention programmes and anti-retroviral treatments, with the drug companies providing the latter – which cost $10,000 per patient in the USA – at cost. The cost of the programme would be $7 billion annually in five years, and the study proposes that the USA meets one-third of it. Given that all health ODA from all bilaterals was $2–4 billion in 1998, the realism of the proposal is open to question.

18. International NGOs account for 5 per cent of all health ODA (WHO, 1999). Public–private partnerships have generated, in some cases, significant resources. The $100 million given by the Bill and Melinda Gates Foundation to a Children's Vaccine Initiative is similar to the annual budget of WHO's Global Programme on Vaccines. Such donations (e.g. Rotarians for Polio Eradication) tend to be focused on highly visible actions with quick results.

19. Projects, whether in health, education, water or any other sector, are not normally administered or implemented by aid agencies, nor by recipient governments, but by universities or other specialized institutions or companies in the North that enter into international competitive bidding, having been shortlisted by the funding agency.

20. OECD (1999) notes that in bilateral agencies there is widespread lack of economists with a background in micro-level analysis to interact with social development advisers and with macroeconomists to ensure a pro-poor bias to sectoral and budgetary support.

21. The World Bank (2000a), citing a Swedish Ministry for Foreign Affairs report (1999), states that many donor practices run against the idea of partnership – for example, maintaining control over the monitoring of resources, emphasizing projects that enable them to 'raise the flag', and tying aid to specific procurements.

22. Thus a DFID White Paper (1997) suggests a similar direction. 'Where we have confidence in the policies and budgetary allocation process and in the capacity for effective implementation of the partner government, we will consider moving away from supporting specific projects to providing resources more strategically in support of sector-wide programmes or the economy as a whole.'

23. The United Nations (2000) also supported this notion of a mechanism for peer review of ODA by users.

24. A DAC Recommendation to untie ODA to the Least Developed Countries entered into force on 1 January 2002. OECD (2005) notes that based on incomplete coverage, about half of total is reported as untied. The Recommendation's contribution to aid effectiveness remains limited, however, by its present coverage (only covering the LDCs and excluding food aid and technical cooperation, for example).

25. Donors have committed themselves to greater coordination among themselves. OECD (2005) says it will measure progress in aid effectiveness in terms of ownership, alignment behind country stategies, harmonization in their procedures and policies, managing for results and mutual accountability against twelve specific indicators.

26. Burnside and Dollar (1997) showed that when aid flows into good policy environments it helps growth; that the reason why there is no simple correlation between between aid and growth is that aid often does not flow to countries with good policy environments; and, finally, that aid does not induce good policy environments to emerge at all.

27. One example from an interview with a senior Government of Malawi official about

the relationship between the government and its donors will suffice: 'We Malawians are very good at writing plans, strategies and reports. It's our national disease! These offices are full of papers saying we should do this, we will do that, but instead of going ahead and doing it we throw it in the cupboard and write another plan instead! The donors are also partly to blame. After this new government took power in 1994 we produced a Poverty Alleviation Plan. Then we wrote the 2020 Vision. Last year we had the PER [Public Expenditure Review]. We have had PFPs [Policy Framework Papers]. Now the World Bank tells us in order to get HIPC debt relief we had to write a PRSP [Poverty Reduction Strategy Paper]. So we must throw everything away and start again, wasting all that work. We have just published the 2020 Vision and already it is a historical document!' (Devereux, 2002).

28. Some agencies see the UK as providing an example of best practice in this area (OECD, 1999). It remains to be seen if the formulation of such policies actually translates into practice in the UK.

29. Such growth depends on the prices of existing exported goods. Developing countries have until recently experienced declines in the prices of their export commodities.

30. At the Singapore Ministerial Meeting to resume a new round of trade negotiations, France, Norway and the USA were making the case for the inclusion of labour standards as a new issue in the trade negotiations – or at the very least, create a working party to discuss the issue.

31. If one were to follow the World Bank's (Collier–Dollar study) recommendations – supporting aid on the basis of policy – countries facing shocks are unlikely to perform well on the policy front, and thus may get less aid. On the other hand, aid may be most needed in these very countries. It has been argued that aid can make a larger difference in such countries, rather than those not suffering from shocks (Guillaumont and Chauvet, 1999).

32. This is not the first time that threats have been held out. In 1986 and 1987 the USA withheld its contribution to WHO's budget, apparently because of its disapproval of WHO policies on breast milk substitutes and essential drugs (Hardon and Kanji, 1992).

33. Thus, Save the Children (2002) points out that the documents prepared by the European Commission for discussion at the EU's 133 Committee call on the other WTO members to open up many service sectors, including those which are public monopolies. Water services are especially targeted for liberalization, given that European companies are big players in that area, as we discussed in Chapter 8.

34. The agreement refers to four possible modes of supplying services: *Cross-border services trade* [Mode 1]. Includes services supplied from one country to another, such as an international telephone call. *Consumption abroad* [Mode 2]. Includes consumers from one country making use of a service in another country, such as tourism. *Commercial presence* [Mode 3]. Includes a company from one country setting up subsidiaries or branches to provide services in another country, such as a bank from one country establishing operations in another country. *Movement of natural persons* [Mode 4]. Includes individuals travelling from their own country to supply services in another country, such as an actress or a management consultant.

35. Hjertholm and White (2000) note that for some smaller donors, allocation and quality of aid flows have been largely, but not wholly, shaped by concern for the development needs of the recipient community. By contrast, the foreign aid of several larger donors has been firmly established as a foreign and commercial policy tool, designed to achieve a range of political, strategic, economic, but also genuinely humanitarian, objectives.

36. Perhaps enlightened self-interest might prevail in not only sustaining and increasing overall ODA and the allocation to basic services, and in changing its character, but also in ensuring consistency between such poverty-reducing aid and international trade policies. A former director of USAID expressed this self-interest well: 'Dangerous infectious

diseases originating in these [poor] countries threaten Americans. Environmental decay and emission of greenhouse gases from nations with huge and growing populations are affecting Americans' weather and health. In worst-case circumstances, poor countries have become recruiting grounds for terrorists. Poverty in all its manifestations constitutes a serious threat to US national interests ... Technical assistance to build democratic institutions and financial systems is an essential part of USAID's contemporary portfolio. These interventions, when combined with more traditional ones in education, health care and environmental preservation, contribute to a freer and more productive society.' It is interesting that Atwood (2001) was making this argument to persuade Senator Jesse Helms, then Senate Foreign Relations Committee chairman, who after the election of George W. Bush to the presidency in 2000 was planning to remove the US government from the aid business, close down USAID, and provide block grants to faith-based charitable organizations through a semi-public foundation.

chapter 11

1. In 1990 the World Bank predicted a decline in the numbers of poor in the world from 1,125 million (1985) to 825 million in 2000. In reality, the number of people living on less than $1 reached 1.2 billion by 1998, including more than 600 million children. Since then, in Africa and Latin America, and elsewhere (except East Asia, most notably China), the proportion of people struggling to survive with income lower than a PPP dollar a day has increased or remained largely constant, despite a moderate rise in output per capita. The fact that these numbers continue to rise, despite their prognostications and the deficiencies in the estimation of the percentage of people whose income falls below the PPP dollar a day standard (see Reddy and Pogge, 2002), should clearly worry not just the governments but also their international advisers and lenders.

2. World Bank, 2000a tries to argue that how growth affects poverty depends on how the additional income generated by growth is distributed; also, that growth can be made more equitable by reducing inequality in access to assets and opportunities.

3. It should also be distinguished from Kuznets's notion of linear stages of development – i.e. that the relationship between income inequality and per capita income may be described by a curve (an inverted U), with an upward phase in which income inequality increases with increases in per capita income, and a downward phase in which income inequality declines with increases in per capita income. Rather, the notion of the second synergy is built upon more recent theoretical and empirical literature, which has demonstrated the benefits for growth of low levels of income inequality.

4. However, we should also note the difference between Rosenstein-Rodan and us. Most classical development economists argued that, in the absence of private entrepreneurship, governments would have to continue to perform the entrepreneurial job while at the same time fostering the development of a cadre of private entrepreneurs able to take over (Adelman, 2000). Although the experience of generating a 'local bourgeoisie' has been quite uneven in most low- and middle-income countries over the past half-century (Chang, 2003), the state has less need now to play entrepreneur. For successful models of industrial policy, for example in East Asia, see Wade, 1990; and Amsden, 1989.

5. For an analysis of why women's capability-enhancement is a necessary condition for triggering the second synergy as well, see Mehrotra, 2002b.

6. Sen's discourse (see Sen, 2000) around the complex functioning of participation has been largely concerned with democracy at the national level (or state level in large federal states), multiparty politics and the role of the opposition in such democracy.

References

Aaron, H., and McGuire, M.C. (1970), 'Public Goods and Income Distribution', *Econometrica* 38/6: 907–20.

Ablo, E., and Reinikka, R. (1998), *Do Budgets Really Matter? Evidence from Public Spending on Education and Health in Uganda*, Policy Research Working Paper No. 1926 (June), Washington DC: World Bank.

Abramovitz, M. (1989), *Thinking about Growth*, Cambridge: Cambridge University Press.

ACC/SCN (2000), *Fourth Report on the World Nutrition Situation*, UN Administrative Committee on Coordination/Sub-committee on Nutrition, Geneva: ACC/SCN with IFPRI.

Addis Ababa Consensus on Principles of Cost Sharing in Education and Health (1997), Forum on Cost Sharing in the Social Sectors of Sub-Saharan Africa, Addis Ababa, 18–20 June.

Adelman, C. (2000), 'A Parallel Universe: Certification in the Information Technology Guild', *Change* 32/3: 20–29.

Agarwal, B. (1994), *A Field of One's Own: Gender and Land Rights in South Asia*, South Asian Studies No. 58, Cambridge: Cambridge University Press.

Agbeyegbe, T., Stotsky, J., and Woldemariam, A. (2004), *Trade Liberalisation, Exchange Rate Changes, and Tax Revenues in Sub Saharan Africa*, IMF Working Paper, WP/04/178, Washington DC. www.imf.org/external/pubs/ft/wp/2004/wp04178.pdf.

Aggarwal, Y. (2000), *Public and Private Partnership in Primary Education in India: A Study of Unrecognized Schools in Haryana*, New Delhi: National Institute of Educational Planning and Administration, March.

Ahluwalia, M.S. (1976), 'Inequality, Poverty and Development', *Journal of Development Economics* 3/4.

Ahluwalia, M.S. (1999), *Reforming the Global Financial Architecture*, Economic Paper 41, Commonwealth Economic Paper Series, Economic Affairs Division of the Commonwealth Secretariat, London.

Ahuja, V., Bidani, B., Ferreira, F., and Walton, M. (1997), *Everyone's Miracle?*, Washington DC: World Bank.

Akesbi, A., Guedira, N., and Zouiten, M. (1998), *Étude du Suivi de L'initiative 20/20*, Rabat: UNICEF–UNDP.

Akin, J., Birdsall, N., and de Ferranti, D. (1987), *Financing Health Services in Developing Countries: An Agenda for Reform*, Washington DC: World Bank.

Alailama, P.J., and Sanderatne, N. (1997), 'Social Policies in a Slowly Growing Economy: Sri Lanka', in S. Mehrotra and R. Jolly (eds), *Development with a Human Face: Experiences in*

Social Achievement and Economic Growth, Oxford: Clarendon Press.

Alesina, A., and Perotti, R. (1994), 'The Political Economy of Growth: A Critical Survey of the Recent Literature', *Worldbank Economic Review* 8: 351–71.

Alfonso, J.R.R., and de Mello, L. (2000), *Brazil: An Evolving Federation*, Washington DC: IMF.

Alur, S., and Jobes, K. (1995), 'Water and Sanitation Sector in the 1990s: The Role of Bilateral Donors', Development and Project Planning Centre, University of Bradford.

Ames, B. (1977), 'The Politics of Public Spending in Latin America', *American Journal of Political Science* 21/1 (February): 149–76.

Amsden, A. (1989), *Asia's Next Giant*, Oxford: Oxford University Press.

Anand, S., and Kanbur, R. (1993), 'The Kuznets Process and the Inequality–Development Relationships', *Journal of Development Economics* 40: 25–52.

Anand, S., and Ravallion, M. (1993), 'Human Development in Poor Countries: On the Role of Private Incomes and Public Services', *Journal of Economic Perspectives* 7/1: 133–50.

Anderson, P.W., Arrow, K.J., and Pines, D. (eds) (1988), *The Economy as an Evolving Complex System: The Proceedings of the Evolutionary Paths of the Global Economy Workshop*, Reading MA: Addison-Wesley.

Arana, M., Chamorro, J.S., De Franco, S., Rivera, R., and Rodrígue, M. (1998), *Gasto Público en Servicios Sociales Básico en Nicaragua*, Managua: UNICEF–UNDP.

Arhin-Tenkorang, D. (2000), *Mobilizing Resources for Health: The Case for User Fees Revisited*, Working Paper Series No. WG3:6, Commission on Macroeconomics and Health, Geneva, November.

Arndt, C. (2000), 'Technical Cooperation', in F. Tare (ed.), *Foreign Aid and Development: Lessons Learnt and Directions for the Future*, London: Routledge.

Arrow, K.J. (1963), 'Uncertainty and the Welfare Economics of Medical Care', *American Economic Review* 538/5: 941–84.

Arrow, K. (1974), 'Economic Analysis and Limited Knowledge', *American Economic Review* 64: 1–10.

Atkinson, A.B. (1989), *Poverty and Social Security*, Brighton: Harvester Wheatsheaf.

Atkinson, T. (1999), 'Macroeconomics and the Social Dimension', in *Experts Discuss Some Critical Social Development Issues*, New York: Division for Social Policy and Development, United Nations.

Atwood, B.J. (2001), 'Bush Too is Going to Need USAID', *International Herald Tribune*, 27 February.

Avila, M., Hoy, D., and Santos, G.C. (1998), *Gasto Público en Servicios Sociales Básico en Belice*, Belmopan: UNICEF–UNDP.

Avritzer, L. (2000), 'Public Deliberation at the Local Level: Participatory Budgeting in Brazil', paper, Experiments for Deliberative Democracy conference, Wisconsin, January.

Baiocchi, G. (1999), 'Participation, Activism, and Politics: The Porto Alegre Experiment and Deliberative Democratic Theory', paper, Department of Sociology, University of Wisconsin–Madison.

Balakrishnan, P., et al. (2006), 'Liberalization, Market Power, and Productivity Growth in India', *Journal of Policy Reform* 9/1: 55–73.

Banerji, A., Mookerjee, D., Munshi K., and Ray, D. (2001), 'Inequality, Control Rights and Rent-Seeking: Sugar Cooperatives in Maharashtra', *Journal of Political Economy* 101/9.

Barbato, Celia (ed.), 2001, *Globalización y políticas macroeconómicas: su incidencia en el desarrollo latinamericano de los años noventa*, Montevideo: Ediciones Trilce.

Bardhan, P. (1984), *The Political Economy of Development in India*, Oxford: Basil Blackwell.

Bardhan, P., and Mookherjee, D. (1999), 'Relative Capture of Local and Central Governments: An Essay in the Political Economy of Decentralization', First Draft 30 November, Department of Economics, University of California at Berkeley.

Bardhan, P., and Mookherjee, D. (2000), 'Capture and Governance at Local and National Levels', paper, January, Department of Economics, University of California at Berkeley/Boston University.

Barnum, H., and Kutzin, J. (1993), *Public Hospitals in Developing Countries: Resource Use, Cost, Financing*, Baltimore and London: Johns Hopkins University Press.

Barros, F.C., Vaughan, J.P., and Victora, C. (1986), 'Why so many Caesarean Sections? The Need for Further Policy Change in Brazil', *Health, Policy and Planning* 1/1: 19–29.

Bashir, S. (1997), 'The Cost Effectiveness of Public and Private Schools: Knowledge Gaps, New Research Methodologies, and an Application in India', in C. Colclough (ed.), *Marketizing Education and Health in Developing Countries: Miracle or Mirage?*, Oxford: Clarendon Press.

Bashir, S., and Ayyar, R.V. (2001), 'District Primary Education Programme', article submitted to the *Encyclopaedia of Indian Education*, National Council of Educational Research and Training, New Delhi.

Bates, R. (1988), 'Contra Contractarianism: Some Reflections on the New Institutionalism', *Politics and Society* 16: 387–401.

Bates, R.H., and Weingast, B.R. (1995), *A New Comparative Politics: Integrating Rational Choice and Interpretivist Perspectives*, Cambridge MA: Center for International Affairs, Harvard University.

Baytelman, Y., Cowan, K., de Gregorio, J., and González, P. (1998), *Gasto Público en Servicios Sociales Básico en Chile*, Santiago: UNICEF–UNDP.

Becker, G. (1994), *Human Capital*, New York: Columbia University Press.

Becker, J. (2001), 'A Calamitous Scale of Water Problems in China', *International Herald Tribune*, 5 January.

Bedi A.S., and Garg, A. (2000), 'The Effectiveness of Private versus Public Schools: The Case of Indonesia', *Journal of Development Economics* 61/2 (April).

Benería, L. (ed.) (1992), *Women and Development: The Sexual Division of Labour in Rural Societies*, New York: Praeger.

Bennel, P. (1995), 'Using and Abusing Rates of Return: A Critique of the World Bank's 1995 Education Sector Review', mimeo.

Bennel, P., and Furlong, D. (1997), *Has Jomtien Made a Difference? Trends in Donor Funding for Education and Basic Education Since the Late 1980s*, IDS Working Paper 51, Institute of Development Studies, Brighton.

Bennett, S. (1997), 'Private Health Care and Public Policy Objectives', in C. Colclough. (ed.), *Marketizing Education and Health Developing Countries*, Oxford: Clarendon Press.

Bennett, S., and Tangcharoensathien, V. (1994), 'A Shrinking State – Politics, Economics and Private Health Care in Thailand', *Public Administration and Development* 14/1: 1–17.

Berman, P., and Rose, L. (1996), 'The Role of Private Providers in Maternal and Child Health and Family Planning Services in Developing Countries', in *Health Policy and Planning* 11/2: 142–55.

Betke, F. (2001), *The 'Family-in-Focus' Approach: Developing Policy-Oriented Monitoring and Analysis of Human Development in Indonesia*, Innocenti Working Paper No. 83, Florence: UNICEF Innocenti Research Centre, www.unicef-icdc.org.

Beynon, J. (1999), '"Assessing Aid" and the Collier/Dollar Poverty Efficient Aid Allocation: A Critique', www.dfid.gov.uk/public.

Bhagwati, J. (1993), *India in Transition: Freeing the Economy*, Oxford: Clarendon Press.

Bharadwaj, K. (1974), *Production Conditions in Indian Agriculture. A Study Based on Farm Management Surveys*, Cambridge: Department of Applied Economics, Occasional Paper No. 33, Cambridge: Cambridge University Press.

Bideau A., Desjardins, B., and Brignoli, H.P. (eds) (1997), *Infant and Child Mortality in the Past*, Oxford: Clarendon Press.

Bird, G. (1999), 'How Important is Sound Domestic Macroeconomics in Attracting Capital Inflows to Developing Countries?', *Journal of International Development* 11: 1–26.

Birdsall, N., and de la Torre, A., with Menezes, R. (2001), *Washington Contentious: Economic Policies for Social Equity in Latin America*, Washington DC: Centre for Global Development.

Birdsall, N., and Londono, J.L. (1997), 'Asset Inequality Matters: An Assessment of the World Bank's Approach to Poverty Reduction', *American Economic Review* 87/2: 32–7.

Birdsall, N., Ross, D., and Sabot, R. (1995), 'Inequality and Growth Reconsidered: Lessons from East Asia', *World Bank Economic Review* 9/3: 477–508.

BIS (Bank for International Settlements) (1996), *Annual Report 1995–1996*, Basle.

Bishop, M.D., Corbin, R., and Duncan, N.C. (1997), 'Barbados: Social Development in a Small Island State', *Development with a Human Face*, Oxford: Oxford University Press.

Black, M. (1996), *Children First: The Story of Unicef, Past and Present*, New York: Oxford University Press.

Blair, H. (2000), 'Participation and Accountability at the Periphery: Democratic Local Governance in Six Countries', *World Development* 28/1: 21–39.

Bloom, G. (1997), 'Financing Rural Health Services: Lessons from China', in C. Colclough (ed.), *Marketizing Education and Health in Developing Countries: Miracle or Mirage?*, Oxford: Clarendon Press.

Bloom, G. (1998), 'Equity in Health in an Unequal Society', *Social Sciences Medicine* 47: 1529–38.

Bond, P. (1998), 'Privatisation, Participation and Protest in the Restructuring of Municipal Services: Ground for Opposing World Bank Promotion of "Public–Private Partnerships"', paper, Graduate School of Public and Development Management, University of the Witwatersrand, South Africa. pbond@wn.apc.org.

Bongaarts, J. (1995), *The Role of Family Planning Programs in Contemporary Fertility Transitions*, Research Division Working Paper No. 71, New York: Population Council.

Bongaarts, J. (1994), 'The Impact of Population Policies: Comment', *Population and Development Review* 20/3.

Bornschier, V., and Chase-Dunn, C. (1985), *Transnational Corporations and Underdevelopment*. New York: Praeger.

Borón, A.A. (2003), *Estado, capitalismo y democracia en América Latina*, Buenos Aires: CLACSO.

Borón, A.A., Gambina, J., and Minsburg, N. (eds) (1999), *Tiempos violentos: neoliberalismo, globalización y desigualdad en América Latina*, Buenos Aires: Consejo Latinoamericano de Ciencias Sociales: EUDEBA

Boulanger, P.M., and Tabutin, D. (eds) (1980), *La mortalité des enfants dans le monde et dans l'histoire*, Liege: Ordina.

Bourguignon, F., Ferreira, H.G., and Leite, P.G. (2002), 'Ex-Ante Evaluation of Conditional Cash Transfers Programs: The Case of Bolsa Escola', paper at conference on The Economics of Child Labour, Oslo. www.ucw-projects.org/events.

Bourguignon, F., and Morrison, C. (1992), *Adjustment and Equity in Developing Countries: A New Approach*, Paris: OECD.

Braunstein, E., and Epstein, G. (2002), *Bargaining Power and Foreign Direct Investment in China: Can 1.3 Billion Consumers Tame the Multinationals?*, CEPA Working Papers 2003–13, CEPA, New School University, New York.

Bray, M. (1997), 'Community Financing of Education: Rationales, Mechanisms, and Policy Implications in Less Developed Countries', in C. Colclough (ed.), *Marketizing Education and Health in Developing Countries: Miracle or Mirage?*, Oxford: Clarendon Press.

Bray, M. (2002), 'The Costs and Financing of Education: Trends and Policy Implications', *Education in Developing Asia*, vol. 3, Asian Development Bank, Comparative Research Centre, University of Hong Kong.

Breman, J. (1996), *Footloose Labour: Working in India's Informal Economy*, Cambridge: Cambridge University Press.

Briscoe, J., and Garn, H.A. (1995), 'Financing Water Supply and Sanitation under Agenda 21', *Natural Resources Forum* 19/1: 59–70.

Brossard, M., and Gacougnolle, L. (2000), *Financing Primary Education for All: Yesterday, Today and Tomorrow*, Paris: UNESCO.

Bruno, M., and Easterly, W. (1995), *Inflation Crisis and Long Run Growth*, NBER Working Paper 5209, National Bureau of Economic Research, Washington DC.

Bruno, M., Ravallion, M., and Squire, L. (1996), *Equity and Growth in Developing Countries: Old and New Perspectives on the Policy Issues*, Policy Research Working Paper No. 1563, Washington DC: World Bank.

Buckland, P., Hofmeyer, J., and Meyer, S. (1993), *Teacher Salaries in South Africa: A Policy Perspective*, Johannesburg: EDUPOL, National Business Initiative.

Budlender, D., and Sharp, R., with Allen, K. (1998), *How to Do a Gender-sensitive Budget Analysis: Contemporary Research and Practice*, Canberra: AUSAID/London: Commonwealth Secretariat.

Bulmer-Thomas, V. (ed.) (1996), *The New Economic Model in Latin America and Its Impact on Income Distribution and Poverty*, London: Macmillan.

Burgess, R., and Stern, N. (1993), 'Taxation and Development', *Journal of Economic Literature*, 31/2: 762–830.

Burgess, R.S.L. (1997), 'Fiscal Reform and the Extension of Basic Health and Education Coverage', in C. Colclough (ed.), *Marketizing Education and Health in Developing Countries: Miracle or Mirage?*, Oxford: Clarendon Press.

Burnside, C., and Dollar, D. (1997), *Aid, Policies and Growth*, Washington DC: World Bank.

Bustelo, E. (1991), *La producción del estado de malestar: ajuste y política social en América Latina*, Buenos Aires: UNICEF Argentina.

Buvinich, M.R., and Reyes, A. (1992), *El gasto social en Honduras y su prioridad hacia el desarrollo humano*, Tegucigalpa: UNICEF–UNDP.

Caines, K., and Lush, L. (2004), *Impact of Public–Private Pattnerships Addressing Access to Pharmaceuticals in Selected Low and Middle Income Countries*, Initiative for Public–Private Partnerships for Health, Global Forum for Health Research, Geneva. www.globalforumhealth.org.

Caldwell, J.C. (1980), 'Mass Education as a Determinant of the Timing of Fertility Decline', *Population and Development Review* 6.

Caldwell, J.C. (1986), 'Routes to Low Mortality in Poor Countries', *Population and Development Review* 12/2.

Carciofi, R., and Cetrángolo, O. (1994), *Tax Reforms and Equity in Latin America: A Review of the 1980s and Proposals for the 1990s*, Innocenti Occasional Paper No. 39, Florence: UNICEF Innocenti Research Centre.

Carnoy, M. (1992), *The Case for Investing in Basic Education*, New York: UNICEF.

Carnoy, M. (1995), 'Structural Adjustment and the Changing Face of Education', *International Labour Review* 134/6: 653–73.

Carnoy, M. (1999), *Globalization and Educational Reform: What Planners Need to Know*, Paris: UNESCO, International Institute for Educational Planning.

Carnoy, M., and Welmond, M. (1996), 'Do Teachers Get Paid Too Much?, Stanford University, Palo Alto CA, mimeo.

Cassen, R. (1994), '*Does Aid Work? Report to an Intergovernmental Task Force*, 2nd edn, Oxford: Clarendon Press.

Castro, B.C., Naranjo, M.B., Pareja, F., and Montufar, M. (1998), *Gasto Público en Servicios Sociales Básico en Ecuador*, Quito: UNICEF–UNDP.

Castro-Leal, F., Dayton, J., Demery, L., and Mehra, K. (1998), *Public Social Spending in Africa: Do the Poor Benefit? Poverty Reduction and Economic Management*, Washington DC: World Bank, mimeo.

Chabot, J., Harnmeijer, J.W., and Streefland, P.H. (eds) (1995), *African Primary Health Care in Times of Economic Turbulence*, Amsterdam: Royal Tropical Institute.

Chafani, L., Moussa, F., and Abdou-Saleye, M. (1997), *L'Initiative 20/20: Examen des Possibilités de Mobilisation de Ressources Additionnelles en Faveur des Services Sociaux Essentiels*, Niamei: UNICEF–UNDP.

Chafani, L., and Inack, S. (1998), *L'Initiative 20/20: Possibilités de Mobilisation des Ressources Additionnelles en Faveur des Services Sociaux Essentiels par la Restructuration des Dépenses Dudgétaires de L'état et de l'Aide Publique au Developpement*, Yaounde: UNICEF–UNDP.

Chakravarty, S. (1982), *Alternative Approaches to a Theory of Economic Growth: Marx, Marshall and Schumpeter*, New Delhi: Orient Longman.

Chakravarty, S. (1987), *Development Planning: The Indian Experience*, Oxford: Clarendon Press.

Chang, H.J. (2002), *Kicking Away the Ladder: Development Strategy in Historical Perspective*, London: Anthem Press.

Chang, H.J. (ed.) (2003), *Rethinking Development Economics*, London: Anthem Press.

Charmes, J. (1998), 'Informal Sector, Poverty and Gender: A Review of Empirical Evidence', background paper for *World Development Report 2001*, Washington DC: World Bank.

Chatterjee, M., and Vyas, J. (2000), 'Organising Insurance for Women Workers', in R. Jhabvala and R.K.A. Subrahmanya (eds), *The Unorganized Sector: Work Security and Social Protection*, New Delhi: Sage.

Chen, M.A., Jhabvala, R., and Lund, F. (2002), *Supporting Workers in the Informal Economy*, Working Paper on the Informal Economy No. 2, Geneva: ILO.

Chenery, H., Ahluwalia, M.S., Bell, C.L.G., Duloy, J.H., and Jolly, R. (1974), *Redistribution with Growth*, Oxford: Oxford University Press.

Chenery, H., and Srinivasan, T.N. (eds) (1988), *Handbook of Development Economics*, vol. 1, Amsterdam: North-Holland.

Chudnovsky, D., and López, A. (eds) (2002), *Integración regional e inversión extranjera directa: el caso del MERCOSUR*, Buenos Aires: Banco Interamericano de Desarrollo, Departamento de Integración y Programas Regionales, Instituto para la Integración de América Latina y el Caribe, BID–INTAL.

Clunies-Ross, A. (1999), 'Sustaining Revenue for Social Purposes in the Face of Globalization', Division of Social Policy and Development, Department of Economic and Social Affairs, New York: United Nations.

Coase, R. (1988), 'The New Institutional Economics', *American Economic Review* 88/2.

Cochrane, S. (1979), *Fertility and Education: What Do We Really Know?*, Baltimore MD: Johns Hopkins University Press.

Cochrane, S. (1988), *The Effects of Education, Health and Social Security on Fertility in Developing Countries*, Working Paper WPS 93, Population and Health Resources Department, Washington DC: World Bank.

Colclough, C. (1993), *Education and the Market: Which Parts of the Neo-liberal Solution are Correct?*, UNICEF Innocenti Occasional Paper No. 37, Florence: UNICEF Innocenti Research Centre.

Colclough, C. (ed.) (1997), *Marketizing Education and Health in Developing Countries: Miracle or Mirage?*, Oxford: Clarendon Press.

Colclough, C., and Al-Samarrai, S. (2000), 'Achieving Schooling for All: Budgetary Expenditure on Education in Sub-Saharan Africa and South Asia', *World Development* 28/11: 1927–44.

Collins, A., and Bosworth, B. (1996), 'Economic Growth in East Asia: Accumulation versus Assimilation', *Brookings Papers on Economic Activity* 2: 135–91.

Cominetti, R. (1994), 'Fiscal Adjustment and Social Spending', *CEPAL Review* 0/54

Commission of Global Governance (1995), *Our Global Neighbourhood*, New York: Oxford University Press.

Cook, S., and White, G. (2001), 'Alternative Approaches to Welfare Policy Analysis: New Institutional Economics, Politics and Political Economy', in G. Mwabu, C. Ugaz and G. White (eds), *Social Provision in Low-Income Countries: New Patterns and Emerging Trends*, WIDER Studies in Development Economics, Oxford: Oxford University Press.

Cordera, R., and Ziccardi, A. (eds) (2000), *Las políticas sociales de México al fin del milenio: descentralización, diseño y gestión*, México: Universidad Nacional Autónoma de México, Instituto de Investigaciones Sociales: M.A. Porrúa Grupo.

Cornia, G.A. (1990), *Child Poverty and Deprivation in Industrial Countries: Recent Trends and Policy Options*, UNICEF Innocenti Occasional Papers No. 2, Florence: UNICEF Innocenti Research Centre.

Cornia, G.A. (2000), 'Inequality and Poverty in the Era of Liberalisation and Globalisation', paper, UNU Millennium Conference, January.

Cornia, G.A. (ed.) (2004), *Inequality and Poverty in an Era of Liberalization and Globalization,* World Institute for Development Economics Research, Oxford: Oxford University Press.

Cornia, G.A., Addison, T., and Kiiski, S. (2003), *Income Distribution Changes and Their Impact in the Post-World War II Period*, Discussion Paper 2003/28, Helsinki: World Institute for Development Economics Research.

Cornia, G., Jolly, R., and Stewart, F. (eds) (1987), *Adjustment with a Human Face*, Oxford: Oxford University Press.

Cornia, G.A., and Mwabu, G. (1997), 'Health Status and Health Policy in Sub-Saharan Africa: A Long-Term Perspective', Helsinki: UNU–WIDER.

Corsini, C.A., and Viazzo, P.P. (eds) (1993), *The Decline of Infant Mortality in Europe, 1800–1950: Four National Case Studies*, Florence: UNICEF and Innocenti Research Centre.

Cowen, P.J.B. (1997), 'Getting the Private Sector Involved in Water – What to Do in the Poorest of Countries', *Viewpoint Note No. 102,* World Bank, Finance Private Sector and Infrastructure Network.

Cox, D., and Jimenez, E. (1991), 'The Relative Effectiveness of Private and Public Schools: Evidence from Two Developing Countries', *Journal of Development Economics* 34: 99–121.

Creese, A., and Kutzin, J. (1997), 'Lessons from Cost Recovery in Health', in C. Colclough (ed.), *Marketizing Education and Health in Developing Countries: Miracle or Mirage?*, Oxford: Clarendon Press.

Crook, R., and Sverrison, A.S. (2001), *Decentralization and Poverty Alleviation in Developing Countries: A Comparative Analysis or Is West Bengal Unique?*, IDS Working Paper 130, Institute of Development Studies, Brighton.

Damill, M., and Fanelli, J.M. (1994), *La macroeconomía de América Latina: de la crisis de la deuda a las reformas estructurales*, Buenos Aires: CEDES.

Dasgupta, A., and Mookherjee, D. (1997), 'Design and Enforcement of Personal Income Taxes in India', in S. Mundle (ed.), *Public Finance: Issues for India*, New Delhi: Oxford University Press.

Dasgupta, A., and Mookherjee, D. (1998), *Incentives and Institutional Reform in Tax Enforcement: An Analysis of Developing Country Experience*, New Delhi: Oxford University Press.

Dasgupta, A., and Mookerjee, D. (2000), 'Reforming Indian Income-Tax Enforcement', in S. Kähkonen and A. Lanyi (eds), *Institutions, Incentives and Economic Reforms in India,* New Delhi: Sage.

Dasgupta, P. (1993), *An Inquiry into Well-Being and Destitution*, Oxford: Oxford University Press.

Davies-Adetugbo, A., Adetugbo, K., Orewole, Y., and Fabiyi, A.K. (1997), Breast-feeding Promotion in a Diarrhoea Programme in Rural Communities', *Journal of Diarrhoeal Diseases Research* 15/3 (September).

De Bruyn, J., McIntyre, D., Mthethwa, N., Naidoo, F., Ntenga, L., Pillay, P., and Pintuse-witz, C. (1998), *Public Expenditure on Basic Social Services in South Africa*, Cape Town: UNICEF–UNDP.

De Janvry, A., and Sadoulet, E. (2002), 'Land Reforms in Latin America: Ten Lessons towards a Contemporary Agenda', Land America World Bank Land Policy Seminar, Mexico.

De Sousa Santos, B. (1998), 'Participatory Budgeting in Porto Alegre: Toward a Redistributive Democracy', *Politics and Society* 26/4.

Deininger, K. (1999), 'Asset Distribution Inequality and Growth', Washington DC: World Bank Development Research Group.

Deininger, K., and Squire, L. (1996), 'A New Data Set Measuring Income Inequality', *World Bank Economic Review* 10/3: 565–91.

Delamonica, E., Mehrotra, S., and Vandemoortele, J. (2004), 'Education for All: How Much Will it Cost?', *Development and Change* 35/1 (January).

Demery, L., and Squire, L. (1996), 'Macroeconomic Adjustment in Africa: An Emerging Picture', *World Bank Research Observer* 11: 39–59.

Deolalikar, A., and Vashishta, P. (1996), *The Health and Medical Sector in India: Potential Reform and Problems*, India Working Paper No. 9, University of Maryland.

Dermer, A. (1997), Breastfeeding: Good for Babies, Mothers, and the Planet, *The Medical Reporter*, February.

Dermer, A. (2001), 'A Well-kept Secret: Breastfeeding's Benefits to Mothers', *New Beginnings* 18/4: 124–7.

Dervis, K., and Birdsall, N. (2006), *A Stability and Social Investment Facility for High-Debt Countries*, Working Paper No. 77, January, Washington DC: Centre for Global Development.

Dervis, K., with Ozer, C. (2005), *A Better Globalization: Legitimacy, Governance, and Reform*, Washington DC: Center for Global Development.

Devarajan, S., and Swaroop, V. (1998), *The Implications of Foreign Aid Fungibility for Development Assistance*, Policy Research Working Paper No. 2022, Washington DC: World Bank.

Devarajan, S., Dollar, D., and Holmgren, T. (1999), 'Aid and Reform in Africa', Washington DC: World Bank Development Research Group, mimeo.

Devarajan, S., Miller, M.J., and Swanson, E.V. (2002), *Goals for Development: History, Prospects and Costs*, Policy Research Working Paper No. 2819, Washington DC: World Bank.

Development Alternatives (1998), 'External Assistance for Education and Sectoral Programmes', UNICEF New York, Education Section, mimeo.

Development Research Bureau (1999), *Report on a Study on the Compact 20/20 Initiative in Nigeria*, Lagos: UNICEF.

Devereux, S. (2002), 'Safety Nets in Malawi: The Process of Choice', paper prepared for the IDS Conference on Surviving the Present, Securing the Future: Social Policies for the Poor in Poor Countries, Institue of Development Studies, Brighton, March.

DFID (Department for International Development) (1997), *Eliminating World Poverty: A Challenge for the 21st Century*, White Paper, London: HM Government.

DFID (Department for International Development) (2000), *Making Globalisation Work for the Poor*, White Paper on International Development, London: HM Government.

DFID (Department for International Development) (2001), *Understanding and Reforming Public Expenditure Management, Guidelines for DFID*, Version 1, March, London: HM Government.

Diamond, P., and Mirlees, J. (1971), 'Optimal Taxation and Public Production', *American Economic Review* 61: 8–27, 261–78.

Dommen, B., and Dommen, E. (1997), 'Mauritius: The Roots of Success 1960–1993', in S. Mehrotra and R. Jolly (eds), *Development with a Human Face. Experiences in Social Achievement and Economic Growth*, Oxford: Clarendon Press.

Drèze, J. (1999), 'Militarism, Development and Democracy', lecture given at the University of Baroda.

Drèze, J. (2001), 'Starving the Poor', *The Hindu*, 28 February.

Drèze, J., and Sen, A. (eds) (1989), *Hunger and Public Action*, Oxford: Clarendon Press.

Drèze, J., and Sen, A. (eds) (1998), *Indian Development, Selected Regional Perspectives*, study prepared for WIDER, Delhi: Oxford University Press.

Duffy, J. (1990), *The Sanitarians: A History of American Public Health*, Urbana: University of Illinois Press.

Duncan, T., Jefferis, K., and Molutsi, P. (1997), 'Botswana: Social Development in a Resource-rich Economy', in S. Mehrotra and R. Jolly (eds), *Development with a Human Face: Experiences in Social Achievement and Economic Growth*, Oxford: Clarendon Press.

Dutt, A.K. (1990), *Growth, Distribution, and Uneven Development*, New York: Cambridge University Press.

Dutt, R.C. (1903), *Economic History of India*, vol. 2: *In the Victorian Age*, New York: Burt Franklin.

Easterly, W. (1999), *Life During Growth: International Evidence on Quality of Life and Per Capita Income*, Working Papers, Macroeconomics and Growth, Stabilization, Monetary/Fiscal Policy, Washington DC: World Bank.

Eatwell, J. (1997), 'International Capital Liberalization: The Impact on World Development', *Estudios de Economica* 24/2 (December): 219–61.

Eatwell, J., and Milgate, M. (eds) (1983), *Keynes's Economics and the Theory of Value and Distribution*, London: Duckworth.

Economy and Finance Ministry, UNDP/UNICEF (1999), *Initiative 20/20 au Burkina Faso: L'Allocation des Ressources Budgétaires aux Services Sociaux de Base Pour les Années 1990 à 1997, 1998*, Ouagadougou: UNICEF–UNDP.

Elson, D. (1995), *Male Bias in the Development Process*, Manchester: Manchester University Press.

Elson, D., and Catagay, N. (2000), 'The Social Content of Macro-economic Policies', *World Development* 28/7.

Engle, P. (1999), 'The Role of Caring Practices and Resources for Care in Child Survival, Growth, and Development: South and Southeast Asia', *Asian Development Review* 17/1–2.

Escuder, J.A., Peguero, R.M., and Gómez, A.M. (1998), *Gasto Público en Servicios Sociales Básico en República Dominicana*, Santo Domingo: UNICEF–UNDP.

Esman, M.J., and Uphoff, N. (1984), *Local Organisations: Intermediaries in Rural Developmen*, Ithaca: Cornell University Press.

FAO, ILO and IUF (2005), *Agricultural Workers and Their Contribution to Sustainable Agriculture and Rural Development*, joint report, Rome: FAO.

FAO/ILSI (1997), *Preventing Micronutrient Malnutrition: A Guide to Food-based Approaches: A Manual for Policy Makers and Programme Planners*, Washington DC: International Life Sciences Institute (ILSI).

Farell, J., and Oliveira, J. (eds) (1993), *Teachers in Developing Countries: Improving Effectiveness and Managing Costs*, Washington DC: World Bank.

Felix, D. (1994), 'Industrial Development in East Asia: What Are the Lessons for South America?', UNCTAD Discussion Paper No. 84 (May).

Ferber, M.A., and Nelson, J.A. (eds) (1993), *Beyond Economic Man: Feminist Theory and Economics*, Chicago: University of Chicago Press.

Fields, G.S. (1980), *Poverty, Inequality, and Development*, Cambridge: Cambridge University Press.

Filmer, A. (1995), 'Inequality, Poverty, and Growth: Where do We Stand?', in M. Bruno and B. Pleskovic (eds), *Annual World Bank Conference on Development Economics*, Washington DC: World Bank.

Filmer, D., Hammer, J., and Pritchett, L. (1997), *Health Policy in Poor Countries: Weak Links in the Chain*, Policy Research Working Papers No. 1874, Washington DC: World Bank.

Filmer, D., and Pritchett, L. (1997), *Child Mortality and Public Spending on Health: How Much Does Money Matter?*, DECRG, World Bank Research Working Paper No. 1864, Washington DC: World Bank.

Fine, B. (2001), 'Neither the Washington nor the post-Washington Consensus', in B. Fine, C. Lapavitsas and J. Pincus (eds), *Development Policy in the Twenty-first Century*, London: Routledge.

Fine, B., Lapavitsas, C., and Pincus, J. (eds) (2001), *Development Policy in the Twenty-first Century*, London: Routledge.

Finnegan, W. (2002), 'The World is Running out of Fresh Water, and the Fight to Control it has Begun', *New Yorker*, April.

Fishlow, A. (1966), 'Levels of Nineteenth Century American Investment in Education', *Journal of Economic History* 26/4.

Fishlow, A. (1991), 'Some Reflections on Comparative Latin American Economic Performance and Policy', in T. Banuri (ed.), *Economic Liberalization: No Panacea*, Oxford: Clarendon Press.

Fishlow, A. (1995), 'Inequality, Poverty and Growth: Where Do We Stand?', in M. Bruno and B. Pleskovic (eds), *Annual World Bank Conference on Development Economics*, Washington DC: World Bank.

Fisman, R., and Gatti, R. (2002), 'Decentralization and Corruption: Evidence across Countries', *Journal of Public Economics*, March.

Fogel, R. (1994), 'Economic Growth, Population Theory and Physiology: The Bearing of Long-Term Processes on the Making of Economic Policy', *American Economic Review* 84/3: 369–95.

Foster, M., Brown, A., Norton, A., and Naschold, F. (2000), *The Status of Sector-Wide Approaches*, London: Overseas Development Institute.

Foster; M., and Merotto, D. (1997), 'Partnership for Development in Africa: A Framework for Flexible Funding', London: DFID, Africa Economics Department.

Franceys, R. (2001), 'Patterns of Public Private Partnerships', in regional conference The Reform of the Water Supply and Sanitation Sector in Africa: Enhancing Public–Private Partnership in the Context of the Africa Vision for Water (2025), Kampala, Uganda, 26–28 February, *Proceedings*, vol. II, Papers & Presentations.

Fukuda-Parr, S., Lopes, B., and Malik, K. (1996), *Capacity for Development: New Solutions to Old Problems*, London: Earthscan/UNDP.

Fundação Friedrich Ebert–Instituto Latino-Americano de Desenvolvimento Econômico e Social (2003), *As mulheres na reforma da previdência: o desafio da inclusão social*, Brasília: CFEMEA.

Garegnani, P. (1970), 'Heterogeneous Capital, the Production Function and the Theory of Distribution', *Review of Economic Studies* 37/3: 407–36.

Garnier., L., Grynspan, R., Hidalgo, R., Monge, G., and Trejos, J.D. (1997), 'Costa Rica: Social Development and Heterodox Adjustment', in S. Mehrotra and R. Jolly (eds), *Development with a Human Face: Experiences in Social Achievement and Economic Growth*, Oxford: Clarendon Press.

Gbayoro, B., Mamadou, K., Dangbé Todjou Idrissa Ouattara (1997), *Financement des secteurs sociaux de base en Côte d'Ivoire*, UNICEF–UNDP Country Study.

Gereffi, G. (1994), 'The Organization of Buyer-driven Global Commodity Chains: How U.S. Retailers Shape Overseas production Networks', in G. Gereffi and M. Korzeniewicz (eds), *Commodity Chains and Global Capitalism*, Westport CT: Praeger.

Gertler P., and Van der Gaag, J. (1990), *The Willingness to Pay for Medical Care: Evidence from Two Developing Countries*, Baltimore: Johns Hopkins University Press.

Gertler, P., and Molyneaux, J. (1997), *Experimental Evidence on the Effect of Raising User Fees for Publicly Delivered Health Care Services: Utilization, Health Outcomes, and Private Provider Response*, Santa Monica, CA: RAND.

Ghose, A. (2004), 'The Employment Challenge in India', *Economic and Political Weekly*, 27 November.

Ghosh, D.N. (2005), 'FDI and Reform: Significance and Relevance of Chinese Experience', *Economic and Political Weekly*, 17 December.

Gilson L., and Mills A. (1995), 'Health Sector Reforms in Sub-Saharan Africa: Lessons of the Last 10 Years', *Health Policy* 32.

Gilson, L., Sen, P.D., Mohammed, S., and Mujinja, P. (1994), 'The Potential of Health Sector Nongovernmental Organizations: Policy Options', *Health Policy and Planning* 9/1: 14–24.

Glewwe, P., and Jacoby, H. (1992), *Estimating the Determinants of Cognitive Achievement in Low-Income Countries: the Case of Ghana*, Living Standards Measurement Study Working Paper No. 91, Washington DC: World Bank.

Cómez, A.S., Delgado, L.C., and Reyes Gonzalo, C.E. (1998), *Gasto Público en Servicios Sociales Básico en Colombia*, Bogota: UNICEF–UNDP.

Gopalakrishnan, R., and Sharma, A. (1999), *Education Guarantee Scheme*, Government of Madhya Pradesh, Bhopal.

Gore, C., and Figueiredo, J.B. (1997), *Social Exclusion and the Anti-poverty Policy: A Debate*, Geneva: International Institute for Labour Studies, ILO.

Govinda, R. (ed.) (2002), *India Education Report – A Profile of Basic Education*, New Delhi: Oxford University Press.

Grabel, I. (2003), 'Internationa Private Capital Flows and Developing Countries', in H.J. Chang (ed.), *Rethinking Development Economics*, London: Anthem Press.

Graham, E.M., and Wada, E. (2001), 'Foreign Direct Investment in China: Effects on Growth and Economic Performance', in P. Drysdale (ed.), *Achieving High Growth: Experience of Transitional Economics in East Asia*, Oxford: Oxford University Press.

Green, A. (1987), 'The Role of Non-Governmental Organisations and the Private Sector in the Provision of Health Care in Developing Countries', *International Journal of Health Planning and Management* 2: 37–58.

Green, A. (1990), *Education and State Formation: The Rise of Education Systems in England, France and in the USA*, New York: St. Martins Press.

Green, A., and Matthias, A. (1995), 'Where Do NGOs Fit In? Developing a Policy Framework for the Health Sector', *Development in Practice* 5/4: 313–23.

Griffin, C. (1992), *Health Care in Asia: A Comparative Study of Cost and Financing*, Washington DC: World Bank, Regional and Sectoral Studies.

Grindle, M.S., and Thomas, J.W. (1991), *Public Choices and Policy Change: The Political Economy of Reform in Developing Countries*, Baltimore and London: Johns Hopkins University Press.

Grootaert, C., (1992), *The Evolution of Welfare and Poverty during Economic Recession and Structural Change: The Case of Côte d'Ivoire*, Washington DC: World Bank, Poverty and Social Policy, mimeo.

Gross, R.N., and Tilden RL. (1998), 'Vitamin A Cost-effectiveness Model', *International Journal of Health Planning Management* 3: 225–40.

Guillaumont, P., and Chauvet, L. (1999), 'Aid and Performance: A Reassessment', CERDI, CNRS and University of Auvergne, mimeo.

Gupta, S., Schiff, J., and Clements, B. (1996), *World-wide Military Spending, 1990–95*, International Monetary Fund Working Paper 96/64, Washington DC: IMF.

Gupta, S., Verhoeven, M., and Tiongson, E. (2002), 'The Effectiveness of Government Spending on Education and Health Care in Developing and Transition Economics', *European Journal of Political Economy* 18: 717–37.

Gwilliams, K.M., and Shalizi, Z.M. (1997), 'Road Funds, User Charges and Takes', World Bank Discussion Paper, April, Washington DC.

Habte, A. (1999), 'The Future of International Aid to Education: A Personal Reflection', in K. King and L. Buchert (eds), *Changing International Aid to Education: Global Patterns and National Contexts*, Paris: UNESCO Publishing/NORRAG.

Halstead, S.B., Walsh, J.A., and Warren, K.S. (1985), *Good Health at Low Cost*, New York: Rockefeller Foundation.

Hanmer, L., Lensink R., and White H. (1999), 'Infant and Child Mortality in Developing Countries: Analysing the Data for Robust Determinants', mimeo.

Hannaway, J. (1991), 'The Organization and Management of Public and Catholic Schools: Looking inside the "Black Box"', *International Journal of Educational Research* 15/5: 463–81.

Hansen, H., and Tarp, F. (2000), 'Aid Effectivenes Disputed', in F. Tarp, *Foreign Aid and Development*, London: Routledge.

Hao, Y., Suhua, C., and Lucas, H. (1997), 'Equity in the Utilization of Medical Services: A Survey in Poor Rural China', *IDS Bulletin* 28/1, Institute of Development Studies, Brighton.

ul-Haq, M. (1997), *Human Development in South Asia*, Karachi: Oxford University Press.

ul-Haq, M., Kaul, I., and Grunberg, I. (eds) (1996), *The Tobin Tax: Coping with Financial Volatility*, Oxford: Oxford University Press.

Hardon, A., and Kanji, N. (1992), 'New Horizons in the 1990s', in N. Kanji et al., *Drugs Policy in Developing Countries*, London: Zed Books.

Hausmann, R., and Purfield, C. (2004), *The Challenge of Fiscal Adjustment in a Democracy*, IMF Working Paper, WP/04/168, Washington DC, September.

Held, D. (1995), *Democracy and the Global Order: From the Modern State to Cosmopolitan Governance*, Stanford: Stanford University Press.

Helleiner, G. (2000), 'Towards Balance in Aid Relationships: Donor Performance Monitoring in Low Income Developing Countries', Toronto: University of Toronto.

Hemson, D. (1997), 'Privatisation, Public–Private Partnerships and Out-sourcing: The Challenge to Local Governance', cited in M. Webster and K. Samsom (eds), 'Public–Private Partnership and the Poor: An Initial Review', *Task* 164 (March), Loughborough University, www.lboro.ac.uk/well/.

Heng L.C., and Hoey, T.S. (1997), 'Malaysia: Social Development, Poverty Reduction and Economic Transformation, in S. Mehrotra and R. Jolly (eds), *Development with a Human Face: Experiences in Social Achievement and Economic Growth*, Oxford: Clarendon Press.

Heymann, D., and Kosacoff, B. (2000), *La Argentina de los noventa: desempeño económico en un contexto de reformas*, Buenos Aires: Eudeba and ECLAC

Heyneman, S.P. (1999), 'Development Aid in Education: A Personal View', in K. King, Kenneth and L. Buchert (eds), *Changing International Aid to Education: Global Patterns and National Contexts*: Paris: UNESCO.

Heytens, P., and Zebregs, H. (2003), 'How Fast Can China Grow?', in W. Tseng and M. Rodlauer (eds), *China: Competing in the Global Economy*, Washington DC: International Monetary Fund.

Hill, T., Kim-Farley, R., and Rohde, J. (1993), 'Expanded Programme on Immunization: A Goal Achieved towards Health for All', in J. Rohde et al., *Reaching Health for All*, Delhi: Oxford University Press.

Hinchliffe, K. (1996), *Monetary and Non-Monetary Returns to Education in Africa*, World Bank Staff Working Paper, World Bank: Washington DC.

Hirschman, A.O. (1958), *The Strategy of Economic Development*, New Haven: Yale University Press.

Hirschman, A.O. (1970), *Exit, Voice and Loyalty: Responses to Decline in Firms, Organizations and States*, Cambridge MA: Harvard University Press.

Hirschman, A.O. (1977), *The Passions and the Interests: Political Arguments for Capitalism before its Triumph*, Princeton NJ: Princeton University Press.

Hirschman, A.O. (1981), *Essays in Trespassing*, Cambridge: Cambridge University Press.

Hjertholm, P., Laursen, J., and White, H. (2000), 'Foreign Aid and the Macroeconomy', in F. Tarp and P. Hjertholm (eds), *Foreign Aid and Development: Lessons Learnt and Directions for the Future*, London: Routledge.

Hobsbawm, E. (1969), *Industry and Empire*, Pelican Economic History of Britain, vol. 3, Harmondsworth: Penguin.

Holsey, C.M., and Borcherding, T.E. (1997), *Why Does Government's Share of National Income Grow? An Assessment of the Recent Literature on the U.S. Experience*, Cambridge, New York and Melbourne: Cambridge University Press.

Hsiao, C. (2003), *Analysis of Panel Data Analysis*, 2nd edn, Cambridge and New York: Cambridge University Press.

Human Development Centre (1997), *Human Development Report of South Asia*, Islamabad: Oxford University Press.

Human Development Centre (1998), *Human Development in South Asia: Education*, Islamabad: Oxford University Press.

IEO (Independent Evaluation Office) (2003a), *Evaluation of the Prolonged Use of IMF Resources*, Washington DC: IMF, Independent Evaluation Office.

IEO (Independent Evaluation Office) (2003b), *Fiscal Adjustment in IMF-Supported Programmes. Evaluation Report*, Washington DC: IMF, Independent Evaluation Office.

IEO (Independent Evaluation Office) (2004), *Evaluation of PRSPs and PRGFs*, Washington DC: IMF, Independent Evaluation Office.

IFAD (2002), 'Strategic Framework for Ifad 2002–2006', www.ifad.org.

IFC (International Finance Corporation) (2002b), *Investing in Private Health Care: Strategic Directions for IFC*, Washington DC: International Finance Corporation.

IFC (International Finance Corporation) (2002a), *IFC Strategic Directions*, Washington DC: International Finance Corporation.

IIPS (International Institute of Populations Studies) (1995), *National Family Health Survey (MCH and Family Planning), India 1992–93*, Bombay: IIPS.

IIPS (International Institute of Population Sciences) (2000), *National Family Health Survey, 1998–9*, Mumbai: International Institute of Population Sciences.

ILO (International Labour Organization) (1991), 'Teachers: Challenges of the 1990s', Joint Meeting on Conditions of Work of Teachers, Geneva.

ILO (International Labour Organization) (2005), *World Employment Report 2005–05: Employment, Productivity and Poverty Reduction*, Geneva: ILO.

IMF (1999a), 'Heavily Indebted Poor Countries (HIPC) Initiative – Strengthening the Link between Debt Relief and Poverty Reduction', paper prepared by the Bank–Fund Joint Implementation Committee, Washington DC: International Monetary Fund/World Bank.

IMF (1999b), 'Military Spending Continues to Stabilize; Some Countries Increase Social Spending', *IMF Survey* (June).

IMF (2001), *External Comments and Contributions on IMF Conditionality*, September 2001: 147.

IMF (2003), 'Aligning the Poverty Reduction and Growth Facility (PRGF) and the Poverty Reduction Strategy Paper (PRSP) Approach: Issues and Options', www.imf.org/external/np/prsp/2003/eng/042503.htm.

IMF (2004), *Global Monitoring Report 2004*, Washington DC: IMF.

IMF and IDA (2002), 'Review of the Poverty Reduction Strategy Paper (PRSP) Approach: Early Experience with Interim PSRSPs and Full PRSPs', New York: IMF and World Bank.

Institute for Sustainable Development (1998), *Analysis of Budget and Aid Restructuring in Nepal for Monitoring the 20/20 Compact*, Kathmandu.

Iriart, C., Elias, E.M., Waitzkin, H. (2001), 'Managed Care in Latin America: The New Common Sense in Health Policy Reform', *Social Science & Medicine* 52/8: 1243.

Iyer, A., and Sen, G. (2000), 'Health Sector Changes and Health Equity in the 1990s in India', in S. Roghuram (ed.), *Health and Equity*, Technical Report Series 1.8, Bangalore: HIVOS.

Jaguaribe, H. (2002), *Brasil: alternativas e saída*, São Paulo: Paz e Terra.

Jajoo, U.N. (2000), 'Health Insurance for the Poor: Innovations in Primary Health Care', in R. Jhabvala and R.K.A. Subrahmanya (eds), *The Unorganized Sector: Work Security and Social Protection,* New Delhi: Sage.

Jarrett, S.W., and Ofusu-Amaah, S. (1992), 'Strengthening Health Services for MCH in Africa: The First Four Years of the "Barnako Initiative"', *Health Policy and Planning* 7/2: 164–76.

Jayarajah, C., Branson, W., and Sen, B. (1996), 'Social Dimensions of Adjustment: World Bank Experience, 1980–1993', *World Bank Operations Evaluations Study*, Washington DC: World Bank.

Jellife, D.B., and Jellife, F.P. (1978), *Human Milk in the Modern World*, Oxford: Oxford University Press.

Jhabvala, R., and Subrahmanya, R.K.A. (eds) (2000), *The Unorganized Sector: Work Security and Social Protection*, New Delhi: Sage.

Jimenez, E. (1986), 'The Public Subsidization of Education and Health in Developing Countries:

A Review of Equity and Efficiency', *World Bank Research Observer* 1/1: 110–29.

Jimenez, E. (1987), *Pricing Policy in the Social Sectors: Cost Recovery for Education and Health in Developing Countries*, Baltimore: Johns Hopkins University Press.

Jimenez, E., and Lockheed, M. (1995), *Public and Private Secondary Education in Developing Countries: A Comparative Study*, World Bank Discussion Paper No. 309, Washington DC: World Bank.

Jimenez, E., Lockheed, M., Luna, E., and Paqueo, V. (1991a), 'School Effects and Costs for Private and Public Schools in the Dominican Republic', *International Journal of Educational Research* 15: 393–410.

Jimenez, E., Lockheed, E., and Paqueo, V. (1991b), 'The Relative Efficiency of Private and Public Schools in Developing Countries', *World Bank Research Observer* 6, 205–18.

Jolly, R. (1997), 'Profiles in Success: Reasons for Hope and Priorities for Action', in S. Mehrotra and R. Jolly (eds), *Development with a Human Face: Experiences in Social Achievement and Economic Growth*, Oxford: Clarendon Press.

Jomo K.S. (2005), 'Economic Reform for Whom?', *Post-autistic Economics Review* 35.

Jomo K.S., and Fine, B. (2005), *The New Development Economics: After the Washington Consensus*, London: Zed Books.

Jones, P. (1992), *World Bank Financing of Education: Lending, Larning and Development*, London: Routledge.

Kähkonen, S., and Lanyi, A. (eds) (2000), *Institutions, Incentives and Economic Reforms in India*, New Delhi, Sage Publications.

Kakwani, N., Khandker, S., and Son, H. (2004), *Pro-Poor Growth: Concepts and Measurements with Country Case Studies*, International Poverty Centre Working Paper 1, Brasilia: UNDP, August.

Kamanga, I. (1998), *A Proposal on Monitoring the 20/20 Compact on Budget and Aid*, Lusaka: UNICEF–UNDP Country Study.

Kanbur, R. (2000), 'Aid, Conditionality and Debt in Africa', in F. Tarp and P. Hjertholm (eds), *Foreign Aid and Development: Lessons Learnt and Directions for the Future*, London: Routledge.

Kanbur, R. (2001), 'Economic Policy, Distribution and Poverty: The Nature of Disagreements', *World Development* 29/6: 1083–94.

Kanbur, R., and Todd, S., with Morrison, K. (1999), *The Future of Development Assistance: Common Pools and International Public Goods*, Policy Essay 25, Washington DC: Overseas Development Council.

Kanbur, R., and Squire, L. (1999), *The Evolution of Thinking about Poverty: Exploring the Interactions*, Department of Agricultural Resource, and Managerial Economics, Working Paper 99–24, Ithaca NY: Cornell University.

Kanji, N., Hardon, A., Harnmeijer, J., Mamdani, M., and Walt, G. (eds) (1992), *Drug Policy in Developing Countries*, London: Zed Books.

Kar, S.B., Pascual, C.A., and Chickering, K.L. (1999), 'Empowerment of Women for Health Promotion: A Meta-Analysis', *Social Science and Medicine* 49: 1431–60.

Kayani, L., and Papenfuss, A. (2005), *Do the PRSPs Really Help Reduce Poverty? A Critical Analysis of the Tanzanian Poverty Reduction Strategy Paper (PRSP) Process and Its Impact on Child Poverty*, New York: UNICEF Working Paper.

Kelley, C. (1997), 'Teacher Compensation and Organization', *Educational Evaluation and Policy Analysis* 19/1: 15–28.

Kent, G. (1991), *The Politics of Children's Survival*, New York: Praeger.

Khan, A.H. (1997), 'The Sanitation Gap: Development's Deadly Menace', *Program of Nations*, New York: UNICEF.

Khan, M.H. (2001), 'The New Political Economy of Corruption', in B. Fine, C. Lapavitsas and J. Pincus (eds), *Development Policy in the Twenty-first Century: Beyond the Post-Washington Consensus*, London and New York: Routledge.

Khattri, G.B., and Friedan, T. (2002), 'Controlling Tuberculosis in India', *New England Journal of Medicine* 347/18: 1420–25.

Khundker, N., Kibria, R., Ghulam Hussain, A.K.M., Syed, I.A., and Nazneen, K. (1999), *Aid and Budget Restructuring in Bangladesh*, Dhaka: UNICEF–UNDP.

King, E. (1995), 'Does the Price of Schooling Matter? Fees, Opportunity Costs and Enrollment in Indonesia', World Bank, mimeo.

King, K., and Buchert, L. (eds) (1999), *Changing International Aid to Education: Global Patterns and National Contexts*, Paris: UNESCO/NORRAG.

Kingdon, G.G., and Muzammil, M. (2001), 'A Political Economy of Education in India: The Case of U.P.', *Economic and Political Weekly* 36/32.

Kingdon, G.G. (1994), 'An Economic Evaluation of School Management Types in Urban India – A Case Study of Uttar Pradesh', D. Phil. thesis, University of Oxford.

Knox, R.A. (1993), *Germany: One Nation With Health Care for All*, Washington DC: Faulkner & Gray's Healthcare Information Center.

Koivusalo, M. (1999), *World Trade Organization and Trade-Creep in Health and Social Policies*, GASPP Occasional Papers No. 4.

Komives, K. (1998), 'Designing Pro-Poor Water and Sewer Concessions: Early Lessons from Bolivia', Washington DC: World Bank, Private Sector Development Division, mimeo.

Korbi, W. (2000), 'Welfare States, Economic Growth, and Scholarly Objectivity', *Challenge* 43/2: 49–66.

Kremer, M. (2003), 'Evidence from a Study of Vouchers for Private Schooling in Colombia', background paper for the *World Bank Development Report 2004*.

Kremer, M., Muralidharan, K., Chaudhury, N., Hammer, J., and Rogers, H. (2004), 'Teacher Absence in India', working draft, Washington DC: World Bank.

Krishnan, T.N. (1997), 'The Route to Social Development in Kerala: Social Intermediation and Public Action', in S. Mehrotra and R. Jolly (eds), *Development with a Human Face. Experiences in Social Achievement and Economic Growth*, Oxford: Clarendon Press.

Kuczynski, P.-P., and Williamson, J. (eds) (2003), *After the Washngton Consensus: Restarting Growth and Reform in Latin America*, Washington DC: Institute for International Economics.

Kumar, D. (1965), *Land and Caste in South India*, Cambridge: Cambridge University Press.

Lai Pingyao (2002), 'Foreign Direct Investment in China: Recent Trends and Patterns', *China and World Economy* 2.

Lal, D., and Myint, H. (1996), '*The Political Economy of Poverty, Equity and Growth: A Comparative Study*, Oxford: Clarendon Press.

Lancaster, H.O. (1990), *Expectation of Life: A Study in the Demography, Statistics and History of World Mortality*, New York: Springer Verlag.

Landes, D.S. (1969), *The Unbound Prometheus: Technological Change and Industrial Development in Western Europe from 1750 to the Present*, London: Cambridge University Press.

Lavy, V., and Germain, J.-M. (1994), *Quality and Cost in Health Care Choice in Developing Countries*, LSMS Working Paper No. 105, Washington DC: World Bank.

Lazo, J.F. (1998), *Gasto Público en Servicios Sociales Básico en El Salvador*, San Salvador: UNICEF–UNDP.

Lee, T.R. (2002), 'Improving the Management of Water Supply and Sanitation Systems in Latin America', *The Water Page*, Santiago, Chile: ECLAC.

Lee, T.R., and Jouravlev, A. (1998), 'Prices, Property and Markets in Water Allocation', Santiago, Chile: ECLAC.

Leipziger, D., and Foster, V. (2003), 'Is Privatisation Good for the Poor?', Washington DC: International Finance Corporation.

Lensink, R., and White, H. (2000), 'Assessing Aid: A Manifesto for Aid in the 21st Century', *Oxford Development Studies* 28/1 (February).

Lesourne, J., and Orléan, A. (eds) (1998), *Advances in Self-Organization and Evolutionary Economics*, Paris: Economica.

Levine, R., and Radelet, D. (1992), 'Cross-country Growth Regressions', *American Economic Review* 84/2: 942–63.

Levy-Bruhl, D., Soucat, A., Osseni, R., Ndiaye, J.-M., Dieng, B., de Bethune, X., Diallo, A.T., Conde, M., Cisse, M., Moussa, Y., Drame, K., and Knippenbery, R. (1997), 'The Bamako Institute in Benin and Guinea: Improving the Effectiveness of Primary Health Care', *International Journal of Health Planning and Management* 12 (Suppl.1): S49–S79.

Lewis, W.A. (1955), *The Theory of Economic Growth*, London: Allen & Unwin.

Lewis, W.A. (1978), *The Evolution of the International Economic Order*, Princeton NJ: Princeton University Press.

Li, H., and Zou, H. (1998), 'Income Inequality is Not Harmful for Growth: Theory and Evidence', *Review of Development Economics* 2/3: 318–34.

Lindblom, C.E. (1959), 'The Science of 'Muddling Through'', *Public Administration Review* 19: 79–88.

Lindert, P.H. (1994), 'The Rise of Social Spending, 1880–1930', *Explorations in Economic History* 31/1 (January).

Lindert, P.H. (2000), 'What Drives Social Spending, 1980–2020', University of California–Davis, mimeo.

Lindert, P.H. (2001), *Democracy, Decentralisation and Man Schooling Before 1914*, Working Paper No. 104, Agricultural History Center, University of California–Davis.

Lindert, P.H. (2004), *Growing Public: Social Spending and Economic Growth since the Eighteenth Century*, Cambridge: Cambridge University Press.

Lindert, P.H., and Williamson, J.G. (1983), 'English Workers' Living Standards during the Industrial Revolution: A New Look', *Economic History Review* 36/1 (February): 1–25.

Lipton, M., and Ravallion, M. (1994), 'Poverty and Policy', in J. Behrman and T.N. Srinivasan (eds), *Handbook of Development Economics*, vol. III, Amsterdam: North-Holland.

Litvack, J., and Bodart, C. (1993), 'User Fees Plus Quality Equals Improved Access to Health Care: Results of a Field Experiment in Cameroon', *Social Sciences and Medicine* 37/3.

Loayza, M., Santa Cruz, J., and Pereira, R. (1998), *Gasto público en servicios sociales básico en Bolivia*, La Paz: UNICEF–UNDP.

Lobina, E., and Hall, D. (1999), 'Public Sector Alternatives to Water Supply and Sewage Privatisation: Case Studies', PSIRU Report, presented at 9th Stockholm Water Symposium, August.

Lockheed, M., Verspoor, A., et al. (1991), *Improving Primary Education in Developing Countries*, Oxford: Oxford University Press.

Loewenson, R., and Chisvo, M. (1997), 'Rapid Social Transformation despite Economic Adjustment and Slow Growth: the Experience of Zimbabwe', in S. Mehrotra and R. Jolly (eds), *Development with a Human Face. Experiences in Social Achievement and Economic Growth*, Oxford: Clarendon Press.

Maddison, A. (1982), *Phases of Capitalist Development*, Oxford and New York: Oxford University Press.

Malkin, J., and Wildavsky, A. (1991), 'Why the Distinction between Private and Public Goods Should be Abandoned', *Journal of Theoretical Politics* 3: 355–78.

Mamdani, M. (1996), *The Political Economy of Democratic Decentralization*, Kampala: Fountain Publishers.

Manasan, R.G., and Llanto, G.M. (1994), *Financing Social Programmes in the Philippines: Public Policy and Budget Restructuring*, Manila: UNICEF–UNDP.

Mann, Susan (1990), *Agrarian Capitalism in Theory and Practice*, Chapel Hill: North Carolina University Press.

Marcus, R., and Wilkinson, J. (2002), *Whose Poverty Matters? Vulnerability, Social Protection and PRSPs*, London: Childhood Poverty Research and Policy Centre.

Marglin, S. (1984), *Growth, Distribution and Prices*, Cambridge MA: Harvard University Press.

Marshall, A. (1920), *Principles of Economics*, 8th edn, London: Macmillan.

Mason, S., et al. (1980), *The Economic and Social Modernization of the Republic of Korea*, Cambridge, MA: Harvard University Press.

Masuy–Stroobant, G. (1999), 'Infant Health and Infant Mortality in Europe: Lessons from the Past and Challenges for the Future', in C.A. Corsini and P.P. Viazzo (eds), *The Decline of Infant Mortality in Europe, 1800–1950: Four National Case Studies*, Florence: UNICEF and Innocenti Research Centre.

McCloskey, D., and Ziliak, T. (1996), 'The Standard Error of Regression', *Journal of Economic Literature*, March: 97–114.

McGillivray, M., and Morrissey, O. (2001), 'Aid Illusion and Public Sector Fiscal Behaviour', *Journal of Development Studies* 37/6.

Mcginn, N., and Borden, A.M. (1994), *Framing Questions, Constructing Answers: Linking Research with Policy in Developing Countries*, Cambridge, MA: Harvard Institute for International Development.

McKeown, T. (1976), *The Modern Rise of Population*, London: Edward Arnold.

McKinley, T. (2004), 'MDG-Based PRSPs Need More Ambitious Economic Policies', UNDP Discussion Paper, New York: UNDP.

McPake, B., Asiimwe, D., Mwesignye, F., et al. (1999), *The Economic Behaviour of Health Workers in Uganda: Implications for Quality and Accessibility of Public Health Services*, PHP Departmental Publication No. 27, London School of Hygiene and Tropical Medicine.

Mead, D.C., and Liedholm, C. (1998), 'The Dynamics of Micro and Small Enterprises in Developing Countries', *World Development* 26/1: 61–74.

Meerman, J. (1979), *Public Expenditures in Malaysia: Who Benefits and Why?*, New York: Oxford University Press.

Mehrotra, S. (1990), *India and the Soviet Union: Trade and Technology Transfer*, Cambridge: Cambridge University Press.

Mehrotra, S. (1996), 'Domestic Liberalization Policies and Public Finance: Poverty Implications', in *Globalisation and Liberalisation: Effects of International Economic Relations on Poverty*, New York and Geneva: UNCTAD.

Mehrotra, S. (1997), 'Health and Education Policies in High-Achieving Countries: Some Lessons', in S. Mehrotra and R. Jolly (eds), *Development with a Human Face: Experiences in Social Achievement and Economic Growth*, Oxford: Clarendon Press.

Mehrotra, S. (1998a), 'Mitigating the Social Impact of the Economic Crisis: A Review of the Royal Thai Governments Responses', Bangkok: UNICEF–UNDP, mimeo.

Mehrotra, S. (1998b), 'Education for All: Policy Lessons from High Achieving Countries', *International Review of Education* 44/5–6: 461–84.

Mehrotra S. (1999), 'Improving Cost-Effectiveness and Mobilizing Resources for Primary Education in Sub-Saharan Africa', *Prospects* 28/3.

Mehrotra, S. (2000), *Integrating Economic and Social Policy: Good Practices from High-Achieving Countries*, Innocenti Working Papers No. 80, Florence: UNICEF Innocenti Research Centre.

Mehrotra, S. (2002a), 'Some Methodological Issues in Determining Good Practices in Social Policy: The Case of High-Achieving Countries', in E. Oyen et al. (eds), *Best Practices in Poverty Reduction: An Analytical Framework*, London: Zed Books.

Mehrotra, S. (2002b), 'The Capabilities and Human Rights of Women: Towards and Alternative Framework for Development', paper at conference on Women and Capabilities, St Edmund's College, Cambridge University, http://santoshmehrotra.org.

Mehrotra, S. (2004a), *Improving Child Well-being in Developing Countries: What Do We Know? What Can Be Done?*, Chip Report No. 9, Childhood Poverty Research and Policy Centre, London.

Mehrotra, S. (2004b), 'Child Malnutrition and Gender Discrimination in South Asia: Is the Worst Malnutrition Linked to the Worst Gender Discrimination in the World', in R. Thakur and O. Wiggen (eds), *South Asia in the World: Problem Solving Perspectives on Security, Sustainable*

Development, and Good Governance, Tokyo: United Nations University Press.

Mehrotra, S. (2004c), 'Job Law Can Sharply Cut Poverty this Decade', *Economic and Political Weekly* 39/5 (December).

Mehrotra, S. (2005b), 'Governance and Basic Social Services: Ensuring Accountability in Service Delivery through Deep Democratic Decentralisation', *Journal of International Development* 18/2.

Mehrotra, S. (ed.) (2006a), *The Economics of Elementary Education in India: The Challenge of Public Finance, Private Provision and Household Costs*, New Delhi: Sage.

Mehrotra, S. (2006b), 'Democracy, Decentralization and Access to Basic Services: An Elaboration on Sen's Capability Approach', in S. Alkire, F. Gormin and M. Qizilbash (eds), *The Capability Approach: Concepts, Measures and Applications*, Cambridge: Cambridge University Press.

Mehrotra, S. (2006c), 'Governance and Access to Basic Social Services: Ensuring Accountability in Service Delivery through Deep Democracy', *Journal of International Development* 18/2.

Mehrotra, S., and Biggeri, M. (2002a), *The Subterranean Child Labour Force: Sub-contracted Home Manufacturing in Asia*, Innocenti Working Paper No. 96, Florence: UNICEF Innocenti Research Centre.

Mehrotra, S., and Biggeri, M. (2002b), *Social Protection in the Informal Economy: Home-based Women Workers and Outsourced Manufacturing in Asia*, Innocenti Working Paper No. 97, Florence: UNICEF Innocenti Research Centre.

Mehrotra, S., and Biggeri, M. (2005), 'Can Industrial Outwork Enhance Home Workers' Capabilities: Evidence from South Asian Clusters', *World Development* 33/10.

Mehrotra, S., and Biggeri, M. (2006), *Asian Informal Workers: Global Risks, Local Protection*, London: Routledge.

Mehrotra, S., and Buckland, P. (1998), *Managing Teacher costs for Access and Quality*, Evaluation, Policy and Planning Working Paper No. 4, New York: UNICEF.

Mehrotra, S., and Delamonica, E. (1998), 'Household Costs and Public Expenditure on Primary Education in Five Low Income Countries: A Comparative Analysis', *International Journal of Educational Development* 18/1: 11–61.

Mehrotra, S., and Jarrett, S. (2002), 'Improving Health Services in Low-Income Countries: Voice for the Poor', *Social Science and Medicine* 54: 1685–90.

Mehrotra, S., and Jolly, R. (eds) (1997), *Development with a Human Face: Experiences in Social Achievement and Economic Growth*, Oxford: Clarendon Press.

Mehrotra, S., Baek, H.J., and Park, I.-H. (1997), 'Social Policies in a Growing Economy: The Role of the State in the Republic of Korea', in S. Mehrotra and R. Jolly (eds), *Development with a Human Face: Experiences in Social Achievement and Economic Growth*, Oxford: Clarendon Press.

Mehrotra, S., Panchamukhi, P.R., Srivastava, R., and Srivastava, R. (2005), *Universalizing Elementary Education in India: Uncaging the 'Tiger' Economy*, New Delhi: Oxford University Press.

Mills, A. (1997), 'Improving the Efficiency of Public Sector Health Services in Developing Countries: Bureaucratic versus Market Approaches', in C. Colclough (ed.), *Marketizing Education and Health in Developing Countries: Miracle or Mirage?* Oxford: Clarendon Press.

Minsky, H.P. (1975), *John Maynard Keynes*, New York: Columbia University Press.

Mirrlees, J. (1976), 'Optimal Tax Theory: A Synthesis', *Journal of Public Economics* 6/4: 327–58.

Mitchell, B.R. (1980), *European Historical Statistics 1750–1975*, 2nd edn, London: Macmillan.

Mitchell-Weaver, C., and Manning, B. (1991–92), 'Public–Private Partnerships in Third World Development: A Conceptual Overview', *Studies in Comparative International Development* 26/4: 45–67.

Mkandawire, T. (ed.) (2004), *Social Policy in a Development Context*, New York: Palgrave Macmillan.

Mookherjee, D. (1997), 'Incentive Reforms in Developing Country. Bureaucracies: Lessons from Tax Administration', paper published for the Annual World Bank Conference on Development Economics, International Bank for Reconstruction and Development/World Bank.

Moore, B. (1966), *The Social Origins of Dictatorship and Democracy: Lord and Peasant in the Making of the Modern World*, Boston MA: Beacon Press.

Moore, B. (1988), *Horizontalists and Verticalists: The Macroeconomics of Credit Money*, New York: Cambridge University Press.

Moore, M. (1998), 'Death without Taxes: Democracy, State Capacity and Aid Dependence in the Fourth World', in M. Robinson and G. White (eds), *The Democratic Developmental State: Political and Institutional Design*, Oxford: Oxford University Press.

Moore, M., et al. (2005), 'Signposts to More Effective States: Responding to Governance Challenges in Developing Countries', Centre for the Future State, Institute of Development Studies, Brighton.

Morrison, K. (1999), 'Don't Make Debt Relief a Burden', *ODC Viewpoint*, Washington, DC: Overseas Development Council, September.

Moyo, S. (2004), 'Dominance of Ethnic and Racial Groups: The African Experience', background paper to *Human Development Report 2004*, New York: UNDP.

Mukand, S.W., and Rodrik, D. (2002), 'In Search of the Holy Grail: Policy Convergence, Experimentation and Economic Performance', *American Economic Review* 95/1: 374–83.

Mundy, K. (1998), 'Educational Multilateralism at a Crossroads', in K. King and L. Buchert (eds), *Changing International Aid to Education*, UNESCO Publishing/Norrag.

Muzammil, M. (1989), *Financing of Education*, New Delhi: Ashish Publishing House.

Mwabu, G., Ainsworth, M., and Nyamete, A. (1993), 'Quality and Medical Care and Choice of Medical Treatment in Kenya: An Empirical Analysis', *Journal of Human Resources* 29/4: 838–62.

Mwabu, G., Ugaz, C., and White, G. (eds) (2001), *Social Provision in Low-Income Countries: New Patterns and Emerging Trends*, Oxford: WIDER Studies in Development Economics and Oxford University Press.

Myrdal, G. (1953), *The Political Element in the Development of Economic Theory*, London: Routledge & Kegan Paul.

Narayan, D. (2000), *Voices of the Poor*, Washington DC: World Bank.

Narayan, D., with Patel, R., Shaff., R.A., and Koch-Schulte, S. (2000), *Voices of the Poor: Can Anyone Hear Us?*, Oxford: Oxford University Press for the World Bank.

National Economic and Social Development Board (Office of the Prime Minister), Kanok Wattana Consultant Co., *Assessment of Basic Social Services Financing in Thailand*, Bangkok: UNICEF–UNDP.

National Report (1998), *Government of Vietnam Basic Social Services in Vietnam: An Analysis of State Public and Donor Expenditures*, Hanoi: UNICEF–UNDP.

Naughton, B. (1994), *Growing Out of the Plan: Chinese Economic Reform, 1978–1993*, Cambridge: Cambridge University Press.

Nayyar, D. (ed.) (2002), *Governing Globalization: Issues and Institutions*, New York: Oxford University Press.

Nell, E. (1992), *Transformational Growth and Effective Demand*, New York: New York University Press.

Nell, E. (1998), *General Theory of Transformational Growth*, Cambridge: Cambridge University Press.

Nelson, J. (1996), *Feminism, Objectivity and Economics*, London and New York: Routledge.

Nelson, R., and Winter, S. (1982), *An Evolutionary Theory of Economic Change*, Cambridge MA: Harvard University Press.

Neri, M.C., Carvalho, A.P., Abrahão de Castro, J., Datrino, M.F., Macedo, M., Nascimento, M.C., Piola, S., Ribeiro, J.A., and Filho, J.S. (1998), *Gasto Público en Servicios Sociales Básico en Brasil*, Brasilia: UNICEF–UNDP.

Nganda, B.M., and Ong'olo, D.O. (1998), *Public Expenditures on Basic Social Services in Kenya*, Nairobi: UNICEF–UNDP.

Nigam, A., Gujja, B., Bandyopadhyay, J., and Talbot, R. (1997), *Fresh Water for India's Children and Nature*, New Delhi: World Wildlife Fund and UNICEF, December.

Nigam, A., and Rasheed, S. (1998), 'Financing of Fresh Water for All', *UNICEF Staff Working Papers*, EPP-EVL 98–003.

NIPCCD (1992), *National Evaluation of Integrated Child Development Scheme*, New Delhi: National Institute of Public Cooperation and Child Development.

Nittaramphong, S., and Tsangcharoensathien, V. (1994), 'Thailand: Private Health Care Out of Control?', *Health Policy and Planning* 9/1: 31–40.

Nolan, P. (1995), *China's Rise, Russia's Fall: Politics, Economics and Planning in the Transition from Stalinism*, London: Macmillan.

Nolan, P. (2003), *China at the Crossroads*, Cambridge: Polity Press.

Normand, C. (1997), 'Health Insurance: A Solution to the Financing Gap?', in C. Colclough (ed.), *Marketizing Education and Health in Developing Countries: Miracle or Mirage?*, Oxford: Clarendon Press.

North, D.C. (2001), 'The Process of economic Change', in G. Mwabu, C. Ugaz and G. White (eds), *Social Provision in Low-Income Countries: New Patterns and Emerging Trends*, Oxford: WIDER Studies in Development Economics and Oxford University Press.

Nussbaum, M. (2000), *Women and Human Development: The Capability Approach*, Cambridge: Cambridge University Press.

Ocampo, J.A. (ed.) (2004), *El desarrollo económico en los albores del siglo XXI*, Bogotá: Alfaomega.

Ocampo, J.A., and Taylor, L. (1998), *Trade Liberalization in Developing Economies: Modest Benefits but Problems with Productivity Growth, Macro Prices, and Income Distribution*, Center for Economic Policy Analysis Working Paper No. 8, March.

OECD (1996a), *Shaping the 21st Century: The Contribution of Development Cooperation*, Development Assistance Committee (DAC), Paris: OECD.

OECD (1996b), *Development Cooperation, Efforts and Policies of the Members of the Development Assistance Committee, 1995 Report*, Paris: OECD.

OECD (1999), *Opportunities and Constraints for Better Donor Reporting on Social Services*, Paris: OECD.

OECD (2000), 'Measuring Aid to Basic Social Services', DAC Secretariat contribution to the World Summit for Social Development (WSSD + S), Geneva, June.

OECD (2001), *The DAC Journal Development Cooperation Report 2000*, Paris: OECD.

OECD (2005), *Economic Survey of China 2005*, Paris: OECD.

OECD/DAC (1999), *The DAC Journal Development Cooperation Report 1999*, Paris: OECD.

OECD/DAC (2002), *The DAC Journal Development Cooperation Report 2002*, Paris: OECD.

OECD/DAC (2003), *The DAC Journal Development Cooperation Report 2003*, Paris: OECD.

OECD/DAC/DCR (1998), *Shaping the 21st Century: The Contribution of Development Co-operation*, Paris: OECD.

Oey-Gardiner, M., Suleeman, E., Brodjonegoro, B., Tjandraningsih, I., Hartanto, W., Wijaya, H., and Sejahtera, I.H. (2001), *Women and Children Home-based Workers in Selected Sectors of Indonesia*, Florence: UNICEF Innocenti Research Centre.

Opio, F., Kalibwani, K., and Tumukwasibwe, E. (1998), *Uganda's Basic Social Services Achievements: Monitoring the 20/20 Compact. A Report on Allocation of National Resources And Donor Aid, and Proposals for Possible Restructuring, in Support of Basic Social Services*, Kampala: UNICEF–UNDP.

Or, Z. (2000), 'Determinants of Health Outcomes in Industrial Countries: A Pooled, Cross-country, Time-series Analysis', *OECD Economic Studies* 30/1: 53–77.

Orshansky. M. (1965), 'Counting the Poor: Another Look at the Poverty Profile', *Social Security Bulletin* 28/1 (January): 3–29.

Osmani, S.R. (1997), 'Poverty and Nutrition in South Asia', *Nutrition and Poverty*, ACC/SCN Policy Paper No. 16, Geneva: SCC/CAN.

Oxfam International (2000), *HIPC Leaves Poor Countries Heavily in Debt: New Analysis*, 23 September, www.oxfam.org.

Oxfam International (2004), *Trading Away Our Rights: Women Working in Global Supply Chains*, www.oxfam.org.

Oxford Policy Management (1997), *Sector Investment Programmes in Africa: Issues and Experiences*, Oxford: Oxford Policy Management.

Pachauri, S. (1994), *Reaching India's Poor: Non-Governmental Approaches to Community Health*, New Delhi: Sage.

Pack, H. (1992), 'Endogenous Growth Theory: Intellectual Appeal and Empirical Shortcomings', *Journal of Economic Perspectives* 8 (Winter).

Palley, T. (1998), *Plenty of Nothing: The Downsizing of the American Dream and the Case for Structural Keynsianism*, Princeton: Princeton University Press.

Parry, T.R. (1997), 'Achieving Balance in Decentralization: A Case Study of Education Decentralization in Chile', *World Development* 25/2: 211–25.

Patnaik, U. (2005), 'Principal Task on the Agrarian Front', in S.V. Rangacharyulu (ed.), *Guaranteed Employment for the Rural Poor*, vol. 2, Hyderabad: National Institute for Rural Development.

Paul, S. (1992), 'Accountability in Public Services: Exit, Voice and Control', *World Development* 20/7: 1047–60.

Pittok, J. (2002), 'The Johannesburg Summit: More Pipes Will Not Solve the World's Water Crisis', *International Herald Tribune*, 13 August.

Planning Commission (2002), *The Tenth Five Year Plan 2002–2007*, vol. 1, New Delhi: Government of India.

Polak, B., and Williamson, J.G. (1991), *Poverty, Policy and Industrialization: Lessons from the Distant Past*, World Bank Working Paper No. 645, April.

Polanyi, K. (1944), *The Great Transformation: The Political and Economic Origins of Our Times*, New York: Rinehart.

Portes, A. (1990), 'When More Can Be Less: Labour Standards, Development, and the Informal Economy', in S Herzenberg and J. Perez-Lopez (eds), *Labour Standards and Development in the Global Economy*, Washingon DC: US Department of Labor.

Potter, B., and Diamond, J. (1999), *Guidelines for Public Expenditure Management*, IMF, www.imf.org/external/pubs/ft/expend/index.htm.

Prabhu, K.S. (1995), 'Structural Adjustment and Financing of Elementary Education: The Indian Experience, *Journal of Educational Planning and Administration* 9.

Prennushi, G. (1999), *Nepal: Poverty at the Turn of the Twenty-first Century'*, South Asia Region Discussion Paper No. 174, Washington DC: World Bank.

Preston, S.H. (1976), 'The Changing Relationship between Mortality and Level of Economic Development', *Population Studies* 29/2: 231–47.

Preston, S.H., and Haines, M.R. (1991), *Fatal Years: Child Mortality in the Late Nineteenth Century America*, Princeton NJ: Princeton University Press.

Pritchett, L. (1994a), 'Desired Fertility and the Impact of Population Policies', *Population and Development Review* 20/1.

Pritchett, L. (1994b), 'The Impact of Population Policies: Reply', *Population and Development Review* 20/3.

Pritchett, L., and Woolcock, M. (2002), *Solutions when the Solution is the Problem: Arraying the Disarray in Development*, Working Paper No. 10, Washington DC: Center for Global Development.

PROBE (1999), *Public Report on Basic Education in India*, Delhi: Oxford University Press.

Pronk, J. (2001), 'Aid as a Catalyst', *Development and Change* 32/4: 6111–29.

Prost, A. (1981), *Histoire générale de l'enseignement en France, 1800–1967*, Paris: Armand Colin.

Psacharapolous, G., Tan, J.P., and Jimenez, E. (1986), *Financing Education in Developing Countries*, Washington DC: World Bank.

Psacharapoulos, G., and Woodhall, M. (1990), *Education for Development: An Analysis of 'Investment' Choices*, Oxford: Oxford University Press.

Putnam, R. (1993), *Making Democracy Work: Civic Traditions in Modern Italy*, Princeton NJ: Princeton University Press.

Pyatt, G. (1999), 'Poverty versus the Poor', Dies Natalis Address, Institute of Social Studies, 1996, reproduced in G. Pyatt and M. Ward (eds), *Identifying the Poor: Papers on Measuring Poverty to Celebrate the Bicentenary of the Publication in 1797 of the State of the Poor by Sir Frederick Morton Eden*. Amsterdam: IOS Press.

Radwan, I. (1997), *Monitoring the 20/20 Compact*, Windhoek: UNICEF–UNDP.

Ramachandran, V. (1998), 'The Indian Experience', in *Bridging the Gap Between Intention and Action: Girls' and Women's Education in South Asia*, New York: UNESCO.

Ramachandran, V., and Sethi, H. (2000), *Rajasthan Shiksha Karmi Project: An Overall Appraisal*, New Education Division Documents No. 7, Stockholm: Swedish International Development Cooperation Agency (SIDA).

Ramalingaswami, V., Jonsson, U., and Rohde, J. (1996), 'The Asian Enigma', *Program of Nations*, New York: UNICEF.

Ramsey, F. (1927), 'A Contribution to the Theory of Taxation', *Economic Journal* 37/45: 47–61.

Ranis, G., and Stewart, F. (2000), 'Economic Growth and Human Development', *World Development* 28/2: 197–219.

Rannan-Eliya, R., Senagama, R., Weerakoon, D., and Aturupane, H. (1998), *Monitoring the 20/20 Compact on Budget and Aid Restructuring: Sri Lanka, Colombo*: UNICEF–UNDP.

Rao, M.G. (2000), 'Fiscal Decentralization in Indian Federalism', Bangalore: Institute of Economic and Social Change, mimeo.

Rao, M.G., and Singh, N. (2005), *Political Economy of Federalism in India*, New Delhi: Oxford University Press.

Ravallion, M. (1997), 'Good and Bad Growth: The Human Development Reports', *World Development* 25/5: 631–8.

Ravallion, M. (2004), *Pro-poor Growth: A Primer*, Development Research Group, Washington DC: World Bank.

Ravallion, M., and Chen, S. (1997), 'What Can New Survey Data Tell Us about Recent Changes in Distribution and Poverty?', *World Bank Economic Review* 11, May.

Reddy, S., and Miniou, C. (2002), 'Stagnation! Growth Failures, Coping Strategies and Human Development: Cross-Country Evidence and Policy Implications', background paper for UNDP *Human Development Report 2003*.

Reddy, S., and Pogge, T. (2002), 'How Not to Count the Poor', Columbia University, New York.

Reddy, S., and Vandemoortele, J. (1996), *User Financing of Basic Social Services: A Review of Theoretical Arguments and Empirical Evidence*, Evaluation, Policy and Planning, Working Paper No. 6, New York: UNICEF.

Reinert, E. (2003), 'Increasing Poverty in a Globalized World: Marshall Plans and Morgenthau Plans as Mechanisms of Polarization of World Incomes', in H.J. Chang (ed.), *Rethinking Development Economics*, London: Anthem Press.

Reinikka, R., and Svensson, J. (2002), *Assessing Frontline Services Delivery*, Development Research Group, Washington DC: World Bank.

Robinson, J. (1956), *The Accumulation of Capital*, London: Macmillan.

Robinson, M., and White, G. (2001), 'The Role of Civic Organization in the Provision of Social Services: Towards Synergy', in G. Mwabu, C. Ugaz and G. White (eds), *Social Provision in Low-Income Countries: New Patterns and Emerging Trends*, Oxford: WIDER Studies in Development Economics and Oxford University Press.

Rodgers, G.B. (1979), 'Income and Inequality as Determinants of Mortality: An International Cross-Section Analysis', *Population Studies* 33: 343–51.

Rodrik, D. (1998), 'Why Do More Open Economies Have Bigger Governments', Kennedy School of Government, www.ksg.harvard.edu/rodrik.

Rodrik, D. (1999a), 'Governing the Global Economy: Does One Architectural Style Fit All?', paper for the Brookings Institution Trade Policy Forum, April. www.ksg.harvard.edu/rodrik.

Rodrik, D. (1999b), *The New Global Economy and Developing Countries: Making Openness Work*, Washington DC: Overseas Development Council.

Rodrik, D. (2000), 'Development Strategies for the 21st Century', paper for conference on Developing Economies in the 21st Century, Japan, January. www.ksg.harvard.edu/rodrik

Rodrik, D. (2002), *Institutions, Integration and Geography: In Search of the Deep Determinants of Economic Growth*, www.ksg.harvard.edu/rodrik.

Rodrik, D. (2004), 'Industrial Policy for the Twenty-First Century', Kennedy School of Government, Harvard University, Cambridge MA. www.ksg.harvard.edu/rodrik.

Rohde, J. Chatterjee, M., and Morley, D. (1993), *Reaching Health for All*, Delhi: Oxford University Press.

Rohde, J.E., and Vishwanathan, H. (1995), *The Rural Private Practitioner*, New Delhi: Oxford University Press.

Rosati, F., and Tzannatos, Z. (2000), *Child Labour in Vietnam: An Economic Analysis*, World Bank Working Paper, Washington DC: World Bank.

Rosenstein-Rodan, P. (1943), 'Problems of Industrialization of Eastern and South-Eastern Europe', *Economic Journal* 53: 202–11.

Rostow, W.W. (1959), 'The Stages of Economic Growth', *Economic History Review* 12/1: 1–16.

Rostow, W.W. (1960), *The Stages of Economic Growth*, Cambridge: Cambridge University Press.

Roy, B. (1999), 'The Politics of Waste and Corruption', *Lokayan Bulletin* 16/1, July–August.

Russell, S., and Gilson, L. (1997), 'User Policies to Promote Service Access for the Poor: A Wolf in Sheep's Clothing', *International Journal of Health Services* 27/2: 359–79.

Ryan, A., and Taylor, B. (1999), 'Bangladesh: Non-formal Primary Education (NFPE), Phase II 1996–1999, Final Evaluation', unpublished report presented to the BRAC Donor Consortium, Dhaka, mimeo.

Szreter, S. (1994), 'Mortality in England in the Eighteenth and the Nineteenth Centuries: A Reply to Sumit Guha', *Social History of Medicine* 7/2: 269-82.

Sachar, R. (1999), 'Right to Information – The Constitutional Aspect', *Lokayan Bulletin* 16/2, September–October.

Sachs, W. (2005), *The End of Poverty: Economic Possibilities for Our Time*, New York: Penguin.

Sader, E., Gentili, P., and Borón, A. (1995), *Pós-neoliberalismo: as políticas sociais e o Estado democrático*, São Paulo: Paz e Terra.

Sahn, D., and Bernier R. (1995), 'Has Structural Adjustment Led to Health Sector Reform in Africa?', in P. Berman (ed.), *Health Sector Reforms in Developing Countries: Making Health Development Sustainable*, Boston MA: Harvard School of Public Health.

Saith, A. (1996), 'Reflections on South Asian Prospects in East Asian Perspective', discussion paper, Geneva: ILO.

Samoff, J. (1995), 'Which Priorities and Strategies for Education?', Oxford International Conference on Education and Development, mimeo.

Samoff, J. (1996), 'Which Priorities and Strategies for Education?', *International Journal of Educational Development* 16/3: 249–71.

Sanderson, M. (1983), *Education, Economic Change and Society in England, 1780–1870*, London: Macmillan.

Sauma, P., and Diego, J. (1998), *Trejos Gasto Público en Servicios Sociales Básico en Costa Rica*, San Jose: UNICEF–UNDP.

Save the Children (2002), *Globalisation and Children's Rights: What Role for the Private Sector?*, London: Save the Children.

Saxena, N.C. (1997), *Policy and Legal Reforms for the Poor in India*, Monograph Series No. 1, Mussoorie: LBS National Academy of Administration.

Scheetz, T. (1985), 'Gastos militares en Chile, Perú y la Argentina', *Desarrollo Economico* 25/99.

Schick, A. (1998), *A Contemporary Approach to Public Expenditure Management*, Washington DC: World Bank Institute, www.worldbank.org/publisector/pe.

Schiefelbein, E. (1997), *School-related Economic Incentives in Latin America: Reviewing Drop-out and Repetition and Combating Child Labour*, Innocenti Occasional Papers, Florence: UNICEF.

Schneider, P.E. (1998), *Gasto Público en Servicios Sociales Básico en Guatemala*, Guatemala City: UNICEF–UNDP.

Schofield, R., and Reher, D. (1991), *The Decline of Mortality in Europe*, Oxford: Clarendon Press.

Schultz, T.W. (1961), 'Investing in Human Capital', *American Economic Review* 51/1.

Schumpeter, J. (1934), *The Theory of Economic Development*, Cambridge MA: Harvard University Press.

Segall, M., Tipping, G., Lucas, H., Truong, D., et al. (2000), *Health-care Seeking by the Poor in Transitional Economics: The Case of Vietnam*, IDS Research Report 43, Institute of Development Studies, Brighton.

Selowsky, M. (1979), *Who Benefits from Government Expenditure?* New York: Oxford University Press.

Semega-Janneh, I.J. (1998), *Breastfeeding: From Biology to Policy*, ACC/SCN Nutrition Policy Paper No. 17.

Sen, A. (1982), *Choice, Welfare and Measurement*, Oxford: Basil Blackwell.

Sen, A. (1985), *Commodities and Capabilities*, Oxford: Oxford University Press.

Sen, A. (1989), *Hunger and Public Action*, Oxford: Oxford University Press.

Sen, A. (1994), 'Economic Regress: Concepts and Features', *Proceedings of the World Bank Annual Conference on Development Economics 1993*, Washington DC: World Bank.

Sen, A. (1995), 'Mortality as an Indicator of Economic Success and Failure', Innocenti Lectures, Florence: UNICEF.

Sen, A. (1998), 'Radical News and Moderate Reforms', in J. Drèze and A. Sen, *Indian Development, Selected Regional Perspectives*, study prepared for WIDER, Delhi: Oxford University Press.

Sen, A. (1999), 'Investing in Health', General Keynote Speech at 52nd World Health Assembly, May.

Sen, A. (2000), *Development as Freedom*, Oxford: Clarendon Press.

Seshadri, S. (1997), 'Nutritional Anaemia in South Asia', in Stuart Gillespie (ed.), *Malnutrition in South Asia: A Regional Profile*, Kathmandu: UNICEF, Regional Office for South Asia.

SEWA (2000), 'A Comprehensive Approach to Health Care', in R. Jhabvala and R.K.A. Subrahmanya, (eds), *The Unorganized Sector: Work Security and Social Protection*, New Delhi: Sage.

Shaikh, A. (1974), 'Laws of Algebra and Laws of Production: The Humbug Production Function', *Review of Economics and Statistics* 61/1.

Shapiro, S., Schlesinger, E.R., and Nesbitt, R.E.L., Jr. (1968), *Infant, Perinatal, Maternal and Childhood Mortality in the US*, Cambridge MA: Harvard University Press.

Shetty, P.S., and James, W.P.T. (1994), *Body Mass Index: A Measure of Chronic Energy Deficiency in Adults*, Food & Nutrition Paper 56, Rome: Food and Agriculture Organization.

Simon, H. (1991), 'Organizations and Markets', *Journal of Economic Perspectives* 5: 25–44.

Singh, A. (2000), 'Participatory Micro-Planning for Universal Primary Education, Year 2000 Assessment – Education for All, Ministry of Human Resource Development, Government of India and National Institute of Educational Planning and Administration, New Delhi.

Singh, A. (1994), 'Openness and the Market Friendly Approach to Development: Learning the Right Lessons from Development Experience', *World Development* 22/4.

Singh, A., Dutt, A., and Kim, K. (eds) (1994), *The State, Markets and Development*, Cheltenham: Edward Elgar.

SIPR (2001), *Stockholm International Peace Research Institute Yearbook*, Stockholm: Stockholm International Peace Research Institute.

Sitthi-Amorn, C., Somrongthong, R., and Janjaroen, W.S. (2001), 'Some Health Implications of Globalizaton in Thailand', *Bulletin of the World Health Organization* 79/9: 889–90.

Skocpol, T. (1992), *Protecting Soldiers and Mothers: The Political Origins of Social Policy in the United States*, Cambridge MA: Harvard University Press.

Smith, A. (1937), *The Wealth of Nations* [1776], New York: Random House.

Smith, R. (1977), Military Expenditure and Capitalism', *Cambridge Journal of Economics* 1/3.

Smith, R. (1978), 'Military Expenditure and Capitalist Stability', *Cambridge Journal of Economics* 2/3.

Sohail, M., and Cotton, A. (2001), *Public–Private Partnerships and the Poor, Interim Findings – Part A*, Water Engineering and Development Centre, Loughborough University. http://wedc.lboro.ac.uk/publications.

Solow, R. (1997), *Learning from 'Learning by Doing': Lessons for Economic Growth*, Stanford: Stanford University Press.

Sosola, R., Mwase, T., Mserembo, P., Chilima, C., Ballo, B.B., Coulibaly S., Konate, A., Traore, N., Keita, M., Drave, E.H., Traore, S., and Coulibaly, S. (1998), *Suivi de L'initiative 20/20: Financement des Secteurs Sociaux Essentiels au Mali, Contribution Essentielle à la Lutte Contre la Pauvreté*, Bamako: UNICEF–UNDP.

Sraffa, P. (1960), *Production of Commodities by Means of Commodities*, Cambridge: Cambridge University Press.

Srinivasan, T.N. (1985), 'Agricultural Production, Relative Prices, Entitlements and Poverty', in J. Mellor and G.M. Desai (eds), *Agricultural Change and Rural Poverty*, Baltimore and London: Johns Hopkins University Press.

Srinivasan, T.N. (1994), 'Database for Development Analysis: An Overview', *Journal of Development Economics* 44/1.

Srinivasan, T.N. (2000), 'The Washington Consensus a Decade Later: Ideology and the Art and Science of Policy Advice', *The World Bank Research Observer* 15/2: 265–70.

Srivastava, R. (2001), 'Access to Basic Education in Rural Uttar Pradesh', in A. Vaidyanathan and G. Nair (eds), *Elementary Education in Rural India*, Delhi: Sage.

Srivastava, R. (2005), 'Public Expenditure on Elementary Education', in S. Mehrotra et al., *Financing Elementary Education in India: Uncaging the 'Tiger' Economy*, New Delhi: Oxford University Press.

Srinivasta, R., and Amar Nath, H.K. (2001), *Central Budgetary Subsidies in India*, New Delhi: National Institute of Public Finance and Policy.

Stalker, P. (2000), *Beyond Krismon: The Social Legacy of Indonesia's Financial Crisis*, Florence: UNICEF Innocenti Research Centre. www.unicef-icdc.org.

Standing, G. (2000), 'Brave New Words: A Critique of Stiglitz's World Bank Rethink', *Development and Change* 31: 737–63.

Stein, R. (2001), 'Reforming the Water and Sanitation Sector in Africa', in regional conference on The Reform of the Water Supply and Sanitation Sector in Africa: Enhancing Public–Private Partnership in the Context of the Africa Vision for Water (2025), Kampala, 26–28 February, *Proceedings*, vol. II: *Papers and Presentations, Reform of the Water Supply and Sanitation in Africa*.

Stephens, W.B. (1998), *Education in Britain, 1750–1914*, New York: St. Martin's Press.

Stern, N. (2001), 'Open the Rich Markets to Poor Countries Exports', *International Herald Tribune*, 25 January.

Stewart, F. (1974), 'Technology and Development', *World Development*, March.

Stewart, F., and Wang, M. (2003), 'Do PRSPs Emporer Poor Countries and Disempower the World Bank, or is it the Other Way Round', QEH Working Paper 108, Queen Elizabeth House, University of Oxford.

Stiglitz, J. (1991), 'Development Strategies: The Roles of the State and the Private Sector', in *Proceedings of the World Bank's Annual Conference on Development Economics 1990*, Washington DC: World Bank

Stiglitz, J. (1997), 'The Role of Government in Economic Development', *Proceedings of the World Bank's Annual Conference on Development Economics 1996*, Washington DC: World Bank.

Stiglitz, J. (1998a), 'More Instruments and Broader Goals: Moving Toward the Post-Washington Consensus', *Annual Lecture 2* (January), Helsinki: World Institute for Development Economics Research (WIDER).

Stiglitz, J. (1998b), 'Redefining the Role of the State: What Should it do? How Should it do it? And How Should these decisions be made?', paper presented on the 10th Anniversary of MITI Research Institute (March).

Stiglitz, J. (1998c), *Towards a New Paradigm for Development: Strategies, Policies and Processes*, 9th Raoul Prebisch Lecture (October), Geneva: UNCTAD.

Stiglitz, J. (2000), 'What I Learned at the World Economic Crisis, The Insider', mimeo, April.

Stiglitz, J. (2002), *Globalization and Its Discontents*, New York: W.W. Norton.

Stiglitz, J., et al. (1989), 'The Economic Role of the State', in A. Heertje (ed.), *The Economic Role of the State*, Oxford: Basil Blackwell.

Streeten, P. (1993), 'Market and State: Against Minimalism', *World Development* 21/8: 1281–98.

Streeten, P., et al. (1981), *First Things First: Meeting Basic Needs in Developing Countries*, New York: Oxford University Press.

Sundrum, R.M. (1990), *Income Distribution in Less Developed Countries*, New York: Routledge.

Szreter, S. (1988), 'The Importance of Social Intervention in Britain's Mortality *c.* 1850–1914', *Social History of Medicine* 1/1: 1–38.

Szreter, S. (1994), 'Mortality in England in the Eighteenth and Nineteenth Centuries: A Reply to Sumit Guha', *Social Hostory of Medicine* 7/2: 269–82.

Tabatabai, H. (1996), *Statistics on Poverty and Income Distribution: An ILO Compendium of Data*, Geneva: International Labour Organization.

Tabélé-Omichessan, C., Séphou, M., Tomènou, E., Débourou, D., Gbayé, Y., Kotchoffa S., Agbota A., Faton, P., and Estève, A.R. (1998), *Bénin: Financement des Services Sociaux Essentiels*, Cotonou: UNICEF.

Tan, J.P., et al. (1984), *User Charges for Education: The Ability and Willingness to Pay in Malawi*, World Bank Staff Working Paper No. 661, Washington DC: World Bank.

Tanzi, V. (1995), *Taxation in an Integrating World*, Washington DC: Brookings Institution.

Tanzi, V. (1996), 'Is There a Need for a World Tax Organization?', paper at the International Institute of Public Finance, 52nd Congress, Tel Aviv.

Tanzi, V., and Schuknecht, L.(2000), *Public Spending in the 20th Century: A Global Perspective*, Cambridge: Cambridge University Press.

Tarp, F., and Hjertholm, P. (eds) (2000), *Foreign Aid and Development: Lessons Learnt and Directions for the Future*, London: Routledge.

Tavares Soares, L. (2003), *O desastre social*, Rio de Janeiro: Editora Record.

Tavares Soares, L. (2004), *Governo Lula: decifrando o enigma*, São Paulo: Viramundo.

Taylor, L. (1984), 'Social Choice Theory and the World in Which We Live', *Cambridge Journal of Economics* 8: 189–96.

Taylor, L. (1991), *Income Distribution, Inflation and Growth*, Cambridge MA: MIT Press.

Taylor, L. (2006), *Reconstructing Macroeconomics: Structuralist Proposals and Critiques of the Mainstream*, Cambridge MA: Harvard University Press.

Taylor, L., Mehrotra, S. and Delamonica, E. (1997), 'The Links Between Economic Growth, Poverty Reduction and Social Development: Theory and Policy', in S. Mehrotra and R. Jolly (eds), *Development with a Human Face: Experiences in Social Achievement and Economic Growth*, Oxford: Clarendon Press.

Tendler, J. (1997), *Good Governance in the Tropics*, Baltimore: Johns Hopkins University Press.

Tendler, J. (2004), 'Why Social Policy is Condemned to a Residual Category of Safety Nets and What to Do about It', in T. Mkandawire (ed.), *Social Policy in a Development Context*, New York: Palgrave Macmillan.

Tendler, J., and Freedheim, S. (1994), 'Trust in a Rent-Seeking World: Health and Government Transformed in Northeast Brazil', *World Development* 22/12: 1771–92.

Thakur, R., and Wiggen, O. (eds) (2004), *South Asia in the World: Problem Solving Perspectives on Security, Sustainable Development, and Good Governance*, Tokyo: United Nations University Press.

Thobani, M. (1983), *Charging User Fees for Social Services: The Case of Education in Malawi*, World Bank Staff Working Paper No. 572, Washington DC: World Bank.

Tilak, J.B.G. (1997), 'Lessons from Cost Recovery in Education', in C. Colclough (ed.), *Marketizing Education and Health in Developing Countries: Miracle or Mirage?*, Oxford: Clarendon Press.

Tilak, J.B.G. (2002), 'Public Subsidies in Education In India', paper presented in the Conference on India: Fiscal Policies to Accelerate Economic Growth, National Institute of Public Finance and Policy, New Delhi.

Tilak, J.B.G., and Nalla Gounden, A.M. (2006), 'The Cost and Financing of Elementary Education in a High-achieving State: Tamil Nadu', in S. Mehrotra (ed.), *The Economics of Elementary Education in India: The Challenge of Public Finance, Private Provision and Household Costs*, New Delhi: Sage.

Tilak, J.B.G., and Sudarshan, R.M. (2001), 'Private Schooling in India', paper prepared under the Research in Human Development of National Council of Applied Economic Research Programme, New Delhi.

Tobin, J. (1974), *The New Economics One Decade Older*, Eliot Janeway Lectures on Historical Economics in Honor of Joseph Schumpeter, 1972, Princeton: Princeton University Press.

Tooley, J. (1999), *The Global Education Industry: Lessons from Private Education in Developing Countries*, Studies in Education No. 7, London: Institute for Economic Affairs.

Tornqvist, N., Wenngren, B., Nguyen, T.K.C., et al. (2000), 'Antibiotic Resistance in Vietnam: an Epidemiological Indicator of Inefficent and Inequitable Use of Health Resources', in P.M. Hung et al. (eds), *Efficient Equity-Oriented Strategies for Health: International Perspectives – Focus on Vietnam*, CIMH: University of Melbourne.

Tsai, P.-L. (1995), 'Foreign Direct Investment and Income Inequality: Further Evidence', *World Development* 23/3: 469–83.

Tseng, W., and Zebregs, H. (2003), 'Foreign Direct Investment In China: Some Lessons For Other Countries', in W. Tseng and M. Rodlauer (eds), *China: Competing in the Global Economy*, Washington DC: International Monetary Fund.

Tsoka, M. (1998), *The 20/20 Initiative: Malawi Country Study*, Lilongwe: UNICEF–UNDP.

Tulsidhar, V.B. (1996), *Government Health Expenditure in India*, International Health Policy Programme Working Paper, Washington DC.

Turner, M., and Hulme, D. (1997), *Government, Administration and Development*, West Hartford CT: Kumarian Press.

UNCTAD (1996), *Globalisation and Liberalisation: Effects of International Economic Relations on Poverty*, New York and Geneva: UN Conference on Trade and Development.

UNCTAD (1999), *Trade and Development Report 1999*, New York and Geneva: UN Conference on Trade and Development.

UNCTAD (2001), *Trade and Development Report 2001*, Geneva: UN Conference on Trade and Development.

UNDP (1990), *Human Development Report: Concept and Measurement of Human Development*, New York: Oxford University Press.

UNDP (1995), *Human Development Report 1995: Gender and Human Development*, New York: Oxford University Press.

UNDP (1998), *Human Development Report 1998*, New York: Oxford University Press.

UNDP (1999a), *Human Development Report 1999*, New York: Oxford University Press.

UNDP (1999b), *Poverty Report*, New York: United Nations Development Programme.

UNDP (2000), *Poverty Report*, New York: United Nations Development Programme.

UNDP (2002), *Human Development Report 2002*, New York: Oxford University Press.

UNDP (2003), *Human Development Report 2003: Millennium Development Goals*, New York: Oxford University Press.

UNDP (2004), *Human Development Report 2004: Cultural Liberty in Today's Diverse World*, New York: Oxford University Press.

UNDP (2005), *Human Development Report 2005: International Cooperation at a Crossroads*, New York: Oxford University Press.

UNDP, UNESCO, UNFPA, UNICEF, WHO and the WORLD BANK (1998), *Implementing the 20/20 Initiative: Achieving Universal Access to Basic Social Services*, New York: UNICEF.

UNESCO (1996), *Statistical Yearbook*, Geneva: UNESCO.

UNESCO (2002), *EFA Global Monitoring Report 2002*, Paris: UNESCO Publishing.

UNESCO (2003), *Global Monitoring Report 2003/4. Gender and Education for All: The Leap to Equality,* Paris: UNESCO Publishing.

UNICEF (1995a), *A UNICEF Strategy for the Water and Sanitations Sector*, New York: Oxford University Press.

UNICEF (1995b), *State of the World's Children*, New York: Oxford University Press.

UNICEF (1998a), *Malawi: A Success Story in Education*, New York: Oxford University Press.

UNICEF (1998b), *State of the World's Children (Focus on Nutrition)*, New York: Oxford University Press.

UNICEF (1999), *State of the World's Children (Focus on Education)*, New York: Oxford University Press.

UNICEF (2000), *Poverty Reduction Begins with Children*, New York: Oxford University Press.

UNICEF (2001), *State of the World's Children (Focus on Early Childhood Care)*, New York: Oxford University Press.

United Nations (1999), *World Population Prospects 1998*, New York: United Nations.

United Nations (2000a), *Progress Made in Providing Safe Water Supply and Sanitation for All During the 1990s*, Report of the Secretary General, Commission on Sustainable Development, E/cn.17/2000/13s.

United Nations (2000b), 'Official Development Assistance in the 21st Century: Raising Confidence in the Process', Department of Economic and Social Affairs, New York, mimeo.

United Nations (2005), *Investing in Development: A Practical Plan to Achieve the Millennium Development Goals*, New York: United Nations.

Uphoff, N. (1993), 'Grassroots Organizations and NGOs in Rural Development: Opportunities with Diminishing States and Expanding Markets', *World Development* 21/4.

Uplekar, M. (1989), *Implications of Prescribing Patterns of Private Doctors in the Treatment of Tuberculosis in Bombay, India*, Research Paper No. 41, Takemi Programme in International Health, Harvard School of International Public Health, Boston.

Uvin, P. (2002), 'On High Moral Ground: The Incorporation of Human Rights by the Development Enterprise', *Praxis* 17: 19–26.

Vaidyanathan, A., and Nair, G. (eds) (2001), *Elementary Education in Rural India*, Delhi: Sage Publications.

Van de Walle, D., and Nead, K. (eds) (1995), *Public Spending and the Poor: Theory and Evidence*, Baltimore: Johns Hopkins University Press for the World Bank.

Van der Hoeven, R., and Shorrocks, A. (eds) (2003), *Perspectives on Growth and Poverty*, Delhi: Bookwell.

Vandemoortele, J. (2000), *Absorbing Social Shocks, Protecting Children and Reducing Poverty. The Role of Basic Social Services*, UNICEF Staff Paper EPP-00–001 (January), New York: UNICEF.

Vandemoortele, J., and Delamonica, E. (2000), 'Education 'Vaccine' against HIV/AIDS', *Current Issues in Comparative Education* 3/1.

Van Lerberghe, W., Coneceicao, C., Van Damme, W., and Ferrinho, P. (2002), 'When Staff is Underpaid: Dealing with Individual Coping Strategies of Health Personnel', *Bulletin of the World Health Organization* 80/7: 581–4.

Vásquez, E., Cortez, R., Parodi, C., Montes, J., and Riesco, G. (1998), *Gasto Público en Servicios Sociales Básico en Perú*, Lima: UNICEF–UNDP.

Velasquez, G., Madrid, Y., and Quick, J. (1998), *Health Reform and Drug Financing: Selected Topic – Health Economics and Drugs'* DAP Series No. 6, WHO/DAP/98.3, Geneva: World Health Organization.

Verspagen, B. (1992), 'Endogenous Innovation in Neo-classical Growth Models: A Survey', *Journal of Macroeconomics* 4/14.

Vos, R., et al. (2003), *Can Poverty Be Reduced? Experience with Poverty Reduction Strategies in Latin America*, project commissioned by Sida, The Hague: Institute for Social Studies.

Wade, R. (1985), 'The Market for Public Office: Why the Indian State is Not Better at Development', *Word Development* 13/4: 467–97.

Wade, R. (1989), 'Politics and Graft: Recruitment, Appointment, and Promotion to Public Office in India', in P.M. Ward (ed.), *Corruption, Development and Inequality: Soft Touch or Hard Graft?*, London: Routledge.

Wade, R. (1990), *Governing the Market: Economic Theory and the Role of Government in East Asian Industrialization*, Princeton NJ: Princeton University Press.

Walley, J.M., Tefera, B., and McDonald, M.A. (1991), 'Integrating Health Services – The Experience of NGOs in Ethiopia', *Health Policy and Planning* 6/4: 327–35.

Watkins, K. (2000), *The Oxfam Education Report*, London: Oxfam International.

Webster, C. (ed.) (1993), *Caring for Health: History and Diversity*, Health and Disease Series Book 6, Buckingham: Open University Press.

Webster, M., and Sansom, K. (1999), 'Public–Private Partnership and the Poor: An Initial Review', WELL Study, Loughborough University. www.lboro.ac.uk/well/.

Weisbrot, M. (2005), 'The IMF Has Lost Its Influence', *International Herald Tribune*, 22 September.

Weissman, S., and Foster, M. (2000), *World Bank Instruments and New Initiatives*, London: Overseas Development Institute.

Werner D., and Sanders, D. (1997), *Questioning the Solution: The Politics of Primary Health Care and Child Survival*. Palo Alto CA: Healthwrights.

West, E.G. (1994), *Education and the State*, Indianapolis: Liberty Fund.

Whaites, A. (2000), *PRSPs: Good News for the Poor? Social Conditionality, Participation and Poverty Reduction*, Milton Keynes: World Vision International.

White, H., and Anderson, E. (2000), 'Growth versus Distribution: Does the Pattern of Growth Matter?', Institute of Development Studies, Brighton, mimeo.

Whitehead, M., Dahlgren, G., and Evans, T. (2001), 'Equity and Health Sector Reforms: Can Low-Income Countries Escape the Medical Poverty Trap?', *The Lancet* 358/9284: 833–6.

WHO (1994), *World Health Report*, Geneva: World Health Organization.

WHO (1999), *World Health Report*, Geneva: World Health Organization.

WHO (2000), *World Health Report*, Geneva: World Health Organization.

WHO Commission (2001), *Macroeconomics and Health: Investing in Health for Economic Development*, Report of the Commission on Macroeconomics and Health, World Health Organization, December.

Wiener, M. (1995), *The Child and the State in India*, New York: W.W. Norton.

Wilkinson, R. (1994), 'Health Redistribution and Growth', in A. Glyn and D. Miliband (eds), *Paying for Inequality: the Economic Cost of Social Injustice*, London: IPPR/Rivers Oram Press.

Williamson, J. (1990), 'What Washington Means by Policy Reform', in J. Williamson (ed.), *Latin American Adjustment: How Much Has Happened?*, Washington DC: Institute of International Economics.

Williamson, J.G. (1982), 'Was the Industrial Revolution Worth It? Disamenities and Death in 19th Century British Towns', *Explorations in Economic History* 19: 221–45.

Wood, A. (1994), *North–South Trade, Employment and Inequality: Changing Fortunes in a Skill-driven World*, Oxford: Clarendon Press.

World Bank (1980), *World Development Report 1980: Poverty and Human Development*, Washington DC: World Bank.

World Bank (1986), *Financing Education in Developing Countries: An Exploration of Policy Options*, Washington DC: World Bank.

World Bank (1990a), *World Development Report 1990: Poverty*, Washington DC: World Bank.

World Bank (1990b), *Financing Health Services in Developing Countries: An Agenda for Reform*, Washington DC: World Bank.

World Bank (1991), *Feeding Latin America's Children: An Analytical Survey of Food Programmes*, Washington DC: World Bank.

World Bank (1993a), *World Development Report: Investing in Health*, Washington DC: World Bank.

World Bank (1993b), *The East Asian Miracle: Economic Growth and Public Policy*, Washington DC: World Bank.

World Bank (1994a), *World Development Report 1994: Infrastructure for Development*, Washington DC: World Bank.

World Bank (1994b), *Better Health in Africa*, Washington DC: World Bank.

World Bank (1995), *World Development Report 1995: Workers in an Integrating World*, Washington DC: World Bank.

World Bank (1996a), *India: Primary Education Achievement and Challenges*, South Asia Country Department II, Report No. 15756–IN, Washington DC: World Bank.

World Bank (1996b), *World Development Report 1996: From Plan to Market*, Washington DC: World Bank.

World Bank (1997a), *World Development Report 1997: The State in a Changing World*, Washington DC: World Bank.

World Bank (1997b), *The World Bank and Poverty Reduction,* Washington DC: World Bank.

World Bank (1997c), *China: Higher Education Reform*, Washington DC: World Bank.

World Bank (1998), *Public Expenditure Management Handbook*, Washington DC: World Bank.

World Bank (1999a), *Public Expenditure Management Handbook*, Washington DC: World Bank.

World Bank (1999b), *World Development Report 1998–99: Knowledge for Development*, Washington DC: World Bank.

World Bank (2000a), *World Development Report 1999/2000: Entering the 21st Century*, Washington DC: World Bank.

World Bank (2000b), *The HIPC Debt Initiative*, www.worldbank.org/hipc.

World Bank (2000c), *World Development Indicators*, Washington DC: World Bank.

World Bank (2001a), *World Development Report 2000/2001: Attacking Poverty*, Washington DC: World Bank.

World Bank (2001b), *World Development Indicators*, Washington DC: World Bank.

World Bank (2002), *Private Sector Development Strategy – Directions for the World Bank Group*, April, Washington DC: World Bank.

World Bank (2004), *World Development Report 2004: Making Services Work for Poor People*, Washington DC: World Bank.

World Bank (2005), *World Development Report 2005: A Better Investment Climate for Everyone*, Washington DC: World Bank.

World Bank/Government of India (1997), V. Rehoej, E. Glennie, S. Abeyratne, J. Sjorslev, 'Rural Water Supply and Sanitation', Draft Report, India, Water Resources Management Sector.

Wratten, E. (1995), 'Conceptualising Urban Poverty', *Environment and Urbanization* 7/1.

WTO (2001), *Market Access: Unfinished Business – Post Uruguay Round Inventory and Issues*. Geneva: World Trade Organization.

Yang, B.M. (1993), 'Medical Technology and Inequity in Health Care: The Case of Korea', *Health Policy and Planning* 8/4: 385–93.

Yashar, D. (2004), 'Citizenship and Ethnic Policits in Latin America: Building Inclusive Societies', background paper for *Human Development Report 2004*, www.undp.org/hdr

Yasheng Huang (2003), *Selling China: Foreign Direct Investment during the Reform Era*, Cambridge: Cambridge University Press.

Yesudian, C.A.K. (1994), 'Behaviour of the Private Sector in the Health Market in Bombay', *Health Policy and Planning* 9/1: 72–80.

Yokozeki, Y., and Sawamura, N. (1999), 'Redefining Strategies of Assistance: Recent Trends in Japanese Assistance to Education in Africa', in K. King and L. Buchert (eds), *Changing International Aid to Education. Global Patterns and National Contexts*, Paris: UNESCO/NORRAG.

You, J. (1995), 'Income Distribution and Growth in East Asia', paper presented at UNCTAD conference on Income Distribution and Development, December, mimeo.

Yusof, Z.A., Razali, N., Guan, L.H., and Muda, R. (1999), *An Assessment of Public Spending on Social Development in Malaysia*, Kuala Lumpur: UNICEF–UNDP.

Zebregs, H. (2003), 'Foreign Direct Investment and Output Growth', in W. Tseng and M. Rodlauer (eds), *China: Competing in the Global Economy*, Washington DC: International Monetary Fund.

Zedillo Report (2000), report submitted to the UN Financing for Development Conference, Monterrey, Mexico, March.

Zeitlin, M.F., and Guldan, G. (1987), *Bangladesh Infant Feeding Observations*, preliminary report submitted to the Office of International Health and the Asia and Near East Bureau of the United States Agency for International Development, Washington DC, 7 September.

Zhang, M. (1997), *Conceptions and Choices: A Comparative Study on Student Financial Support Policies*, Beijing: People's Education Press.

Zuckerman, E., and de Kadt, E. (eds) (1997), *The Public–Private Mix in Social Services: Health Care and Education in Chile, Costa Rica and Venezuela*, Social Policy Agenda Group, Washington DC: Inter-American Development Bank.

Zymelman, M., and DeStefano, J. (1993), 'Primary School Teacher Salaries in Sub-Saharan Africa', in J. Farrell and J. Oliveira (eds), *Teachers in Developing Countries: Improving Effectiveness and Managing Costs*, Washington DC: World Bank.

Index

accountability, 178, 214, 224, 233, 364, 366; local, 175; types, 313; watsan, 185

Africa, 63; agriculture, 204; extra-budgetary funds, 309; francophone, 176; health sector cost recovery, 286; hunger increase, 9; national budgets, 119; NGO health services, 256–7; private schools, 239; sub-Saharan, *see* sub-Saharan; unequal land control, 64

agriculture, 62–6; Africa, 204; subsidies, 343–4

Aguas del Tunari, International Water subsidiary, 263

Ahluwalia, M.S., 93

aid, basic education, 334; BSS allocation, 342; dependence, 319, 341, 345; donor needs, 196, 337; efficiency, 173; fungibility issue, 332; poverty focus, 322; primary health care, 335; project, 321, 339

Alfonso, J.R.R., 308

Alma Ata 1978 conference, 335; Declaration, 167

Anand, S., 101

Angola, rural health, 196

Argentina, 35, 267; Buenos Aires hospitals, 251; economic recovery, 91–2; health, 249; public hospitals, 252; tax revenues, 300

Asia: agriculture, 66; BSS spending increase, 124; financial crisis 1997, 30, 59; health spending, 169; mass schooling, 239

Asian Monetary Fund, proposed, 92

Atkinson, A.B., 303

Atkinson, T., 13–14, 317–18

Bamako Initiative, 170–72, 231–2, 287

Bangladesh: BRAC schools, 247; education, 245; health spending, 142; malnutrition rates, 207; subsidies, 295; teacher absenteeism, 237

Barbados, the state, 213

Bashir, S., 244

basic social services (BSS), 2–4, 7, 15, 31, 38; complementarities, 106; –debt service ratio, 291; defence spending ratio, 121–2; efficiency/inefficiency, 132, 154; ethnic disparities, 136; GDP share, 130; global resource requirements, 278; global spending on, 347; higher-level services bias, 280; industrialized world's history, 364; inelastic demand for, 156; labour-intensive, 115, 320; ODA, 326, 350; outcome disparities, 134; per capita spending, 121–2; private sector promotion, 349; public spending share, 113, 116, 123–4, 152, 210; sectoral approach, 337; spending inequalities, 148–50; state provision, 99, 107, 109–10; travel time for, 151; UN assistance, 327; universalist, 236; user charges, 170; wage levels, 114

Bechtel corporation, 263–4

Benin, 146, 172, 179; Bamako Initiative, 232; BSS deficiencies, 135; defence spending, 288; generic drugs policy, 194

Bennett, S., 249–51, 253, 256

Bentham, Jeremy, 42

Birdsall, N., 89–91, 94

Bismarck, Otto von, 48

Bolivia, 262; neoliberal policy, 263; water co-op, 269; water privatization, 264

Bosworth, B., 58

Botswana, 36, 180; public schooling success, 239

Braunstein, E.,73

Bray, M., 247

Brazil, 36, 108, 179, 315, 344, 362, 366; BSS disparities, 135; Ceara state decentralization, 222–3; condoms distribution, 257; drug production, 345–6; earmarked taxes, 308; federal structure, 226; health, 249; Partido dos Trabalhadores, 224; private health, 250; public hospitals, 252; Watsan Programme, 186

Bruno, M., 20, 25

budget deficits, 18, 242, 297, 299, 309; social benefit, 20

Burgess, R., 303

Burkina Faso, 199, 294; health budgets, 192; textbook production, 181

Cambodia: health budgets, 192; rural health, 196; teachers' wages, 175

Cameroon, 119; defence spending, 288

'capabilities' approach/enhancement, 1, 18, 55, 154, 214–15, 233, 359–60

capital markets: herd behaviour, 28; short-term flows, 83, 90

Caribbean, the, PPPs, 258

Carnoy, M., 244

Central African Republic, 199

Chang, H.J., 31, 69, 86

Chartism, 45

children: labour, 160; malnutrition, 203, 205, 223, 299; mortality rates, 9, 144–6, 202, 292, 335; poverty, 28

Child Survival Revolution, UNICEF, 168

Chile, 24, 251, 262; defence spending, 288; education, 245; health sector, 142, 249; tax revenues, 300, 306; the state, 213; watsan success, 267–9

China, 9, 16, 30–31, 36, 60, 63, 66, 69, 83, 85, 343, 348, 358–9, 362; earmarked taxes, 308; essential drugs access, 194; export-processing industries, 74; FDI policies, 71–3; growth rates, 24; land, 64; poverty decline, 8; private sector, 75; public health cuts, 250; secondary schooling, 243; VAT, 306; water, 164, 266–7

cholera, Kwazulu Natal, 266

civil service composition, 296

Côte d'Ivoire, 119, 179, 343; BSS disparities, 135; education, 137, 139, 141, 175; gender gap, 152; generic drug policy, 194; health budget, 193; water provision, 186

Cochabamba, water conflict, 263–4

Colclough, C., 244

Collins, A., 58

Colombia: education, 244–5; taxes, 304, 306

colonialism, state legacy, 212–13, 217; surplus extraction, 213

commodity prices, fall, 344

commodity-chains, buyer-driven, 78

conditionalities, 341; increase, 30; interlocking, 271; social, 8

Consultative Group of Donors, 1

contraception, 102, 104, 199, 202

Convention on the Rights of the Child, 238

Cornia, G., 24, 26, 101

corruption, 218; aid, 341; sanitation, 187

Costa Rica, 111, 130, 239; education distribution, 137, 179; health spending, 142; infant mortality decrease, 109; public spending, 312; tax reform, 304; the state, 213

Covenant on Economic, Social and Cultural Rights, 238

Cowen, B., 263

Cox, D., 244;

Creese, A., 170, 286

Cuba, 108, 180

currency transaction (Tobin) tax, 316

De Janvry, A., 65

De Mello, L., 308

decentralization, 185, 214–15, 218; accountability, 222, 224; debate, 216; deep democratic, 7, 108, 110, 221, 230, 234, 366; 'despotism', 219; local elite capture, 220; public health systems, 231; state authority need, 219; training need, 217; varied outcomes, 197

defence expenditure, 109

Deininger, K., 25

demographic pressures, 76–7

Deolalikar, A., 254

Dervis, K., 28, 84, 87–91, 94

development: agencies, 342; theory, 5

Diamond, P., 303, 308

Dominican Republic, 147; education, 244; health sector, 146, 192; tax revenues, 300

donors, aid: autonomy, 340; primary education, 180; –recipient relationship, 341

dual synergy, 5, 55–6, 59, 360–61

earmarked (hypothecated) taxes, 307–8, 315, 368

East Asia, 16, 25, 26, 31, 58: capital accumulation, 67; FDI, 70–71; IMF 1997 deal, 345; industrial policy, 68–9; land reform, 62; PPPs, 258; protective barriers, 83; 'tigers', 85

east Europe, water privatization protests, 265

Easterly, W., 20, 32

economic growth, 24, 56, 358; endogenous models, 19; GNP per capita, 33; pre-1973, 59; 'pro-poor', 31, 59–60, 361

economics: leader–follower model, 14; state intervention, 22; neoclassical, 16–17, 21, 26, 236, 359

economies of scale, BSS provision, 107, 237, 365

Ecuador: health, 249; IMF conditionality, 131; tax reform, 304; teacher absenteeism, 237

education: accountability, 178; basic, 364; community financing, 247; compulsory, 51; curriculum flexibility, 273; decentralized, 229; developed world subsidized, 239; enrolment rates, 243; Ethiopia studies, 184; Germany, 48; girls, 104–6; health synergies, 102–3, 109–11; IDA lending to, 328; India, 226; inequalities, 137; ministries, 14; NGO provision, 238, 246; nineteenth-century UK, 41, 45–7; ODA provision, 182, 351–3; out-of-pocket expenses, 181; per-pupil expenditure, 282; primary, *see* primary; private, 138–9, 160; salaries, 175; school feeding programmes, 206–7; secondary, 151; spending distribution, 140, 156–9; state provision, 43, 54; subsidies maldistribution, 152; teaching materials, 180; technical efficiency, 174; tertiary, 160, 282–5; user fees/eliminations, 161, 281; voucher systems, 244; Western world spending, 54; World Bank funding, 333

Education for All, commitments, 328

efficiency: health spending definition, 127; technical, 155

Egypt, education budget bias, 149

employment: children, 160; informalization, 68, 363; infrastructural, 77, 166; women, 112–13

enclosures, 41

Epstein, G., 73

Esman, M.J., 233

Established Anglican Church, 44

Ethiopia, education, 184

Europe, social security systems, 53

European Union: Common Agricultural Policy, 344; ODA, 325

exchange rates, fixed, 58

external debt service expenditure, 84, 118, 289–90, 292–3, 363

externalities, 97, 101; model of, 98; positive, 360; treatment of, 106

family planning, 104

famine, income determinant, 204

fertility, reductions, 202

Filmer, D., 100

fiscal policies, 34; pro-cyclical, 90

Fisher, Irving, 52

Fogel, Robert, 56

food, buffer stocks, 205

foreign direct investment (FDI), 71; –growth relationship, 73; China, 74–5; East Asia, 70; mergers and acquisitions, 85; tax concessions, 306

foreign exchange: fixed rates, 58; reserves, 91

France, 54; dispensary clinics, 50; water PPP model, 259, 261

Franceys, R., 261

freedom of information, 230–31, 341

Free Trade Area of the Americas (FTAA), proposed, 349

Freire, Paulo, 246

'functionings', 15, 38, 40, 215; enhancement, 34–7; women's, 55

G20, establishment of, 93

G7, 93, 292, 362

gender: discrimination, 136, 152; education differentials, 139, 182; equality consequences, 55, 202–3, 361; health inequality, 170

Germany, 343; nineteenth-century government role, 48; welfare benefits, 50

Ghana, 169, 343; decentralization, 197; education, 137, 139; health budget, 149; health spending inequality, 143; school fees impact, 151

Gilson, L., 256

global environment taxes, 315, 318

Global Lottery, notion of, 317

Green Revolution, 164

'growth-mediated' strategy, 38–9

Guinea, 172; Bamako Initiative, 232; health spending, 142–3

Gupta, S., 127

Gwilliams, K.M., 310

Haines, M.R., 52

Haiti, 293

Hanmer, L., 101

Hannaway, J., 243

health services, 49, 146, 151; allocative inefficiency, 167; budgets, 43, 100–101, 126, 142–3, 193; charges, 150; child clinics, 53; church organization provision, 256; community financing, 172; cost recovery, 285, 366; doctor–nurse ratios, 194–6; donor assistance to, 329; education synergies, 102, 109–11; health agents, 222–3; hospitals' spending, 47, 145; industrial, 51; insurance varieties, 49, 248; military concern with, 52; ministries, 14, 197; NGO management systems, 257; nutrition deficiency consequences, 104–5; ODA, 354–5; prepayment, 173; primary care, 144, 167–8; private sector, 249; reproductive, 4, 199–201, 207, 321, 356; rural practitioners, 255; spending 'efficiency', 127; spending distribution, 147–8; technical efficiency, 189; transnationalization, 249; UK nineteenth-century public, 47–8; user fees, 169–71, 286; vested interests, 192; –water synergy, 163; 'willing to pay for', 101

Helleiner, G., 339

Highly Indebted Poor Countries, (HIPCs), 298, 341, 344; Initiative, 291–4, 320

Himachal Pradesh, India, education accountability, 231

Hirschmann, A.O., 298

HIV/AIDS, 9, 35, 199, 321, 335; education impact, 103

Honduras, 180; education wages, 175; watsan provision, 269

Human Development Index (HDI), 162

Hungary, local council water service, 269

hygiene education, 186

IMF (International Monetary Fund), 1, 17, 22, 59, 83, 87, 90–91, 93, 236, 270, 291, 293, 303, 309, 342, 362; –Argentina confrontation, 92; Compensatory and Contingency Finance facility, 345; Extended Structural Adjustment Facility (ESAF), 299–301; gold reserves, 294; inflation concern, 89; Internal Evaluation Office (IEO), 23, 27–30, 94, 130–31, 341; Poverty Reduction and Growth Facility (PRGF), 88, 132, 292; PRSPs, see PRSPs; programme targets, 325; prolonged fund users, 324; public expenditure caps, 197; Special Drawing Rights, 316
immunization, 98–9, 145, 167–8, 222
import-substitution policies, 57–8, 76
income distribution, 21, 27; –growth relationship, 25–6; government policy, 33–4
India, 16, 30, 58, 60, 65, 169–70, 230, 252, 359, 362, 366; budget deficit, 297; decentralization, 216; District Primary Education Programme, 174; earmarked taxes, 308; economic growth, 24, 358; education, 227, 243, 245–6, 282; federal structure, 226; health sector, 253–5, 286; Integrated Child Development Schemes, 207; interest rates, 82; literacy/illiteracy, 281; malnutrition, 203; medical drugs, 194, 345; NGO hospital services, 257; performance budgeting, 313; poverty decline, 8; scavengers, 187; self-employment, 66; social insurance, 81; subsidies, 295–6; taxes, 299–306; teacher absenteeism, 237; water privatization protest, 265; water scarcity, 164; West Bengal, 64, 220
Indonesia, 35, 239; decentralization, 216; education, 243; tax reforms, 302; teacher absenteeism, 237
industrial outwork, 78
inequalities: assets, 61; fiscal widening, 118; income, 55, 358; interregional, 107, 238; intra-country, 134; privatization reinforcement, 84, 87; within-country, 24, 25, 60
inequities, inefficiency consequences, 133
infant industry protection, 86
inflation, 20, 89
informal economy, 76–80
interest rates, 20, 58; global differences, 90; income redistribution, 91
'internal wars', cost, 290, 293
International Conference on Population and Development, 199
International Finance Facility, 317
international finance institutions, 14, 21, 26, 91, 171, 278; governance, 88, 94; prescriptions, 16
intra-uterine growth retardation, 205
Iraq, debt write-off, 294

Italy, regional differences, 217

Jakarta, water privatization, 267
Jamaica, education, 243
Japan, low inequality, 67
Jimenez, E., 243–4
Jolly, R., 26
Jomtien Conference, 328; commitments, 182

Kakwani, N., 31
Kanbur, Ravi, 341
Karachi, Orangi sanitation, 188
Kenya, 119, 293; harambee schools, 247; health budgets, 142, 192; school fees elimination, 281
Kerala, India, 108, 227; health sector, 248
Keynesianism, 310
Korea, Republic of (South), 30, 35, 77, 111, 239, 250, 363; BSS, 108; earmarked taxes, 308; education, 162, 245, 283; infant mortality decrease, 109; low inequality, 67
Krugman, Paul, 17
Kutzin, J., 170, 286
Kuznets, S., 55

labour: national market development, 41–2; international cost advantages, 68; supply, 21
land: access to, 61, 358, 362; concentration, 65; reforms, 62–4, 85
Latin America, 31, 63, 84; decentralization, 216; earmarked taxes, 308; economic performance, 24, 58; education, sector, 160, 181, 239, 246, 283–5; FDI, 70–71; health multinationals, 248–9; health sector, 251–2; land issues, 64–5; minimal state, 213; national budgets, 119; per capita income, 23; performance budgeting, 313; PPPs, 258–62; structuralist view, 57; taxes, 301–4; teachers wages, 175; urban sanitation, 166; VAT contribution, 306; water privatization, 265
Lesotho, school fees elimination, 281
Levine, R., 32
Lewis, W.A., 76
Liedholm, C., 79
life expectancy, 108, 136
literacy/illiteracy, 3, 9, 32, 43–4, 53–4, 136, 241–2, 281, 364; Europe nineteenth-century, 45, 49; female, 125–6; Rajasthan state, 228
local governments, 197, 287
Lockheed, E., 179, 243
Lok Jumbish project, India, 228
low birth weight (LBW), 205–6
Luxemburg, ODA targets met, 323
Lyonnaise des Eaux, 261

Madagascar, tax revenues, 300
Madhya Pradesh, India, 226–30
malaria, 9

Malawi: health sector, 248; intra-sectoral reallocations, 314; school fees elimination, 150, 161, 281
Malaysia, 196; education, 243; performance budgeting, 313; public spending, 312
Mali, health budgets, 192
Mamdani, J., 219
Manila, water privatization success, 266
manufacturing: employment elasticity, 76; export-oriented, 72
market, the, idealized, 14–19; social policies, 235; state created economies, 57
Marshall, Alfred, 202
Matthew Effect, the, 149, 151
Maurice Pate prize, UNICEF, 222
Mazdoor Kisan Shakti Sangathan, Rajasthan, 220
McGillvray, M., 332
McKeown, T., 52
Mead, D.C., 79
medical drugs: affordable, 232; companies, 346; essential, 172; generic, 194, 345; Indian production, 254; irrational use, 252–5; shortages, 193
Medium Term Expenditure Frameworks, 326
Meerman, J., 116
Mehrotra, S., 243
Mexico: hospitals, 192; taxes, 300, 304; unnecessary drugs, 253; VAT, 306
Millennium Development Goals (MDGs), 2, 6, 8, 10, 61, 81–2, 87–9, 94, 198, 278, 315, 317–22, 324, 327, 332–3, 335–6, 343, 349–50, 363, 368
military spending, 290
Mirlees, J., 303
monopolies, 19
Monterrey Consensus, 325, 344
Morley, D., 24
Morocco, education wages, 175
Morrissey, O., 332
mortality rates: child, 52–3, 127, 144–6, 202–3, 292, 335; developed countries, 130; France, 50; infant, 109, 148; maternal, 329; neonatal, 53; nineteenth-century Europe, 44–5; under-5, 37, 126
Mozambique, 199; health sector, 192, 220, 248
multilingualism, 181–2
Mumbai Dharavi slum sanitation, 188
Mwabu, G., 101

Namibia, 199, 310; tax revenues, 300
Nash equilibrium, 22
National Education Statistical Information Systems, 178
Nayyar, D., 94
Nepal, 179; BSS disparities, 134; budget deficits, 297; earmarked taxes, 308; health budget, 193; rural health, 196

Netherlands, ODA targets met, 323
newly industrialized countries (NICs), 69–70
NGOs, Africa health provision, 256
Nicaragua, 35, 180; education wages, 175
Niger, 294; budget deficit, 297; generic drugs policy, 194
Nigeria, 175
Nussbaum, Martha, 18, 56, 360
nutrition, 52, 103–4; determinants, 204; global malnutrition, 9; protein-energy, 206; school feeding programmes, 207
official development aid (ODA), 7–8, 29, 88–9, 290, 300, 317–18; bilateral, 23; BSS aid, 320; composition, 327, 333; donor monitoring, 340; education, 182, 328–9; net flows, 323; rural projects share, 336
oil, 1973 price shock, 57–8
Or, Z., 130
Organization for Economic Cooperation and Development (OECD), 326; Development Assistance Committee (DAC), 320–21, 324, 330, 339, 342

Pakistan, 58, 65; information availability, 230; religious schools, 246; water privatization protest, 265
panchayat, Indian village councils, 227–8
Papua New Guinea: decentralization, 219; teacher absenteeism, 237
parent–teacher associations, 177
Pareto optimality, 18
Paris Declaration process, 340
Parry, T., 244
participatory budgeting, 223–5
performance budgeting, 312–13
Peru, 179; teacher absenteeism, 237; VAT, 306
Philippines, the, 196; decentralization, 216; defence spending, 288; earmarked taxes, 308; education, 244; performance budgeting, 313; tax reform, 302; social insurance, 81
Pigou, A.C., 97
Polanyi, Karl, 42, 57, 85
population growth, 198, 202
Porto Alegre, Brazil, 223–5
Potter, B., 308
Poverty Reduction and Growth Facility (PRGF), 23, 27, 132, 301
poverty: child, 28; –growth relationship, 32, 37, 40; income, 3, 8, 23, 39, 359; rural, 62
pregnancy: management, 167; nutrition, 206
Preston, S.H., 52
primary education, 174, 179; community management, 227; drop-outs, 179, 181; enrolment, 9; fees, 162; subsidies, 152
Pritchett, L., 32, 100
private schools, 138–9, 160, 239–46
privatization, 7, 19–20, 24, 84–5, 87, 277, 365; Russia, 59; social services, 22; urban watsan,

185, water, 166, 186, 259, 264-7, WTO
  push, 347
pro-cyclical policies, 26
PRSPs (Poverty Reduction Strategy Papers),
  1–2, 27–8, 87–9, 132, 270–71, 293, 298, 326
Prussia, military success, 46
public goods, notion of, 98–101
Public Services International Research Unit, 269
public spending: allocation differences, 124; child
  mortality link, 127; –GDP ratio, 128–9, 283,
  310–11, 314, 364; inter-sector reallocation,
  287; intra-sector reallocation, 280, 296
public universities, 'social development', 285
public–private partnerships (PPPs), 7, 258–62
punishment, costs of, 45
Putnam, R., 217
Pyatt, G., 135

Radelet, S., 32
Rajasthan, India, 226, 230; Village Education
  Committees, 229
Ramalingaswami, V., 254
Ramsey, F., 303
Rao, G., 295
Ravallion, M., 25, 31, 101
regression analysis, 40, 131
rent-seeking, state functionaries, 213, 366
Rodrik, D., 20, 24, 58–9, 69, 79, 84
Rosenstein-Rodan, P., 55, 360
Rostow, W.W., 55, 360
Rotarians, Expanded Programme of
  Immunization, 257
Russia, 31; privatization, 59
Sadoulet, E., 65
Scandanavia, ODA targets met, 323
school uniforms, cost, 161–2
Self-Employed Women's Association (SEWA),
  173
Selowsky, M., 118
Sen, Amartya, 2, 14–15, 18, 38–9, 56, 110, 215,
  298, 360
Senegal, 9; tax revenues, 300
Shalizi, Z.M., 310
Shiksha Karmi project, India, 228
SMEs, (small and medium enterprises), clusters
  of, 76, 78–9
Smith, Adam, 42
social insurance, 80–81
'social overhead capital', 298
South Africa, 174, 310, 312, 344; contraception,
  199; education, 140; generic drugs policy,
  194; health spending, 147–9; HIV/AIDS
  drugs, 346; land reform, 64; PPPs, 262;
  private health, 250; tax revenues, 300;
  teachers' salaries, 178–9; water privatization
  protest, 265–6
South Asia, 63, 319; defence spending, 288;
  education spending, 160; gender differentials,

182; low birth weight, 205; PPPs, 258;
  private health providers, 287; subsidies, 295;
  tertiary education, 284
Southeast Asia, 30; health user charges, 286;
  PPPs, 261
Spencer, Herbert, 43
Sri Lanka, 35, 108, 180, 230, 239, 293, 310;
  defence spending, 288; health sector, 193,
  196, 248; performance budgeting, 313
Srivastava, R., 295
stagflation, 23
state, the: authority need, 219; BSS provision
  failures, 108, 211, 214–15; budgets, 114–18;
  apitalism, 57; complementarity role, 106, 272;
  developmental functions, 58, 213; industrial
  policies, 67–70; minimal, 216; nineteenth-
  century intervention, 49–51, 53; post-
  colonial, 212, 233; regulatory, 43; role, 56, 277
Stern, N., 303
Stewart, F., 26
Stiglitz, J., 26–7, 30
structural adjustment policies, 87, 169, 235–6,
  287
subcontracting, role of, 77–8
Sub-Saharan Africa, 36, 169, 177–8, 300, 319,
  333; bilateral assistance, 340; deforestation,
  164; education spending, 160; foreign
  exchange reserves, 325; gender differentials,
  182; HIV/AIDS, 199; low birth weight, 205;
  malnutrition, 203; PPPs, 258; teachers' wages,
  175; tax revenues, 301
subsidies, 294; inequitable, 295–6, 298; irrigation,
  163
Sulabh International, Indian NGO, 187
supermarkets, power of, 65
surplus labour, rural, 65
Swaziland, tax revenues, 300

Taiwan, 58, 363; small-scale industries, 77; low
  inequality, 67
Tanzania, 196, 340; budget deficits, 297;
  education, 244; health sector, 248; school
  fees elimination, 281
Tanzi, V., 305
taxes, 18–19, 51, 71, 73, 82, 132, 172–3, 292,
  297, 341, 367; administration reform, 305,
  315; earmarked, 309; evasion, 277, 302;
  excise, 307; –GDP ratio, 300–301; local, 47;
  optimal theory, 303; progressive/income,
  285, 304; tariff revenues, 84, 301, 306, 344;
  VAT, 306
TB (tuberculosis), 9
teachers: absenteeism, 21, 177, 237; female,
  182–3, 365; need for, 175; promotions, 180;
  salaries, 176–9, 242, 246
Tendler, J., 79, 222
Thailand, 9, 199, 250, 344, 346; drug
  production, 345; education, 243, 251; private

health sector, 250

Thames Water, Shanghai sewerage plant, 266

Thobani, M., 162

trickle-down mechanisms, 22; failure, 25

Tseng, W., 73

Tucuman, Argentina, water protests, 265

20 Country Policy and Institutional Assessment, 28

20/20 Initiative, 28

Uganda, 9; decentralization, 197; education, 231; intra-sectoral reallocations, 314; school fees elimination, 281; tax revenues, 300; teacher absenteeism, 237

UK (United Kingdom), 86, 261; nineteenth-century state role, 41–7; economic growth, 56; education, 239, 245; National Health Service, 189; White Papers on International Development, 342

Ukraine, weak state, 219

'unaimed opulence', 38–9, 242

UN (United Nations), 14; Declaration on Human Rights, 107; Development Cooperation Reports, 330; FAO, 9; International Drinking Water and Sanitation Decade, 164; Millennium Project Report, 88; UNDP, 113, 327, 344; UNESCO, 329, 334; UNICEF, 6, 113, 134, 160, 168, 185, 222, 336; UNICEF GOBI–FFF approach, 168

Universal Campaign for Immunization, 335

Uphoff, N., 233

Uplekar, M., 250

urban–rural inequalities: BSS, 135, 154–5; education, 139–40; health, 145–6, 196, 207; income, 60; watsan, 165, 191

urbanization, 163; sanitation, 166; water systems, 186

Uruguay Round, trade agreements, 30

Uruguay, the state, 213

USA (United States of America), 86, 178, 346, 348–9; agriculture subsidies, 343–4; Civil War, 46; education earmarked taxes, 308; government industrial policy, 68; House of Representatives, 171; mercantilist policies, 52; nineteenth-century education, 50–51; ODA targets, 325

USSR (Union of Soviet Socialist Republics), 57, 84

utilitarianism, 42, 361

vaccination, 221

Vashista, P., 254

Verspoor, A., 179

Vietnam, 30, 348, 359; health spending, 149; hospital costs, 252

Vivendi Water, 261, 265

'voice', local collective, 212, 214, 223–6, 228, 231, 233–4, 366

Wagner's Law, 310

Wal-Mart, 78

watsan (water and sanitation), 4, 105; appropriate technology, 184–8; British and French companies, 261; groundwater overuse, 164; infrastructure, 185, 189; ODA share, 327, 330–31, 336, 357; PPPs, 258, 260, 262–3, 367; privatization, 258, 366; rural area user committees, 259; rural deficiencies, 165, 191; rural sanitation, 163, 166; safe drinking water, 9, 163; sanitation efficiency, 48, 189; South Africa privatization, 266; urban sanitation, 167; water sellers, 259; water systems auction, 263; wastewater treatment, 188

welfare: pluralism, 235; 'socialism', 49

women: agency of, 359–61; child nutrition, 205; education consequence, 106; literacy/illiteracy, 125–6; marginalized, 232; reproductive rights, 203; social reproduction work, 21; status, 110, 112; water infrastructure, 185; water maintenance, 189

World Bank, 1, 29, 68, 81, 87, 89, 92–3, 118, 130–32, 161–2, 170–71, 204, 236, 262, 264, 281, 285–6, 291, 293–4, 324, 339, 345, 362; education attitudes, 333–4; education lending, 184; health policy, 249, 335; International Development Agency, 271, 327; International Finance Corporation, 251, 265, 270–71; PPPs pressure, 270; PRSPs, see PRSPs; Public Expenditure Reviews, 114, 287, 297; Roads Management Initiative, 309; Sector Investment Programmes (SIPs), 337–8; welfare pluralism attitude, 248; World Development Indicators, 23

World Development Report 2006, 358

World Health Organization (WHO), 197, 255, 335

World Summit for Social Development, 278

World Summit on Sustainable Development, Johannesburg, 165

WTO (World Trade Organization), 31, 348; GATS (General Agreement on Trade in Services), 236, 270, 342, 346–9; manoeuvre space, 362; privatization push, 368; TRIPS (Trade-Related Intellectual Property Rights), 342, 345–6

Year 2000 Health for All, 172; targets, 232

Zambia: external debt, 292; HIV/AIDS, 281; teachers' absenteeism, 175, 237

Zebregs, H., 73

Zedillo Report, 318

Zimbabwe, 179; doctor–nurse ratio, 194; education, 243; multilingualism, 182; private health sector, 250 teachers' salaries, 176